Containing the proceedings of Helion & Company's inaugural 2022 Naval History Conference, this volume includes chapters from scholars experienced and young, and from across the world, on various aspects of the naval history of the Age of Reason and Revolution.

This work contains its fair share of high seas action and naval operations, representing British, Spanish, French, and Italian perspectives: Mauro Difranceso explores the operations and effectiveness of the Venetian *Armata grossa* during the Second Morean War, and Albert Parker explores first how Spain utilized seapower during the 1730s-1740s, and then second assesses the French and Spanish Bourbon operations to supply and support the 1745 Jacobite Rising. Olivier Aranda pitches in to assess the success of the French Navy's flying squadrons of the early 1790s, long neglected by French and English historiography.

A particular focus is on naval operations in North American waters, and on the wider significance of those operations. R.N.W. Thomas provides an analysis of the North American Station in the 1760s/1770s, exploring how the navy was maintained and how it was utilized to enforce imperial policies in the pre-American Revolutionary period. Thomas Golding-Lee then examines the 'Nile that wasn't' and the French missed opportunity at the Battle of St Lucia (1778), and Nicholas James Kaizer highlights the historical lessons learned from three single ship actions of the War of 1812 where the Royal Navy displayed an appalling lack of leadership and skill in action, including a challenge to preeminent narratives of the Royal Navy in that conflict.

Of course, naval administration, recruitment, and other aspects of manpower are well served. On the strategic level, Paul Leyland assesses the role played by Antwerp in British and French naval strategies and wider foreign policy. Andrew Young then examines the herculean role played by Anson as First Lord of the Admiralty in building up of the Royal Navy's administrative capacity. Joseph Krulder examines the state of affairs in 1754-1755, at the start of the Seven Years War, demonstrating that this process was far from complete by this stage, all while placing this period into its proper social context. Andrew Johnston explores the changing trends in naval law through courts martial held from 1812-1818, demonstrating the navy rapidly moving away from 'rum, soddomy, and the lash.'

Next, three chapters address topics related to the social/cultural history of the Royal Navy: Jim Tildesley examines the career of Consul John Mitchell and his contributions to manning the fleet and supplying intelligence. Andrew Lyter explores the careers of black pilots serving with HMS *Poictiers*, long forgotten by history, and how they leveraged their vital knowledge to carve out identities as free maritime professionals. Finally, Callum Easton examines the careers and demographics of the Greenwich pensioners, veterans of the French Revolutionary and Napoleonic Wars, and provides a fascinating picture of how society's views and stereotypes of these Jack Tars changed in the decades following the long eighteenth century.

Nicholas James Kaizer is a Canadian scholar and teacher, who studies the cultural history of the Royal Navy during the Napoleonic era. In particular, he is interested in the Anglo-Canadian responses to single ship losses of the War of 1812. He has a MA from Dalhousie University and is the author of *Revenge in the Name of Honour*, also published by Helion. He has written for *Warships: IFR*, the *Cool Canadian History* podcast, the *Napoleon Series*, the *War, Literature, and the Arts* journal, the *Trafalgar Chronicle*, and the Navy Records Society.

Sailors, Ships and Sea Fights

Proceedings of the 2022 'From Reason to Revolution 1721–1815' Naval Warfare in the Age of Sail Conference

Edited by Nicholas James Kaizer

Helion & Company

To the team of wonderful scholars, young and old, who contributed to this volume

Helion & Company Limited
Unit 8 Amherst Business Centre
Budbrooke Road
Warwick
CV34 5WE
England
Tel. 01926 499619
Email: info@helion.co.uk
Website: www.helion.co.uk
Twitter: @helionbooks
Visit our blog at http://blog.helion.co.uk/

Published by Helion & Company 2024
Designed and typeset by Mach 3 Solutions (www.mach3solutions.co.uk)
Cover designed by Paul Hewitt, Battlefield Design (www.battlefield-design.co.uk)

Text © Individual contributors 2024
Maps as individually credited.

Cover: 'The Brave Captain Tyrrill in the Buckingham of 66 Guns and 472 Men, Defeating the Florissant, Aigrette & Atalante, Three French Ships of War, 3rd November, 1758'. Print by Banazech after Francis Swaine. (Yale Center for British Art)

ISBN 978-1-804513-44-6

British Library Cataloguing-in-Publication Data.
A catalogue record for this book is available from the British Library.

For details of other military history titles published by Helion & Company Limited, contact the above address, or visit our website: http://www.helion.co.uk

We always welcome receiving book proposals from prospective authors.

Contents

List of Plates

List of Maps

Contributors' Biographies

Olivier Aranda is a PhD candidate in History at the University Paris 1 Panthéon-Sorbonne, working mainly on the French navy during the revolutionary wars. He currently teaches as a *professeur agrégé* in History, and works for the Institut d'Histoire Moderne et Contemporaine, which has received funding from the French Ministère des Armées.

Mauro Difrancesco studies Italian naval history in the long eighteenth century. He has published several articles and is working towards completing a masters thesis entitled '*Le navi del re: costruzioni e politica navale del Regno di Sardegna nell'età della Restaurazione (1815-1819).*' He graduated from the University of Genoa, there researching the sailing warships of the Order of St John, which is in the process of publication as '*Sotto la croce di Malta: le campagne navali dell'Ordine di San Giovanni nelle memorie del cavaliere fra' Afranio Petrucci, maggiore dei vascelli (1715-1717).*' He serves as a member of the association Arma Virumque and SISM (Società Italiana di Storia Militare), directed by Professor Virgilio Ilari. He has served in the Italian Carabinieri as a non-commissioned officer since 2011.

Callum Easton is a Caird Research Fellow at the National Maritime Museum, Greenwich, studying the Greenwich Seaman's Hospital. His contribution here is the first stage of an effort to produce the first academic social and economic history of the institution. Previously, Callum completed his PhD at the University of Cambridge in July 2020, which provided a new interpretation of the 1797 fleet mutinies that emphasised the importance of fairness to their causation and trajectory. His work highlighted how this event can reveal a myriad of aspects of the wider British society during the 'Age of Revolutions.'

Thomas Golding-Lee is a professional military operational analyst working in the private defence and security sector. Having been interested in naval history from an early age, he attended Pangbourne College, then studied War Studies at King's College London, following it with a Master of Arts in Intelligence in International Security. During his time at university Thomas focused his studies on British Imperial Strategy and military operations as well as intelligence in counter insurgency operations. In his spare time Thomas is an avid wargamer and rugby player and enjoys wandering through the Hertfordshire countryside with his wife Sarah.

Andrew Johnston is a PhD student in history at the University of Victoria, studying crime and punishment in the nineteenth-century British Royal Navy. His dissertation work continues that of his MA, conducting a digital analysis of courts martial and legal reform of the navy between 1815 and 1889, with a specific interest in the relationship between military and criminal law and the developments therein.

Nicholas James Kaizer (editor) is a Canadian teacher and independent scholar, who studies the cultural history of the Royal Navy during the Napoleonic era. In particular, he is interested in the Anglo-Canadian responses to single ship losses of the War of 1812. He has a MA from Dalhousie University and is the author of *Revenge in the Name of Honour*, also published by Helion. He has written for *Warships: IFR*, the *Cool Canadian History* podcast, the *Napoleon Series*, the *War, Literature, and the Arts* journal, the *Trafalgar Chronicle*, and the Navy Records Society.

Joseph Krulder is a cultural historian specializing in the greater Atlantic world throughout the Long Eighteenth Century. He is currently a professor at Butte College and has taught previously at Yuba College and on board two United States Navy vessels through Central Texas College. He is the author of *The Execution of Admiral John Byng as a Microhistory of Eighteenth-Century Britain*, which examines the cultural, social, and political pulse of eighteenth-century British society through the notorious execution of Admiral Byng.

Paul Leyland gained a passion for history from an early age, reveling in the family war stories of his paternal grandfather Norman and then discovering his maternal grandfather Joe's silent horror was caused by the loss of five of his six uncles and the horrendous wounds sustained by his father and remaining uncle during the First World War. Paul's childhood passion was nurtured by a fantastic history department at Hutton Grammar School, equipping him to gain a First in History from Leicester University, where he wrote his dissertation on French strategy and finance during the Seven Years War, under the incomparable Reverend-Professor Richard Bonney. Ten years as a financial analyst in the City of London helped to instill the logic of 'follow the money' as well as a deep understanding of what happens when operational capabilities fail to live up to strategic ambition, an approach which helps to give a different perspective on more thematic approaches to history. Paul has maintained a keen academic interest in history throughout his 20-year professional career, regularly using historical analogy in his role as a strategy advisor. This is his first chapter for publication.

Andrew J. Lyter is the Executive Director and Curator for the Lewes Historical Society in Lewes, Delaware. He is an avid maritime historian and sailor, having crewed traditionally rigged tall ships in both the United States and Great Britain. He holds a BA in history from West Chester University and an MA in naval history from the University of Portsmouth, Great Britain. As a maritime historian, Lyter specializes in maritime identities of the Revolutionary Atlantic and the social history of sailors, c. 1770-1815. He most recently curated the Lewes Historical Society's current exhibitions: "With a Splendid Breeze: Lewes Maritime Art Ashore & Afloat", "Jacob Jones – Lewes' Own", and "Breaking Britannia's Grasp: Lewes, the Royal Navy, and the Legacy of 1812". He is currently completing his forthcoming book, *Going Among the English Sailors – American Tars & HMS Belvidera, 1809–1813*.

Albert Parker earned his PhD in history at Washington University, St Louis, Missouri. During a career as a sample survey research professional, he pursued naval history as an avocation. He has been investigating the naval campaigns of the 1730s and 1740s since 2002. He presented an earlier version of 'Spanish Use of Sea Power' to the 2017 McMullen Naval History Symposium at the US Naval Academy in Annapolis, Maryland, and of 'From Ferrol and Flanders' to Helion's 'The Jacobite Rising of 1745 – 275th Anniversary Conference' in 2021. A two-volume work, *All the Seas of the World: The First Global Naval War, 1739–1748*, will be published by Helion in 2024. Another volume from the same project, *Baltic and Barents: Sweden Versus Russia at Sea, 1741–1743*, is pending.

Jim Tildesley has had a career working in education, museums, and local authorities. He retired as Director of the Scottish Maritime Museum in 2012. A Member of the National Historic Ships Committee for seven years, Jim also co-ordinated the saving of the clipper ship *City of Adelaide* and her transfer from Scotland to South Australia. Over the last 20 years, Jim has concentrated on researching the Royal Navy of the eighteenth century. Publications include the critically acclaimed biography of Admiral John Inglis and, most recently, a reassessment of the influence of John Clerk of Eldin on British fleet tactics during the Napoleonic War.

R.N.W. Thomas has a PhD in Archaeology from Southampton University. His monograph *'No Want of Courage': The British Army in Flanders, 1793-1794* was published by Helion in 2022. He is a contributor to the Oxford Dictionary of National Biography and has authored papers published in the *Journal of the Society for Army Historical Research*, the *International History Review* and in the *Proceedings of the Consortium on Revolutionary Europe*. He edited the letters of Colonel Daniel George Robinson, Bengal Engineers, for the Army Records Society. He works in the shipping industry.

Andrew Young is a former Royal Navy officer, specialising in professional military education. He has worked at the Royal United Services Institute on Whitehall and lectured on courses at Britannia Royal Naval College Dartmouth, Commando Training Centre Royal Marines, Joint Services Command and Staff College, and RAF College Cranwell. He is currently the Fellowships Officer for the Royal Navy Strategic Studies Centre. He is a PhD candidate at King's College London.

Comparison of Ranks

At first glance, a comparison of ranks between navies might seem simple. Today, when western navies are designed to operate together through organizations such as NATO, roles and ranks do often have a direct equivalence. That was not necessarily the case in the long eighteenth century, however. The individual ranks and titles used by the navies that are covered in this volume did have rough equivalents, but these ranks did not always come from the same tradition, nor did they perform the same duties. The British Royal Navy, for example, shared a similar system of flag officers with other European navies, such as the French and Dutch. Here there were three basic ranks of admiral (or *amiral*), with very similar terminology. Both the French and British had an additional higher-tier rank for a senior officer. In Britain, this was the Admiral of the Fleet, awarded to the seniormost actively serving flag officer. An equivalent title in the French navy was that of *Amiral de France*, which was more akin to a title of honour. Spain, by contrast, did not yet use the term 'admiral' for its flag officers, preferring the terminology conventionally used by armies (general). Another outlier is the British use of 'commodore' for naval captains temporarily given the responsibilities of flag rank – command of individual squadrons.

Table of Ranks – Circa 1790s

British Royal Navy	French *Marine du Roi / Nationale* *	Spanish *Real Armada*
Admiral of the Fleet	*Amiral de France* †	*Capitán General de la Armada*
Admiral	*Amiral*	*Capitán General* ‡
Vice Admiral	*Vice-amiral*	*Teniente General*
Rear Admiral	*Contre-amiral*	*Jefe de Escuadra*
Commodore §	---	*Brigadier* ‖
Post Captain	*Capitaine de vaisseau* *Capitaine de frégate* ¶	*Capitán de navío* *Capitán de fragata* ¶

Notes

* The ranks of the pre-Revolutionary *Marine du Roi* were different, and for much of the period *Vice-amiral* was the seniormost flag officer.

† Rank in abeyance during the Revolutionary period (1790s). It was resurrected under Napoleon Bonaparte (1804).

‡ *Capitán General* and the senior equivalent were both introduced in the 1750s, following the period covered in both chapters by Albert Parker in this volume during which *Teniente General* was the highest rank.

§ Temporary flag rank awarded to post captains.

‖ Like British commodores, Spanish brigadiers flew pennants, but typically did not command detached squadrons or subdivisions of fleets. Instead, they commanded the largest ships of the line of a fleet. In terms of seniority, they fell between the British equivalent of 'post captain' and 'rear admiral.'

¶ Both the Spanish and French navies had distinct ranks for commanders of ships of the line and frigates.

Most of the chapters of this volume – reflecting the interest of most English-language naval historiography – are focused on the British Royal Navy. This volume does include several chapters dealing with aspects of French and Spanish naval operations, namely those of A. Parker, O. Aranda, and T. Golding-Lee. Additionally, one chapter (M. Difrancesco) covers the navy of the Republic of Venice, which had a very different naval command structure. Firstly, the structure of command differed during peacetime than during wartime. During the Second Morean War (or Seventh Ottoman-Venetian War), overall command of the Venetian fleet was entrusted to the *Capitano general da Mar*. Beneath this officer, however, the fleet was divided into squadrons based upon types of vessels. One squadron, the senior, consisted of the oared galleys (*Armata sottile*), while another consisted of sailing vessels (*Armata grossa*). Unlike in the navies of northwestern Europe, the body of officers employed by Venice were not dedicated professional officers, and many held a variety of civil and military posts throughout their career. They were patricians first, and served in positions in command because it was their right and duty to do so. A table of the three seniormost 'admirals' of the Venetian navy during the Second Morean War, including titles, translations, and roles, is provided below.

Table of Ranks – Republic of Venice, circa 1720

Rank	Translation	Role
Capitano general da Mar	Captain General of the Sea	Commander-in-Chief of the Venetian Fleet
Provveditore d'armata	Superintendent of the fleet	Commander of the Galley Squadron
Capitano Straordinario delle Navi	Captain Extraordinary of the Sailing Ships	Commander of the Sailing Squadron

Introduction

Halifax (and its wider municipality) has always been a naval town. The Royal Naval Yard was established there just a decade after the town was founded, and the heart of the city has beat to the tune of naval and maritime life ever since. Today, that yard continues to serve as the home of the Royal Canadian Navy's Atlantic Fleet, and tonnes and tonnes of maritime traffic of all stripes continues to flow through the Narrows. Just as, in decades past, the arrival of a particularly important man-of-war sparked discussion and buzz throughout Halifax, so too did the arrival in September 2019 of HMS *Queen Elizabeth*, an aircraft carrier too big to even make it to the naval base itself, reverberate interest among many in Halifax.

It is also a city home to many bookshops. Imagine my frustration, however, that even finding works in Halifax bookshops exploring naval or maritime history continues to be a challenge. In the mass market publishing world, naval and maritime history has always taken a backseat to other genres, particularly land-based military history. Not that the world of military non-fiction publishing is always ideal, for the selections available are still typically based upon twentieth century stories.

However, it cannot be said that the world of naval historiography reflects this dearth. In 2008, after being commissioned by the *Historical Journal* to write an article highlighting the current state of British naval historiography, N.A.M. Rodger quipped that 'it is not very likely that the editor of the *Historical Journal*, or any other scholarly publication, would have asked for such an article as this twenty-five years ago.'[1] He added that, in 2008, naval history had entered one of its periodic golden ages, after being effectively shunted out of the realm of academia and professional historians for many years. Today, in 2023, naval historiography continues to bask in that glow. And now, thanks to the rise of specialist and online book retailers and publishers (such as Helion & Company), readers – and there are many such avid readers – can now grasp dozens of titles. Besides fresh approaches on conventional topics – represented by numerous biographical, operational, and technical histories – historians are applying the latest trends to the naval world. Important works have helped to explore the social, cultural, administrative, and political aspects of naval history. Armed with new historical techniques and methodologies, historians have taken advantage of the internet and the tools which it has enabled to explore a range of niche and once-obscure topics; many have appeared in one of Helion's excellent series.

---

1   N.A.M. Rodger, 'Recent Work in British Naval History, 1750-1815,' *The Historical Journal*, 51:3 (2008), p.741.

In the From Reason to Revolution series thus far there have been more than a dozen covering different aspects of naval history – including two from contributors to this volume. These works are broad in their scope and in their methodology. They include operational and social histories, and even works of reference, such as *Royal Navy Officers of the Seven Years War*, which offers biographical data on every naval officer who served in that conflict. Several volumes examined the strategic role and use of seapower in conflicts such as the American Revolutionary War (*All at Sea*, John Dillon) and wars against Revolutionary and Napoleonic France (*Far Distant Ships*, Quintin Barry). There is also a biography of Admiral Sir Pulteney Malcolm, an often forgotten but long-serving officer (*The Sea is my Element*, Paul Martinovich), and a biographical work on the contributions of North Americans to Nelson's Navy (*From Across the Sea*, Sean M. Heuvel and John A. Rodgard). My own title explores the social and cultural history of the Royal Navy through the events of the War of 1812 (*Revenge in the Name of Honour*). Helion's naval works also span the globe. There are a number which examine the American Revolutionary War and the War of 1812, and even one translated work exploring the operations of the Russian Mediterranean Fleet (*Northern Tars in Southern Waters*, Vladimir Bronevskiy translated by Darrin Boland) a fleet that many English-speaking history buffs likely will not have heard of.

This volume will offer a selection of historical research with broader a scope than Helion's current selection. All of the chapters – aside from one excellent late addition – were first presented at the inaugural 2022 Helion Naval Warfare in the Age of Sail Conference, generously hosted by the From Reason to Revolution series editor, Andrew Bamford. It was held online and attracted a diverse group of scholars, young and old, from across the world. If the logistics of running such an international conference were a challenge, the outcome was well worth it.

The 14 chapters, authored by 13 scholars, have been divided into sections. Parts I and II present new research into an old sphere: naval operations. Once, virtually every work of naval history (and military history, for that matter) was confined to the realm of operations. Even as historians today have moved away from this narrower approach, scholars continue to breath new life into the genre by introducing new sources, methodologies, and topics. Included here are chapters focused on the Venetian, Spanish, and French navies, as well as examinations of British operations exploring neglected theatres and battles. In Part III, four chapters are devoted to different aspects of naval administration, now recognized as one of the most important factors in the success – or failure – of any naval operation. Finally, Part IV presents work in the realm of naval social history, including discussions of careers of various kinds of naval professionals hereto neglected by wider naval historiography.

Nicholas James Kaizer
Halifax, 2023

Part I

Naval Operations: European Waters

Were you to peruse a bookshelf of naval history in the later nineteenth century, you would be hard pressed to find a title not devoted to naval operations. Throughout the *Pax Britannica*, many authors produced an extensive collection of naval history works detailed all aspects of the operational history of the Royal Navy, and the Napoleonic era was a favourite. Often, these works were meant to inform policy in strategy in an era where sea power was identified as a key aspect of projecting a state's power and influence; Mahan's work, cited in this volume, was a key and influential example. These works typically went through battle after battle, campaign after campaign, in painstaking detail, and were often chiefly concerned about British triumphs at sea. Some, such as William James' seminal work, were dedicated to celebrating British victories and explaining away British losses.

Today, many of the best operational narratives examine long-neglected actions or the use of seapower from non-British perspectives; this section will highlight the use of seapower by Venetian, Spanish, and French powers. Firstly here is an excellent analysis of the *Armata grossa*, or 'sailing fleet,' of the Venetian Navy during the Second Morean War by Mauro Difrancesco, an Italian scholar. This is an area rarely discussed in the English language, but the Venetian Republic remained an important naval power throughout the period, and Difrancesco's examination of the organization, operations, and effectiveness of the sailing arm of a fleet still dedicated to galleys is a welcome addition to the historiography.

If the role of the Venetian navy during the eighteenth century has been neglected in English historiography, so too has the Spanish *Real Armada* and the use of seapower by the newly legally-united Kingdom of Spain in that century. In his first chapter, Albert Parker counters prevailing English assumptions about the Spanish navy, namely that theirs was an ineffective fleet which mostly stayed at anchor, only coming out to be defeated in detail by the Royal Navy. He demonstrates, in fact, that the Spanish navy did play an important role in using Spanish sea power in many ways. He highlights how a materially inferior navy can be used to advantage in wars against much stronger naval powers. In his second contribution, Parker examines how Bourbon Spain and France both utilized sea power in support of the 1745 Jacobite Rising. While he demonstrates that Spain's smaller contribution was without success, France's much more extensive support did prove profitable to the French, even if Charles Stuart's campaign was a failure. France, though not winning any significant naval actions against the British, nonetheless employed sea power effectively.

Finally, French historian Olivier Aranda turns to long-neglected naval operations in 1794. Narratives of this period, in both French and English historiography, are dominated by major events like the Glorious First of June, and have little to say about the resourcefulness of the French navy and Committee of Public Safety. However, two sorties of 'flying squad-rons' of well-sailing ships of the line did prove effective at assaulting British commerce, which Aranda highlights. So neglected are these operations that even N.A.M. Rodger confused these sorties with the winter 1794-1795 sortie of the French Atlantic Fleet. In his account, Aranda examines the operations and the forces involved, arguing that these opera-tions demonstrate that the French revolutionary navy could be employed effectively, a point often lost in narratives of the naval war against Revolutionary and Napoleonic France that focuses on the major fleet actions.

1

Venetian and 'Auxiliary' Vessels in the Second Morean War: Failures and Successes of a Mediterranean Navy in the Age of Sail (1714-1718)

Mauro Difrancesco

The modern age of naval warfare was a period of great transformation. Until the end of the sixteenth century, the main vessel of naval fleets was without doubt the galley. These oared warships were the heir to an ancient naval tradition and the subject of centuries of development and improvement that reached an almost definitive stage between the eighteenth century and the early nineteenth, when it was still in use by a number of navies.[1] The sailing ship – large, round, and high-sided ships powered primarily by square and lateen sails – went through its own evolution, establishing itself as a capital ship during the seventeenth century.[2] However, the evolutionary path that led it to operate alongside and gradually replace the galley began in the fifteenth century.

Fifteenth-century ships had certain qualities that made them superior to galleys: the height of their sides, their greater autonomy and firepower, as well as a significantly smaller though highly specialised crew that greatly reduced running costs. But set against these advantages were certain limitations that still made such vessels unsuited to war: they were designed for ocean navigation in particular and for the high seas more generally. They were

---

1   France and Spain only stopped employing their own galley squadrons, as independent entities, in 1748; the Kingdom of Naples abolished its squadron in 1779 and Venice in 1797, when the old aristocratic republic fell; Sweden stopped building galleys in 1749, although it replaced them with other types of sailing and rowing boats; Russia kept some galleys in service until the early nineteenth century; the Kingdom of Sardinia kept one galley in operation until 1810, and built two more half-galleys in 1815 that it kept in service until 1836. Otto von Pivka, *Navies of the Napoleonic Era* (Devon: Newton Abbot, 1990), pp.196-197, 206-210; Ciro Paoletti, 'La marina sabauda dal 1798 alla Restaurazione', *Bollettino d'Archivio dell'Ufficio Storico della Marina Militare*, (2011), p.5; Giuseppe Tommaso Spinola, *Cronaca delle principali memorie relative all'Arsenale marittimo di S.M. Sarda in Genova* (Genoa: Unknown Publisher, 1837), p.38.
2   Henceforth, 'ship' will refer to specifically to full rigged sailing vessels of the period, as per the contemporary definition of ship.

therefore less than ideal for contemporary naval operations, which primarily took place along the coasts, and for operating in the Mediterranean, with its peculiar weather and sea conditions, a region of considerable importance.

Moreover, the restricted manoeuvrability of ships, which became especially clear when sailing in formation with other vessels, compromised their usefulness in the *guerre d'escadre*.[3] By contrast, it was precisely the manoeuvrability and the small draft of the galleys that made them perfect for Mediterranean operations, as they were the only type of vessel capable of moving easily between the numerous islands and inlets, of patrolling the coast, of carrying out rapid amphibious assaults, and of disengaging from battle even in the absence of wind. But, while limited in its usefulness in the Mediterranean, the ship was able to deploy its full potential on the oceans, where its firepower, combined with the ability to exploit the consistent winds and its ample operational autonomy, gave it a key role in European expansion and in the wars waged by the principal Atlantic and northern European powers: between the fifteenth and sixteenth centuries ships and caravels made a crucial contribution to the Portuguese success in the Indian Ocean; the Spanish fleets that shuttled along the Atlantic routes between America and Europe were mainly formed by galleons; the wars in the Baltic — which involved the Scandinavian monarchies, the trading city of Lübeck and Poland — were fought by combined fleets of ships and galleons; finally, ships and galleons were also the main weapons in the clash between Spain and England, which culminated in the failed invasion of the kingdom of Elizabeth I in 1588, and in the consequent disaster for the 'Invincible Armada'.

In the fifteenth century Mediterranean ships had essentially established themselves, at an operational level, in a support and defensive capacity; during naval campaigns they served as part of the logistical force that followed the fleet, while during battles they were positioned in front of the galleys in order to use their artillery power to break through enemy formations. Then the fight between galleys ensued: the 'ram' (a protruding iron rostrum at the end of the bow) was used to immobilise opposing vessels so that they could be boarded and their crews overpowered. However, naval battles such as Zonchio (1499) and Preveza (1538) highlighted the extreme difficulty of getting ships and galleys to work together. During the latter, fought on 27 September 1538, the difficulty of manoeuvring ships within a combined fleet became clear: after the defeat and retreat of the galleys of the Holy League, some Spanish-Venetian ships and galleons were unable to remain in formation, and were attacked by numerous Ottoman galleys. While proving themselves firm in defence, some ships, having become separated from the rest of the formation, were captured or sunk.[4] Even so, between the second half of the sixteenth century and the early years of the seventeenth, a number of important innovations started to tip the balance in favour of the ship: Iberian builders on the Atlantic coasts developed the galleon, a type of sailing ship that finally

---

3   This type of 'over-the-horizon' war was fought between large naval formations in more or less decisive battles. While the major naval powers were able to choose between the *guerre d'escadre* and the *guerre de course*, depending on their preferred strategies and the enemy they were facing, the smaller states were often forced to opt for the second path, granting corsair licenses to captains of private ships tasked with causing as much damage as possible to the opposition's maritime trade.

4   Guido Candiani, *I vascelli della Serenissima. Guerra, politica e costruzioni navali a Venezia in età moderna, 1650-1720* (Venice: Istituto Veneto di scienze, lettere ed arti, 2009), pp.7-8.

seemed to offer good manoeuvrability without compromising firepower, making it both an effective merchant vessel, thanks to its high load capacity, as well as a formidable warship.

In northern Europe, meanwhile, the Dutch were the first to construct a fleet of sailing ships with wide-ranging operational capabilities, while also introducing the tactic known as 'line-of-battle' combat. Although it is still debated, it seems that the first military use of this formation was in the Battle of the Downs in 1639, fought by a Dutch formation against a Spanish fleet. In 1653 the English navy codified the 'Fighting Instructions', which established the use of 'in line', or 'line of battle' deployment for the fleet; in a short time this type of formation became a staple of European naval tactics, influencing naval design and leading to a clear but previously absent distinction between ships used for military purposes and merchant vessels, even though the latter could be adapted for use in war.[5] The Eighty Years War (1568–1648), waged by the rebel United Provinces against Spanish rule, was the fundamental test bed for the construction of a new type of sailing unit of about 300 tons armed with around 40 guns, which became known as 'frigate'. This ship, with its low sides and refined lines, was used successfully against the heavy galleons of the Iberian fleets on several occasions, proving its worth. The construction qualities of the Dutch frigate also made it capable of adapting to the particular conditions of the Mediterranean, and the infamous Barbary States of Algiers, Tunis and Tripoli were among the first to appreciate its potential. The new type of ship seemed able to meet the needs of corsairs thanks to its high degree of autonomy, which made it possible to carry out raids over a wider range, while its powerful armament and smaller crew made it superior to the other vessels used up to that point. In the early seventeenth century, the Barbary States co-opted some unemployed Dutch, and possibly English, privateers and acquired their naval know-how. The result was the gradual but substantial evolution of their fleets towards the decisively greater use of sailing ships – the Venetian sources call them 'bertoni' – rather than oar-propelled craft. This resulted in prolonged operational use even in the winter season and in a much wider range of action than the previously used rowing vessels, which had been strongly limited by their coastal use, the need for good weather conditions, the shallowness of their sides and their inability to contain large quantities of supplies. The Algiers fleet alone, the largest of the Barbary fleets, numbered 35 galleys and 30 galliots in 1571, but in 1624 contained around 100 'round vessels' and only six galleys. Other sources tell of an Algerian fleet which, in the sixteenth and seventeenth centuries, could call on a naval force composed of various types of vessels numbering 60 and 80 units.[6]

The Italian states and the Ottoman Empire were instead more reluctant to abandon the use of galleys as the nucleus of their fleets. The Republic of Venice was probably the first Italian power to develop its own shipbuilding industry focused on the construction of large warships, conscious of the fact that to maintain dominance of the seas against the Barbary States and Ottomans it was necessary to supply its armed forces with the most modern

---

5   Candiani, *I vascelli*, p.115; Geoffrey Parker, *La rivoluzione militare* (Bologna: il Mulino, 2014), pp.176-177; Arturo Pacini, 'Le marine italiane', in P. Bianchi-P. Del Negro (eds), *Guerre ed eserciti nell'età moderna* (Bologna: Il Mulino, 2018), p.292.
6   Alberto Tenenti, *Venezia e i corsari, 1580-1615* (Rome: Laterza, 1961), pp.73, 88; Salvatore Bono, *Corsari nel Mediterraneo* (Milan: Mondadori, 1993), pp.89-94; Marco Lenci, *Corsari. Guerra, schiavi, rinnegati nel Mediterraneo* (Rome: Carocci, 2006), p.113.

technical and operational solutions (which did happen, albeit incrementally and sometimes with unsatisfactory results). The Ottoman Empire followed the example of its traditional rival with some delay, only beginning to build sailing ships in 1649.

Whereas the establishment of the sailing ship as the primary vessel of navies took place during the seventeenth century – first in northern Europe, then in the Mediterranean – it was in the eighteenth century that, in a far from linear way, naval warfare underwent a transformation and the European states reorganised their military apparatus. That century saw the definitive formation of permanent navies, comprising battle fleets of ships of the line and smaller vessels (such as frigates, sloops, brigs, but also galleys, galliots and half-galleys, as well as a certain number of armed mercantile vessels) in charge of maritime policing, commerce-raiding, and other auxiliary operations. It is important, however, to note that not all Mediterranean states followed the same path to establishing their own complement of ships.

While the major powers favoured the development and maintenance of national fleets based on a formation divided between ships and galleys (like Venice, which created the new 'Armata grossa' composed of ships, to go alongside the traditional 'Armata sottile' made up of galleys), the smaller states chose to encourage the development of private shipbuilding for the construction of merchant vessels equipped with a good number of cannon, chartering them from their owners in times of greatest need. This was the approach of the Republic of Genoa: in 1651 the government of the Republic decided to form a small sailing ship squadron – defined as 'squadra delli vascelli tondi' or 'nuovo armamento' by the Genoese sources of the period – composed of at least four differently rated vessels, commissioned for construction in the Dutch shipyards on the island of Texel. After many years of escort service to the convoys, organised by the Republic, which shuttled between Genoa and Spain, it became impossible to support the economic burden of a naval fleet of ships and galleys; therefore, the Genoese government decided to incentivise the establishment of private shipyards along the Ligurian coast (particularly around Sampierdarena, Foce and along the western coast), capable, even starting from the 1680s, of fitting out and launching a large number of well-armed merchant ships that could defend themselves when on a voyage.[7]

The military and naval history of the Republic of Venice is one dominated by its fleet of galleys and with the successes it achieved in the many naval campaigns of the Middle Ages and the early modern age. This was a well-organized and large fleet, about which much scholarship been written, and which will not be dealt with here. The focus of this study will instead be the sailing component of the Venetian navy, the aforementioned *Armata grossa*,

---

7   Giacomone Piana, 'La squadra del Commendatore de Langon: cavalieri di Malta su vascelli genovesi nella guerra di Corfù (1716)', in Josepha Costa Restagno (ed), *Riviera di Levante tra Emilia e Toscana. Un crocevia per l'Ordine di San Giovanni* (Genova-Bordighera: Istituto Internazionale di Studi Liguri, 2001) p.238. On Genoese shipbuilding between the seventeenth and eighteenth centuries see the interesting work by Luciana Gatti, 'Le navi di Angelo M. Ratti "imprenditore" genovese del XVIII secolo', *Quaderni del centro di studio sulla storia della tecnica del Consiglio Nazionale delle Ricerche*, 18 (2001) and the recent study by Paolo Calcagno, 'Un arsenal en dehors de la ville. La construction des vaisseaux de guerre sur la plage du ponant de Génes (seconde moitié du XVIIe siècle)', in Caroline Le Mao (ed), *Les Arsenaux de la Marine. Du XVIe siècle à nos jours* (Paris: Sorbonne Université Presses, 2021), pp.163-164.

and the role that it played during the Second Morean War (1714–1718).[8] Although the brunt of this conflict was borne by Venice's public fleet, a certain number of vessels armed by other Christian powers – described as 'auxiliaries' by contemporary sources[9] – augmented the navy of the Republic between 1715 and 1717. The ancient Order of Malta supplied four ships in 1715-1716 and two in 1717. In 1716 Pope Clement XI had the idea, albeit unsuccessful, of chartering five private merchant ships '*armate in guerra*' (equipped for war), and entrusted their command to the knight-officers of the Order of Malta. Philip V of Spain provided a squadron of six ships in 1716, placed under the command of the Genoese patrician Stefano de Mari. Finally, between 1716 and 1717 the Kingdom of Portugal sent a powerful formation of 11 vessels, including ships, *brulotti* (fire ships), and minor craft.

The auxiliary ships provided by the Order of Malta and the Republic of Genoa are the most significant for this historical study, first because the production and operations of their forces are better documented, and second because the Maltese were the most active auxiliary component during the conflict, participating in three of the four years of the war. The papal contingent, while used with little success only during the Corfu campaign of 1716, was commanded by some of the knight-officers who served on the ships of the Order and who had already collaborated with their Venetian colleagues in the 1715 campaign.[10]

In the course of its long naval history, the Republic of Venice made frequent use of warships propelled exclusively by sail, but up to the seventeenth century their presence was rather sporadic, and did not follow a linear progression. It is possible to fix the starting point of the development of a sailing component in the War of Candia (1649–1665), or even earlier, in the Adriatic crisis surrounding the Duke of Osuna, Viceroy of Naples (a semi-official conflict fought between 1616 and 1620). In the years of the crisis, Venice made extensive use of chartered ships – in particular Dutch and English ones – in order to establish an elite squadron as a means of countering the Spanish-Neapolitan squadron composed of numerous galleons. During the war, Venice deployed a fleet of about 40 warships, of which only two were public, presumably the *Santa Maria Torre di Mar* and *Padre Eterno* galleons. The construction of these two galleons had begun in the early seventeenth century, but had been delayed due to high costs. They were finished only in 1617, entering service the following year.[11] After the end of the crisis and the consequent dismissal of all the foreign units that had made up the core of this high seas fleet, the Republic chose both to encourage

8   In English Historiography, this conflict is often referred to as the Seventh Ottoman–Venetian War.

9   The term was used by the Venetians to refer to all the Christian states that supported the war in the Levant with finance or manpower, even though they were not officially at war against the Ottoman Empire nor were formally allied to Venice.

10   One of these knights, Afranio Petrucci, wrote a detailed account of the Order's naval campaigns during the conflict, compiling the squadron's activities into a manuscript titled '*Diario di viaggio 1715–1717*'. Piana, 'La squadra del Commendatore de Langon', p.168; Anton Quintano, *The Maltese-Hospitaller Sailing Ship Squadron 1701-1798* (PEG: San Gwann, 2003), pp.161, 287, 289-292; Mauro Difrancesco, *Sotto la croce di Malta: le campagne navali dell'Ordine di San Giovanni nelle memorie del cavaliere fra' Afranio Petrucci, maggiore dei vascelli (1715-1717)* (Viareggio: La Villa, 2023), forthcoming.

11   The *Santa Maria Torre di Mar* had 36 cannons, 32 of which were large-calibre, while the *Padre Eterno* had 26 cannons, 23 of which were heavy. Candiani, *I vascelli*, pp.12-14.

private shipbuilding, by offering subsidies, and to follow an approach based on charters, which had proved successful and relatively inexpensive.

However, there was no equivalent initiative for the creation of a pool of publicly owned vessels. At the outbreak of the War of Candia, Dutch units, whose ships and crews were particularly valued, were once again chartered, along with English ones, while the only private Venetian ship deemed suitable was the *Madonna della Salute* (a 50-gun vessel): a clear indication that the Venetian shipbuilding industry had not reached the level of quality required for the construction of large sailing ships.[12] The long conflict over Candia saw the deployment of two distinct naval formations: while galleys and galleasses made up the traditional *Armata sottile*, the numerous chartered vessels were brought together in the new *Armata grossa*, which was quite distinct from the former not only because of the type of craft, but also for the composition of its crews: the sailors and soldiers of the *Armata sottile*, composed of state units, were mostly Venetian subjects, while the sailing ships, formed from private units, were almost exclusively manned by foreign personnel. The extensive use of foreign units, however, aroused concern within Venetian political and military circles, and also risked undermining the prestige of a city with ancient naval traditions. Little by little, the idea was gaining ground of creating a brand-new battle squadron made up of state ships, which could still have been augmented by chartered units, but in a decidedly reduced number compared to the past.

However, the navy with which Venice fought the First Morean War in 1684 was very different, being the product of an impressive shipbuilding programme that took place between 1675 and 1683: 'Having abandoned the policy of chartering armed merchant ships for both reasons of costs and of the evolution of the military fleet, the Serenissima had undertaken the construction of its own battle squadron of warships, and also adopted the new tactic of the line of battle.'[13]

After the War of Candia, even Constantinople recognised the urgent need of establishing a modern programme of naval rearmament and focused decisively on the construction of large sailing ships and on the preparation of highly trained crews. There was an appreciable qualitative leap during the First Morean War: the new fleet of 'sultanas',[14] with a large number of Barbary vessels sailing alongside, was able to keep up with the Venetian counterpart, winning some battles and offsetting the balance of power on the sea. Ultimately, while the Venetians were defeated in the War of Candia but still managed to re-establish their supremacy on the sea, the first war for the Morea turned the situation on its head: the two navies were once again equal in qualitative terms, but the fleet of sultanas had considerably increased in number, a factor that would decisively influence Venice's strategic decisions in the opening stages of the Second Morean War.

---

12   The policy of state subsidies for the construction of large sailing ships had already been enacted by the Venetian Senate at the end of the fifteenth century, and resumed in the seventeenth century. Candiani, *I vascelli*, pp.5, 18-19.

13   Candiani, 'Vele, remi e cannoni: l'impiego congiunto di navi, galee e galeazze nella flotta veneziana, 1572-1717', in Guido Candiani, Luca Lo Basso (eds), *Mutazioni e permanenze nella storia navale del Mediterraneo secc. XVI-XIX* (Milan: Angeli, 2010), p.150.

14   A term generally used to refer to ships in the Ottoman imperial fleet.

Organisation of the *Armata grossa* between the two Morean Wars

In the years of peace between the two Morean Wars, the Venetian authorities had to determine how best to manage the fleet of national ships still in service in 1699. They had to decide how many ships to keep active, which to disarm, and which type to prioritise. The majority of the *Capi da Mar* (the highest-ranking officers of the fleet) were in favour of keeping the smallest ships (the second and third-rate vessels) in service, those best adapted to the task of policing the Adriatic and for hunting down the corsairs who infested its waters, while a few large, first-rate units would serve as flagships. The Senate fixed the number of ships to retain in service at 16 of the 29 still active, of which four were first-rate, five were second-rate and seven third-rate, but the composition of the various squadrons – of the *Golfo*, or rather the Adriatic, of the lower Ionian and of the Morea – was not defined, as neither was their operating function.

Furthermore, certain problems of a structural nature – it was discovered, for example, that the covered aquatic construction areas of the Arsenal were not high enough to accommodate the larger ships – jeopardised the prospects of the *Armata*, and when the number of ships in service reached the planned quota of 16 in 1701, almost all were first-rate, while most of the smaller vessels were already laid up. It was thus necessary to use the large ships for purposes other than what was originally intended – the hunt for corsairs and patrol of the Adriatic – thereby subjecting them to wear and tear that led to losses, so much so that only 12 units remained in service by 1714, just a year before the war against the Ottomans reignited.[15]

At the end of the war most of the sailors returning to Venice were unable to collect their pay for the service they had rendered. The huge accumulation of debts and inability to immediately pay the veterans was exploited by the government of the Republic in order to persuade the sailors to remain in Venice, with the promise that they would be compensated in due course when the credit slips issued to them during the conflict could be cashed in. In this way the Republic sought to create a pool of valuable veterans, already highly trained at the state's expense, who could be readily recruited for future operations.

However, this financial policy risked driving many families into severe hardship, pressuring the sailors to sell their credit slips to profiteers, often at a huge loss, or to emigrate for a better life. This affected the Venetian government in two negative ways: not only did it lose men who had undergone arduous training, but the public debt accumulated during the conflict remained completely or mostly untouched. Furthermore, the Venetian failure to institutionalise a permanent corps of manpower benefited the navies of the main foreign powers – France, Holland, Britain and Spain – which often offered better conditions of engagement, above all to experienced and technically trained men: 'The profession [...] operated in a restricted and therefore particularly competitive market, where navies vied with each other to acquire the services of seafarers of any origin.'[16]

In addition to the sailors, the role of officers was also impacted by the lack of a framework clearly defined by the state structures. Venice suffered from the effects of placing its

---

15   For information on the size of the Venetian public fleet and for further details on its organisation between the two wars of the Morea, see Candiani, *I vascelli*, pp.415-420.

16   Candiani, *I vascelli*, p.426.

long naval tradition firmly in the hands of the urban patriciate, which guarded it jealously. But members of the Venetian aristocracy belonged to the political class and during their careers held numerous civil and military offices, and thus became increasingly distant from that figure of the professional and specialised military man that was establishing itself in other European navies, which were already consolidating around a category of officers well-integrated within state structures and distinct from their merchant counterparts.[17]

While the patricians, or noblemen, held the most prestigious appointments, the role of ship's captain was given to men who did not belong to the nobility, a factor which prevented them from rising to higher positions and which made their appointment precarious: they were in fact dismissed when their ships returned to Venice. While the patricians and captains were part of the higher officialdom – referred to as the 'stato maggiore'[18] – lower officialdom was instead composed of officer-sailors of lower social backgrounds, specialised in the various on-board duties and from whose ranks the ship captains were drawn.

After having mentioned the numerical and organisational situation of the ships and crews of the Armata grossa, it is necessary to briefly introduce the matter of the construction of new ships and the new model of rigging first introduced in 1712. In the years from 1700 to the Second Morean War, Venetian policy was essentially focused on the construction of a certain number of large, first-rate ships to maintain the fleet's efficiency and to form effective battle squadrons, in keeping with the logic of the guerre d'escadre. As that policy was being applied an initiative to renew the ships' rigging was being championed by the patrician Fabio Bonvicini.[19] From 1700 to 1702, Bonvicini presented a text to the Senate concerning the strictly technical aspects of construction and the management policy of public ships, but his proposals were rejected, mainly because of the increase in costs that the reforms would have entailed. However, Bonvicini's ideas were not completely discarded, but were in fact presented again in 1711.

The main criticism of the existing system – summarised at the beginning of this section – concerned the delays in payment and the captains' mismanagement of their crews. There was also an emphasis on the persistent dual role of staff officers, who should have been 'of the navy and soldiers, not of trade and traffic.' The system proposed by Bonvicini had certain identifiable, non-negotiable points, namely making the captain responsible for military functions alone, while economic matters, catering and the procurement of goods, were assigned to two publicly appointed scriveners, where previously the position was the prerogative of the captain who would appoint only one of them. Bonvicini also proposed

---

17   On the training of officers serving in the main European navies and on the professionalisation and bureaucratisation of their role, see Glete, Warfare at Sea, pp.71-83.

18   While the differences between the Venetian and foreign navies were significant when it came to the organisation and management of 'stato maggiore' officers, those relating to the 'sailor-officers', that is, the lower officers, were not so big. Candiani, 'La gestione degli equipaggi nei vascelli veneziani tra sei e settecento', in Alessandra Dattero, Stefano Levati (eds), Militari in età moderna. La centralità di un tema di confine (Milan: Cisalpino, 2006), pp.171-195.

19   Fabio Bonvicini (1660–1715) came from a family from Rovato, in the province of Brescia, which became part of the Venetian patriciate during the War of Candia by purchasing a noble title, a practice which had been established above all to replenish the state coffers in times of greatest need. Candiani, I vascelli, pp.249-250, 457; Giacomo Diedo, Storia della Repubblica di Venezia dalla sua fondazione sino l'anno MDCCXLVII (Venice: stamperia di Andrea Paoletti, 1751), vol. IV, p.104.

an increase of officers and the division of sailors into three classes. The new system was tested on the *Corona*, a ship built according to technical instructions outlined by Bonvicini himself, but it was extended to other ships in the same category only in 1714, after which it served as the paradigm for all first-rate ships.[20]

Auxiliaries: The Squadron of the Order of St John and the Papal-Genoese Vessels

In the early eighteenth-century Malta began to modernise its navy by means of the formation of a sailing ship squadron. Compared to other states in Europe and the Mediterranean the decision to establish its own complement of sailing ships was overdue, and it had become urgently necessary in order for the island to be capable of repulsing attacks by the many high-sided ships that made up the fleets of the Barbary States and of the Ottoman Empire. The adoption of sailing ships by the Maltese navy, however, actually dated back to the sixteenth century, when it made occasional use of large carracks well equipped with artillery to transport goods and foodstuffs.[21]

The seventeenth century also witnessed the use of ships and galleons, albeit still on an occasional basis, with only a few units and in fact sometimes just one.[22] This ended up undermining the formation of a permanent squadron of sailing ships until the beginning of the eighteenth century, as the specific tasks of the Maltese navy – privateer warfare and maritime policing – rendered heavy galleons unsuitable. The history of the Maltese sailing ship squadron began in all probability in 1697, when a knight with strong maritime experience and particular interest in the introduction of sailing ships, Raimondo Perellos y Roccaful, was elected Grand Master.[23]

Three years later, on 31 March 1700, Perellos appointed a committee to examine the idea of rigging a certain number of vessels that would comprise the new squadron. In January 1701, the knights of the committee declared themselves in favour, thus allowing the creation of a new squadron to sail alongside the traditional galleys. The new squadron's organisation partly followed the model adopted by the galleys starting from 1596. By 1701 the Congregation of the Vessels had already been established, as a parallel to the Congregation of the Galleys. Similar to what happened in other Mediterranean navies, the Maltese one remained faithful to tradition, ensuring that the rank of Captain General of the Galleys remained higher than the Lieutenant General of the Vessels: the latter had the role of second in command whenever the two squadrons had to operate together.[24] Once the establishment of the squadron was decided, the authorities of the Order initially turned to the famous Coulomb family of Toulon, renowned for its shipbuilding projects. Francois

---

20   Candiani, *I vascelli*, pp.463-476.
21   Francesco Frasca, 'La squadra dei vascelli dell'Ordine di Malta', *Rivista Marittima*, 4, (2016), pp.68-74.
22   'Before 1701 the Order's navy had already had sailing warships in commission, but these were few and single units, never organised into a squadron; and although they were heavily armed, their presence had mainly been for transport rather than bellicose purposes'. Quintano, *The Maltese-Hospitaller*, p.12.
23   Quintano, *The Maltese-Hospitaller*, p.36.
24   Giovanni Scarabelli, *La squadra dei vascelli dell'Ordine di Malta agli inizi del Settecento* (Taranto: Centro Studi Melitensi, 1997), pp.50-51.

Coulomb (1654–1717) was commissioned to build at least two vessels: the *San Giovanni*, with 64 cannon and 440 crewmen, and the *San Giacomo*, with 58 cannon and a crew of 392.[25] A third ship, named *Santa Caterina*, equipped with 56 cannon and a crew of 392 men, was built directly in Malta with the contribution of French workers.[26] A vessel classified as a 'magistral frigate' was fully financed by the Grand Master, fitted out in Malta and incorporated into the squadron in 1704 under the name of *Santissima Vergine del Pilar e San Giuseppe*. This latter vessel had a somewhat short life due to her bad construction: she was built in Malta by craftsmen previously used to make galleys, and their lack of experience in building such large vessels led to numerous defects that afflicted the frigate during its time in operation, such as the arrangement of the gun ports: the artillery pieces, which originally should have numbered 40, were reduced to 20 as the lower deck battery was never installed since the ports were too low relative to the waterline, and opening them would have brought the risk of flooding.[27]

The shipbuilding proceeded quickly, so that already by 1705 the Grand Master was able to preside over the ceremonial consignment of the new ships to the commendatore Fra Francoise Castel de Saint Pierre, who was placed in command of the squadron. The vessels became fully operational soon after and began their patrols of the Mediterranean. In the years between the formation of the initial nucleus of the new squadron and the Second Morean War, some of the units were decommissioned and replaced by other vessels, as was the case with the *San Giuseppe*, which was substituted in 1706 by the *Santa Croce*, another ship in the same category.[28] This had a rather short life, given that by 1714 its place in the squadron had already been taken by the new vessel *San Raimondo*, which was also classified as a frigate and armed with 40 cannons and crewed by 307 men. The Order took part in the first two years of the war, when the complete squadron was placed under the orders of the knight commander Jean-Francois de Chevestre Cintray, while in 1717 both the *San Giovanni* and the *San Giacomo*, deemed no longer seaworthy, were laid up. The final naval battle in the Levant was thus fought by a reduced Maltese contingent, being able to deploy only the *Santa Caterina* and the *San Raimondo* frigate while the 'Balì' of the Order,[29] Jacques-Auguste Maynard de Bellefontaine, took command of the squadron, including all the other auxiliary vessels.

---

25   Rif Winfield, Stephen S. Roberts, *French Warships in the Age of Sail, 1626–1786. Design, Construction, Careers and Fates* (Barnsley: Pen and Sword, 2017), pp.130, 139.

26   Scarabelli, *La squadra dei vascelli*, pp.39-46.

27   Joseph Muscat, *The Maltese Vaxxell – The Third Rates of the Order of St. John 1700-1798* (Pietà: Pubblikazzjonijiet Indipendenza, 2000), p.6.

28   This was *La Rosa*, the former flagship of the privateer fleet of Tunis, which was captured on 3 May 1706 off the Peloponnese. Despite the lack of information on this vessel it is known that, after being refitted in Malta, it was equipped with 36 guns, twelve-pounders in its first battery, and eight-pounders in its second. It replaced the *San Giuseppe* in 1710. Tommaso Braccini, *Afranio Petrucci, Giornale di viaggi 1705-1709* (Pistoia: Spazzavento, 2005), p.1.

29   The rank of Balì, as well as those of Commodore and Gran Croce, were honorary titles; moreover, the Balì title was conferred on holders of important military commands. Bellefontaine had reached the top of the French navy, and his appointment as lieutenant-general of all the auxiliary squadrons derived from an apostolic brief from Pope Clement XI dated 23 April. Candiani, *I vascelli*, p.545.

In the course of its history, the navy of the Papal States included very few sailing units, but could count on a small nucleus of galleys and other rowing craft whose management was entrusted, starting from 1587, to the *Congregazione pro classe paranda et servanda ad Status Ecclesiastici defensionem*, a body similar to a modern ministry created by Pope Sixtus V in the context of the reorganisation of the ecclesiastical institutions via the bull *Immensa Aeterni Dei*. The reorganisation of the papal naval component became necessary to repress criminal and smuggling activities as well as the continuous corsair assaults that plagued the Roman coast.[30] On the outbreak of the Second Morean War, having been told that the Ottoman navy was able to arm a mighty fleet of vessels, Pope Clement XI decided to equip his own squadron of ships. After having obtained the assent of the Order of Saint John to provide officers, an apostolic brief of 20 January 1716 declared the acquisition of four ships from private shipowners. The prior Fra Francesco Maria Ferretti,[31] governor-general of the papal galleys, oversaw negotiations and soon was able to charter the four vessels from Genoa,[32] placing them under the orders of the knight-commander Fra Adrien de Langon, and other Maltese officials. Thanks to the study carried out by Giacomone Piana, we know that the vessels chartered in Genoa were the following: *Nostra Signora del Monte e Sant'Antonio*, with 50 cannon and under the command of Captain Giovanni Antonio Oneto; the *Nostra Signora della Speranza e Sant'Antonio da Padova*, also known as the *Burlandina*, with 50 cannon and under Captain Giovanni Maria Isola; the *Porco Spino*, with 44 cannon, captained by Pietro Maria Boero, and the *Nostra Signora della Guardia*, also known as the *Molinari*, with 32 cannon under Giovanni Battista Molinari.

The fitting out of the ships was completed by early May 1716 and the squadron sailed from Genoa on the 9th or 10th of that month, arriving in Civitavecchia on the 19th. After having taken on board the infantry contingents and equipment, the squadron set out towards Malta on 1 June, where it moored on the 28th, joining a fifth papal unit from Ancona. This last was the vessel *Fenice Risorta*, also referred to as the *Fenice d'Oro*, *Fenice Rinnovata* or *Radì*; a large ship armed with 62 cannon. During the 1716 campaign it was placed under the command of the Knight Hospitaller de Sabran. According to Petrucci's diary it may have been chartered in Venice.

Once the squadron reached the island of Corfu, the Venetian commanders strongly criticised the Genoese ships, as did the Maltese knight-commanders. Petrucci declared the Papal-Genoese squadron to be 'too weak to be sent into the armada, both for its quality and for the strength of the ships, which were more suited to commerce than war.'[33] All the Genoese ships, with the exception of the *Fenice*, which was put into the line of battle, were disarmed or relegated to auxiliary tasks, with the best elements of the ship's company being transferred to the Venetian ship *San Lorenzo Giustinian* and the *Fenice*.

---

30   Fabrizio Filioli Uranio, *La squadra navale pontificia nella repubblica internazionale delle galere: secoli XVI-XVII* (Ariccia: Aracne, 2016).

31   Francesco Maria Ferretti, Grand Prior of the Order of Malta and Governor-General of the Papal Galleys under Clement XI; Alberto Guglielmotti, *Storia della marina pontificia: Gli ultimi fatti della squadra romana, da Corfù all'Egitto, 1700-1807* (Rome: Tipografia Vaticana, 1893), pp.4-5.

32   Piana, 'La squadra del commendatore de Langon', pp.247-248.

33   Mauro Difrancesco, *Sotto la croce di Malta* (publication pending, pagination unavailable).

The Papal-Genoese squadron nevertheless remained in the zone of operation until early September 1716, returning to Malta on the 21st of the same month before then being dispersed. The experience of the 1716 campaign had considerable repercussions for the relationship between Pope Clement XI, who was aware that the effort to establish the squadron of ships had proved particularly expensive and of very little use, and the Venetians, who reproached the pontiff for having squandered precious resources that could have been better used as financial support for the Serenissima.[34]

Naval Warfare Between 1715 and 1718: Strategy, Objectives, and Results.

The final part of this chapter is dedicated to an analysis of the strategic and operational foundations underlying Venetian action in the naval war of 1715–1718, and of certain organisational and tactical details that emerged during the course of the conflict. The war of 1684–1699, despite having given Venice a new possession, had also forced it to make a considerable financial sacrifice to make good the drastic conditions of the Kingdom of Morea. The need to install an effective administration, upgrade its defences and encourage economic recovery came to weigh heavily on the Republic's finances, which were already drained by the recently concluded conflict. The financial, as well as the diplomatic, situation was made even worse by the outbreak of the War of the Spanish Succession (1701–1713). Resorting to a policy of neutrality, Venice did not side with either of the opposing blocs (the French and Spanish kingdoms on one side, the English, Dutch, Austrian and Piedmontese on the other), and thereby ended up politically isolated and burdened by the costs of maintaining a substantial military force to ensure its territorial integrity in the domains of the mainland. What is more, in the early eighteenth century a severe food crisis made Venice's weakness even more evident.

The Ottoman Empire, on the other hand, appeared to have largely recovered from the defeats suffered in the previous century. The reconstitution of its military power was such that it had enabled a clear victory in the Russo-Ottoman War of 1710–1711, through which the Sublime Porte recovered the city of Azov and control of the Black Sea, as well as considerable international prestige.[35] Massive land and naval preparations for hostilities against Venice were already under way as early as spring 1714, to be completed in the December. The pretext for launching an offensive was the capture of a Turkish vessel accused of piracy by Venetian shipping, to which Sultan Ahmed III reacted by declaring war and starting military operations.

The 1715 campaign saw the Ottoman forces take the initiative in a decisive way, and while the army, calculated at between 80,000 and 120,000 men, breached the Morea via the Isthmus of Corinth, the navy provided communications and logistical support from the sea. Although it is by no means easy to reconstruct the extent of the naval forces that Istanbul deployed during the conflict, the imperial fleet was to appear as a grand sight: Roger C. Anderson reports the figures of 48 ships of the line, 30 galleys, 70 galliots, and five fireships;

34   Piana, 'La squadra del Commendatore de Langon', p.258.
35   Nicholas Dorrel, *Peter the Great Humbled: The Russo-Ottoman War of 1711* (Warwick: Helion & Co., 2018).

Map of the Levant during the last Second Morean War (1715 – 1718), showing the Venetian dominions and the places where the battle fleets of the Republic and the Ottoman Empire faced each other. (George Anderson © Helion and Company 2023)

Mario Nani Mocenigo, a historian of the Venetian navy, provides the same numbers with some negligible differences in the number of galleys and galliots; Candiani instead mentions 40 vessels (sultanas), 12 armed merchant ships, the same number of Barbary ships, and five fireships, to which must be added about 20 galleys, 30 galliots and 60 fuste (light galleys).[36] As Dyonisios Hatzopoulos has written, 'The Ottoman Navy, under efficient command,

---

36   Roger Charles Anderson, *Naval Wars in the Levant (1559-1853)* (Princeton: Princeton University Press, 1952), p.244; Mario Nani Mocenigo, *Storia della Marina Veneziana da Lepanto alla caduta della Repubblica* (Rome: Ufficio Storico della Regia Marina, 1935), p.318; Candiani, *I vascelli*, p.498-499.

imposed its presence in the Aegean'[37] and used its sheer numerical strength to crush any attempt by the Venetian fleet to oppose the invasion. The cities of the Morea, protected by modern fortifications but defended by an insufficient number of troops, could not withstand the assault and gradually fell, one after the other: Corinth was captured on 2 July, Nauplia on the 20ht, while Modon capitulated on 17 August and Malvasia on 7 September. Other cities and fortresses were simply abandoned.

On the maritime front the first Venetian fortress to be overthrown was the island of Tinos, where a sizeable contingent of troops disembarked on 5 June, obtaining the garrison's surrender with a promise of immunity; the islands of Aegina and Cerigo fell soon after. In the hope of receiving reinforcements from the sea, the fortresses of Souda and Spinalonga, the last bastions of the ancient Venetian dominion on the island of Candia (Crete) prepared for a siege, but were forced to concede defeat on 23 September and 7 October respectively, with no Venetian ship ever appearing on the horizon. The total success of the land and naval operations of 1715 was a clear sign of a skilfully prepared and implemented Ottoman strategy: while the army conquered the Venetian fortresses in the Morea, the fleet had to ensure supplies to the troops, transport heavy equipment and contingents assigned to occupy the islands, while all the time keeping open lines of communication and maintaining control of the sea against possible incursions by the Venetian fleet.

For its part, Venice sought to safeguard its battle fleet by using it as little as possible, but was unable to protect its possessions when they came under attack. At the start of the war, the Venetian patrician Daniele IV Dolfin, appointed *Capitano Generale da Mar* (the commander-in-chief of the navy), was aware that the number of ships at his disposal was greatly inadequate, but had argued that it was necessary to attempt to defend at least Modon. He therefore moved the *Armata grossa* towards the fortress. The relief efforts, however, were frustrated by bad weather and by the Ottoman fleet, which was firmly positioned along the coast to prevent any access from the sea. After the fall of the stronghold, Dolfin retreated towards the Ionian Islands, thinking only of keeping the fleet intact in case the Turks tried to break open the gates of the Adriatic, whose defensive cornerstone was the island-fortress of Corfu.

Nevertheless, a desperate attempt to engage the enemy fleet was made in October, after receiving the reinforcements of some new Venetian vessels and four Maltese ships. On 13 October Dolfin, in agreement with the council of the Capi da Mar, launched an incursion intended to take the joint Venetian-auxiliary fleet into the South Aegean.[38] However, by then the advanced season and treacherous winds of the Aegean made it inadvisable to continue beyond the island of Cerigo, where, however, the Maltese abandoned the campaign and returned home. On this last part the sources differ substantially; although the Venetian ones speak of the abandonment by the auxiliaries as a 'surprise', Petrucci's diary sheds a

---

37   Dionysios Hatzopoulos, 'An Overview of Naval Strategy during the 1714–1718 War between the Ottoman Empire and the Venetian Republic', *Nuova Antologia Militare*, 3:1 (2022), p. 317.

38   Mocenigo states there were 22 ships, 33 galleys, two galleons and 10 galliots, while Candiani estimates that the sailing component of the fleet was about 30 vessels, between the Venetians and the Maltese auxiliaries. A further source comes in the form of the handwritten diary of Petrucci, which reports the presence of 33 sailing units between the public ships, armed merchant ships and Maltese vessels, 15 of which were Venetian, five Maltese, four Papal and two Tuscan, as well as two galleys, eight galliots and 16 brigs. Nani Mocenigo, *Storia della Marina Veneziana*, p.318; Candiani, *I vascelli*, p.501; Difrancesco, *Sotto la croce di Malta*.

The city of Corfu with its fortifications at the beginning of the eighteenth century and, at anchor, Venetian vessels and galleys; artist unknown. (Public Domain)

different light on the matter: the intention to disengage from the Venetian fleet, at least as regards the Maltese vessels, had previously been made known to Dolfin, alongside a request for supplies that were never forthcoming. Moreover, Petrucci mentions the possibility that the Venetian *Capitano Generale* had deliberately hidden the news of the loss of the final Venetian strongholds in the Aegean from the auxiliary commanders, which he had become aware of well before them. Dolfin refrained from passing on the terrible news before starting the offensive, fearing that the auxiliaries would somehow feel authorised to return to their bases and abandon the campaign, considering that the reason for which they had joined in the war effort, the defence of the Morea, had now failed. It is plausible that the Venetian commanders – and Dolfin in particular – then wrote their own reports on the disastrous 1715 campaign, and attempted to offload part of the responsibility for the failed operation onto the shoulders of the auxiliaries, who supposedly abandoned the campaign for their own reasons, leaving the Venetian fleet at the mercy of superior Turkish forces.[39]

If the first year of the war had ended in disaster, 1716 began with foreboding, for a new Ottoman offensive was a launched towards the island of Corfu, and if that stronghold were to fall, the entire defensive system of the Ionian Islands would collapse, opening the way to the Adriatic for the Turks. In the early days of July, the Ottoman fleet ferried an army of around 30,000 men from the coast of Albania to the island opposite, beginning the disembarkation without opposition. The Venetian fleet, under the command of the new *Capitano Generale* Andrea Pisani – Dolfin had been replaced the year before – was further south, between Corfu and the strait that separated Zakynthos from Cephalonia.

---

39   Difrancesco, *Sotto la croce di Malta.*

The *Capitano Generale da mar* Andrea Pisani; he replaced Daniel IV Dolfin at the end of the 1715 campaign and remained in charge until the end of the war, in 1718. (Public Domain)

This was the position of the *Armata grossa* of the *Capitano Straordinario delle Navi* (commander) Andrea Corner and the *Capitano Ordinario* (second-in-command) Ludovico Flangini, to whom we will return later. On 8 July, after they had sailed back up the coast, Corner marshalled the ships in battle formation and engaged the enemy fleet in the Straits of Corfu, managing for a time to interrupt the lines of communication between Albania and the army besieging the island. On 20 August, just as Pisani was preparing a new attack, a violent storm broke out and damaged both fleets, but mostly the Ottoman one, forcing the invading army to abandon the siege. Re-embarkation operations began on 22 August without the Venetian fleet being able to oppose them since it was held back by unfavourable winds. By the time Corner's ships finally managed to form a line of battle, the Turks were already retreating to the north.

After debating whether to pursue the enemy or sail south to block the path to its bases in the Aegean, Pisani opted to let the *Armata sottile* stop in Corfu to replenish its provisions, while Corner's and Flangini's ships set out to hunt down the enemy fleet. But precious time had been lost and it was too late to intercept the Turks. The indecision shown by the Venetian commanders caused particular discontent among the Maltese knights, who were eager to meet the enemy in battle. Petrucci, in his memoirs, writes that the Venetians seemed minded to let the Turks withdraw, while it would have been more appropriate to attack them during the re-embarkation operations, in the moment of their greatest vulnerability: 'the Venetian lords seemed more inclined to build them a golden bridge, and to widen the passage, rather than block their retreat'. [40]

Despite missing the opportunity for a decisive battle that could have inflicted significant losses on the Ottoman fleet, Venetian naval forces had at least finally been able to confront their adversary, at times taking the initiative and managing to re-establish a certain balance

---

40 Difrancesco, *Sotto la croce di Malta.*

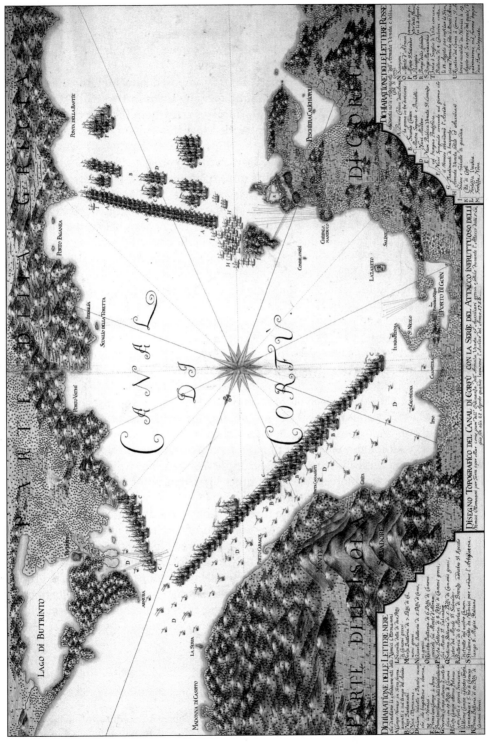

Contemporary topographic map of the Corfu channel during the siege of 1716: we can see the Ottoman-Barbary fleet (left) and the Venetian one together with the auxiliaries (right). (Public Domain)

between the two fleets. The 1716 campaign thus ended with a substantial reversal of fortunes on the part of the Serenissima, which in the following year would seek to exploit the advantage gained by pursuing a concentrated offensive strategy in which its ships and galleys were used to their full potential.

At the end of 1716, the council of the *Capi da Mar* proposed launching the offensive in the following spring, dividing their forces and deploying them in two main operations: after dismissing the idea of using galleys and galleasses so early in the year in the treacherous waters of the northern Aegean, it was decided that the *Armata sottile* would attack the Ottoman strongholds in Albania, while the ships of the *Armata grossa* would set sail no later than April towards the Strait of the Dardanelles in order to block it and thus preempt the exit of the Ottoman fleet, preventing it from joining the Barbary vessels and integrating its crews with the Greek sailors of the Aegean. Despite the intentions of the Venetian commanders, the fleet lacked sailors and officers and it was not possible to deploy full crews until late April, thus compromising the chance to enter the Aegean before the Turks had completed their military preparations. Some members of the council therefore called for the cancellation of the planned offensive, but a large group of commanders was still convinced of the merits of a direct attack on the Dardanelles: they would have moved the theatre of battle to the enemy's home waters, at the same time removing the danger for the Venetian bases in the Ionian.

The main supporter of the offensive was the newly promoted *Capitano Straordinario delle Navi* Ludovico Flangini (1677-1717), who had replaced Corner as the commander of the *Armata grossa* and who it is necessary to consider briefly. Like the unfortunate Bonvicini, Ludovico was a new arrival into the ranks of the patriciate, and had linked his career prospects to his service in the *Armata grossa*, making a passionate contribution to it and bringing to it his distinctive tactical approach (as Bonvicini had done on the organisational level); his premature death was certainly a heavy blow and, together with that of Bonvicini in 1715, weighed heavily on the organisational, managerial and tactical development of the public ships of Venice.[41] Although opposed by the *Capitano Generale* himself, Flangini obtained permission to set off with his ships to blockade the Dardanelles, while Pisani remained in the Ionian awaiting reinforcements from other Christian powers. During the voyage, Flangini issued a series of instructions aimed at improving the *Armata grossa*'s effectiveness: he drew up an order of battle divided into three divisions, each distinguished by a colour – red for that of the *Capitano Stroardinario* in overall command of the forces; yellow for the central division under the command of the *Almirante*;[42] and blue for those of the *Capitano Ordinario* in command of the rearguard – but he also divided these into two further 'squadrons' of two units each, thus creating a fleet of six smaller formations that could offer greater tactical flexibility in battle. A fourth division was added when the Maltese and Portuguese auxiliary vessels joined the Venetians near Cape Matapan, forming a powerful fleet which, according to Petrucci, included 'up to 60 [units] without including lateen sails; and with

---

41   Ludovico di Girolamo Flangini was born in Venice to a family originating from Cyprus. Candiani, *I vascelli*, pp.501, 515, 538, 544.

42   This was the third-highest rank in the *Armata grossa*, after the *Capitano Straordinario* and the *Capitano delle Navi*.

the *Armata sottile* that appeared in the evening with 23 other small ships we were close to a hundred sails'.[43]

In addition to this, Flangini called for improved training of gunners and crews to prepare the men and ships for the battles which they would have to undertake sooner or later. While the ships stopped in Zante, a *Libro d'Ordini* (Book of Orders) was also published. Its four parts covered ships orders, orders and warnings while in port, orders while in navigation and in battle, and orders for use at night. It contained 44 articles, which corresponded to a specific signal communicated with its relative flag.[44]

The hopes of catching the Turks in a state of unpreparedness were finally shattered when the *Armata grossa* reached the island of Imbros on the evening of 8 June and weighed anchor while awaiting news of the opposing fleet. When the exploratory ships discovered the Turks anchored in the Dardanelles, they reported seeing over 30 sultanas, as well as some Barbary units, a sign that the Venetian offensive manoeuvre had failed to prevent the latter from joining up with the Ottoman fleet. The *Armata grossa* therefore found itself involved in two clashes (on 12 and 16 June) in the northern Aegean – between the island of Imbros, the Chalkidiki peninsula and the Dardanelles – that were as bloody as they were inconclusive, if not for the painful loss of Flangini himself, who was wounded during the battle of 16 June and died six days later while directing the ships to attack again.

After Flangini's death command passed to the *Capitano Ordinario* Marcantonio Diedo, who withdrew to Cape Matapan, in the Laconian Gulf, where he could shelter the fleet from enemy attacks and await the arrival of reinforcements under the command of Pisani, which appeared at the beginning of July. A few days later the Turkish fleet also arrived in front of Cape Matapan, but without giving signs of wanting to attack. Only on 19 July, when the Venetians and auxiliaries once more set sail towards the Aegean, did the Turks bar their passage and engage in battle. In addition to the Venetian vessels, there were the Maltese *Santa Caterina* and *San Raimondo* and a powerful Portuguese squadron under the command of Lopo Furtado de Mendoça, first count of Rio Grande, made up of seven vessels of different rates, two fireships, a fluyt and a transport tartane.[45]

The *Armata sottile*, which during the clash found itself in the wake of the *Armata grossa*, made no contribution, but rather found itself driven against the coast, risking annihilation, which forced Diedo to constantly change course in order to protect it, thus preventing him from achieving any significant success against the Ottomans. The galleys, which the ageing Bellefontaine would have liked to have employed actively, proved incapable of working with the modern vessels, which were often concerned with protecting the former and were thus unable to devote all their attention to fighting enemy ships. At the end of the battle, both the public ships and the sultanas once again recorded enormous damage and human losses, but even in this instance it was not possible to declare an outright winner, and

---

43   Difrancesco, *Sotto la croce di Malta*.
44   The order of battle written by Flangini is published in the work by Nani Mocenigo, *Storia della Marina Veneziana*, p.348, and is also cited by Candiani, who writes about Flangini's instructions in detail. It is also worth noting that Flangini's *Libro d'Ordini* came only a few years after the first example of such works, the *English Signal Book*, the earliest surviving copy of which dates back to 1711; Candiani, *I vascelli*, pp.539-540.
45   Difrancesco, *Sotto la croce di Malta*.

the 1717 campaign ended shortly afterwards when both fleets returned to their bases. The final operations consisted of a few amphibious assaults conducted exclusively by Pisani's *Armata sottile* against the coast of Epirus, thanks to which some coastal strongholds were conquered, including Preveza (23 October) and Vonitsa (2 November).

The year 1718 saw only one major battle in the waters between the island of Cerigo and the Laconian Gulf. After a series of manoeuvres aimed at identifying the enemy and finding a favourable position, the two fleets (26 public ships against 36 sultanas, as reported by Hatzopoulos),[46] made contact in the early afternoon of 20 July 1718 and the battle continued until the 22nd, pausing only during the night. After three days of intense fighting the two fleets disengaged, heading to their respective homes to repair the damage suffered. While the cannon still thundered in the eastern Mediterranean, on 21 July the Peace of Passarowitz was signed between Venice, Vienna and Istanbul, bringing an end to the conflict and returning the Morea to the Ottoman Empire. Venice had to settle for maintaining control over a number of strongholds in Dalmatia and regaining possession of Cerigo.

Conclusion

The strategies pursued by Venice and the Ottoman Empire during the Morean War derived from naval doctrines that mirrored each other in some ways, both being centred on the creation and maintenance of a sizeable fleet of large vessels essential for conducting large-scale operations against the adversary and for guaranteeing dominion of the sea, either by shows of force (as the Ottomans did in 1715) or by arriving at eventual clashes in a position to annihilate or severely undermine the fighting capacity of the enemy. In the first year of the war, and partly in 1716, Venice's naval strategy was in fact loosely based on the 'fleet in being' concept, in the hope that the mere existence of the fleet, anchored in the safety of its bases in the Ionian Sea, would be enough to influence Ottoman strategic choices, deterring any attempt to attack. This concept was theorised for the first time by Sir Arthur Herbert, Earl of Torrington (1648–1716) and the commander of the Royal Navy during the Nine Years War (1688–1697). Faced with a numerically superior French fleet cruising the English Channel, Torrington proposed not to engage the enemy except in situations of absolute superiority, while keeping the fleet safe in its own ports so that it could pose a constant threat to the French ships, which would be forced to keep the bulk of their forces in the area and thus be unable to deploy them elsewhere. The fleet in being strategy contrasts sharply with that of the 'command of the sea', which was based instead on the intensive use of the navy to annihilate the adversary and take control of lines of maritime communication by force.

The fleet in being concept, however, can be successfully applied only when naval forces are ready and able to strike the enemy's weak spots, such as their lines of communication, or to show up in force when the enemy is at a disadvantage. As we have seen, the theory, when used within the Venetian strategy, bore no fruit other than that of revealing the weakness and lack of confidence in the Republic's own naval assets – its fear of losing ships, which

---

46   Hatzopoulos, 'An Overview of Naval Strategy', p.329.

left the Ottoman fleet free to make a move towards the Adriatic, was always seen as a valid reason not to undertake risky operations – which allowed the Ottomans to conquer islands and strongholds practically unchallenged. The year 1716 might be considered a turning point, since from that moment, and thanks to the successful defence of Corfu, the Venetian commanders reverted to promoting an offensive strategy aimed at achieving command of the sea in the Levant, by fully committing their forces. The Venetian doctrine of the end of the seventeenth century involved keeping in service enough public ships to be able not only to control the whole of the Levant, by keeping the Ottomans and the Barbaries in a state of subjugation, but also to re-establish the ancient command of the sea on the regional level, so as to increase the Republic's power and its prestige among the other European states. [47]

The idea of sending the *Armata grossa* into the Aegean and challenging the Turks directly near the Dardanelles bases could certainly have produced results, but the offensive lacked adequate logistical support: it is interesting to consider what might have happened if, following behind Flangini and Diedo's ships, there had also been a force of transport ships and galleys capable of launching amphibious assaults against the islands in the archipelago. It seems obvious that merely trying to anticipate the moves of the Turks so as to prevent them threatening the Ionian islands would not enable the Venetians to gain dominion over the sea, especially if this aim was not inspired by the prospect of conquering islands and fortresses in the Aegean, wresting them from enemy hands and re-employing them as centres of operations that could permanently constrain the activities of Ottoman ports and other strategically important targets. And this is without forgetting that it was in fact Venice's inaction during the Turkish offensive of 1715 which led to the losses of the last Aegean bases that could have been vital support points for the refuelling and replenishing of the fleet.

The forward operating bases could also have been made use of by corsair ships that were sometimes armed and used against Ottoman traffic in the Levant, albeit with little success. In 1716, the Pope armed a frigate called *Concordia* in Genoa, granting it a corsair licence to prey on Ottoman shipping,[48] while in 1717, again in Genoa, the *Nostra Signora della Guardia e la Libertà* was given a crew of 118 men and 36 soldiers under the command of the Genoese nobleman Lelio Maria Priaroggia, a renowned seaman who sailed the Mediterranean both as a privateer and as an officer in the British Royal Navy.[49]

The ships suited to corsair warfare were also needed to escort convoys heading from Venice to the Ionian Sea, as well as to counter the piracy of the *Dulcignotti*, ancient subjects of the Ottoman Empire living in the Albanian cities of Ulcinj and Valona who carried out raids in the Adriatic. For this task Venice also sought to use some of the vessels of the Papal-Genoese squadron left idle after the 1716 campaign. Captains Oneto and Molinari were initially authorised by the Genoese government to charter its ships, as well as to hire 800 sailors, but the negotiations failed, chiefly because the Venetians could not guarantee compensation and insurance for any losses.[50]

---

47   Candiani, *I vascelli*, p.121.
48   Difrancesco, *Sotto la croce di Malta*.
49   Candiani, *I vascelli*, p.491; Gatti, 'Le navi di Angelo M. Ratti', pp.36-37.
50   Piana, 'La squadra del commendatore de Langon', pp.258-259.

Together with the other auxiliary squadrons, the Papal-Genoese force helped to swell the ranks of the *Armata grossa*, but a close analysis of the wartime effectiveness and the responsibility assumed by this 'extrinsic' component during the conflict, reveals a picture somewhat different from what the Venetians had probably expected: in the three years during which the Order of St John, the Papal States and the other powers (the kingdoms of Spain and Portugal in particular) supplied their ships for the war in the Levant, but the only battle they took part in was that of 19 July 1717, near Cape Matapan, where the vessels of the combined Lusitanian-Maltese squadron formed the reaguard, and when engaged by the division of the Kapudan Paşha Ibrahim Hogia managed to repel his attack.[51]

In 1715 the Maltese ships' belated appearance made little difference to the outcome of the naval campaign which was in any case conducted in the defensive and with the hope of minimising the loss of ships, as has already been described. The sole battle of 1716 saw only the *Armata grossa* in action, while the Maltese and Spanish auxiliaries arrived too late to take an active role in the defence of Corfu and the Portuguese squadron turned up after the campaign has concluded. The final campaign of 1718 was instead distinguished by the complete absence of auxiliaries for military, political or material reasons: the Venetian Capi da Mar were conscious of the fact that, although the squadrons provided by other Christian powers could help to swell the feet and thus impress the Turks, they nevertheless remained outside of their direct control, while for their part the auxiliary captains assumed they had plenty of room for manoeuvre within the joint fleet, an attitude that antagonised the Venetians and often led to resentment and friction that might have seriously compromised operations.

With the conclusion of the 1718 campaign the long history of Turkish-Venetian conflicts also ended, leaving the stage for the playing out of another drama, for which new actors had already appeared on the Mediterranean scene in preparation of ousting the local navies from their centuries-old dominion of the sea.[52]

Select Bibliography

Published Sources
Anderson, Roger C., *Naval Wars in the Levant (1559–1853)* (Princeton: Princeton University Press, 1952)

Bono, Salvatore, *Corsari nel Mediterraneo* (Milan: Mondadori, 1993)

Candiani, Guido, *I vascelli della Serenissima. Guerra, politica e costruzioni navali a Venezia in età moderna, 1650–1720* (Venice: Istituto Veneto di scienze, lettere ed arti, 2009)

Candiani, Guido, Lo Basso, Luca (eds), *Mutazioni e permanenze nella storia navale del Mediterraneo secc. XVI–XIX* (Milan: Angeli, 2010)

Glete, Jan, *Warfare at Sea, 1500–1650. Maritime Conflicts and the Transformation of Europe* (London: Routledge, 2002)

---

51   A native of Negroponte; in the past he had held the role of *kapudan*, that is to say the commander of the Ottoman navy; Candiani, *I vascelli*, p.541.

52   The War of the Spanish Succession had invested England as ruler of the Mediterranean trade routes – above all through its acquisition of numerous strategic bases such as the Rock of Gibraltar and the island of Menorca – while the Dutch and French still retained a presence but of much lower economic and military importance.

Guglielmotti, Alberto, *Storia della marina pontificia. Gli ultimi fatti della squadra romana, da Corfù all'Egitto, 1700–1807* (Rome: Tipografia Vaticana, 1893)

Mahan, Alfred T., *L'influenza del potere marittimo sulla storia* (Rome: Ufficio Storico della Marina Militare, 1994)

Nani Mocenigo, Mario, *Storia della Marina Veneziana da Lepanto alla caduta della Repubblica* (Rome: Ufficio Storico della Regia Marina, 1935)

Parker, Geoffrey, *La rivoluzione militare* (Bologna: il Mulino, 2014)

Quintano, Anton, *The Maltese-Hospitaller Sailing Ship Squadron 1701–1798* (PEG: San Gwann, 2003)

2

Spanish Use of Sea Power, 1731-1748

Albert C.E. Parker[1]

The Spanish navy in the long eighteenth century appears in English-language naval history mostly in discrete episodes in histories of the British Royal Navy, usually defeats, from the Battle of Cape Passaro in 1718 through Trafalgar in 1805. These defeats reinforce the 'Black Legend' based on sixteenth-century propaganda, that Spaniards were '*uniquely* cruel, bigoted, tyrannical, obscurantist, lazy, fanatical, greedy, and treacherous', not to mention cowardly, subject to most human vices.[2] An anonymous British Marine officer was not being complimentary when he wrote of British performance in the 1744 Battle of Toulon:

> [A] Stranger coming to look on at that Instant of Time, from the great Character we have acquired in maritime Affairs, and the contrary so much decry'd in the Spaniards, would have concluded the Spanish Ships by their Behaviour to be the English, and the English, from their Irresolution, want of Order, and bad Conduct, to be the Spanish ...[3]

1   The author wishes to thank Mark A. Campbell for his comments and suggestions on an earlier draft of this paper.

2   William S. Maltby, *The Black Legend in England: The Development of Anti-Spanish Sentiment, 1558–1660* (Durham: Duke University Press, 1971); Joseph P. Sánchez, *The Spanish Black Legend: Origins of Anti-Hispanic Stereotypes/La Layenda Negra Española: Orígines de los estereotipos antihispánicos* (Albuquerque: National Park Service, Spanish Colonial Research Center, 1990), p.7; Charles Gibson, *The Black Legend: Anti-Spanish Attitudes in the Old World and the New* (New York: Alfred A. Knopf, 1971), p.13; Philip Wayne Powell, *Tree of Hate: Propaganda and Prejudice Affecting United States Relations with the Hispanic World* (Albuquerque: University of New Mexico Press, 1971), p.11 (quotation, italics in original); John L. Robinson, 'Anti-Hispanic Bias in British Historiography', *Hispania Sacra*, 44:89 (January 1992), p.21. The 'cowardly' component of the Black Legend was an element of demands for war by Britain against Spain in the late 1730's: Philip Woodfine, *Britannia's Glories: The Walpole Ministry and the 1739 War with Spain* (Woodbridge: The Boydell Press, 1998), pp.130, 140, 201, 241.

3   Anon., *A Particular Account of the Late Action in the Mediterranean, with the Line of Battle of Both Fleets* (London, T. Tons, 1744), p.12. The twenty-first-century equivalent of 'character' here would be 'reputation'.

The Spanish line of battle in this action was not actually well formed, and a few ships left it without good cause, but the lieutenant was generally correct that a resolute but outnumbered and overmatched squadron did not act as the British expected: the ships stood their ground, closed up around their admiral, and beat off a British attack that was not pressed home. That 'Irresolution, want of Order, and bad Conduct' were characteristic of the Spanish navy expresses a long-standing theme in English-language naval history and popular literature.[4] But if the Spanish could not beat the British at sea, what was the purpose of their navy?

The impression given by British naval history that the Spanish mostly stayed in port, only occasionally emerging to be soundly defeated by the British Royal Navy, is based not only on some genuine British victories and on the Black Legend, but also on lack of knowledge of Spanish naval operations beyond the sight of British officers. In 1973, this could be blamed by a Spaniard on the paucity of Spanish naval history and by what little there was being unknown outside Spain.[5] In the past few decades, however, there has been a great expansion in eighteenth-century Spanish naval history, including operational history, permitting a much more complete assessment of the role and activities of the Spanish navy in the age of sail. Spanish naval operations between 1731 and 1748 demonstrate how a materially inferior navy was used to advantage even in a war against one twice its size.

In the eighteenth century, the Spanish navy was usually outnumbered by more than 2-1 by the British Royal Navy. In number of ships of the line or in total warship displacement tonnage, between 1720 and 1805 Spain had more than half the strength of the British less than a quarter of the time, and sometimes was less than 40 percent as large as the British by both measures.[6] Spain could not contend, on her own, with Great Britain for general mastery of the sea in large-scale fleet actions, and Spanish navy officers knew it.[7] France, also, was always in a position of material inferiority to the British.[8] With monarchs from the same dynasty and equal clashes of interest with Great Britain, the logical solution to the naval materiel problem for Spain and France was to combine their fleets. However, only during the War of American Independence did the Spanish and French navies cooperate effectively. Although France was friendly to and supportive of Spain during the war that began in 1739, she remained a neutral at sea until 1744. After the Battle of Toulon on 22

4   Lowell Newton, 'La Leyenda Negra y la historia de la fuerza naval española: Algunos comentarios', *Archivo hispalense*, 56:171–173 (1973), pp.219–232.

5   'A.C.', item on Newton in *Indice historico español (publicación cuatrimestral*, 19:67 (May-Aug. 1973), p.275.

6   Data from Jan Glete, *Navies and Nations: Warships, Navies and State Building in Europe and America, 1500–1860*, Stockholm Studies in History, 48:1–2 (Stockholm: Almqvist & Wiksell International, 1993), vol.1, pp.260, 268–269, 278, 280, 311, vol.2, pp. 376, 396 (Spanish strength exceeded 50 percent of British at four of 17 five-year intervals, not always at the same points for both measures). Tonnage limited to warships of more than 300 metric tonnes displacement, including ships of the line, frigates, sloops-of-war or corvettes, and mortar vessels, but not minor units.

7   Agustín Ramón Rodriguez González, 'Les objectifs de la marine espagnole', in Olivier Chaline, Philippe Bonnichon, and Charles Philippe de Vergennes (eds), *Les marines de la guerre d'indépendance américaine*, vol.1, *L'instrument naval* (Paris: Presses de l'université Paris-Sorbonne, 2013), p.141; María Boudot Monroy, 'Julián de Arriaga y Rivera: Una vida al servicio de la marina (1700–1776)' doctoral diss., Universidad Nacional de Educación a Distancia, [2005], p.195.

8   John Robert McNeill, *Atlantic Empires of France and Spain: Louisbourg and Havana, 1700-1763* (Chapel Hill: University of North Carolina Press, 1985), pp.77–78.

February 1744,[9] recriminations between French and Spanish naval officers and Spanish suspicions about French good will prevented naval cooperation, and Louis XV's unwillingness to support his navy financially reduced its ability to send its ships to sea. British attention to the French navy in strategic planning and operations did provide opportunities for a Spanish navy reduced by losses earlier in the war, which Spain duly exploited.

But if Spain could not wage a general war at sea against Britain with prospects of success, she still had uses for a strong navy, whether at war with Britain or not.

- When at war with Britain, Spain could exploit the British Royal Navy's inability to be in superior strength everywhere and all the time, exerting temporary local or even long-term domination of selected areas, to maintain important lines of communications.
- When not at war with Britain, Spain could use her navy, which was still the third strongest European navy, to carry out amphibious operations of strategic importance against nations with lesser naval power.

Exploiting British Limitations: The War of Jenkins' Ear

Between 1714 and 1739, disputes arose over British trade privileges with Spanish America and the manner in which Spain enforced its internal imperial trade regulations to prevent what it viewed as smuggling. These disputes led to a crisis between the two countries. In January 1739, Spain agreed to compensate Britain for questionable Spanish seizures of their vessels, partially offset by payment by the British South Sea Company of duties in arrears to the King of Spain. But when the South Sea Company balked at its payment, the Spanish government withheld its payment to the British government. To increase pressure on Spain, on 10 July 1739 the British government ordered the seizure of Spanish ships and their cargoes by navy ships and authorized the granting of letters of marque and reprisal to privateers. Britain had already authorized her American colonial governors to issue letters of marque and reprisal and had sent orders to the West Indies and Mediterranean to begin hostilities. When Spain still refused its payment, Great Britain declared war on 3 November 1739. The resulting 'War of Jenkins' Ear'[10] merged into the War of the Austrian Succession at sea after the French declaration of war on Great Britain in early 1744. For Spain, the war with Great Britain continued until news of the Peace of Aix-la-Chapelle reached America in early October 1748.

During the 1739–1748 war with Great Britain, the principal successful use of the Spanish navy was to maintain lines of communications in three areas:

---

9   The 'new style' Gregorian calendar, in use in Spain and 11 days ahead of the British calendar, is used here, even for British government decisions and British naval operations.

10   For an excellent summary of the causes of the War of Jenkins' Ear, see Paul W. Mapp, *The Elusive West and the Contest for Empire, 1713–1763* (Chapel Hill: University of North Carolina Press for Omohundro Institute of Early American History, 2011), pp.270–71. On the reasons for war in Great Britain, including other issues, Woodfine, *Britannia's Glories*.

- The Atlantic Ocean, for the transfer of government and privately-owned Spanish silver from America to Europe;
- The West Indies, for communications among the Spanish islands and the Florida outpost, and between them and mainland Mexico;
- The Mediterranean, where connections between Spain and her armies in Italy were maintained and communications with North African outposts had to be guarded against other threats.

Assuring the Trans-Atlantic Silver Flow

If the communications between Spain and America could be cut, and if, in particular, the Spanish galleons could be intercepted on their way out or home, or seized in Cartagena harbor, the remittance of the King of Spain's treasure would be stopped – and this had justly been one of the main objectives in every Anglo-Spanish war since the sixteenth century.[11]

The Spanish government's largest source of revenue was the ordinary customs duties, not silver from Peru and Mexico.[12] However, 'American precious metal ... help[ed] offset the deficits being run up elsewhere. It was in fact possible to balance the books precisely because of this monetary input.'[13] The King was entitled to 10 percent of everything mined in his domains; the rest of the silver was privately owned, mostly used to pay for imports to Spanish America, predominantly from France, but vital to the Spanish economy nevertheless. The silver was an important government and national resource that the Spanish navy went to considerable trouble to defend. British proponents of war argued in 1739 that capturing Spanish silver would make the war self-financing.[14]

The British had three ways to achieve the strategic economic objective of interfering with or even 'stopping' the Spanish trans-Atlantic silver flow. They could:

---

11   Richard Pares, 'War and Trade in the West Indies, 1739–1748', *Revue d'histoire des colonies*, 20:85 (January–February 1932), p.52. For a more extensive statement, based on the War of the Spanish Succession (1701–1714), but equally applicable to the 1739–1748 war, Shinsuki Satsuma, *Britain and Colonial Maritime War in the Early Eighteenth Century: Silver, Seapower and the Atlantic* (Woodbridge: The Boydell Press, 2013), pp.47–48.

12   Stanley J. Stein and Barbara H. Stein, *Silver, Trade, and War: Spain and America in the Making of Early Modern Europe* (Baltimore: The Johns Hopkins University Press, 2000), p.232. Of the specie imported into Spain, 1736–49, 95.6 percernt was silver, 4.3 percent was gold: Antonio García-Baquero González, *Cádiz y el Atlántico (1717–1778): El comercio colonial español bajo el monpolio gaditana* (Seville: Escuela de estudios hispano-americanos de Sevilla, 1976), vol. 2, p.251. Hereafter, 'silver' includes small amounts of gold, not separately accounted for in general studies of the specie flow.

13   Agustín González Enciso, 'A Moderate and Rational Absolutism: Spanish Fiscal Policy in the First Half of the Eighteenth Century', in Rafael Torres Sánchez (ed.), *War, State and Development: Fiscal-Military States in the Eighteenth Century* (Pamplona: Ediciones Universidad Navarra, S.A., 2007), p.129.

14   Philip Woodfine, 'Ideas of Naval Power and the Conflict with Spain, 1737–1742', Jeremy Black and Philip Woodfine (eds), *The British Navy and the Use of Naval Power in the Eighteenth Century* (Atlantic Highlands, N.J., Humanities Press International, Inc., 1989), pp.71–73; Woodfine, *Britannia's Glories*, pp.174–176.

- Seize a port where Spanish silver accumulated before shipment to Europe; Havana and Cartagena de Indias were the most important.
- Capture eastbound shipments of silver on the high seas.
- Prevent the shipment of mercury, vital to silver refining in Mexico,[15] from Spain to America. (Peru had mercury mines, but the Mexican mines produced the majority of American silver by the eighteenth century).

Capturing Spanish Silver Ports

The British tried to capture Spanish silver ports in America during the early stages of the war. Vice-Admiral Edward Vernon seized Porto Bello, Panama, in 1739, but there was little silver there. The largest European army sent to the West Indies to date spectacularly failed to capture Cartagena in 1741, with heavy loss of life to disease. Remnants of the expedition made unsuccessful attempts on Santiago de Cuba and Panama.[16]

Intercepting Spanish Treasure at Sea

The defense of Cartagena was a military operation to which sailors on shore contributed; protection of eastbound silver or westbound mercury in the Atlantic was a naval matter. Table 1 shows the flow of Spanish silver across the Atlantic during the war.[17] The amounts for captures are probably too low, but available immediate reports often give only the value of an entire cargo without specifying how much of that was gold and silver. Although only 34 percent of the specie shipped between 1739 and 1748 went in naval ships or convoys escorted by warships, 42 percent of the specie that reached Spain or its allies (including specie landed directly in France) crossed the Atlantic under the auspices of the navy, and 68 percent of the 'King of Spain's treasure' arrived in navy ships and convoys. None of the gold and silver committed to the navy's care was lost to enemy warships or privateers. The dispersed private shipments were much riskier: by value, over a quarter were captured by

---

15   Marqués de la Ensenada (navy minister) to Duque de Huéscar (Spanish ambassador to France), 9 November 1747, in Didier Ozanam and Diego Téllez Alarcia, *Misión en Paris: Correspondencia particular entre el Marqués de la Ensenada y el Duque de Huéscar (1746–1749)* (Logroño: Govierno de La Rioja, Instituto de Estudios Riojanos, 2010), p.336: 'without this material there is neither silver nor Indies'.

16   Richard H. Harding, *Amphibious Warfare in the Eighteenth Century: The British Expedition to the West Indies, 1740–1742* (Woodbridge: The Boydell Press, 1991), is the modern English-language study from the British point of view.

17   García-Baquero González, 'Remesas', pp.229–230, 239–243; Michel Morineau, *Incroyables gazettes et fabuleux métaux: Les Retours des trésors américains d'après les gazettes hollandaises (XVIe–XVIIIe siècles)* (Cambridge: Cambridge University Press, 1985), pp.372–385. Ship-by-ship details in García-Baquero González, 'Remesas', pp.239–243 and Morineau, *Incroyables gazettes*, pp.373–374, 384–385. García-Baquero González broke down the official data according to whether the arriving silver belonged to the Royal Treasury or to individuals. His 'proposed final numbers', including his corrections from Morineau for all years for which he made revisions except for 1742, were used here, including corrections from the official figures for 1740, 1741, 1743, and 1747. Captures are 'arrivals' in Britain according to Morineau, *Incroyables gazettes*, pp.376–377 (1741–1745 only), plus one capture in 1739 and one in 1742. It is assumed that the Spanish official records were accurate concerning the King's own silver and all of García-Baquero González' corrections have been added to his tabulations of specie arrivals owned by individuals.

British privateers or warships. However, the navy's complete success reduced the overall loss rate to about one-sixth. If Royal Treasury silver constituted the same percentage of captures as it did of private shipments that got through, the King lost only 585,500 pesos to capture, or 10.1 percent of Royal Treasury shipments. The British were thus a long way from 'stopping' 'remittances of the King of Spain's treasure' between 1739 and 1748. The King's 14 percent share of the 'private' funds, plus the King's own silver (10 percent of everything mined), amounted to over 12.3 million pesos, and the silver transported across the Atlantic during the war would have paid for all or nearly all of the navy's budget.[18] Given the role of American silver in the Spanish economy and Spanish government finances, providing almost 20 percent of the government revenues in the pre-war years,[19] the maintenance of the wartime movement of Mexican silver from Veracruz to Spain was an important but unrecognized naval victory of the war of 1739–1748, one that required both daring and resourcefulness. How did the Spanish navy achieve its 100 percent success rate?

Table 1: Known Trans-Atlantic Transfers of Spanish-American Silver and Gold, 1739–1748

	Amount (pesos)	Percent of all specie shipped	Percent of specie reaching Spain
Silver and Gold Shipped from America			
By navy ships and convoys	23,353,500	34.7	42.4
By independent ships	43,955,700	65.3	
Reached Spain or allies	32,607,700	48.4	57.6
Captured by British	11,348,000	16.4	
Total	67,309,200	100.0	100.0
Specie Reaching Spain and Allies			
Royal Treasury	5,266,700	7.8	9.4
In navy ships and convoys	3,569,000	5.3	
Belonging to individuals	50,694,400	75.3	90.6
Total	55,961,200	83.1	100.0

Note: '1739' data from August–December only, when British orders to seize Spanish shipping were in effect.

Including the period of rising tensions in the summer of 1739 when the British were trying to ambush *Jefe de Escuadra* José Pizarro's convoy, the Spanish navy made seven trans-Atlantic silver transfers in warships or in merchantmen under navy convoy (Table 2).[20]

18   Didier Ozanam, 'La politica exterior de España en tiempo de Felipe V y de Fernando VI', translated by José Luis López Muñoz in Francisco Cánovas Sánchez, et al., *La época de los primeros Borbones*, Part 1, *La nueva monarquía y su posición en Europa (1700–1759)*, Vol.29, Part 1 of Ramón Menéndez Pidal and José María Jover y Zamora, *Historia de España* (42 vols in 61 parts; Madrid: Espasa-Calpe, 1935–2005; vol. in 1985), p.469; González Enciso, 'Moderate', pp.122, 129.
19   Christopher Storrs, *The Spanish Resurgence, 1713–1748* (New Haven: Yale University Press, 2016), p.105.
20   García-Baquero González, 'Remesas', 239–41.

Table 2: Spanish Navy Trans-Atlantic Silver Transport Operations, 1739-1748

Port of Origin	Arrival Port	Arrival Date	Commander; Ships	Amount of Silver (pesos)*
Havana	Santander	14 August 1739	Pizarro; *Léon* (70), *Guipúzcoa* (60), *Castilla* (60), *Esperanza* (50)	5,209,300
Buenos Aires	Ferrol	14 April 1740	*San Esteban* (50), *Hermiona* (50)	158,500
Veracruz/Havana	Cadiz	25 July 1743	*Conde de Chinchon* (frigate)	679,300
Havana	La Coruña	5–9 Jan. 1745	Torres; *Glorioso* (70), *Castilla* (60), *Europa* (64), and convoy	10,282,600†
Buenos Aires	Corcubión	20 January 1746	Pizarro; *Asia* (64)	572,400
Veracruz	Corcubión	14 August 1747	*Glorioso* (70)	3,910,300
Havana	Cadiz	9 Jan. 1748	Castelain; *Reina* (70) and convoy	2,541,100
Total				23,353,500

Notes:

* For consistency, amounts are from García-Baquero González, 'Remesas', pp.239–241, and may differ from amounts given elsewhere from other sources. Values may include gold and un-minted silver but do not include merchandize or products such as cochineal and indigo, often also carried in 'silver' convoys.

† Unofficial estimates of the value of this convoy range up to 12 million pesos (Morineau, *Incroyables gazettes*, p.374).

Spanish combat strength on these voyages was always less than what the British could assign to interception. Therefore, besides carrying silver in warships or escorting merchantmen, the Spanish navy took additional measures to ensure its safe arrival:

- Use of outports. Only two of the convoys arrived at the usual peacetime silver port, Cadiz. Two arrived at Ferrol, another naval base, or its nearby commercial port, La Coruña. One came in to Santander, and two shipments were landed at the small, remote port of Corcubión in northwest Spain. The Ferrol battle squadron escorted the 1746 shipment from Corcubión to Ferrol;[21] *Glorioso*'s silver was put ashore at Corcubión and moved overland.[22]
- Evasive routing. In 1739, Pizarro, warned at the Azores about British squadrons lurking off Cape Finisterre and Cape St Vincent, went all the way to Ireland and then to Santander.[23]

---

21   Jorge Cerdá Crespo, 'La guerra de la oreja de Jenkins: Un conflicto colonial (1739–1748)', (Doct. diss., University of Alicante, 2009), p.314; Francisco de Paula Pavía y Pavía, *Galeria biografica de los generales de marina, jefes y personajes notables que figuraron en la misma corporación desde 1700 á 1868* (Madrid: F. Garcia, y Ca. Mayor, 1873–1874), vol.3, p.193.

22   Agustín Pacheco Fernández, *El 'Glorioso'* (3rd ed., [Valladolid], Galland Books Editorial, 2016), pp.133–144.

23   Baudot Monroy, 'Julián', p.198; Cerdá Crespo, 'Guerra', p.81; Dionisio de Alsedo y Herrera, *Piraterías y agresiones de los ingleses y otros pueblos de Europa en la América española desde el siglo XVI al XVIII*, (ed. Justo Zaragoza) (Madrid: Manuel G. Hernández, 1883), pp.318–319

• Mid-ocean rendezvous. Elaborate arrangements were made to meet the very valuable Torres convoy at the Azores with French battle squadrons based at Cadiz.[24] These arrangements were unsuccessful,[25] as was an attempt by the Ferrol squadron to meet Pizarro in 1746, but the incoming convoys made port without interception.

Only one of these navy shipments was attacked by British warships. In 1747 *Glorioso* beat off an accidental interception by a British convoy escort off the Azores and a small force off Corcubión.[26]

Defending the Spanish Mercury Shipments
Westbound mercury shipments escorted by the navy were suspended between 1740 and 1747, although there was at least one private shipment which was intercepted. Therefore, the Spanish navy put together a mercury convoy in late 1747 and added over 20 merchantmen. The British navy sent out two small squadrons under Rear-Admiral Sir Edward Hawke and Captain Thomas Cotes to intercept it. Cotes found it on 18 March. The convoy commander, *Jefe de escuadra* Francisco de Liaño, bluffed Cotes into thinking the escort was much more powerful than was the case; Cotes captured five merchantmen but did not molest the mercury, which reached Veracruz on 2 June, boldly passing Jamaica before the British commander there knew of the convoy.[27]

Protecting Lines of Communications in the West Indies
Although Spain could not seize and keep control of the Atlantic Ocean or escort regular convoys across it, she had enough ships of the line and other warships to keep open some of the sea lines of communications among her American possessions, especially among Florida and the Antilles.

---

24   Baudot Monroy, 'Julián', pp.249–50; Cerdá Crespo, 'Guerra', pp.305–06.
25   Clément de Taffanel, 5th Marquis de la Jonquière, *Le Chef d'escadre M[arqu]is. de la Jonquière, gouverneur général de la Nouvelle-France et le Canada de 1749 à 1752* (Paris: Garnier Frères, 1896), pp.61–62; V[incent] Brun, *Guerres maritimes de la France: Port de Toulon, ses armaments, son administration, depuis son origine jusqu'à nos jours* (Paris: Henri Plon, 1861), vol.1, pp.306–308; [François Marie Joseph Georges] Costet, *La Communications de la France avec ses colonies des Antilles pendant les guerres de succession d'Autriche & de sept ans (1744–1763)* ([Paris], École supérieure de guerre navale, [1929]), p.15.
26   Pacheco Fernández, *El 'Glorioso'*, has the most detailed account of the 1747 voyage of Glorioso, but for the encounter off the Azores, Robert Kirke, *Minutes of the Proceedings of a Court-Martial Held on John Crookshanks, Esq, formerly Captain of His Majesty's Ship the Lark* (London: S. Bladen and S. Leacroft, 1772) is essential. Less detailed treatments: Agustín Ramón Rodríguez González, 'La gesta del Glorioso', *Revista general de marina*, May 2001, pp.613–617; Agustín Ramón Rodriguez González, *Victorias por mar de los españoles* (Madrid, Grafite Ediciones S.L., 2006), pp.177–184; Cerdá Crespo, 'Guerra', pp.320–325; Román Piñón Bouza, 'El *Glorioso*, un navío que hizo honor a su nombre', *Revista general de marina*, 243:8–9 (Aug.–Sept. 2002), pp.383–389; León Arsenal and Fernando Prado, *Rincones de historia española* (Madrid, EDAF, 2008), pp.225–235. There is no published English-language account of the whole voyage except a chapter in the author's *All the Seas of the World: The First Global Naval War, 1739–1748* (Helion & Company, forthcoming), vol.2, ch.10.
27   John Amrhein, *The Hidden Galleon: The True Story of a Lost Spanish Ship and the Legendary Wild Horses of Assateague Island* ([Kitty Hawk, N.C.]: New Maritima Press, 2007), p.311.

During the War of Jenkins' Ear (1739–1743), the British and Spanish battle squadrons *de facto* divided control of West Indian waters. The Spanish stayed out of the Caribbean Sea itself, south of Cuba, Hispaniola, and Puerto Rico, and west of the Windward and Leeward Islands, but the British did not send their ships of the line into the Gulf of Mexico or north of the Antilles, except when they were escorting a homebound convoy through the Windward Passage between Cuba and Hispaniola. This division of the West Indies protected three Spanish lines of communications:

- Between Veracruz, Mexico, and Havana, Cuba;
- Between Havana and St. Augustine, Florida;
- Between Havana and the eastern Greater Antilles, Santo Domingo and Puerto Rico.

The battle squadron at Havana also served as a 'fleet in being', pinning the British Jamaica squadron at Port Royal and preventing it from undertaking operations against Spanish America after the failure of the 1741–1742 expedition at Cartagena, Santiago, and Panama, and an unsuccessful attack from the Leeward Islands on Venezuela in 1743.

The most important of the American lines of communications was between Mexico and Havana. Peruvian silver remained cut off from Spain by British occupation of the Caribbean, except for independent merchantmen that tried to make the crossing all the way from the Pacific or from Buenos Aires. However, if Mexican silver could get to Havana, it could be shipped to Spain. Mexico also provided important support for the naval base at Havana and its garrison, including silver to pay the troops, food, and masts.

Spanish ships of the line and large 50-gun 'frigates' were usually used to carry the silver, and sometimes even the masts. They could be met off the southwest coast of Florida by the serviceable ships of the Havana battle squadron, in case of a British interception attempt from Jamaica.[28] This happened only once, at the very end of the war, and brought on the Battle of Havana on 12 October 1748.

Between 1740 and 1748, Spanish navy warships made at least 10 voyages, one or two per year, between Veracruz and Havana.[29] At least seven of these voyages carried over 18 million pesos (almost £4 million) to Cuba, mostly for transshipment to Europe.[30] One of the Havana-Veracruz voyages carried the *Capitán General* of Cuba, newly promoted to Viceroy of New Spain.

The boundary between Georgia and Florida had been a secondary issue during the 1730s, and during the early years of the War of Jenkins' Ear Britain and Spain each made attempts

---

28   Ignacio José de Urrutia y Montoya, 'Teatro histórico, jurídico y politico militar de la isla Fernandina de Cuba y principalmente de su capital La Habana', [unpub., 1791], in Rafael Cowley and Andrés Pego, (eds.), *Los tres primeros historiadores de la isla de Cuba* (Havana: A. Pego, 1876–1877), vol.2, p.367; Antonio de Acedo, *Diccionario geográfico-histórico de las Indias occidentales o América* (Madrid: Manuel González, 1789), vol.5, p.186.

29   Based on mentions in operational ship histories in Gómez Cañas, *Historiales*; Cerdá Crespo, 'Guerra', pp.284–285; Pacheco Fernández, *El 'Glorioso'*, p.117.

30   It is known that the second voyage of 1744 carried silver, but not how much. The other three voyages might have carried small amounts. The total in the six voyages where the amounts are known is 17,970,000 pesos. Pound sterling conversion based on exchange rate for peso coins, since most of the silver was in that form.

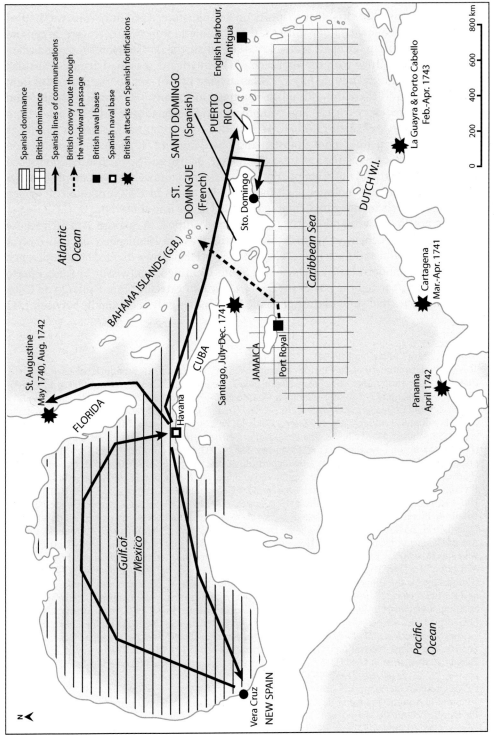

The war of Jenkins's Ear in the West Indies: Britain versus Spain 1739-1748. (George Anderson © Helion and Company 2023)

on the other's outposts. The first British attack on St Augustine, April–July 1740, was baffled by the presence of shallow-draft Spanish craft in the inland waterway that were larger and more heavily armed than the boats available to the British; the invasion force retreated when offshore support withdrew with the approach of the hurricane season. A fruitless Spanish counterattack on Georgia in June–July 1742 was covered by two ships of the line out of sight of British officers and therefore of English-language historians.[31] Transports for the land forces included three navy frigates and two of the Havana squadron's prizes, crewed from the ships of the line. A British raid in 1742 included four small navy warships as well as eight colonial vessels; neither it nor a mostly land-based raid in 1743 made an impression on Castle San Marcos, St Augustine's fortress. Thereafter, British and Spanish attention turned elsewhere. The Spanish did not attempt another attack on Georgia, but their supply convoys to St. Augustine were not molested,[32] although a false alarm in 1747 prompted an armed convoy of light vessels manned by stripping the ships of the line at Havana.[33]

Cuba was not the only island or isolated mainland outpost in Spanish America whose connections with the centers of Spanish power in the Western Hemisphere depended on at least occasional local sea control. East of Cuba stretched Hispaniola, divided between French Saint-Domingue (modern Haiti) and Spanish Santo Domingo, and wholly Spanish Puerto Rico. French ships carried the pay of the Santo Domingo garrison from Santiago de Cuba in 1741,[34] but France had ships of the line in the West Indies only occasionally between 1742

---

31   Baudot Monroy, 'Julián', pp.240–241.
32   This very brief summary of the Florida campaigns is based on J[ulian] G. Braddock, *Wooden Ships – Iron Men: Four Master Mariners of the Colonial South* (Charleston, S.C.: VJB Press, 1996), p.45; Cerdá Crespo, 'Guerra', pp.127–130, 290–291; John Charnock, *Biographia Navalis; or, Impartial Memoirs of the Lives and Characters of Officers of the Navy of Great Britain, from the Year 1660 to the Present Time* (London: R. Faulder, 1794–1798. repr. Uckfield, East Sussex. Naval & Military Press, [ca. 2005]), vol.4, p.58; William Laird Clowes, *The Royal Navy, A History from the Earliest Times to the Present* (London: Sampson Low, Marston and Company, 1897–1903, repr. New York, AMS Press, 1967), vol.3, pp.268–270; James P. Herson, Jr., *A Joint Opportunity Gone Awry: The 1740 Siege of St. Augustine* (Fort Leavenworth, Kans.: U.S. Army Command and General Staff College, 1997); Larry E. Ivers, *British Drums on the Southern Frontier: The Military Colonization of Georgia, 1733–1749* (Chapel Hill, University of North Carolina Press, 1974), pp.92–134, 151–183; Salvador Larrúa-Guedes, 'La Batalla de Bloody Marsh: Una victoria de la Florida española durante la guerra de la oreja de Jenkins', *Camino real*, 2:3 (2010), pp.89–105, 96–97; David F. Marley, *Wars of the Americas: A Chronology of Armed Conflict in the New World, 1492 to the Present* 2nd ed. (Santa Barbara, Cal.: ABC-Clio, 2008), vol.1, pp.381–387; W.E. May, 'His Majesty's Ships on the Carolina Station', *South Carolina Historical Magazine*, 71:3 (July 1970), pp.162–169; H[erbert] W. Richmond, *The Navy in the War of 1739–48* (Cambridge: At the University Press, 1920), vol.1, pp.6–7, 31, 50–51; W. Roy Smith, *South Carolina as a Royal Province, 1719–1776* (New York: The Macmillan Company, 1903), pp.188–191; Phinizy Spalding, *Oglethorpe in America* (Chicago: University of Chicago Press, 1977, repr. Athens, University of Georgia Press, 1984), pp.110–150; *The Spanish Official Account of the Attack on the Colony of Georgia, in America, and of Its Defeat on St. Simons Island*, Collections of the Georgia Historical Society, Vol. 7, Part 3 (Savannah, Georgia Historical Society, 1913); Ricardo Torres-Reyes, *The British Siege of St. Augustine in 1740* (Denver: Denver Service Center, Historic Preservation Team, 1972), pp.2–9, 19–29, 40–47, 62–71, 82–95.
33   Cerdá Crespo, 'Guerra', pp.335–336.
34   *Vice-amiral* Antoine-Françoise de Pardaillan, marquis d'Antin to Navy Minister Jean-Frédéric Phélypeaux, comte de Maurepas, Feb. 6, 1741, quoted in Adrien Dessalles, *Histoire générale des Antilles* (Paris: Libraire-Éditeur, 1847–1848), vol.4, p.131.

and 1748, to escort merchant convoys, so the Spanish were generally on their own regarding sea communications with Santo Domingo and Puerto Rico. Although the Havana squadron commanders sent battleships east of the Windward Passage less often than into the Gulf of Mexico, Spanish ships of the line did periodically cruise as far as San Juan.[35]

The ships of the line of the Havana squadron also patrolled around Cuba and in the Yucatan Channel to chase off British privateers.[36] The Havana squadron had a few smaller warships and these, too, probably were used for this purpose sometimes, but their activities have not been documented well.

Throughout the 1739–1748 war, the naval shipyard at Havana was a major Spanish asset. Both navies encountered difficulties keeping warships 'serviceable' in the Caribbean theater, where the Teredo shipworm and tropical heat and humidity ravaged hulls and rigging. The British commander at Jamaica sometimes had to cannibalize rigging to get some of his ships of the line to sea.[37] The British had royal dockyards, at English Harbor, Antigua, and Port Royal, Jamaica, but they found it difficult to recruit and retain skilled labor. The Havana dockyard was better equipped, and completed three 70-gun and three 60-gun ships of the line during the war. Five of six Spanish ships of the line at the Battle of Havana in 1748 had been built there.

The Havana squadron had included 12 ships of the line after the arrival of *Teniente general* Torres in the spring of 1741, but the return of ships to Spain with silver convoys, and other losses, outpaced the yard's ability to build replacements, and the squadron was down to two 70-gun and four 60-gun (one of them leaky) ships of the line by September 1748. Nevertheless, the Havana squadron was always regarded as a threat by the British commander at Jamaica.[38] Spain did have ambitions to reconquer Jamaica, but did not make any definite plans for an invasion during the 1739–1748 war. However, conservative British commanders generally kept their ships of the line concentrated and close to Port Royal except to escort convoys through the Windward Passage or when they were ordered to try to intercept French convoys to or from Saint-Domingue.

Protecting Lines of Communication in the Mediterranean

Two Spanish lines of communications ran across the Mediterranean, one to the North African outpost of Oran and one to the armies operating in Italy in pursuit of a major strategic objective of the War of the Austrian Succession, control of territory in northern Italy to constitute an appanage for Queen Elizabeth de Farnese's younger son, Prince Philip.

---

35   J[ohn] C[harles] M[artin] Ogelsby, 'Spain's Havana Squadron and the Preservation of the Balance of Power in the Caribbean, 1740-1748', *Hispanic American Historical Review,* 49:3 (August, 1969), pp.473–488, 482; Cerdá Crespo, 'Guerra', pp.306–307, 335; Gómez Cañas, *Historiales.*

36   Gómez Cañas, *Historiales.*

37   For the British, Duncan Crewe, *Yellow Jack and the Worm: British Naval Administration in the West Indies, 1739-1748* (Liverpool: Liverpool University Press, 1993); Richmond, *Navy,* vol.1, pp.241, 243; Geoffrey Ward, 'Nowhere is Perfect: British Naval Centres on the Leeward Islands Station during the Eighteenth Century', *Caribbean Connections,* 1:1 (February 2011), <http://journal.fieldresearchcentre. org/Ward%202011.pdf> (accessed June 18, 2013). There is no specific discussion for the Spanish comparable to Crewe, but the same problems are referred to by Cerdá Crespo; Baudot Monroy, 'Julián'; and Ogelsby, 'Spain's Havana Squadron', p.481.

38   Ogelsby, 'Spain's Havana Squadron', pp.482–488.

Communications with Oran were under continuous threat from raiders from Algiers, from which the city had been seized in 1732, and from British privateers based at Gibraltar or Port Mahon. Once a Spanish army had been landed in Italy, interdicting its supplies and reinforcements was the principal mission of the British Mediterranean fleet, and they were also a potential target for British privateers.

Spain had exploited British naval overstretch to get two contingents of troops to Italy from Spain in 1741–1742. The British Mediterranean fleet concentrated at Gibraltar in the fall of 1741 to counter a Spanish concentration at Cadiz.[39] This permitted a convoy escorted by only three ships of the line to take 14,000 soldiers from Barcelona to Orbitello, Italy, 3–20 November 1741.[40] British Vice-Admiral Nicholas Haddock intercepted the Cadiz squadron off Cartagena on 19 December just as it was joined by the French Toulon fleet under *Lieutenant-général* Claude-Élisée de Court de la Bruyère. Haddock and his officers were uncertain about de Court's intentions; outnumbered 28-15, they let the combined fleet proceed toward Barcelona and went to the British base at Port Mahon, Minorca, after a storm.[41] Concentration there allowed the Franco-Spanish fleet to escort a second troop convoy from Barcelona to La Spezia, Italy, 14–30 January 1742.[42] Due to storm damage, the Spanish fleet then had to put in to the French naval base at Toulon.

The Spanish squadron was still at Toulon when Haddock's successor, Admiral Thomas Mathews, instituted a tight blockade of the coast between Toulon and Genoa in the spring of 1742, attacking coasters trying to carry reinforcements, supplies, and money to Italy;[43] sending parties ashore to destroy Spanish stockpiles;[44] and forcing Genoa to transfer

---

39   Spanish concentration at Cadiz: Josef de Vargas y Ponce, *Vida de D. Juan Josef Navarro, primer marqués de la Victoria* (Madrid: La Imprenta Real, 1808), pp.135–136; José Ignacio González-Aller Hierro, 'Navío Real Felipe', *Revista de historia naval*, 4:14, (1986), pp.47–52. British concentration at Gibraltar: Richmond, *Navy*, vol.1, pp.159–69.

40   Reed Browning, *The War of the Austrian Succession* (New York: St. Martin's Press, 1993), p.81; Richard Harding, *The Emergence of Britain's Global Naval Supremacy: The War of 1739–1748* (Woodbridge: The Boydell Press, 2010), p.114; Juan Gómez Vizcaíno, 'El departamento marítimo de Cartagena de Levante (1750–1753) y el teniente general Francisco Liaño y Arjona', *Revista general de marina*, 253 (July 2007), p.21; *Mercurio [de España]*, Vol. 47 (Nov. 1741), p.114; Ignacio Rivas Ibáñez, 'Mobilizing Resources for War: The British and Spanish Intelligence Systems during the War of Jenkins' Ear (1739–1744)', (PhD diss., University College, London, 2008), p.250.

41   Vargas y Ponce, *Vida*, pp.139–146; Richmond, *Navy*, vol.1, pp.167–171; *Mercure de France*, Dec. 1742, p.212; Robert Beatson, *Naval and Military Memoirs of Great Britain, from 1727 to 1783* (London: Longman, Hurst, Rees and Orme, 1804, repr. [n.p.], Elibron Classics, [ca. 2002]), vol.1, pp.116–117; council of war resolutions, 7 Dec. 1741, enclosed with Haddock to Corbett, *Marlborough* at sea, 9 Dec. 1741, TNA, ADM 1/380; nine British captains' journals in TNA, ADM 51.

42   Vargas y Ponce, *Vida*, pp.148–149; José Campo-Raso, *Continuacion a los comentarios del marques de S. Felipe desde el año de MDCCXXXIII* (Madrid: Imprenta Real, 1793), vol.4, pp.181–183; Brun, *Guerres*, vol.1, p.287.

43   Examples: Beatson, *Naval*, vol.1, pp.154, 169–172; Richmond, *Navy*, vol.1, p.207; Frederic Hervey, *The Naval History of Great Britain, from the Earliest Times to the Rising of the Parliament in 1779* (London: J. Bew, 1779), vol.4, pp.167, 169.

44   Examples: David Spinney, *Rodney* (London: George Allen and Unwin Ltd., 1969), pp.53–54; *London Gazette*, No. 8160 (Oct. 9, 1742), p.4. British landings on Genoese territory searching for Spanish victuals, forage, and munitions: *Le Courrier* (Avignon), 1742, No. 78 (Sept. 28), pp.[1–2], No. 79 (Oct. 2), pp.[2–3].

Spanish munitions to Corsica.[45] Mathews was reinforced and the French Toulon squadron was demobilized, marooning the Spanish under *Jefe de Escuadra* Don Juan Navarro.

This blockade was the principal contribution of Great Britain to the pro-Austrian coalition in Italy. Some supplies leaked through but there were losses, and trained soldiers were too valuable to risk in vulnerable coastal convoys. The direct route straight east from Barcelona being interdicted, the Spanish sent supplies on a roundabout voyage south to the Barbary Coast and then to the territory of the defenseless Papal States.[46]

Again with French help, the Spanish navy did break Mathews' blockade for a short time in February and March, 1744. A combined fleet sailed on 20 February and was engaged on 22 February by a numerically equal British fleet with superior combat power.[47] The British attack was not pressed, and all three contingents retired to their nearest bases. Briefly, the sea lane from Barcelona to Italy was open to Spanish shipping. However, as early as 23 March three 50-gun British ships were back on the Riviera interrupting coastal commerce.[48] Mathews and his successor, Vice-Admiral William Rowley, kept up a close blockade of the coast between Toulon and Genoa until 16 October 1744,[49] and the Spanish did not transport an army across the Mediterranean for the rest of the war.[50]

The lifting of the tight blockade of Toulon in the spring and summer of 1744 also enabled Spain to retrieve the four two-decker frigates that Navarro had left in February because he could not man them. Crews were brought from Barcelona and the ships sailed to Cartagena in September.[51] Navarro took the 10 remaining ships of his squadron to sea in July and again in August and September.[52] It was probably in August that he was reportedly ordered to

45   Ciro Paoletti, 'La marina inglese contro Genova durante la guerra di successione Austriaca', *Bollettino d'archivio dell'ufficio storico della marina militare* (June 2012), pp.71–96, at <http://www.marina.difesa. it/documentazione/editoria/bollettino/Documents/2012/5_Paoletti_La_ Marina_inglese_contro_ Genova_pg_71_96.pdf> (accessed 21 November 2013), pp.71–96; Richmond, *Navy*, vol.1, pp.230–231; *London Gazette*, No. 8244 (26 July 1743), pp.3–4.

46   Paoletti, 'Marina', p.77; *Amsterdam, avec privilege de nos seigneurs les Etats de Holland et de West-Frise*, 1743, No. 76 (Sept. 20), report from Rome dated Aug. 3 (n.s); *A Narrative of the Proceedings of His Majesty's Fleet in the Mediterranean, and the Combined Fleets of France and Spain, from the Year 1741, to March 1744 . . . by a Sea-Officer* (London: J. Millan, 1744), p.38.

47   Each fleet had 28 ships in its line of battle. The British had advantages of about seven percent in total displacement of their ships and 10 percent in 'weight of metal' or total throw weight of the broadsides of the ships in their line. They also had six additional 50-gun ships, at least as heavily armed as some of the ships in the Franco-Spanish line of battle.

48   Spenser Wilkinson, *The Defence of Piedmont, 1742–1748: A Prelude to the Study of Napoleon* (Oxford: Clarendon Press, 1927), p.115.

49   No published account gives a complete chronology of British operations under Mathews and Rowley on the French coast and the Riviera from 30 March/10 April until the end of 1744. The present author has pieced one together from Richmond, *Navy*, vol.2, pp.122–235; Ruddock F. Mackay, *Admiral Hawke* (Oxford: Clarendon Press, 1965), pp.36–39; and two French newspapers, *Le Courrier* (Avignon) and *Gazette* (Paris; Lyon ed.); see *All the Seas of the World*, vol. 1, ch.20.

50   Wilkinson, *Defence*, pp.104–105.

51   Amrhein, *Hidden*, p.487; Gómez Cañas, *Historiales*, vol.1, pp.177, 216, 351, vol. 2, p.94.

52   Vargas y Ponce, *Vida*, p.219; Gómez Vizcaíno, 'Departamento', pp.21–22; Juan Antonio Gómez Vizcaíno, 'El teniente general Blas de Barreda y Campuzano y el departamento marítimo de Cartagena de Levante (1761–1767)', *Revista de Historia Naval*, 33:131 (2015), p.78. Vague mentions of both cruises: Cesáreo Fernández-Duro, *Armada española desde la union de los reinos de Castilla y de Aragón* (Madrid: Est. Typografico «Sucesores de Rivadeneyra», 1901, repr. Madrid, Museo Naval,

cover a convoy of Spanish troops from Majorca, reinforcements for the army in Italy, to the North African coast and then on to the Neapolitan coast.[53] The summer cruises captured a few neutral merchantmen carrying supplies to Port Mahon and presumably reminded the British commanders in the Mediterranean that they had a strong squadron on the flank of their own line of communications; the Cartagena squadron can be considered a second layer of the 1744 blockade of victuallers and storeships in Lisbon, requiring strong escorts for any convoys between Gibraltar and Port Mahon and posing a risk to unescorted convoys, small squadrons, and single warships. However, there is no evidence of deliberate coordination between the French and Spanish to provide a 'blockade in depth'.

The Spanish navy maintained the maritime line of communications to Oran and operated against the other North African cities and commerce raiders based there. *Teniente general* Rodrigo Torres y Morales bombarded Tunis or Tangier and Algiers and captured three xebecs and a settee.[54] *Jefe de escuadra* Ignacio Dautevil took eight ships of the line on a mission of state to Algiers in May 1744.[55] Early in 1745 *Jefe de escuadra* Cosme Álvarez took four frigates on a mission to Algiers, Tunis, and Tripoli.[56] Cruises like these were meant to remind the Barbary states of the naval power of European states, in this case, that even during a war with Great Britain, Spain could exert naval power on the African coast.

In October 1747 *León*, 70, made a voyage, probably accompanied by two 50-gun frigates, to the Canaries, Balearics, Toulon, and several North African cities while the British Mediterranean fleet was elsewhere.[57] The commander of converted merchantman *Brillante*, serving temporarily as a ship of the line, is reported as making a voyage, as part of a squadron or alone, to Trieste, Palermo, Naples, La Spezia, Genoa, Toulon, Port Mahon, Majorca, and Cartagena.[58]

After 1744, the British Mediterranean fleet was less successful in interdicting the Spanish line of communications to Italy. British admirals reported their interceptions,

---

1973,) vol.6, p.305; for a reference to the July cruise, Pilar San Pío Aladrén and Carmen Zamarrón Moreno, *Cátalogo de la colección de documentos de Vargas Ponce que posee el Museo Naval* (Madrid: Instituto Histórico de Marina, 1979), vol.1, p.389.

53   *Mercure historique et politique,* 117 (August 1744), p.230, (September 1744), p.258; *Gaceta de Madrid,* No. 51 (Dec. 22, 1744), p.416, report from Genoa of the arrival there of a tartan with troops from Cartagena and of the capture near the Strait of Bonifacio (between Corsica and Sardinia) by an English frigate of a Majorcan vessel that had already landed its troops at Naples.

54   *Enciclopedia general del mar,* vol.6, p.527, 'Torres y Morales, Rodrigo'; Pavía y Pavía, *Galeria,* vol.2, p.429. *Enciclopedia* has Tunis and Algiers, Pavía y Pavía has Tangier and Algiers. Mission not mentioned in the brief Antonio del Solar y Taboada, *Don Rodrigo de Torres: Primer Marqués de Matallana* (Badajoz: Ediciones Arqueros, 1930).

55   Pavía y Pavía, *Galeria,* vol.4, p.72.

56   This mission is mentioned only by Pavía y Pavía, *Galeria,* vol.4, p.10, in his biography of Álvarez; date or other details not available. The mission had to be undertaken in about the first quarter of 1745 because by June Álvarez was in Ferrol in command of the squadron of four ships of the line there.

57   Gómez Cañas, *Historiales,* vol.1, p.284, vol.2, p.94; Cerdá Crespo, 'Guerra', p.330, mentions the arrival of these ships at Cartagena on 5 November.

58   Pavía y Pavía, *Galeria,* vol.1, p.123. Although the source says that this officer, Blas de Barreda y Campuzano, was appointed to *Brillante* in June 1747 and mentions different service in 1748, the inclusion of Port Mahon in 1747 voyages is suspicious because Port Mahon was an enemy naval base until October 1748 Gómez Vizcaíno, 'Teniente general Blas de Barreda', p.78, mentions an 'intense cruise' ('*una intensa campaña*') by *Brillante* in 1747 but does not name any ports of call.

and Herbert Richmond has emphasized them in his account of British naval operations in the Mediterranean from 1745 to 1748.[59] But it is clear from European newspapers and comments by local British officials that Spain maintained a steady flow of provisions, munitions, money, and even reinforcements by sea to Genoa from staging points at Naples and Barcelona. The traffic was mostly in coastal vessels and made frequent stops at intermediate ports in allied or neutral territory. Some troops and material went from Spain eastward to Naples before heading north, exploiting the absence of British cruisers in the intervening waters. When an Austrian army overran the Genoese Riviera and invaded Provence, city residents expelled the Austrian garrison, leading to an Austrian siege. The city was supplied by sea with food, munitions, and professional French and Spanish troops.[60]

Notices of these convoys do not mention the Spanish navy, and it appears that civil authorities or the Spanish army chartered the coasters and organized the convoys for the traffic from Barcelona; in Naples, a prominent noble merchant who had contracted with the Spanish government before the war was employed as an agent victualler.[61] Possibly, junior navy officers were detailed to the convoys to provide navigational expertise and enforce royal authority.

However, the British consistently overestimated the combat power and effectiveness of the ships at Cartagena. In 1746 the government in Madrid ordered strict economies at the Cartagena naval base in July, and in November transferred the fleet's administrative officers to the navy department based at Cartagena. Clearly, no operational use of the ships at Cartagena was intended.[62] The Spanish might have left their ships of the line rigged to maintain the appearance of a squadron ready for sea, and they seem to have planted exaggerated information about it on the British. By thus functioning as a 'fleet in being', the Cartagena squadron occupied the attention of the British commanders-in-chief in the Mediterranean and caused them to concentrate their ships of the line to blockade Cartagena or be immediately available to counter a sortie by a strong squadron. This left insufficient small warships to interdict Spanish coastal traffic; in particular, the route from Spain to Naples was left entirely unmolested by the British Royal Navy.

59   Richmond, *Navy*, vol.2, pp.134–253, vol.3, pp.152–177.
60   These conclusions are based mostly on reports of convoy departures and arrivals in newspapers *Amsterdam, Le Courier* (Avignon), *Gaçeta de Madrid, La Gazette* (Paris), *London Gazette*, and *Nouvellees extraordinaires des divers endroits* (often referred to as 'Gazette de Leide'), and monthlies *La Clef du cabinet, Mercure historique et politique,* and *Suite de la clef.* Additional references to the traffic may be found in the correspondence between the British representative in the Grand Duchy of Tuscany, Horace Mann, in Horace Walpole, *Horace Walpole's Correspondence with Sir Horace Mann,* ed. W.S. Lewis, Warren Hunting Smith, and George L. Lam (New Haven: Yale University Press, 1954–1971), vols 1–2 (vols 17–18 of *The Yale Edition of Horace Walpole's Correspondence*).
61   Storrs, *Spanish Resurgence*, p.50; *London Gazette*, No. 8462 (27 Aug. 1745), p.1; Heinrich Benedikt, *Das Königreich Neapel unter Kaiser Karl VI: Eine Darstellung auf Grund bisher unbekannter Documente aus den Österreichischen Archiven* (Vienna: Manz Verlag, 1927), p.449; Charles III, King of Spain, *Lettere ai sovrani di Spagna, Carolo di Borbone,* ed. Imma Ascione (Rome: Ministero per i beni e le attività culturali, Direzione generale per gli archive, 2001–02), vol.3, p.237n.
62   Gómez Vizcaíno, 'Departamento maritimo de Cartagena', pp.22–23.

Use of Sea Power Against Minor Powers

Spain had interests that could be advanced by the use of sea power against nations other than Great Britain. Table 3 shows that despite having a navy less than half the size of Great Britain's, in 1730–1740 Spain was tied with France as the second-ranking naval power in Europe and had a larger navy than any European state besides Britain or France. Moreover, four of the next five naval powers (the Netherlands, Denmark, Sweden, and Russia) were in northern Europe where Spain had neither expansionary ambitions nor defensive concerns.

Table 3: Strengths of European Navies, 1730–1740

Nation	1730		1735		1740	
	No. of battleships	Total Displacement	No. of battleships	Total Displacement	No. of battleships	Total Displacement
Great Britain	105	189	107	191	101	195
Spain	*39*	*73*	*44*	*88*	*43*	*91*
France	38	73	43	82	47	91
Netherlands	38	62	42	74	35	65
Russia	38	62	34	60	20	37
Denmark	25	47	28	53	26	48
Ottoman Empire	27*	~60	27*	~50	27*	~40
Sweden	19	31	24	38	23	38
Venice	22	35†	17	28†	9	14‡
Portugal	14‡	29	8‡	23	13‡	28
Austria	4	6	6	9	—	—
Naples	—	—	—	—	2	3
Malta (Knights)	4	6	4	6	4	6

Source: Glete, *Navies*, vol.1, p.311, vol.2, pp.549–695. Displacements in thousands of metric tonnes; excludes warships of less than 300 tonnes and galleys.
*Daniel Panzac, 'Armed Peace in the Mediterranean 1736–1739: A Comparative Survey of the Navies', *Mariner's Mirror*, 84:1 (February 1997), p.43. (50–108 guns, '1735–1740').
†Battleships only.
‡Ships displacing more than 1,000 metric tonnes.

Spain had ambitions in the western Mediterranean, especially for restoration of former possessions in southern Italy and on the North African coast.[63] Although Great Britain had gone to war in 1718 to prevent Spanish expansion in the Mediterranean, the ministry of Sir Robert Walpole did not favour further continental involvement in the 1730s. Therefore, two Spanish initiatives dependent on sea power faced local opposition only: the conquest

---

63   Christopher Storrs, 'The Spanish Risorgimento in the Western Mediterranean and Italy, 1707–1748', *European History Quarterly*, 42:4 (Oct. 2012), pp.555–577; María Baudot Monroy, 'No siempre enemigos: El viaje del infante Don Carlos de Borbón y la expedición naval hispano inglesa a Italia en 1731', *Obradoiro de Historia Moderna*, 25 (2016), pp.244–248.

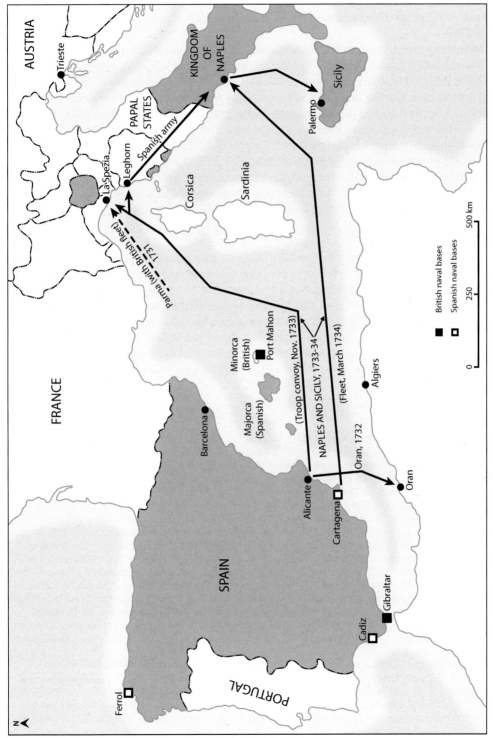

Spanish Expeditions in the Western Mediterranean, 1731-1734. (George Anderson © Helion and Company 2023)

of Oran in 1732 and the conquest of the Two Sicilies (the Kingdoms of Naples and Sicily) in 1734–1735.

Before these expeditions, an international diplomatic arrangement backed by Great Britain allowed the oldest son of Elizabeth Farnese, consort of King Philip V of Spain, to inherit the Duchy of Parma. Habsburg Emperor Charles VI opposed the agreement.[64] To suppress any local resistance, a Spanish army of 7,500 men sailed from Barcelona to Leghorn, escorted by a fleet of 18 Spanish and 12 British ships of the line, four Spanish two-deckers (46–54 guns), nine smaller warships (three Spanish, six British), and seven Spanish galleys.[65] Although the Spanish had previous experience with amphibious expeditions, the 1731 mobilization and voyage provided immediate practice for the larger and riskier 1732–1735 operations. It also enabled King Philip V to demonstrate the recovery of his navy from the 1718 disaster at Cape Passaro. During the 1731 preparations, Spain sent a squadron of six ships of the line to Genoa to enforce a withdrawal of funds that the King had deposited in a Genoese bank.[66]

Conquest of Oran

Oran, on the North African coast west of Algiers, had been occupied by the Spanish in 1509 along with other North African ports as an extension of the recently completed *reconquista* of Spain from the Moslems. But it had been lost to an Algerian siege in 1708 while Spain was engaged in the War of the Spanish Succession. Its reconquest would restore a heritage of Ferdinand and Isabella, possibly reopen a lucrative seventeenth-century trade, shut down British trade, including victuals that supported British ships based at Gibraltar, provide a base for operations against Barbary corsairs, and deny it as a base to those raiders.[67] Therefore, an expedition was prepared to recapture Oran. The preparation of the expe-

---

64   For a review of the historiography, Baudot Monroy, 'No siempre', p.251–252.
65   Fernández Duro, *Armada*, vol.6, pp.196–199. Beatson, *Naval and Military*, vol.3, p.7, and Isaac Schomberg, *Naval Chronology, or an Historical Summary of Naval & Maritime Events, from the Time of the Romans, to the Treaty of Peace 1802* (London: T. Egerton, 1802), vol.4, p.188, each has a list of Wager's fleet that includes 18 British ships of the line, four 50-gun two-deckers, and three smaller warships (40 guns each), but María Baudot Monroy, 'El regreso de Felipe V a Italia después de la Guerra de Sucesión: La expedición anfibia hispano-inglesa a la Toscana de 1731', *Revista Universitaria de Historia Militar – RUHM*, 5:10 (2016), p.76n, and Baudot Monroy, 'No siempre', p.262, cites a list in the Spanish archives with an English-language header for the smaller number. The Beatson-Schomberg list might be of the ships initially assigned to Wager, later modified. An identical list of Wager's fleet as it left England on July 27 [n.s.?] in *Mercurii Relation oder Wochentliche Ordinari-Zeitung* (Munich), extra ed., Aug. 11, 1731, [8] and in *Kurz-gefaßter Historischer Nachrichten Zum Behuf Der Neuern Europäischen Begebenheisen auf das Jahr 1731* (Regensburg), No. 33, p.518, includes 12 ships of the line by name and rate, corresponding to Baudot Monroy's count by rate, but has a 50-gun in place of a 20-gun ship; the German newspaper lists account for some of the extra ships on Beatson's list by saying that, with others, they stayed behind at Spithead under Vice-Admiral Sir George Walton.
66   Baudot Monroy, 'Regreso', p.73; Gregorio Sánchez Doncel, *Presencia de España en Orán (1509–1792)* (Toledo: Estudio Teólogico de San Ildefonso, 1991), p.254; Fernández Duro, *Armada española*, vol.6, p.199n.
67   Sénchez Doncel, *Presencia*, pp.252–253; Luís Fernando Fé Cantó, 'El desembarco en Orán en 1732: Aproximación analítica a una operación compleja', *Revista Universitaria de Historia Militar – RUHM*, 5:10 (2016), pp.90–99; Storrs, *Spanish Resurgence*, pp.1, 4–6.

dition was no secret, but there was good strategic security, with European governments speculating about objectives from Gibraltar to Italy.[68]

The expedition included a well-equipped landing force of about 28,500 (including 5,100 cavalry and dragoons), 110 artillery pieces, and 60 mortars, with associated munitions and victuals.[69] The naval escort covering the convoy and providing fire support during the landing when local troops appeared consisted of eight ships of the line (60–80 guns), two lightly armed 50-gun ships, two mortar vessels, two dispatch vessels, and nine galleys.[70] The transport convoy included 214 vessels as troop transports and 213 carrying artillery, victuals, and munitions, plus 57 that were specially modified as landing craft, for a total of over 600 'sail'.[71] Algiers, by contrast, did not have a state 'navy', because all but one of the armed vessels there were privately owned and commanded, but the ship owners would have found a large, lumbering convoy an attractive target.[72] In 1724 there had been six ships of 40–52 guns and 17 smaller armed vessels. In 1732 six ships of 36–52 guns were still supposed to be present.[73] They could have been organized into a respectable cruiser force, but could not have contended with the battle squadron that Spain sent to sea.

This was a different kind of operation than a trans-Atlantic cruise or a fleet action at sea, but a classic exercise of sea power nonetheless, one that required a professional navy. A colonial governor and some New England merchants without professional naval experience were able to organize a well-prepared and successful amphibious landing of 4,100 men and about 30 artillery pieces in 1745 at Louisbourg on Cape Breton Island,[74] but the Orán landing was a much larger and more complex operation (several times as many troops and guns, cavalry, inshore fire support, larger and more heavily armed ships to guard against). The operation was also larger than the British expedition to Lorient in 1746 that did not include cavalry; it was more like the 1756 French attack on Minorca, and owed much of its success to the speed with which the troops were put ashore. The Spanish navy had a considerable institutional history since 1680 of conducting amphibious operations, even before

68   Sánchez Doncel, *Presencia*, p.254; Anon., *The Spanish Conquest, or a Journal of Their Late Expedition … to the Taking of Oran* (London: J. Roberts, [1732]), pp.1–3; The Bey of Algiers seems also to have been taken by surprise: the only opposition to the landing was a small cavalry force.

69   Fé Cantó, 'Desembarco', pp.107–109; [Jacques Philippe] Laugier de Tassy, *Histoire du Royaume d'Alger* (Amsterdam: Henri du Sauzet, 1725), pp.167–171.

70   Sánchez Doncel, *Prsencia*, p.261; Fé Cantó, 'Desembarco', pp.109–110; Laugier, *Historia*, p.172. Both lists include two ships, credited with 50–70 guns, not on a list of the Spanish navy in 1737 nor on modern comprehensive lists of eighteenth-century Spanish ships of the line and frigates. Both are shown *ibid.*, pp.174–175, as 'paquebots', which were usually lightly armed vessels for carrying dispatches. They might have been large merchantmen chartered for the occasion.

71   Laugier, *Historia*, p.173; Fé Cantó, 'Desembarco', pp.105–106; Fernández Duro, *Armada*, vol.6, p.200n.

72   Glete, *Navies*, vol.2, p.540: 'Alger had a medium size or small cruiser navy up to … 1830'; Laugier de Tassy, *Histoire*, pp.261–262.

73   [Philippe] Laugier de Tassy (Trans. Antonio de Clariana), *Historia del reyno de Argel* (Madrid: Pantaleon Aznar, [1750–1800?]), pp.274–75 (1724; even the 50s had no artillery heavier than 12-pounders); Thomas Shaw, *Travels or Observations Relating to Several Parts of Barbary and the Levant* (Oxford: Printed at the Theatre, 1738), p.70 (1732).

74   Artillery: Robert Emmet, Jr. Wall, 'Louisbourg, 1745', *New England Quarterly*, 37:1 (March 1964), pp.64–83, 73. The number of men is well known in the literature.

the 1731 transfer of troops to Italy.[75] Two Oran expedition flag officers, Marquis Marí and Blas de Lezo, had been captains in the 1715 operation against Majorca,[76] and flag officers in the 1731 fleet, and some of the junior naval officers in the 1715 expedition were captains in 1731–1732.[77]

Once Oran was captured, the navy had to continue cruising and fighting to keep open the line of communications to Oran. *Jefe de escuadra* Blas de Lezo, one of Spain's greatest fighting seamen, cruised off the Algerian coast during the winter of 1732–33, and on 7 February 1733, pursued an Algerian ship into the harbor of Mostaganem. In the kind of action that 'Anglo-Saxon writers usually consider exclusive to their sailors', Lezo sent his boats in past shore batteries to scuttle her at a cost of seven killed and 33 wounded. Even as the navy was concentrating on preparations for the conquest of Naples in 1733, *Jefe de escuadra* Gabriel Pérez de Alderete y Alba had to make a cruise to Algiers, Tunis, and Tripoli 'to contain the depredations of the Moors', and during the 1734 conquest of Sicily he sank a 40-gun Algerian frigate off Cartagena and captured one of three xebecs he chased in the Strait of Gibraltar in 1734. In 1735, two of the navy's galleys, not sent to Italy, captured two Barbary corsairs.[78]

Conquest of Naples

From the end of the fifteenth century until 1707, the kingdoms of Naples and Sicily had been ruled by the Kings of Aragon and then of Spain until the War of the Spanish Succession. An attempt to reclaim these territories in the War of the Quadruple Alliance had failed, in part due to a devastating defeat of an overmatched Spanish fleet off Cape Passaro, Sicily, by a British fleet (11 August 1718). The resulting Treaty of the Hague (1720) had cost Spain not only Sicily but also Sardinia; however, a new opportunity for Spain arose during the War of the Polish Succession.

When King Augustus II of Poland died in February 1733, preparation of a fleet was already under way in Spain, apparently to undertake a punitive expedition, without troops,

75   Armando Albero Romá, 'La expedición contra Orán del año 1732: El embarque de tropas por el Puerto de Alicante', *LQNT – Patrimonio Cultural de la Ciudad de Alicante*, 1 (1993), pp.191–199; Baudot Monroy, 'Regreso'; Fé Cantó, 'Desembarco', p.99; and the following articles in *Revista Universitaria de Historia Militar – RUHM*, 5:10 (2016): Manuel Días-Ordóñez, 'Presentación dossier: La logística anfibia: el poder naval del Imperio español en el Mediterráneo durante el siglo XVIII', pp.10–22; Eduardo Pascual Ramos, 'Formación e instrucciones de la expedición anfibia para la conquista de Mallorca (1715)', pp.46–66; Antonio José Rodríguez Hernández, 'Reclutamiento y operaciones de enlace y transporte militar entre España y Milán a finales del siglo XVII (1680–1700)', pp.23–45; Storrs, *Spanish Resurgence*, p.65.
76   Pascual Ramos, 'Formación', p.51.
77   Junior officers of the Mallorca expedition included *Capitán de navío* Beníto Spínola (Pavía y Pavía, *Biografia*, vol.3, pp.538–539), and two commanders of ships of the line, *Capitán de fragata* Francisco Liaño (Pavía y Pavía, vol.2, pp.377–378); and *Capitán de navío* Conde de Bena-Masserano (Pavía y Pavía, *Biografia*, vol.1, pp.454–455).
78   Agustín Ramón Rodríguez González, 'Otro gran triunfo de Blas de Lezo: Orán, 1732-33', <http://abcblogs.abc.es/espejo-de-navegantes/2014/11/11/otro-gran-triunfo-de-blas-de-lezo-oran-1732-33/> (accessed 15 July 2017) (first quotation); Pavía y Pavía, *Biografia*, vol.1, p.390 (second quotation); Fernández Duro, *Armada*, vol.6, p.207; Storrs, *Spanish Resurgence*, p.64.

against Algiers as a sequel to the seizure of Oran.[79] The preparations were redirected toward an invasion of Italy. In a foreshadowing of the War of the Austrian Succession, France, Sardinia (ruled by Charles Emmanuel III of the House of Savoy), and Spain all took advantage of Austrian military involvement north of the Alps to attack Austrian domains in Italy.

The Spanish conquest of Naples and Sicily required carrying a considerable army across the sea from Spain during the brief period when the Austrian Habsburgs had a Mediterranean navy to protect troop convoys between Trieste and Naples and to keep in check North African raiders who might attack shipping from Trieste. This navy included six 'ships of the line', at least one of which had only 40 guns,[80] which could have disputed the passage of an unescorted troop convoy. They did not do so, but would not have had much chance of success against the fleet that Spain sent as a covering force.[81]

The conquest of Naples required gathering ships from Ferrol and Cadiz on the Atlantic as well as Cartagena in the Mediterranean. Preparations had begun at Cadiz and Ferrol in January 1733 and were completed at Alicante between August and October. Nine infantry battalions in 13 transports escorted by four warships left Alicante on 9 November and landed at Leghorn on 22 November. A larger contingent, including 15 warships, was scattered by a storm and arrived piecemeal at La Spezia and Leghorn between December 1733 and mid-January 1734. Some of the transports, covered by a regular warship and several 'tartans' (small vessels, lightly armed), went to Antibes to pick up cavalry that had marched through southern France but was by December 1733 blocked by the Alps. These movements enabled the Spanish to assemble an army of 30,000 men in Tuscany, including the garrison

---

79   Agustín González Enciso, 'La marina a la conquista de Italia (1733–1735)', in *Expediciones navales españoles en el siglo XVIII*, Instituto de historia y cultura naval, Cuaderno monográfico No. 69 (March 2014), pp.23–26; María Baudot Monroy, 'La expedición naval contra Argel de 1733', in Rafael Torres Sánchez (ed.), *Studium, magisterium, anicitia: homenaje al professor Agustín González Enciso* ([Pamplona]: Eunate D.I., 2018), at https://www.academia.edu/41034880/2018_LA_EXPEDICI%C3%93N_NAVAL_CONTRA_ARGEL_DE_1733 (accessed 3 Oct. 2019), pp.1–4.

80   Jean Bérenger, 'Les Habsbourg et la mer au XVIIIe siècle', in Martine Acerra et al., (eds), *État, Marine et Société* (Paris: Presses de l'Université de Paris-Sorbonne, 2005), p.30; Karl Gogg, *Österreichs Kriegsmarine, 1440–1848* (Salzburg: Verl. Das Bergland-Buch, 1972), p.55; 'Die früheren Entwicklungsphasen der Oesterreichischen Kriegsmarine', *Abendblatt der Oesterreichische Kaiserlichen Wiener Zeitung*, No. 149 (3 July 1857), pp.593–595; Claudia Reichl-Ham, 'Le origini della marina austriaca', *Bollettino d'Archivio dell'Ufficio Storico della Marina Militare*, September 2012, 119–121, at <http://www.marina.difesa.it/conosciamoci/editoria/bollettino/Documents/2012/04_reichl.pdf> (accessed June 2017); Robert Haidinger, 'Kaiser Karl VI und die Marine', (Doct. diss., Vienna University, 2013), p.72, presents lists from Gogg, *Össterreichs*; Alfred Koudelka, *Unsere Kriegsflotte 1556–1906* (Vienna: Ig. v. Kleinmayr & Fed. Bamberg, 1908); and Wladimir Aichelburg, *Register der k.u.k. Kriegsschiffe* (Vienna: Neuer Wissenschaftlicher Verlag, 2002), showing six, three, and four ships of the line, respectively, and concludes (p.71), 'The exact size of the fleet cannot be determined.'

81   No complete list of the Spanish fleet has been found, and the ships involved probably varied over time. González Enciso, 'Marina', p.24, has a list of 12 ships of the line, one of the big 50-gun 'frigates', one mortar vessel, and two small vessels (one officer, 28 crew; perhaps galleys without their rowers), at Alicante in August 1733, and mentions one other large frigate at sea. Fernández Duro, *Armada*, vol.6, p.203, mentions a squadron of 16 ships of the line; the detachment of four that escorted the first contingent was probably drawn from this squadron. The Spanish squadron that appeared off Naples in March 1734 included nine ships of the line and two 'pinks', a term usually applied to transports that probably refers here to two smaller warships such as frigates or xebecs: Michelangelo Schipa, *Il Regno di Napoli al tempo di Carlo di Borbone* (Naples: Luigi Pierro e Figlio, 1904), p.112.

that had been brought over in 1731. This army conducted some preliminary clearing operations in Tuscany in December and marched south in the spring across Papal territory and into the Kingdom of Naples, ruled by a viceroy on behalf of Habsburg Holy Roman Emperor Charles VI.[82]

As the Spanish army approached, the Spanish naval squadron blockaded Naples and occupied its offshore islands. Four Austrian galleys tried to attack the blockading ships of the line during a calm on 25 March 1734, but, as often happened in such attacks, a breeze eventually enabled the sailing ships to bring their superior firepower to bear after, according to the Austrian admiral, suffering some damage and casualties on their flagship. An incomplete 60-gun ship of the line was run aground to prevent her being captured intact by the Spaniards. The galleys eventually made a foggy nighttime escape to Brindisi and arrived at Trieste on 17 June.[83] Prince Charles entered Naples on 10 May and the Spanish army defeated the Austrian army near Brindisi on the Adriatic coast on 25 May. The Spanish put four ships in the Adriatic to cut off reinforcements and supplies to coastal garrisons. After the surrender of the mainland fortresses, another amphibious operation involving 225 transports escorted by five ships of the line took part of the Spanish army to Sicily on 29 August 1734, using the same beach near Palermo as in 1718. The ships were later joined by the four from the Adriatic. However, there was no great-power fleet to defeat the Spanish at sea and isolate their army on Sicily. Spanish Prince Charles, now King Charles VII of Naples, entered Messina on 9 March 1735 and was proclaimed King of Sicily at Palermo.[84] This wide-ranging seaborne expedition had been a complete success.

Conclusion: Use of Sea Power by a Second-Ranked Navy

Between 1732 and 1748 Spain exploited strategic spaces left by the overstretched British Royal Navy. In 1739–1748, Britain's interests were too extensive even for a navy twice as large as Spain's, and she either ignored areas like the Gulf of Mexico or was unable to be present in sufficient force all the time in others. Great Britain had stopped the Spanish attempt to conquer Sicily in 1718 by sending a strong fleet to the Mediterranean that defeated the Spanish fleet at sea (Battle of Cape Passaro). Britain *could* have done the same in defense of Oran in 1732 or of Austrian possessions in Italy in 1733 but chose not to. European speculation that the 1732 expedition under preparation might be aimed at Gibraltar or Minorca

---

82   González Enciso, Marina', pp.24–25; Austria, Kriegsarchiv, *Feldzuge des Prinzen Eugen von Savoyen* (Vienna: Verlag des K. und K. Generalstabs, 1876–1891), vol.19 (1891), pp.76–77; Fernández Duro, *Armada*, vol.6, pp.203–204.

83   Franz Pesendorfer, *Österreich – Großmacht im Mittelmeer? Das Königreich Neapel-Sizilien unter Kaiser Karl VI (1707/20–1734/35)* (Vienna: Böhlau, 1998), p.195; Schipa, *Regno*, p.112–13; Haidinger, *Kaiser* pp.69–70; Count Luca Pallavinci to Prince Eugene of Savoy, Trieste, 24 Oct. 1734, in Joseph Rechberger von Rechkron (ed.), *Österreichs Seewesen in dem Zeitraume von 1500–1797*, vol.1 of *Geschichte der K.K. Kriegs-Marine* (Vienna: Verlag des K.K. Reichs-Kriegs-Ministeriums, Marine-Section, 1882), Appendices, pp.2–3; Gogg, *Österreichs*, p.30. No Spanish mention of the action in the Bay of Naples, which might have been more perfunctory than the Austrian admiral's report suggests, has been found.

84   This paragraph from Fernández Duro, *Armada*, vol.6, pp.204–05; Pesendorfer, *Österreich*, p.195.

was obviously not taken seriously by the British government, which did not mobilize its navy to stop it.[85] Britain's aloofness from the War of the Polish Succession left an opportunity that a competent, rebuilt Spanish navy could exploit.

If the Spanish navy was only useful where the British fleet was absent (in a war with Great Britain) or against states that had practically no navy at all (and in whose favor the British declined to intervene), it might seem that Spain's 40-odd ships of the line in the 1730s, much less the 50–75 of 1770–1800, were an excessive waste of resources. The initial force served as a fleet-in-being threat against Great Britain in the early years of the war, when Spain defended her American colonies against British attack by threatening an invasion of the British Isles in conjunction with France or, by herself, of British-held Minorca in the Mediterranean.[86] Moreover, although there is no evidence that Spain deliberately overbuilt to offset expected attrition, war is hard on a navy: the 42 ships of the line Spain had in January 1739 had shrunk to 18 by January 1749 despite construction or acquisition of 16 new ships,[87] The gross loss of 40 almost equaled the number of battleship hulls in the navy on 1 January 1739. A smaller initial navy would not have been able to successfully defend the 1748 mercury convoy. Before 1739, Spanish policymakers hoped that a large navy would force France and Britain to bid against each other for Spanish favour, France because she needed more naval force against Britain than she could provide on her own, Britain to prevent the Spanish navy from combining with the French.

Contrary to longstanding myth underpinned by the Black Legend and losses in fleet actions to the British Royal Navy, the Spanish navy was neither inactive nor incapable during the eighteenth century. Spanish naval operations between 1732 and 1748 demonstrate how a navy that is only half the size of its main rival can use sea power even in a war with that power. When an even larger navy is not involved, a large but not dominant navy can exert sea power against other states with smaller navies or none at all; the British expedition to recapture the Falklands in 1982 is probably the most recent example. A smaller navy may be deterred from intervening or invasion convoys and lines of communications may be guarded against irregular light forces in the absence of regular state naval forces. In wartime, even facing a 2-1 adverse force ratio, a navy may find strategic spaces it can dominate when its enemy cannot be superior everywhere, all the time. These spaces can be guarded against raids by enemy light forces operating in the absence of main battle forces. In the eighteenth century, these forces included both the cruisers of state navies and privateers. Although the latter have been prohibited in international law since 1907, in a war against a superior navy a materially inferior navy might still find employment against light raiding forces or non-state naval forces.

85   Anon., *Spanish Conquest*, pp.2–3.
86   Rivas Ibáñez, 'Mobilizing', pp.110–117, 234–36; on the temporary credibility of both threats, Harding, *Emergence*, pp.65–67, 71–74.
87   Author's counts based on the list of Spanish ships of the line by Christian de St. Hubert, in John Harbron, *Trafalgar and the Spanish Navy* (Annapolis: Naval Institute Press, 1988), pp.164–173, and *Warship*, 10:37 and 10:38 (1989). Glete's counts and displacement estimates are used elsewhere for consistency in comparison with other navies. Glete counted 43 Spanish 'battleships' on 1 January 1740, and 15 on 1 January 1750. Both counts include 50-gun two-deckers that the Spanish classified as 'frigates'. Spain had at least five of these in 1739–1740; only one remained by 1749–1750.

Select Bibliography

Anon. *The Spanish Conquest, or a Journal of Their Late Expedition . . . to the Taking of Oran* (London: J. Roberts, [1732]).

Baudot Monroy, María. 'Julián de Arriaga y Rivera: Una vida al servicio de la marina (1700–1776)' (doct. diss., Universidad Nacional de Educación a Distancia, [2005]).

Baudot Monroy, María, 'No siempre enemigos: El viaje del infante Don Carlos de Borbón y la expedición naval hispano inglesa a Italia en 1731', *Obradoiro de Historia Moderna*, 25 (2016), pp.243–275.

Baudot Monroy, María, 'El regreso de Felipe V a Italia después de la Guerra de Sucesión: La expedición anfibia hispano-inglesa a la Toscana de 1731', *Revista Universitaria de Historia Militar – RUHM*, 5:10 (2016), pp.67–88.

Beatson, Robert, *Naval and Military Memoirs of Great Britain, from 1727 to 1783* (London: Longman, Hurst, Rees and Orme, 1804, repr. [n.p.], Elibron Classics, [ca. 2002]).

Cerdá Crespo, Jorge, 'La Guerra de la Oreja de Jenkins: Un conflicto colonial (1739–1748)' (doct. diss., University of Alicante, 2009) [His *Conflictos coloniales: La guerra de los nueve años, 1739–1748* (Alicante: Publicaciones de la Universidad de Alicante, 2010) is almost entirely unrevised text from 'Guerra' but without the dissertation's useful reproductions of contemporary documents, lists of ships, and document transcriptions in footnotes and appendices].

Fé Cantó, Luís Fernando, 'El desembarco en Orán en 1732: Aproximación analítica a una operación compleja', *Revista Universitaria de Historia Militar – RUHM*, 5:10 (2016), pp.89–110.

Fernández-Duro, Cesáreo, *Armada española desde la union de los reinos de Castilla y de Aragón* (Madrid: Est. Typografico «Sucesores de Rivadeneyra», 1901, repr. Madrid, Museo Naval, 1973).

García-Baquero González, Antonio, 'Las remesas de metales preciosos Americanos en el siglo XVIII: Una aritmética controvertida', *Hispania: Revista española de historia*, 56:192 (Jan.–Apr. 1996), pp.204–262

Gómez Cañas, Santiago, *Historiales de los navíos de línea españoles (1700–1850)* ([Roquetas de mar, Spain]: Círculo Rojo Editorial, 2021).

González Enciso, Agustín, 'La marina a la conquista de Italia (1733–1735)', in *Expediciones navales españoles en el siglo XVIII*, Instituto de historia y cultura naval, Cuaderno monográfico No. 69 (March 2014), pp.15–35.

Morineau, Michel, *Incroyables gazettes et fabuleux métaux: Les Retours des trésors américains d'après les gazettes hollandaises (XVIe–XVIIIe siècles)* (Cambridge: Cambridge University Press, 1985).

Ogelsby, J[ohn] C[harles] M[artin], 'Spain's Havana Squadron and the Preservation of the Balance of Power in the Caribbean, 1740–1748', *Hispanic American Historical Review*, 49:3 (August, 1969), pp.473–488.

Pacheco Fernández, Agustín, *El 'Glorioso'*, 3rd ed. ([Valladolid], Galland Books Editorial, 2016).

Pavía y Pavía, Francisco de Paula, *Galeria biografica de los generales de marina, jefes y personajes notables que figuraron en la misma corporación desde 1700 á 1868* (Madrid, F. Garcia, y Ca. Mayor, 1873–1774).

Richmond, H[erbert] W., *The Navy in the War of 1739–48* (Cambridge: Cambridge University Press, 1920).

Sánchez Doncel, Gregorio, *Presencia de España en Orán (1509–1792)* (Toledo: Estudio Teológico de San Ildefonso, 1991).

Satsuma, Shinsuki, *Britain and Colonial Maritime War in the Early Eighteenth Century: Silver, Seapower and the Atlantic* (Woodbridge: The Boydell Press, 2013).

Schipa, Michelangelo, *Il Regno di Napoli al tempo di Carlo di Borbone* (Naples: Luigi Pierro e Figlio, 1904).

Storrs, Christopher, *The Spanish Resurgence, 1713–1748* (New Haven: Yale University Press, 2016).

Vargas y Ponce, Josef de, *Vida de D. Juan Josef Navarro, primer marqués de la Victoria*, (Madrid: La Imprenta Real, 1808).

Wilkinson, Spenser, *The Defence of Piedmont, 1742–1748: A Prelude to the Study of Napoleon* (Oxford: Clarendon Press, 1927).

3

From Ferrol and Flanders: Bourbon Seaborne Support for the 1745 Jacobite Rising

Albert C.E. Parker

When James II, King of England, Scotland, and Ireland, had been ousted in 1688, his replacement by 'William (III) and Mary (II)' as sovereigns in the British Isles had not been universally accepted, especially by Scottish nationalists (James was a member of the long-time ruling house in Scotland, the Stuarts) and Catholics (James was a Catholic). William had defeated James and his army in Ireland, and James had died in 1701. His son, called 'James III' by his supporters, had visited Scotland in 1708 but had failed to inspire a rebellion in his favour. He had returned in 1715 during an uprising (known in Scotland and history as The '15) in that year, but that too had been defeated: James had returned to France, and rebel leaders had gone into exile. Spain had sent a small army to Scotland in 1719, but only a few of the troops actually arrived and they had been forced to surrender. The failures of these risings had taught the Stuart supporters, or 'Jacobites' (from the Latin form of 'James'), that they needed substantial outside professional military support to avoid another failure with its attendant executions and exile.

Britain and France formally went to war again in 1744. The French army prepared an invasion force to land in southeast England and march on London with support from English Jacobites, but the French navy was unable to provide the necessary protection for the required crossing of the North Sea. James III's son, Prince Charles Edward Stuart, set out for Scotland on 21 June/2 July 1745,[1] in hope that beginning another rebellion would finally break the standoff between Jacobites who were afraid to rebel without a French invasion and a French government unwilling to mount another invasion of Britain without a

---

1   Because of the use of separate calendars in Great Britain vs. France and Spain, all dates are given in dual format, the date in British calendar followed by the date in the French and Spanish calendar. The dates cited in footnotes are whatever the source used. All years are based on a 1 January–31 December year. However, British official documents, including *The London Gazette* and the logs and journals of navy officers, began the year on 25 March, and thus gave a '1745' year to dates between 1 January and 24 March 1746. Issues of *The London Gazette* must be searched for under the official year in which the day after 31 December1745 is 1 January 1745 and the day after 24 March 1745 is 25 March 1746.

rebellion actually under way. Since Charles had departed without the support and overt knowledge of the French government, no arrangements for an immediate French invasion or other support were in place.[2] However, before leaving France Charles had written to both Bourbon kings. These appeals announced that Charles was going to Scotland and asked for arms for the men he expected to heed his call for an anti-Hanoverian uprising, money to pay them and to purchase supplies in Great Britain, and professional troops to add force to the revolt he intended to lead.

Eventually, the French government prepared an invasion of Kent by a fully equipped professional army, but called off the project before the transport vessels sailed. The focus here is not on the invasion of England but on the attempts of the two Bourbon monarchies to provide money, munitions, and professional troops to aid Prince Charles in the 1745 Jacobite Rising (The '45). This aid had to come by sea; therefore, preventing its delivery was a task for the British Royal Navy. Spanish shipments sailed from Ferrol and ports on the Biscay coast for the west coast of Scotland. French assistance was dispatched to the east coast across the North Sea from ports in Flanders. Of the two, the French support was the more significant. The Spanish efforts were smaller, and did not include Spanish army support. France provided support and manpower, and shipped it from ports near the invasion marshalling point; therefore, it received more attention from the British government and later historians.[3]

The French and Spanish aid efforts took place in the context of a much wider and multi-faceted naval campaign in British home waters. Besides trying to intercept the aid shipments, the British navy had to intercept or otherwise prevent the invasion the French were planning across the Strait of Dover, guard against an invasion attempt elsewhere in the British isles, prevent potential rising participants from moving from the Hebrides onto the Scottish mainland, prevent the rebels from transporting troops and supplies by water on the eastern coast, and assist the British Army in its operations.

The Jacobites won several battlefield victories in Scotland, recruited a larger Scottish army than previous risings, and even invaded England. It was recognized at the time as a more serious threat than James III's brief visit in 1709 or 1715. Both the British government and the Bourbons scored successes if that is measured by successful interception of aid shipments (British success) or their delivery to the Jacobites (Bourbon success). Strategically, only suppression of the rebellion would be a victory for the Hanoverian regime, and that is what happened. On the Bourbon side, delivering enough assistance to keep the rebellion going long enough to divert British troops from Flanders could count as a strategic success. The rest of this chapter will describe the Bourbon aid efforts and evaluate their success.

2   Daniel Szechi, *The Jacobites: Britain and Europe, 1688–1788* (Manchester: Manchester University Press, 1994), p.99.
3   John S. Gibson, *Ships of the '45: The Rescue of the Young Pretender* (London: Hutchinson & Co., 1967), pp.17–26, chronicles the French attempts from both British and French sources; F[rank] J[ames] McLynn, 'Sea Power and the Jacobite Rising of 1745', *Mariner's Mirror,* 67:2 (1981), pp.163–167, revolves around a list of French attempts in the Maurepas papers but omits some sorties.

Spanish Support

On 10/21 July, 1745, before any results of Charles' expedition could be known in Spain (he did not write further to Spain from Scotland until 17/28 August), Philip V's ministers met to decide how to respond to Charles' initial appeal. The result was a royal order to send four shiploads of money and weapons to Scotland, and 50 officers from Spain's Irish regiments.[4] This was much less than the 5,000 troops of 1719 (of whom only a few hundred arrived), and might have been the minimum that Philip and his advisors thought would satisfy Philip's nephew, Louis XV.

What became of this decision, and whether there were other efforts from Spain to help the Scottish Jacobites, is obscure. McGarry says that four ships (the number covered by Philip's promise to Louis XV) were 'funded' by 'Spanish-based Jacobites'.[5] The commander of Spain's Ferrol squadron, *Jefe de escuadra* Cosme Álvarez, received orders to cover a voyage to Scotland, or its initial stage, by two privateer frigates from San Sebastián on the north coast of Spain, *San Ciríaco* and *La Peña de Francia*.[6] Álvarez was to put a navy lieutenant in command of each ship, and the local intendant reported that he had provided the frigates with 90,000 pesos (about £18,000 at the commercial exchange rate), 5,000 muskets, 300 quintals (nearly 14 long tons or metric tonnes) of shot, and 200 quintals (about 10 long tons or metric tonnes) of powder.[7] The commander of *San Ciríaco* was given a letter of marque as a cover and ordered to scout the Azores for British warships after delivering his cargo. Although it is not clear whether the money was entirely for delivery to the rebels or included costs of the expedition such as the chartering of the two privateers, the muskets, powder, and shot alone would have been a significant asset for Prince Charles. If all the money was intended for Charles, it would have amounted to nearly half of what the French tried to deliver to him at Loch nan Uamh in June 1746, and more than they sent him from Flanders in March 1746.

How far Álvarez covered the ships from Ferrol is unknown. *San Ciríaco*, with 12 guns (probably 3- or 4-pounders), four swivels, a crew of 60 and a commissioned officer in command, was captured on 30 September/11 October about 450 miles (720 kilometres) west of Ushant by privateer *Tryal* of Bristol. She had on board exactly half the muskets (2,500) and half the shot (150 quintals), 100 barrels of powder, other munitions, horseshoes, flints, and £6,000 in money (about 30,000 silver pesos).[8]

---

4   Charles Petrie, *King Charles III of Spain: An Enlightened Despot* (New York: The John Day Company, 1971), p.347 and his source, María Josefa Carpio, *España y los ultimos Estuardos* (Madrid: Facultad de Filosofia y Letras, Seminario de Historia Moderna, 1952) pp.284–285; also mentioned by John Cornelius O'Callaghan, *History of the Irish Brigades in the Service of France* (Glasgow: Cameron and Ferguson, 1870; repr. Shannon: Irish University Press, 1969), p.395.

5   Stephen McGarry, *Irish Brigades Abroad: From the Wild Geese to the Napoleonic Wars* (Dublin: History Press Ireland, 2013), p.111.

6   The full name of the first, *San Ciríaco y la Flecha* has given rise to the false conclusion that she was two ships. Antonio Laborda, and Luis Santiago Rodríguez Aedo, 'Barcos auxiliarios de la Real Armada en la guerra del asiento: La fragatilla *San Ciriaco y la Flecha*', *Revista de Historia Naval*, 37:145 (2019), pp.61–65.

7   María Baudot Monroy, 'Julián de Arriaga y Rivera: Una vida al servicio de la marina (1700–1776)' (Doctoral diss., Universidad Nacional de Educación a Distancia, [2005].), p.257.

8   *London Gazette*, No. 8474 (8 Oct. 1745), p.9. The *Gazette* report was repeated in *Gentleman's Magazine*, Vol. 15 (Oct. 1745), p.557, and *Scots Magazine*, Oct. 1745, p.493, and summarized in *London Magazine* (Oct. 1745), p.515.

The Spanish ambassador in Paris reported that two of the four ships were lost, one wrecked on the coast of Ireland, the other captured by a privateer.[9] O'Callaghan says or assumes that all were dispatched from La Coruña, the commercial port adjacent to El Ferrol, and accounts for them as follows:[10]

- *San Ciríaco*, captured;
- One that reached Scotland;
- One wrecked on the coast of Ireland;
- One 'not heard of'.

A ship named *San Pedro* was captured in early/mid-December, about 500 miles (800 kilometres) west of Rochefort (about 46°N), where she had been driven by storms that forced her to jettison her guns after having reached 47°28′N. Like *San Ciríaco*, she also carried 2,500 muskets, plus powder, ball, and flints, and was reported by the privateer *Ambuscade* to have jettisoned the 60,000 pistoles or 120,000 pesos (£24,000) on board.[11] (The amount might have been exaggerated by the crew to taunt their captors). This was too much later than *San Ciríaco* to have been part of the same sailing; since the Spanish ambassador reported only one ship captured, *San Pedro* would seem to be from another aid project, but the ambassador's report might have been too early to include the fate of all four ships. The prisoners told their captors that there were three more vessels at Ferrrol laden with 'Arms and Ammunition, bound for Scotland'.[12]

A Spanish vessel landed 2,500 muskets and accoutrements plus some cash on the island of Barra in October or November 1745.[13] This was probably *Peña de Francia*. McGarry says that one named '*Corunno*' ('from La Coruña') with 16 guns and 60 men 'arrived safely in Scotland',[14] while Gibson describes arms on Barra from a 'Spanish ship from San Sebastian.' The amount of money is variously reported as 4,000 Spanish 'dollars' or pesos and as £4,000; the difference is substantial, since 4,000 pesos were worth about £800 at the current

---

9   Carpio, *España y los ultimos Estuardos*, pp.286–287.

10   O'Callaghan, *History of the Irish Brigades*, p.395. The same number and distribution of outcomes is mentioned by Horace Walpole to Horace Mann, 21 Oct. 1745, in Horace Walpole (W.S. Lewis, Warren Hunting Smith, and George L. Lam eds), *Horace Walpole's Correspondence with Sir Horace Mann*, Vols. 17–27 of 48 vols of The Yale Edition of Horace Walpole's Correspondence (New Haven: Yale University Press, 1954–1971), vol.17, pp.137–138.

11   *London Gazette*, No. 8494 (17 Dec. 1745), p.1; Lord Vere Beauclerk (a commissioner of the Admiralty) to Adm. Edward Vernon, Admiralty-office, Oct. 8, 1745, in B[rian] McL Ranft (ed.), *The Vernon Papers* ([London]: Navy Records Society, 1958.), pp.483–84; Samuel Boyse, *An Historical Review of the Transactions of Europe, from … 1739, … 1745* (Reading: D. Henry, 1747), vol. 2, App. p.119; O'Callaghan, *History of the Irish Brigades*, p.395.

12   *London Gazette*, No. 8494 (Dec. 17, 1745), p.1.

13   Christopher Duffy, *Fight for a Throne: The Jacobite '45 Reconsidered* (Solihull: Helion & Company Limited, 2015), 523; John Lorne Campbell, *A Very Civil People: Hebridean Folk, History and Tradition* (ed. Hugh Cheape) (Edinburgh: Birlinn Ltd, 2000), p.99, and Campbell, 'The Macneils of Barra in the Forty-Five', *The Innes Review*, 17:2 (Autumn 1966), p.86; Keith Branigan, *From Clan to Clearance: History and Archaeology of the Isle of Barra, c. 850–1850*, Sheffield Environmental and Archaeological Research Campaigns in the Hebrides, vol. 6 (Oxford: Oxbow Books, 2005), unpaginated.

14   McGarry, *Irish Brigades*, p.111.

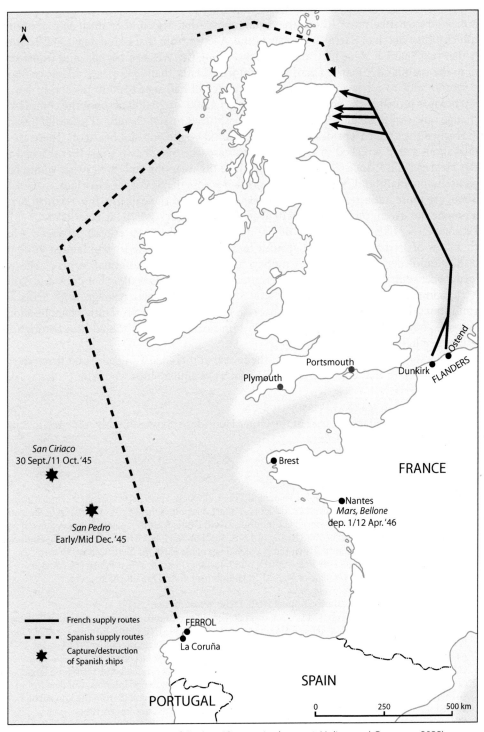

N

San Ciriaco
30 Sept./11 Oct. '45

San Pedro
Early/Mid Dec. '45

Portsmouth

Plymouth

Dunkirk   Ostend   FLANDERS

Brest

FRANCE

Nantes
Mars, Bellone
dep. 1/12 Apr. '46

———— French supply routes
- - - - Spanish supply routes
✳ Capture/destruction
    of Spanish ships

FERROL
La Coruña

SPAIN

PORTUGAL

0   250   500 km

Bourbon sailings in support of the '45 . (George Anderson © Helion and Company 2023)

commercial exchange rate.[15] There are vague reports that a second Spanish ship arrived at South Uist (just north of Barra) at the same time. A letter from that island dated 14 December says that two Spanish ships had 'arrived lately among the Western Islands' and transferred men to the mainland.[16] Prince Charles was informed later that £380 was available on Barra and sent an aide to retrieve it, and the local clan chief had sent £500 to his son-in-law, so 4,000 pesos is probably the correct amount,[17] but £4,000, or 20,000 pesos at the commercial exchange rate, would be more like the amount captured in *San Ciríaco*. If a second Spanish ship reached the Outer Hebrides late in 1745, it could be the one 'not heard of'. There are no details about a ship wrecked in Ireland. In any case, the one or two ships that reached the Outer Hebrides did Prince Charles no good, since the weapons and money that would have been useful on 'mainland' Scotland never made it across the Sea of the Hebrides.

There are more definite, but also incomplete, reports of the capture of a 'Spanish privateer', name not given, on 3/14 February 1746 by *Bridgewater*, 20/24, at Peterhead, 27 miles (44 kilometers) NNE of Aberdeen. Before being captured the Peterhead privateer, a brig with a crew of 35 that had arrived around 16/27 January, reportedly had landed 'nine tun [sic] of gunpowder, three chests of money, and several chests of small arms'.[18] She was armed, because *Bridgewater* took out her guns and powder as well as her crew and sails.[19] Her captain said that that there were '4 or 5 sail more on their passage, with arms and ammunition, that [were] to go to some port on the west coast of Scotland, where he should have gone', but that the weather had driven him north and thus forced him through the Pentland Firth.[20]

This ship, too, could have been part of the four that included *San Pedro* and three she left behind at Ferrol. In that case, the fates of the four December ships would be:

- One captured at sea (*San Pedro*);
- Two that delivered their cargo in the Outer Hebrides and presumably returned to Spain;
- One captured at Peterhead.

15   Branigan, *From Clan to Clearance* (unpaginated); J.L. Campbell, *Very Civil People*, p.99, and 'McNeils of Barra', pp.85–86; David Wemyss, Lord Elcho, *A Short Account of the Affairs of Scotland in the Years 1744, 1745, 1746* (ed. Evan Charteris) (Edinburgh: David Douglas, 1907), p.360; James A Stewart Jr, 'Highland Motives in the Jacobite Rising of 1745–46: "Forcing Out," Traditional Documentation and Gaelic Poetry', in Benjamin Bruch (ed.), *Proceedings of the Harvard Celtic Colloquium*, vol. 21 (Cambridge: Harvard University Press, 2001), p.153; Joshua Dickson, *When Piping Was Strong: Tradition, Change and the Bagpipe in South Uist* (Edinburgh: John Donald, 2006), p.94.
16   Dickson, *When Piping Was Strong*, p.94.
17   Branigan, *From Clan to* Clearance, unpaginated; Elcho, *Short Account*, 360n.
18   *Gentleman's Magazine*, 16 (Feb. 1746), p.94, from 20 Feb. 1746 extraordinary issue of *London Gazette* not now available; *Scottish Magazine*, 8 (Jan. 1746), p.44 (quotation); R[amon] P[hilip] Fereday, *Orkney Feuds and The '45* (Kirkwall:, Kirkwall Grammar School, 1980) p.153; master's log, *Bridgewater*, TNA, ADM 52/551; James, Allardyce (ed.), *Historical Papers Relating to the Jacobite Period, 1699–1750* (Aberdeen, New Spalding Club, 1895), vol.1, pp.262, 264. 'Tun' was originally the term for a large cask. Later descriptions of the Spanish brig's cargo say 'nine tons' of gunpowder. Arrival date from J.E. Tocher (ed.), *The Book of Buchan* (Peterhead: The Buchan Club 1910), p.306, from the journal of a loyalist minister in Aberdeen, about 27 miles (45 kilometers) away as the seagull flies.
19   Master's log, *Bridgewater*, 3 Feb. 1745/6, TNA, ADM 52/551.
20   *Gentleman's Magazine*, 16 (Feb. 1746), p. 94, from *London Gazette*, extraordinary issue.

Whether the December sailings were a government project or a private effort by Spanish Jacobites is unknown.

One final fleeting reference to Spanish support states that 'Early in March 1746 a Spanish ship reached Montrose with supplies', presumably munitions.[21] This seems too late to be the Peterhead ship.

Thus, the Spanish efforts to provide assistance were wholly ineffectual. Some of the ships sent did not reach Scotland. The munitions and money landed by those that did never got to Charles or his forces where they could support his rebellion. French support was more extensive and persistent, and made a positive contribution to the military aspect of the rebellion.

French Support

While the British had been organizing naval forces in home waters, including the North Sea, to isolate the rebellion, the French had begun sending the assistance to Prince Charles that he had hoped to provoke by raising a rebellion in Scotland. After landing at Loch nan Uamh, Charles had written a letter to Louis XV, following up on the missive that he had left behind at Nantes for delivery after he had sailed. The second letter announced Charles' successful disembarkation and appealed for assistance. The ship that had brought him raided British shipping before putting in at Amsterdam on 23 August/3 September. Her owner proceeded to Paris to deliver Charles' second letter and report in person that he had delivered the Prince to Scotland.[22]

Charles' presence in Scotland was already known in France, and French government ministers had already begun considering how to react during August (in their calendar).[23] The Foreign, Navy, and War (army) Ministries analysed and debated the advantages and disadvantages to France of various responses, including an invasion of Ireland, and the administrative details of various schemes, including their monetary costs. The first reaction was not to mount a major assistance effort or an invasion but to send a well-travelled Provençal lawyer, Alexandre-Jean-Baptiste Boyer, Marquis d'Éguilles, to Scotland to investigate the potential of a rising. D'Éguilles received his instructions on 13/24 September, and proceeded immediately to Dunkirk. However, as early as 3/14 September Navy Minister Maurepas had written to the navy commander at Dunkirk, *Chef d'escadre* François-Cornil Bart, warning him to be ready to support a new invasion attempt, and two days later ordered him to begin chartering vessels for the transfer of money and arms to Scotland. Maurepas was sceptical of the strength of the English Jacobites and therefore of the prospects of a

---

21   J. de Courcey Ireland, Note about McLynn, 'Sea Power', *Mariner's Mirror*, 67:3 (1981), p.289, including a discussion of a study of Irish participation in The '45 by the president of the Military History Society of Ireland in the 1950s, probably referring to Charles Petrie, 'Irishmen in the Forty-Five', *Irish Sword*, 2:8 (1956), pp.275–82 (not available for this project).

22   Gibson, *Ships*, pp.15–16; Henri Malo, 'Le prétendant Charles-Édouard et les corsaires', *The Anglo-French Review*, 1:6 (July 1919), p.518.

23   F[rank] J. McLynn, *France and the Jacobite Rising of 1745* (Edinburgh: Edinburgh University Press, 1981), p.61.

French invasion of England to overthrow the existing Hanoverian regime. Throughout the '45, he successfully avoided involving the navy itself and its warships. Since he did not think that a small French invasion army would result in the replacement of the Hanoverian George II by a Stuart king in Britain, he reserved his limited budget for refitting his warships for the 1746 campaign he hoped to mount to recover Louisbourg on Cape Breton Island, captured by a New England expedition earlier in the year. By the end of summer in 1745, the French navy still owed private ship-owners their charter fees from the 1744 invasion attempt, had no credit, and could just pay its current bills. Although the costs of supporting Prince Charles were charged to the army, Maurepas complained in October 1745 that the navy had incurred expenses for the shipments already made to Scotland and those then under preparation.[24]

With the British not yet watching the coast, four small vessels carrying d'Éguilles, weapons for about 2,400 men (including muskets, flints, powder, musket balls, and sabres), six light field artillery pieces, and £4,200 (4,000 guineas) or £6,000 sailed individually as they were ready, between 26 September/7 October and 11/22 October. Their sorties, and those of later vessels carrying aid to Prince Charles or seeking to evacuate him from Scotland, are listed in Table 1. The map shows the relative positions of the ports of embarkation and debarkation for the French aid effort in the North Sea. D'Éguilles left with the money and some volunteer army officers on *Espérance,* a privateer chartered by the navy, on 26 September/7 October, after the capture of Edinburgh and the victory at Prestonpans that drove the British army over the Scottish border to Berwick-on-Tweed, but before news of these favourable events had reached France. Since it was not known that Edinburgh and its port, Leith, were under rebel control, this was a risky operation, and *Espérance* was almost intercepted by a British squadron while trying to put in to the Firth of Tay, which would have taken her to Dundee. However, she found a merchantman with a Jacobite captain on board who brought her into Montrose, about 60 miles (100 kilometres) northeast of Edinburgh, on 6/17 October. Three other chartered vessels, merchantmen *Hareng Couronné* and *Sainte-Geneviève* and privateer *Neptune,* sailed on 2/13 October and 11/22 October with the arms and equipment that *Espérance* had been too small to carry. *Hareng Couronné* also delivered her share of the munitions at Stonehaven on 7/18 or 15/26 October,[25] and *Neptune* and *Sainte-Geneviève* at Montrose and at Stonehaven, another 20 miles (33 kilometres) up the coast, somewhat later in October. These ships also delivered £2,000–5,000.[26] All four vessels were able to return to Dunkirk, *Neptune* on 21 November/2 December.[27] They brought dispatches from d'Éguilles,

24   McLynn, *France and the Rising,* pp.61–69, 77; Germain Lefèvre-Pontalis, 'La mission du marquis d'Éguilles en Écosse auprès de Charles-Édouard (1745–1746)', *Annales de l'École Libre des Sciences Politiques,* 2 (1887), pp.248–249; [Fernand René] Lamorte, 'L'Action de la France contre les Îles Britanniques pendant la guerre de succession d'Autriche' ([Paris]: École de guerre navale, [1933]) p.31; James Pritchard, *Anatomy of a Naval Disaster: The 1746 French Naval Expedition to North America* (Montreal & Kingston: McGill-Queen's University Press, 1995), p.34; Comte Estienne [Antoine Charles] de Chabannes-La Palisse, 'Camp de Boulogne (1745)', *Revue des questions historiques,* 64:3 (issue 252) (May 1936), p.37.
25   Jean E[sther] McCann, 'The Organisation of the Jacobite Army, 1745–1746' (PhD diss., Univ. of Edinburgh, 196), p.154, cites correspondence supporting both dates.
26   McCann, 'Organisation', p.54, who thinks *Hareng Couronnée* was followed by only one or two ships.
27   McLynn, *France and the Rising,* p.68; Lefevre-Pontalis, 'Mission du Éguilles', pp.247, 253, 254n;

appeals from Jacobites, and a personal emissary from Charles, Sir James Stuart. Of the four, only *Neptune* made another voyage.

Table 1: French Aid Shipments to Jacobite Rebels, 1745–1746

Date	Origin	Ships (tons)*	Fate	Content †
1745				
26 Sep./7 Oct.	Dunkirk	Espérance/Soleil (120)	Ar. Montrose, 6/17 Oct.	Marquis d'Éguilles, £4,400–6,000
2/13 Oct.	Dunkirk	Hareng Couronné (110–120)	Ar. Montrose	Arms, equipment for 2,400 infantry; 6 field pieces
11/22 Oct.	Dunkirk	Neptune (90)	Ar. Montrose/ Stonehaven	
		Ste.-Geneviève (80)	Ar. Montrose, 24 Oct./4 Nov.	
16/27 Nov.c	Dunkirk	*Fine* (900 disp.)	Destroyed Montrose, 27 Nov./8 Dec.	300 infantry (RE)
		Renomée (150)	Ar. Montrose, 24 Nov./5 Dec.	150 infantry (RE), 6 cannon
		St.-Bernard (20)		?
17/28 Nov.	Dunkirk	Jeanneton (?), Paix (?)	Ar. Peterhead & Stonehaven	Inf.: 400 (RE) + 50 (D)
		Saint-Thérèse (120) ‡		?
		Louis XV (45) ‡	Capt. by *Milford*	200 inf. (Be, Bu, C, R)
		Espérance/Soleil (120) ‡	Capt. by *Sheerness*	150 infantry (RE)
1746				
8/19 Feb.	Ostend	Bourbon (220), Charité (?),	Turned back	359 cavalry (FJ), £5,000
		Prince de Nassau/Sophie	Ar. Aberdeen	130 men (FJ), cav. equip.
18 Feb./1 Mar.	Dunkirk	*Aventurier* (55)	Burned Peterhead harbour	46 infantry (Be)
		Eméraude (900 disp.), Neptune (90) Ste.-Thérèse (120), Confiance (100), Comte de Maurepas (180)	Reached Scottish coast, did not land anything, returned to Dunkirk	600 infantry (Be, C)
20 Feb./3 Mar.	Ostend	*Bourbon* (220), *Charité* (?)	Capt. by *Hastings* and consorts.‖	359 cavalry (FJ), £5,000
	Ostend	Comte de Lowendal§, Saint Pierre§, Fortune§, St. Louis Dogre§, Sirène§	Did not sail	600 infantry

O'Callaghan, *Irish Brigades*, p.385; Malo, 'Prétendant', pp.518–519; 254n; *Courrier* (Avignon), No. 101 (Dec. 17, 1745), p.4, *Neptune* identified by the name of her captain as given by Malo, 'Prétendant', p.519.

Date	Origin	Ships (tons)*	Fate	Content †
14/25 Mar.	Dunkirk	*Prince Charles* (273 burthen)	Capt. by *Sheerness*	£12–13,000, 100 men (Be)
20 Apr./1 May	Nantes	Mars (300), Bellone (350)	Battle of Loch nan Uamh	ca. £35,000, munitions
3/14 May	Dunkirk	Hardi Mendicant (55)	Returned to Dunkirk	Rescue of Pr. Charles
28 May/8 Jun.	Dunkirk	Levrier Volante (30)	Returned to Dunkirk	Rescue of Pr. Charles
31 May/11 Jun.	Dunkirk	*Bien Trouvé* (small)	Capt. by *Glasgow, Trial*	Rescue of Pr. Charles
8/19 Jun.	Dunkirk	Hardi Mendicant (55)	Returned to Dunkirk	Rescue of Pr. Charles
18/29 Jun.	Ostend	Comte de Lowendal (300), Comte de Maurepas (180)	Returned to France	Rescue of Pr. Charles
31 Jul./11 Aug.	St. Malo	Heureux (300), Prince de Conti (180)	Brought Pr. Charles from Loch nan Uamh to Roscoff	Rescue of Pr. Charles

Source: Base list from McLynn, 'Sea Power', p.171, from Maurepas Papers, Cornell Univ.; origin, fate details, content from scattered sources. This table does not include voyages only to carry dispatches, such as one by *Prince Charles* after her capture from the British or a round trip by *Bien Trouvé* in March 1746 mentioned by Gibson, *Ships*, p.25. Ships in italics did not return to France, others returned, date and port not shown.

The heavy rules delineate the period in which the sorties analysed by Lavery, Shield, p.60, occurred.

* French measurement tons, indicative of cargo capacity; 'disp.' indicates displacement in French tonneaux.

† French regiment abbreviations: Be = Berwick; Bu = Bulkeley; C = Clare; D = Dillon; FJ = Fitzjames (cavalry); L = Lally; R = Rothe; RE = Royal Écossais

‡ Left overnight, perhaps the next calendar day after midnight.

§ Not on McLynn's list

‖ Triton, Salamander, Vulcan

D'Éguilles met Charles and his small army and wrote a report to French Foreign Affairs Secretary, the Comte d'Argenson, at Edinburgh between 16/27 and 19/30 October. By 23 October/3 November, Charles had about 9,400 armed men at Edinburgh and was expecting another 3,600. D'Éguilles stayed in Scotland and continued to report back to France, sending dispatches on returning arms runners or troop transports. His earliest accounts, and news of the victory at Prestonpans on 20 September/2 October, convinced the French government to make a more substantial investment in Prince Charles and the Stuarts by signing the Treaty of Fontainebleau with representatives of Prince Charles' father, who claimed the titles of King James III of England and King James VIII of Scotland, on 13/24 October. The treaty pledged military support to England and Scotland as domains of King James. With the treaty came the decision to send professional French army troops to Scotland and to invade England.[28]

---

28   Lefèvre-Pontalis, 'Mission du Éguilles', in p.258n; McLynn, *France and the Rising*, pp.86–87; Eveline Cruickshanks, *Political Untouchables: The Tories and the '45* (New York: Holmes & Meier Publishers, Inc., 1979), p.83.

Although the invasion of southern England involved more troops, they were to move as a concentrated corps, whereas the plan to aid Prince Charles directly admitted sending several contingents. The Scottish plan was to send the French army's 'Irish' brigade, regiments raised in Ireland during the war of 1688–1697, and recruited since from expatriate Irish nationalists who wanted to continue to fight King William III and Queen Mary II, and their successors. The first unit to be sent was the 'Royal Écossais' (Royal Scottish) regiment. Two 28-gun French navy frigates that had been hired out to private entrepreneurs for commerce-raiding, *Fine* and *Eméraude,* had put in to Dunkirk to repair rigging damage incurred in an action with a British warship off Yarmouth.[29] They were chartered to provide escorts for more lightly-armed merchantmen and privateers, so Louis XV paid for the use of his own ships. Only *Fine* escorted the Royal Écossais regiment; perhaps *Eméraude*'s repairs had not yet been completed.

Like the October/early November shipment, the Royal Écossais convoy also left Dunkirk in separate groups, although each consisted of two or three ships instead of just one, and they were close together. *Fine, Renommée,* and *Saint Bernard* left on the night of 16/17–27/28 November; *Jeanneton* and *Paix* sailed on the afternoon of 17/28 November; and *Espérance, Louis XV,* and *Sainte-Thérèse* sailed that night, 17/28–18/29 November. These vessels were attempting to transfer the entire Royal Écossais regiment with all its equipment and most of its officers (a few had gone ahead on the October ships), plus some 300 men comprising one 'picquet' from each regiment of the Irish regiments, with their equipment. *Fine* and *Renommée* were detailed as escorts as well as transports.[30] However, in the face of the developing British blockade, it was decided not to risk the Fitzjames cavalry regiment, so *Eméraude,* the regiment's transport, did not sail.[31]

The first contingent was scattered by a storm in the North Sea that had already sunk British frigate *Fox*, 20/24, with all hands, and wrecked sloop *Trial*, 10, on Holy Island (Lindisfarne), both on 14/25 November (*Trial* was salvaged). *Fine* delivered her troops at Montrose on 26 November/7 December but ran aground trying to avoid attack by *Milford*, 44 (formerly *Advice*, 50; sometimes called a '40' in the literature of the '45).[32] and was wrecked. *Milford* also ran aground but got off. *Renommée, Saint Bernard, Jeanneton, Paix,* and *Sainte Thérèse* delivered their troops and supplies (*Renommée* at Montrose, 24 November/5 December, the others at Peterhead and Stonehaven) and returned to Dunkirk. In getting in to Montrose, *Renommée* trapped a small British warship, *Hazard*, 16, assisted by the field artillery she had just landed, and turned her over to the rebels. They repaired her damage with stores scavenged from *Fine* and insouciantly renamed her *Prince Charles*. However *Espérance*, after jettisoning guns in the North Sea gale, encountered *Sheerness*, 24, near the Dogger Bank on 22 November/3 December and had to surrender with 150 soldiers on board; and *Louis XV,* with 200 men (including 16 officers and six non-combatants) from three of the Irish

29   Malo, 'Prétendant', p.519, and Henri Malo, *Les Dernièrs corsaires: Dunquerque (1715–1815).* (Paris: Émile-Paul Frères, Éditeurs, 1925), pp.17–18.

30   Thomas Hindley, 'Le régiment Royal Ecossais durant la campagne d'Ecosse, 1745–1746' (Master's thesis, University of Paris IV, 2014), p.119; McLynn, *France and the Rising*, p.110.

31   McLynn, *France and the Rising,* p.111.

32   Rif Winfield, *British Warships in the Age of Sail, 1714–1792: Design, Construction, Careers and Fates* (Barnsley, South Yorks.: Seaforth Publishing, 2007), p.142.

regiments was taken by *Milford* off Montrose on 28 November/9 December.[33] British histories and contemporary accounts indicate that *Espérance* had previously been named *Soleil,* and some contemporary and later accounts use only that name for her; but there is no trace of a name change in French mentions.

After the French attempt to invade Kent was ended by the cancellation of a sailing scheduled for 2/13 January 1746, the French government reaffirmed its decision to continue sending men and munitions to Scotland.[34] Three expeditions were planned from different ports. There is confusion in the accounts, not helped by the fact that sailings occurred close together but at separate ports, or on nearly the same date but in the two different British and French calendars.

The first of these expeditions was an attempt to carry a fully-equipped heavy cavalry regiment, Fitzjames, with all of its equipment, from Ostend, an Austrian Netherlands port captured by the French in August 1745. The troopers and their 'horse furniture' were loaded onto three transports and initially sailed on 8/19 February.[35] The larger ships, *Bourbon* and *Charité,* turned back when confronted by British warships. A third vessel, possibly unarmed, named either *Sophie* or *Prince de Nassau* (one of these possibly a former name) did get away into the North Sea and landed two companies (130 men) with their saddles and other equipment. A fourth unnamed vessel is mentioned in connection with this sailing. McLynn and Malo say she was captured shortly after departure by a British warship, Lamorte says that she returned safely to Ostend.[36] The best date for the arrival of *Sophie/Prince de Nassau* at Aberdeen is 22 February/5 March 1746.[37]

Bourbon and *Charité* made a second attempt to take the rest of the regiment to Scotland on 20 February/3 March. However, they were captured almost immediately by Commodore Charles Knowles in *Hastings*, 44. Knowles' initial report said there were '5 or 600 of Fitz-James' Regiment, with all their Saddles, Arms and Horse-Furniture, and some Ammunition', and 500 has been published in some later accounts, but lists of the officers with counts of

---

33   Duffy, *Fight for a Throne*, pp.527–528; McLynn, *France and the Rising*, p.111; Hindley, 'Régiment Ecossais', p.119; Brian Lavery, *Shield of Empire: The Royal Navy and Scotland* (Edinburgh: Birlinn, 2012), pp.53–54; *London Gazette*, No. 8487 (Nov. 23, 1745), p.7, No. 8490 (Dec. 3, 1745), p.2, No. 8491 (Dec. 7, 1745), p.2. .

34   Lamorte, 'Action de la France', p.35; Chabannes-La Palisse, 'Camp de Boulogne (1745)', p.51.

35   Lavery, *Shield of Empire*, p.58; McLynn, 'Sea Power', p.171, Malo, 'Prétendant', p.522, and *Dernièrs corsaires*, p.24.

36   Lavery, *Shield of Empire*, p.58; Mairead McKerracher, *The Jacobite Dictionary* (Glasgow: Neil Wilson Publishing Ltd, 2007), p.206; McGarry, *Irish Brigades*, p.116; Stuart Reid, *1745: A Military History of the Last Jacobite Uprising* (Staplehurst: Spellmount, 2001), p.116; Stephen Wood, *The Auld Alliance: Scotland and France, the Military Connection* (Edinburgh: Mainstream Publishing, 1989), p.82; V[alentine John] Hussey-Walsh, 'A Projected Jacobite Invasion', *Quarterly Review*, No. 433 (October, 1912), p.389; McLynn, *France and the Rising*, pp.189–190; McLynn, 'Sea Power', 171; Malo, 'Prétendant', pp.522–523 and *Dernièrs corsaires*, p.24; Lamorte, 'Action de la France', p.36.

37   Jacqueline Riding, *Jacobites: A New History of the '45 Rebellion* (New York: Bloomsbury Press, 2016), pp.374–375; Wood, *Auld Alliance*, 82. F[rancis] Douglass and W[illiam] Murray (eds.), *The History of the Rebellion in 1745 and 1746, Extracted from the Scots Magazine* (Aberdeen: F. Douglass and W. Murray, 1755), p.150, and George Charles, *History of the Transactions in Scotland, in the Years 1715–16, and 1745–46* (Leith: George Charles, 1817), vol.2, p.255, quote a report by the Duke of Cumberland of an unnamed ship that matches *Prince de Nassau/Sophie* landing 130 men at Stoneheaven on 22 Feb./5 Mar.

enlisted men, published only a week later, show 199 on *Bourbon* and 160 on *Charité*, for a total of 359.[38] Although some accounts have indicated that the regiment was or was supposed to be accompanied by its horses, they are not mentioned in Knowles' report or summaries of the prize papers at The National Archives.[39] In fact, the regiment was equipped to serve as infantry, with infantry muskets but without the carbines used by cavalry. Since horses could only be found in Scotland for the 46 or so men of the regiment landed there by dismounting an extemporized local cavalry unit, sending a 400-man heavy cavalry regiment with its expensive 'horse furniture' in case mounts were found in Scotland was a misallocation of resources and would not have provided Prince Charles and his army with a valuable cavalry arm; *Sophie/Prince de Nassau*, *Bourbon*, and *Charité* would have been better devoted to transporting more Irish Brigade infantry.

The second sailing of Fitzjames followed by a couple of days a sortie from Dunkirk with 650 men of the Berwick and Clare Regiments from the Irish Brigade. The men were on five vessels, *Aventurier*, *Confiance*, *Eméraud*, *Neptune*, and *Sainte-Thérèse*, to be escorted by privateer *Comte de Maurepas*, 16. The convoy put to sea in a fog on 18 February/1 March 1746 and was not intercepted in the North Sea, but was unable to stay together. *Aventurier* landed 46 Berwick Regiment men at Peterhead on 25 February 258 March but was chased onto a shoal at Cruden Bay, 20 miles (32 kilometres) NNE of Aberdeen, by *Gloucester*, 50; *Eltham*, 44; and *Winchelsea*, 24. *Gloucester* sent in her boats and burned *Aventurier*. *Comte de Maurepas* landed some money but not her contingent of soldiers, and had to beat off a British sloop, *Vulture*, 10, in the Moray Firth after evading *Glasgow*, 24. Meanwhile, *Eméraude* and *Neptune* had rendezvoused at Aberdeen on 24 February/7 March but when a boat was sent to investigate the situation ashore, the men in it were warned that the Duke of Cumberland and his army would be in Aberdeen by evening. The convoy commander, *Lieutenant de Vaisseau* Saint-Allouarn (commander of *Eméraude*), tried to take the convoy north about to land the troops on the west coast, still under Jacobite control, but some of the ships could not make headway against adverse winds and *Confiance* lost her main topmast. As *Aventurier*'s fate and the encounters by *Comte de Maurepas* had shown, remaining on the east coast was a dangerous proposition, and on 27 February/10 March the military and overall commander, the Marquis de Cimarron, decided to return to France. *Comte de Maurepas* returned to Ostend on 6/17 March, the others to Dunkirk between 4/15 and 6/17 March, with a third of *Eméraude*'s crew sick. The dangers for the French ships were shown by the experience of *Comte de Maurepas*. The day before she made Ostend, she was chased

---

38   Lavery, *Shield*, p.58; Reid, *1745*, p.116; McLynn, 'Sea Power', p.171; Knowles' report from the Downs, 21 February 1745, *London Gazette*, No. 8512 (22 Feb. 1746); Winfield, *British Warships*, p.169. Officer lists in *London Gazette*, No. 8514 (Feb. 25, 1745), p.2, in *The British Chronologist, Comprehending Every Material Occurrence . . . from the Invasion of the Romans to the Present Time* (London: G. Kersley, 1775), vol.2, p.391.

39   A[rchibald] McKenzie Annand, 'FitzJames's Horse in the '45', *The Irish Sword*, 16:65 (Winter 1986), p.274; Christian Aikman, *No Quarter Given: The Muster Roll of Prince Charles Edward Stuart's Army, 1745-46* ([Glasgow]: Neil Wilson Publishing, 2012), p.40; British National Archives, High Court of Admiralty, Prize Papers, HCA 32/100/11, summary at <https://discovery.nationalarchives.gov.uk/details/r/C14512570> (accessed 26 June 2019); Andrew Bamford, *The Lilies and the Thistle: French Troops in the Jacobite '45* (Warwick: Helion, 2018), p.67.

by a British warship; in the chase, her foremast was damaged becoming 'unserviceable', four men were killed, and the wounded included two who lost legs.[40]

Another troop convoy had been prepared at Ostend to take men of the Rothe Regiment to Scotland, including *Comte de Lowendal* as escort and transports *Fortune, St. Louis Dogre, Sirène,* and *Saint Pierre.* Baffled by contrary winds and British cruisers (which presumably appeared whenever the wind would be favourable for a sortie), this convoy either never sailed or sailed but returned to port shortly without losing ships to capture by the British and without reaching the coast of Scotland.[41]

The French made one more effort to assist the Jacobite rebellion in the spring of 1746. *Prince Charles* (formerly British *Hazard*), 10, had made several round trips to France with dispatches. In March 1746 she was returning not only with messages but with 140 soldiers of the Berwick Regiment and £12,000–13,000 in gold coins. So far, troop pay and supply purchases for Charles' army had been financed by seizure of government funds in towns the Jacobite forces had occupied (money that Charles considered at his disposal as regent for the rightful sovereign), but those funds were running out. The ports north of the Firth of Tay, principally Montrose, Aberdeen, and Peterhead, had by this time been occupied by the British army under the Duke of Cumberland, so *Prince Charles* got through the Pentland Firth and put in to the Kyle of Tongue, a bay on the north coast. This was a remote, thinly inhabited region, but the specie and the troops were put ashore. However, they were captured by the militia of a clan that supported the Hanoverian government, not Prince Charles, and on 23 March/3 April *Prince Charles* herself ran aground and was recaptured by *Sheerness,* 24. Charles' paymaster estimated that the £35,000–£36,000 landed later at Loch nan Uamh would have paid 7,000 men for six months at £5 per man or 16s 8d per month (a British infantry private's pay was 18s 8d per 28-day month); thus the capture by loyalists of the money on *Prince Charles* deprived the ship's namesake of sufficient specie to pay 7,000 men for two months, and forced Charles to stand and fight at Culloden rather than see his army dribble away in desertions from lack of food and pay.[42] (The French royal regiments brought their pay with them).

In his appeals to the Bourbon kings for assistance, Charles did not ask for specific numbers of troops or amounts of money against which the success or failure of the French and Spanish support efforts could be measured. The '45 clearly failed to restore the Stuarts to the throne of Great Britain or even the throne of an independent Scotland, so the French effort self-evidently failed to achieve that. But there are other ways to evaluate the French project.

---

40   *Courrier* (Avignon), No. 20 (11 Mar. 1746), dispatch from Paris, 5 Mar.; *London Gazette,* No. 8519 (15 Mar. 1745), p.1, 'Hague, March 22, N.S.'; No. 8520 (18 Mar. 1745), p.5, 'Hague, March 29'; Duffy, *Fight for a Throne,* p.529; McLynn, *France and the Rising,* p.192; Malo, 'Prétendant', p.523 and *Dernièrs corsaires,* pp.24–25.

41   Malo, 'Prétendant', p.523 and *Dernièrs corsaires,* p.24; McLynn, *France and the Rising,* pp.189, 193; Gibson, *Ships,* p.24; Reid, *Scottish Jacobite Army,* p.30; Lamorte, 'Action de la France', p.36.

42   Doron Zimmerman, *The Jacobite Movement in Scotland and in Exile, 1746–1759* (Basingstoke: Palgrave Macmillan, 2003), p.27; Gibson, *Ships,* p.25; John Roberts, *The Jacobite Wars: Scotland and the Military Campaigns of 1715 and 1745* (Edinburgh: Polygon at Edinburgh [Edinburgh University Press], 2002), p.149; Lavery, *Shield of Empire,* pp.59–60.

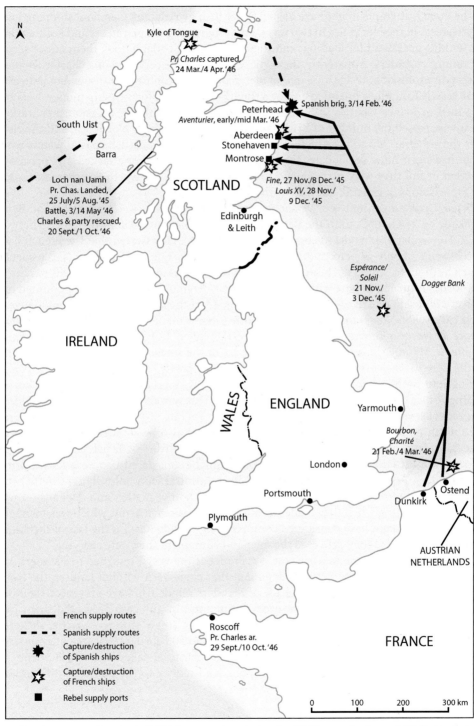

N

Kyle of Tongue
Pr. Charles captured,
24 Mar./4 Apr. '46

South Uist

Barra

Loch nan Uamh
Pr. Chas. Landed,
25 July/5 Aug. '45
Battle, 3/14 May '46
Charles & party rescued,
20 Sept./1 Oct. '46

SCOTLAND

Peterhead
Spanish brig, 3/14 Feb. '46
Aventurier, early/mid Mar. '46
Aberdeen
Stonehaven
Montrose
Fine, 27 Nov./8 Dec. '45
Louis XV, 28 Nov./
9 Dec. '45

Edinburgh
& Leith

*Espérance/
Soleil*
21 Nov./
3 Dec. '45

Dogger Bank

IRELAND

ENGLAND

Yarmouth

*Bourbon,
Charité*
21 Feb./4 Mar. '46

WALES

London

Ostend
Portsmouth
Dunkirk

Plymouth

AUSTRIAN
NETHERLANDS

——— French supply routes
- - - Spanish supply routes
Capture/destruction
of Spanish ships
Capture/destruction
of French ships
Rebel supply ports

Roscoff
Pr. Charles ar.
29 Sept./10 Oct. '46

FRANCE

0   100   200   300 km

Bourbon support routes in British home waters during the '45. (George Anderson © Helion and
Company 2023)

The French attempts might have helped the British by reducing merchant shipping losses to privateers in the North Sea in two ways. First, chartering the privateers and holding them at Dunkirk or Ostend for loading, and their voyages to Scotland, took them out of service as commerce raiders. Apparently, the owners preferred the certainty of a charter fee to the uncertain profits of a voyage in search of merchantmen to capture or ransom, but it diverted their vessels from their intended use for a time. Second, the efforts to ship money, weapons, and men to Prince Charles in Scotland, in combination with the invasion preparations, greatly increased the number of British warships in the southern North Sea, and the rising plus the aid effort led to the establishment of a squadron in Scottish coastal waters where there had been none previously. The ships involved would have attacked any privateers, whether or not they were carrying aid to Charles, making the North Sea more hazardous for French ships in general, not just for the aid effort vessels.

Brian Lavery has analysed 19 sorties attempted between 'the resumption of Byng's blockade on 26 October until the Battle of Culloden six months later' (departures between 15/26 November 1745 and 14 February/25 March 1746). He asserted that the French had a 'success rate' of only 37 percent (seven sorties) and a 'loss rate' of 37 percent (seven sorties), which he thought 'would not be an acceptable level of losses in any conflict'.[43] (His remaining five sorties returned to port without landing their cargo in Scotland.) Lavery counted only delivery *and* safe return as a 'success'. However, 13 of the 19 sorties, 68 percent, delivered their cargo (*Fine, Renommée, Jeanneton, Sainte-Thérèse* on 26 November, *Paix, St. Bernard, Prince de Nassau, Eméraude, Neptune, Sainte-Thérèse* on 18 February/1 March, *Confiance, Comte de Maurepas, Aventurier*), while only six of the sorties, 32 percent, resulted in loss of the vessel (*Fine, Espérance, Louis XV, Bourbon, Charité, Aventurier*), with two vessels falling into both categories (*Fine, Aventurier*). Lavery's period should include 20 sorties, adding *Prince Charles'* departure on 14/25 March. This was an unsuccessful loss, making a loss rate of seven out of 20 or 35 percent and a success rate of 14 of 21 or 67 percent. From the French point of view, the first three voyages must also be counted as successes, for a success rate of 17 of 24 or 71 percent. While preventing delivery of 32 percent of the cargoes during the most active interception operations might be considered a 'success' for the British commanders, Admiral Edward Vernon and Rear Admiral Hon. John Byng, whether that, and the losses, were 'unacceptable' to the French is another matter, and depends on what they were expecting when they made the attempts. The French army, which was managing the shipments, might have considered compensating ship owners for the loss of their small vessels worthwhile if they delivered the men and equipment they were carrying.

Lavery counted a sortie as a 'success' for France if the vessel returned to Flanders; that includes the ships with the Berwick Regiment that came back without landing the troops they were carrying. The British blockade of Flanders might also have prevented the Rothe Regiment convoy of five ships from even sailing, and in any case prevented them from landing anybody. Counting each attempt to sail by a single ship as a sortie, including *Bourbon* and *Charité* twice for their 8/19 February and 20 February/3 March attempts, and *Émeraude* and consorts with the Rothe Regiment that never sailed as a single 'sortie', the French made 25 attempts to get men, weapons, and money to the east coast of Scotland.

---

43   Lavery, *Shield of Empire*, p.60.

Between *Espérance*'s first sortie and the end of 1745, 10 of 12 sorties delivered their cargoes, only *Louis XV* and *Espérance* on her second voyage being captured, for a delivery rate of 83 percent. *Fine* delivered her troops of the Royal Ecossais regiment but was wrecked at Montrose. Of the 1,250 troops that set out from Flanders, 900 made it to Scotland, a delivery rate of 72 percent. These figures are displayed in Table 2.

Table 2: French North Sea Delivery Rates, September 1745–March 1746

Period	Sorties	Deliveries	Men Carried			Delivery Rate, %		% of men captured
			Sortied	Delivered	Captured	By Sortie	By Men	
Sep.–Nov. 1745	12	10	1,250	900	350	83	72	28
Feb.–Mar. 1746	13	2	2,194	176	459*	15	8	21*
Overall	25	12	3,444	1,076	809	48	31	23

Note: Sorties, deliveries, and men include *Comte de Lowendal* and four consorts, which did not sail from Ostend, as one sortie with 600 men, no delivery.
*Includes 100 men captured after landing from *Prince Charles* at Kyle of Tongue, 24 Mar./4 Apr. 1746.

The 1745 missions took place while the British government was still assessing the situation in Scotland and then organizing a naval response in the North Sea. By early 1746, that organization had been completed, with a flag officer in Scotland (Byng) reporting to the commander-in-chief at the Downs (Vernon) and an increase in the number of ships committed to the coasts of both Scotland and Flanders. In 1746, two of 13 sorties (15 percent) succeeded in landing their soldiers in Scotland. Of the 2,194 men the French hoped to deliver, only 176 were actually put ashore: 130 cavalrymen on *Prince de Nassau/Sophie* and 46 infantry of the Berwick Regiment on *Aventurier*. Only 459 (the Fitzjames cavalrymen on *Bourbon* and *Charité* and 100 from *Prince Charles* taken prisoner ashore) were captured (21 percent), but only eight percent were delivered, because 44 percent of the men designated for delivery were on ships that turned back, and 27 percent were on ships that did not sail.

There is an even larger disparity between delivery rates for the money the French were trying to send to Prince Charles. In 1745, all of the money, £4,000–6,000, was delivered, in the very first sortie that also delivered the Marquis d'Éguilles. In 1746, none of the £21,000–24,000 sent reached Charles, and over 70 percent was captured.

If the French had been able to maintain a 72 percent delivery rate into 1746, Prince Charles would have received another 1,400 experienced French soldiers; if they had been infantry who arrived with their weapons, they might have made a difference in the outcome of the Battle of Culloden: Cumberland would still have had the larger number of disciplined, professional infantry, but not to the same extent as was actually the case on 16/27 April 1746. Christopher Duffy has suggested that the presence of the Irish troops that were neither captured nor landed 'would have given the Duke of Cumberland pause for some very serious thought.'[44] About 100 men and £12,000–13,000 on *Prince Charles* were a 'delivery' from the

44   Duffy, *Fight for a Throne*, p.529.

naval point of view, but neither the money nor the troops reached Charles or his army, and the chase of *Prince Charles* by frigate *Sheerness* forced their delivery into the hands of a pro-Hanoverian clan militia. The British interdiction campaign had thus achieved an important tactical success.

For the British, any Bourbon sortie that failed to deliver money, weapons, or professional soldiers to the Jacobites was a tactical success, whether that came about through interception and capture before delivery, a return without delivery because of fear of interception, or a failure even to sail because of the same fear. By that criterion, the British in the North Sea had a success rate of only 17 percent in 1745 but 85 percent in 1746. The capture of the money and 100 troops on *Prince Charles*, after they were landed, by a pro-regime militia was also a tactical success, and one for which the navy, which forced *Prince Charles* to take refuge in an area not under Jacobite control, can take partial credit.

The losses in the North Sea and failure of the late February/early March convoy to deliver more than a handful of France's Irish Brigade, followed by the loss of the ports north of the Firth of Tay to the Duke of Cumberland's army, cut off further attempts to send troops, arms, and money to Prince Charles from Flanders. However, during the spring of 1746, at the behest of Louis XV and his navy minister, Jacobite exiles Antoine Walsh and his brother François fitted out two more privateers, *Mars* and *Bellone*, to carry money and weapons for Charles from Nantes to the west coast of Scotland. These were larger and more powerful ships than had been used in the North Sea, with good chances because 'it does not appear that the English have frigates strong enough on this [west] coast to oppose' them.[45]

When the ships left Nantes on 31 March/11 April 1746,[46] Charles' retreat north beyond Edinburgh in the face of the Duke of Cumberland's army was known, and the two privateers had orders to evacuate Charles if they found that the rebellion had been defeated and Charles was on the run. There is uncertainty about what the two ships were carrying, although there is agreement on a quantity of brandy and 3,000 muskets. The gold amounted to 852,000–888,000 French *livres*, in *louis d'or* coins.[47] At slightly varying commercial exchange rates, they would have been worth nearly £36,000 or over £37,000, but £35,000 is usually given as the amount. Had Charles' army still been in the field, this money could have paid 7,000 men for six months.[48]

Mars and *Bellone* arrived at Loch nan Uamh on 29 April/10 May 1746, two weeks after the Battle of Culloden, where the muskets would have been useful to those Highlanders who did not have firearms. A score of Charles' officers came on board with news of the defeat, but the French

45   Joannes Tramond, *Manuel d'histoire maritime de la France, des origins à 1815* (Paris: Société d'Éditions Géographiques, Maritimes et Coloniales, 1947), p.167n; L[ouis] A[ugustine] Boiteux, 'Un baroud d'honneur: le "Mars" et la "Bellone" en Ecosse (mai 1746)', *Revue historique diplomatique*, 63 (Oct.–Dec. 1959), p.307; quotation from Sir Thos Sheridan to Col Wm O'Brien, Inverness, 2 Mar. 1746, in A. and H. Tayler, *Stuart Papers*, p.144; 'Affaires d'Angleterre et d'Ecosse', April 1746, Archives nationales, Paris (henceforth, AN), Marine, B1-64, fo. 26.

46   'Affaires d'Angleterre et d'Ecosse', AN Marine, B1-64, fo. 26; Boiteux, 'Un baroud d'honneur', p.307; S[tephane] de La Nicollière-Teijeiro, *La Course et les corsaires du port de Nantes: Armaments, combats, prises, pirateries, etc.* (Paris: Honoré Champion, 1896; repr. Marseille: Lafitte Reprints, 1978), p.176; Lamorte, p.36.

47   Lamorte, 'Action de la France', 36; 'Affaires d'Angleterre et d'Ecosse', AN Marine, B1-64, fo. 26

48   Charles' paymaster, Æneas Macdonald: Zimmerman, *The Jacobite Movement*, p.27.

began landing the muskets and brandy; after some hesitation over the money, Charles' former secretary persuaded the French commander that he had authority to receive it (this 'treasure of Arkaig' has never been found).[49] Charles had been close to the Loch a few days before but had moved on to the Hebrides ahead of the British government troops looking for him.

Just after dawn on 3/14 May, the French ships were attacked at anchor by a small *ad hoc* squadron gathered by the senior British naval officer in the Hebrides, Captain Thomas Noel of *Greyhound*, 24, accompanied by snow *Baltimore*, 14, and sloop *Terror*, 10. The two larger French ships beat off the attack with some damage and loss, and sailed the next morning, going round north of the island of Lewis and reaching Nantes on 2/13 June.[50]

Once it was known that Charles was a fugitive, the French government sent out six expeditions with a total of eight sailings, six from Dunkirk and Ostend and the last two from St Malo, to rescue him from potential beheading at the Tower of London. *Heureux* and *Prince de Conti* delivered the Prince and some of his followers to Roscoff on the north coast of Brittany on 29 September/10 October 1746.[51]

Robert and Isabelle Tombs have suggested that France's investment in the '45 was 'far from profitless' for France: for a 'small investment of arms, men, and money (less than 5 million livres)' they captured Brussels, with 20 million livres, while troops that might have opposed them were in Britain. This enhanced the long-term success in Flanders that secured them the post-war return to the *status quo ante* and restored Louisbourg. Moreover, the British Royal Navy had been distracted for a time from hunting French privateers, which had made many prizes.[52] The money and munitions captured on the high seas, as well as that landed in Scotland, were just part of this diversion. Finally, the captured French soldiers were exchanged for British prisoners in French hands.

49   La Nicollière-Teijeiro, *La Course*, p.176; Boiteux, 'Un barroud d'honneur', p.307; 28 April: Elcho, *Short Account*, p.439; Hugh Douglas and Michael J. Stead, *The Flight of Bonnie Prince Charlie* (Phoenix Mill, England: Sutton Publishing Limited, 2000), p.2.

50   The battle of Loch nan Uamh will be fully described in the author's account of naval operations, 1739–1748, to be published by Helion, based on 'Relation du combat des corsaires de Nantes la Bellone, capitaine Lory, et le Mars, capitaine Rouille, contre trois frégates anglaises près Kilmore en Écosse', AN Marine, B4-58, fo. 4–6, partly quoted by [Léonard Léonce de Bonfils de Lablénie-Rochon de Lapeyrouse], Comte de Lapeyrouse Bonfils, *Histoire de la marine française* (Paris: Dentu, 1845), vol.2, pp.283–88; Boiteux, 'Un barroud d'honneur', pp.307–314; La Nicollière-Teijeiro, *La Course*, pp.180–89, quoting *Relation de ce qui s'est passé dans le voyage qu'ont faite les frégates le Mars et la Bellone en Écosse* (Nantes: N. Verger, 1746); *Greyhound*, captain's journal, 1–4 May 1746, TNA, ADM 51/0418; *Baltimore*, captain's journal 1–4 May 1746, TNA, ADM 51/0080; *Terror*, captain's journal, TNA, ADM 51/1009; *Greyhound*, master's log, 1–4 May 1746, TNA, ADM 52/0602; *Terror*, master's log, 1–4 May 1746, TNA, ADM 52/0731; Gibson, *Ships*, pp.38–39; Captain Noel's reports in *London Gazette*, No. 8536 (17 May 1746), p.6, and No. 8538 (24 May 1746), p.10; *Scots Magazine*, 8 (May 1746), p.238.

51   Gibson, *Ships*, pp.66–146.

52   Robert Tombs and Isabelle Tombs, *That Sweet Enemy: The French and British from the Sun King to the Present* (New York: Alfred A. Knopf, 2007), p.37. James Cable, *The Political Influence of Naval Force in History* (New York: St. Martin's Press, 1998), pp. 46–47: the French 'obtained a substantial return on their small investment', including withdrawal of British ships from the Mediterranean in addition to withdrawal of troops from Flanders. However, Richard Harding, *The Emergence of Britain's Global Naval Supremacy: The War of 1739–1748* (Woodbridge, England: Boydell Press, 2010), pp.235–78, charts the shift of ships from the Mediterranean to home waters but does not mention any specific decision to do so in his discussion of the strategic effects of the '45.

Select Bibliography

Archives
The National Archives, Kew, London (TNA)
    ADM 51 (captains' journals).
    ADM 52 (masters' logs).
    on-line index to series HCA 32 (High Court of Admiralty, prize papers).
AN Marine: Archives nationales, Paris, Marine (navy), Sous-serie B1 (Decisions), B4 (campagnes)

Newspapers
Boston Evening Post, Boston.
Le Courrier, Avignon.
The Gentleman's Magazine and Historical Chronicle, London.
London Magazine, London.
The London Gazette, London.
Scots Magazine, Edinburgh.
Mercure de France, Paris.

Published Sources

Bamford, Andrew, *The Lilies and the Thistle: French Troops in the Jacobite '45* (Warwick, England: Helion & Company Limited, 2018).

Barr, William, 'From Wager Bay to the Hebrides: The Duties of an Eighteenth-Century Bomb Vessel', *The Musk-Ox*, No. 16 (1975), pp.32–52.

Baudot Monroy, María, 'Julián de Arriaga y Rivera: Una vida al servicio de la marina (1700–1776)' (Doctoral diss., Universidad Nacional de Educación a Distancia, [2005]).

Boiteux, L[ouis] A[ugustine], 'Un baroud d'honneur: le "Mars" et la "Bellone" en Ecosse (mai 1746)', *Revue historique diplomatique*, vol. 63 (Oct.–Dec. 1959), pp.305–314.

Branigan, Keith, *From Clan to Clearance: History and Archaeology of the Isle of Barra, c. 850–1850* Sheffield Environmental and Archaeological Research Campaigns in the Hebrides, vol.6 (Oxford: Oxbow Books, 2005).

Campbell, John Lorne, *A Very Civil People: Hebridean Folk, History, and Tradition* (Edinburgh: Birlinn, 2014).

Carpio, María Josefa, *España y los ultimos Estuardos* (Madrid: Facultad de Filosofia y Letras, Seminario de Historia Moderna, 1952).

Chabannes-La Palisse, Comte Estienne [Antoine Charles] de, 'Camp de Boulogne (1745)', *Revue des questions historiques*, 64:3 (issue 252) (May 1936), pp.3–57.

Dickson, Joshua, *When Piping was Strong: Tradition, Change and the Bagpipe in South Uist* (Edinburgh: John Donald, 2006).

Douglass, F[rancis] and W[illiam] Murray (eds.), *The History of the Rebellion in 1745 and 1746, Extracted from the Scots Magazine* (Aberdeen: F. Douglass and W. Murray, 1755).

Duffy, Christopher, *Fight for a Throne: The Jacobite '45 Reconsidered* (Solihull: Helion & Company Limited, 2015).

Elcho, David Wemyss, Lord, *A Short Account of the Affairs of Scotland in the Years 1744, 1745, 1746* (ed. Evan Charteris) (Edinburgh: David Douglas, 1907).

Gibson, John S., *Ships of the '45: The Rescue of the Young Pretender* (London: Hutchinson & Co., 1967).

Lamorte, [Fernand René,] Lieutenant de vaisseau, 'L'Action de la France contre les Îles Britanniques pendant la guerre de succession d'Autriche' ([Paris]: École de guerre navale, [1933]).

La Nicollière-Teijeiro, S[tephane] de la, *La Course et les corsaires du port de Nantes: Armaments, combats, prises, pirateries, etc.* (Paris: Honoré Champion, 1896; repr. Marseille: Lafitte Reprints, 1978).

Lavery, Brian, *Shield of Empire: The Royal Navy and Scotland* (Edinburgh: Birlinn, 2012).

Lefèvre-Pontalis, Germain, 'La mission du marquis d'Éguilles en Écosse auprès de Charles-Édouard (1745–1746)', *Annales de l'École Libre des Sciences Politiques*, vol. 2 (1887), pp.239–262, 423–452; vol. 3 (1888), pp.99–119.

Malo, Henri, *Les Derniers corsaires: Dunquerque (1715–1815)* (Paris: Émile-Paul Frères, Éditeurs, 1925).

Malo, Henri, 'Le prétendant Charles-Édouard et les corsaires', *The Anglo-French Review*, 1:6 (July 1919), pp.513–558.

McCann, Jean E[sther], 'The Organisation of the Jacobite Army, 1745–1746' (Ph.D. diss., University of Edinburgh, 1963).

McGarry, Stephen, *Irish Brigades Abroad: From the Wild Geese to the Napoleonic Wars* (Dublin: History Press Ireland, 2013).

McLynn, F[rank] J[ames], *France and the Jacobite Rising of 1745* (Edinburgh: Edinburgh University Press, 1981).

McLynn, F[rank] J[ames], 'Sea Power and the Jacobite Rising of 1745', *Mariner's Mirror*, 67:2 (1981), pp.163–167.

O'Callaghan, John Cornelius, *History of the Irish Brigades in the Service of France* (Glasgow: Cameron and Ferguson, 1870; repr. Shannon: Irish University Press, 1969).

Reid, Stuart, *1745: A Military History of the Last Jacobite Uprising* (Staplehurst, Kent: Spellmount, 2001).

Wood, Stephen, *The Auld Alliance: Scotland and France, the Military Connection* (Edinburgh: Mainstream Publishing, 1989).

Zimmerman, Doron, *The Jacobite Movement in Scotland and in Exile, 1746–1759* (Basingstoke: Palgrave Macmillan, 2003).

4

An Unsung Success: The French Flying Squadrons in the Atlantic, 1793-1795

Olivier Aranda

'It is not only on the borders of the republic that the defenders of the fatherland obtain success. The French navy in its frequent cruises crushes and destroys the trade of our enemies. The rich and numerous prizes which it brings each day in our ports, while depriving the tyrants of the most powerful resources, circulate in our country abundance and life.'[1] In his November 1794 issue, the author of the *Annales républicaines de Brest* painted a striking picture of one of the elements of Republican naval strategy: the hunting of enemy trade, not by privateers but by units of the regular fleet, notably squadrons of half a dozen 74-gun ships of the line with great sailing abilities. Indeed, on this date, a squadron of five ships of the line and light units had just returned to Brest with numerous prizes, especially merchant ships.[2] The Brest newspaper therefore seized this opportunity to restore the reputation of the Republican navy, which had little to show against the victories of the French armies at the same time.[3] This was obviously wishful thinking, since British trade was not disrupted to the extent announced in the *Annales républicaines*; the most important thing was perhaps the hope that French trade would recover thanks to the prizes' cargoes.[4] If the success of these undertakings is therefore to be put into perspective, it is nevertheless worth taking an interest in them, all the more so as they are part of a long-term practice that spans important political breaks such as the fall of Robespierre on 9 Thermidor II (27 July 1794). From the start of the war on 1 February 1793 until the summer of 1795, there were several instances of light squadrons being used from Brest, without being attached to a fleet.

---

1   *L'ami des principes, ou annales républicaines de Brest*, n°1, 1er frimaire an III (21 November 1794), p.3.
2   *Réimpression de l'Ancien moniteur*, vol. XXII, pp.487-488. National Convention session of the 22 Brumaire an III (12 December 1794).
3   Hervé Drévillon (ed.), '3. Guerre, violence et Révolution', in Hervé Drévillon *et. al.*, *Histoire militaire de la France. I. Des Mérovingiens au Second Empire* (Paris: Perrin, 2018), pp.507–535.
4   Karine Audran, 'Course, Marine et approvisionnements sous la Révolution. Les prises et les cargaisons terries à Brest au début de la Convention (1793-an II) : un chantier historique à mener', in Anne de Mathan, Pierrick Pourchasse and Philippe Jarnoux (eds), *La mer, la guerre et les affaires. Enjeux et réalités maritimes de la Révolution française* (Rennes: PUR, 2017), pp.113–123.

However, there is hardly any mention of these squadrons in the French historiography of the revolutionary navy. Only *Contre-Amiral* Nielly's second sortie in the autumn of 1794 has attracted attention, as it resulted in the rare event of the capture of a British ship of the line, the *Alexander*, by French units.[5] The underlying trend has not been taken seriously: for most of French historiography, the revolutionary period is associated with the destruction of the French navy; due to a supposed incompatibility between the revolutionary way of thinking and the management principles of a war navy.[6] As a result, the revolutionary navy has hardly been studied in depth in France and even less its strategy; the best works about it are generally written by foreign authors.[7] But in the particular instance of these cruises, they lack documentation because of the very success of these enterprises. For once, most of the papers stayed in French hands, and it is only possible from a British point of view to trace some raids by the loss of merchants. Hence the confusion often made between the flying squadrons and the sortie of the bulk of the French fleet in the winter of 1794-1795, an error made for example by N.A.M. Rodger.[8]

It is therefore important to place these cruises in the context of a deliberate policy of the revolutionary government to employ light and fast squadrons with the aim of harassing the adversary, within the framework of an indirect strategy led by the *Comité de salut public* (Committee of Public Safety). This strategy was aimed at the attrition of the enemy's will to fight, while waiting for the development and massive production of marine shells.[9] Indeed from 1793 to 1795, in Meudon-la-Forêt near Paris, a secret commission was testing and producing marine shells and incendiary munitions, another little-known aspect of the French revolutionary navy.[10] Once these weapons were produced *en masse*, the Committee of Public Safety thought France could again dream of commanding the sea, even against such a formidable coalition as the one the Republic was facing at that time.

But while waiting for these 'miracle weapons' (which eventually proved unsuccessful), strategic caution was indeed the order of the day for the revolutionary navy at the beginning of the conflict; French strategy cannot be simplistically summed up in the sequence of a period of squadron warfare and of '*guerre de course*'. The study of the cruises of the light squadrons also requires the cross-referencing of various sources: firstly, the decrees of the Committee of Public Safety, in particular the secret operational decrees; but also the

---

5   Louis Édouard Chevalier, *Histoire de la marine française sous la première république* (Paris: Hachette, 1886), pp.164–165.

6   Joseph Martray, *La destruction de la marine française par la Révolution* (Paris: France-Empire, 1988).

7   Norman Hampson, *La marine de l'an II : mobilisation de la flotte de l'Océan, 1793-1794* (Paris: Marcel Rivière, 1959).

8   N.A.M. Rodger, *The Command of the Ocean. A Naval History of Britain, 1649-1815* (London: Allen Lane, 2004), p.432.

9   Olivier Aranda '"Pour visiter Pitt en bateau": les canons de la République', *Annales historiques de la Révolution française*, 393:1 (2018), pp.35–55.

10   This scheme is explained in length in an ongoing doctoral dissertation: Olivier Aranda *La marine de la République à Brest et dans l'Atlantique. Direction politique, stratégie, opérations 1792-1799*, Paris 1-Panthéon Sorbonne [unpublished work], (2023). See also, for the technical and scientific aspects of the program, Patrice Bret, *L'État, l'armée, la science : L'invention de la recherche publique en France (1763-1830)* (Rennes: PUR, 2002) and Charles Coulston Gillispie, 'Science and Secret Weapons Development in Revolutionary France, 1792-1804: A Documentary History', *Historical Studies in the Physical and Biological Sciences*, 23:1 (1992), pp.35–152.

correspondence of the officers, and finally the logbooks, which make it possible to locate these cruises at sea. This information can occasionally be cross-referenced or challenged with British data, in particular during contacts between the two navies.

A Silver Lining in the Dark Autumn of 1793: Van Stabel's and Kérangen's Cruises

The declaration of war by Republican France against Great Britain on 1 February 1793, and then against the United Provinces and Spain, placed the French navy in a difficult situation. With only 65 ships of the line, it was impossible to contest the command of the sea with the British, who had more than a hundred of them alone; not to mention the dozens of Dutch, Spanish and even Portuguese ships of the line, too often forgotten, which must be added to this total. Contemporaries were perfectly aware of this balance of power; the Girondin deputy Barbaroux stated to the Convention on 23 March 1793 that: 'France must rely on its sailors as on its soldiers; but, if we have courage on our side, our enemies have the number of their ships of the line on theirs.'[11] Despite this reality, the French navy initially envisaged the conflict in a traditional manner, with in particular the prospect of an expedition to India.[12] It was not until the Vendean and Chouan insurrection that it took a resolutely defensive stance. Faced with the mortal risk for the Republic of a junction between the insurrection and foreign forces, the French navy in the Atlantic was given the task of establishing a naval blockade of the Vendée.[13] The latter quickly became the only objective of the navy, which was reduced to the defensive, and all the ships were directed towards Belle-île, to the windward of the Vendée, as soon as their fitting out was completed.[14] Any attempt to command the sea is explicitly rejected in the general plan of 24 June 1793; on the other hand, the need for harassment of the enemy trade is reaffirmed.[15] A few days earlier the use of light squadrons had been mentioned for the first time in a report of the 1st division of the ministry of the navy: 'General Landais addresses to the minister rather extended observations on the mission of which he is charged. First of all, he thinks that at least three ships of the line are needed to make up a light squadron intended for cruising … he therefore asks whether the minister still intends him to command this light squadron.'[16] This mission had probably been discussed before the events of the Vendée broke out. In June 1793, nevertheless, this last theatre focuses all the attention, hence a temporary cancellation of the mission: 'I think that the current events having required the employment of all our forces, it will be the circumstances which will decide those to give to the *Contre-Amiral* Landais as well as his mission

---

11   *Archives parlementaires de 1787 à 1799 (1ère série). Recueil complet des débats législatifs et politiques des chambres françaises* (Paris: Imp. Nat., 1867-2009) vol. LX, p.498, 23 March 1793.
12   Executive Council session of 7 March 1793. Alphonse Aulard (ed.), *Recueil des actes du Comité de salut public avec la correspondance des représentants en mission et le registre du conseil exécutif provisoire* (Paris: Imp. Nat., 1889-1971), vol. II, p.275.
13   Service Historique de la Défense-Marine Vincennes (SHD-MV), BB1 4 f°162, 24 March 1793.
14   SHD-MV, BB1 5 f°80, 15 April 1793.
15   SHD-MV, BB4 14 f°34, naval force disposition plan 'adopted by the Council on 24 June'.
16   SHD-MV, BB1 6 f°23, « 1ère division. Brest », 9 June 1793.

which is delayed ... The present circumstances cannot allow the assembly of a light fleet separated from the large fleet.'[17]

These circumstances soon changed, however. Indeed, at the end of the summer of 1793, the fleet returned to Brest after having fulfilled its role as an interposition force between the Vendée coast and the British fleet. The fleet also underwent a major mutiny, based on the demand to return to Brest; for fear that the Brest arsenal would suffer the same fate as that of Toulon, as well as because of the difficulty of cruising.[18] Contrary to what one can read here and there, this mutiny did not lead to a paralysis of operations once the fleet had returned. The units being again available, the need for harassing the enemy was reaffirmed by the Committee of Public Safety; on September 24, it asked the Minister of the Navy for a table of the cruises to be established for the winter, by asking that they are able to 'protect the trade of France, to worry that of the enemy, and especially to support the arrival of the ships either French, or foreign, in charge of supplies for the Republic.'[19] Indeed, preventing food shortages was one of the major missions of the French Navy until 1795. In response, the minister Dalbarade proposed the constitution of a double chain of light units all along the Atlantic coast.[20] There is no mention of sending a light squadron in these measures; nevertheless, the context was favourable to the resumption of the scheme mentioned in June. This is nevertheless done in different political conditions: *Contre-Amiral* Landais had been dismissed and put in compulsory retirement following the mutiny of the summer of 1793, where he appeared to be overwhelmed by events.[21] As a consequence, the command of the light squadron was entrusted to Pierre Jean Van Stabel, who had been appointed *contre-amiral* on 16 November 1793.[22] Indeed, this officer had made a name for himself by maintaining strict discipline on board during the mutiny, and had skilfully capitalised on the situation by having a speech written by him testifying to the loyalty of his crew sent to the Convention, which was passed on to the minister and then to the Committee of Public Safety.[23] Like most of the newly promoted officers, he did not come from the 'Great Corps' of noble officers of the *Ancien Régime*, but from auxiliary officers to whom the Revolution ensured fast promotion, and who were far from all incapable, as the case of Van Stabel illustrates perfectly.

The sources on the departure of his squadron are fragmentary: in particular, there are no real continuous logbooks that would allow the ships to be located precisely. Nevertheless, it is possible to reconstruct the essentials. The squadron comprised six 74-gun vessels: *Jean Bart*, *Aquilon*, *Révolution*, *Tourville*, *Tigre* and *Impétueux*; accompanied by the frigates *Sémillante* and *Insurgente* and the corvettes *Espiègle* and *Ballon*.[24] Setting out on 15 November towards the north-west, the squadron captured several merchant ships and inspected neutral ships,

17   SHD-MV, BB1 6 f°23, « 1ère division. Brest », 9 June 1793, apostille to the report.
18   William S. Cormack, *Revolution and Political Conflict in the French Navy 1789-1794* (Cambridge: Cambridge University Press, 2002), p. 224.
19   Aulard (ed.), *Recueil des actes*, vol. VII, p.31. Decree of 24 September 1793, by Jeanbon Saint-André.
20   SHD-MV, BB4 14 f°41, « tableau des croisières d'hiver », 24 Vendémiaire an II (15 October 1793).
21   Léon Lévy-Schneider, *Le conventionnel Jeanbon Saint-André* (Paris: F. Alcan, 1901), pp.510-513.
22   Aulard (ed.), *Recueil des actes*, vol. VIII, p.455. Decree of 6 Brumaire an II (16 November 1793).
23   SHD-MV, BB4 17 f°237, letter from Van Stabel to the Minister of the Navy, 18 September 1793.
24   SHD-MV, BB4 27 f°116, 'Rapport sur la croisière de la Corvette l'Espiègle', 12 Frimaire an II (2 December 1793).

particularly American ones, as the French law of the sea at the time allowed.[25] Only three days after its departure, on 18 November, the French squadron found itself in the presence of the British fleet. Indeed, while chasing an unknown sail in a strong southerly wind, the *Tigre* commanded by Van Stabel recognised 38 sails, including 26 ships of the line, to the north-east at 9:30 a.m.[26] Very quickly, the order to set full sail was given, and a chase began in a southerly direction, as close to the wind as possible on different tacks, a very demanding point of sail for the ships. When the British frigate *Latona* approached the *Semillante*, a little after midday, the *Tigre* took up an intermediate position to defend her, successfully, using the artillery on her upper deck; the lower deck certainly being closed due to the fairly rough sea.[27] Van Stabel having made the manoeuvre independent so that each ship could choose the point of sailing that best suited her, the frigate *Sémillante* and the corvette *Espiègle* separated from the rest of the squadron; the latter eventually being captured.[28] During the night, the 74-gunners *Impétueux* and *Tourville* also separated and made an independent return to Brest.[29]

This episode has been noted several times by both French and English historiography. William James notes Van Stabel's manoeuvre to protect his frigate, and adds that two British ships lost one or more of their topmasts during the pursuit, an information confirmed by the French admiral's account.[30] The important point about this successful escape of the squadron is that it is generally credited to the superiority of French naval construction by early works, notably that of *Amiral* Edmond Jurien de la Gravière.[31] David Hannay, too, believes that the French escape was due to the greater scientific nature of French naval construction, which ensured speed.[32] But this vision of the French navy is now dated and has been called into question, in line with recent developments in history of science. In reality, the idea of a superior French construction is largely artefactual and proceeds from a considerable overestimation of the importance and impact of theoretical advances on concrete naval construction: 'The reality is that the French indeed placed a high value on pure science, but the mathematicians still knew far too little to be of any practical use to naval constructors.'[33] But in this case, how did the French ships manage to escape from the British in November 1793? A careful observation of the ships that made up the squadron can give an element of answer:

25   SHD-MV, BB4 27 f°116, 'Rapport sur la croisière de la Corvette l'Espiègle'.
26   SHD-MV, BB4 17 f°248/249, 'Evénemens remarquables qui ons eus lieu pendant la croisière du contre-amiral Van Stabel', 14 Frimaire an II (4 December 1793).
27   SHD-MV, BB4 17 f°248/249, 'Evénemens remarquables qui ons eus lieu pendant la croisière du contre-amiral Van Stabel', 14 Frimaire an II (4 December 1793).
28   SHD-MV, BB4 18 f°285, 'Rapport des raisons qui ont nécessité ma séparation ...' by Captain Le Mancq of the *Sémillante*, 19 November 1793.
29   SHD-MV, BB4 17 f°248/249, 'Evénemens remarquables qui ons eus lieu pendant la croisière du contre-amiral Van Stabel', 14 Frimaire an II (4 December 1793). SHD-MV, BB4 17 f°250, letter from Van Stabel to the Minister of the Navy, 12 Frimaire an II (2 Fecember 1793). SHD-MV, BB4 17 f°253, letter from Van Stabel to the Minister of the Navy, 21 Frimaire an II (11 December 1793).
30   William James, *The Naval History of Great Britain* (London: Harding-Lepard, 1826), vol.1, p.87.
31   Edmond Jurien de la Gravière, 'Nelson, Jervis et Collingwood, Études sur la dernière guerre maritime 01'. *Revue des deux mondes*, 16 (1846), p.408.
32   David Hannay, *A Short History of the Royal Navy 1217-1815 / Volume II 1689-1815* (London: Methuen and Co., 1907), p.300.
33   Nicholas Rodger, 'Recent work in British naval history, 1750–1815', *The Historical Journal*, 51:3 (2008), p.750.

Table 1: Composition of Van Stabel's Light Squadron, November 1793

Ship	Captain	Construction Date	Sailing Qualities	Class
Jean Bart	Coëtnempren	1790	'*Marche supérieure*' [Superior sailing]	*Téméraire* (Class 1782)
Aquilon	Henry	1789		*Téméraire* (Class 1782)
Révolution	Trinqualéon	1790	'*Marche très bien*' [Very good sailing]	*Téméraire* (Class 1782)
Tourville	Bonnefoux	1788	'*Marche bien*' [good sailing]	*Téméraire* (Class 1782)
Tigre	Van Stabel	1793		*Tigre* (New class 1793)
Impétueux	Lévêque	1787		*Téméraire* (Class 1782)

Source: Alain Demerliac, La marine de la Révolution : nomenclature des navires français de 1792 à 1799 (Nice: Omega, 1996). For sailing qualities, see also SHD-MV, BB5 6, 'Inventaire de l'armée navale', undated.

In reality, it was the coherence of the composition of the squadron that allowed it to escape effectively. The ships were all lined and bolted in copper, and were only three-and-a-half years old on average, which was a major factor in their speed; moreover, they were chosen from among the 74s constructed post-1782, and therefore from the standardised classes of the Borda-Sané plans, including the most recent one that was inaugurated by the *Tigre*. If these units were not strictly speaking faster than the British ships, they nevertheless had a certain uniformity of movement, which is essential in the case of a flight in squadron.[34] It was therefore the strategic choices of the Committee of Public Safety, in conjunction with the Ministry of the Navy, that made this success possible, rather than a supposed golden age of French shipbuilding.

Van Stabel's cruise in itself only resulted in the capture of 15 merchant ships, mostly British.[35] Nevertheless, by escaping Admiral Howe's fleet, Van Stabel achieved a real stunt. As a result, the Committee of Public Safety chose him to carry out the next delicate mission: to bring back to France the merchant fleet of Saint-Domingue which had taken refuge in the United States, after having loaded it with flour bought locally. During this time, the war effort in the arsenal had to be maximal, to prepare the ships for a possible direct confrontation between fleets the following spring. Now, this effort was largely made possible by the large number of prizes landed in Brest; the food cargoes in particular were welcomed with joy by the Republican authorities.[36] The continuation of the raids was therefore not only a means of training the crews, but also of supplying the port and the activity of the arsenal. Unsurprisingly, the local authorities in Brest were therefore in favour of light

---

34   It should be noted that Villaret was convinced of the superiority of the French 74: Lévy-Schneider, *Le conventionnel Jeanbon Saint-André*, p.566.

35   SHD-MV, BB4 17 f°106. SHD-MV, BB4 17 f°248/249, 'Evénemens remarquables qui ons eus lieu pendant la croisière du contre-amiral Van Stabel'. Roger Moriss, *The Channel Fleet and the Blockade of Brest, 1793-1801* (London: Routledge, 2001), p.3.

36   Audran, 'Brest sous la Convention', pp.37-52.

squadron sorties. It was in this context that *Contre-Amiral* Louis Thomas Villaret-Joyeuse, commanding the Brest fleet, ordered a new light division of three ships, commanded by Bertrand Kéranguen, to attack the enemy trade in the latitude of Cape Clear in Ireland. This decision was taken in agreement with the people's *représentants en mission*, Bréard and Jeanbon Saint-André, in mid-December 1793, a little over a month after the previous sortie.[37] The *représentants en mission* were deputies to the Convention who had a control and inspection role over military operations, including naval ones. Nevertheless, upon learning the news, these orders did not turn out to be to the taste of the minister, who deplored the dispersion of the fleet; undoubtedly by fear of a repetition of the cruise of Van Stabel, where the Republic took the risk of losing six ships of the line for the gain of some merchant ships.[38] Villaret, on the other hand, hoped for 'compensation' for this aborted raid.[39] As for Jeanbon Saint-André, he was in favour of an active fleet during the winter, an opinion probably based on the hope that the British fleet had returned to port, which had been the case since 10 December 1793.[40]

In sum, the debate was less about strategic philosophy (there is no question of researching a decisive action here) than about how to conduct indirect strategy, with or without ships of the line. This divide also intersects with a tension over the place and nature of command: should the military and *représentants en mission* in Brest or the politicians in Paris decide on the sortie of units? Finally, the Committee of Public Safety decided for itself at the beginning of January 1794: 'You can see, citizens colleagues, how important it is, in order not to harm the overall operations, that the Committee always knows which vessels it can dispose of. A partial movement would disunite the combinations and break up their development.'[41] There is thus, during year II, no more sorties of vessels without the agreement of the Committee of Public Safety, nor of instructions given by Villaret only, and not the political authorities; as it is the case for the sortie of Bertrand Kéranguen. This raid went off without a hitch while the strategic-political debate continued.

The division was composed of the 74-gun ships *Achille*, *Nestor* and *Northumberland*, accompanied by the frigates *Insurgente* and *Tamise*.[42] The ships do not seem to have been particularly fast, except for the *Nestor*, which came out of the shipyard and was based on the modernised plans of the *Tigre*. The choice of units was therefore probably made according to the schedule of armaments and refits. Kéranguen's squadron began by escorting Van Stabel's ships (sent to pick up the merchant convoy from Saint-Domingue that had been stopped at the Chesapeake) beyond the approaches. This mission was carried out quickly,

37   SHD-MV, BB4 19 f°334, letter from Villaret to the Minister of the Navy, 3 Nivôse an II (23 December 1793).

38   Aulard (ed.), *Recueil des actes*, vol. IX, p.705, letter from Jeanbon Saint-André to the Committee of Public Safety, 7 Nivôse an II (27 December 1793).

39   SHD-MV, BB4 19 f°334, letter from Villaret to the Minister of the Navy, 3 Nivôse an II (23 December 1793).

40   John III Barrow, *The Life of Richard Earl Howe, Admiral of the Fleet* (London: John Murray, 1838), p.215.

41   Aulard (ed.), *Recueil des actes*, vol. X, p.36. Letter from the Comité de salut public to Bréard and Jeanbon Saint-André, 13 Nivôse an II (2 January 1794).

42   SHD-MV, BB4 19 f°334, letter from Villaret to the Minister of the Navy, 3 nivôse an II (23 December 1793).

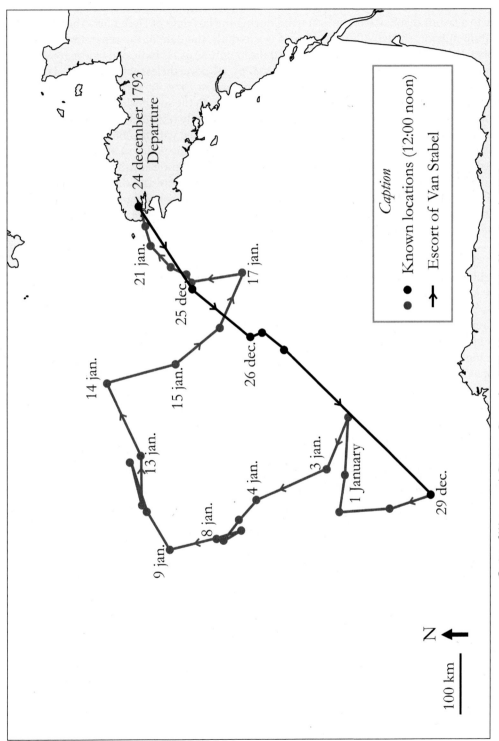

24 december 1793
Departure

21 jan.

17 jan.

25 dec.

26 dec.

14 jan.

15 jan.

13 jan.

4 jan.

3 jan.

8 jan.

9 jan.

1 January

29 dec.

Caption
● Known locations (12:00 noon)
↑ Escort of Van Stabel

N

100 km

Cruise of Kéranguen's Division, December 1793–January 1794.* (© Olivier Aranda 2023)

* SHD-MV, BB4 38 f°8-9, 'Extraits des journaux du vaisseau de la République l'Achille', 5 pluviôse an II (24 january 1794).

due to a favourable East-North-East wind during the last days of December. The commerce raiding mission started after the 29th of this month, the date of the separation with Van Stabel. Bertrand Kéranguen slowly reached the longitude of 11° indicated to him by Villaret, frequently interrupted by the chase of enemy ships. He nevertheless acted with great caution, perhaps aware that his cruise had not been approved in Paris; in particular, he stayed well away from the enemy coast, and made a long diversion to the south when returning to Brest, probably to avoid possible British units. The division finally returned to its home port on 24 January with 14 mainly British prizes, including one loaded with 80,000 piasters in metallic money.[43] The cruise also illustrates the interest of refusing the policy of 'free ships make free goods', which was that of the Republic at this date, since several Danish ships (thus neutral), loaded with grain belonging to powers at war with France, were also diverted towards Brest and their cargo declared a good prize.[44] The absence of British squadrons at sea made for a smooth cruise, which probably encouraged the Commity of Public Safety to send other ships ahead to receive Van Stabel, without fear of a superior enemy force.

Light Squadrons and the Prairial Naval Campaign, May/June 1794: An Ambiguous Role

The next use of a light squadron was during the Prairial campaign, when *Contre-Amiral* Nielly was sent with five ships in the hope of meeting the merchant fleet led by Van Stabel on the high seas and escorting it to safety. The need of reinforcements for the French merchant ships assembled in the United States followed the realisation in Paris that the situation of the convoy was very difficult and required vigorous measures. The cabinet in London was easily and quickly informed of the formation of the convoy in the United States.[45] It finally set sail for France on 17 April 1794, almost exactly two months after the arrival of Van Stabel's division (which included two ships of the line and some light vessels).[46] There were 114 ships at the start, loaded with colonial products and above all 14,000 barrels of flour, for a total of 127 ships on arrival, due to the 10 prizes made during the voyage as well as three French warships rescued from the fighting that joined the convoy.[47]

In France, sticking to a first missive of Van Stabel where he indicated his hope to leave around 15 March,[48] the Committee of Public Safety ordered the departure of *Contre-Amiral* Nielly to go meet him, with a squadron made up of the *Sans-Pareil* of 80 guns, *Trajan*,

---

43   SHD-MV, BB4 37 f°163, letter from Villaret to the Minister of the Navy, 5 pluviôse an II (24 January 1794).

44   SHD-MV, BB4 37 f°163, letter from Villaret to the Minister of the Navy, 5 Pluviôse an II (24 January 1794).

45   SHD-MV, BB4 43 f°50, letter fromVan Stabel to the Minister of the Navy, 16 Germinal an II (5 April 1794).

46   SHD-MV, BB4 43 f°56–59, 'Raport fait au Ministre de la Marine par le contre amiral Van Stabel', Prairial an II (May-June 1794).

47   SHD-MV, BB4 43 f°59–60, 'tableau de situation des bâtiments composant le convoi parti de la rade d'Hampton', undated.

48   SHD-MV, BB4 43 f°42, letter from Van Stabel to the Minister of the Navy, 19 Ventôse an II (8 March 1794).

Téméraire, *Patriote*, and *Audacieux* of 74, with six lighter ships.[49] The departure was planned for 28 March but due to headwinds it did not take place until 10 April.[50] Nielly headed for the rendezvous (47-48° north, 12° 46' west), and reached it on 18 April, almost exactly at the same time as Van Stabel's actual departure from the United States, '4,500 kilometres away' as Hampson notes.[51] Nielly then showed great tenacity by remaining at his post for almost a month and a half, despite the difficult weather, in particular the 'heavy wind … and the rains that brought disease to the division'.[52] It is within this operational framework that the main British and French fleets came into play from May 1794 onwards, and it is not for us to dwell on them: their operations have already been analysed in detail. *Contre-Amiral* Villaret on the French side and Admiral Howe on the British each had 26 ships of the line, and made contact on 28 May 1794.

Before coming to the confrontation itself, it is nevertheless necessary to insist on the role of Nielly's squadron in the transmission of information, notably through the question of prizes. Indeed, both Nielly's and Villaret's units were eager to capture ships, not only for the sake of gain but also as part of the state privateering responsible for a great part in supplying the Atlantic ports. The importance of these prizes is illustrated by the enthusiastic reception they were given in the ports; for example, the *représentant en mission* at Rochefort, Topsent, wrote to his colleague Guezno: 'I am pleased to inform you, dear colleague, of the arrival in this port of the Dutch frigate the *Vigilante*, of 26 guns, accompanied by 15 other prizes made by the Nielly division, loaded with various goods and in particular with 560 boucauts of sugar; these scoundrels must continue to supply us.'[53] The shortages (particularly those linked to the civil war in the west) therefore had an impact on operations, as it was through the recaptures that the position of Villaret's fleet and Nielly's squadron was revealed. The British, for their part, were careful enough to burn their prizes.[54]

After the actions of 28 and 29 May 1794, the light squadron we are dealing with, that of Nielly, joined up with the rest of the Brest fleet. One ship of this squadron, the *Patriote*, had already met the main fleet before the beginning of the fighting against the British.[55] On the morning of 30 May, the rest of the squadron, the vessels *Sans-Pareil*, *Trajan* and *Téméraire* joined the main fleet.[56] This junction may seem welcome, since during the day of the 29th, the vessels *Montagnard* and *Indomptable* were separated from the main fleet due to major damage and returned to France. It testifies to the tenacity of Nielly, who was able to remain at his post when his British counterpart, Montagu (who had six ships of the line), returned to refresh at Portsmouth during the crucial period at the end of May, even though he knew

---

49 Aulard (ed.), *Recueil des actes, Suppléments*, vol. III, p.36. Decree of Comitee of public safety of the 2 Germinal an II (22 March 1794). Lévy-Schneider, *Le conventionnel Jeanbon Saint-André*, p.762.

50 Lévy-Schneider, *Le conventionnel Jeanbon Saint-André*, p.762.

51 Norman Hampson, *La stratégie française et britannique pendant la campagne du printemps de l'an II* [unpublished], Bibliothèque de l'Institut d'Histoire de la Révolution Française (Z 177), p.8.

52 SHD-MV, BB4 39 f°395, logbook of the *Trajan*.

53 Aulard (ed.), *Recueil des actes, Suppléments*, vol. III, p.247. Letter from Topsent to Guezno, 22 Prairial an II (10 June 1794).

54 James, *Naval History*, vol.1, p.182.

55 Jeanbon Saint-André, *Journal sommaire de la croisière de la flotte de la république* (Paris: Imprimerie nationale, 1794), p.5.

56 Saint-André, *Journal sommaire*, p.21.

the French fleet was at sea.[57] With this squadron, the Brest fleet regained its strength of 26 ships of the line. English-language historiography has generally interpreted this event in a positive sense; thus Mahan states: 'These four fresh ships replaced the four disabled ones that had parted company.'[58]

However, this is a mistaken contribution. Indeed, Nielly's ships were far from operational; they were badly hit by disease, in this case typhus.[59] This situation was not specific to the squadron, even if the relatively long stay at sea (almost two months) and the difficult weather conditions already mentioned did not help the situation. Indeed, Van Stabel's squadron, another French squadron stationed at Cancale, and many other units were affected by this epidemic, attributed in particular to the unhealthy state of the bilges, which had not been renewed for a long time.[60] It is likely that the collapse of discipline during the early years of the revolution contributed to this health disaster, although the Republican authorities, far from ignoring the situation, had always insisted on the importance of hygiene on board.[61] In any case, the situation on Nielly's ships was dramatic; it was indeed a real epidemic: the *Trajan* had more than 80 patients; the *Sans-Pareil* had 150.[62] At the end of the Battle of Prairial – the action known to the British as the 'Glorious First of June', the naval health committee of Brest inspected the *Patriote* and noted 'that the stowage of the vessel has not been renewed for two years, that the vessel has not made water and that that of the bilge had not been renewed since that time…, that some of these parts having been ventilated lately the foreman of the hold who was doing this operation was asphyxiated and on the point of perishing.'[63] Moreover, in its quest for captures, Nielly's squadron formed numerous prize crews, which weakened its vessels; the British frigate *Castor*, in particular, was given a crew of 200 men but was eventually recaptured.[64]

In short, these ships were unfit for combat, and this had serious consequences for the main confrontation, the Battle of Prairial itself, which took place on 1 June 1794. At dawn the fleets were uncovered at close range and Howe ordered a general attack on the French line, which could be done without difficulty as he had previously gained the weather gauge. Much attention has been paid by literature to the manoeuvre chosen by the British admiral, which included for the first time a deliberate breaking of the line, with passage to the stern

57   Michael Duffy, 'The man who missed the grain convoy' in *Les marines françaises et britanniques face aux Etats-Unis, 1776-1865*, VIIème journées franco-britanniques d'histoire de la marine (Vincennes: SHD, 1999), pp.160–161.
58   Alfred Thayer Mahan, *The Influence of sea power upon the French Revolution and Empire: 1793-1812* (London: S. Low, Marston & co, 1893), vol.1, p.135.
59   SHD-MV, BB1 8 f°03, 'Rapport au Comité de salut public sur la maladie épidémique de Philadelphie', Germinal an II (March April 1794).
60   SHD-MV, BB4 34 f°42, letter from Valteau to the Commissaire de la marine Dalbarade, 14 Thermidor an II (1 August 1794).
61   This point is discussed in detail in: Olivier Aranda, 'Affreux, sales... et malades ? La campagne navale française du printemps 1794 au prisme de l'hygiène et de la santé', *Revue d'histoire maritime*, publication pending.
62   SHD-MV, BB4 39 f°249, 'Procès-verbal de la prise du vaisseau le Sans-Pareil', 13 Messidor an II (1 July 1794).
63   SHD-MV, BB4 37 f°217, minutes of the health committee, 12 Messidor an II (30 June 1794).
64   SHD-MV, BB4 36 f°148–149, letter from Nielly to the Commissaire de la Marine, 21 Messidor an II (9 July 1794).

of the opponent and fighting downwind.[65] However, little analysis has been made of the individual and non-individual confrontations that followed the manoeuvre. By entering into the details of the battle, it is possible to understand the considerable weight of the presence of very weakened ships in the French battle line. Two pieces of information must first be cross-referenced: the initial positions in the line of battle and the fate of the ships.

Table 2: French Battle Line on 1 June and Fate of the Ships

Number in the Line	Ship	Squadron	Post-Battle Status
1	*Convention*	Van	Little damage
2	*Gasparin*	Van	Damaged
3	*América*	Van	**Captured**
4	*Téméraire*	**Nielly**	Little damage
5	*Terrible*	Van	Dismasted
6	*Impétueux*	Van	**Captured**
7	*Mucius*	Van	Dismasted
8	*Éole*	Van	Little damage
9	*Tourville*	Van	Little damage
10	*Trajan*	**Nielly**	Little damage
11	*Tyrannicide*	Centre	In tow
12	*Juste*	Centre	**Captured**
13	*Montagne*	Centre	Damaged
14	*Jacobin*	Centre	Damaged
15	*Achille*	Centre	**Captured**
16	*Vengeur du Peuple*	Centre	Sunk
17	*Northumberland*	Centre	**Captured**
18	*Patriote*	**Nielly**	Little damage
19	*Entreprenant*	Rear	Little damage
20	*Neptune*	Rear	Little damage
21	*Jemmapes*	Rear	Dismasted
22	*Trente et un mai*	Rear	Damaged
23	*Républicain*	Rear	Very damaged
24	*Sans Pareil*	**Nielly**	**Captured**
23	*Scipion*	Rear	Dismasted
24	*Pelletier*	Rear	Little damage

Sources: SHD-MV, BB4 37 f°192–193 'Ordre de bataille naturel de l'armée de la République dans le combat du 13 prairial', undated; BB4 39 f°296, logbook of the frigate Tamise.

Firstly, Villaret was certainly aware of the great weakness to which the illness had reduced Nielly's ships, for he dispersed them in his squadrons, certainly hoping that they would be supported by ships more able to fight. He also spared them any crucial roles, as first or last

---

65   Rodger, *The Command of the Ocean*, p.430.

ship of the line, or the full centre of it, around the flagship, the *Montagne*. Secondly, a pattern is spotted twice, the vessel preceding a captured ship is one of Nielly's, the latter having very little damage itself. This confirms what other accounts suggest: the ships of Nielly's squadron fought very little, and quickly retreated leeward of the battle.[66] As a result they released a British ship, which went up the line to place the next French ship in a crossfire; this ship logically surrendering to the enemy outnumbering them. The pattern of ship-to-ship duels evoked by historiography, like that of the *Vengeur du Peuple* and the *Brunswick*, is therefore not the most common.[67] The ships of Nielly's squadron were not the only ones to withdraw; but of the eight ships that left the line prematurely, three belonged to Nielly's squadron, to which must be added another that was in tow of a ship of that squadron.[68] The latter was therefore responsible for half of the line breaks, although it only accounted for 15 percent of the fleet's total strength (four ships out of 26). Of Nielly's four ships, three left their positions in the line and the fourth was captured. As the French line disintegrated, local numerical superiorities emerged; the 80-gun *Juste*, in particular, was attacked to windward and leeward by two three-deckers: her surrender in this context was not surprising.[69] In this light, the traditional explanations of the French tactical defeat should also be put into perspective; namely, the supposed carelessness of the strategy of the Committee of Public Safety, the poor quality of the officers, the negligence of artillery.[70]

Without being the only explanatory element of the French defeat, the state of Nielly's ships is therefore a central element in the outcome of the confrontation: six French ships captured, and a seventh, the *Vengeur du Peuple*, sunk.[71] The latter foundered at the end of a prolonged confrontation; it should be noted that it was bolted in iron, and that the probable galvanisation likely accelerated its submersion.[72] Her resistance up to the moment of sinking is only the most spectacular of the many examples of prolonged refusal to surrender in the French fleet that day; the Republicans thus partly succeeded in changing, qualitatively, the modalities of naval combat.[73] The toll could have been even higher, for in the afternoon Villaret reconstituted a solid line of battle and managed to get several dismasted ships out of the fray with the help of frigates sent to tow the disabled units.[74] The battle did not resume later in the day. At this point, however, while the fighting between the fleets was over, the fate of the convoy was not yet determined; but Howe's decision to return to port, among other elements, allowed Van Stabel to arrive safely. The role of Nielly's light squadron was

---

66   Saint-André, *Journal sommaire*, p.27.
67   Mahan, *The Influence of sea power*, vol.1, pp.141–142.
68   Olivier Aranda, *La bataille de Prairial : le Fleurus de la marine républicaine?*, MA thesis, Paris I Panthéon Sorbonne, p.207.
69   SHD-MV, BB4 38 f°179, minutes of the surrender of the *Juste*, 13 Prairial an II (1 June 1794).
70   Chevalier, *Histoire de la marine française*, p.162.
71   The ships captured were the 74-gun *América*, *Impéteux*, *Northumberland*, *Achille*, *Sans-Pareil*, and the 80-gun *Juste*.
72   Demerliac, *La marine de la Révolution*, p.23.
73   Olivier Aranda, 'Combattre et mourir en républicain sur les mers: la bataille du 13 Prairial an II, au-delà du *Vengeur du Peuple*' in Walter Bruyère-Ostells, Benoît Pouget and Michel Signoli (eds), *Des chairs et des larmes: combattre, souffrir, mourir dans les guerres de la Révolution et de l'Empire (1792-1815)* (Aix-en-Provence: Presses universitaires de Provence, 2020), pp.31–42.
74   Sturges Jackson, *Logs of the Great Sea Fights* (London: HardPress, 1899), p.135.

therefore complex during this period, both remarkable for its tenacity but ultimately of little help at the time of the battle and even a burden. However, this commander was soon given a chance to redeem himself.

The Unknown Successes: Autumn 1794

The timid attitude of the British admirals, both Howe during the Glorious First of June and Montagu throughout the campaign, may have emboldened the Committee of Public Safety in their desire to attack British trade.[75] Perhaps as a result, the 1793 pattern of sending a light squadron of ships at the end of a naval campaign was repeated, despite the fall of Robespierre and the reshuffling of the Committee of Public Safety during the summer. This political rupture did not have military effects at first; the general plan of operations of 24 June 1794, which provided the use of a light squadron, thus continued to be applied.[76] On 29 August 1794, the minister of the navy wrote to Villaret: 'the Committee seems to want you to make an exit after the gales; the fleet must not lack anything at this time'.[77] The minister also specified in the same letter: 'it would be well that six ships of 74 of the best sailing qualities had for six months of stores on board,... by there we would have ships ready to go for some missions or raids'.[78] These ships are to be entrusted, again, to *Contre-Amiral* Nielly. The quantity of foodstuffs mentioned indicates the ambition of a distant project, such as an Indian expedition, which was a long-running project of the revolutionary period. Nevertheless, it was finally the hunting of British convoys to which the light squadron was tasked; one arriving from India, and one leaving for the West Indies.[79] On 5 September 1794, the Committee of Public Safety ordered that the squadron should go some distance off Cape Clear, and 'be disposed in such a way as to see and recognise any vessel that might pass between the 52nd and 48th degrees of north latitude', which meant that there was a considerable area to cover. The units were to remain for a month in search of the two British convoys. Here again, the confidence of the Committee of Public Safety was also based on the new shells and incendiary balls developed at Meudon.[80]

The squadron entrusted to *Contre-Amiral* Nielly was made up of 74-gun ships with great qualities of sailing, which is not surprising, the authorities of the port knowing Howe's fleet being at sea:

---

75 Duffy, 'The man who missed the grain convoy', p.159.

76 Aulard (ed.), *Recueil des actes, Suppléments*, vol. III, p.222–225. Secret decree of the Committee of Public Safety, 6 Messidor an II (24 June 1794).

77 SHD-MV, BB4 37 f°84, letter from the Minister of the Navy to Villaret, 12 Fructidor an II (29 August 1794).

78 SHD-MV, BB4 37 f°84, letter from the Minister of the Navy to Villaret, 12 Fructidor an II (29 August 1794).

79 Aulard (ed.), *Recueil des actes, Suppléments*, vol. III, p.353. Secret decree of the Committee of Public Safety, 19 Fructidor an II (5 September 1794).

80 Aulard (ed.), *Recueil des actes, Suppléments*, vol. III, p.353. Secret decree of the Committee of Public Safety, 19 Fructidor an II (5 September 1794).

Table 3: Nielly's Squadron During its Sortie in September–October 1794

Ship	Captain	Construction date	Sailing qualities	Class
Zélé	Nielly	1763	'*L'un des meilleurs voiliers de la flotte*' [One of the finest sailing ships of the fleet]	
Droits de l'Homme	Trinqualéon	1794		*Tigre* (New class 1793)
Jean Bart	Pilet	1790	'*Marche très bien*' [Very good sailing]	*Téméraire* (Class 1782)
Nestor	Monnier	1793	'*Marche bien*' [good sailing]	*Tigre* (New class 1793)
Tigre	Matagne	1793		*Tigre* (New class 1793)
Marat	Le Franck	1794	'*Marche supérieure*' [Superior sailing]	*Tigre* (New class 1793)

Sources: SHD-MV, BB4 36 f°139, 'Division commandée par le Contre Amiral Nielly', undated; for the sailing quali-ties, see SHD-MV, BB5 6, 'Inventaire de l'armée navale', undated, and SHD-MV, BB4 72 f°177, 'Remarques ou devis sur les qualités du vaisseau le Marat', undated.

Four of the most recent vessels in the French fleet were selected: this shows the impor-tance of the criterion of age. But it is not the only one of importance: the exception of the *Zélé* can be explained by its remarkable nautical qualities which justified its overhaul in 1786. Moreover, among the recent ships, those based on the updated Borda/Sané plans (those of the *Tigre*) are numerous. This cautious choice almost proved essential, as it did for Van Stabel's squadron, because the British fleet was at sea at the same time, from 7 to 22 September.[81] Nielly's squadron left on 11 September 1794, accompanied by the frig-ates *Précieuse*, *Fraternité* and *Surveillante*.[82] The latter saw the British fleet, according to the *représentants en mission* Faure and Tréhouard, during a chase; but the envoys reassured the Committee of Public Safety by specifying that 'the six vessels have a superior course. They made the advantage of the mainsheet to the frigate, which however outpaced the best sailing English ships.'[83] Of these frigates, the *Précieuse* and the *Surveillante* had to return to Brest because of damage.[84] The main squadron nevertheless continued on its way after having learned of the presence of the British fleet at sea on 28 September; this led to a redou-bling of gunnery training on the squadron.[85] A few days later, on 2 October 1794, Nielly's ships joined the French units already stationed off Cape Clear, namely the frigates *Gentille*, *Driade*, *Cocarde* and *Tribune*; this provided Nielly with a reinforcement of light ships to chase the merchants in all directions. The Minister of the Navy had regretted before the

---

81   Thomas Trotter, *Medicina Nautica, an essay on the diseases of seamen* (London: T. Cadell, Jun. and W. Davies, 1797), p.76.

82   SHD-MV, BB4 36 f°139, 'Division commandée par le Contre Amiral Nielly', undated.

83   SHD-MV, BB3 61, Letter from the representatives of the people to Committee of Public Safety, 4 Sans-Culottides an II (20 September 1794).

84   Trotter, *Medicina Nautica*, p.76.

85   SHD-MV, BB4 36 f°190, Signal log of the *Zélé*, 7 and 8 Vendémiaire an III (28 and 29 September 1794).

departure that Nielly's ships were not accompanied by some 20 light units.[86] The squadron nevertheless did not seize any British convoys, but did get hold of 20 isolated prizes; one was recaptured, six were sunk, 12 entered Brest and the others were directed towards Lorient, a mixed result for more than a month's cruise.[87]

However, the captures were not the only interest of this type of operation; as the *représentants en mission* in Brest wrote, 'We also think that these short and repeated cruises, by worrying the enemy infinitely, are very necessary to train our sailors of first requisition and to exercise the officers, who need it.'[88] It is thus these same representatives who ordered a new departure of the light squadron only a few days after the return of Nielly, which illustrates again the multiplicity of the decision centres in the republican navy.[89] The departure took place very quickly, on 25 October 1794.[90] This precipitation probably explains the composition of the new squadron, more motley than the previous ones; if one finds the 74s *Jean Bart*, *Droits de l'homme*, *Marat*, *Tigre*, and *Pelletier*, it is necessary to note the presence of a ship of 80 guns, the *Caton*, which is more surprising. The ship had just been refitted, but was still performing very poorly. After having been dismasted, she had to leave the squadron on 5 November 1794.[91] Despite this event, the cruise was the most successful of all those in the beginning of the Revolutionary Wars. Indeed, the following day the squadron saw two British ships of the line at daybreak, which were quickly chased.[92] Only the *Alexander*, under Captain Richard Rodney Bligh, was caught after a half-dozen-hour chase downwind, under studding-sails, and a brief battle.[93] Her companion, the *Canada*, chased by the *Pelletier* and the *Tigre*, managed to escape after having shed a good part of her equipment.[94] In view of the very poor performance of the *Alexander*, which was revealed when it was retaken over the following year, the action was far from a French masterstroke from a tactical point of view; it is reasonable to think that a more efficient squadron would have taken the two ships.[95] However, there is no mention of Republican losses of lives, including in the press, which is consistent with a pursuit scenario where combatants tend to target the rigging in order to slow down the opponent. After this success, Nielly only thought of bringing his prize back to Brest, as the history of his movements shows; he arrived in this port on 19 Brumaire (9 November 1794).

On land, a political and military whirlwind awaited him. The capture of the *Alexander* was announced with a form of relief by the *représentants en mission*, who at last had an

86   SHD-MV, BB4 37 f°104, le Commissaire la Marine à l'amiral Villaret, 3ème jour des Sans-Culottides an II (19 September 1794).
87   SHD-MV, BB4 38 f°160, captain of the *Gentille* to the Minister of the Navy, undated.
88   Aulard (ed.), *Recueil des actes*, vol. XVII, p.471. Letter from Faure and Tréhouard to the Committee of public safety, 25 Vendémiaire an III (16 October 1794).
89   SHD-MV, BB4 36 f°151, letter from Nielly to the Minister of the Navy, 30 Vendémiaire an III (21 October 1794).
90   SHD-MV, BB4 39 f°93, logbook of the *Pelletier*, 3 to 4 Brumaire an III (24–25 October 1794).
91   SHD-MV, BB4 39 f°96-97, 15 to 16 Brumaire an III (5–6 November 1794).
92   SHD-MV, BB4 36 f°155, Minute from Captain Le Franck of the *Marat*, 16 Brumaire an III (6 November 1794).
93   SHD-MV, BB4 39 f°93-100, logbook of the *Pelletier*.
94   SHD-MV, BB4 39 f°93-100, logbook of the *Pelletier*.
95   SHD-MV, BB4 37 f°240, account of Contre-Amiral Nielly.

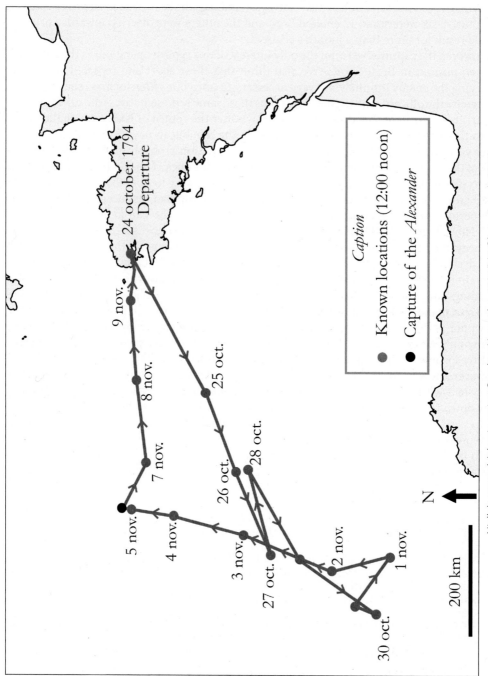

Nielly's second Atlantic cruise, October–November 1794.* (© Olivier Aranda 2023)

* SHD-MV, BB4 39 Fº93–100, logbook of the *Pelletier*.

Caption
● Known locations (12:00 noon)
● Capture of the *Alexander*

24 october 1794
Departure

9 nov.
8 nov.
7 nov.
5 nov.
4 nov.
3 nov.
2 nov.
1 nov.
30 oct.
27 oct.
26 oct.
28 oct.
25 oct.

N

200 km

element to counterpart the success of the armies: 'Fortune, which seemed to have forgotten only the naval army of the Republic, has at last given us a sign of remembrance: we have one more fine ship of 74.'[96] The capture was immediately enlisted in the service of the Thermidorian reaction, that is to say the process of vindicating the fall of Robespierre. Naval success, in a way, validated the political upheaval; thus, the *Annales Républicaines de Brest* reported the words of a member of the popular society of the city, which celebrated Nielly: 'Citizens, victory was only waiting to return to our walls at the moment when the crime had disappeared.'[97] The flag of the *Alexander* left to decorate the vaults of the Convention. This success was a particularly positive conclusion to a sequence of light squadrons raids whose unity generally went completely unnoticed.

Indeed, the light squadron cruises, through the prizes they generated and the experience they allowed crews and officers to accumulate, were a notable success that has not been noted until now. This choice of force employment was not, however, capable of significantly influencing the course of the naval war; but the main point here is to note the relevance of the strategic choices made by the Committee of Public Safety and the Ministry of the Navy, far from the indifference that was supposed to characterise the Republic regarding maritime operations. Conversely, it is the interest shown in naval warfare by civilian institutions, and in particular the Committee of Public Safety, that is striking in the genesis of naval operations. It is important to note that these classic harassment operations took place at the same time as the development of explosive and incendiary shells, which the Committee of Public Safety hoped would turn the tide of the naval war; showing the adaptability of this institution, often portraited as ideological and clueless concerning naval matters. In liaison with the offices of the Navy, the Committee of Public Safety therefore produced an ambitious plan of maritime operations which is the framework of the campaign of the year 1795.

Select Bibliography

Published Primary Sources
Saint-André, Jeanbon, *Journal sommaire de la croisière de la flotte de la république* (Paris: Imprimerie nationale, 1794).
Trotter, Thomas, *Medicina Nautica, an essay on the diseases of seamen* (London: T. Cadell, Jun. and W. Davies, 1797).

Published Sources
Aranda, Olivier, 'Combattre et mourir en républicain sur les mers: la bataille du 13 Prairial an II, au-delà du *Vengeur du Peuple*' in Walter Bruyère-Ostells, Benoît Pouget and Michel Signoli (eds.), *Des chairs et des larmes : combattre, souffrir, mourir dans les guerres de la Révolution et de l'Empire (1792-1815)* (Aix-en-Provence: Presses universitaires de Provence, 2020), pp.31–42.
Aranda, Olivier, '"Pour visiter Pitt en bateau": les canons de la République', *Annales historiques de la Révolution française*, 393:1 (2018), pp.35–55.
Aranda, Olivier, 'Affreux, sales… et malades? La campagne navale française du printemps 1794 au prisme de l'hygiène et de la santé', *Revue d'histoire maritime* [publication pending].

---

96   Aulard (ed.), *Recueil des actes*, tome XVIII, p.57. Letter from Amable Faure to the Committee of public safety, 19 Brumaire an III (9 November 1794).
97   *L'ami des principes, ou annales républicaines de Brest*, n°1, 1er Frimaire an III (21 November 1794), p.7.

Audran, Karine, 'Brest sous la Convention: la course approvisionnante comme processus de résilience' in Christian Borde, *et al. La résilience des villes portuaires européennes: Tome 1. Crises et réinventions (XVIe-XXIe siècle)* (Villeneuve d'Ascq: Presses universitaires du Septentrion, 2022), pp.37-52.

Audran, Karine, 'Course, Marine et approvisionnements sous la Révolution. Les prises et les cargaisons terries à Brest au début de la Convention (1793-an II): un chantier historique à mener', in Anne de Mathan, Pierrick Pourchasse and Philippe Jarnoux (ed.), *La mer, la guerre et les affaires. Enjeux et réalités maritimes de la Révolution française* (Rennes: PUR, 2017), pp.113–123.

Aulard, Alphonse (ed.), *Recueil des actes du Comité de salut public avec la correspondance des représentants en mission et le registre du conseil exécutif provisoire* (Paris: Imp. Nat., 1889-1971).

Barrow, John, *The Life of Richard Earl Howe, Admiral of the Fleet* (London: John Murray, 1838).

Chevalier, Louis Edouard, *Histoire de la marine française sous la première république* (Paris: Hachette, 1886).

Demerliac, Alain, *La marine de la Révolution : nomenclature des navires français de 1792 à 1799* (Nice: Omega, 1996).

Drévillon, Hervé (ed.), '3. Guerre, violence et Révolution', *Histoire militaire de la France. I. Des Mérovingiens au Second Empire* (Paris: Perrin, 2018), pp.507–535.

Duffy, Michael, 'The man who missed the grain convoy' in *Les marines françaises et britanniques face aux Etats-Unis, 1776-1865*, VIIème journées franco-britanniques d'histoire de la marine (Vincennes: SHD, 1999), pp.155-167.

James, William, *The Naval History of Great Britain* (London: Harding-Lepard, 1826).

Jurien de la Gravière, Edmond, 'Nelson, Jervis et Collingwood, Études sur la dernière guerre maritime 01' in *Revue des deux mondes*, vol. XVI (1846), pp.385-431.

Hampson, Norman, *La marine de l'an II: mobilisation de la flotte de l'Océan, 1793-1794* (Paris: Marcel Rivière, 1959).

Hampson, Norman, *La stratégie française et britannique pendant la campagne du printemps de l'an II*, [unpublished], Bibliothèque de l'Institut d'Histoire de la Révolution Française (Z 177).

Hannay David, *A Short History of the Royal Navy 1217-1815 / Volume II 1689-1815* (London: Methuen and Co, 1907).

Jackson, Sturges, *Logs of the Great Sea Fights* (London: HardPress, 1899).

Lévy-Schneider, Léon, *Le conventionnel Jeanbon Saint-André* (Paris: F. Alcan, 1901).

Mahan, Alfred Thayer, *The Influence of sea power upon the French Revolution and Empire: 1793-1812* (London: S. Low, Marston & Co, 1893).

Martray Joseph, *La destruction de la marine française par la Révolution* (Paris: France-Empire, 1988).

Moriss Roger, *The Channel Fleet and the Blockade of Brest, 1793-1801* (London: Routledge, 2001).

Rodger, Nicholas A.M., *The Command of the Ocean. A Naval History of Britain, 1649-1815* (London: Allen Lane, 2004).

Rodger, Nicholas A.M., 'Recent work in british naval history, 1750–1815', *The Historical Journal*, 51:3, 2008, p.741-751.

Theses

Aranda Olivier, *La bataille de Prairial : le Fleurus de la marine républicaine?* MA thesis, Paris I Panthéon Sorbonne.

Part II

Naval Operations: North America

Part I touched on the way in which Spanish sea power was used in the West Indies; here follows a more detailed discussion on the way in which different European powers – the French and the British – exercised sea power and conducted naval operations in North American waters. Studies of Britain's North American naval forces have always been few and far between, and typically there has been little interest outside of Canadian academic circles (although there are some excellent Canadian studies). The first study here actually concerns the use of British sea power during a time of peace: R.N.W. Thomas examines the operations of the Royal Navy in North America from 1767 to 1771, during the period preceding the American Revolution. In this important context of changing relations and attitudes between Great Britain and the colonies, Thomas explores how the Royal Navy was used in exercising peacetime imperial policy regarding trade and public order. He also touches upon the important topic of naval administration (covered in more depth in Part III), through an analysis of the Halifax Naval Yard and the navy's capacity to maintain the peacetime North American Station in operation.

Next, Thomas Golding-Lee turns to the resulting American Revolutionary War and demonstrates a notable failure on the part of the French to effectively employ sea power at the Battle of St Lucia. Golding-Lee describes this action as 'the Nile that wasn't,' an interesting analogy that highlights the tactical and strategic similarities of this action in the West Indies during the American Revolutionary War with the more notable British victory in 1798. Here, a British force is caught at anchor by a more powerful French squadron, but the French commander fails to achieve a victory, largely due to systemic problems stemming from French naval doctrine of the era.

From a French failure in the American Revolutionary War, this volume's editor turns to notable but long neglected British defeats in those same North American waters; three single ship losses of the War of 1812 are examined in detail. Each was the result of under-preparation and an appalling lack of leadership displayed by the respective commanders. The historical significance of these defeats is explored, with respect to questions around general gunnery proficiency amongst naval crews as well as the nature of accountability in a navy used to success. The chapter challenges prevailing historical narratives about the British in the War of 1812 and the period more generally.

5

The Royal Navy in North America, 1767-1771: Trade, Public Order, and the Halifax Naval Yard

R.N.W. Thomas

Trade protection and regulation arguably consumed the majority of the Royal Navy's resources during the eighteenth century. While the primary role of defending the home islands was key during wartime, trade protection was relevant at all times, whether the nation was at war or not, with the added responsibility of attacking an enemy's commercial resources during times of conflict.[1] Subsidiary activities included the maintenance of public order, through the carriage of troops to areas of unrest or by providing visible evidence of state power, and vessel maintenance. These three themes – trade regulation, public order and vessel maintenance – are the topics addressed in this chapter.

As far as North America was concerned, the years between the end of the Seven Years War (1756-1763) and the American War of Independence (1775-1782; hereafter referred to as the 'American War') were characterised by a raft of legislation from London aiming to use trade as a revenue generator to offset the significant national debt accumulated through conflicts during the first half of the eighteenth century. As an important component of imperial power, the Royal Navy played a key role in enforcing these regulations, providing in many cases the actual interface between the colonists and the state. The Navy was therefore important in shaping attitudes on both sides during the critical years leading to the American War. This chapter will examine how the Navy was deployed on the North America Station, the duties undertaken, and the issues faced with the enforcement of an increasing body of trade legislation targeting revenue generation. South Carolina is used to provide a more detailed illustration of affairs during this important period.

---

1   J. Black, 'Naval power and British foreign policy in the age of Pitt the Elder', in J. Black, and P. Woodfine (eds.), *The British Navy and the use of naval power in the eighteenth century* (Leicester: Leicester University Press, 1988), pp.92-93 and 101-102 and J.R. Jones, 'Limitations of British seapower in the French Wars', in *ibid*., p.42.

The North America Station[2]

North America had witnessed significant military activity during the Seven Years War, but following the French failure to retake Quebec in May 1760 and their surrender of Montreal the following September, the number of ships on station reduced heavily as many returned to Britain for repair, to France with paroled prisoners or to the Caribbean to continue the war. The first peacetime deployment following the end of the war consisted of 21 ships commanded by Rear Admiral Lord Alexander Colvill, which proceeded to North America during the summer of 1763, with all vessels already there being ordered home. The command consisted of nine sub-stations extending from the Cape Breton Island to Florida, including the Bahamas. The headquarters was at Halifax, Nova Scotia, a small outpost with few amenities. Colvill was in the process of handing over his command to Vice Admiral Philip Durell, when Durell died in September 1766, shortly after his arrival at Halifax, at which point Colvill himself returned home. The squadron was then commanded by the senior captain until the arrival of Commodore Samuel Hood in July 1767.[3]

The period addressed by this chapter comprises the commands of Hood and his successor, Commodore James Gambier. When Hood arrived in North America, his geographical responsibilities had been drastically reduced, consisting of the coast from the River St Lawrence to New York. The Admiralty Board subsequently extended this as far south as Cape Hatteras in North Carolina in mid-1768, but Hood requested it to be further enlarged to include Cape Florida, given that all the ships stationed in the south used the Halifax navy yard; this rearrangement was made in December 1768.[4] Headquarters remained at Halifax during the majority of Hood's tenure, but increasing civil tension in Boston forced him to relocate there temporarily between November 1768 and August 1769 before the Admiralty Board ordered a permanent move of his headquarters to Boston in July 1770.[5] Hood was succeeded by Commodore Gambier on 10 October 1770. Gambier's tenure in command lasted only until 12 August 1771 when he was relieved by Rear Admiral John Montagu.[6]

By January 1768, Hood's command consisted of 20 vessels, of which five had been ordered home. Of the remaining 15, the largest ship was the fourth rate *Romney*, which served as Hood's flagship and was mostly stationed at Halifax. The only other rated ships were the fifth rate *Launceston* and two sixth rates – the *Fowey* and *Glasgow* – with the remainder consisting of five sloops, five schooners (none of which carried guns) and one armed vessel.

---

2   This naval command is known by several names in the literature: 'North America Station,' 'North American Station,' 'North American Squadron.' The terminology has varied in historical and modern accounts, although historic sources often defaulted to 'North America Station' and less often to 'North American Squadron.' Both 'North America Station' and 'North American Squadron' will be used in this volume.

3   N.R. Stout, *The Royal Navy in America, 1760-1775. A study of enforcement of British colonial policy in the era of the American Revolution* (Annapolis: Naval Institute Press, 1973), pp.13-14, 29 and 56-58.

4   TNA: ADM 1/483 pp.6, 153 and 192-193: Hood to Stephens, 17 May 1767, 23 October 1768 and 26 March 1769 and TNA: ADM 2/94 pp.385-386 and 480-481: Admiralty Board to Hood, 3 August and 16 December 1768.

5   TNA: ADM 1/483 pp.159-160, 228 and 303: Hood to Stephens, 12 November 1768, 7 August 1769 and 25 September 1770 and ADM 2/95 pp.456-458: Admiralty Board to Hood, 16 July 1770.

6   TNA: ADM/1 483 pp.334-335: Gambier to Stephens, 10 October 1771.

All the schooners had been locally procured and commissioned in North America. From north to south, the ships were disposed with the *Romney* and *Glasgow* stationed: 'In the River St. Lawrence on the coast of Nova Scotia, Bay of Fundy and along the coast to Cape Ann', while the sloops *Beaver*, *Senegal* and *Viper* were en route to Halifax in January 1768. Next were the *Launceston* and the schooner *Magdalen* located between the Capes of Virginia and Cape Hatteras. The sloop *Martin* was stationed in North Carolina, between Cape Hatteras and Cape Fear, adjoining the station occupied by the *Fowey*, whose responsibilities extended as far south as St John's River in modern-day Florida. The sloop *Bonetta* and schooner *Chaleur* were responsible for East Florida and the Bahamas. Lastly, the schooners *Gaspee*, *St John* and *St Lawrence* were stationed between the St Lawrence River and the Capes of Virginia with the armed vessel *Canceaux* employed on surveying duties in the '…Northern Districts of America'.[7]

Trade Regulation

A primary function of the North America Squadron was to protect North American trade from French privateers, the threat from which remained undiminished given the strong feelings of *revanche* then prevalent. The French had been granted fishing rights in the peace terms of 1763, with bases on the islands of St Pierre and Miquelon near the southern coast of Newfoundland, which the British feared could be used to raid commercial shipping. A second objective, and one which grew in importance during the years between the end of the Seven Years War and the American War, was to extract revenue from the North American colonies to mitigate the considerable British national debt accumulated during the first half of the eighteenth century.[8] It is this latter responsibility with which this chapter is primarily concerned.

North American Commerce in the Eighteenth Century

Key components of North American trade were the considerable volumes of timber and provisions exported from New England to the West Indies, where they were exchanged for molasses, much of which originated from French islands. The relationship was symbiotic. The West Indies were heavily dependent on sourcing their food and wood from America but had a significant surplus of molasses, particularly in the French islands, as converting this to rum was against the commercial interests of their own wine and spirits producers. On the other hand, American traders found an insufficient market for their goods in the British islands and had a large surplus of damaged fish that was considered fit only for slaves. A blind eye was turned to this trading with the enemy during the early years of the Seven Years War, since Britain needed American support for operations against the French in Canada. However, the Board of Trade launched an investigation in 1759, which found that most goods were exchanged in one of three ways – by straightforward smuggling, on ships used for the exchange of prisoners via cartels and, lastly, by using the port of Monte

---

7   TNA: ADM 8/44: Admiralty List Book, 1768.
8   Stout, *The Royal Navy in America*, pp.14, 25-27, 58-59 and 165-166.

Christi located on the Spanish side of the border between French and Spanish Hispaniola (the modern-day Dominican Republic), thus disguising French goods as Spanish.[9]

Attempts by British authorities to prevent the trade commenced in 1760, when the Prime Minister, William Pitt, wrote to colonial governors denouncing '… this illegal and most pernicious Trade…', stating that it enabled the French to maintain the conflict and thus protract the war. The governors were urged to seek out and punish those individuals engaged in it and use whatever powers they had to prevent any continuation. More practical action was taken by Rear Admiral Charles Holmes, commanding the Jamaica station, who ordered his ships to seize all vessels leaving Monte Christi and ports in French Hispaniola. The home government neither countermanded nor ratified these orders, but left the jurisdiction to prize courts; thus commenced the Royal Navy regulation of trade in the region.[10] The problem with this laissez-faire arrangement, at least from the British Government's perspective, was that the colonial authorities refused to condemn participants. In Philadelphia, both the legal fraternity and the vice-admiralty court judge supported the merchants, arguing that goods became British when purchased by British citizens. It also transpired that the previous governor, William Denny, had made a business of selling numerous flags of truce, thus facilitating one of the identified methods by which illegal trade was conducted.[11] The governors of both Rhode Island and New York stated the merchants would have no money to buy British goods if their West Indian trade via Monte Christi was stopped. Meanwhile, in South Carolina, the vice-admiralty court refused to condemn vessels seized for trading with the enemy, while the custom house could not deny clearances for Spanish ports.[12]

Judicial proceedings in the West Indies initially went more smoothly, with Rear Admiral Holmes' seizures being tried successfully in vice-admiralty courts there. However, these judgements were reversed in early 1761 by the Court of Prize Appeals in London for ships engaged in the Monte Christi trade, which was therefore only checked during the second half of 1760 before being revived in 1761. The Court upheld the decisions of colonial courts on seizures of flag of truce ships, but the potential for smuggling via this method was stopped by an Order in Council of March 1761, which placed the Royal Navy in charge of these exchanges.[13] It was now the turn of the Treasury to take a hand in proceedings in May 1763, by ordering the customs commissioners to improve revenue collection in North America and the West Indies. All customs officers were ordered to return to their posts by 31 August, but many refused to do so, having obtained their positions as sinecures with no

9   Stout, *The Royal Navy in America*, pp.10 and 14-17 and L., Sellars, *Charleston business on the eve of the American Revolution* (London: Macdonald and Jane's, 1974), p.179.
10   Pitt to Governors in North America and the West Indies, in G.S. Kimball, *Correspondence of William Pitt when Secretary of State with colonial governors and military and naval commissioners in America* (New York: Macmillan, 1906), vol.2, pp.320-321 and Stout, *The Royal Navy in America*, pp.17-19.
11   Governor James Hamilton to Pitt, in Kimball, *Correspondence of William Pitt*, vol.2, pp.320-321.
12   Lieutenant Governor Cadwallader Colden to Pitt, 27 October and 11 November 1760, Lieutenant Governor Francis Fauquier to Pitt, 28 October 1760, Governor B. Wentworth to Pitt, 9 December 1760, Governor Stephen Hopkins to Pitt, 20 December 1760 and Lieutenant Governor William Bull to Pitt, 18 February 1761 in Kimball, *Correspondence of William Pitt*, vol.2, pp.348-351, 358-359, 362-363, 373-382 and 394-396.
13   Stout, *The Royal Navy in America*, pp.21-22 and J. Munro (ed.), *Acts of the Privy Council of England* (London: HMSO, 1911), vol.4, p.464.

intention of actually residing in America, let alone undertaking any work. Those failing to respond to the Treasury's order, or not assuming their positions without an acceptable explanation, were dismissed. Aside from attempting to address the personnel issue, the Treasury stopped the practice of 'composition', or out of court settlements between customs officers and merchants trading in smuggled goods, where settlements were typically based on one third of the value of the goods in question plus all duties and costs.[14]

Legislative Background

A key aspect of naval officers' duties in North America was to ensure that trade legislation was implemented:

> In pursuance of the King's Pleasure signified to us by the Earl of Hillsborough, one of His Majesty's Principal Secretaries of State, you are hereby required and directed (with His Majesty's Ship under your Command) when legally called upon, every proper support and Protection in your Power to the Civil Magistrates and to the Officers of the Revenue in the execution of their Duty, and for enforcing a due obedience to the Laws of the Kingdom, the Execution of which has, in several instances been unwarrantably resisted and their authority denied.[15]

Amongst the foremost 'Laws of the Kingdom', as far as trade was concerned, were the Navigation Acts, enacted between 1660 and 1696, and the Molasses Act of 1733, these being the legislation already in place prior to the end of the Seven Years War. Being responsible for implementing this legislation, naval officers, and especially the captains of vessels, required an understanding of the various provisions. The main points related to the persons permitted to conduct trade or the means to trade, and the routeing by which goods were allowed to travel. Regarding the former, only ships owned and navigated by British subjects could trade with British colonies or bring goods from Asia, Africa or America to Britain, and no aliens could act as merchants or factors in British colonies. Regarding the latter, enumerated articles (initially sugar, tobacco, cotton, ginger and dyewoods, but later acts added rice, furs, copper, molasses and naval stores) had to be shipped to Britain before transhipment, but this was subsequently broadened to cover any commodity grown or manufactured in Europe. These measures required documentation, so ships trading with the colonies had to post a bond which was forfeited if the enumerated goods were not brought to Britain or a British possession. Ships entering colonial ports could not unload unless they could prove they were owned and managed by British subjects and a 'cocket', or certified cargo list, presented. Violations might result in the loss of the ship and cargo. Of great importance to the Royal Navy was the division of the proceeds arising from any seizures made. For those on land, proceeds were divided one third each between the King, the colonial governor and the party responsible for the seizure, whereas those made at sea were split equally between the King and the naval officers performing the seizure.[16]

---

14   Stout, *The Royal Navy in America*, pp.11-12 and 31-32.
15   TNA: ADM 2/94 p.384: Admiralty Board to Captains Robinson, Hayward and Wallace, 3 August 1768.
16   'An Act for the encouraging and increasing of shipping and navigation', 12 Charles II, c.18, and 'An

Despite these measures enacted in the first two of the Navigation Acts, enumerated goods continued to be shipped direct to Europe, undercutting the price of those transhipped in Britain, by sailing to another British colonial port where the bonds were redeemed before proceeding onwards. The Navigation Act of 1673 therefore stipulated that bonds issued at loading were to be for discharge in Britain only, or else the equivalent amount had to be paid in 'plantation duties'.[17] An administrative structure was required for their collection, so the same legislation introduced customs officers to the colonies. The final Act, passed in 1696,[18] broadened the powers of colonial customs officers, who were now made responsible for collecting all duties, with the same powers as their colleagues in Britain. Colonial governors also had to take an oath to enforce the Navigation Acts, which annulled any colonial legislation if it was contrary to their provisions. The issue of routeing was addressed by making ships loading enumerated articles post bonds to carry them to Britain or British colonies, even if 'plantation duties' had been paid. Bonds had to be redeemed within 18 months and could only be secured by individuals of known residence and worth to prevent the use of fictitious persons or paupers, as had sometimes been the case previously. The Act also tightened previous legislation relating to the ownership of ships, by introducing stricter registration requirements to keep foreign-built vessels away from imperial trade. Finally, and of the greatest importance for officers serving on the North America Station, violations could now be tried in courts of vice-admiralty, which had no juries and had the same powers as colonial common law courts, since there were no courts of exchequer in America. It also addressed the issue that colonial juries very rarely convicted breaches of the Navigation Acts.[19]

The other relevant legislation existing prior to 1763 was the Molasses Act.[20] This provided significant advantages to West Indian sugar producers supplying molasses (a waste product of sugar manufacturing) to North America, where great demand existed for it as a cheap sweetener or as the principal ingredient of rum. The strong Parliamentary influence exerted by British West India planters resulted in the Act stipulating a duty of 6d per gallon on foreign molasses, thus reducing competition from French sources. In practice, this duty was rarely collected because it suited no one to enforce the Act. Britain needed the colonies to pay for its produce, and local customs officials had no desire to limit trade through their ports.[21]

Act for the encouragement of trade', 15 Charles II, c.7, in D. Pickering (ed.), *The statutes at large* (Cambridge: Joseph Bentham, 1763-1765), vol.7, pp.452-460 and vol.8, pp.160-167.

17   'An Act for the encouragement of the Greenland and Eastland trades, and for the better securing the plantation-trade', 25 Charles II, c.7, in Pickering (ed.), *The statutes at large*, vol.8, pp.397-400.

18   'An Act for preventing frauds, and regulating abuses in the plantation trade', 7&8 William III, c.22, in Pickering, (ed.), *The statutes at large*, vol.9, pp.428-437.

19   R.C. Simmons, 'Trade legislation and its enforcement, 1748-1776', in J.P. Green and J.R. Pole (eds.), *The Blackwell encyclopedia of the American Revolution* (Oxford: Basil Blackwell, 1991), p.162; Stout, *The Royal Navy in America*, p.7.

20   'An Act for the better securing and encouraging the trade of His Majesty's sugar colonies in America', 6 George II, c.13, in Pickering, (ed.), *The statutes at large*, vol.16, pp.374-379.

21   Simmons, 'Trade legislation and its enforcement', p.163; P.D.G. Thomas, 'The Grenville Program, 1763-1765', in Green and Pole (eds.), *The Blackwell encyclopedia*, p.108 and Stout, *The Royal Navy in America*, pp.9-12.

The Navigation Acts and the Molasses Act were all directed at regulation, not revenue. This was to change dramatically from 1763, when the British parliament began enacting legislation that was specifically directed at using trade to generate tax income. The first measure was the Customs Act of 1763, which made the Royal Navy a fully-fledged branch of the customs service, empowering it to enforce trade and revenue laws. Naval officers were deputised as members of the customs service, taking an oath before a colonial governor or a surveyor general of customs. The division of revenue from seizures at sea remained as per the Navigation Acts, though an order in council of 1 June 1763 stated the squadron commander would receive 50 percent of the King's share. The Act targeted smaller ships of less than 50 tons (subsequently increased to 100 tons) used to land smuggled goods in shallow waters, by making such craft liable to seizure if they were found to be hovering within two leagues of the shore. Most importantly in the American context, where the threat of litigation against Government officials was common, the Act protected customs officials from action in the civil courts by removing their liability to prosecution for damages, so long as probable cause was certified by a judge. This meant the burden of proof was placed on the owner of the seized goods, who also had to post security to cover the costs of the suit.[22]

Directly targeting the West India trade was the Revenue or Sugar Act of 1764, which stiffened the colonial enforcement regime by establishing a new vice-admiralty court with jurisdiction over all America, in order to mitigate the problems experienced hitherto with colonial vice-admiralty courts. This was established in Halifax during the autumn of 1764. Another important measure was a reduction of duty on imported molasses from 6d per gallon to 3d, which aimed to encourage the volume of legitimate trade by making smuggling less attractive. The Sugar Act set out in some detail the documentation required for each shipment, and it was this that officers of the customs and their deputised naval colleagues had to check. It included a certificate that ships loading British sugar, rum and molasses were required to have signed by a magistrate showing the origin, quantity and quality of the product before the vessel could depart the loading port. On completion of the voyage, the cargo could not be discharged until the certificate had been presented to a customs collector. Any cargo not on the certificate was considered foreign and subject to import duty. If this included rum, the ship could be seized. A bond also had to be taken out before any part of the cargo could be loaded, including non-enumerated goods, which was an attempt to prevent foreign molasses being loaded during a voyage and then landed in a British port. Finally, a cocket or cargo list had to be prepared before any part of the cargo was loaded, showing the quality and quantity of the goods, any marks on packages, the names of the shippers and consignees for each cargo item and when and by whom duties had been paid. This largely went against the custom of the trade, whereby cargo was usually loaded continuously as it arrived at the wharf, since many ports had no warehouses. Often the loading places were distant from the customs house, making it impractical for documentation to be obtained in

---

22   'An act for the further improvement of his Majesty's revenue of customs; and for the encouragement of officers making seizures; and for the prevention of the clandestine running of goods into any part of his Majesty's dominions', 3 George III, c.22, in Pickering, (ed.), *The statutes at large*, vol.25 part 1, pp.345-351; Munro, *Acts of the Privy Council*, vol.4, pp.560-562; Simmons, 'Trade legislation and its enforcement', p.164; Stout, *The Royal Navy in America*, pp.27-29 and Sellars, *Charleston business*, p.193.

the manner prescribed. Crews habitually traded small volumes of goods on a personal basis, but these now became liable to seizure if they were not entered on the cocket. The Sugar Act also further eased pressures on customs officers, since all seizures could be prosecuted and an accused party could not defend the case until a £60 security had been posted to cover costs. The accused also had to pay court costs, even if he won the case, if there was deemed to be probable cause for the seizure, and could not sue any informer for damages. The Act also tightened up existing measures regarding the vessels engaged in commercial activities as, with certain exceptions, ships loading in Britain for the colonies were not permitted to call first at a foreign port, and any foreign ships found within two leagues of a British colony could be seized', if they did not depart within 48 hours.[23]

More overtly designed for revenue generation was the Stamp Act of 1765, which aimed at '… further defraying the expenses of defending, protecting and securing…' the British colonies. This established a duty chargeable on all official documents, including those connected with courts and legal proceedings, land surveys and sales, certificates issued by educational institutions, and even extending to packs of playing cards and pairs of dice. More importantly, as regards commercial matters, cargo documentation such as bills of lading also fell under the terms of the Act, though it has been argued this may have had more to do with fraud prevention than generating revenue. Demonstrations against the legislation started in Boston on 14 August 1765, and by the time the Act was to go into effect on 1 November all stamp distributors had resigned throughout the North American colonies. The Act was ultimately repealed by Parliament on 18 March 1766 after solid opposition from the colonists and merchants in England, so was never actually implemented.[24]

As the ships of Commodore Hood's squadron were preparing for their voyage to North America, Parliament was busy enacting a series of five measures collectively known as the 'Townsend Acts' between May and June 1767.[25] These consisted of the Customs Act, Revenue Act, Indemnity Act, New York Restraining Act and the Vice Admiralty Court Act, which collectively aimed to replace revenue lost by the repeal of the Stamp Act the previous year and were written by a committee of the whole House.[26] Import duties were imposed

23 'An act for granting certain duties in the British colonies and plantations in America', 4 George III, c.15, in Pickering, (ed.), *The statutes at large*, vol.26, pp.33-52; Sellars, *Charleston business*, pp.179-180; Simmons, 'Trade legislation and its enforcement', pp.164-165 and Stout, *The Royal Navy in America*, pp.34-38.

24 'An act for granting and applying certain stamp duties, and other duties, in the British colonies and plantations in America', 5 George III, c.12, in Pickering, (ed.), *The statutes at large*, vol.26, pp.179-204; Simmons, 'Trade legislation and its enforcement', p.165; Thomas, 'The Grenville Program', pp.109-111 and Stout, *The Royal Navy in America*, pp.91-92. The Stamp Act was repealed by 6 George III, c.11. See Pickering, (ed.), *The statutes at large*, vol.27, p.19.

25 The Hon. Charles Townshend (1725-1767), of Adderbury, Oxon., served as Chancellor of the Exchequer from July 1766 until his death and was the prime mover of this legislation: see <https://www.historyofparliamentonline.org/volume/1754-1790/member/townshend-hon-charles-1725-67>, accessed 23 August 2023.

26 [Customs Act] 'An act to enable his Majesty to put the customs, and other duties, in the British dominions in America, and the execution of the laws relating to trade there, under the management of commissioners to be appointed for that purpose, and to be resident in the said dominions, 7 George III, c.41, [Revenue Act] 'An act for granting certain duties for British colonies and plantations in America', 7 George III, c.46, [Indemnity Act] 'An act for taking off the inland duty of one shilling

on a wide range of commodities, with powers given to customs officers to search properties they suspected might contain smuggled goods through 'writs of assistance', a measure that violated American sensibilities since it potentially removed a citizen's right to remain secure in his private property. A drawback on English import duties was available for tea re-exported to the colonies, making the commodity cheaper and more able to compete with smuggled goods. Of further direct relevance to naval operations was the establishment of an American Board of Customs Commissioners, with the same powers to enforce trade legislation as their equivalent in Britain. This new Board was to be located in Boston, thus enabling local resolution of issues which might otherwise be delayed by reference to Britain. This tightening of the enforcement regime inevitably led to increased conflict with the colonists. Also of direct relevance was the establishment of a vice-admiralty court for all America, which was a superior court to those in each of the colonies. Adverse reaction to this legislation was swift. On 11 February 1768, the Massachusetts General Assembly passed the 'Massachusetts Circular letter' calling on all other colonial assemblies to unite in opposition to the Townsend Acts, thus forcing a redeployment of the North America Squadron, as discussed further below.[27]

The Enforcers

Before looking in some detail at how trade legislation was enforced by the Royal Navy, it would be worth considering the administrative structure responsible for regulation. Prior to the Townshend Acts, primary responsibility lay with the Lords Commissioners of Trade and Plantations, otherwise known as the Board of Trade, which was the major repository of information on the colonies within the executive branch. The Board had power delegated by the King to accept or reject colonial laws and, though it only had advisory powers, its advice was usually followed. The Board's medium of communication with the King was the Secretary of State for the Southern Department, who formulated policy with the Board and transmitted the King's orders to the colonies. The Secretary of State also held the power of patronage, appointing colonial governors and lesser officials. The Board of Customs Commissioners, a subsidiary of the Treasury Board, was responsible for the number and location of customs districts together with various personnel issues including the appointment and disciplining of colonial customs officers; they also ruled on revenue questions until the establishment of a vice-admiralty court in America and were the primary source of information on colonial trade. As far as the individual colonies were concerned, royal governors had an absolute veto over any measures enacted in their local legislature, also possessing extensive powers of patronage. Further down the administrative scale were surveyors general in each of the northern, middle and southern colonies, who supervised

per pound weight on all black and singlo teas consumed in Great Britain, 7 George III, c.56, [New York Restraining Act] 'An act for restraining and prohibiting the governor, council, and house of representatives of the province of New York', 7 George III, c.59, [Vice-Admiralty Court Act] 'An act for the more easy and effectual recovery of the penalties and forfeitures inflicted by the acts of parliament relating to the trade or revenues of the British colonies and plantations in America', 8 George III, c.22 in Pickering, (ed.), *The statutes at large*, vol.27, pp.447-449, 505-512, 600-605 and 609-610 and Pickering, (ed.), *The statutes at large*, vol.28, pp.70-71.

27   R.J. Chaffin, 'The Townshend Act crisis, 1767-1770' in Green and Pole (eds.), *The Blackwell encyclopedia*, pp.126-145.

the district customs officers and acted as intermediaries between them and the Board of Customs in London. Lastly, customs personnel consisted of a collector and, usually, a comptroller in each district who had reciprocal powers of oversight; reporting to them were searchers, surveyors and tidewaiters.[28]

After 1763, administration of the customs service and the structure of vice-admiralty courts was made more cohesive, with a superior court established in Halifax from 1764, and the Customs Commissioners in Boston from 1767. This was followed in 1768 by a middle tier of vice-admiralty courts being set up in Boston, Philadelphia and Charleston. Although these measures aimed to make operations more efficient by providing locally based administrative oversight for the customs service, together with higher courts where appeals from the provincial level could be heard, they also meant that control previously exercised by colonial governors weakened considerably due to their loss of patronage and from the revenues potentially generated by enforcement.[29]

Royal Navy Involvement

It was a widely held belief in the Royal Navy that smuggling was endemic in America. Only 18 days after arriving at Charleston, Captain Robinson of the *Fowey* wrote to the Admiralty Board asking for a schooner of 40 tons to be put under his command, stating: 'I find a great deal of smuggling carried on in this Country by the means of so many little inlets, and small barr'd places, that it is impossible for the *Fowey* to come near, and where there are no Custom house or Boats to prevent it'.[30] Almost identical views were held by both Commodores Hood and Gambier. Hood noted: 'The Business of illicit Trade, is very great over all the Coast of America',[31] stating the number of ports and inlets were so numerous that a significantly greater number of small ships would be needed to police them. Over two years later, in January 1771, Commodore Gambier reported exactly the same thing, proving that the authorities in Britain had done nothing to address the issue:

> ... the amazing illicit Trade which is carried on all along this coast which ... can only be sensibly and effectually checqued, and in a great degree prevented, by having a number of small craft from the nature of the coast abounding with numberless Bays and Creeks all along it the limits for seizing being at so small a distance from the shore ...'[32]

Occasionally, the authorities received advance information of illicit cargoes and attempted to establish an interception. Such was the case in November 1770 when the Customs Commissioners in Boston gave Gambier: '...an account of a very great illicit Trade carried on between Holland and America, particularly to New York'.[33] Gambier immediately sent the sixth rate *Deal Castle* from New York and the schooner *Sultana* from Rhode Island

---

28   Stout, *The Royal Navy in America*, pp.5-8.
29   Simmons, 'Trade legislation and its enforcement', pp.164-166.
30   TNA: ADM 1/2388: Robinson to Stephens, 15 November 1767.
31   TNA: ADM 1/483 p.54: Hood to Stephens, 28 March 1768.
32   TNA: ADM 1/483 pp.361-362: Gambier to Stephens, 21 January 1771.
33   TNA: ADM/1 483 pp.334-335: Gambier to Stephens, 16 November 1770 and enclosure.

to cruise for 14 days to intercept the merchant ships, one of which, the sloop *Helen*, was supposed to have '400 large Chests of Tea' concealed in rice barrels. This attempt to catch the ships was unsuccessful.[34] Some months later, Gambier learned that many vessels attempting to smuggle illicit goods were expected from the West Indies and Europe, so he stationed the vessels under his command as best he could to intercept them.[35] There is no evidence to suggest they were successful, and the loss of most of the vice-admiralty court records makes it difficult to assess the effectiveness of the Royal Navy in cases like this. It is therefore inconclusive whether there was a significant increase in seizures by the Royal Navy after the American Board of Customs Commissioners assumed responsibility for enforcement.[36]

The techniques used by the mercantile community to counter increased Royal Navy involvement consisted of compromising warship manning levels, developing alternative methods of smuggling and outright violence.

One of the merchants' best defences was to keep naval vessels short-handed by openly encouraging desertion amongst their crews. This was a constant headache for both Commodores Hood and Gambier, and the commanders of individual ships. Hood complained to the Admiralty Board in March 1768 that he was: '... sorry to acquaint their Lordships, that the *Senegall* [sic] has lost by Desertion almost the whole of her working men...' as the ship was 29 seamen short from a complement of 90 when mustered at Rhode Island on 20 March 1768.[37] Hood once more voiced his frustration in July 1769, informing the Admiralty of the high incidence of desertion. The problem persisted throughout the years addressed in this chapter, with Gambier reporting in February 1771 that: '... the seamen of His Majesty's Ships here [are] being daily seduced to desert....'.[38]

Gambier's solution was to issue a proclamation in December 1770 stating that seamen deserters who returned to their ships by 1 February 1771 would not be prosecuted, which avoided the necessity of pressing men '... a mode so obnoxious in the Colonies', and hopefully removed the fear of punishment that may have deterred men from re-joining.[39] This measure had met with little success by late January 1771, so recruiting parties were ordered to Boston offering bounties of £3 for every able seaman or 30/- for ordinary seamen and landsmen. Again, this produced very few men but Gambier hoped it would convince the population that only very real necessity would lead the navy to take further steps that could be regarded as prejudicial to the colonists' trading interests and personal liberties.[40] It was well known what could happen if the Royal Navy resorted to impressment, for Lieutenant Panton of the sixth rate *Rose* had been killed while leading a boarding party in April 1769, as related to the Admiralty Board by Commodore Hood:

> On the 22d past off Cape Ann, he visited a Brig called the *Pitt* Packet, from Cadiz bound to Marble-head, when four of her Crew betook themselves to a sort of Fish

34   TNA: ADM/1 483 p.342: Gambier to Stephens, 5 December 1770.
35   TNA: ADM/1 483 pp.391-392: Gambier to Stephens, 9 May 1771.
36   Stout, *The Royal Navy in America*, pp.130-131 and 138.
37   TNA: ADM 1/483 pp.55 and 365: Hood to Stephens, 28 March 1768 and enclosure.
38   TNA: ADM 1/483 p.219: Hood to Stephens, 28 July 1769 and Gambier to Stephens, 27 February 1771.
39   TNA: ADM/1 483 pp.334-351: Gambier to Stephens, 21 December 1770 and enclosure.
40   TNA: ADM/1 483 p.363: Gambier to Stephens, 25 January 1771.

room in the Hold armed with a Musquet, Ax, Harpoon & Fishgig, and would not suffer Lieutenant Panton to make search as an officer of the Customs for fear of being impressed. He therefore ordered a Board of the Partition to be taken down and on his attempting to go in, he was struck in the throat with the Harpoon, and died immediately.[41]

Merchants could also refuse to pay full wages for the last commercial voyage undertaken by men who joined the Royal Navy, which provided a strong disincentive for them to enlist. This was achieved by an interpretation of the Piracy Act of 1721,[42] by which half the wages were paid in cash and the other half as a bill of exchange redeemable when the vessel reached Britain. The issue was not just an inconvenience to the man concerned, but also occupied the time of his officers in resolving the matter. Captain Robinson of the *Fowey* stated the problem to the Admiralty in August 1768 after he had gone to the trouble of obtaining the opinion of a lawyer at Charleston. This he forwarded to the Admiralty Board requesting their advice for his future guidance, but no reply has been found.[43]

Aside from widespread attempts to manipulate the manning of Royal Navy ships, mercantile interests could also arrange for smuggled goods to be transferred from ocean going vessels into smaller craft whilst still out at sea, thus limiting the cost of seizures if made.[44] This was one of the specific issues addressed by the Customs Act of 1763, discussed above, but the continued lack of naval ships of a similar size greatly limited the extent to which smaller craft could be intercepted and their landing places watched. Finally, in extreme cases, merchants and their followers could resort to outright violence. An example of this during the period under review concerned the revenue cutter *Liberty*, which was severely damaged and scuttled in Newport Harbour, Rhode Island, on 17 July 1769. After attacking the vessel's commander, Captain William Reid, while he was on shore, the mob then made various demands relating to individual crew members and two ships seized by the *Liberty* for alleged breaches of trade regulations, after which they boarded the vessel and disabled it. While such incidents were rare, they indicate what could happen following strict enforcement by the Royal Navy.[45]

The Case of South Carolina

The frigate *Fowey* was stationed in South Carolina during the period addressed in this chapter, arriving at Charleston on 28 October 1767.[46] The following table shows how the ship was deployed during each complete calendar year of its service in North America:

---

41   TNA: ADM 1/483 p.209: Hood to Stephens, 5 May 1769.
42   'An act for the more effectual suppressing of piracy', 8 George I c.24. in Pickering, (ed.), *The statutes at large*, vol.14, pp.468-472.
43   TNA: ADM 1/2388: Robinson to Stephens, 26 August 1768 and Stout, *The Royal Navy in America*, pp.138-139.
44   Stout, *The Royal Navy in America*, pp.139-140.
45   TNA: ADM 1/483 pp.219-227: Hood to Stephens, 25 July 1769 and enclosures.
46   TNA: ADM 1/375: Captain's Log of the *Fowey*, June 1767-June 1770, entry for 28 October 1767.

Table 1: Deployment of the Fowey, 1 January 1768–31 December 1770

Calendar Year	Days in Port	Days at Halifax careening wharf	Days at Sea
1768	237	45	83
1769	266	34	65
1770	273	26	66

Source: TNA: ADM 7/574: Abstracts of ships' journals, 1761-1776 and TNA: ADM 1/375: Captain's Log of the Fowey, June 1767-June 1770.

The table shows an average of 70.9 percent of days were spent in port, 9.6 percent of days at the careening wharf at Halifax and 19.5 percent of days at sea between 1 January 1768 and 31 December 1770. In this context, it is worth mentioning the Admiralty Board's instructions to captains: 'Commanders of His Majesty's Ships formerly stationed in America have sometimes taken unwarrantable Liberties of loitering in Port thereby neglecting the Guard of the Coast & Trade for which they were appointed, to the dishonour of His Majesty's Service'.[47] Why, then, did the Fowey spend such a high proportion of time in port? Some clue may be gained from examining customs statistics for the volume of merchant traffic utilising ports in South Carolina:

Table 2: Number of Vessels Entered Inwards, South Carolina, 1768

Origin	Topsails	Sloops &c	Tonnage
Britain	147	0	18,850
Ireland	10	1	1,010
Southern Europe	18	1	2,123
Africa	0	0	0
West Indies	51	86	8,623
Newfoundland	0	0	0
Quebec	0	0	0
Nova Scotia	0	0	0
13 Colonies	30	111	5,221
Bahamas	0	24	415
Bermuda	1	10	338
Total	257	233	36,580

Source: TNA: CUST 16/1 pp.1-2

The table shows that over half the tonnage entering the port of Charleston was from Britain (51.5 percent), with a much smaller volume from the West Indies (23.6 percent) and the Thirteen Colonies (14.3 percent). It is perhaps unsurprising that the number of larger ships ('topsails') was overwhelmingly from Britain (57.2 percent) and the West Indies (36.9 percent), whereas smaller craft were mainly from the Thirteen Colonies. Of the greatest

---

47   TNA: ADM 2/94 pp.126-129: Admiralty Board to Captain Mark Robinson, 7 August 1767.

relevance to the Royal Navy and the customs service, a total of 490 vessels entered ports in South Carolina in 1768, or about 41 vessels per month.

Table 3: Number of Vessels Entered Outwards, South Carolina, 1768

Origin	Topsails	Sloops &c	Tonnage
Britain	130	3	16,968
Ireland	0	0	0
Southern Europe	48	0	5,515
Africa	0	0	0
West Indies	47	79	6,410
Newfoundland	0	0	0
Quebec	0	0	0
Nova Scotia	0	0	0
13 Colonies	19	102	3,682
Bahamas	0	25	405
Bermuda	0	11	353
Total	244	220	33,333

Source: TNA: CUST 16/1 pp.3-4.

The data for ships departing ports in South Carolina shows, once again, that the dominant trading partner was Britain, accounting for 50.9 percent of tonnage compared to 19.2 percent proceeding to the West Indies and 16.5 percent to Southern Europe. The trade to Britain and Southern Europe was dominated by 'topsails', in contrast to sailings to the Thirteen Colonies and the West Indies, which were mostly in sloops or smaller craft. A total of 464 vessels departed ports in South Carolina, or about 39 per month.

Prescribed documents relating to an average of 80 merchant vessels per month therefore required processing and checking by the Royal Navy and their customs colleagues, at least in 1768, and this must go some way to explain why the *Fowey* spent so many days in port.

Two examples of customs enforcement in South Carolina serve to illustrate the work of the Royal Navy in America. The first concerned the regulation of the considerable coasting trade, which was brought to prominence by the arrest of the merchant schooner *Active* by Commander James Hawker of the *Sardoine*, in May 1767. The second was the seizure of the merchant schooner *Bellmore* in February 1769 on suspicion of smuggling. The case highlighted several issues faced by officers and men of the Royal Navy while supporting the customs authorities. To appreciate the details of these two cases, some outline must first be given of commerce in South Carolina.

Commodities were transported to or from the interior of the state via three main waterways. From north to south these were the Peedee River, which meets the coast at Georgetown on Winyah Bay, some 65 miles north of Charleston. Next is the Santee River located in the centre of the state, also meeting the sea at Winyah Bay, while to the south the Savannah River ends at the town of the same name in Georgia. The extent of the coasting trade was dictated by the nature of the ports at which goods either entered or departed these river systems. Most ports were restricted, meaning that ocean going vessels were unable to utilise them, or had to do so when not fully loaded. Georgetown, for example, was only suitable for ships with a draft of between 10-12 feet, while Wilmington in North Carolina had dangerous shoals at the port entrance. Port Royal, located near the border with Georgia, was situated on an island and disconnected from the inland waterway system, while Savannah was not well developed at this period. Port restrictions therefore meant that commodities from all these ports had to be shipped on coastal vessels to or from Charleston, being the only location in the region where they could be loaded or discharged from larger ocean-going ships.

South Carolina was primarily an exporter, dominating overall shipments from the Thirteen Colonies of rice, deer hides and indigo. Shipments of piemento (chilli pepper), while relatively small in volume terms, were also significant in relation to the Thirteen Colonies as a whole.

Table 4: South Carolina Exports, 1768

Commodity	Unit	13 Colonies	South Carolina	% South Carolina
Rice	Barrels	138,230	135,288	97.87%
Hides	Number	1,757	1,115	63.46%
Deer Hides	Pounds weight	131,547	50,073	38.06%
Deer Hides	Casks	2,123	188	8.86%
Deer Hides	Number	6,739	1,108	16.44%
Deer Hides	Hogsheads	625	315	50.40%
Indian Corn	Bushels	1,108,112	41,268	3.72%
Piemento	Pounds weight	23,060	12,560	54.47%
Indigo	Pounds weight	523,764	497,988	95.08%
Indigo	Casks	554	196	35.38%

Source: TNA: CUST 16/1 pp.13-25.

In contrast, imports to South Carolina were minimal. This was especially important given the relatively insignificant volumes of imported foreign molasses and rum, in contrast to the more northerly provinces, meaning the issues discussed above affecting the smuggling of these commodities concerned South Carolina far less.

Table 5: South Carolina Imports, 1768

Commodity	Unit	13 Colonies	South Carolina	% South Carolina
British Cotton	Pounds Weight	186,036	5,400	2.90%
Foreign Molasses	Gallons	2,775,613	64,832	2.34%
British Mahogany	Feet	407,600	130,000	31.89%
Rum	Gallons	2,076,876	125,838	6.06%
West Indies Salt	Bushels	436,416	26,156	5.99%

Source: TNA: CUST 16/1 pp.3-6.

One notable absence from the available customs data are slaves, who were imported into South Carolina in great numbers. This was especially the case during 1765, when 7,184 were imported, an unusually high number resulting from a prohibitive level of duty anticipated from 1 January 1766. Importation effectively stopped during the three year period covered by this duty, but 4,612 were imported in 1769, after it ended. The following two years were quiet, since slaves were included under the resolutions of non-importation adopted as a protest to the Townshend Acts, so the trade did not revive until 1772 when 4,865 slaves were landed.[48] A survey of the population of Charleston undertaken during the summer of 1770 revealed a total of 5,831 negro compared to 5,030 white inhabitants, with the former, '... employed as Domestic Servants & Mechanics'.[49]

Returning to the case of the merchant schooner *Active*, the ship had been arrested since it appeared to be an ocean-going vessel yet had none of the cargo documentation required by the Sugar Act of 1764. The case was tried at the Court of Vice-Admiralty in Charleston by Judge Egerton Leigh, who ruled that coasting vessels such as the *Active* did not require these documents, but that Commander Hawker had probable cause for the seizure under the terms of the Customs Act of 1763. The Charleston merchants were therefore eager to avoid a repetition of this incident on the arrival of Captain Mark Robinson, the new commander of the South Carolina station, in October 1767, writing to him at some length and outlining all the details of the case.[50] The coasting trade was of great importance in the province of South Carolina, and the judgement handed down in the case of the *Active* was critical in removing a potential flashpoint between the Royal Navy and the mercantile community.

The case of the *Bellmore* was different, ending in frustration for both the enforcement authorities and mercantile interests. The vessel was boarded outside Charleston on 3 February 1769 en route from St Eustatius. It ostensibly carried a cargo of molasses, but was found to have 60 gallons each of brandy and rum, five cases of gin and sundry other cargo including china, glass tumblers, cayenne peppers and candles, without the relevant documentation. The crew attempted to destroy the evidence by throwing some of the cargo over the ship's side and drilling holes in the hogsheads containing the liquor, but were detected in the attempt. As with the merchant ship *Pitt* and the revenue cutter *Liberty*, discussed above, the Royal Navy boarding party despatched from the frigate *Fowey* was met with violence when the merchant captain James Rogers:

> ... presented his Pistol, (which he said was loaden with a brace of Ball) to my Mouth, with many oaths and execrations, swearing whether the Schooner was seized or not, the first time he saw me on shore, he would blow my Brains out, and tear me Limb, from Limb, like a Frog with many other Threatnings of Violence, whenever he should catch me on shore.[51]

---

48   Sellars, *Charleston business*, p.134.
49   TNA: CO 5/409 pp.94-95: Lieutenant Governor William Bull to the Earl of Hillsborough, 30 November 1770.
50   TNA: ADM 1/2388: Robinson to Stephens, 10 December 1767 with enclosure.
51   TNA: ADM 1/2388: John Berry to Captain Mark Robinson, 4 February 1769.

Legal proceedings were initiated against the owners of the *Bellmore*, but the vessel had to be returned to them in April 1769 when the time limitation for such action was exceeded. The problem was due to the absence of a Vice Admiralty Court judge to try the case, since Sir Augustus Johnson did not reach Charleston until May.[52]

While the *Active* and *Bellmore* cases were noteworthy, they were very much the exception in South Carolina. The *Active* set a legal precedent for the subsequent handling of coastal trading by the authorities, and no further conflict arose from this source during the period under study. The relative lack of imported goods to South Carolina meant the *Bellmore* was an isolated example of smuggling, and there is no further evidence of cases occurring prior to 1771, though the circumstances may have been little different to other examples elsewhere in the American colonies.

In contrast to the received image of conflict between the authorities and the colonists, it is noteworthy that Captain Mark Robinson was given five grants of land in December 1770, shortly before his departure from South Carolina.[53] This was followed shortly afterwards by a warm address from the mercantile community:

> Your regard to the Welfare of this Country and the constant attention you have shown during your Command here to our Navigation entitle you to the warmest thanks of your fellow subjects and to the approbation of Government.
>
> Impressed with sentiments of the highest esteem for you, the Merchants of South Carolina intreat your Acceptance of their unfeigned acknowledgements and grateful Sense of the Obligations you have conferred on them, as a body, by your unremitted care of the Trade of the Province.
>
> In whatsoever part of the World you may be called by the duties of your Station you will be always attended by our fervent wishes for your health, honour, & prosperity.[54]

These sentiments suggest harmonious civil-military relations, at least in the years up to early 1771.

Public Order Duties

The Royal Navy's involvement in maintaining public order comprised two activities: the conveyance of troops and attempts to discourage civil disturbance. An example of the former occurred in October 1768 when the *Fowey* transported a detachment of the 1st Battalion,

---

52   TNA: ADM 1/2388: Robinson to Stephens, 14 April 1769 with enclosures and W.R. Smith, *South Carolina as a Royal province* (London: Macmillan, 1903), pp.149-150.

53   Land Grant Office, Raleigh, North Carolina: Book 20, pp.638-639: Grants 363 and 364, 640 acres each in Bladen County on both sides of Fryers Swamp; Grant 365, 640 acres in Bladen County on both sides of Great Slap Arse Swamp; Grant 366, 640 acres in Brunswick County on both sides of the Gum Swamp and Grant 367, 640 acres in Brunswick County joining on the north east side of the Wagana [sic] Lake. All grants dated 24 December 1770.

54   *South Carolina Gazette*, Thursday, January 31, 1771.

60th Regiment from Charleston to New York in the interests of speed and economy.[55] At almost the same time, Commodore Hood informed the Admiralty:

> I was under a necessity of laying hold of the Southern Ships[56] as well as those under my command, for Transporting Troops to Boston, which was a saving to Government of near £3,000 … and if I had not been prepared with King's Ships to receive them, they could not have been sent at all from hence, as there was a difficulty to procure sufficient vessels for the women, children and baggage.[57]

Hood's deployment of his squadron was therefore dictated, for periods at least, by the need to support the army, as he explained in November 1768: '… for if Troops should be required to be carried from this Province [Virginia] to any other, or from any other to this it is a service not to be effected but in his majesty's ships, as Transport Vessels cannot be hired'.[58]

Examples of ships being used to overawe a refractory populace primarily concerned increased deployments to Boston, the theory being that a demonstration of state power would ensure the safety of customs and revenue officers, while also protecting government property. These deployments commenced in early 1768, caused by increasingly violent opposition to the Townsend Acts, leading the Customs Commissioners to request a frigate at the port, with a sloop to cruise in Canso Bay. Hood ordered the fourth rate *Romney* to Boston, where it sailed on 6 May 1768, thus providing a refuge for the Customs Commissioners following a serious riot on 10 June. The situation at Boston was sufficiently grave for Hood to proceed there himself to assess what naval force should be deployed during the winter, but this was decided for him by the Admiralty Board, directing that one frigate, two sloops and two schooners should be retained there to support the Customs Commissioners until further notice.[59]

The public order situation at Boston continued to affect the deployment of naval vessels for the remainder of the period under study. The aftermath of the 'Boston massacre' of 5 March 1770, when soldiers under the command of Captain Thomas Preston of the 29th Regiment killed three men and wounded eight (two mortally) of a mob harassing them, led

---

55   TNA: ADM 1/2388: Robinson to Stephens, 30 October 1768. Captain Robinson identified these troops as being from 'His Majesty's Sixty first Regiment', but this unit was quartered in England. The 1st Battalion 60th Regiment had one captain, one lieutenant, two sergeants, one drummer and 18 men stationed in Charleston, together with one sergeant and 18 men at Fort Charlotte. Other detachments were stationed in Georgia at Forts Augusta, Prince George and Frederica. The main body of the unit, six companies, was based in Montreal (TNA: WO 379/1: Dispositions and movement returns, 1737-1800).

56   Hood detained the 5th rate *Launceston* which had disembarked its lower deck guns at Halifax in order to make room for troops being conveyed to Boston. The vessel had to return to Halifax for its guns before proceeding to its station in Virginia (TNA: ADM 1/483 pp.131-132: Hood to Stephens, 15 September 1768).

57   TNA: ADM 1/483 pp.153-155: Hood to Stephens, 23 October 1768.

58   TNA: ADM 1/483 pp.169-171: Hood to Stephens, 22 November 1768.

59   TNA: ADM 1/483 pp.59 and 61: Customs Commissioners to Hood, 12 February and 4 March 1768, enclosed in Hood to Stephens, 28 March 1768; TNA: ADM 1/483 pp.84, 93-96, 144 and 154: Hood to Stephens, 30 May, 23 June, 12 and 23 October 1768 and TNA: ADM 2/94 pp.340-341: Admiralty Board to Hood, 15 June 1768.

the Admiralty Board to order Commodore Hood to be, '…very attentive to what passes at Boston'.[60] He therefore sent the frigates *Mermaid* and *Hussar*, followed by the sloops *Bonetta* and *Martin*, to the town.[61] After Commodore Gambier assumed command of the squadron from October 1770, he discovered that ships had to be constantly called off their stations and sent to Boston, meaning he had few opportunities to supervise the Halifax naval yard.[62] By January 1771, the fourth rate *Salisbury*, the sloops *Beaver* and *Senegal* and the schooner *Gaspee*, were all stationed at Boston.[63]

Ship Maintenance

Aside from regulating commerce and engaging in public order duties, ships of the North America Squadron spent significant amounts of time under maintenance. Much of this consisted of daily routine tasks undertaken by the crew, but always involved an annual visit to the careening wharf at Halifax, where more extensive repairs were also undertaken.[64] This was the only state owned repair facility then existing in North America, and we have already noted that just under 10 percent of the *Fowey*'s time was spent there, undergoing maintenance and repairs. This was in compliance with the Admiralty Board's instructions to captains proceeding to North America:

> … you are to proceed to Halifax once in every year at such time as the service you are employed upon will best admit of it and not oftener in order to have the Ship you command cleaned & refitted: or to repair with her to England in case she shall appear to stand in need of any considerable works, for our further directions.[65]

Authorisation for the Halifax Naval Yard had been given in 1757, with a suitable site being chosen by Commodore Philip Durell the following year. Construction commenced in 1759, and by the *Fowey*'s first visit in 1768, facilities included a capstan house, a mast house and pond, a boat house, storehouses, a watering wharf, an anchor wharf, two careening wharves and a blacksmith's shop. Importantly, there was no dry dock, hence no vessel construction or major refits were possible; in common with similar facilities in the western hemisphere at English Harbour, Antigua, and Port Royal, Jamaica, Halifax was not a dockyard.[66]

Despite being of relatively recent construction, the yard suffered greatly from the effects of a rigorous winter climate and was in considerable disrepair when Commodore Hood

---

60   TNA: ADM 2/95 p.402: Admiralty Board to Hood, 27 April 1770.
61   TNA: ADM 1/483 p.292: Hood to Stephens, 29 June 1770.
62   TNA: ADM 1/483 pp.326 and 338-339: Gambier to Stephens, 29 October and 8 December 1770.
63   TNA: ADM 8/47: Admiralty List Book, 1771.
64   'Careening is used to heave one of the ship's sides so low in the water, as that her bottom, being elevated above its surface on the other side, may be cleaned from any filth, which adheres to it'. W. Falconer, *An universal dictionary of the marine* (London: T. Cadell, 1784).
65   TNA: ADM 2/94 pp.78-80 and 131: Admiralty Board to Captains Mark Robinson and Thomas Hayward.
66   J. Gwyn, *Ashore and afloat: the British Navy and the Halifax Navy Yard before 1820* (Ottawa: University of Ottawa Press, 2004), pp.3-13.

arrived in mid-1767. A severe frost during the preceding winter and succeeding heavy rains had caused extensive damage to the wharves and naval stores. In addition, the timber from which many buildings were constructed needed replacing.[67] Matters hardly improved the following year, when Hood informed the Admiralty that the condition of the careening yard '... becomes more & more ruinous every week: a great part of the watering wharf is washed away, by the heavy rains succeeding the Frost'.[68] He reported further extensive damage to the careening wharf caused by a severe gale on 1-2 April 1768.[69] Ongoing repairs caused by the weather were a constant feature of the Halifax yard, with Hood outlining in November 1769 the considerable work needed to the capstan house, sea defences, boat slip, both careening wharves, cooperage, watering and anchor wharves. Some protection for yard facilities was hoped to result from a stone wall built around the careening yard in January 1770 at a cost of £2780,4,6 and for naval stores by the construction of a suitable building at the rear of the capstan house for £2867,3,9.[70] Adding to these problems was a shortage of labour, meaning that ships' crews had to be utilised for repair works to yard facilities.[71]

Conclusion

The primary tasks of the Royal Navy in North America were the protection of trade and the enforcement of trade and revenue legislation. This aimed at increasing revenue for the customs service by reducing the incidence of smuggling, evidenced by the direct trade between both Europe and the West Indies to America.[72] The widespread view in Britain that America was full of smugglers did not only emanate from West Indian Planter interests, but was common amongst officers of the Royal Navy, who strongly believed that smuggling was endemic.[73]

Although a lack of complete data from local vice-admiralty courts makes a quantitative assessment of the Royal Navy's efforts problematic, it is clear that various difficulties existed with the enforcement of trade regulations. A main cause was friction between customs officers and the Royal Navy over the division of prize money. This arose from inconsistency between the Navigation Acts, and then from 1763 when the Customs Act officially allowed a significant share to the Royal Navy that had, at least in part, previously been enjoyed by the customs service. The division of revenue from seizures also led to conflict between the Royal Navy and colonial governors, who formed another interested party in the division of spoils arising from enforcement. Issues such as this often led to a lack of motivation amongst naval officers, who realised the opportunities for profit were slim.[74]

---

67   TNA: ADM 1/483 pp.8-9, 10-22 and 30: Hood to Stephens, 28 July, 5 September and 13 October 1767.

68   TNA: ADM 1/483 p.50: Hood to Stephens, 10 March 1768.

69   TNA: ADM 1/483 p.73: Hood to Stephens, 4 April 1768.

70   TNA: ADM 1/483 pp.236-238 and 259-262: Hood to Stephens, 23 November 1769 and 17 January 1770.

71   TNA: ADM 1/483 pp.8-9 and 120-121: Hood to Stephens, 28 July 1767 and 2 August 1768.

72   J. Gwyn, 'The Royal Navy in North America, 1712-1776', in Black and Woodfine (eds.), The British Navy and the use of naval power in the eighteenth century, p.141

73   TNA: ADM 1/483 pp.54 and 330: Hood to Stephens, 28 March 1768 and Gambier to Stephens, 6 November 1770 and Stout, The Royal Navy in America, pp.12 and 41.

74   Gwyn, 'Royal Navy in North America', pp.141-142 and Stout, The Royal Navy in America, pp.8-9 and 50-55.

Smooth civil-military relations were not helped by some officers, such as Rear Admiral Lord Colvill, who tended to show an overall contempt for officials during his tenure on the North America Station between October 1763 and September 1766, though both his successors, Commodores Hood and Gambier, enjoyed generally good relations with both local officials and the colonists. More junior officers, in nearly all cases representing the actual interface between the state and the mercantile community, could also cause difficulties. A case in point was Commander James Hawker of the *Sardoine*, based at Charleston between August 1766 and November 1767, who was overly confrontational and adopted a too literal interpretation of the trade regulations. Legal difficulties followed Hawker around America, starting in December 1763 in New York, continuing in Philadelphia in June 1764, before his seizure of the *Active* in Charleston in May 1767 actually caused mob violence.[75]

Difficulties with enforcement were also caused by an insufficient number of small vessels able to enter the many draft restricted creeks and inlets habitually used for landing illicitly traded goods. Commodore Gambier stated in November 1770 that he had seven schooners, one of which was permanently located in the Bahamas, to cover 600 leagues of coast. He requested six more. A misplaced need for economy by the Admiralty thus restricted enforcement of the very acts designed to raise revenue.[76] In mitigation, smaller vessels could suffer unduly during their passage across the Atlantic, as Commodore Hood informed the Admiralty in October 1767: '... his Majesty's Sloop *Viper* is just arrived here after a passage of two months from Plymouth, in which she has been very severely buffeted by contrary Gales of wind, and is a near wreck'.[77]

The success or otherwise of the enforcement regime greatly depended on maintaining the serviceability of the naval craft deployed. The Halifax Yard was the only maintenance facility in North America at this time, yet its' infrastructure suffered considerably from the exigencies of the weather. The use of inappropriate construction materials, in a misconceived attempt to save costs, proved uneconomic and often distracted the attention of officers commanding the North America Station, since they had responsibility for maintenance and repairs.

The creation of the American Board of Customs Commissioners by the Customs Act of 1767 was designed to ease the burden on the English taxpayer by increasing revenue collections in America. There is little evidence the Royal Navy was any more successful than previous arrangements and most of the duties imposed in 1767 were soon repealed. The expected revenues therefore never accrued and more money was expended in enforcement than was covered by collections. The Royal Navy was thrust into an increasingly demanding role after 1763, being given too many tasks to perform for the resources allowed by a parsimonious ministry. This represented a failure of Government policy, with the result that officers and men of the Royal Navy were left to enforce the unenforceable.

---

75 Simmons, 'Trade legislation and its enforcement', pp.166-167 and Stout, *The Royal Navy in America*, pp.41, 45-46, 75-77 and 81-84.
76 TNA: ADM/1 483 pp.330-331: Gambier to Stephens, 6 November 1770; Gwyn, 'Royal Navy in North America', p.143; Stout, *The Royal Navy in America*, pp.127-128.
77 TNA: ADM 1/483 p.30: Hood to Stephens, 13 October 1767.

Select Bibliography

Archives
The National Archives, Kew (TNA)
    ADM 1/375 Captain's Log of the *Fowey*, June 1767-June 1770.
    ADM 1/483 Flag Officers' Letters, North America, Commodores Hood and Gambier, 1767-1772.
    ADM 1/2388 Captain's Letters, 1764-1771, names beginning with R.
    ADM 2/94 Admiralty Board out-letters, May 1767-March 1769.
    ADM 2/95 Admiralty Board out-letters, April 1769-September 1770.
    ADM 8/44 Admiralty List Book, 1768.
    ADM 8/47 Admiralty List Book, 1771.
    CO 5/409 South Carolina, Letters to Secretary of State, 1767-1772.
    CUST 16/1 Ledgers of imports and exports, America, 1768-1773.
    WO 379/1 Dispositions and movement returns, 1737-1800.
Land Grant Office, Raleigh, North Carolina
    Land Patent Book 20.

Newspaper
South Carolina Gazette.

Published Primary Sources
Kimball, G.S. (ed.), *Correspondence of William Pitt when Secretary of State with colonial governors and military and naval commissioners in America* (New York: Macmillan, 1906).
Munro, J. (ed.), *Acts of the Privy Council of England* (London: HMSO, 1911).
Pickering, D. (ed.), *The statutes at large* (Cambridge: Joseph Bentham, 1763-1765).

Published Sources
Black, J. and Woodfine, P. (eds.), *The British Navy and the use of naval power in the eighteenth century* (Leicester: Leicester University Press, 1988).
Falconer, W., *An universal dictionary of the marine* (London: T. Cadell, 1784).
Green, J.P. and Pole, J.R. (eds.), *The Blackwell encyclopedia of the American Revolution* (Oxford: Basil Blackwell, 1991).
Gwyn, J., *Ashore and afloat: the British Navy and the Halifax Navy Yard before 1820* (Ottawa: University of Ottawa Press, 2004)
Sellars, L., *Charleston business on the eve of the American Revolution* (London: Macdonald and Jane's, 1974)
Smith, W.R., *South Carolina as a Royal Province* (London: Macmillan, 1903).
Stout, N.R., *The Royal Navy in America, 1760-1775. A study of enforcement of British colonial policy in the era of the American Revolution* (Annapolis: Naval Institute Press, 1973).

6

The Nile That Wasn't: D'Estaing, Barrington, and the Battle of St Lucia, 1778

Thomas Golding-Lee[1]

The Battle of St Lucia (or the Battle of Grand Cul De Sac Bay), fought on 15 December 1778, bore striking similarities to the Battle of the Nile (1-3 August 1798). Indeed, Alfred Thayer Mahan made the parallel in his seminal work, *The Influence of Seapower Upon History.*[2] An outnumbered British squadron was caught at anchor and at the mercy of a superior French force. The British fleet's loss would have meant the end of the wider St Lucia campaign (13–28 December 1778) with the loss of 5,000 crack troops. Why, then, did the British fleet not suffer the same fate as that of the French fleet at Aboukir Bay, 20 years later? This chapter will examine the battle fought between British force under the command of Rear-Admiral the Hon. Samuel Barrington and French fleet under *Vice-Amiral* Charles Henri Hector, Comte d'Estaing, and argue that the French admiral proved to be no Nelson.

This chapter will aim not only to recount the details of this interesting and unique engagement, in order to bring it to its deserved attention as a victory of note for the Royal Navy, but will also re-examine the engagement and reappraise the efforts of both the British and French navies to give a more full, accurate and fair holistic picture of the battle.

The Admirals: Jean Baptiste d'Estaing and Samuel Barrington

Vice-Amiral Jean Baptiste Charles Henri Hector, Comte d'Estaing, was born in 1729 and at the age of nine he joined (on paper, it must be said) the famed Mousquetaires du roi. From a young age d'Estaing had a close relationship with the French Royal Family and had been educated alongside the Dauphin Louis (father of the ill-fated Louis XVI); this would both make his career but also eventually sign his death warrant.

---

1   In loving Memory of Robin Brodhurst. *Fortier ac Fideliter.*
2   Alfred Thayer Mahan, The *Influence of Sea Power Upon History, 1660-1783* (Boston: Little, Brown, and Company, 1898), p.366.

By the age of 19, he was a colonel in command of a regiment and served during the War of Austrian Succession. After the end of the war, d'Estaing was considered a leading military reformer in command of a 'model' regiment. He continued to serve in diplomatic and military posts. While serving as an officer of the French East India Company during the Seven Years War (following his capture and paroling at the Siege of Madras), d'Estaing was stationed in the Indian Ocean where he captured several prizes in the Persian Gulf as well as destroyed an East India Company factory. He then crossed to Sumatra, capturing three British forts and raiding numerous other British positions on the island. For his naval success was made a *maréchal de camp* (major general).

D'Estaing was finally made a *chef d'escadre* (rear-admiral) in 1762, without ever having proceeded through the naval hierarchy, in preparation for an expedition to South America that came to nothing due to the peace of 1763. He served in numerous staff postings following his return, before receiving his American command (again likely due to his personal connections). Following his contribution to the American War d'Estaing saw no more active service after 1779. He later supported the reforms of the French Revolutionaries, but despite his support for liberal reforms, he remained loyal to the Royal family he had known for so long. He spoke on behalf of Marie Antoinette at her trial and was himself executed in 1794.[3]

D'Estaing has received much criticism for failing to crush Barrington's force at St Lucia, and for his naval command more widely. A significant aspect of this criticism is that d'Estaing lacked naval experience and credentials. Naval historians are want to paint him as a landlubber.[4] The criticism then generally follows that he should have overwhelmed the small British force with aggressive close action, in the manner of Nelson at the Nile. The French force was vastly superior in both numbers and firepower and should have been able to overcome Barrington's force. The fault therefore lay with d'Estaing's poor command and not weather, geography, or his captains.[5]

D'Estaing's military career was of mixed success but he was a quintessentially enlightenment figure who was very much a man of the age. To compare d'Estaing to Barrington or even Nelson in anything other than a tactical sense, removes the historical reality of the man. It obscures our understanding of the man by placing him in a context not his own. It ignores his evident qualities as a soldier, poet, author, and liberal minded politician. When viewed in the round, d'Estaing is clearly a quite shining example of the sort of enlightened polymath renowned across continental Europe during the eighteenth century.

Rear-Admiral Samuel Barrington could not stand in greater contrast to the continental enlightenment aristocrat d'Estaing. Though the fourth son of a viscount and the brother of the Bishop of Llandaff, Barrington had been at sea practically his entire life, first serving at

---

3   This narrative of d'Estaing's life is drawn from the J.J.R. Calmon-Maison, *L'Amiral d'Estaing 1729-1794* (Paris: Calmann-Levy, 1910). It is the only full-length biography of this remarkable figure of the enlightenment and there is no edition available in English, leaving this author to struggle on with the aide of his prep school French and significantly better-educated wife.

4   Sam Willis, *The Struggle for Sea Power: A Naval History of the American Revolution* (London: Atlantic Books, 2015), p.232.

5   Sir Charles Ekins, *The Naval Battles of Great Britain: From the Ascension of the Illustrious House of Hannover to the Throne to the Battle of Navarin* (London: Baldwin and Craddock, 1828), pp.91-94; Willis, *The Struggle for Sea Power*, p.232.

11 and becoming a post captain at 18, in no small part due to the influence of his brother William, an Admiralty Lord. He was seemingly at sea continuously for 22 years between 1741 and 1763.[6]

Despite his rise being indisputably aided by patronage and familial connections, Barrington is an excellent example of the solid, instinctive, and lifelong sea-officer that the Royal Navy had been developing over the course of the long eighteenth century. His behaviour at the Battle of St Lucia is an example of the career spanning, and indeed inter-generational, learning cycles that would culminate in the famous victories of Jervis, Duckworth and Nelson. At St Lucia, Barrington and the men under his command demonstrated the technical seamanship capabilities and cool courage that became expected of the Royal Navy in later years.

Opening Moves

Following the signing of the Franco-American alliance in February 1778, d'Estaing left Toulon with a French fleet on 13 April to cross the Atlantic and engage the British fleet in North America under Vice-Admiral Howe. D'Estaing was ordered to pursue Howe's forces across North America and deliver an 'outstanding' victory. This was both to provide advantage to the Continental Army but also to bring glory to the French Navy, the subtext being that it would be revenge for French naval defeats during the Seven Years War.[7]

For the French navy – la Royale – this was a new doctrine.[8] In contrast to the British, French naval doctrine was in many ways fundamentally defensive, and was centred on the preservation of naval force. French commanders were instructed not to place their valuable fleets at risk of destruction or serious damage. To this end the French fought cautiously, in defensive formations, and tended not to initiate combat with British fleets. This doctrine was not wholly unreasonable. As a continental power with continental commitments, France traditionally could not afford to commit wholesale to a naval arms race and the loss of many ships of the line that could not easily be replaced.[9]

During the 15 years between the end of the Seven Years War and the French intervention in the war between the Thirteen Colonies and Britain, the French government had enacted a series of naval reforms. The purpose of these reforms was to professionalise the French navy to increase the chance of victory against the Royal Navy and to prevent the crippling effect of one or two decisive defeats.[10] This was supported by legislative changes to engender a culture of aggression in the French fleet. A new law offered 600 livres of what

---

6   Hugh Chisholm, *Encyclopædia Britannica* (Cambridge University Press, 1911) 'Barrington, Samuel', <https://en.wikisource.org/wiki/1911_Encyclop%C3%A6dia_Britannica/Barrington,_Samuel> accessed 23 February 2023.

7   'Amiral Charles-Henri Comte d'Estaing's Summary of the Supplement to His Instructions', M.J. Crawford, D.M. Conrad, E.G. Bowen-Hassell, M.L. Hayes (eds), *Naval Documents of the American Revolution* (Washington DC: Naval History and Heritage Command, 2013), vol.XII, p.518

8   Willis, *The Struggle for Sea Power*, p.231.

9   James Tritten, *Navy and Military Doctrine in France* (Norfolk, Virginia: US Navy, Naval Doctrine Command, 1994), pp.2-10.

10   Willis, *The Struggle for Sea Power*, pp.207-210, 224

the British called gun money (money paid per gun carried by every ship taken, burnt or sunk).[11] The desire was for a decisive naval battle, an engagement later generations would describe as Nelsonian. D'Estaing was being sent to America in this new spirit of aggressive action. His orders went further than simply beating the British in battle. D'Estaing was in effect required to render strategic (potentially war winning) effects through decisive tactical victory and to break British sea power and colonial control in the Americas. However, the change was by diktat. A desire for revenge, sweeping legal change, and financial incentives could not overturn in a moment decades of established naval doctrine.

D'Estaing's voyage to the Americas was far from a feat of seamanship. The journey from Toulon to America took 85 days, a considerable time in which news of d'Estaing's arrival reached the British.[12] The poor sailing and handling qualities of d'Estaing's ships (in terms of both ships and crews) in this crossing in many ways foreshadow their poor performance at St Lucia. It is not in the scope of this chapter to cover the frankly lacklustre campaign mounted by d'Estaing and his squadron against the British fleet commanded by Howe, however a study of that campaign would show several episodes which foreshadow many of the operational difficulties the French would experience at St Lucia. On numerous occasions d'Estaing failed to engage British forces that were inferior to his own. Both in terms of numbers and firepower. D'Estaing was fearful of British reinforcements and neither himself nor his captains wished to place their ships at risk.

Battered by storms and enemy action, d'Estaing withdrew from Rhode Island in August to Boston for repairs. After lying for some months at anchor in Boston (where the French fleet posed a significant challenge to the city's food supply), d'Estaing elected to sail for the West Indies. Hurricane season was now over and d'Estaing saw an opportunity to strike a blow at Britain's lucrative sugar islands. On 4 November the French fleet set sail for the West Indies. Coincidentally this was precisely the same day that Commodore Hotham escorting 5,000 British troops set sail from New York also bound for the Caribbean.[13]

Hotham had been delayed by the hurricane season of 1778, but was bound on an important task. To appropriate a somewhat anachronistic term, the British government wished to open another front against France, shifting the focus of the war from Europe and North America to the Caribbean in an attempt to gain the strategic initiative. St Lucia was selected as the target for strategic and operational reasons, rather than economic gain: these being the island's proximity to Martinique and good anchorages.

St Lucia had been captured during the Seven Years War in 1762, as part of the incredibly successful island-hopping campaign conducted by the British Army and Royal Navy in that year. It was clear then that St Lucia offered significant advantages to the Royal Navy in its attempt to blockade Martinique, France's major Caribbean naval base. The harbour at Fort-Royal (now Fort-de-France) is visible from St Lucia on a clear day – meaning British ships would not have to be exposed to prolonged periods of sea keeping (with all the damage and attrition to naval stores that would entail).[14] The island was handed back to France at the

---

11   Willis, *The Struggle for Sea Power*, p.231.
12   Willis, *The Struggle for Sea Power*, p.233.
13   Willis, *The Struggle for Sea Power*, pp.246-251.
14   G.R. Barnes & J.H. Owen (eds), *The Private Papers of John, Earl of Sandwich, 1771-1782* (Abingdon: Routledge for the Navy Records Society, 2019), Vol.1, p.326.

peace talks exceedingly reluctantly and was identified as the desirable target of a strategic shift by Captain Lord Mulgrave, a member of the Board of Admiralty. Mulgrave accurately assessed that control of St Lucia would result in 'obvious and permanent' advantage for Britain as it would result in, effectively, the blockade of Martinique.[15]

In addition to the advantages presented by the prospect of St Lucia to Britain, there is suffi-cient evidence to believe that the British government was relatively certain that the expedi-tion would succeed. Lord Germain wrote to Major General James Grant in July stating that 'the King's Servants' (that is to say, spies) in the French West Indies had reported not only that the islands were poorly garrisoned but also that the French plantocracy were willing to pledge allegiance to Britain. Germain treated the reports with something close to the scepticism they deserved, but nevertheless it appears that this 'intelligence' formed part of the justification for the plan.[16]

The plan itself was for Commodore Hotham to sail to for Barbados with four ships of the line (though only two would accompany the expedition), three fourth rates of 50-guns and four frigates (again only one seems to have accompanied Hotham to Barbados), escorting 60 transports carrying around 5,000 troops. There he was to rendezvous with the newly-appointed Rear-Admiral Barrington before proceeding to St Lucia. If Barrington was not there, then Hotham was to sail alone. Initially it was planned that Hotham would sail before the hurricane season, but the onset of the season and the reticence of British senior officers in New York prevented the dispatch of the expedition.[17]

Hotham sailed for Barbados in accordance with his orders as d'Estaing set course for Martinique. D'Estaing believed Hotham was headed for Antigua. While historians have lambasted d'Estaing for not pre-empting the destination of Hotham's squadron, Barrington himself understood that d'Estaing's plan was to attack all the British colonies in the Caribbean, starting with Antigua.[18] Additionally, given that Barrington was at Antigua around that time it is entirely reasonable to assume that d'Estaing had very good reasons to believe that Hotham was sailing to reinforce him at the dockyard at English Harbour. It is easy to jump to a conclusion of poor seamanship when the decision may well have been a perfectly understandable intelligence failure.[19] The master of Barrington's flagship, Charles Stuart, who was admittedly not with Hotham but as a master of a flagship in the Royal Navy must nonetheless be considered a reliable authority, stated that the two fleets were separated by no more than 40 or 50 leagues. In fact, it should have been apparent to d'Estaing that he was rather close to the British.[20]

15   Lord Mulgrave's Proposal for an Attack on the W.I. Islands (no date), Barnes & Owen (eds), *The Private Papers of John, Earl of Sandwich*, Vol.1, pp.357-358.
16   Germain to Grant, 29 July 1778, Barnes & Owen (eds), *The Private Papers of John, Earl of Sandwich, 1771-1782*, Vol.2, p.339.
17   Palliser to Sandwich, 9 November 1778, Barnes & Owen (eds), *The Private Papers of John, Earl of Sandwich*, Vol.2, p.342; Gambier to Sandwich 22 September 1778, *ibid.*, p.313.
18   G.A. Ballard (ed), 'Some Letters of Admiral the Hon Samuel Barrington; Enclosure I of Ramsay's of 18 February 1779, Rev. James Ramsay to the Bishop of Llandaff', *Mariner's Mirror* 19:4 (1933), p.386.
19   Willis, *The Struggle for Sea Power*, p.256.
20   Stuart to ?, 8 January 1779, Barnes & Owen (eds), *The Private Papers of John, Earl of Sandwich*, Vol.2, p.355.

Had d'Estaing intercepted Hotham's force at sea then it is probable that the latter would have been destroyed or captured in large part or whole. While d'Estaing had failed and would fail again to destroy smaller British forces, Hotham's ships were undermanned, outgunned and outnumbered. It would have ended the British attempt to seize St Lucia, cost Britain of some of the Army's best troops and left the entire British West Indies incredibly vulnerable in the short term.

The distance of 40-50 leagues (104-130 nautical miles) may not seem particularly close, it was a distance that even at the relatively slow speed of three knots could be covered in under two days. Naval operations in the age of sail often saw vast distances being covered in relatively short periods of time.[21] While d'Estaing would have to maintain that speed in addition to the speed of the Hotham's convoy in order to overhaul them, and adopt the correct course to intercept the British, a concerted effort would certainly have made it possible. Hotham's main concern would have been to keep his convoy together, rather than sailing as fast as possible. Locating the British squadron over such a large area would have been difficult, but not impossible. D'Estaing could have deployed his frigates as a reconnaissance screen. A masthead lookout would have been able to see the topsails of another vessel around 20 nautical miles away, at the very least enabling the squadron to set course after the British.[22] While poor weather and contrary winds may have prevented d'Estaing from catching Hotham, a concerted effort would have at least enabled him to discern Hotham's destination and perhaps would have enabled him to sweep up straggling transports. It would certainly by no means be an easy feat of seamanship or command but attempting to force an action was within d'Estaing's power.

To illustrate this proximity, in the last week of November, a transport ship carrying horses was blown off course during a storm and failed to keep up with Hotham's orders. It was captured by d'Estaing the next day, but once again poor seamanship meant d'Estaing's storm-battered ships were in no real condition to do anything but limp for safety.[23] Allegedly a dog from a British ship that had jumped overboard was rescued by d'Estaing's flagship. The dog was later spotted by a British officer during ceasefire negotiations. While this tale may be a classic Victorian embellishment, it is nevertheless a good illustration of what a colossal missed opportunity this was for d'Estaing.[24]

Hotham sent the frigate *Venus* ahead to Barbados. She arrived on 23 November, reporting that Hotham's ships were low on both men and supplies. Hotham arrived on 10 December with the remaining 59 transports, with some colourful names such as *Roman Emperor* and *Charming Nelly*. Escorting them were two third rates, three fourth rates and the bomb vessel *Carcass*.[25] There they rendezvoused with Rear-Admiral Barrington. Barrington had set sail for the West Indies in the May of 1778 on board the *Prince of Wales* (74). He arrived at

---

21   Sam Willis, *Fighting at Sea in the Eighteenth Century: The Art of Sailing Warfare* (Woodbridge: Boydell Press, 2008), pp.37-38.
22   Calculated based on the visible horizon from a masthead of a frigate to the topgallant yard of similarly sized vessel.
23   Major General Grant to the Secretary of State, 31 December 1778, D. Bonner-Smith (ed.), *The Barrington Papers: Selected from the Letters and Papers of Admiral The Hon. Samuel Barrington* (Abingdon: Routledge for the Navy Records Society, 2019), Vol.2, p.167.
24   Ekins, *The Naval Battles of Great Britain*, p.89
25   Barnes & Owen (eds), *The Private Papers of John, Earl of Sandwich*, Vol.2, p.335.

Barbados a month later and was joined in a few weeks by the *Boyne* (70). He failed to prevent the fall of Dominica in September and left with the two ships of the line and the frigate *Aurora* to spend the hurricane season at English Harbour on Antigua. Barrington and his squadron stayed for a month and returned to Barbados on 18 November, having spent some time blockading Martinique. Their return was only days ahead of the *Venus.*[26]

Descent on St Lucia

When Hotham arrived, Barrington wasted little time. He had received intelligence that a French fleet was close at hand, and in order to (in his own words) 'save time and prevent confusion', Barrington gave Hotham responsibility for the convoy, and told him to continue to utilise the existing signal book. This demonstrates a keen understanding of the nuances and procedures that governed fleets under sail and the resulting confusion that could result in the alteration of non-standard signals.[27]

Barrington was ready to sail on 11 December but Grant asked for a days delay to allow some of his officers to re-board their ships. The British weighed anchor on the 12th, arriving at St Lucia on the 13th. Barrington dispatched some of his unrated vessels and the frigate *Ariadne*, to clamp a hold on Gros Islet (now Rodney Bay), Castries and the north of the Island.[28]

Due to its excellent properties as an anchorage and light defences, the British chose Grand Cul de Sac Bay as the disembarkation point. Barrington and Hotham began disembarking the troops and despite only reaching the bay at 3:00 p.m. they managed to land 3,000 troops by sunset.[29] The redcoats met little resistance, and the landings continued on the 14th. However, d'Estaing had not been idle. The French had sailed from Martinique, and to say they were confident would be something of an understatement. According to Barrington the French on Martinique spoke of the British as if they were rats or mice caught in a trap.[30] One of the officers of d'Estaing's fleet (in a letter scathing of the admiral) wrote that 'the capture of the squadron, the transports and army was certain'.[31] This prognostication was to prove woefully poor.

At 5:00 p.m. *Ariadne*, acting as a scout, signalled that d'Estaing's fleet had been sighted and at 6:00 p.m. Captain Thomas Pringle went aboard the flagship, reporting that around a dozen sail of the line were standing in for St Lucia, bound from Martinique. *Ariadne* was a small sixth rate, at 20 guns the smallest ship that could be commanded by a post captain, but she would find herself defending a critical point in the line within 24 hours. The British fleet was facing heavy odds at Grand Cul de Sac Bay.[32]

26 Barnes & Owen (eds), *The Private Papers of John, Earl of Sandwich*, Vol.2, pp.333-335.
27 Journal, 11 December 1778, Bonner-Smith (ed.), *The Barrington Papers*, Vol.2, p.115.
28 Journal, 13 December 1778, Bonner-Smith (ed.), *The Barrington Papers*, Vol.2, p.116.
29 Journal, 13 December 1778, Bonner-Smith (ed.), *The Barrington Papers*, Vol.2, p.116.
30 Ballard (ed), 'Some Letters of Admiral the Hon Samuel Barrington', p.386.
31 Ballard (ed), 'Some Letters of Admiral the Hon Samuel Barrington', p.389.
32 Journal, 14 December 1778, Bonner-Smith (ed.), *The Barrington Papers*, Vol.2, pp.117-119.

The Geography

Grand Cul de Sac Bay was a wide deep-water anchorage at the mouth of a river valley and flanked on both sides by forested hills. The prevailing winds at St Lucia tend to blow across the island from the East. Due to the high mountains, cut with deep valleys that can block or channel the wind (seemingly at random to those unaccustomed to the coast), sailing to the lee of the island can be challenging. In the context of warfare under sail this poses a significant issue in handling a single ship, let alone a squadron or fleet in complex manoeuvres with unpredictable wind: especially while in contact with the enemy.[33] One can see the remarkable difficulty by sailing the area directly, as the author has. While a small catamaran might lack yards, spars, miles of rope, and (in the case of this author) a well-trained crew, the changeable winds and the impact of the topography of the island can be severe and rather jarring.[34]

On 15 December 1778 this wind was blowing directly from the north, over the hills and mountains that ringed the entrance to the bay. In the lee of the island's mountains, any attempt to attack the British position would be difficult.[35] Marshalling a squadron in changeable winds for such an attack, even more so. Therefore, the wind and terrain would play a decisive role in the Battle of St Lucia. Other than a passing reference by Mahan, historians have not given this critical factor the attention it deserves.[36]

Preparations

The two fleets that opposed each other in the waters around St Lucia in December 1778 were greatly mismatched. D'Estaing commanded 12 ships of the line and 12 frigates (given by Barington as 'several' and the *Prince of Wales*' master Charles Stuart as 12), not to mention a host of unrated vessels with American privateers in attendance. The British fleet was significantly weaker. Not only numerically, but also in terms of the weight of metal in the fleet's broadsides. Barrington commanded seven ships of the line but only one, his flagship, mounted 74 guns. Three were fourth rates and were armed with only 50 guns, a lighter armament than d'Estaing's smallest ship of the line. Barrington's fleet was reinforced by three frigates and four unrated vessels.

---

33 'Saint Lucia – Climate', *GlobalSecurity.org* <https://www.globalsecurity.org/military/world/caribbean/st-climate.htm>, accessed 26 February 2023.
34 This perhaps explains this author's sympathy with d'Estaing. Being dismasted a few hundred yards from jagged volcanic rock is an experience that one does not rush to repeat.
35 Journal, 15 December 1778, Bonner-Smith (ed.), *The Barrington Papers*, Vol.2, p.124.
36 Mahan, *Influence of Sea Power Upon History, 1660-1783*, p.366.

Table 1: French Ships of the Line at St Lucia

Ship	Captains and Flag Officers	Guns
Languedoc	Henri-Louis de Boulainvilliers de Croy (*Capitaine de vaisseau*), Jean Baptiste Charles Henri Hector Comte d'Estaing (*Vice-amiral*)	80
Tonnant	Paul-Jacques de Bruyères-Chalabre (*Capitaine de vaisseau*), Pierre-Claude Haudeneau de Breugnon (*Chef d'escadre*)	80
César	Jean-Baptiste de Moriès de Castellet (*Capitaine de vaisseau*), Jean-Joseph de Rafélis de Broves (*Chef d'escadre*)	74
Guerrier	Louis-Antoine Comte de Bougainville (*Capitaine de vaisseau*)	74
Hector	Pierre de Moriès-Castellet (*Capitaine de vaisseau*)	74
Marseillais	Louis-Armand de La Poype de Vertrieux (*Capitaine de vaisseau*)	74
Protecteur	Étienne-Joseph de Saint-Germain d'Apchon (*Capitaine de vaisseau*)	74
Zélé	Jacques-Melchior Saint-Laurent, Comte de Barras (*Capitaine de vaisseau*)	74
Fantasque	Pierre Andre de Suffren (*Capitaine de vaisseau*)	64
Provence	Victor-Louis Desmichels de Champorcin (*Capitaine de vaisseau*)	64
Vaillant	Joseph-Bernard de Chabert-Cogolin (*Capitaine de vaisseau*)	64
Sagittaire	François Hector d'Albert de Rions (*Capitaine de vaisseau*)	54

Source: Onésime-Joachim Troude, *Batailles navales de la France* (Paris: Challamel Aîné, 1867), p.19. It has not been possible to compile a complete list of French frigates. Those frigates identified were *Chimère* (32), *Engageante* (26), *Alcmène* (26), *Aimable* (26) and *Iphengie* (32).

Table 2: The British Fleet at St Lucia

Ship	Captains and Flag Officers	Guns
Prince of Wales	Benjamin Hill (Captain) Samuel Barrington (Rear-Admiral)	74
Boyne	Herbert Sawyer (Captain)	70
Nonsuch	Walter Griffith (Captain)	64
St Albans	Richard Onslow (Captain)	64
Centurion	Richard Braithwaite (Captain)	50
Isis	John Raynor (Captain)	50
Preston	Samuel Uppleby (Captain) William Hotham (Commodore)	50
Venus	James Ferguson (Captain)	36
Aurora	James Cumming (Captain)	28
Ariadne	Thomas Pringle (Captain)	20
Ceres	James Richard Dacres (Commander)	18
Barbadoes	Sir George Home of Blackadder, 7th Baronet (Lieutenant)	12
Snake	Billy Douglas (Commander)	12
Pelican	John Hardy (Lieutenant)	unrated

Source: Bonner-Smith (ed.), *The Barrington Papers*, Vol 2, pp.30, 58.

Following the report of Captain Pringle, Barrington reacted to the news with his characteristic sang-froid. The British were anchored in the outer reaches of Grand Cul de Sac Bay, with the 59 transports having disembarked almost all British troops.[37] The Admiral decided to warp the transports behind the line of warships that would be anchored across the mouth of the bay.[38] For the seamen of Barrington's fleet it would have been back-breaking work. Working on the tween decks of a cramped ship by lantern light, in temperatures well in excess of 25 degrees Celsius, reeking of sweat and tar. It would have taken hours for the men to manoeuvre heavily laden merchantmen into position.

However, Barrington did not have enough ships to completely close off the bay's entrance. Barrington placed *Isis* (50) along with his three frigates at the northern end of his line. The frigates were usually considered far too small to stand in the line of battle but were given the key task of preventing French warships from forcing their way through the northern passage into the bay, but the lee of the island and coastline made that difficult. *Ariadne* of 20 guns would soon find herself exchanging fire with ships of the line carrying four times as many guns of far greater weight of shot.

Barrington positioned his strongest warships at the southern end of his line. He assessed that given the short length of the line, the vessels at the leeward end of the line were in the most vulnerable position. However, it have been hard to rake those vessels, or to tack between or around the rear of the line, due to the confines of the bay and northerly wind. It was a brilliant defensive trick and essentially meant that the French lacked a realistic way to outflank the British. Barrington's deployment was the result of experience gained from a lifetime at sea. While his ships were vulnerable, they were as safe as they could be under the circumstances. The British were outnumbered at St Lucia, in qualitative terms the advantage squarely lay with the Royal Navy. D'Estaing may not have been the hapless amateur that he has been portrayed as, but he lacked Barrington's decades of experience. This enabled the Royal Navy to turn small tactical decisions into a battle winning formula. At Grand Cul de Sac Bay the defenders (the British) possessed these advantages while the attackers (the French) did not. Two decades later at Aboukir Bay, these advantages were possessed by the attacker. A crucial difference.

Still, Barrington's preparations were ultimately a last-ditch attempt to save his fleet from destruction, seemingly with little to no hope. As his men laboured to reposition nearly four score ships within the bay, Barrington was met after nightfall by Lieutenant Richard Hawford, an hour and a half after having received the news of d'Estaing's arrival by Captain Pringle. Hawford was the Second Lieutenant of the *Boreas*, a frigate that had accompanied Barrington in the West Indies earlier in the year. Barrington had ordered the vessel to Antigua when he had set sail with Hotham's convoy to St Lucia. However, the frigate had sprung her topmast and had been forced to return to Barbados. There she had been joined by the *Pearl*, a sloop bearing a letter from Vice-Admiral Byron in North America. The letter carried the news that d'Estaing had left the coast of North America and was thought to be heading for the West Indies. The letter also declared Byron's intent to follow d'Estaing to the Caribbean as soon as he could be sure that the French had indeed left North America.

37   Journal, 14 December 1778, Bonner-Smith (ed.), *The Barrington Papers*, Vol.2, pp.117-118.
38   Stuart to ?, 8 January 1779, Barnes & Owen (eds), *The Private Papers of John, Earl of Sandwich*, Vol.2, p.345.

Captain Linzee had sailed from Rhode Island on 17 November, only two days ahead of Byron's planned date of departure.[39]

The *Pearl* had suffered during the passage from Rhode Island to Barbados, both her topmast and bowsprit being badly damaged, and Captain Thompson of the *Boreas* undertook the duty of delivering the news to St Lucia. However, Thompson found that he could not safely pass the French fleet under d'Estaing lying in the St Lucia channel. What followed was an episode of considerable daring do, as Thompson strove to ensure the dispatches reached Barrington, dashing under the cover of night to place the dispatches into Barrington's hands.[40] While it is unclear exactly where on the coast d'Estaing's squadron was that night, the most likely place given the events of the following day is somewhere around the north of the island, around what is now Rodney Bay. To reach Barrington's position in Grand Cul de Sac Bay from the most southerly point of Rodney Bay is a journey in excess of eight and half nautical miles. The British position was no longer as hopeless as it had seemed earlier in the day. If Barrington and his men could hold out against D'Estaing's overwhelming numerical advantage, they would be relieved.

Day of Reckoning

As the day dawned on 15 December the confidence felt by French sailors was not without cause. Not only were the British outnumbered in terms of number of ships and weight of broadsides, but Hotham's ships had been stripped of men before leaving New York.

The crews of Barrington's ships had worked through the night and made great progress but at dawn they had not finished their preparations. It made complete sense for D'Estaing not to offer battle at night. At the Nile in 1798, Nelson did offer battle after dark, at considerable peril to his fleet; however, the sandy bottom and flat environs of Aboukir Bay made it a less dangerous prospect than a pell-mell action in the dark amongst transports and warships, with jagged black rocks on both windward and leeward shores.

What is more surprising however is d'Estaing's decision not to immediately launch an attack on the British position after sunrise. Instead, the fleet headed for the Carenage (Castries Harbour) to land d'Estaing's troops. However, after a brief exchange of fire between d'Estaing's flagship *Languedoc* and British shore batteries, the French withdrew. While the abortive attempt to land at Castries, rather than pouncing on Barrington's disorganised squadron, has been another source of criticism of d'Estaing's command during the St Lucia campaign, it was not an entirely unreasonable course of action. D'Estaing apparently believed that the town and its fortifications had not fallen to the British. However, both Castries and the formidable fortifications on the Morne Fortune had been taken without a fight on the 14th – not long at all before D'Estaing attempted to enter the harbour. D'Estaing presumably sought to reinforce the garrison and militia with the troops accompanying his

---

39   Journal, 14 December 1778, Bonner-Smith (ed.), *The Barrington Papers*, Vol.2, pp.119; Captain Linzee to Barrington, 13 December 1778, Bonner-Smith (ed.), *The Barrington Papers*, Vol.2, pp.120-121; Captain Thompson to Barrington, 14 December 1778, Bonner-Smith (ed.), *The Barrington Papers*, Vol.2, p.121.
40   Journal, 14 December 1778, Bonner-Smith (ed.), *The Barrington Papers*, Vol.2, p.119.

fleet and prevent the very thing that had happened the previous day without his knowledge; an understandable but not optimal decision.[41]

D'Estaing's subsequent actions demonstrate that while he may not have been a landlubber, he was not a sailor with Barrington's lifelong experience. Not aided by poorly trained crews or damage suffered during the crossing from North America, the admiral struggled to form his squadron in the strong coastal currents and highly changeable breezes created by the mountains and valleys of the island. Major General Grant described the French as being 'much disconcerted and at a loss how to act'.[42]

By the time the French were able to form into a line of battle it was around 11:30 a.m. and Barrington's squadron had largely completed its defensive preparations, the men having worked for over 16 hours to warp the warships and transports into position. Despite the remarkable physical labour of the British tars, some of the transports were not able to withdraw behind the protective screen of warships. Barrington dispatched his unrated vessels *Pelican*, *Snake*, *Ceres* and *Barbadoes* to cover those transports which had fallen behind.[43]

D'Estaing's plan was consummately Nelsonian. The French had been ordered to heave to or anchor at point blank range from the British ships. The idea was to batter the outnumbered British into submission with sheer weight of fire power. Any French ship that could not anchor was ordered to break into the bay and cause mayhem and destruction amongst the unprotected transports.[44] If it was practical the French captains were authorised to lay alongside the British and carry their ships in a boarding action.[45] D'Estaing's instructions were bold and entirely in accordance with his orders to annihilate a British force in American waters. They also placed his fleet at risk of considerable damage, something that differed from the traditional (and understandable) French practice of trying to preserve the physical manifestation of their naval power.

The French however were only able to form 10 ships into a line of battle for the initial descent on the British, scarcely outnumbering Barrington. A rather famous painting by Dominic Serres captures the moment the fleets clashed, exchanging broadsides at close range with remarkable vividness. While Serres' work has undoubted artistic qualities, it draws a veil over the reality of the French attack on the British line.

Whether it was because d'Estaing could not form a larger number of ships into line or because the unreliable winds in the lee of the mountains of St Lucia and the poor training of his sailors made manoeuvring into close battle with the British impossible (this seems the most plausible reason, given the trouble d'Estaing had in forming his squadron in the first place), d'Estaing abandoned his Nelsonian plan. Instead, the 10 French men of war bore down on the British, with d'Estaing's flagship the *Languedoc* in the lead, and made to pass along the entire line, opening fire at the woefully ineffective range of a mile. Hardly the close battle depicted by Serres.[46]

---

41   Major General Grant to the Secretary of State, 31 December 1778, Bonner-Smith (ed.), *The Barrington Papers*, Vol.2, p.167.

42   Major General Grant to the Secretary of State, 31 December 1778, Bonner-Smith (ed.), *The Barrington Papers*, Vol.2, p.167.

43   Journal, 15 December 1778, Bonner-Smith (ed.), *The Barrington Papers*, Vol.2, p.125.

44   Willis, *The Struggle for Sea Power*, p.260; Troude, *Batailles navales de la France*, pp.19-20.

45   Troude, *Batailles navales de la France*, p.19.

46   Journal, 15 December 1778, Bonner-Smith (ed.), *The Barrington Papers*, Vol.2, p.124.

Charles Stuart, given far more to purple prose than Barrington, described the fire as 'Very Hot' but Barrington simply stated that the two fleets exchanged fire.[47] According to accounts passed from the Navy to the Army after this first engagement, the British suffered not a single casualty.[48] It took the French fleet an hour to pass along the British line. During this time the three frigates would have been hotly engaged with French sail of the line such as *Languedoc* of 80 guns and *César* of 74 guns. The smaller vessels were spared from harm by the extreme range.

Some of these ships had met in combat before. On 12 August off Rhode Island, *Isis* (50) had engaged *Guerrier* (74) for two hours at pistol shot range. *Guerrier*'s superior weight of broadside told, and fire from *Isis* slackened. However, a well-aimed or lucky shot shattered the helm of the French vessel. Unable to steer effectively, *Isis* was able to escape *Guerrier*. Not only had their helm been shot away and their quarry escaped, but *Guerrier*'s captain at the time, Raymondis, lost his right arm in the fighting.[49]

After completing their ferocious but ineffective cannonade, each French ships turned in succession and tacked north after they had passed Barrington's *Prince of Wales*. Neither Stuart or Barrington detail British losses from the first French attack, and by all accounts the British appear to have weathered the initial French storm well. It took the French time to beat against the northerly wind, to reform and were joined by two further ships of the line. Captain Francis Downman of the Royal Artillery rather dryly remarked in his diary that the delay was caused by the need of the French officers to have lunch and indeed drink rather more wine than was usual, to prepare them for a second attack.[50] It took the French fleet agonising hours to re-form for its second, and presumably final, hammer blow.

The high expectations the French had for their quick and decisive strike had been dashed, and if their confidence was dented the British were reportedly veritable grey hounds in the slips. According to Charles Stuart the British sailors wanted to pursue d'Estaing as he retreated upwind and when the second French attack came 'nothing was heard but our dear country, England forever, and a general resolve to sell our little fleet as dear as possible'.[51] Jack Tar was clearly ready for the fight, even if he did not expect victory. There is a tendency amongst more modern historians to dismiss this sort of thing as hyperbole, which Stuart's account admittedly strays into at times. However, given the industry with which Barrington's sailors conveyed the army ashore and supported it there and the tenacity they displayed in engaging the French it is fair to say that the British espirt de corps was excellent and proved a foundation for Barrington's victory alongside skill.

D'Estaing commenced his second assault around 4:00 p.m. having again struggled to re-form his line and martial it into a position to attack the snug British position at closer

---

47   Stuart to ?, 8 January 1779, Barnes & Owen (eds), *The Private Papers of John, Earl of Sandwich*, Vol.2, p.347 & Journal, 15 December 1778, Bonner-Smith (ed.), *The Barrington Papers*, Vol.2, p.125.

48   Lieutenant Colonel Francis Downman & Colonel F.A. Whinyates (eds), *The Services of Lieut.-Colonel Francis Downman, R.A. In France, North America, and the West Indies, Between the Years 1758 and 1784* (Woolwich: Royal Artillery Institute, 1898), p.95.

49   Troude, *Batailles navales de la France*, p.15.

50   Downman & Whinyates (eds), *The Services of Lieut.-Colonel Francis Downman*, p.96.

51   Stuart to ?, 8 January 1779, Barnes & Owen (eds), *The Private Papers of John, Earl of Sandwich*, Vol.2, p.347.

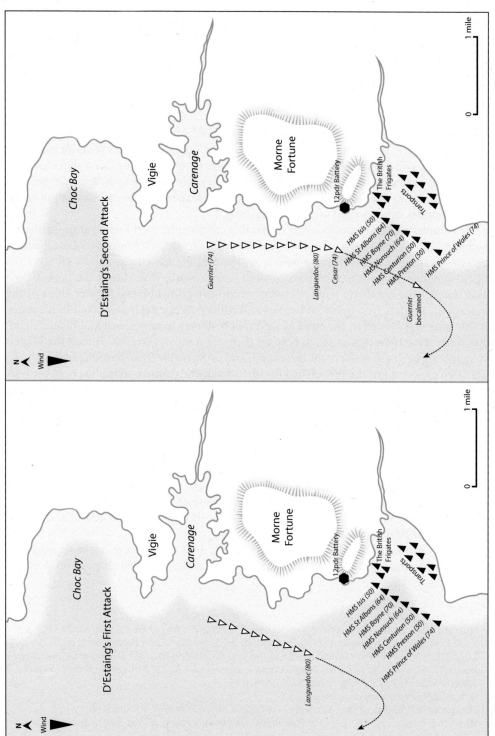

Plans of the Engagements between the British and French Squadrons on 15 December 1778. Left: The First French Attack. Right: The Second French Attack. (George Anderson © Helion and Company 2023)

range.[52] The British, not unreasonably, assumed that d'Estaing's initial assault was a reconnaissance in force, designed to assess the strength of the British squadron before launching a decisive thrust. As 12 sail of the line bore down on the British, while undoubtedly apprehensive Jack Tar appeared resolute. Assuming the French would commit to a single pitched battle, the British were determined to make sure that it was as costly an affair as possible and to sell their lives and ships dearly.[53]

However, the second French attack, in much the same way as the first, failed to live up to the hopes of French commanders. The French sailed in to engage the British line, this time closer at three-quarters of a mile, but not the pistol shot range envisaged in d'Estaing's plan for the battle. According to a letter written by a French officer present at the battle, as the French squadron stood in to attack the British line a particularly thick rain squall dissuaded d'Estaing from forcing a decision. Instead, the admiral altered his signals and the attack proceeded in the same fashion as the first.[54] This second failure to engage in a yardarm to yardarm smashing match lends credence to the theory that it was the inability of French crews to handle their ships sufficiently well in difficult winds, rather than a want of numbers or courage, that prevented the French seeking a decisive stroke. Once again, the French passed along the British line of battle, with d'Estaing's ship this time third in the line of battle: the ship that led the attack was probably the *César* (74) flying the flag of *Chef d'escadre* Jean-Joseph de Rafélis de Broves.[55]

While the range of this second French attack was shorter, it was still a comparatively long ranged gunnery duel. Nevertheless, as the French once again passed down the line of British warships, the exchange of fire was much more fierce and certainly worthy of the descriptor 'hot' in the language of the day. This time the fire from both sides caused damage and casualties, but the British considered the gunnery of the French to be quite poor. Sailors reported that the French had fired high, shooting away the rigging on British vessels, but relatively few shots struck home against the hulls of the ships to cause battle winning damage and casualties.[56] The *Boyne* suffered only two strikes against her hull, and the only casualties aboard her were two men wounded by the explosion of their own powder.[57] Even the little *Ariadne*, exchanging broadsides with two-decked ships of the line, suffered only one man wounded. The flagship *Prince of Wales*, in theory Barrington's most vulnerable ship, had only two fatal casualties and seven wounded men.[58]

---

52   Stuart to ?, 8 January 1779, Barnes & Owen (eds), *The Private Papers of John, Earl of Sandwich*, Vo.2, p.347 & Journal, 15 December 1778, Bonner-Smith (ed.), *The Barrington Papers*, Vol.2, p.125.

53   Stuart to ?, 8 January 1779, Barnes & Owen (eds), *The Private Papers of John, Earl of Sandwich*, Vol.2, p.347.

54   Ballard (ed), 'Some Letters of Admiral the Hon Samuel Barrington', p.389.

55   Journal, 15 December 1778, Bonner-Smith (ed.), *The Barrington Papers*, Vol.2, p.125, Troude, *Batailles navales de la France*, p.19.

56   Stuart to ?, 8 January 1779, Barnes & Owen (eds), *The Private Papers of John, Earl of Sandwich*, Vol.2, p.347.

57   Stuart to ?, 8 January 1779, Barnes & Owen (eds), *The Private Papers of John, Earl of Sandwich*, Vol.2, p.347.

58   Stuart to ?, 8 January 1779, Barnes & Owen (eds), *The Private Papers of John, Earl of Sandwich*, Vol.2, p.347; Journal, 15 December 1778, Bonner-Smith (ed.), *The Barrington Papers*, Vol.2, p.125.

This did not mean the French fire was not intense. The Royal Navy were, after all, deployed in a screen covering the vital transports. While the aim of d'Estaing's ships may have been too high to smash through the hulls of the British men of war, the shot fell with deadly effect amongst the British transports. The transport ship *Lord Howe* had all her cables and anchors shot away. She was carrying vital artillery supplies for Grant's army.[59] While Barrington reported that only two men were killed and one wounded aboard the transports, the more dramatic account of Charles Stuart paints a far darker picture. According to his account, 18 men and two women were killed onboard the transports.[60] While Stuart's account is far more hyperbolic in places than Barrington's professional naval diary, the letter was written some weeks later, so it is plausible that his recollection of that part of the story had the benefit of some hindsight.

British sailors later found shot from French guns a quarter of a mile inland.[61] The inference in contemporary British accounts is that the French gunnery was poorly aimed and thus largely whistled over the decks of the warships, only causing relatively light casualties amongst the transports. It is understandable that the British, who favoured close range fire aimed directly into the hulls of the enemy vessels to cripple them, would view French gunnery in this way. But French gunnery was as much a natural development of French doctrine as British gunnery was of the doctrine of the Royal Navy. The French focus on the preservation of naval force (to maintain sea lines of communication, defend commerce and convey armies) had led to the development of a gunnery practice very different to the British. The tendency to fight at range, to prevent a fleet-crippling smashing match, led to different practical demonstrations of gunnery.[62] French gunners would aim their broadsides high, into the rigging of British ships, disabling them. Just over six months after the battle at St Lucia, d'Estaing's fleet inflicted a stinging defeat on the Royal Navy off Grenada, by firing high into the masts and rigging of the British ships, preventing them from engaging the French closely. Nine British ships were left essentially crippled due to damage to their masts and rigging.[63] It would seem that no-matter the heady sums of gold offered to the French sailors for the capture and destruction of British ships, years if not decades of doctrine could not be overcome by a royal decree and a desire to engage the enemy more closely.

It was the French themselves who would suffer the most grievous damage in the engagement. D'Estaing's vessels appeared to be ravaged by British gunnery in the second attack. At St Lucia it was British gunnery that struck the rigging of the French ships to devastating effect. The sternmost ship in d'Estaing's line of battle, *Guerrier*, was under 'perpetual fire' having become becalmed in front of the British line. The unlucky French vessel suffered a further pounding when the yard supporting her main topsail was shot away.[64] So badly damaged was her rigging that, after passing the British line, she was unable to make sail for

59   Journal, 15 December 1778, Bonner-Smith (ed.), *The Barrington Papers*, Vol.2, p.125.
60   Stuart to ?, 8 January 1779, Barnes & Owen (eds), *The Private Papers of John, Earl of Sandwich*, Vol.2, p.347.
61   Stuart to ?, 8 January 1779, Barnes & Owen (eds), *The Private Papers of John, Earl of Sandwich*, Vol.2, p.347.
62   Willis, *Fighting at Sea in the Eighteenth Century,* pp.129-141.
63   Willis, *The Struggle for Sea Power*, pp.308-309.
64   Stuart to ?, 8 January 1779, Barnes & Owen (eds), *The Private Papers of John, Earl of Sandwich*, Vol.2, p.348; Calmon-Maison, *L'Amiral d'Estaing 1729-1794*, p.232.

two hours. Other French vessels had suffered such bad damage aloft that they were forced to strike yards from their masts and replace them. As a result of this, the British believed they had inflicted significant damage on the French vessels, which appears confirmed by the claim of Stuart that each French ship suffered on average 12 fatal casualties and many more wounded.[65]

The Little Ships

As the battle raged between the lines of battle and Barrington's squadron fought for its life against seemingly overwhelming odds, a simultaneous engagement carried on throughout the day – one that has received strangely little attention in retellings of the battle. While Barrington's preparations had largely been carried out by the time d'Estaing struck, not all of the transports had been able to retreat behind the screen of warships. Some transports that were anchored further from the shoreline in deeper water had fallen to leeward of the squadron and been unable to warp themselves into position in time.

As previously mentioned, Barrington dispatched his sloops to defend these ships as d'Estaing's sail of the line fell on the main body of the British force. The *Pelican, Ceres, Snake* and *Barbadoes* were tasked with the duty at not inconsiderable risk. D'Estaing's powerful force of ships of the line was accompanied by 12 frigates and a 'great number of sloops and schooners'.[66] Barrington noted that throughout the duration of the French assault on his line, several of the frigates and some vessels belonging to American privateers 'paraded' themselves at a distance from the fighting, but only one made any motion to engage the lightly defended transports. This ship was described by Barrington as a cutter, commanded by 'the pirate Cunningham'.[67] The small vessel engaged the *Pelican*, with both ships opening fire on each other.

This cutter was the *Revenge*, captained by Gustavus Conyngham, an Irish born officer in the Continental Navy. Conyngham had started the war as a smuggler of arms and was actually arrested by the French in 1777 for attacking British vessels in the English Channel. Freed, he began a campaign of raiding in the mid-Atlantic and 'infested the coast of Portugal'.[68] Conyngham had been ordered by the agent of the Continental Congress in Martinique to inform the French of the presence of Barrington's squadron and crucially to attack any of Commodore Hotham's vessels that had been blown off course. The orders were dated 29 November, before Hotham arrived in Barbados, which suggests that the French and Americans on Martinique had intelligence that Hotham's force was bound for the Windward Islands.[69] Conyngham was a very successful privateer captain, his actions alleg-

---

65   Journal, 15 December 1778, Bonner-Smith (ed.), *The Barrington Papers*, Vol.2, p.125.
66   Stuart to ?, 8 January 1779, Barnes & Owen (eds), *The Private Papers of John, Earl of Sandwich*, Vol.2, p.346; Journal, 15 December 1778, Bonner-Smith (ed.), *The Barrington Papers*, Vol.2, p.124.
67   Journal, 15 December 1778, Bonner-Smith (ed.), *The Barrington Papers*, Vol.2, p.125.
68   Journal, 15 December 1778, Bonner-Smith (ed.), *The Barrington Papers*, Vol.2, p.124; Robert Neeser (ed.), *Letters and Papers Relating to the Cruises of Gustavus Conyngham – A Captain of the Continental Navy 1777-1779* (Grizzell Press, 2012), ebook, unpaginated.
69   William Bingham to Gustavus Conyngham, Neeser (ed.), *Letters and Papers*, ebook, unpaginated.

edly drove up shipping insurance in the English Channel by 28 percent, but this swashbuckling raider was unable to find success at St Lucia on 15 December.[70]

The Valuable Army

As the battle lines clashed and privateers stalked vulnerable stragglers in search of a prize, the British troops on St Lucia were not idle spectators to the fighting. While later maps and French accounts imply that the British had batteries on both the north and south promontories of the bay, it is clear from British accounts that the Royal Artillery and Royal Navy did not have time to erect batteries at the entrance to Grand Cul de Sac Bay before the arrival of the French fleet.[71]

Despite this, the Royal Artillery had been able to re-commission a battery of four 12-pounder cannon, that guarded the northern end of the bay, and had fired on the British when they first anchored on the 13th. The French had spiked these guns, but Lieutenant Garstin and his men were able to bring them back into service. These guns supported the three British frigates and the fourth rate *Isis* in guarding the northern entrance to the bay from d'Estaing's attack. Garstin's service was considered so valuable that Barrington thanked him publicly after the battle.[72]

The Aftermath

When d'Estaing's ships beat their way northward for a second time on the evening of 15 December, the Royal Navy did not realise it but they had won a victory against seemingly insurmountable odds. Fighting on St Lucia and in the waters around the island would continue for the better part of two weeks, but 15 December was the only day on which d'Estaing pitted his fleet against Barrington's in as close to open battle as the British would allow. Barrington had led his small force, in a strange and forgotten but rather remarkable action.

While none of the seamen and officers in either fleet knew it, when d'Estaing hauled his wind and retreated and the *Guerrier* had endured her mauling at the hands of the *Prince of Wales*, the grand fleet action between the ships of the line was finished. However naval combat in the waters around St Lucia carried on as the tense standoff continued.

On 16 December little occurred: d'Estaing appeared to be making sail for the British line but withdrew, electing to anchor off Gros Islet with his transports. Barrington had feared that the French, venturing to the south, would try and take possession of the southern end of the bay in order to force the British out to sea. However, the characteristically fantastic relationship between Barrington and Grant (the evident mutual respect and friendship

---

70   Robert Neeser (ed.), *Letters and Papers*, ebook, unpaginated.
71   Journal, 17 December 1778, Bonner-Smith (ed.), *The Barrington Papers*, Vol.2, p.127; Stuart to ?, 8 January 1779, Barnes & Owen (eds), *The Private Papers of John, Earl of Sandwich*, Vol.2, p.349.
72   Downman & Whinyates (eds), *The Services of Lieut.-Colonel Francis Downman*, p.95.

clear from their letters), saw a detachment of troops secure the position from any potential French assault.[73]

The following day saw a resumption of the fighting at sea. Barrington was attempting to strengthen his defensive position, warping deeper into the bay, so that his limited number of ships could hold a line that could not be outflanked. As the transports were withdrawing deeper into the bay, those which had spent the battle being protected by Barrington's unrated vessels were attacked by the *Iphengie* (32), the *Sagittaire* (54) and one other frigate around 10:00 a.m. *Ceres* (18), commanded by Commander James Dacres. baited the *Iphengie* and *Sagittaire* into chasing her, away from the transports. *Snake*, *Barbadoes* and *Pelican* were able to shepherd the majority of the transports into the shelter of the British lines. One transport however was not so lucky. The remaining pursuing frigate was able capture the *Admiral Shuldham*. Barrington was unconcerned with the capture of the transport as it contained no stores of military value. However, somewhat distressingly, the ship was noted as containing not only the baggage of officers, but also women who were presumably their wives.[74]

The *Ceres* led her pursuers on a merry chase, indicating a failure on the part of the French to ignore the bait by sending two much larger vessels in pursuit of a single sloop of war. Dacres and his officers did what they could, but with such overwhelming odds he was forced to strike his colours after an hour and a half chase. Dacres' career did not suffer for the loss of his ship, and he eventually rose to flag rank; his son (also called James) would go down in history as the unhappy captain of the *Guerriere* in her epic duel with the USS *Constitution*.[75]

That same day d'Estaing decided to break the deadlock by landing troops, who combined with French forces already on the island and on the 18th launched an attack on an isolated British position at the Vigie Peninsula. They were stunningly repulsed by heavily outnumbered British grenadiers, fusiliers, and light infantry. This battle is not in the scope of this chapter but is a fascinating engagement in its own right, also prefiguring many characteristics of battles in the wars of the French Revolution and Napoleon.

On Christmas Eve an American privateers, the *Bunker Hill* (18), was revealed by the rising of the sun well within the range of Barrington's guns. She struck her colours and was quickly hauled within the defensive circle of the British line before the French could respond. Shortly after at 10:00 a.m., d'Estaing finally weighed anchor and appeared to be forming his squadron for an attack. Strangely, d'Estaing again declined to press the issue against Barrington's reinforced position and returned to his anchorage between Gros Islet and Castries.[76]

On 29 December the island's French garrison surrendered. D'Estaing had reembarked his troops under the cover of night and shortly after dawn sailed for Martinique.[77] The Battle of St Lucia was over. Against all the odds, the Royal Navy was victorious.

---

73 Journal, 16 December 1778, Bonner-Smith (ed.), *The Barrington Papers*, Vol.2, p.126.
74 Journal, 17 December 1778, Bonner-Smith (ed.), *The Barrington Papers*, Vol.2, p.127; Captain Dacres to Barrington 29 December 1778, *ibid.*, Vol.2, p.187.
75 From Captain Dacres to Barrington 29 December 1778, Bonner-Smith (ed.), *The Barrington Papers*, Vol.2, p.187.
76 Journal, 23 December 1778, Bonner-Smith (ed.), *The Barrington Papers*, Vol.2, p.135.
77 Journal, 29 December 1778, Bonner-Smith (ed.), *The Barrington Papers*, Vol.2, p.140.

Conclusion: The Man Who Wasn't Nelson

Why, then, did d'Estaing fail at St Lucia where Nelson succeeded at the Nile? D'Estaing has been criticised by English speaking historians and faced the contempt of officers under his command. Pierre de Suffren served as one of d'Estaing's captains and excoriated d'Estaing for not attempting to 'anchor upon their buoys' and carry the British ships by boarding. Suffren reckoned the French would be superior in such a contest and, given the dilapidated state of British crews due to disease, he may well have been right.[78]

Perhaps the most significant factor that enabled Nelson to annihilate the French fleet at the Battle of the Nile was the fact he was possessed excellently trained crews and his captains known as the band of brothers. Indeed, where Nelson was loved by his Band of Brothers, the animosity between d'Estaing and his officers was at times open.[79] D'Estaing had no such luxury. Indeed, while he was beloved by his men, many of his subordinate naval officers viewed him with contempt for leapfrogging the naval hierarchy due to his royal connections.[80] Suffren's criticisms of d'Estaing after St Lucia were repeated after later events at Grenada.[81] While d'Estaing's courage was never questioned, his professional competence was. Unlike Nelson he did not seek counsel with his officers, and it must have been painfully apparent that while not a complete novice in the nautical realm he lacked experience and was the beneficiary of patronage.[82]

The slow sailing time of his fleet and its poor performance in North America, clearly shows why the French had a difficult time forming for battle in the strangely channelled breezes and leeward calms of the St Lucian mountains. So too was French doctrine not optimised for the sort of climatic annihilation battle d'Estaing wanted to fight. While the French admiralty had specifically ordered d'Estaing to annihilate the British fleet in American waters, and offered ludicrous subsidies to its sailors if they could do so, a decree does not change the institutionalised attitudes from decades of French doctrine requiring admirals to economise their fleets. The survival and good condition of ships therefore was the ultimate concern. Not even the vaunted Suffren was going to risk his ship to run in shore of the enemy line to outflank them, like Foley of the *Goliath* at the Nile. With the strange conditions created by the prevailing winds, valleys, and mountains around St Lucia. It would have been hard to seek a close action with the line, especially with the end of the line defended by the *Isis*, the towering cliffs deadening the wind. It would have been fool hardy to try and force a passage. The volcanic shore would have shown little mercy.

Forming the squadron itself, with poorly trained crews, into an orderly formation to conduct combined fleet manoeuvres to bring about a close engagement would also have been very difficult and could explain the decision to conduct long range cannonades. It is possible that nothing else was practical, especially after the ships had been damaged in the initial exchange of fire. It is a critical issue that is often overlooked even in ideal conditions: fleet manoeuvres were difficult, let alone in an area with changeable winds, close to a shoreline

---

78   Mahan, *Influence of Sea Power Upon History*, p.426.
79   Andrew Lambert, *Nelson: Britannia's God of War* (London: Faber and Faber 2010), pp.106-134.
80   Willis, *The Struggle for Sea Power*, pp.264-265.
81   Willis, *The Struggle for Sea Power*, p.309.
82   Willis, *The Struggle for Sea Power*, p.232.

with an enemy in a defensive position. Wind and topography mattered immensely in battles under sail and there is not enough appreciation for the decisive effect of the elements in sea fights.

D'Estaing was aware of British reinforcements under Vice-Admiral Byron, which might explain his desire not to risk his ships. Even with all these constraints he could have done it, but the result would have looked more like Copenhagen than the Nile: ships, laid alongside at pistol shot, battering the other and their crews into shattered wrecks. Crucially for the French it would make any follow up campaign or battle with Byron an impossibility. Such a battle was not something the French navy would contemplate, even if it was supposedly their mission.

Historians have been harsh on d'Estaing. His task was formidable. Other than numerical advantage, he held far fewer cards than Nelson did at the Nile. He was not a fool, a coward or someone who did not understand the sea. But he was an enlightened courtier, not a life-long sea-officer and that is one the key factors that determined the outcome of the battle. D'Estaing understood sea power, and its ability to project force to influence the strategic and political balance of a conflict. But it is not unfair to say that his skill in managing the confluence of operational challenges that was a fleet engagement under sail, was often found wanting, and at key points declined to place his fleet at risk to force a decisive engagement.

While the withdrawal of the fleet under d'Estaing left St Lucia in the hands of the British, Barrington still possessed a numerically inferior squadron and the French had already captured Dominica. Relief arrived on 6 January, in the pre-dawn light, when Vice-Admiral Byron anchored in Grand Cul de Sac Bay with nine ships of the line, two frigates and two sloops. Byron's arrival did little to brighten the fortunes of the British in the West Indies. By the middle of 1779 d'Estaing had received reinforcements and launched rapid thrusts to capture St Vincent and Grenada. On 6 July 1779 the fleets met again off Grenada. D'Estaing's French fleet was victorious. No ships were lost on either side, however, and the animosity between d'Estaing and his officers that undoubtedly contributed to the French defeat at St Lucia was on display.[83]

Yet had d'Estaing committed to a Copenhagen-like battle against Barrington, battering the small but resolute British squadron and then carrying them by boarding as the fire eating Suffren wished, such a victory would have been impossible. This point is easy to miss in the drama of the capture of St Lucia and the subsequent shock of the British defeat at Grenada. Risk averse French doctrine had clear benefits. It meant the Navy retained the capability to utilise seapower against the enemies of France. Britain may have taken St Lucia, but she had lost St Vincent and Grenada in turn.

For all the faults of d'Estaing, it would be easy to write the Royal Navy as passive actors in the Battle of St Lucia. They had little choice but to fight tenaciously, or the fleet and Grant's army would be destroyed. But that would be a mistake, below the surface appearance of a story of a plucky stand is the result of a deep and lifelong technical understanding of fighting a battle under sail and a dogged commitment to achieving victory in spite of the odds. Whether that be the clever positioning of the *Prince of Wales* in the line, the boats that

---

83   Willis, *The Struggle for Sea Power*, p.309.

rowed guard at night to prevent ambush, the well-aimed gunnery that so mauled the larger French ships, or a midnight dash past the enemy to deliver welcome news of reinforcements.

Alongside the qualitative differences between Nelson and d'Estaing's captains it is a key differentiator between the outcomes of St Lucia and the Nile. Nelson faced a fleet scarred by years of political turmoil and defeat. D'Estaing was facing a fleet that, while sapped by disease, was crewed and officered by deeply competent men with high morale.

Barrington's victory at St Lucia deserves to be remembered for more than a French failure to win a Nile-like victory. It should be remembered as shining example of the quiet professionalism and technical brilliance that would deliver Britain command of the seas in the wars against the Revolution and Napoleon.

Select Bibliography

Published Primary Sources
Barnes G.R. & Owen J.H. (eds), *The Private Papers of John, Earl of Sandwich, 1771-1782* (Abingdon: Routledge for the Navy Records Society, 2019).
Bonner-Smith D. (ed.), *The Barrington Papers: Selected from the letters and papers of Admiral the Hon. Samuel Barrington* (Abingdon: Routledge for the Navy Records Society, 2019).

Secondary Sources
Calmon-Maison, J.J.R, *L'Amiral d'Estaing 1729-1794* (Paris: Calmann-Levy, 1910).
Troude, Onésime-Joachim, *Batailles navales de la France* (Paris: Challamel Aîné, 1867).
Willis Sam, *The Struggle for Sea Power: A Naval History of the American Revolution* (London: Atlantic Books, 2015).

7

Unprepared and Unaccountable? The Historical Significance of the Loss of His Majesty's Sloops *Peacock*, *Boxer*, and *Epervier*, 1813-1814

Nicholas James Kaizer[1]

William James did not plan to enter the world of naval historiography in 1812. He was then a practicing lawyer, but had the misfortune of finding himself travelling in Philadelphia when the War of 1812 broke out. James found himself for some time behind enemy lines, as the astounding news came of the destruction of HMS *Guerriere* in an action with USS *Constitution*. It was a shocking event, for the British world – including Halifax, where James eventually found refuge – was not used to hearing of naval defeats. The vast majority of naval actions of all scales over the last two decades had been British victories; in the War of 1812, however, the British lost most of the single ship actions that were fought against the United States Navy.

In the aftermath of the war, James wrote a short pamphlet which aimed to refute many of the narratives spreading surrounding the shocking defeats of several British frigates and sloops in that conflict.[2] This was a particular problem in Halifax, as often the only accounts of actions that occurred in North America were sources from American papers. James, like the residents of Halifax where the piece was published, was a proud Briton and sought to restore the honour of his beloved national navy.[3] Many were outraged by the defeats, and

---

1   The analysis presented here is based upon research first undertaken for my MA dissertation and subsequent Helion volume, *Revenge in the Name of Honour*. Here, I have asked new questions of this research

2   First, James produced a short piece while in Halifax. Following his return to London, he published a longer and more comprehensive book: William James, *A Full and Correct Account of the Chief Naval Occurrences of the late war between Great Britain and the United States of America*, published in 1817. This chapter consulted a republished version: William James, *Naval Occurrences of the War of 1812: A Full and Correct Account of the Naval War Between Great Britain and the United States of America, 1812-1813* (London: Conway Maritime Press, 2004).

3   So proud were contemporary Haligonians of their Britishness that James managed to sell nearly 2,000 copies in Halifax, then a town of just 5,000. Lambert, quoted in foreword to James, *Naval Occurrences*, pp.vi-vii.

Constitution crossing *Guerriere*'s bows, *Not the Little Belt.* (Elizabetha Tsitrin, https://bluenautilusart.com/)

sought comfort in the disparity in force between the defeated British frigates – *Guerriere*, *Macedonian, Java* – and their American counterparts – *Constitution* and *United States*.

In the words of historian Andrew Lambert,[4] 'after examining every engagement in which a ship had been taken [James] concluded "no British ship has been captured by an American one of equal force."'[5] He was vilified by the Americans and lauded by the British, and when 'James died, in May 1827, it was widely acknowledged that he had single-handedly corrected the American version of the War of 1812.'[6] Indeed, British historiography has more-or-less accepted James' thesis ever since.[7] In the words of N.A.M. Rodger – a true giant of the field – historians generally consider 'the disparity in force [to be] a sufficient explanation' for the losses in 1812.[8]

---

4   Lambert has published excellent scholarship on this subject in his own right: Andrew Lambert, *The Challenge: Britain against America in the Naval War of 1812* (London: Faber and Faber, 2013).

5   Lambert, quoted in foreword to James, *Naval Occurrences,* pp.i-ii.

6   Lambert, quoted in foreword to James, *Naval Occurrences,* p.v.

7   For a more detailed examination of this historiography, see Nicholas James Kaizer, *Revenge in the Name of Honour: The Royal Navy's Quest for Vengeance in the Single Ship Actions of the War of 1812* (Warwick: Helion & Company, 2020), xx-xxi and Nicholas James Kaizer, 'Regret, Determination, and Honour: The Impact of the Single Ship Losses in North American Waters on the British Royal Navy, 1812-1813' (MA Thesis, Dalhousie University, 2018).

8   N.A.M. Rodger, *The Command of the Ocean: A Naval History of Britain, 1649-1815* (New York: W.W.

James was largely correct in many of his assessments. The three British fifth rate frigates were vastly outgunned by their American counterparts and likely had no prospect of success, even if many serving naval officers at the time refused to accept this point. They were balanced out by three additional single ship action victories, where British ships defeated evenly matched opponents due to superb training and seamanship.[9] In other words, when the Royal Navy and the United States Navy met on even terms, the British acquitted themselves admirably and demonstrated the very best they had to offer. The problem with this historical assessment, however, is the case of three other single ship actions; namely the losses of His Majesty's Sloops *Peacock*, *Boxer*, and *Epervier* in 1813 and 1814. These sloops and the actions in which they fought are often left out of British historical accounts of the War of 1812 altogether, and the reason is readily apparent: on paper they were not significantly outgunned, and faced American sloops of war of relatively similar armament. Their defeats could not be sufficiently explained by 'the disparity in force.' Rather, these three sloops were defeated largely because of the lack of preparedness and competency of their commanders and crew. These actions have largely been ignored by British historiography, but this does not mean they are of no historical importance. Indeed, they raise interesting and significant questions about the Royal Navy in the immediate post-Nelson era.

During the War of 1812, there were a little more than a dozen clashes that can be described as single ship actions (or something close to). These were very rare events in naval warfare. Most naval actions occurred between forces of quite uneven dimensions and force, based upon how warships tended to operate.[10] Single ship actions were notable because they were rare; naval officers coveted the opportunity for a captain and crew to test themselves against an opponent of equal strength, and the potential outsized fame and reward that came with it. Between 1793 and 1814, Royal Navy frigates fought 45 such actions against frigates of the French *Marine Nationale;* of these, the British won 35 outright, seven were inconclusive, and only three were clear French victories.[11] A comparative record for the War of 1812 – a much shorter conflict, involving far fewer ships – makes a stark contrast. Eleven were fought between single British and American ships of vaguely the same class that can without controversy be classified as single ship actions. Of these, all but two were American victories. In three of these cases, the British defeat can be blamed upon a severe lack of preparation, training, and leadership on the part of the captains and officers; the aforementioned sloops *Peacock*, *Boxer*, and *Epervier*.

The fact that, of the well over 100 ships employed in North American waters throughout the War of 1812, this small sample size included three starkly poor commanders, raises an interesting question: did the Royal Navy – long understood to have a uniquely effective corps of officers which contributed to a spectacular reign of successes from 1793-1815 – have some degree of trouble with quality control on individual ships?

Norton, 2005), p.568.

9   *Shannon* versus *Chesapeake*, *Pelican* versus *Wasp*, and *Endymion* versus *President*. Some, such as Lambert, also credit *Pheobe*'s victory over *Essex* as a single ship contest.

10   Mark Lardas, *British Frigate vs. French Frigate: 1973-1814* (London: Osprey Publishing 2013), pp.4-5, 69-70.

11   Lardas, *British Frigate vs. French Frigate*, p.69.

Led by the well-trained officers of the Royal Navy, British warships throughout the French Revolutionary and Napoleonic Wars were near consistently able to outperform their French and Spanish counterparts in crucial aspects of naval warfare: seamanship and manoeuvrability, and the speed and accuracy of gunfire, which together decided many engagements.[12] That the same did not happen when the limited ships of the United States Navy met their British counterparts is interesting, and complicates general narratives of the Royal Navy of this period. The standard historical narrative, stretching back to William James and his very loyal Halifax readers, does not fully reflect the actual record of the Royal Navy in this conflict. The unique circumstances of the War of 1812 – a limited naval war, owing to the small United States Navy and its frequent strategy of lone cruisers – resulted in over a dozen single ship (or approximately single ship) engagements, and the resulting defeats open questions of the issue of quality control within the Royal Navy, the level of preparedness of its commanders, and the nature of naval accountability.

Peacock, *Boxer*, and *Epervier*: **Worst in the Fleet?**

HMS *Peacock*, an 18-gun *Cruizer*-class brig sloop, was nicknamed 'the Yacht.' Her reputation, under the command of Commander William Peake, was based upon her captain and crew's dedication to spit and polish. According to James, she:

> …had long been the admiration of her numerous visitors, for the tasteful arrangement of her deck, and had obtained, in consequence, the name of the *yacht*. The breechings of the carronades were lined with white canvass; the shot-lockers shifted from their usual places; and nothing could exceed, in brilliancy, the polish upon the traversing-bars and elevating screws.[13]

She was described as 'deservedly styled one of the finest vessels of her class in the British navy' by none other than Master Commandant James Lawrence,[14] who on 24 February 1813 in USS *Hornet* brought *Peacock* to battle and sank her in less than half an hour of gunnery.[15]

---

12   Douglass W. Allen, 'The British Navy Rules: Monitoring and Incompatible Incentives in the Age of Fighting Sail', *Explorations in Economic History*, 39 (2002), p.209; Michael Duffy, 'The Gunnery at Trafalgar: Training, Tactics, or Temperament?' *The Journal for Maritime Research*, 7:1 (2005), p.145.

13   James, *Naval Occurrences*, p.100.

14   It is unclear if Lawrence is referring to her reputation as a trim and pretty ship, or suggesting she was a sloop with a good fighting reputation in the Royal Navy. The former is more likely, given 'the Yacht's' well known reputation, but the latter is also possible. Lawrence was always interested in his own glory, and would have the incentive to exaggerate his victory. For more on Lawrence's attitudes and personal search for glory, see Voelcker, 'Victories or Distractions, Honour or Glory?' in Tim Voelcker (ed.), *Broke of the Shannon and the War of 1812* (Barnsley: Seaforth Publishing, 2013), pp.57-73.

15   Master Commandant James Lawrence to Secretary of the Navy William Jones, 19 March 1813, in William S. Dudley, Christine F. Hughes, and Tamara Moser Melia (eds), *The Naval War of 1812: A Documentary History* (Washington: Naval Historical Center, Dept. of Navy, 1985), Vol.I, pp. 70-72; Library and Archives Canada (LAC), MG12 ADM 1 1/503, C-12854, Lieutenant Frederick Wright to Vice Admiral John Warren, 26 March 1813.

Table 1: Comparison of the Dimensions and Force of *Hornet* and *Peacock*

	Hornet	*Peacock*
Length of deck	112 ft	100 ft
No. of carronades / main battery	18 guns (32-pdrs)	18 guns (24-pdrs)
Broadside weight	297 lbs	198 lbs
Tonnage	450	386
Initial crew / survivors	165/160	122 /101

Source: James, *Naval Occurrences*, pp.101-103. *Hornet* was a better-armed vessel, although the speed in which *Peacock* was destroyed and the relative lack of damage suffered by *Hornet* was too great to be explained by this disparity alone.

It was evident very early in the action that *Hornet*'s gunnery was superior. *Peacock*'s hull was smashed by the first broadside, and in response her smaller guns had done little but cut away some of her opponent's rigging and a handful of men aloft. Her rigging was quickly shot away, her rudder compromised, and Peake himself was seriously wounded early in the action. Lieutenant Frederick Wright, who subsequentially took command, stated that:

> [A]t this period of the Action Captain Peake was wounded by a Musquet Shot and by a Splinter which knocked him down he continued however to retain the Command of the Ship for some Minutes longer when he gallantly fell nobly defending his Ship by a Cannon Shot which instantly deprived him of Life, and the Service of a Meritorious and brave Officer.[16]

Somewhere between 14 and 30 minutes after the first gun was fired,[17] Wright surrendered and signalled to the enemy that his ship was in a state of distress; her crew was evacuated to *Hornet* with no time to spare before she sank. *Hornet* had suffered very little damage.[18]

In the wake of any loss of ship, Royal Navy captains (or acting captains, such as Lieutenant Wright) were subjected to a process of accountability, ending with a court martial. First, an official report was dispatched to the captain's commanding officer, in this case to Vice Admiral John Warren, commander-in-chief of the North American Squadron. These accounts were very frequently published in a number of British and American papers, even for defeats. Notably, Wright's letter never was, and so when James wrote his analysis of the action, there was no official report available.[19] The reason, in hindsight, is obvious.

---

16   LAC, MG12 ADM 1 1/503, C-12854, Wright to Warren, 26 March 1813.

17   Lawrence's account suggests the action was much quicker than Wright's account.

18   LAC, MG12 ADM 1 1/503, C-12854, Wright to Warren, 26 March 1813; Kevin D. McCranie, *Utmost Gallantry: The U.S. and Royal Navies at Sea in the War of 1812* (Annapolis: Naval Institute Press, 2011), p.83; Theodore Roosevelt, *The Naval War of 1812 or the History of the United States Navy during the last war with Great Britain* (New York: G.P. Putnam's Sons, 1882), pp.166-169.

19   It was preserved within the Admiralty's records, as part of the dispatches sent by the commander-in-chief. It is available within ADM 1/503, and microfiche copies were made in the early 1900s by then-Dominion Archives, now Library and Archives Canada, and are available online (MG12 ADM 1 1/503, C-12854).

Wright's task was to defend the conduct of himself, his fellow officers and crew, and of his deceased captain. Chief among those responsibilities was to demonstrate that the sloop had not been surrendered lightly. He began by explaining that they were in a dire situation when he took command; much of the crew had been killed or wounded, four guns were out of action, the sloop was un-manoeuvrable, and was taking on dangerous quantities of water. Still, Wright asserted that he was not immediately ready to surrender:

> [Y]et as the fire was briskly kept up by the Waist Guns I was determined to support the honor of the British Flag *as long as defense was practicable* but the Main Mast going close by the board a few minutes afterwards and the Enemy again taking up his raking position and the Vessel an unmanageable and sinking wreck, I was at length to save the lives of the remaining Crew however reluctant and painful it was compelled to wave my hat in acknowledgment of having struck the ensign having fallen with the Gaff into the water.[20]

Wright asserted that he initially wanted to continue the action, 'with an ardour characteristic of British Seamen', but as he came to realize the unmanageable state of the ship and his inability to mount an effective resistance to the enemy off his quarter, he concluded that victory was no longer a possibility.[21]

As to why *Peacock* found herself in such a situation, Wright emphasized the enemy's superiority in force:

> [W]e came to compare the disparity of Force between the two Vessels with the extraordinary Number of Men on board the Enemy which allowed them to keep a large number in their Tops who supported an incessant galling and destructive Fire.[22]

He concludes with the assertion that his crew would have prevailed had they 'not been opposed to an overwhelming force under more favorable circumstances and with anything like equality of Guns or Men have ensured success...'[23]

Wright does not comment on the state of his crew's gunnery, but this was something that interested the following court martial. They discussed the apparent ineffective fire of *Peacock* at length. One of her officers attributed this poor fire to the rough seas, as *Peacock* was a small vessel and the rocking of the sloop made loading and aiming difficult. However, she was not substantially smaller than *Hornet*, whose gunnery seemed to have been unhindered by the choppy waves. More telling is the account of *Peacock*'s gunner, who revealed a poor gunnery training regime onboard 'the yacht.'[24] The disproportionate damage and loss of life suffered by *Peacock* were quickly attributed by the court to 'the want of skill in

20   LAC, MG12 ADM 1 1/503, C-12854, Wright to Warren, 26 March 1813.
21   LAC, MG12 ADM 1 1/503, C-12854, Wright to Warren, 26 March 1813.
22   LAC, MG12 ADM 1 1/503, C-12854, Wright to Warren, 26 March 1813.
23   LAC, MG12 ADM 1 1/503, C-12854, Wright to Warren, 26 March 1813.
24   McCranie, *Utmost Gallantry*, p.83.

'The *Hornet* and *Peacock*, or, John Bull in Distress.' In one of America's earliest political cartoons, the small but mighty American hornet is assaulting Britain, represented by a mashup of the traditional John Bull and a peacock, representing the defeated sloop. (Yale University Art Gallery)

directing the fire in consequence of the crew not having practised the use of the guns for three years.'[25]

Later that year, following two British successes in the *Shannon* versus *Chesapeake* and *Pelican* versus *Argus* actions, another British sloop was engaged and defeated by a similarly armed opponent on 5 September 1813. HMS *Boxer*, under the newly promoted Samuel Blyth, encountered USS *Enterprise*, under Master Commandant Burrows, north of Boston. Both were relatively small vessels, each armed with 18-pounder carronades, and the crews of both vessels were eager for action; cheers erupted from both as the brig-sloops approached, and Commander Blyth ordered his ensign to be nailed to the mast, proclaiming to his crew that the colours would never be struck whilst he stood. This was true, for he was killed early in the action (as was Burrows) and it was Lieutenant McCrery who offered his sword to the American Lieutenant Edward McCall, after *Boxer* had been dismasted and her crew began deserting their posts.[26] Master Commandant Burrows was still on deck, although too wounded to have been in command, and was only moved below after *Boxer* had surrendered.

---

25   TNA: ADM 1/5436, CM *Peacock*, Verdict.
26   McCranie, *Utmost Gallantry*, pp.192-193; Roosevelt, *Naval War of 1812*, pp.214-215.

USS *Enterprise* against HMS *Boxer*, the latest in a series of shocking defeats for the British, painting by Michel Corne. (Naval History and Heritage Command)

According to Theodore Roosevelt, Burrows simply said 'I am satisfied. I die contented...' before being taken below.[27]

Both William James and Theodore Roosevelt argued that *Enterprise*'s superior armament and crew size sufficiently explained her victory, and while James admitted that the Americans' guns were handled with more skill, Roosevelt asserts that the two forces fought with equal skill, pointing to the fact that the casualties on both sides were close to equal.[28] By contrast, the *Boxer*'s court martial took a different view:

> The court is of the opinion that the capture of H.M. brig *Boxer*, by the U.S. vessel of war *Enterprise*, is to be attributed to a superiority in the enemy's force, principally in the number of men, as well as to a greater degree the skill in the direction of her fire, and the destructive effects of her first broadside.[29]

Enterprise had two additional guns than *Boxer*, and otherwise the two sloops were armed with the same main battery. The court martial was not very interested in this relatively insignificant advantage in firepower. They were more concerned with the larger crew on board *Enterprise*, which went into action with nearly double the men. Contemporary accounts of naval officers Captain William Tremlett, Captain Sir William Dillon, and Lieutenant Henry Edward Napier all make the case that larger and better trained crews were more significant

---

27   Roosevelt, *Naval War of 1812*, p.215.
28   Jon Latimer, *1812: War with America* (Cambridge, Massachusetts: Harvard University Press, 2007), p. 239; Roosevelt, *Naval War of 1812*, p.216.
29   ADM 1/5440, CM *Boxer*, Verdict.

advantages than heavier broadsides.[30] More concerning for the Royal Navy, though, was the finding that *Boxer* suffered from less skilful and effective gunnery, as had been the case with *Peacock*. It was a disturbing pattern.

Table 2: Comparison of the Dimensions and Force of *Enterprise* and *Boxer*

	Enterprise	*Boxer*
Length of deck	97 ft	84 ft
No. of carronades / main battery	16 guns (18-pdrs)	14 guns (18-pdrs)
Broadside weight	135 lbs	114 lbs
Tonnage	245	179
Complement	163	66

Source: James, *Naval Occurrences*, pp.132-133. Like with *Peacock*, *Boxer* was less heavily armed than her opponent, but the most important factor was the size and skill of the enemy's crew.

To echo a point made in Andrew Johnston's chapter, 'given the threat of American attacks in North American waters during that stage of the War of 1812, it seems that a competent commander would have taken it on himself to prepare his crew for the relatively likely occurrence of combat.'[31] By the end of April, 1814, seven British men of war (three frigates and four sloops) had been taken or sunk in one-on-one action with the enemy. It is almost certain that Commander Richard Wales, in command of HMS *Epervier* on the North American Squadron, would have heard of the defeats. News and gossip travelled fast among naval officers and the communities in which they operated, such as Halifax, where Wales had spent much time with his sloop. Unfortunately for her crew, the captain of *Epervier* appears not to have been a competent commander.

This *Cruizer*-class brig sloop (the same class as *Peacock* and a number of sloops which operated in this conflict) had had a very unlucky career thus far in North America. Her officers complained at length over the poor quality of their small crew and the defective state of the brig herself. According to William James, Wales himself complained about the state of his crew – possibly on the verge of mutiny – directly to the senior officer in Halifax.[32] Worse, the sloop had sunk at anchor during a storm in Halifax Harbour, and had remained under water for some time before being raised. On her current voyage, a storm had resulted in a sprung bowsprit. Wales would have done well to avoid action when she encountered USS *Peacock* – named after *that Peacock* – whilst escorting a southward-bound convoy. But Wales had the weight of the Royal Navy tradition and its urge for revenge upon his shoulders, his responsibility to protect the several merchantmen under his protection, not to mention nearly $120,000 worth of specie on board his own ship. Though he carried a smaller armament – sixteen 32-pound carronades and a pair of lighter long guns to *Peacock*'s twenty 32s – and a much smaller crew,

---

30 Kaizer, *Revenge in the Name of Honour*, pp.98-99.
31 See Andrew Johnston, 'War and Peace: Trends in Royal Navy Courts Martial, 1812-1818', in this work #add cross-reference once paginated#
32 James, *Naval Occurrences*, p.170.

Wales knew his duty was to engage the enemy, and so stood in for *Peacock* and cleared for action.[33]

Things went awry immediately. Under the pressure of recoil, several of *Epervier's* 32-pounder carronades snapped from the sides and went caravanning along the deck. Their breeching bolts were corroded, likely due to exposure to the saltwater while the ship was submerged, and the impact of recoil caused them to break. Men had to be diverted with every discharge to catch and restrain the guns, stretching the demoralized men to their limits as they tried to keep up with the Americans' rate of fire. The morale of the *Epervier's* crew deteriorated over the next half-hour, and men began to abandon their posts and flee below decks. The senior lieutenant, John Hackett, attempted to rally the men, but was struck in the arm by enemy shot, which carried his elbow joint clean off. All the while, *Peacock's* fire was relentless – nothing at all like that of her namesake. *Epervier* was shot to pieces, and, with his ship unmanageable and his crew in shambles, Wales was forced to strike his colours. He was content only that his convoy had scattered and escaped.[34]

Table 3: Comparison of the Dimensions and Force of *Peacock* and *Epervier*

	Peacock	*Epervier*
Length of deck	97 ft	84 ft
No. of carronades / main battery	22 guns (32-pdrs)	18 guns (32-pdrs)
Broadside weight	338 lbs	274 lbs
Tonnage	539	382
Complement	185	117

Source: James, *Naval Occurrences*, pp.172-175. Of the three single ship actions examined, on paper these adversaries were the most evenly matched. It may have in reality been the least fair contest, owing to Wales' failed command.

The two vessels were evenly matched on paper, but *Epervier* really did not stand a chance. James makes this case in his analysis, when he questions the motivation for *Peacock's* captain, Warrington, for not highlighting *Eperiver's* catastrophic issues with her guns:

> The reader now sees, what were Captain Warrington's reasons for concealing the state of *Epervier's* guns? Had he told the truth, it would have appeared, that he had been engaging an almost defenseless vessel; a vessel whose guns, for any use they were, might as well have been made of wood, as of iron.[35]

James correctly argus that *Epervier* was not effectively of equal force to her opponent, as American commentors claimed, as a result of the defective state of her guns and the general inadequacies of her crew.[36] The reason, however, that *Epervier* was not a sufficiently fair

---

33   McCranie, *Utmost Gallantry*, p.204; Roosevelt, *Naval War of 1812*, p.313; Lambert, *The Challenge*, unpaginated.

34   LAC, MG12 ADM1/506, Admiral's Dispatches, North America, C-12855, Commander Richard Wales to Vice Admiral Alexander Cochrane, 8 May 1814.

35   James, *Naval Occurrences*, p.171.

36   James, *Naval Occurrences*, p.174.

match for *Peacock* was one of her captain's own making, as shown at the subsequent court martial.

The court had questioned Wales on the state of training of his crew, and on the cause of the carronades chaos:

> Q: Have the crew generally speaking exercised in the use of the great guns?
> A: They were frequently exercised, but there were many who were not so expert as I thought they ought to have been, from the time they had been exercised.
> ...
> Q: Did the [fighting] bolts ever come out of their places in a similar manner when the guns were exercised?
> A: No[37]

According to Wales, though the guns had been exercised frequently, no defect in the carronade fastenings had yet been discovered. The reason soon became apparent, though, when Lieutenant Hackett admitted they had only ever fired one live round in practice.

> Q: Did the same circumstance ever occur when the guns were exercised?
> A: No, as we *never exercised with powder* and I conceived it was from the concussion of the guns.
> Q: From the time of your appointing to the *Epervier* until the Day of the Action was the weather frequently [unintelligible] as to have allowed your exercising with powder, and frequently at a mark?
> A: After we went to sea, I think the latter end of January or the beginning of February there was so much to do from the brig being lately fitted out, that we were obliged to take every opportunity of putting the rigging in order during the first cruise when we went out the second time with convoy for Bermuda, and the West Indies during that voyage after leaving the convoy we certainly had frequent opportunities of firing at a mark although the ship now was in a bad state from the bowsprit and heel of the foremast being sprung.
> Q: Were the men well acquainted with the use of the great guns?
> A: They were
> Q: How often were they *exercised without powder*?
> A: *Every evening for an hour when the weather would permit.*[38]

The second lieutenant, John Harvey, confirmed this in his testimony, while also criticizing the quality of his crew:

> Q: Were the *Epervier*'s crew generally speaking expert in the exercise of the great guns?

---

37   TNA, ADM 1/5447, CM *Epervier*: Testimony of Commander Richard Wales.
38   TNA, ADM 1/5447, CM *Epervier*: Testimony of Lt. John Hackett; author's emphasis

A: They were, *considering the strength of the Men, they were not strong men, and to appearance very unhealthy men.*

Q: Were they frequently exercised at the great guns?

A: Every evening when the weather would permit, for an hour.

Q: When at sea, *had they been exercised powder and shot?*

A: *Once, one gun only.*

Q: Were there opportunities of their being so exercised or of firing at a mark?

A: *The weather would frequently permit*

Q: Were the Men from the different guns brought to that one gun which was fired?

A: No, it was to try the end breechings that had been just fixed.[39]

Harvey admitted that while there were frequent opportunities to fire the guns in drill, they never were. The one live-fire round was expended for the purposes of testing one gun's breechings. The ship went into action with nothing more than pantomime gunnery drills and not having tested her gun's fittings, even after having been submerged in Halifax Harbour.

Worse, perhaps, the officers of *Epervier* attempted to place the blame for their loss on the quality of the crew. William Pearson, quartermaster, expressed this when asked about his view on the men's gunnery:

Q: Were the crew of the *Epervier* expert in the use of the great guns?

A: No, I believe not, several of those at my gun did not perform in the firing properly.

Q: Were they frequently exercised?

A: yes, every night when the weather permitted.

Q: How do you account for their being not expert?

A: I believe it was for want of headpiece

Q: Were the Crew of the *Epervier* generally speaking strong and healthy men, or a weak Ship's Company?

A: They were a very indifferent Ships Company.[40]

The senior lieutenant, Hackett, listed several crewmen he accused of cowardice, whom he chased out of the forehold during action, and Harvey had called the men weak and unhealthy. The master, too, complained about the weak character of the crew. Wales had publicly complained about his crew before, and it is of little surprise that he made his complaints clear during the court martial. They were not 'so expert as I thought they ought to have been', according to the captain's testimony, and they were described as 'a weak crew and *not bred as seamen*'.[41]

The problem with this defence is the obvious culpability of Wales and his officers, as those responsible for training and leading their men. It is not for the present author, as a practicing teacher, to suggest that a lack of student achievement is *always* the fault of the teacher,

---

39   TNA, ADM 1/5447, CM *Epervier*: Testimony of Lt. John Harvey; author's emphasis.

40   TNA, ADM 1/5447, CM *Epervier*: Testimony of William Pearson, Quartermaster

41   TNA, ADM 1/5447, CM *Epervier*: Testimonies of Capt Wales; Lt. Hackett; Lt Harvey; David Genlan, Master; and William Pearson, quartermaster; author's emphasis.

A carronade of USS *Constitution*, 32-pounder, of the same type and calibre as used on *Eperiver* and *Peacock*.
(Author's photograph)

but here the results of Wales' lack of training and preparation speak for themselves. Apart from the matter of training their men in seamanship and gunnery, they had neglected to even test the ship's equipment after she had spent days under water in Halifax Harbour. Indeed, a full reading of the court martial makes it clear that Commander Wales' lack of leadership was largely responsible for *Epervier*'s loss.

These three sloops have the distinction of being amongst the worst-prepared and worst-led ships in the service during the conflict. In each case, a man of war had been lost as a result of downright incompetence. Men had been killed and wounded. Trained seamen, a precious resource for an overstretched Royal Navy, had been taken captive. And each defeat added to the collective crisis of morale throughout the British world.

'Pantomime' vs Live Drill: Naval Preparedness in an Age of Success

In March 1813, Admiral Warren issued a memorandum to the captains of the North American Squadron on behalf of the Lords Commissioners of the Admiralty, in which he reminded his captains that:

> Their Lordships trust that all of the Officers of His Majesty's Naval Service must be convinced that upon the good discipline and the proper training of their Ships Companies to the expert management of the Guns, the preservation of the high character of the British navy most essentially depends, and that other works on which it is not unusual to employ the Men are of very trifling importance, when Compared with a due Preparation (by instruction and practice) for the effectual Services on the day of Battle.[42]

The Admiralty of 1813 was preoccupied with the danger posed to the reputation of the British Royal Navy. Politicians and newspapers across the country were shocked by the losses suffered in 1812; George Canning, the future Prime Minister, declared in the House of Commons that 'the sacred spell of invincibility of the British navy was broken.'[43] The threat of the American navy, though small, was powerful. Every defeat imposed significant harm on British naval morale.[44] The Admiralty were also preoccupied, it seems, with the prospect that crews of Royal Navy vessels were not being fully prepared for action, and that it was 'not uncommon' for crews to be employed in other work 'of very trifling importance.' Just as the Admiralty dispatched the memorandum to their commander-in-chief in North America, one Royal Navy sloop had demonstrated just how detrimental a lack of proper gunnery training could be; within a year, the captains of *Boxer* and *Epervier* failed to heed this advice.

Why was this the case? One reason was that gunpowder was expensive. Men like Peake, Blyth, and Wales were not alone in rarely firing their guns, instead relying on pantomime drill – running through the motions of loading, pointing, and firing the guns, without expending expensive powder.[45] Admiralty supplies were seen by many officers as insufficient for regular gunnery drill, as complained about in publications such as *The Naval Chronicle*; Captain William Tremlett, who wrote to the *Chronicle* to add his voice to the public discourse following the losses of 1812, argued that the losses showed that American gunnery was superior, as evident from the British suffering higher casualties and more extensive rigging damage in each action.[46] He explained this by suggesting that:

---

42   'Admiral Sir John Warren, R.N., Standing Order on the North American Station, Bermuda, 6 March 1813,' *Naval War of 1812*, Vol.2, p.59.

43   Historic Commons Hansard, HC Debate 18 February 1813, col.643, Hon. George Canning, MP. *Historic Hansard Index, UK Parliament*. <https://api.parliament.uk/historic-hansard/index.html> (accessed 6 November 2019).

44   Kaizer, *Revenge in the Name of Honour*, p.86.

45   Martin Bibbings, 'A Gunnery Zealot: Broke's Scientific Contribution to Naval Warfare,' in Voelcker (ed.), *Broke of the Shannon*, p.116.

46   'Tremlett to the Editor, 21 May 1813,' *The Naval Chronicle, for 1812: Containing a General and Biographical History of The Royal Navy of the United Kingdom; with a variety of original papers on*

[American] seamen have been more exercised in firing at a mark than ours – their government having given their commanders leave to exercise whenever they think proper, and to fire away as much ammunition as they please. By the rules of our navy, we are not allowed a sufficient quantity of powder in one year to exercise the people one month (notwithstanding we try, by every means in our power, to add to this allowance).[47]

Here, Tremlett highlighted the importance of live-fire drill and effective gunnery practice, something generally lacking in British ships but consistently applied in American vessels.

Popular understanding of the Royal Navy's tradition of live gunnery practice has become considerably exaggerated. According to Michael Duffy, this is a result of a focus on a handful of exceptionally efficient officers whose accounts have overshadowed the norm.[48] Some captains, such as Philip Broke, maintained well-drilled crews. Broke's own approach to gunnery, which was unique in its scientific nature, had turned his frigate HMS *Shannon* into one of the most efficient fighting machines of the Royal Navy.[49] Broke, however, was the exception; most captains did not dedicate as much time and resources to gunnery training. Some, such as Peake, Blyth, and Wales, did not consider such training a priority at all.

The problem with pantomime exercises – carrying out all of the moves of loading and firing a gun without actually burning any of their gunpowder – was that it resulted in inexperienced crews unused to the reality and chaos of gunnery duels. Such crews would go into action and be shocked by the noise and commotion of the guns, which hampered their morale and effectiveness in action. Confusion on board a ship, in as cramped a space as a gun deck, was not conducive to safety or efficiency.[50]

Another problem was that, prior to 1813, official Admiralty regulations and instructions on gunnery drill were often quite vague. Live fire was not technically required, and captains were given considerable – and understandable – leeway to not hold drills in times of poor weather, when the men were needed to keep their ship safe and on course.[51] This meant that officers had great leeway to avoid formal gunnery drill when conditions were not 'convenient.'

These points were made in Halifax newspaper *The Acadian Recorder* in 1814, saying of American ships 'it is not, that they fire so uncommonly well; but that we fire so wretchedly bad! In the *Shannon* and *Chesapeake*, our performance was a master-piece: in the *Pelican* and *Argus*, notwithstanding the equality of force, the difference of execution was as 5 to 1.' Excuses were made to explain a pitiful performance, comparatively, in the cases of *Boxer* and *Epervier*.[52] In December 1814, the paper reflected again on the poor state of gunnery in the lost ships:

Nautical Subjects. Vol.28: July to December (London: Joyce Gold, 1812), p.465.

47   'Tremlett to the Editor, 21 May 1813,' *Naval Chronicle* Vol 28, p.465.

48   Duffy, 'The Gunnery at Trafalgar' pp.140-145.

49   Gwyn, *Frigates and Foremasts*, p.143; Bibbings, 'A Gunnery Zealot,' pp.103-126; Martin Bibbings, 'The Battle', in Voelcker (ed), *Broke of the* Shannon, pp.127-128; McCranie, *Utmost Gallantry*, pp.150-151.

50   Duffy, 'The Gunnery at Trafalgar' pp.140-145.

51   Julian Gwyn, *Frigates and Foremasts: The North American Squadron in Nova Scotia Waters, 1745-1815* (Toronto and Vancouver: UBC Press, 2003), p.143; Bibbings, 'A Gunnery Zealot,' pp.103-126; Duffy, 'The Gunnery at Trafalgar' pp.140-145.

52   Nova Scotia Archives (NSA), *Acadian Recorder*, 4 June 1814, 2:23; Haligonians were very reluctant to

Nothing here said is intended, however to [excuse] the miserable gunnery exhibited, in nine cases out of ten, on board our national vessels. Yet, neither the crews, nor the commanders, of our ships can help this. The fault lies *higher-up*.... And, as few commanders in the navy can afford to furnish at their cost (as they have in some instances) powder and shot, to expend in exercising their men in firing at marks, an ample allowance of that necessary article in a fighting ship, should be served out; and means taken to compel its being properly used.[53]

It was understood, then, amongst some in the press – albeit in a naval town like Halifax, where journalists would have little trouble finding a naval officer to complain to them at length about inadequate supplies of gunpowder – that the losses of sloops like *Peacock*, *Boxer*, and *Epervier* could be blamed on a lack of proper preparation. They did not blame the officers, but they did recognize the problem.

Captains of the calibre of Peake, Blyth, and Wales could not have been too rare. Throughout the War of 1812 there were hundreds of ships stationed in North American waters, and dozens of sloops of war. If these three sloops were wholly unique, it would mean that the Royal Navy was exceptionally unlucky during the conflict, that these exceptions were among the very few engaged. Single ship actions were, after all, rare events, and only a small proportion of naval captains ever fought one. It is more likely that a small but not insignificant proportion of commanders and captains, tempted by the expense of gunpowder and loose regulations around drilling, had sacrificed gunnery training for pursuits of more 'trifling importance'.

The losses of *Peacock*, *Boxer*, and *Epervier* offer a view into the dangers of ill-prepared and poorly led Royal Navy ships' companies. In these three cases, a failure to adequately train and lead resulted in defeat to opponents of relatively equivalent strength in number and weight of armament, and it is argued that a hidden cadre of such poor commanders must have lurked within the Royal Navy, hidden by an otherwise stellar record of success across the board. Why, however, did these inadequate captains not cause such defeats earlier in wars? The answer may be in the state of their main opponents: even if there were some woefully unprepared Royal Navy ships' companies deployed, the average French or Spanish opponent in this period had their own deficiencies. The problems of the French and Spanish navies in the French Revolutionary and Napoleonic Wars, with respect to their warfare with the British, has often been exaggerated and poorly understood, but analysis of the results of naval action throughout the period shows a clear pattern. At Trafalgar, where the allies arguably performed at their best, it is clear that the ships of the British Mediterranean Fleet suffered little damage in their slow approach on the Franco-Spanish line of battle, and suffered many fewer casualties throughout the battle.[54]

The United States Navy was not the navy of Revolutionary and Napoleonic France, and it took gunnery training and preparation very seriously.[55] In part, this came down to the

---

criticize their naval heroes.
53   NSA, *Acadian Recorder*, 31 December 1814, 3:1.
54   Duffy, 'Gunnery at Trafalgar,' p.145.
55   Robert W. Neeser, 'American Naval Gunnery: Past and Present,' *The North American Review*, 196:685 (1912), pp.780-782.

small size of the American navy; supplying their few ships with ample stores of powder was not a huge expense. Also, they had not suffered such setbacks as had their continental counterparts throughout the period. They did not have an established reputation of victory and invincibility as the British did, but they did have lots of powder and guns to fire. In the eyes of British naval officers on the eve of the conflict, American captains and crews could be expected to put up fair and tough fights; their defeat, therefore would be a greater source of honour and glory than the typical French opponent of this period.[56]

The tendency, then, of some Royal Navy captains to neglect their gunnery drills for the sake of more 'trifling' shipboard activities caused few major operational problems for the Royal Navy until the outbreak of war with the United States and the single ship actions of that conflict. As British frigates and sloops were destroyed or captured by their American counterparts, a growing crisis of national honour took hold within the British state and the Royal Navy. It was a result of this that the Admiralty and the navy took matters of gunnery drill more seriously.

A Question of Accountability

The verdicts in some of the court martials that followed the losses of 1812 can seem harsh. Captain John Carden, who lost his frigate HMS *Macedonian* after a long and bitter duel with USS *United States* in November 1812,[57] was criticized by his own first lieutenant, David Hope, for failing to bring about a close engagement with the enemy whilst attempting to hold the weather gauge.[58] The court agreed, chiding Carden for this missed opportunity:

> [P]revious to the commencement of the action, from an over anxiety to keep the weather gage an opportunity was lost at closing with the enemy, and that owing to this circumstance the *Macedonian* was unable to bring the *United States* to close action until she had received material damage... [59]

The court which tried the surviving officers of *Peacock* 'was of opinion that the loss of the said Sloop was owing to the want of skill in directing the fire in consequence of the crew not having practised the use of the guns for three years.'[60] The captains of *Boxer*'s court martial concluded that her loss was owing to the greater skill in gunnery of her opponents.[61] In the case of *Epervier*, the court:

---

56   Wade Dudley, *Splintering the Wooden Wall: The British Blockade of the United States, 1812-1815* (Annapolis: Naval Institute Press, 2003) pp.44-50.
57   Ironically, it is suggested by some accounts that Carden once met with *United States*' Captain Stephen Decatur during the peace, and there each had toured and discussed each other's ships at length. Carden is reported to have brushed aside the 24-pounder main batter of *United States* and her sisters as needless and of little value compared to the more dependable 18-pounders standard on British frigates.
58   TNA ADM 1/5436, CM *Macedonian*, Lieutenant David Hope's Testimony.
59   TNA ADM 1/5436, CM *Macedonian*, Verdict.
60   TNA ADM 1/5436, CM *Peacock*, Verdict.
61   TNA ADM 1/5440, CM *Boxer*, Verdict

Agreed that the cause of the capture of His Majesty's late Sloop *Epervier*, was the very superior force of the enemy, the unsecure manner in which the breeching bolts of the *Epervier* were fitted, and the breeching bolts decaying … and the inefficiency of her crew…[62]

That said, the captains trying Wales also concluded that:

[T]he said Captain Richard Wales took the *Epervier* into action in a very skilled manner… and did judge the said Captain Richard Wales and the other officers and ship's company (except the persons before mentioned to have deserted their quarters) to be fully and honourably acquitted.[63]

The surviving officers of *Peacock* and *Boxer*, too, were honourably acquitted. In fact, as is argued by Johnston elsewhere in this volume, captains, commanders, and other officers of ships lost to enemy action or the elements were seldom officially reprimanded.[64] Courts martials were willing to criticize, but rarely actually placed blame on any particular officer. In the three courts martials examined here, each decided that a lack of proficiency in gunnery – stemming from a lack of training – resulted in the losses of His Majesty's Sloops, but none directly challenged the commanders and officers who were the primary cause of that lack of training.

Beyond these implicit but unspoken critiques, only one officer involved in any of the single ship actions of the War of 1812 was reprimanded and dismissed from the service: Lieutenant Andrew Duncan, who allegedly deserted his duty during the *Essex* versus *Alert* action early in the war.[65] Some non-commissioned members of the crew of *Boxer* were reprimanded for cowardice, but none of the officers.[66] The rest were honourably acquitted. The rest, though seemingly having failed in their duty as leaders, demonstrated courage and bravery during the actions themselves. Each convinced the courts that they had done their utmost to fight their ships so long as they had a reasonable prospect for success. Publicly, that mattered more than what had transpired *before* the actions. The reputation of the service as a whole mattered more.[67]

As William James noted, to his frustration, official reports of the losses of *Peacock*, *Boxer*, and *Epervier* were not available publicly as was typical of the time. It was common for the press – principally the *London Gazette* and the *Naval Chronicle* – to run official letters and even minutes of court martials for even prominent losses, such as the three frigate losses in 1812. In these three instances, however, little made its way into the press and subsequent world of naval historiography. Court martial verdicts, which frequently were published, could only serve as an embarrassment in the cases of these three defeats. It was the collective

---

62   TNA ADM 1/5447, CM *Epervier*, Verdict.

63   TNA ADM 1/5447, CM *Epervier*, Verdict.

64   See Johnston, 'War and Peace.'

65   *Naval Chronicle*, Vol 28, p. 506; David Syrett and R.L. DiNardo, *The Commissioned Sea Officers of the Royal Navy, 1660-1815* (Aldershot: Scholar Press for the Navy Records Society, 1994) p.135.

66   ADM 1/5440, CM *Boxer*, Verdict

67   Kaizer, *Revenge in the Name of Honour*, pp.204-206.

honour and reputation of the Royal Navy that mattered, and the various courts martial involved were content to highlight bravery and zeal, and to leave accountability to someone else.

When accountability came, if it came at all, it came indirectly and *after* the court martial. The Royal Navy of this period had too many officers at every level, but particularly too many lieutenants and commanders. Towards the end of the conflict, there were twice as many commanders as sloops to be commanded, and many lieutenants could only hope for advancement as a gift in retirement.[68] Reputation and connections were key to gainful employment, and even more crucial during the peace. The commanders involved in the defeats typically fared worse than those involved in the victories, and ended their careers in obscurity and half pay: a notable exception was Richard Wales, who had strong familial connections in the Royal Navy, who still nonetheless never reached flag rank. Peake, commander of 'the Yacht,' of course was killed in action. Blyth of *Boxer* also was killed in action, although his lieutenant was not helped by the defeat and never reached the rank of commander. His counterpart from *Peacock*, Wright, also appears to have disappeared from the records following the action, suggesting a lack of active service. Both of Wales' lieutenants from *Epervier*, however, continued to serve after the action.[69] Compared with officers involved in the several successes of the War of 1812, the record was poorer, but not as starkly so as may be assumed.[70]

Conclusion

The War of 1812 is often left out of general survey histories of the Royal Navy, of the warfare of the Napoleonic era, or of European military history more generally. The naval war of 1812 is even less covered, the single ship actions less so still. Many British and Canadian historians mention the losses in 1812 in passing; shocking though they were to contemporaries, they were sufficiently explained by the sheer disparity in force of the monstrous American heavy frigates that *Guerriere*, *Macedonian*, and *Java* faced. William James had set out to demonstrate that in no actions fought during the War of 1812 did the Americans triumph against an evenly matched opponent. It was a view shared by his fellow Britons, including those of Halifax who purchased his pamphlets in droves. While it contains a great deal of truth, it does not tell a complete story of the naval War of 1812.

Among the naval captains who participated in the conflict, we see some superb examples of zeal and professionalism: Captains Philip Broke of *Shannon*, and Henry Hope of *Endymion*, were both excellent commanders and drilled their crews into considerable fighting machines. However, other commanders we see in this conflict were perhaps among the worst that put to sea for the Royal Navy: Commanders Peake and Wales in particular, whose crews were utterly ill prepared for action. Whereas the common conclusion of British and Canadian scholars is that the British won actions against the Americans when both

68   Evan Wilson, 'Social Background and Promotion Prospects in the Royal Navy, 1775-1815', *English Historical Review* CXXXI, no. 550 (2016), p.538.
69   Syret and Dinardo, *Commissioned Sea Officers*, pp.193, 206, 288, 454.
70   Kaizer, *Revenge in the Name of Honour*, pp.204-206.

were on even terms, both Peake and Wales lost their sloops in actions that were, on paper, evenly matched. They were not defeated by a superior force of the enemy, but instead by their own inability to train and lead their men. They complicate the story of the Royal Navy during this period, opening new questions into the true picture of levels of preparedness and competency amongst the commanders and captains of the navy as a whole, and offer a window into the nature of naval accountability.

Select Bibliography

Archives
Library and Archives Canada (LAC): Admiralty Records (Microform Copies), MG12 ADM 1
  ADM 1/503, C-12854: Admiral's Dispatches, North America, 1812-1813
  ADM 1/504, C-12854: Admiral's Dispatches, North America, 1813
  ADM 1/505, C-12855: Admiral's Dispatches, North America, 1814
  ADM 1/506, C-12855: Admiral's Dispatches, North America, 1814
The National Archives, Kew (TNA)
  ADM 1/5436, Court Martial *Macedonian* / Court Martial *Peacock*
  ADM 1/5440, Court Martial *Boxer*
  ADM 1/5447, Court Martial *Epervier*

Newspapers
Acadia Recorder, Halifax, NS, 1813-1815, Nova Scotia Archives

Published Primary Sources
Dudley, William S., Christine F. Hughes, and Tamara Moser Melia (eds), *The Naval War of 1812: A Documentary History* (Washington: Naval Historical Center, Dept. of Navy, 1992).
The Naval Chronicle, for 1812: Containing a General and Biographical History of The Royal Navy of the United Kingdom; with a variety of original papers on Nautical Subjects, Vol. 28-34 (London: Joyce Gold, 1812-1815)

Published Sources
Duffy, Michael, 'The Gunnery at Trafalgar: Training, Tactics, or Temperament?' *Journal for Maritime Research*, 7:1 (2005), pp.140-169.
Lambert, Andrew, *The Challenge: Britain against America in the Naval War of 1812* (London: Faber and Faber, 2013).
Kaizer, Nicholas James, *Revenge in the Name of Honour: The Royal Navy's Quest for Vengeance in the Single Ship Actions of the War of 1812* (Warwick: Helion & Company, 2020).
McCranie, Kevin D., *Utmost Gallantry: The U.S. and Royal Navies at Sea in the War of 1812* (Annapolis, Naval Institute Press, 2011).
Roosevelt, Theodore, *The Naval War of 1812 or the History of the United States Navy during the last war with Great Britain* (New York: G.P. Putnam's Sons, 1882).
Voelcker, Tim (ed.), *Broke of the Shannon and the War of 1812* (Barnsley: Seaforth Publishing, 2013).
Wilcox, Martin, '"These peaceable times are the devil:" Royal Navy Officers in the post-war slump, 1815-1825', *The International Journal of Maritime History*, Vol.26, No.3 (2014), pp.471-488.
James, William, *Naval Occurrences of the War of 1812: A Full and Correct Account of the Naval War between Great Britain and the United States of America, 1812-1815* (London: Conway Maritime Press, 2004).
Wilson, Evan, 'Social Background and Promotion Prospects in the Royal Navy, 1775-1815.' *English Historical Review*, Vol.CXXXI, No.550 (2016).

Part III

Naval Administration

The administration of the Royal Navy – or any navy – was of little interest to historians writing during the *Pax Britannica*, and yet the successful apparatus developed and deployed by Britain to finance, man, supply, and maintain its fleet was one of the most important factors in the success of the British navy in the eighteenth century. The building of this apparatus was a long and less-than-straightforward process, and is well-covered by the chapters provided in this volume.

Firstly, Paul Leyland examines the importance of geography and naval infrastructure in the development of sea power and foreign policy, chiefly respecting the Belgian port of Antwerp. This port, sitting very close to Britain at the eastern end of the Channel, was a port of paramount importance both to Britain and to any powers seeking to contest British sea power, as Leyland highlights. This chapter examines the role of Antwerp both as a port and as a tool of foreign policy from the Armada through the whole of the Long Eighteenth Century, arguing that the port was Britain's 'Achilles Heel,' one which Britain could not afford to fall into the hands of its chief rival France. The strategic importance of this port was recognized by both British and French leaders, and it influenced operations and policy throughout the wars of the 'Second Hundred Years War'.

Turning from the 'career' of one port throughout the period, Andrew Young presents the career of one man, Admiral George Anson. Anson's career was remarkable both for his operational exploits but also for his role as an administrator. The navy which he inherited in the 1740s had a very mixed record indeed, but two decades later was a very effective and well-run naval machine. Young's chapter highlights the role played by Anson in developing the administrative apparatus that allowed Britain to effectively project sea power in the latter half of the Long Eighteenth Century.

Joesph Krulder then focuses in on the rather chaotic state of the Royal Navy at the start of the Seven Years War, during the first of Anson's terms as First Lord of the Admiralty, demonstrating that the process of reform and institution-building was still far from complete by 1755. Indeed, at this time foreign heads of state quipped that the Royal Navy was ill-equipped, undermanned, and in disrepair. Krulder also highlights the wider social, cultural, and political context exhibited in the archival record. The Royal Navy did not exist in a vacuum, after all. This chapter harmonizes naval history with wider societal points of view.

Finally, Andrew Johnston concludes this section with an examination of naval courts martial at the very conclusion of the long eighteenth century. The final years of the

Napoleonic Wars and the years succeeding this long conflict saw a dramatic change of trends in naval law and accountability, set into the context of a very gradual change in law and attitudes between the 1749 Articles of War and the Naval Discipline Act in 1860. A great deal of change occurred during this century; much of it from 1812-1818. This period saw, among other trends, greater proportions of offenses coming to courts martial and a reduction in capital and corporal publishments – hanging and extreme floggings – a process that continued through the *Pax Britannica*, and the Royal Navy trending away from the vibrant stereotypes prevalent in the nineteenth and twentieth centuries, characterized by Winston's Churchill's quips about 'rum, buggery, and the lash'.

8

Antwerp: Britain's Achilles Heel

Paul Leyland

Between 1721 and 1815 Britain cemented its position as a Great Power and laid the foundations to become the first global superpower. While British armies often fought on the Continent during this period, British success is typically attributed primarily to state financial strength and the Royal Navy.[1] These forces drove British commercial-imperial expansion and allowed targeted Coalition-based interventions in Continental wars to further British interests, later referred to as a 'Blue Water' policy.[2] However, a point often missed by history is that France had the solution to directly challenge Britain's maritime superiority sitting quite literally on its doorstep. Just 80 miles from France's northern border is the port-city of Antwerp on the River Scheldt, with the Dutch-Belgian border cutting through the estuary. Antwerp was Britain's Achilles Heel, as the prospect of its occupation and use by France or other hostile powers threatened to undermine Britain's Blue Water strategy and therefore to threaten Britain's Great Power status. Britain could not be safe unless Antwerp and the Scheldt could be defended.

The Greatest Port in Christendom: The Armada and the End of Antwerp's Golden Age

Today, Antwerp is the second largest port in Europe, behind only nearby Rotterdam in the Netherlands. But while Rotterdam requires industrial dredging to maintain, Antwerp is a natural deep-water harbour. During the mid-sixteenth century Antwerp was the largest port in the world, handling around 2,500 ships per week.[3] To put Antwerp's Renaissance

---

1   See John Brewer, *The Sinews of Power: War, Money and the English State* (Cambridge: Harvard University Press, 1989); which explained and popularised this thesis.

2   See Daniel A. Baugh, 'Great Britain's Blue Water Policy, 1689-1815,' *The International History Review*, 10:1 (1988), pp.33-58.

3   D.J.B. Trim, 'Medieval and Early-Modern Inshore, Estuarine, Riverine and Lacustrine Warfare,' in D.J.B. Trim and Mark C. Fissel (eds) *Amphibious Warfare 1000-1700: Commerce, state formation and European Expansion* (Boston: Brill, 2006), pp.357-419.

maritime scale into context, the whole of England had only 1,642 registered merchant ships in 1582 (excluding small coastal vessels), growing to 3,281 in 1701, and a British total of around 7–8,000 in the 1750s through 1780s.[4] Similarly, Antwerp's mid-sixteenth century population of around 100,000 rivalled London and dwarfed Amsterdam. Antwerp's position at the mouth of the Rhine estuarine system made it easy to supply as well as an ideal entrepot. Antwerp is also only 140 miles from the English coast, less than a day's sailing in seaworthy vessels with a following wind. Antwerp in the hands of a Great Power could therefore develop a significant commercial, naval, and military threat to Britain.

When parts of the Low Countries revolted against Philip II of Spain's rule in the late 1560s, the English government feared that France would put England at a structural maritime disadvantage by seizing Antwerp and the coastal provinces. Lord Burghley, Elizabeth I's senior minister, wrote a memorandum in July 1580 which explained the nature of the potential French risk to England; advice that would remain relevant two centuries later:

> ...it is very probable the countries will be annexed to the Crown of France in time to come, notwithstanding any limitations to the contrary. It is also likely that the Crown and realm of England which have of old been confederate with those countries for their mutual defence against France, will by this alteration be weakened, and for lack of the ancient league become subject to the power of France. Besides, by this 'adjunction' of the Low Countries to France, especially of the islands [Walcheren]; as Holland, Zealand, and the other maritime countries, as Flanders and Brabant [Antwerp], England will be at the command of France for the usual traffic by sea, and will also become inferior to France in navigation and power by sea; whereas now England is known to be far superior to France.[5]

However, in August 1585, the Spanish Army of Flanders secured control of Antwerp after a year-long siege.[6] In just five years, the main threat to England had shifted from the risk of France capturing parts of the Low Countries to Spain mounting a credible invasion from them.

The English response to this increased Spanish threat was the Treaty of Nonsuch, agreed between England and the Netherlands in July-August 1585, as Antwerp fell. The treaty promised 7,400 men and financial support for the rebels, as well as English military leadership. The English government was also given direct control over Flushing (Vlissingen) and Fort Rammekens on Walcheren as well as the port of Brill (Brielle) near Rotterdam. Flushing, Rammekens and Brill were known at the time and since as the 'Cautionary Towns' since their ostensible purpose was to keep the Dutch government honest in paying Elizabeth's

4   Abbott Payson Usher, 'The Growth of English Shipping 1572-1922', *The Quarterly Journal of Economics*, 42:3 (1928), pp.465-478.
5   'Elizabeth: July 1580, 6-10', in Sophie Crawford Lomas (ed.), *Calendar of State Papers Foreign: Elizabeth, Volume 19, August 1584-August 1585* (London: His Majesty's Stationery Office, 1916), pp.341-352.
6   'Elizabeth: August 1585, 1-10', in Lomas (ed.), *Calendar of State Papers Foreign: Elizabeth, Volume 19, August 1584-August 1585*, pp.643-655.

loans back.[7] However, any number of towns further away from Spanish forces could have been more safely chosen, whereas the strategic rationale for an English occupation of the Cautionary Towns was both compelling and decisive. Flushing was the only major deep-sea harbour on the Dutch-Belgian coast (Sluis had a very narrow entrance due to sand banks), while the guns of Fort Rammekens prevented large fleets from sailing safely into the deep but confined Scheldt estuary to get to Antwerp. However, while these key strategic locations on Walcheren could be easily held thanks to Anglo-Dutch coastal sea control, they could not be easily supplied and Walcheren was an infamously sickly island. The occupation of Brill solved this problem by securing a supply of fresh food and water from the mainland, as well as an entrepot for English deployment inland. The Treaty of Nonsuch therefore denied key maritime infrastructure to the enemy, ensured that the garrison could be kept supplied and healthy, and ensured that England's vital interests could not be betrayed or let down by local forces. Around 4,000 English troops flooded into Walcheren immediately the treaty was agreed.[8]

The rapid deployment of an English garrison to Walcheren in 1585 effectively sealed the fate of the Armada three years before it sailed. It is well known that when the Armada reached the Channel-North Sea junction in August 1588 it had no port that it could use to meet the Army of Flanders, since the seaward approach to Dunkirk-Ostend where the troops were concentrated was too shallow for ocean-going ships. The waiting Army of Flanders dwindled due to sickness, the Armada was running perilously short of supplies and was scattered by fireships from an exposed anchorage off Calais; the two forces were never able to combine.[9] The use of Antwerp would have solved Spain's combined operations problems: the soldiers could be kept supplied using river traffic, the fleet could be refitted and resupplied without being exposed, and the army could embark from a large port. It has never been recognised that the key to the strategic failure of the Armada was the denial of Antwerp by a small but brilliantly placed English garrison.

After 1585, the English garrison on Walcheren and the Dutch navy prevented Antwerp's use as a port by blockade. Merchants and trade diverted to hitherto much smaller Dutch ports, and this became the major contributor to the Dutch Golden Age.[10] Antwerp was contested between Spanish and Dutch forces throughout the Eighty Years War, which contributed to the port's decline. Lacking international traffic and suffering from on-and-off warfare, the city's population fell from around 100,000 in the 1560s to less than 50,000 by the mid-eighteenth century and its maritime infrastructure disappeared.[11] However,

7   W. Frischy, 'A "Financial Revolution" Reconsidered: Public Finance in Holland during the Dutch Revolt 1568-1648', *The Economic History Review*, 56:1 (2003), pp.57-89.
8   'Elizabeth: August 1585, 1-10,' in Lomas (ed.), *Calendar of State Papers Foreign: Elizabeth, Volume 19, August 1584-August 1585*, pp.643-655.
9   Colin Martin and Geoffrey Parker, *Armada: The Spanish Enterprise and England's Deliverance in 1588* (New Haven: Yale University Press, 2022), p.58; 'Elizabeth: August 1585, 1-10,' Lomas (ed.), *Calendar of State Papers Foreign: Elizabeth, Volume 19, August 1584-August 1585*, pp.643-655.
10   Oscar C. Gelderblom, 'From Antwerp to Amsterdam: The Contribution of Merchants from the Southern Netherlands to the Commercial Expansion of Amsterdam (c. 1540 – 1609)', *Review*, 26:3 (2003), pp.247-282.
11   Bruno Blondé and Ilja van Damme, 'Retail growth and consumer changes in a declining urban economy: Antwerp (1650 – 1750)', *Economic History Review*, Vol.3 (2010), pp.638-663.

Antwerp's latent potential as a natural port remained if a Great Power could control both the city and the Scheldt estuary.

By the beginning of the eighteenth century, the strategic brilliance of the Treaty of Nonsuch had long been forgotten. The campaigns of William III and the Duke of Marlborough to prevent Louis XIV's France from over-running Belgium and the Netherlands were seen as dangerously Continentalist by many British politicians and commentators, rather than as a key to Britain's maritime security. Queen Anne turned her back on such costly 'adventures' to adopt a supposedly 'traditional' Blue Water strategy, as she explained in her Queen's Speech in March 1714, shortly after the Peace of Utrecht:

> I congratulate my own subjects, that they are delivered from a consuming Land War and entered on a Peace, the good effects whereof nothing but intestine divisions [internal politics] can obstruct. It was the glory of the wisest and greatest of my predecessors to hold the balance of Europe and to keep it equal by calling in their weight as necessity required. By this conduct they enriched the Kingdom and rendered themselves dreadful to their enemies, and useful to their friends. I have proceeded on the same principle and I doubt not that my successors will follow these examples. Our situation points to us our true interest, for this country can only flourish by trade and will be most formidable by the right application of our naval force.[12]

Nevertheless, British statesmen could not ignore the security of Belgium, so they came up with a seductively cheap fix. By the terms of the Treaty of Utrecht and contemporaneous Barrier Treaties (1709-1715), Britain effectively outsourced the defence of Belgium to Habsburg Austria (which acquired the Habsburg territories in the Low Countries following the Bourbon accession in Spain), supported by a fortified Barrier on the Franco-Belgian border, maintained, and manned by Dutch money and troops.[13]

Georgian Britain had therefore inherited a security policy that relied upon the power and willingness of Austria and the Netherlands to defend Belgium in line with British interests. However, this outsourced security policy carried the very risk that the Treaty of Nonsuch was designed to eliminate with a permanent English garrison on Walcheren: Austria and the Netherlands might not always be willing or able to defend Belgium from a resurgent France.

A Great Incapacity to Hurt Us: France's Structural Maritime Flaws

Without access to a harbour of the scale and capability of Antwerp, France's ability to exercise sea power, or to mount an invasion of Britain, was severely compromised. As Burghley noted in 1580, England's maritime advantages over France were significant and maritime

---

12   'House of Lords Journal Volume 19: 2 March 1714,' in *Journal of the House of Lords: Volume 19, 1709-1714* (London: His Majesty's Stationery Office, 1767-1830), pp.624-628.

13   Randall Lessaffer 'Fortress Belgium: The 1715 Barrier Treaty,' *Oxford Public International Law*, <https://opil.ouplaw.com/page/520> (accessed 1 March 2023).

geography had not materially changed into the eighteenth century. When considering ports from a strategic perspective, there is a tendency to assess purely naval questions such as how many ships can be held, the depth of water, and the defensibility of the anchorages.[14] These are vital characteristics, but other attributes must be added to understand a port's ability to hold the large numbers of sailors and soldiers needed for an invasion or even to hold a fleet for any length of time:

- proximity to large population centres for easy access to fresh food and water;
- access to sufficient seaworthy vessels and competent crews to provide transport;
- the ability to supply the invasion forces with sufficient naval and military stores without interdiction;
- for invasion, proximity to the British Isles and prevailing winds.

When these additional attributes are factored in, the reason why France was never able to mount a successful invasion of Britain, or even keep a battlefleet together for any length of time becomes clear.

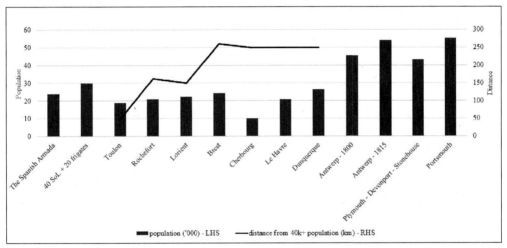

French port capacity, c.1800.

France's best naval base was Toulon. While the port was not especially defensible – as the French navy found to its cost during the sieges of 1707 and 1793 – and with a population of around 20,000 in 1800 was not big enough to sustain a significant body of men, Toulon is just 42 miles from Marseilles, which had a population of nearly 100,000 in 1800, and was serviced by large volumes of coastal shipping, which the Royal Navy struggled to interdict thousands of miles from home bases and some 250 miles from Menorca or Sardinia. Toulon proved its combined arms capability impressively: in 1756, 15,000 men invaded Menorca;[15]

---

14   For example, see Quinton Barry, *Far Distant Ships: The Blockade of Brest 1793-1815* (Warwick: Helion & Company, 2022), pp.4-5.

15   Daniel Baugh, *The Global Seven Years War, 1754-63: Britain and France in a Great Power Contest*

in 1798, 38,000 men invaded Egypt.[16] The 1798 French Egyptian campaign deployed a single-lift amphibious force of a scale that Britain only matched once before its own 1882 invasion of Egypt – to seize Walcheren in 1809 (with 40,000 men in 600 ships).[17] Toulon was also a key source of French warship construction. The ability of France to exploit Toulon's maritime strengths is significant because it demonstrates that where the right port infrastructure existed, France could exercise sea power. However, since Toulon was in the Mediterranean, it served little purpose as a direct threat to the British Isles, while British control of Gibraltar limited its Blue Water value.

France's main Atlantic naval base was Brest, promisingly close to the entrance to the Channel. Brest has a large, deep, natural harbour and was defensible.[18] Brest had a population of around 25,000 in 1800, but, unlike Toulon, it is hundreds of miles from any large cities; the regional capital Rennes was only the same size as Brest and some 150 miles away by road; Brest's riverine network also leads nowhere useful from a supply and logistics perspective. Given these constraints, the only way to keep Brest supplied was with coastal traffic, which became extremely challenging in wartime given the near-constant British naval blockade established from the Seven Years War onwards. Napoleon tried to fix Brest's logistical limitations by ordering the Brest-Nantes canal during a brief period of Anglo-French peace in 1802, but this was barely started during his turbulent reign due to manpower shortages. There was no commercial logic to building a 240-mile canal along a navigable coastline. The canal's purpose was military, to allow barges of supplies to get to Brest without interdiction, but it was not finished in time to be used in anger. Brest's remoteness meant that while more than 50 ships were often kept in the port, fewer than 20 were typically fully manned.[19]

Brest's remoteness was not the end of its problems as a port from which to develop sea power. For the Brest fleet to support an invasion, it would have to rendezvous in the Channel. However, the prevailing winds in the Channel are westerly, and an extension of the Gulf Stream system. The 'sou'westers', as they were colloquially called, kept French ships in port while they blew but allowed British ships to keep station off Brest. To get out of Brest, a French fleet would need an easterly wind, but this was the wrong wind to then tack into the Channel; an easterly wind also blows most reliably in the winter due to seasonal high pressure in Siberia (the Siberian anticyclone), when destructive storms are far more likely. Due to the unpredictability of easterly winds and the likely stormy conditions that accompanies them, synchronising operations between Brest and the Channel during the Age of Sail was all but impossible, with all the attendant risks that the escorting fleet and the invasion force would be unable to link up, become wrecked, or be defeated in detail. Brest's problems with prevailing winds were well known, as the polemicist Sir Richard Steele wrote in defence of British policy to prevent Dunkirk from being turned into a naval base in 1714:

     (London: Routledge, 2014), p.173.

16   Andrew Roberts, *Napoleon the Great* (London: Penguin 2015), p.209.

17   Robert M. Fiebel, 'What Happened At Walcheren: the primary medical sources', *Bulletin of the History of Medicine*, 42:1 (1968), pp.62-79.

18   Barry, *Far Distant Ships*, pp.4-5.

19   Barry, *Far Distant Ships*.pp.4-5: a chronic lack of sailors in France was another contributing factor, but this was also a direct result of limited maritime infrastructure, which in turn limited the number of commercial mariners from which to draw naval crews.

Brest lies without [that is to say, outside] the Channel, under this great Incapacity to hurt us, that the same Wind which carried our trade down the Channel prevents the ships of Brest from coming into it….If ships from Brest are appointed to way-lay our ships in the Channel, they must take the opportunity of Westerly Winds, to come into it; and wait the coming of an Easterly Wind to carry our ships down it; by this means they must all the time be at Sea, exposed to all the dangers for want of a Port in which to harbour their Men-of-War, or return to Brest, which they cannot do with the Wind that brought them out.[20]

France's subsidiary Atlantic naval bases of Rochefort and Lorient were even worse than Brest in terms of size, supply-chain limitations, and distance from Britain, while they faced the same wind issues due to their geography.

France had several Channel ports: Saint-Malo, Cherbourg, Le Havre, Dieppe, Boulogne, Calais, and Dunkirk. However, all were small and all but Le Havre, which is on the Seine estuary, were cut off from easy supply; they were largely self-contained fishing communities that could not cope with the prolonged presence of a major fleet or a large body of men. The structural limitations of these ports were revealed by Napoleon's invasion scheme of 1803-1805: Napoleon deployed his massive invasion force of some 150,000 men between Boulogne and Ostend.[21] An army that would concentrate to around seven miles frontage in battle was strung out across 120 miles of coastline. The problems of trying to coordinate ships and men across these distances would have been felt keenly at sea and on enemy shores, but the emperor had no choice but to plan based upon the available logistics. Further, because the French Channel ports were relatively small and isolated, they were vulnerable to British attack. For example, during the Seven Years War, British troops raided Rochefort, Saint-Malo (unsuccessfully), Cherbourg, and Le Havre.[22] In 1804, during the invasion scare, the Royal Navy bombarded and attacked the barges being assembled in Boulogne, albeit with limited success.[23] Even unsuccessful attacks presented considerable problems for the French, who were largely without the means to feasibly respond in kind.

The most serviceable French port in the Channel was Dunkirk, which is why the Treaty of Utrecht required that it could not be fortified.[24] However, because of the treacherous sandbanks that surrounded the harbour entrance, Dunkirk was only suitable for low-draft vessels, just as it was in 1940 once modern port facilities had been destroyed by bombing (hence the 'Little Ships'). Dunkirk was suitable for fishing boats, coasters, and privateers, but not for launching a large-scale invasion (or an evacuation for that matter), unless small vessels could carry men and equipment to bigger ships waiting in the Channel. Such a ferrying operation to anchored warships and transports would have been impossible with an alert Royal Navy from the 1740s onward, which obviously did not have to worry about the *Luftwaffe*.

---

20   Sir Richard Steele, 'The French Faith in the Present State of Dunkirk', Letter to the Editor, *The Examiner* (1714), pp.7-8.
21   Roberts, *Napoleon the Great*, p.200.
22   Baugh, *The Global Seven Years War*, pp.262-268, 308-311, 424.
23   Roberts, *Napoleon the Great*, p.411.
24   Sir Richard Steele, 'The French Faith in the Present State of Dunkirk', Letter to the Editor, *The Examiner* (1714), pp.7-8.

Because French Channel trade was fragmented and mostly coastal, the French Channel ports could only provide the merchant shipping to transport in the region of 30,000 men in one go.[25] While 30,000 men might have been enough to catch Britain by surprise as war was declared, or to support a rebellion, it was not enough to defeat Britain if it was prepared. Consequently, a French invasion force large enough to be decisive would require specially constructed transport vessels. During the Age of Sail, 'specialist transport vessels' amounted to little more than flat-bottomed barges with a limited sailing rig and a few oars operated by grudging and untrained landlubbers.[26] Some barges had large guns mounted to offer theoretical defensive capabilities, but firing even medium artillery from a small, unstable, and hastily constructed platform at sea would probably have been more dangerous to the crew than to the target.

The Channel is a deceptive body of water which can be deadly for unseaworthy vessels or untrained crews. Popular historians tend to focus on the narrow 20 mile choke-point as an easy crossing point, but only the port of Calais is close, just 27 miles from Dover. Calais was a relatively small port during the Age of Sail, which could not support a large force. France's other Channel ports are much further from Britain: Dunkirk is 45 miles, Boulogne 47 miles, Ostend 66 miles, Cherbourg 80 miles, and Le Havre – logistically France's best Channel port – is 125 miles away from the British coast. A barge propelled by limited sail and oars would take around eight hours to make a 45-mile crossing in calm conditions and a following wind, but could take over 12 with contrary winds and conditions.[27] Combined with the time taken to load supplies and embark thousands of soldiers this amounted to a days-long process, which would alert vessels watching the Channel coast. Unless a French fleet had diverted or destroyed the Channel Fleet and other regional commands, the barge flotilla would have been extremely vulnerable to interdiction, even by frigates, sloops, and privateers. However, the Royal Navy would probably not have had to fire a shot to destroy a barge flotilla in the Channel. Barges were unseaworthy and poorly manned by definition. The chances of eight to 12 daylight hours of fine weather and a following wind in the Channel are slim even during the summer; anything else was likely to have proved fatal to the expedition and many of the men involved. If any barges lost course due to winds, currents, or navigational errors, especially coming from the shortest point around the Calais region, they might end up in the relatively open North Sea, which would have doomed them if not promptly rescued. A strong headwind would prevent a crossing, a squall or rising seas would cause many to flounder, a storm would likely have caused severe losses, especially if the barges were already miles from shore.

A quick comparison to Britain's maritime infrastructure is instructive. London and its subsidiary ports like Chatham had all the naval supplies, fresh food, and fresh water a fleet and even an army could possibly need. It might be difficult for a fleet based in the Thames to get into the Channel if a sou'wester was blowing, but it could defend the capital with

---

25   This figure can be deduced from the fact that enough shipping existed to transport 30,000 men in the planned invasion of 1778, but that the 1759 invasion plan for 60,000 men required specialist barges to be constructed; both of these invasion plans are discussed in the next section.

26   For example, see Roberts, *Napoleon the Great*, p.387.

27   A calculation accurately made by Parma in 1586 and unchanged in Napoleon's time; see Martin and Parker, *Armada*, p.169.

relative ease. Britain had two major ports directly on the Channel to counter any French move from Brest or the Channel ports: Portsmouth (including Portsea and Gosport), and Plymouth (including Devonport). Both main British Channel ports were large urban conurbations with over 40,000 people each in 1801 and were teaming with coastal traffic of every sort.[28] Plymouth could be used as a base to guard the Atlantic mouth of the Channel and blockade Brest directly; Portsmouth was a point of resupply and sea control mid-Channel, protected by the Isle of Wight. Beyond these, there were many smaller ports and anchorages that could be used as points of supply and refuge for the Channel Fleet. France had nothing to compare to these ports for effectively deploying and sustaining a navy into the Channel. However, France's severe maritime limitations were more significant in shaping the outcome of the great Anglo-French maritime contest than Britain's relative advantages: French efforts often simply defeated themselves.

Pre-1804 Blue Water security and Continental Commitments

France quickly re-emerged as a territorially acquisitive Great Power after the wars of Louis XIV during the War of the Polish Succession (1733-1738). However, French strategy was not to attack the vulnerable Austrian Netherlands to ensure that Austria was isolated from its theoretical allies Britain and the Dutch Republic.[29] The French plan worked and Britain chose not to support its Austrian ally and key security partner, leading to Austria's defeat. Similarly, when Frederick II of Prussia seized Silesia from Austria in 1740, Britain initially did nothing to support its Austrian ally until Prime Minister Robert Walpole was ousted in late 1741.[30]

Frederick II's attack had exposed Austria as weak and vulnerable. Louis XV's government saw an opportunity to destroy Habsburg Austria as a Great Power, especially given Britain's insouciance in the face of Austrian desperation and the distraction of a war with Spain (Jenkins' Ear). However, the new British government was alert to its vital interests in Belgium. In 1742, Britain sent 16,000 troops to Ostend, in response to fears that France might widen the war by attacking the Austrian Netherlands.[31] While 16,000 men were unlikely to turn the tide, it at least signalled Britain's willingness to fight and in any event it was the only force Britain could muster. In a telling logistical twist to the British deployment plan, the deep-water Scheldt could not be used because the Dutch Republic was determined to remain neutral in the coming conflict and so would not give the Royal Navy access. The inability to use deep-water ports had important and severely limiting operational implications: the British merchant vessels used to carry the army to Ostend had to be under 200

28   British urban population figures taken from the 1801 Census available via <www.visionofbritain. uk> (accessed February 2023).

29   John L. Sutton, *The King's Honor and the King's Cardinal: the War of the Polish Succession*, (Lexington: University of Kentucky Press, 1980), p.19

30   Reed Browning, *The War of the Austrian Succession* (New York: St Martin's Press, 1993), p.100.

31   David Syrett, 'Towards Dettingen: The Conveyancing of the British Army to Flanders in 1742,' *Journal of the Society for Army Historical Research*, 84:340 (2006), pp.316-326.

tons burden in order to navigate the treacherous waters off southern Belgium.[32] Therefore, in 1742, all Britain could do in the face of a potential French threat that would likely number over 100,000 men was to send a small army into the broader theatre, making it essentially dependent upon the Austrian forces it was there to support. This was precisely the problem that the 1585 Treaty of Nonsuch solved by ensuring that English vital interests were directly and sustainably defended by English troops.

In late 1743 France and Britain rapidly headed towards formal war. French policymakers attempted a 'quick win' solution to stop Britain's proxy support for Austria: France would launch a surprise pro-Stuart invasion of Britain while a large portion of the available British Army was still on the Belgian-German border. By January 1744 France had concentrated 12,000 men at Dunkirk, for which there was enough organic coastal shipping to lift them to Britain as one body. The Brest fleet sailed in support of the invasion, only loosely coordinated due to the challenges of distance, weather, and the need to maintain surprise. The escort fleet was caught by a British squadron and a storm, which forced it to turn back. The French transport ships were also caught in a storm, which sank 12. It remains doubtful that 12,000 French soldiers could have achieved much had they landed, but they did not get more than a few miles into the treacherous Channel before the invasion was destroyed by an alert British squadron and the weather.[33]

The failure of the 1744 invasion highlights three key factors which French control of Antwerp and the Scheldt would have solved:

- The separation of the Brest fleet from the invasion force made it vulnerable to interception or weather damage before it could carry out its escorting duty; the Scheldt provided ample space and resources for the invasion flotilla and the escorting fleet to assemble as one force.
- It would remain tempting for French forces to sail in dangerous weather (although this time winter was a diplomatic choice), partly due the prevalence of easterly winds necessary to exit Brest, partly because it gave the best chance to evade British naval forces; exiting the Scheldt on an easterly wind would allow an invasion of Britain to occur in one swift movement while providing an easy point of retreat if a strong sou'wester blew, the easterly needed to exit and invade would also make it very challenging for any blockading forces to stay on station
- France's lack of sufficient maritime infrastructure in the Channel meant that it was impossible to lift large bodies of men quickly and a small invasion force would need to be backed by a successful revolution to have any hope of success; it would take just a few years of investment for the Scheldt to produce all the commercial and naval shipping France could need, as both Renaissance history and the Napoleonic future would demonstrate.

Despite this failed invasion attempt, the inherent problem of outsourced Belgian security arrangements of the Peace of Utrecht now revealed itself. France assembled a force of

---

32   Browning, *War of the Austrian Succession*, pp.134-140.
33   Browning, *War of the Austrian Succession*, pp.156-158.

over 100,000 men to attack the Austrian Netherlands in 1744. A combination of superior numbers, the planned distraction of the 1745 Jacobite Rebellion for British forces, and a renewed Prussian offensive against Austria in 1744-1745, ensured that France was able to gain the upper hand in Belgium and take Antwerp in 1746. By 1748, French forces had captured Bergen-Op-Zoom from the Dutch on the north bank of the Scheldt, and were poised to invade the Netherlands. Louis XV was on the cusp of gaining a major deep water port for France, with the Netherlands powerless to stop the unblocking of the Scheldt in the face of a threatened French invasion. To resolve this dangerous situation, British security policy introduced a new actor into the defence of the Low Countries: Russia. The slow progress of a 37,000 man Russian army from Eastern Europe to the Netherlands, largely financed by Britain, was one of the reasons why France decided to make peace in 1748.[34]

A combination of war-weariness, the imminent arrival of a new enemy, and mounting financial concerns led Louis XV to accept the return of his colonies taken by Britain and to give Belgium back to Austria through the Treaty of Aix-la-Chapelle.[35] By giving up Belgium for colonies, Louis XV and his advisors missed the point that was clear to Lord Burghley in 1580 when Antwerp was still a major port: by controlling Belgium and threatening a weak Netherlands for access to the Scheldt, France could develop the capability reconquer its colonies in later wars using a much stronger maritime economy. The Treaty of Aix-la-Chapelle seemed to reinforce the security status quo for Habsburg Belgium at great cost to Britain, Austria and the Dutch Republic. However, Austria's foreign and security policy now firmly pivoted to Central Europe and Italy, with the Austrian Netherlands seen as little more than a tempting pawn to give away to anyone that could help to fulfil Austria's strategic priorities.

The convoluted diplomatic and miliary manoeuvrings which led to the Diplomatic Revolution and the outbreak of the Seven Years War contained two elements that directly related to Belgium and therefore Antwerp. First, in 1755 the Austrian government insisted that Britain subsidise a Russian army to counter the threat from Prussia if Austria were to be expected to defend Belgium from France again, since France was still allied to Prussia and becoming increasingly antagonistic towards Britain over unresolved colonial disputes. The Austrian government was making it clear that it was no longer prepared to defend Belgium with its own resources. However, Austria took over the Russian subsidy treaty in January 1757 to bring Russia into the war against Prussia and against British interests, under a transformed geopolitical situation.[36]

Second, in May 1757 France and Austria signed the Second Treaty of Versailles to bring France directly into the war against Prussia, alongside Russia. At this time, Britain and France had been formally at war for a year (and for several years at war unofficially in North America), but the only major action in Europe between the two maritime powers had been the French seizure of Menorca. By the terms of the Second Treaty of Versailles, French soldiers were allowed to occupy the previously Dutch-manned Barrier Fortress towns on the Franco-Belgian border (Chimay, Beaumont Ypres, Furnes, and Mons) as well as the Belgian North Sea ports of Nieuwpoort and Ostend, which denied Britain direct maritime access to Belgium. Belgium was therefore immediately rendered defenceless. However,

---

34   Browning, *War of the Austrian Succession*, pp.199-206, 240-244, 279-285, 302-316, 337-341, 352.
35   Browning, *War of the Austrian Succession*, p.353.
36   Franz A.J. Szabo, *The Seven Years War In Europe* (London: Routledge, 2013), pp.13-48.

the major prize would be that if Austria, France, Russia, and Sweden were successful in wresting Silesia from a surrounded and heavily outnumbered Prussia, then Belgium would become Bourbon under Philip Bourbon-Farnese, Duke of Parma.[37] Belgium would therefore be taken out of its ancient Habsburg orbit as a counter to France and effectively made a defenceless French satellite state under a Bourbon dynasty. As an added incentive for France to escalate a European war, the French military route to Prussia was through Hanover, which would provide another powerful bargaining chip to add to Menorca, since George II would almost certainly want his electorate back and the British government had already proved willing to hand back colonial gains to achieve the European status quo in 1748.

French strategy for 1757 can therefore be seen as far more sound than is typically presented, and it contained a military-diplomatic endgame which would have challenged British maritime superiority through effective French control of Belgium. With Belgium in play, British maritime security now depended on the security of Hanover and the staying power of Prussia. However, despite the sound strategy, France botched the execution of the 1757 campaign after a promising start; Hanover and Prussia were saved from defeat.[38]

In 1759, with the Seven Years War now going badly for France, the French government once more planned to invade Britain to secure a quick and decisive victory. Unlike in 1744, Britain was on a war footing, with an active naval blockade of Brest, an ever-expanding army, and a sizeable militia. It was not possible to threaten Britain with 12,000 men, but British forces could be more credibly challenged by Choiseul's plan for a 40,000-man invasion of England, supported by a further 20,000 landing in Scotland. However, France did not have the shipping to move such a large body of men, meaning hundreds of barges were built as transports and concentrated at Le Havre. Choiseul understood the need for concentration and speed, but his plan had serious operational and logistical flaws:

- realizing the inability to coordinate an escort due to the blockade of Brest, Choiseul initially ruled out any naval escort, relying instead on surprise;
- the main invasion force concentrated in Le Havre, which was France's biggest and easiest port to supply on the Channel, but for that reason it was watched by the Royal Navy and raided in July; there could be no surprise (in August the Duc de Belle-Isle hoped to mount the invasion from Ostend instead; a movement easier to undertake for the soldiers than the assembled shipping);
- the lack of surprise was a problem, since the distance from Le Havre to Britain is at least 125 miles, which would take a barge travelling at approximately five miles per hour an entire 24 hours to make the crossing, including all the perils of being forced to sail during the night (collisions, getting lost), sudden changes in the weather, and the devastating encroachments of the Royal Navy on a practically undefended flotilla.

Finally, a watered-down plan was settled upon, involving fewer than 20,000 men being transported in seagoing vessels from Britany escorted by a squadron from Brest, in the hope that it could trigger a rebellion or diversion.[39] In other words, French strategy was to

---

37   Szabo, *The Seven Years War*, pp.48-51.
38   Szabo, *The Seven Years War*, pp.77-79.
39   Baugh, *Global Seven Years War*, pp.424-426; the volume of available shipping and crews to lift the

attempt a re-run of the disastrous 1744 invasion attempt against a more prepared enemy. The Brest fleet could only put to sea in October, when the weather was bad enough to drive the Royal Navy away from its blockading stations, but it was soon caught and destroyed while trying to seek shelter in Quiberon Bay on the French Atlantic coast in November 1759.[40] The Quiberon disaster came far too late in the season to attempt an invasion even with seaworthy transports, as the 1744 experience had demonstrated 15 years before with the loss of transports. The same problems revealed in 1744 and 1759 would have been largely fixed by the same solution: control of Antwerp and the Scheldt. The absence of suitable port logistics on the French Channel coast continued to give a decisive naval advantage to Britain.

A generation later, France and Spain were allied with the Thirteen Colonies fighting the War of American Independence. The French Navy had been rebuilt and expanded, and critically an alliance with Spain was agreed before the French navy could be defeated in detail, as had happened in the Seven Years War. In 1779 a powerful Franco-Spanish 'Armada' of 66 ships of the line gained effective sea control of the Channel; for a few weeks in the summer, the Royal Navy was outnumbered and initially off station. However, this potentially decisive operational success was made strategically irrelevant by two related factors. First, the Franco-Spanish fleet was poorly provisioned and lacked a major port to put into to resupply: Brest inevitably had insufficient supplies for such a large fleet given its remoteness, while entering Brest would have meant leaving the Channel and ceding the initiative to the Royal Navy, as Sir Richard Steele had explained. Due to the lack of a major Channel-North Sea port, the Franco-Spanish fleet could not stay in the critical theatre of operations for long. Second, while some 30,000 men had been assembled for the capture of Portsea Island (now part of Portsmouth), no attempt was made to coordinate this force with the fleet, which meant that temporary naval ascendancy in British home waters could not be exploited in time.[41] While the failure to coordinate land and sea assets was a French own goal, it also once more demonstrated the extreme difficulties in conducting combined arms operations without a major port in the Channel. France simply lacked the port infrastructure to resupply a fleet or keep 30,000 men in readiness on transports to exploit what could only be a structurally fleeting moment of maritime superiority in British home waters.

By the late 1700s, the Low Countries had declined in importance in Austrian foreign policy, and they even considered trading some or all of the region for Bavaria during the Bavarian succession crisis (though the conflict ended with a status quo mediation).[42] While Austria's interest in the region declined, so too did the Dutch Republic's ability to defend it due to losses suffered in the Fourth Anglo-Dutch War (1780-1784). Ironically, the Royal Navy significantly accelerated the decline of the Dutch Republic as a major power, leaving it

---

invasion force had been significantly reduced from peacetime levels by privateering activity.

40   Baugh, *Global Seven Years War*, pp.438-443.
41   Frank McLynn, *Invasion: From the Armada to Hitler: 1588-1945* (London: Routledge and Keegan Paul, 1987), pp.73-79.
42   Karl Otmar Freiherr von Aretin, 'Russia as a Guarantor Power of the Imperial Constitution under Catherine II,' *The Journal of Modern History*, 58, Supplement: Politics and Society in the Holy Roman Empire, 1500-1806 (1986), pp.141-160.

financially crippled, strategically vulnerable, and facing revolution.[43] By the 1780s Belgian security was therefore in a very dangerous position, unable to rely upon either its Habsburg overlords or its once-powerful Dutch neighbour for protection.

In 1792, when the War of the First Coalition broke out, Britain initially remained neutral, despite the likelihood of Belgium becoming a theatre of operations in a war between Austria, allied to Prussia, and France. Even following the defeat at Valmy, the British chose not to intervene. Soon after, however, the French secured control of the Belgian coast after the Battle of Jemappes.[44] Antwerp was under French occupation, and on 16 November 1792 the French government declared that it would open the Scheldt to shipping. Britain had little choice but to go to war in February 1793 as the news of Belgium's occupation and the Scheldt's opening percolated.[45]

Britain tried to lead an Austrian-Dutch-Prussian-British coalition to regain and hold Belgium, but the defence of Belgium only really mattered to an unprepared Britain and a declining Netherlands. France gained the upper hand in the Low Countries campaigns in 1793 and 1794 in no small part because of Britain's lack of military preparedness or competence.[46] The result was that Belgium and then the Netherlands were over-run by the winter of 1794-1795. The Netherlands quickly became a French satellite, allowing French control of the Scheldt-Rhine maritime-commercial system that became and remained the backbone of European trade.[47] In 1795 Austria fully deprioritised the defence of Belgium after Prussia made a separate peace with France, forcing British troops to withdraw from the theatre. The French annexation of Belgium was formalised in the 1797 Treaty of Campo Formio and Austria would never again try to recover its northern-European possessions.[48] Britain now lacked any credible means of removing French forces from Belgium, which was rapidly assimilated into metropolitan France. Britain's largely outsourced defence plan for Belgium had finally met its ignominious end.

However, the British government had one decisive operational advantage in managing the maritime risk of a French Belgium with a Dutch client state that was not available to Elizabeth I. Antwerp had been uninvested as a port since it was blockaded from 1585 and its disuse was legally sanctioned from 1648. The French Revolutionary government might have declared the Scheldt open for trade again, but after over two centuries of disuse it would take considerable sums of money and several years of effort to turn Antwerp into a great port once more, an effort that was beyond embattled Revolutionary France.

In 1801 as Britain once more feared invasion, Admiral Lord St Vincent, who was commander of the Channel Fleet and would soon become one of Britain's most effective

43   H.M. Scott, 'Sir Joseph Yorke, Dutch Politics and the Origins of the Fourth Anglo-Dutch War,' *The Historical Journal*, 31:3 (1988), pp.571-589.
44   R. Hayes, 'General O'Moran and the French Revolution: Part II. The French Invasion of Belgium,' *Studies: Irish Quarterly Review*, 23:89 (1934), pp.42-58.
45   Charles Esdaile, *The Wars of the French Revolution, 1792-1801* (London: Routledge, 2019) p.85.
46   R.N.W. Thomas, 'Wellington in the Low Countries 1794-95,' *The International History Review*, 11:1 (1989), pp.14-30.
47   Robert Mark Spaulding, 'Revolutionary France and the Transformation of the Rhine,' *Central European History*, 44:2 (2011), pp.203-226.
48   Paul W. Schroeder, '"An Unnatural 'Natural Alliance" Castlereagh, Metternich and Aberdeen in 1813,' *The International History Review*, 10:4, (1988), pp.522-540.

professional heads of the navy, famously quipped 'I do not say, my Lords, that the French will not come. I say only they will not come by sea'.[49] It is tempting to read St Vincent's statement as an expression of confidence in beating the French at sea or as morale-boosting bravado, but with Antwerp unusable France still had to plan invasions of Britain using the Channel ports, as Napoleon was to continue in 1803-1805. However, a speech made by the Secretary of State for War Lord Liverpool, in January 1810, suggests that St Vincent and his naval colleagues were acutely aware of the limitations of French ports and the importance of the Scheldt. When defending the government's 1809 attempt to seize Walcheren and Antwerp during the Parliamentary Inquiry into the disaster, Liverpool explained that:

> It was known to be a favourite measure of our enemy to form a naval arsenal and dock at the mouth of the Scheldt, and it had been always admitted by professional men, that if an invasion of this country were ever to be attempted, it could never be effected but from the Scheldt.[50]

A Pistol at England's Heart: Napoleonic Antwerp

For all St Vincent's confidence, there was a clear and obvious risk that Antwerp would be brought into use as soon as France had a chance. As Colonel Crawford MP explained in the House of Commons in December 1803, after the fragile Peace of Amiens of 1802 had collapsed into renewed Anglo-French war:

> Without at all entering into the merits of that treaty [of Amiens], I shall merely say, that, even if after the conclusion of it, the conduct of the French government had been apparently pacific; yet, when we consider that by that treaty we recognized them as legitimate sovereigns of the Netherlands [Belgium], and that the possession of that country, which at any time would have given France a predominant influence in Holland [the Netherlands], does in the present state of Europe give them the absolute command of it; it undoubtedly behoved us to adopt a new and more enlarged military system than had ever before been deemed necessary, and to employ ourselves during the peace in strengthening our means of defence in proportion to the increased means of offence which France would possess in case of a renewal of war.[51]

However, the 'increased means of offence' available to France due to control over the Low Countries that Colonel Crawford referred to could not be immediately deployed and

---

49   Angus Konstam, *Naval Miscellany* (London: Bloomsbury Books, 2009), p.124.
50   Historic Lords Hansard, HL Debate 23 January 1810, vol 15 cc1-37, the Earl of Liverpool. *Historic Hansard Index, UK Parliament.* <https://hansard.parliament.uk/Lords/1810-01-23/debates/edf64572-8d76-4bd2-bd7c-7e7cc4841205/LordsChamber> (accessed 1 August 2023)
51   Historic Lords Hansard, HC Deb 12 December 1803 vol 1 cc261-303 *Historic Hansard Index, UK Parliament.* <https://api.parliament.uk/historic-hansard/commons/1803/dec/12/report-on-the-army-estimate> (accessed 1 August 2023)

Napoleon wanted rapid results. Napoleon's invasion plan of 1803-1805 was therefore a rehash of Choiseul's of 1759, with some notable but still ineffective changes. First, the invasion force was enlarged from 60,000 to 150,000 men, to take into account of the strengthened 'means of defence' available to Britain: 122 regular infantry battalions were stationed in Britain and Ireland in December 1804, with only 50 deployed overseas.[52] Second, an invasion flotilla of some 2,100 barges was brought closer to Britain than Le Havre, but had to be spread between Boulogne and Ostend (with an additional 300 from Dutch ports). Third, rather than sending no escort or a small squadron, a Franco-Spanish fleet would be sent to the West Indies in the hope of creating a diversion before joining forces with the Brest fleet to gain temporary sea control as the invasion flotilla sailed.[53] Napoleon's plan fell apart under the weight of its own complexity and Britain's successful attempt to bring Russia and Austria into the war. However, just as with the invasion attempts of 1744, 1759, and 1779, the lack of a major port near to Britain was the deciding factor in splitting the Franco-Spanish fleet from the key Channel-North Sea theatre, scattering the invasion forces over a very wide front, and relying on potentially lethal barges as troop transports.

By August 1805, Napoleon had abandoned his attempts to invade Britain, and French naval operations continued to be hampered by the lack of major ports and the isolation between the few France had. This is illustrated by the Battle of Trafalgar (21 October 1805). The Franco-Spanish Fleet was decisively defeated, but the actual losses in combat were not catastrophic. Only six of the 18 French ships of the line present were actually lost. However, three were wrecked in a storm shortly after the battle, four were captured off Cape Ortegal in November while attempting to reach French Atlantic bases, and five made it to Cadiz, only to be blockaded by the Mediterranean Fleet and later interned due to the Franco-Spanish War in 1808.[54] Had those ships access to French ports, or had they been able to effect a concentration closer to the English Channel, more may have survived. In other words, while the Royal Navy directly accounted for one third of the French ships of the line at Trafalgar, the lack of suitable port logistics from which to challenge the Royal Navy indirectly, but more decisively, accounted for the loss of two-thirds.

French losses at Trafalgar represented a brutal pattern that had started during the Seven Years War and was re-established over the course of the French Revolutionary wars. Changes in tactics and the growing superiority of British crews meant that the Royal Navy could increasingly engage to capture enemy ships through close combat and boarding actions rather than standing off for less decisive gunnery duels.[55] Between 1791 and 1800 French dockyards purpose-built an impressive 51 ships of the line despite the pressures of the Revolution.[56] However, 46 French ships of the line were lost in just four major engage-

52   Robert MacArthur, 'British Army Establishments During the Napoleonic Wars,' *Journal of the Society for Army Historical Research*, 87:350 (2009), pp.150-172.

53   Nick Lipscombe, 'Napoleon's Obsession – The Invasion of England,' *British Journal for Military History*, 1:3 (2015), pp.115-133.

54   'Battle of Trafalgar, 21st October 1805', *Three Decks*, <https://threedecks.org/index.php?display_type=show_battle&id=157> (accessed 25 August 2023); each ship present is linked to its service history and fate.

55   R. Mackay and M. Duffy, *Hawke, Nelson and British Naval Leadership, 1747-1805*, (Martlesham: Boydell Press 2009), pp.214-215 and *passim*.

56   *Three Decks*: ship search: originating as Purpose Built defined as Ships of the Line belonging to

ments over a roughly corresponding period: 10 at Toulon in 1793, seven at the Glorious First of June in 1794, 11 at the Nile in 1798, and the 18 present at Trafalgar (counting Trafalgar, Ortegal and Spanish internment).[57] France's inability to concentrate and supply sufficient ships of the line close to Britain due to the lack of suitable port infrastructure forced the dissipation of naval assets, leading to an unsustainable rate of attrition on the French navy as they were defeated in detail. Tellingly, during the same decade, Great Britain purpose built only 22 ships of the line; the lower tempo was sustainable because between 1793 and 1805 the Royal Navy captured 72 enemy ships of the line, many of which were brought into British service.[58] While French naval forces remained dissipated and poorly supplied outside the Mediterranean, the Royal Navy's ascendancy was assured.

France's most dangerous and credible attempt to wrest maritime dominance from Britain occurred after Trafalgar for precisely the reason that Lord Burghley warned in 1580: possession of the Low Countries, especially the Scheldt, could tip the maritime balance of power in France's favour. On 4 July 1807, just days after the Peace of Tilsit ended war with Russia, Napoleon wrote to Denis Decrès, his Minister of the Navy and the Colonies: 'The continental war is over. Energies must be turned towards the navy'.[59] Unlike previous invasion schemes, Napoleon's plan from 1807 was simple and dangerously effective. On 30 June 1811, British Admiralty intelligence reported the Emperor believed that 'we shall be able to make peace with safety when we have 150 Ships of the Line – and in spite of the obstacles of War, such is the state of the Empire that we will shortly have that number.'[60] Given that the Royal Navy's strength was then hovering around 110 operational ships of the line and this was seriously testing manning constraints, Napoleon's strategic thinking was robust. Napoleon came close to achieving his strategic aims, with 80 major warships completed by late 1812 and another 35 building: rapidly approaching parity with the Royal Navy.[61]

The entire basis of Alfred Thayer Mahan's later massively influential critique of British maritime success during the Age of Sail was that Britain could and did sustain a battlefleet to contain or defeat much smaller and less effective French squadrons: in simple terms, the battlefleet was the answer to sea power.[62] What Mahan and others only partially recognised

France, from 1791 to before 1801. <https://threedecks.org/index.php?display_type=ships_search> (accessed 30 August 2023)

57   'Siege of Toulon, 29th August 1793 – 19th December 1793', *Three Decks* <https://threedecks.org/index.php?display_type=show_battle&id=994> (accessed 30 August 2023); 'Glorious 1st of June, 1st June 1794', *Three Decks*, <https://threedecks.org/index.php?display_type=show_battle&id=147> (accessed 30 August 2023); 'Battle of the Nile, 1st August 1798', *Three Decks*, <https://threedecks.org/index.php?display_type=show_battle&id=151> (accessed 30 August 2023); 'Battle of Trafalgar, 21st October 1805', *Three Decks*, <https://threedecks.org/index.php?display_type=show_battle&id=157> (accessed 30 August 2023); 'Battle of Cape Ortegal, 4th November 1805', *Three Decks*, <https://threedecks.org/index.php?display_type=show_battle&id=158> (accessed 30 August 2023)

58   *Three Decks*: ship search: originating as Captured defined as Ships of the Line belonging to Great Britain, from 1793 to before 1806. <https://threedecks.org/index.php?display_type=ships_search> (accessed 30 August 2023)

59   Peter Hicks, 'Napoleon, Tilsit, Copenhagen and Portugal', *Napoleonica, La Revue*, 2, (2008), pp.87-99.

60   Richard Glover, 'The French Fleet: Britain's problem; Madison's Opportunity', *The Journal of Modern History*, 39:3 (1967), pp.233-252.

61   Glover, 'The French Fleet', pp.233-252.

62   Alfred Thayer Mahan, *The Influence of Sea Power upon History 1660-1783* (Boston: Little, Brown &

was that this was not a question of inferior French doctrine or state resource allocation, but the iron grip of port logistics and maritime infrastructure. Napoleon had already learned the lesson that Mahan would later teach after his 1803-1805 invasion plan unravelled. To defeat Britain, Napoleon would need a large battlefleet that could be deployed close to British home waters which could not be defeated in detail, and so he sought to build one.

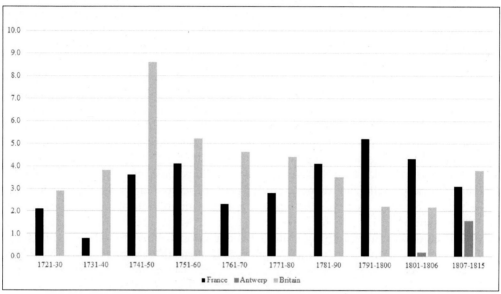

Annual Ship of the Line Output, France, Antwerp, and Britain[63]

Antwerp was key to Napoleon's naval construction programme. Between 1807 and 1814, France and French satellites completed 42 ships of the line, with 14 or 33 percent of these constructed at Antwerp.[64] The building of larger ships of the line occurred from 1810, once the new deep-water docks were ready and after the ill-fated Walcheren expedition had taken place.[65] To this day the Port of Antwerp credits Napoleon's investment for its rebirth as a major port.[66]

Co, 1890).

63   *Three Decks*: ship search: originating as Purpose Built defined as Ships of the Line belonging to France, subset launched at Antwerpen, from 1807 to before 1815. <https://threedecks.org/index.php?display_type=ships_search> (accessed 30 August 2023)

64   *Three Decks*: ship search: originating as Purpose Built defined as Ships of the Line belonging to France, subset launched at Antwerpen, from 1807 to before 1815. <https://threedecks.org/index.php?display_type=ships_search> (accessed 30 August 2023)

65   *Three Decks*: ship search: originating as Purpose Built defined as Ships of the Line belonging to France, subset launched at Antwerpen, from 1807 to before 1815. <https://threedecks.org/index.php?display_type=ships_search> (accessed 30 August 2023)

66   'The history of the port of Antwerp,' *Port of Antwerp*, <https://www.portofantwerpbruges.com/en/our-port/world-port/history-port-antwerp> (accessed 1 May 2023).

As well as becoming the preeminent French port for shipbuilding, Antwerp could provide shelter and supplies for the accumulating ships, other French squadrons, and a large military force, just 140 miles from Britain. The French build-up at Antwerp therefore significantly reduced the risks of split forces, poor logistics and long voyages that destroyed previous French invasion attempts. Crucially, because they were mostly kept in a safe port, these ships were not captured by the Royal Navy and so French shipbuilding began to accumulate. While there was no doubt that British crews were far more experienced than anything Napoleon could bring together from France, the Netherlands, Italy, Denmark, and the German Hanse towns that France then controlled (an impressive list of European maritime regions), numbers start to have a quality of their own, especially if those numbers gave the French navy greater confidence to sortie in strength. Antwerp also had a significant meteorological advantage over Brest: the same easterly wind that would allow French ships to depart for Britain would make it harder for British ships to mount an effective blockade when it blew. The threat of 100 ships of the line concentrated at Antwerp was therefore a completely different order of magnitude to Britain than 20 operational ships of the line at Brest, whatever the Royal Navy's tactical advantages.

The direct British response to Napoleon's naval build-up was the infamous Walcheren Expedition of 1809. However, while the port of Flushing was severely damaged, little was done to slow the tempo of French shipbuilding. Moreover, because British soldiers on Walcheren became sickly without the easy resupply of fresh provisions and ability to cycle troops to the mainland that Brill had provided in 1585, the island had to be evacuated.[67] Walcheren was therefore a major strategic disaster for Britain over and above the operational failure and loss of life to sickness. Without the ability to neutralize Antwerp and the Scheldt, Britain would need Continental allies to free Belgium by defeating France on land. However, Walcheren coincided with another Austrian defeat in 1809 which led to Napoleon marrying a Habsburg princess in 1810, while Russia was technically a French ally since 1807. Due to Napoleon's prolific naval construction, control of the Scheldt, and the reinvested port of Antwerp after Trafalgar, Britain was facing credible maritime competition and potential invasion for the first time, with no obvious means of stopping Napoleon's progress.

Napoleon's invasion of Russia in 1812 did not solve Britain's strategic problem because it did not lead to the inevitable defeat of France as popular histories tend to suggest. Crucially, during the course of 1813, the Eastern Powers (Austria, Russia, Prussia) twice offered peace to Napoleon on the basis of France keeping control of Belgium and the Scheldt. The first occurred in June 1813 at Reichenbach, where peace was offered in return for France abandoning just Poland and Croatia, as Britain was arranging subsidy deals with Russia and Prussia in the same town.[68] Peace was offered a second time at Frankfurt in November in return for France withdrawing from parts of Italy and Germany east of the Rhine; Prince Metternich, Austria's foreign minister, explained his position to British negotiators, who were being left to fight alone in Spain and at sea with no military leverage in northern Europe: 'your special interests are selfish, ours are European'.[69] Napoleon refused both

---

67   Fiebel, 'What Happened at Walcheren', pp.62-79.
68   Michael V. Leggiere, 'From Berlin to Leipzig: Napoleon's Gamble in North Germany, 1813', *The Journal of Military History*, 67:1 (2003), pp.39-44.
69   Schroeder, '"An Unnatural 'Natural Alliance"', pp.522-540.

peace offers, preferring to fight to keep everything he had gained. Napoleon's belligerence gave the Eastern Powers a problem: they could not afford to sustain large armies far from home bases, which would be crucial to defeating France. The power of the British economy and state finance now took on a strategic dimension in freeing Belgium and making Britain safe from invasion. From November 1813 to March 1814, a mere five-month period in wars that had lasted over 20 years, the British government made the price of its newly generous subsidies very clear: Belgium and the Scheldt must be detached from France, with France returned to its 1791 borders.[70]

During the early part of the French Revolution, French finances and military logistics collapsed, a problem exacerbated by the rapid increase in the size of French armies. The French military turned a supply-chain disaster into a military virtue by turning to pillage as a matter of doctrine, thereby significantly reducing the supply chains of their armies and making them far more operationally manoeuvrable than their enemies, who continued to try to supply their armies with food.[71] The need for Coalition allies to compete with France's increasingly competent mass armies created a growing gap between human and financial resources; the most extreme example of this the Russian Empire. While Russia had a population of some 37,000,000 at the end of the eighteenth century, Russian government income was in the region of only 55 million roubles or £12 million.[72] Roughly 30-50 percent of Russia's income was spent on the army, which allowed a theoretical force of 400,000-600,000 men on organic resources.[73] Russia could therefore afford either a large army which it could not pay for on campaign, or a much smaller army which could be supplied but which would be outnumbered by French forces: essentially what happened in 1812 and the first half of 1813. This meant that for the major European powers to field armies on the scale of what Revolutionary and Napoleonic France could muster, financial support from the United Kingdom was necessary.

Between 1793 and 1815, Britain provided £58.5 million in subsidies and loans to allies, although 34 percent of this amount was concentrated between 1813 and 1815, averaging £6.6 million per annum (the average for the previous 20 years was a far from decisive £1.9 million).[74] Whereas previously the British government had spent in the region of £20 per soldier to hire and supply German mercenaries on campaign (including profits for German suppliers), for most of the French Revolutionary and Napoleonic Wars the British government used a 'standard rate' for calculating subsidies of £12-15 per man, a rate which stripped away profit and was more suited to allies contributing part of the costs.[75] By dividing the

70   Editorial comment in J.M. Thompson, *Napoleon's Letters* (London: Prion, 1998), p.273.
71   Paddy Griffith, *The Art of War of Revolutionary France, 1789-1802* (London: Greenhill, 1998), p.52.
72   'Russian revenue and expenditure, 1762-1815,' *European State Finance Database*, <https://www.esfdb.org/table.aspx?resourceid=12064> (accessed 25 August 2023); 'Currency Exchange Rate in 1799: Russia and Muscovy', *The Napoleon Series*, <https://www.napoleon-series.org/research/abstract/miscellaneous/currency/1799/c_1799Russia.html> (accessed 10 March 2023).
73   Walter M. Pinter, 'The Burden of Defense in Imperial Russia,' 1725-1914, *The Russian Review*, 43:3 (1984), pp.231-259.
74   N.J. Silberling, 'Financial and Monetary Policy of Great Britain During the Napoleonic Wars,' *The Quarterly Journal of Economics*, 38:2 (1924), pp.214-233.
75   R. Carr, *Gustavus IV and the British Government 1804-9*, The English Historical Review Vol.60, No. 236 (Jan 1945), pp.36-66; 'First Parliament of George II: Fourth session – begins 21/1/1731,' in *The*

£6.6 million of subsidies provided per annum by the £15 Continental operating cost per soldier, we can estimate that British subsidies of the crucial last nine months of the War of the Sixth Coalition and the following Hundred Days campaign of 1815 paid for, equipped, and supplied approximately 440,000 Coalition soldiers in Europe per annum, representing roughly half of the Coalition armies fielded and more than 100 percent of the cost of the Coalition armies that directly invaded France in 1814.[76] British subsidies therefore ensured that Napoleon was outnumbered by well-supplied and operationally mobile troops, whereas he would not have been without them.

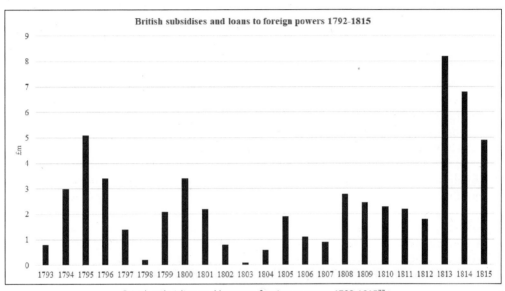

British subsidies and loans to foreign powers, 1792-1815[77]

The need to totally defeat France significantly empowered Britain as the only state wealthy enough to fund a landward invasion of France. However, British subsidies were also a last resort for the Eastern Powers, who tried hard to avoid them through the two separate deals with Napoleon offered during 1813. The willingness of the other Coalition powers to let France keep the Low Countries demonstrated the limitations of British coalition strategy for defending or liberating the Scheldt when not facing an egomaniac who threatened European peace regardless of his country's own best interests.

In February 1814, a desperate Napoleon wrote a letter to his father-in-law, the Austrian Emperor Francis I, in the hope that he could rekindle Austria's anti-British peace deal offered to him just three months before, he explained:

History and Proceedings of the House of Commons: Volume 7, 1727-1733, (London: Chandler, 1742), pp.69-86.

76   Charles Esdaile, *Napoleon's Wars* (London: Penguin, 2007), p.522, which gives an initial allied invasion strength of 350,000.

77   Silberling, 'Financial and Monetary Policy', pp.214-233.

There is not a Frenchman alive who would not rather die than submit to terms that would make us slaves to England and strike France off the list of powers. Such terms can be no part of Your Majesty's intentions: certainly they are not in the interests of your monarchy. England may wish to destroy Antwerp and place a permanent obstacle in the way of any restoration of the French navy. But you, sire, what interest have you in the annihilation of the French navy? By the principles laid down at Frankfort your majesty also becomes a maritime power. Do you wish your flag to be violated and outraged by England, as has constantly happened before? What would Your Majesty stand to gain by putting the Belgians under the yoke of a Protestant prince whose son is destined to mount the English throne? [William of Orange, as part of a new United Netherlands]

...I will never give up Antwerp and Belgium. A peace on the lines of Frankfort can be honestly enforced and will enable France to turn all her attention to rebuilding her fleet, and reestablishing her commerce. Nothing else can. If Your Majesty persists in sacrificing your own interests to the selfish policy of England, or the resentment of Russia, if you will not lay down arms except upon the frightful conditions proposed at the Congress; then Providence and the Genius of France will be on our side.

... Your Majesty will hardly ask why I address myself to you. I cannot turn to the English, whose aim is the destruction of my navy, nor to the Emperor Alexander [of Russia], whose only feelings about me are those of vengeance and passion....[78]

Napoleon's letter demonstrates that he clearly understood how vital Antwerp and Belgium were to France's maritime strength and British security and that 'English politicians' understood that too. Napoleon also revealed that he saw the loss of Antwerp as effectively meaning the loss of his navy, which demonstrates just how limiting Brest and the French Channel ports were from a sea power perspective. However, by February 1814 Napoleon was losing the war, as his plaintive letter effectively admitted. Francis I chose Russian amity and British money over a very risky alternative. British maritime pre-eminence had been salvaged more than it had been saved: Napoleon's maritime strategy against Britain had been defeated by his own impetuous and arrogant personality.

As peace was agreed in April 1814, Belgium was brought into a newly created United Netherlands under King William of Orange, although Napoleon was proved right that the Belgian people would not tolerate a Protestant monarch for long. More specifically, Article XV, Clause 2, of the 1814 Treaty of Paris decreed that 'Antwerp shall for the future be solely a Commercial port.'[79] After over 20 years of conflict Britain had finally achieved its key security objective.

---

78   'Napoleon I to Francis I, 21 February 1814,' in Thompson, *Napoleon's Letters*, pp.273-277.
79   '1814 Treaty of Paris' in the C. Parry (ed.), *Consolidated Treaty Series*, 1969-1980, Vol. 169, p.185, <https://www.icj-cij.org/public/files/case-related/169/169-20171130-REQ-05-00-E.pdf> (accessed 5 May 2023).

Britain's Continental commitment: Wellington and the Defence of Antwerp

The Battle of Waterloo, fought in Belgium on 18 June 1815, just 35 miles from Antwerp, is typically seen as the end of British military Continental commitments for nearly 100 years. However, Napoleon's final *dénouement* did not mark the end of Britain's commitment to the direct defence of Antwerp and Belgium; rather, it interrupted the beginning.

Long term British maritime security policy for Belgium could not afford to rely on subsidising European armies once Napoleon had been finally defeated, nor could it expect the Concert of Europe to remain intact forever. Whereas in 1713 Britain had shortsightedly relied on Dutch and Austrian forces to defend Belgium from a potentially resurgent France, in 1814 Britain did not take such a high-risk outsourced security approach. Instead, Britain and the United Netherlands jointly invested £6.5m in a belt of 21 state-of-the art fortresses which were designed to hold 58,000 men and hundreds of heavy artillery pieces. The forts were largely completed by 1820. As the map below clearly shows, the key purpose and ultimate defensive position of these forts was Antwerp, which was fortified for a garrison of 8,000 men and equipped with 150 heavy guns, 160 field guns, and 40 mortars. The Duke of Wellington himself took personal command of the construction and allied management of the fortress chain, which gave them their name: the Wellington Barrier.[80] Any mobilisation by France could be met by strong fortifications rapidly reinforced by a British field force, initially to be deployed into the port of Antwerp itself, which was now in the same country as the Scheldt estuary.

As far as the soldiers and statesmen in charge of British security policy at the end of the Napoleonic Wars were concerned, the Wellington Barrier ensured that never again would Britain lose control of the only port from which a Continental enemy could hope to launch a successful invasion or develop as a maritime competitor to Britain. The end of the Napoleonic Wars did not therefore mark a shift to 'Blue Water' policies for Britain, but for several years to come Britain opted to maintain a clear Continental military commitment to directly defend Britain's Achilles Heel: Antwerp.

Select Bibliography

Browning, R, *The War of the Austrian Succession* (New York: St Martin's Press, 1993).
Baugh, D.A., *The Global Seven Years War, 1754-63: Britain and France in a Great Power Contest* (Oxford: Routledge, 2014).
Esdaile, Charles, *The Wars of the French Revolution, 1792-1801* (Oxford: Routledge, 2019).
Esdaile, Charles, *Napoleon's Wars* (London: Penguin, 2007).
Glover, Richard, 'The French Fleet: Britain's problem; Madison's Opportunity', *The Journal of Modern History*, 39:3, (1967), pp.233-252.
McLynn, F.J., *Invasion: From the Armada to Hitler: 1588-1945* (London: Routledge and Kegan Paul, 1987).
Martin, Colin, and Parker, Geoffrey, *Armada: The Spanish Enterprise and England's Deliverance in 1588* (New Haven: Yale University Press, 2022).
Sutton J.L., *The King's Honor and the King's Cardinal: the War of the Polish Succession* (Lexingon: University of Kentucky Press, 1980).
Szabo, F.A.J., *The Seven Years War In Europe* (Oxford: Routledge (2013).

---

80   C. Nelson, 'The Duke of Wellington and the Barrier Fortresses after Waterloo', *Journal of the Society for Army Historical Research*, 42:169 (1964), pp.36-43.

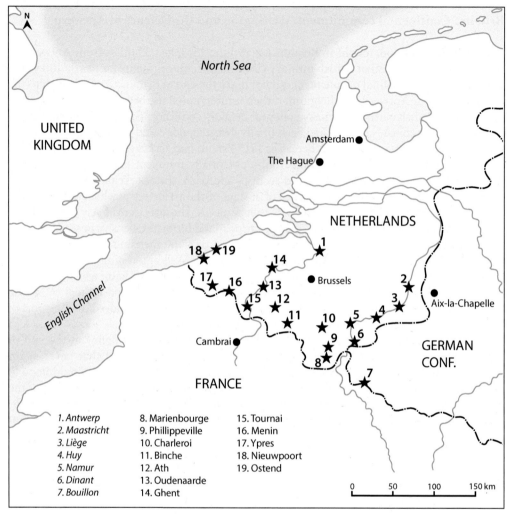

N

North Sea

UNITED
KINGDOM

Amsterdam●

The Hague ●

NETHERLANDS

English Channel

18 ★★19
1 ★
14 ★
17 ★
16 ★
13 ★
15 ★
12
● Brussels
2 ★
3 ★
● Aix-la-Chapelle
11 ★
10 ★
5 ★
4 ★
9 ★
6 ★
Cambrai ●
8 ★
7 ★
GERMAN
CONF.

FRANCE

1. Antwerp
2. Maastricht
3. Liège
4. Huy
5. Namur
6. Dinant
7. Bouillon
8. Marienbourge
9. Phillippeville
10. Charleroi
11. Binche
12. Ath
13. Oudenaarde
14. Ghent
15. Tournai
16. Menin
17. Ypres
18. Nieuwpoort
19. Ostend

0   50   100   150 km

The Wellington Barrier. (George Anderson © Helion and Company 2023)

9

Anson's Legacy: The Man Who Built a Navy, 1751-1762

Andrew Young

How did the Royal Navy come to the exultation to 'Rule the Waves' and to 'conquer Again, and again'?[1] From post-1805 hindsight, it may seem a strange question. Was the Royal Navy not pre-destined to dominate the global seaways?[2] But the Royal Navy's history in the seventeenth century was hardly auspicious. The first three Anglo-Dutch wars had ended at best in stalemate, at worst in abject failure and humiliation, whilst the Nine Years War saw victory and disaster go hand in hand. Even the victories of the War of the Spanish Succession, such as the capture of Gibraltar and Menorca, masked major structural issues that became all too apparent during the War of the Austrian Succession. What is remarkable, therefore, is that from the mixed record of the 1740s the Royal Navy was, less than two decades later, able to project power successfully and effectively from the Americas to the South China Sea. Such progress is of great interest to scholars and practitioners alike, providing case studies in leadership, organisational development, state formation, and institutional theory.[3]

George Anson (later Baron Anson), a man who sat at the heart of naval administration, planning, operations, and strategy, is the central figure in this transformational tale.[4] Anson is an unnatural figure for hero-worship – he was unsociable company and scarred by scurvy – but one whose achievements certainly merit it. The first Briton to lead a circumnavigation of the globe since Drake, capturing the Acapulco treasure galleon to boot, Anson's leadership set him apart from his peers and established a reputation for durability and professionalism. The prize money he garnered funded a political power base; Anson understood the importance of influence 'at the highest levels, in the Cabinet itself...hop[ing] to educate the politicians who directed the Navy in war and funded it in peace'. He had lost 1,300

1   Brian Lavery, *Anson's Navy: Building a Fleet for Empire 1744 to 1763* (Barnsley: Seaforth, 2021), p.7.
2   Paul Kennedy, *The Rise and Fall of British Naval Mastery* (London: Penguin, 2004), pp.102-104.
3   Richard Harding, 'Introduction' & 'The Royal Navy, History and the Study of Leadership' in Richard Harding & Agustin Guimera (eds), *Naval Leadership in the Atlantic World in the Age of Reform and Revolution, 1700-1850* (London: University of Westminster Press, 2017) pp.4-17.
4   Andrew Young, 'Anson: The Man who Built a Navy', *The Naval Review*, 101:4 (2013), pp.410-415.

seamen and marines to scurvy and disease on his epic voyage, and spent the next eighteen years 'dominat[ing] Naval policy, improving every aspect of the service, from health care to tactics, by way of ship design and strategy'.[5] Through this combination of professionalism and political nous, Anson 'left a Fleet well supplied with battle-winning officers, well-found ships, bases and funds'.[6] If there is a modern 'Art of Admiralty' then it was formulated on Anson's watch; a signal lesson of vital importance to naval practitioners today.[7]

Perusing the literature, however, and one might be forgiven for questioning Anson's part at all. As one of his biographers states, 'the more one searches, the more one discovers how much he really did do, and how well he concealed it.'[8] His self-confessed aversion to writing marked his career, even leading his father-in-law (Philip Yorke, Earl of Hardwicke) to complain that 'He loved reading little, and writing or dictating his own letters less'.[9] If ever there was a proponent of the Silent Service, it was he; the naming of the latest *Astute*-class submarine in his honour is doubly appropriate.[10] Although it is hard to establish what role Anson played in the reforms, there is 'indirect evidence to suggest that his influence was crucial',[11] and 'the presence of his guiding hand is easier to sense than to prove.'[12] Perhaps proof-positive of his impact is the knowledge that both the Duke of Bedford and Lord Sandwich, as successive First Lords of the Admiralty, 'entrusted him with the management of the affairs of the Admiralty'[13]; as Corbett described, it was a 'dictatorship' that 'worked admirably'.[14]

This, then, is the reality of the Royal Navy's rise to global pre-eminence. It was not pre-ordained or pre-destined, but rather the result of one man's singular vision, dedication, attention to detail, and driving sense of duty. His example set the tone for the next two centuries. Indeed, it is possible to trace an unbroken patronage line from Anson to Nelson via Hawke, Hood, and Jarvis, and from Nelson to Cunningham via Parker, Hornby and Beatty. It was Anson who laid the foundations for the fleet that, for a century, ensured *Pax Britannica* ruled the world ocean; his reforms to infrastructure, logistical support, personnel management and the very ships set the groundwork for his successors to capitalise.[15] It is a lesson modern naval practitioners and policy makers ignore at their peril.

5   Andrew Lambert, *War at Sea in the Age of Sail 1650-1850* (London: Smithsonian Book, 2005), p.111.
6   Andrew Lambert, *Admirals: The Naval Commanders who Made Britain Great* (London: Faber & Faber, 2008), pp.121-156.
7   James Smith, 'What is the "Art of Admiralty"?', May 15, 2023, at <https://jameswesmith.substack.com/p/what-is-the-art-of-admiralty> (accessed 19 May 2023).
8   Walter Vernon Anson, *The Life of Admiral Lord Anson, the Father of the British Navy, 1697-1762* (London: John Murray, 1912), p.188.
9   John Barrow, *The Life of George Lord Anson* (London: John Murray, 1839), p.401; & Philip Yorke, 1st Earl Hardwicke, quoted in Lavery, *Anson's Navy*, p.14.
10   Anson, *The Life of Admiral Lord Anson*, p.185. The Royal Navy's Submarine Service is referred to colloquially as 'the Silent Service' and provides the primary offensive capability of the maritime forces.
11   Richard Harding, *Seapower and Naval Warfare 1650-1830* (Abingdon: Routledge, 2003), p.206.
12   Nicholas Rodger, *The Wooden World* (London: Penguin Press, 1988), p.30.
13   Barrow, *The Life of George Lord Anson*, p.395.
14   Sir Julian Corbett, *England in the Seven Years War* (London: Longmans, Green, and Co., 1907), Vol I, p.35.
15   Lambert, *Admirals*, pp.119-420.

Anson's Rise

Anson's career prior to 1740 was typical of the period, relying as much on familial connection and loyalty to the political class as merit.[16] Entering the navy during the Spanish Succession, he was fortunate not to be put on to half pay at the subsequent peace.[17] He served under Admiral Norris in the Baltic in 1716, and fought in Admiral Sir George Byng's flagship at Cape Passaro in 1718.[18] He was made master and commander of the sloop HMS *Weazle* in 1722, combatting Dutch smugglers in the North Sea, and then captain of HMS *Scarborough* the following year and ordered to South Carolina to protect commerce from piracy and smuggling.[19] His character and professionalism was set in these years of independent command, from his personal skill at navigation and chart work to keeping his ship and crew at readiness 'on the frontier of Empire, where war, peace and piracy were the norm'.[20] It is likely during this time that he first became theoretically acquainted with the island Juan Fernandez through the works of Defoe; an acquaintance that would be pivotal in later years when, like Crusoe, he would rely on the island's bounty for survival.[21] His good character, success in navigating the complex political geography of the time, and familial connections built during this formative period of putative peace promised much for the future.

In 1739, Anson's patronage networks paid dividends when he was selected to command an independent squadron.[22] Tensions over the *Asiento*, the South Sea Company's intransigence, and public expectation of success all conspired to make war with Spain all but inevitable.[23] Intent on waging a naval war, Parliament and the Admiralty proposed concurrent strikes in the West Indies and the Pacific:[24] Anson was to round Cape Horn and 'attack the Peruvian coast and Manila' and 'shatter the western end of Spain's imperial trade routes'.[25] Meanwhile, another expedition would strike overland towards Panama, and Vernon would follow up on his success at Porto Bello by taking Cartagena.[26] However, between first being apprised of his mission in October and finally receiving his orders in June, Anson's mission had been downgraded from conquest to one of harassment whilst the Panama scheme had been abandoned. No longer was he to take Manila, but rather to 'annoy and distress the Spaniards', to foment rebellion and, if judged prudent, 'to look out for the Acapulco ship'.[27] Only Vernon's expedition, which had received Royal backing, would continue as planned

---

16   Lambert, *Admirals*, p.123.
17   Lavery, *Anson's Navy*, p.12.
18   Lambert, *Admirals*, p.123.
19   Barrow, *The Life of George Lord Anson*, p.9.
20   Anson, *The Life of Admiral Lord Anson* p.3; Lambert, *Admirals*, p.124.
21   Anson, *The Life of Admiral Lord Anson* p.3.
22   Lambert, *Admirals*, p.125.
23   Andrew Lambert, *Crusoe's Island* (London: Faber & Faber, 2016), p.69; Richard Harding, *The Emergence of Britain's Global Naval Supremacy: The War of 1739 – 1748* (Woodbridge: Boydell Press), pp.23-28.
24   Anson, *The Life of Admiral Lord Anson* pp.23-24.
25   Harding, *The Emergence of Britain's Global Naval Supremacy*, pp.62-63.
26   Anson, *The Life of Admiral Lord Anson*, pp.23-24.
27   Barrow, *The Life of George Lord Anson*, pp.29-35.

and would therefore benefit from the accumulation and concentration of resources and manpower: all six regiments of marines, and the regiment of foot originally destined for Manila, would sail for the West Indies.[28]

As it was, the planning, preparation and dispatch of Anson's squadron was the example of what not to do. Manpower throughout the fleet was at a premium, leaving Anson short of some 300 trained sailors.[29] This was an administrative problem: the navy was projected to expand from a peacetime establishment of 16,000 to 35,000,[30] yet the legal methods of doing so (including impressment) were imperfect and beholden on local magistrates with their own local political obligations.[31] With a poor harvest in 1739 and a harsh winter, supplies of salt beef and cheese were later found to be improperly cured and prematurely barrelled, and were subsequently condemned.[32] Moreover, whilst written orders were dated 31 January 1740, they were not received until 28 June – an unconscionable delay.[33] Worse was to come; contradictory orders and the need to convoy the outbound trade meant that the squadron finally made sail in mid-September. Anson chafed at the delays, knowing that each postponement would 'confine his passage round Cape Horn to the most rigorous season of the year.'[34]

Those fears were well founded. Leaving so late in the year meant contending with westerly winds; the passage from St Helens to Madeira, normally a 16-day sail, took 40.[35] Worse was to come. It took three months to beat a passage round the Horn, but the squadron splintered: the Severn and Pearl turned back, whilst the Wager was wrecked.[36] Anson made for the rendezvous at Juan Fernandez, accompanied by the sloop Tryal and later joined by the Gloucester and storeship Anna.[37] Scurvy and other shipboard diseases had run rife in the 148 day passage from Brazil to Juan Fernandez, the consequence of poor diet before the ships departed and long time at sea without Vitamin C rich victuals. They made a sorry sight. Each ship was storm battered, strewn with dead, dying, and survivors clinging on despite being mired in their own desperate filth.[38] Across the three warships (Centurion, Gloucester, Tryal) of the 961 souls who had departed Spithead, only 335 survived, barely enough to crew the Centurion.[39] The invalids and Marines had suffered particularly badly: on the Centurion alone, of 'fifty invalids and seventy-nine marines, there remained only 4 invalids, including officers, and eleven marines; and on board the Gloucester every invalid perished; and out of forty-eight marines only two escaped'.[40] The depleted squadron spent the next 104 days

28   Harding, The Emergence of Britain's Global Naval Supremacy, p.64.
29   George Anson, A Voyage Around the World in the Years 1740-1744, Richard Walter ed. (London: John and Paul Knapton, 1748), p.5.
30   Harding, The Emergence of Britain's Global Naval Supremacy, pp.51-52.
31   Rodger, The Wooden World, p.164.
32   Harding, The Emergence of Britain's Global Naval Supremacy, pp.80-81.
33   Anson, The Life of Admiral Lord Anson, p.24.
34   Anson, A Voyage Around the World, p.6
35   Anson, The Life of Admiral Lord Anson, pp.30-31.
36   Lambert, Admirals, p.125; Lavery, Anson's Navy, p.13.
37   Lambert, Admirals, p.126.
38   Lambert, Crusoe's Island, pp.70-77.
39   Anson, The Life of Admiral Lord Anson, p.41.
40   Anson, A Voyage Around the World, p.160.

recuperating. Anson had gardens planted, sowed fruit trees, and augmented the rations with fresh vegetables, fish and seal meat.[41]

Having broken up the *Anna* and joined her crew to that of the *Gloucester*, Anson's squadron was too depleted to mount the kind of campaign originally envisioned.[42] In September 1741, a year after leaving England, the squadron dispersed to harass the local trade of Chile and Peru, capturing several prizes and sacking the town of Paita.[43] From the prizes, it was learned that Vernon's expedition to Cartagena had been disastrous, rendering the ambition to 'join hands' across the Panama isthmus moot.[44] He instead resolved to go to Acapulco and attempt capture of the treasure galleon, but found himself too late to intercept and the town too heavily guarded.[45] Yet intelligence indicated that the laden galleon would make the outward journey to Manila in the coming months; if Anson could get himself across the Pacific beforehand, he still may have a chance to intercept.[46] Resolved to do so, he scuttled his prizes and, with just the *Gloucester* in company, the *Centurion* struck out across the Pacific.[47]

It was another harrowing voyage. Scurvy, so long at bay during their cruise along the Spanish-American coast where fresh provisions abounded, struck again.[48] The ships began to founder; *Gloucester* was scuttled and her crew transferred to the *Centurion*, adding scarce manpower to her pumps that clattered day and night to keep her afloat.[49] Finally, they made landfall at Tinian in the Marianas in late August 1742, and there repaired the ship and recuperated as best they could, before moving on to Macao to undertake more lasting repairs in the dockyards and hire fresh sailors from the international trade that passed through its port.[50] Even with this latter addition of 23 skilled hands, the *Centurion* mustered only 227 men to take on one, possibly two, galleons with at least 500 apiece.[51] Undeterred, Anson sailed back to the Philippines and there, in June 1743, fell upon the *Nuestra Senora de Cavadonga*; 'the prize of all the oceans'[52] worth 'nearly a million and half of dollars'.[53] It was a masterful display of seamanship and fighting skill: for the loss of 16 dead and 15 wounded, his gunners had killed and wounded a quarter of the Spanish crew.[54] Anson, with the prize in tow, made for Canton where he disposed of the captured crew and the galleon, stored his

41   Barrow, *The Life of George Lord Anson*, pp.52-53; Lambert, *Crusoe's Island*, pp.78-82.
42   Barrow, *The Life of George Lord Anson*, p.53.
43   Alfred Thayer Mahan, *The Influence of Sea Power upon History 1660-1783* (Boston: Little, Brown & Co, 1890), pp.261-262.
44   Anson, *The Life of Admiral Lord Anson*, p.46; Mahan, *The Influence of Sea Power upon History*, p.261.
45   Lambert, *Admirals*, p.127.
46   Anson, *The Life of Admiral Lord Anson*, p.48.
47   Barrow, *The Life of George Lord Anson*, p.63.
48   Lambert, *Admirals*, p.127; Barrow, *The Life of George Lord Anson*, pp.62-64; Anson, *The Life of Admiral Lord Anson*, , pp.49-51.
49   Anson, *A Voyage Around the World*, pp.297-300.
50   Barrow, *The Life of George Lord Anson*, p.66; Anson, *The Life of Admiral Lord Anson*, pp.50-53; Lambert, *Admirals*, p.128.
51   Anson, *The Life of Admiral Lord Anson*, p.55; Lambert, *Admirals*, p.128.
52   Lambert, *Admirals*, p.128.
53   Barrow, *The Life of George Lord Anson*, p.75.
54   Anson, *The Life of Admiral Lord Anson*, pp.56-58; Barrow, *The Life of George Lord Anson*, p.75.

ship and, after a delay of some five months, finally sailed for England in December 1743.[55] He arrived at Spithead on 15 June 1744, one of just 188 original survivors of the ships that had rendezvoused at Juan Fernandez, and of the 1,800 men who had left some three years and nine months earlier.[56]

Anson's voyage was 'leadership on a heroic scale'.[57] If 'by their works shall ye know them', then Anson's leadership is proof of his character: he worked 'impossibilities with impossible material'.[58] It was the making of Anson, in more ways than one.[59] His success also came at an invaluable juncture in the war with Spain and France. Vernon and Wentworth's expedition to Cartagena, launched with such high hopes after the former's successful surprise attack on Porto Bello in 1739, had ended in disaster: of the Marines and American reinforcements dispatched, barely a 'tenth part of the number that had been sent abroad' remained.[60] Mathews and Lestock's disastrous handling of the fleet at Toulon in February 1744 had further sunk the navy's reputation, with Richard Norris (the original captain of the *Gloucester* and son of Admiral Sir John Norris) particularly disgracing himself and his family's reputation.[61] A 'spate of courts martial and parliamentary inquiries'[62] over the next year consumed the Admiralty: Mathews, Lestock and 11 of the 29 ship's captains found themselves fighting for their careers.[63] Throughout this political turmoil, Vernon, Mathews, Lestock and others took to pamphleteering and parliament to advance their versions of events.[64] It was an unedifying spectacle, one which contrasted with Anson's taciturn professionalism where actions spoke louder than words. Parading the Acapulco treasure in 32 wagons through the streets of London was a much-needed morale boost,[65] yet not all shared the *London Evening Post*'s triumphant tone: the *Daily Post* highlighted the human 'tragedy and cost of the voyage, and the fact that none of the money was added to the state's coffers.'[66]

Over the next four years, Anson set about securing his future, although it was not without mishap. Promoted to rear admiral of the blue in June 1744, he immediately refused the commission upon hearing that his recommendation for Piercy Brett, his first lieutenant on *Centurion*, to be gazetted captain had been refused on a matter of precedent.[67] It was, however, a short-lived setback. With the accession of a new ministry in December 1744, the Duke of Bedford's Admiralty Board confirmed his promotion to rear admiral of the white

55   Anson, *The Life of Admiral Lord Anson*, p.61
56   Lambert, *Admirals*, p.129; Anson, *The Life of Admiral Lord Anson*, p.61
57   Lambert, *Admirals*, p.129.
58   Corbett, *England in the Seven Years War*, p.34.
59   Ben Wilson, *Empire of the Deep: The Rise and Fall of the British Navy* (London: Weidenfeld & Nicolson, 2013), p.302.
60   Thomas More Molyneux, *Conjunct Expeditions* (London: R & J Dodsley, 1758), p.183.
61   Mahan, *The Influence of Sea Power upon History*, pp.265-268; Lambert, *Admirals*, p.129.
62   Wilson, *Empire of the Deep*, p.295.
63   Mahan, *The Influence of Sea Power upon History*, p.268.
64   Harding, *The Emergence of Britain's Global Naval Supremacy*, pp.230-232; Wilson, *Empire of the Deep*, pp.295-298.
65   Wilson, *Empire of the Deep*, p.298.
66   Lavery, *Anson's Navy*, p.13.
67   Anson, *The Life of Admiral Lord Anson* pp.64-67.

in 1745, a double promotion.[68] With his share of the prize money, Anson was now so independently wealthy that he could afford to play politics: a necessary pastime for any ambitious officer in the eighteenth century.[69] £91,000 was a considerable sum; for comparison, his pay for the three-year voyage came to £719.[70] He bought the parliamentary seat at Hedon and invested heavily in securing Lichfield for his brother.[71] As a 'staunch Staffordshire Whig family in a predominantly Tory county', the Ansons bridged the political divide.[72] In 1748, he cemented his political connections through marriage to Elizabeth Yorke, daughter of the Lord Hardwicke, the Lord Chancellor.[73]

He would return to sea twice more. First, in 1746 when Vernon was finally dismissed,[74] Anson took command of the newly conglomerated Western Squadron.[75] Anson was not the originator of the idea to combine the various Chanel commands, but did make the squadron an effective strategic instrument and tactical fighting force.[76] He recognised what Vernon had – that a squadron cruising the Western Approaches could: protect the homeland from invasion; protect the home-bound trade; intercept French trade; and effect a distant blockade of the French Biscay and Channel ports, predominantly in Brittany (Brest and the Morbihan).[77] However, given the limited endurance of the fleet and the vast area to be patrolled, the squadron required an effective intelligence network in order to concentrate at the decisive point at precisely the right moment.[78] Moreover, given the rather lacklustre performance of the navy in the war to date, a significant change in tactical method and mindset was also needed.[79] Anson drilled his captains and crews hard, enforcing the daily gunnery drills that had been mandated in 1745.[80] New signals were devised, too, one's that reflected Anson's philosophy of naval battle.[81] When necessary, the line of battle was to be abandoned for general chase, and ships were to engage at extremely close range.[82] He spoke regularly with his second in command, Warren (freshly returned from the capture of Louisburg), and his subordinates, working out a series of 'actions on' that would be recognisable to any modern military practitioner: should the fleet scatter or visual sight of the flagship be lost, then standard operating procedures would dictate the next move.[83] Yet, at the same time, officers were to exercise their own initiative in line with Anson's overall

---

68   Harding, *The Emergence of Britain's Global Naval Supremacy*, p.219; Anson, *The Life of Admiral Lord Anson*, p.72; Lambert, *Admirals*, p.131.
69   Wilson, *Empire of the Deep*, p.301.
70   Lambert, *Admirals*, p.130.
71   Lavery, *Anson's Navy*, p.13; & Lambert, *Admirals*, p.130.
72   Harding, 'Leadership Networks and the Effectiveness of the British Royal Navy', in Harding & Guimera (eds), *Naval Leadership*, p.32.
73   Anson, *The Life of Admiral Lord Anson*, p.109.
74   Barrow, *The Life of George Lord Anson*, pp.130-138.
75   Lambert, *Admirals*, p.132.
76   Wilson, *Empire of the Deep*, pp.300-304.
77   Nicholas Rodger, *The Command of the Ocean* (London: Penguin, 2005), p.251.
78   Wilson, *Empire of the Deep*, p.301.
79   Harding, *The Emergence of Britain's Global Naval Supremacy*, p.288.
80   Lambert, *Admirals*, p.133.
81   Lavery, *Anson's Navy*, p.127.
82   Lambert, *Admirals*, p.133.
83   Wilson, *Empire of the Deep*, pp.301-302.

intent: to find, fight and destroy the enemy.[84] This was doctrine rather than dogma, and mission command before *auftragstaktik* had been conceived.[85] Aggression was the key, and it paid off when Anson successfully intercepted de la Jonquiere's outbound convoy in First Finisterre (3 May 1747 (os)), pocketing him a further £63,000 in prize money and an elevation to the peerage.[86] Anson's methods became the blueprint: Hawke replicated and exploited Anson's advances at Second Finisterre (14 October 1747 (os)).[87]

The second, and last time, Anson took to the sea in command was in 1758. Hawke, in a fit of pique, hauled down his flag: smarting from the failure of the Rochefort descent, he objected to being made a supporting role to Captain Howe's inshore squadron and the proposed descents on St Malo and Cherbourg.[88] He left the Western Squadron at a critical juncture: the navy was suffering a critical shortage in manpower; and the Plymouth vict- ualing yard had yet to achieve full war-time efficiency.[89] Nor was Anson impressed with the quality of the officers and crews under his command:

> When I began to exercise my fleet I never saw such awkwardness in going through the common manoeuvres necessary to make an attack upon an enemy's fleet at all. What we do now in an hour, in the beginning took eight... Most of the captains declared they had never seen a line of battle, and none of them more than once.[90]

Given the rapid turnover in personnel, reduced sea-time, and the use of the fleet to cover inshore operations and descents, this deficiency cannot solely be laid to rest at Hawke's door; Anson's rapid and unprecedented mobilisation and expansion of the fleet must also share some burden of blame.[91] However, Anson took to the challenge or bringing the squadron to a satisfactory state of preparedness with alacrity, partly through professional pride and partly through his intent to draw out the French fleet; he viewed Pitt's descents on the French coast as means of goading Conflans and the Brest squadron into an ill-judged contest.[92] It was not to be, but when Anson returned to his seat at the Admiralty he left Hawke, newly reinstated, with a squadron that was well-prepared for the tests ahead.[93]

---

84   Lambert, *Admirals*, p.133.
85   The German approach to war popularised as 'mission command' is more accurately defined as a command philosophy, one that is predicated on mutual understanding, trust, and initiative. See Donald Vandergriff, 'How the Germans Defined Auftragstaktik: What Mission Command is – AND – is Not', *Small Wars Journal*, 21 June 2018, at <https://smallwarsjournal.com/jrnl/art/how-germans-defined-auftragstaktik-what-mission-command-and-not#_ednref1> (accessed 4 March 2023); Major General Werner Widder, 'The Origins of Auftragstaktik', *Army University Press*, Military Review Sep-Oct 2002, pp.3-9 at <https://www.armyupress.army.mil/Portals/7/Hot-Spots/docs/MC/MR-Sep-Oct-2002-Widder.pdf> (accessed 4 March 2023).
86   Lambert, *Admirals*, pp.134-137
87   Wilson, *Empire of the Deep*, pp.304-306.
88   Corbett, *England in the Seven Years War*, p.268.
89   Wilson, *Empire of the Deep*, p.330.
90   Anson to Hardwicke, in Corbett, *England in the Seven Years War*, p.274.
91   Lambert, *Admirals*, p.148.
92   Corbett, *England in the Seven Years War*, pp.273-274.
93   Lambert, *Admirals*, p.149.

A New Art of Admiralty

Professor Richard Harding views naval leadership as lying 'at the heart of their perceptions of success and failure, organisational design, and the lived experience' of personnel.[94] If we take this to be true, then in Anson's tenure every element underwent significant reform and evolution, if not a full revolution in military affairs. Having secured his power base, burnished his public reputation, and proven his loyalty to his subordinates by standing on a matter of principal, Anson entered the Admiralty with clear intentions.[95] With the experience of fitting-out fresh in his mind and the current poor state of morale amongst an officer corps that had known nothing but disappointment, he was 'determined…to reorganise' the dockyards and supply chain and to 'instil a new spirit' into the navy.[96] Vernon's departure from the Admiralty in 1746 left Anson virtually uncontested as the 'professional head of the navy… His potential competitors had fallen away' in the succession of crises that marked 1740-46.[97]

The administrative system of the eighteenth century Royal Navy was split between the Admiralty and its subordinate boards: Navy, Victualling, and Sick and Wounded. The Admiralty 'was the centre of the Naval system rather than its head,' responsible for 'overall Naval policy, command and discipline.'[98] The Navy Board 'was responsible for finance, dockyards, naval stores and shipbuilding,'[99] whilst the Victuallers dealt with food; the Sick and Wounded Board – medical matters including supplies and appointment of physicians. Separately, gunners drew powder, shot and martial stores from the Ordnance Board, which also supplied the Army.[100] Each guarded its independence fiercely, and attempts by Bedford's Admiralty Board to exert control over the Navy Board were resisted.[101] It was only in the 1740s and early 1750s that the Admiralty and Navy Boards began to cooperate effectively, and then almost entirely due to Anson's reforms to the latter.[102] Reflecting 'practical insight with first-hand knowledge' and by rewarding 'proven quality' rather than 'political convenience', Anson began a system of reform based around people management rather than 'endlessly tinkering with regulations'; evolution through good management rather than wholesale bureaucratic change.[103] In effect, by winning the battle to appoint his own choices based on merit rather than influence, Anson was able to perform an internal coup on the structures and management of the navy's diurnal running.[104] This would encompass: ships; marines; health and victualling; and the manning of the fleet.

94   Harding and Agustin (eds), 'Introduction', in *Naval Leadership*, p.4.
95   Lambert, *Admirals*, pp.130-132.
96   Anson, *The Life of Admiral Lord Anson* p.81.
97   Harding, 'Leadership Networks', p.32.
98   Rodger, *The Command of the Ocean*, p.295; & *The Wooden World*, p.33.
99   Lavery, *Anson's Navy*, p.21.
100 Rodger, *The Wooden World*, pp.35-36.
101 Rodger, *The Command of the Ocean*, p.299.
102 Harding, *Seapower*, p.206.
103 Lambert, *Admirals*, pp.131-137; Wilson, *Empire of the Deep*, p.322.
104 Wilson, *Empire of the Deep*, pp.323-324.

Building a Fleet

Anson had clear experience of ships that were not fit for purpose; he intended to change that. His vision was for ships to 'catch the enemy, to keep the sea, and to fight their guns, in all weathers'.[105] When Anson entered the Royal Navy, the 'Establishments' were just being laid out.[106] These were ships designed for the near battle 'between the Thames and Texel': 'overcrowded with guns, short of space, not desperately seaworthy and found it difficult to open their lower-deck gunports in a seaway'.[107] These ships were ill-suited to the new type of oceanic warfare envisioned by the proponents of a 'sea war':[108] 'they lacked the endurance, stowage, seaworthiness and speed' of their larger French and Spanish counterparts.[109] So behind was British ship design by 1740, that the Spanish *Princessa* (70 guns) was able to compete on equal terms with three British ships of nominally the same rate. Similarly, Mathews' squadron's performance at Toulon proved the superiority of the French 74-gun ship over the British 80.[110] Frankly, whatever the 'stereotypes in which the political nation believed,'[111] it was clear that the Royal Navy's ships were ill-suited to the task in hand.

Part of the problem lay in the restrictive Establishments designed to meet the needs of a different kind of war; a further part in the people who oversaw the design and development of the fleet. This was the preserve of the Navy Board, under whose Surveyor ships were designed and commissioned from the network of Royal and commercial dockyards.[112] Unfortunately, the hexagenerian Sir Jacob Ackworth had been appointed Surveyor 1715, and under him 'conservative design, restricted dimensions, and the dead hand of precedent' stifled innovation.[113] The Duke of Bedford, guided by Anson, attempted to revitalise design in 1745 but with disappointing results. The sea-officers and shipwrights created a series of vessels that were not standardised, that suffered from poor sailing qualities, and did not match the dimensions of their competitors.[114] Ackworth died in 1749, enabling a change in regime,[115] one which Bedford's successor as First Lord, Lord Sandwich, took full advantage of. He took the Admiralty Board on a visit to the Royal Yards, under the pretext that the yards were mismanaged and slow to complete work.[116] It was a bold and unprecedented move, one that in the end caused more damage than it alleviated; the Navy Board dug in its heels, resisting what they perceived to be the Admiralty's over-reach.[117]

Anson became First Sea Lord in 1751. Rather than reopen old wounds, he took a different tack, replacing personages with people he could work with.[118] In 1755, Ackworth's

---

105 Anson, *The Life of Admiral Lord Anson, 1697-1762*, p.185.
106 Lavery, *Anson's Navy*, p.32.
107 Lambert, *Admirals*, p.138.
108 Lavery, *Anson's Navy*, p.32; Harding, *The Emergence of Britain's Global Naval Supremacy*, p.24.
109 Lambert, *Admirals*, p.138.
110 Harding, *Seapower*, p.193.
111 Rodger, *The Command of the Ocean*, p.248.
112 Lavery, *Anson's Navy*, p.21; Roger, *The Wooden World*, p.33.
113 Lavery, *Anson's Navy*, p.38; Lambert, *Admirals*, p.138.
114 Lavery, *Anson's Navy*, p.33.
115 Lambert, *Admirals*, p.13
116 Rodger, *The Command of the Ocean*, p.300.
117 Wilson, *Empire of the Deep*, p.321.
118 Lambert, *Admirals*, p.139.

'disappointing successor', Sir Joseph Allin, was taken ill; there is some evidence to suggest he suffered a mental breakdown.[119] Anson wasted no time in appointing his favourites, Thomas Slade and William Batley.[120] As lead architect for the navy, Slade was an inspired choice.[121] The two had met in 1746 when Anson commanded the Western Squadron, based in Plymouth. Whilst there, Anson handed over several captured French ships to Slade's uncle, and the nephew studied their design extensively.[122] Slade's appointment led to a period 'of rapid transformation': the improved 74-gun ships, starting with the *Dublin* and *Norfolk*, were launched within two years and proved to be the backbone of the navy for the next 50.[123] Evolutionary rather than revolutionary, balancing 'gun power and sailing quali-ties', these ships were capable of standing in the line of battle *or* pursuit, and in all weath-ers.[124] 'Radical' new classes of '28-, 32- and 36-gun frigates' were developed for scouting and blockade work.[125] All combined French ship architecture with robust British construc-tion methods; Slade built ships for 'global conflict; strong, capacious, durable and fast'[126] with increased 'stowage for long cruises'.[127] After 40 years of stagnation, British construc-tion finally caught up with its global ambitions and Slade's masterpiece, *Victory*, has been retained to this day.[128] Perhaps Anson's greatest impact on ship design and development was authorising the coppering of the frigate *Alarm* in 1762.[129] While it may seem prosaic, it was a move which in no small way precipitated the industrial mining of the ore and the revolution that followed: as Daniel Cuhna argues, 'No copper, no Industrial Revolution'.[130] The Royal Navy was the prime recipient of copper for sheathing their ships, and thus Anson could also claim, tenuously, to be the catalyst for the boom that saw Britain dominate markets and technology in decades to come.

Marines

For most of his sea-service career, Anson did without Marines. From their inception under the Duke of York, later James II, prior to the Second Dutch War until their establishment on a permanent basis in 1755, sea-soldiers were raised and disbanded according to the prac-tices of the War Office. Marine regiments were predominantly for hostilities only, although three were retained as regiments of foot after the Treaty of Utrecht (1713). Further, whilst they came under Admiralty control during both the War of Spanish Succession and War of Austrian Succession, they were organised and administered according to foot regiment

119 Lavery, *Anson's Navy*, p.34; Wilson, *Empire of the Deep*, p.322.
120 Lambert, *Admirals*, p.141; Wilson, *Empire of the Deep*, p.322.
121 Lambert, *Admirals*, p.141
122 Lavery, *Anson's Navy*, p.37.
123 Rodger, *The Command of the Ocean*, p.414; Lavery, *Anson's Navy*, p.37; Lambert, *Admirals*, p.141.
124 Lavery, *Anson's Navy*, p.34; Wilson, *Empire of the Deep*, p.322; Rodger, *The Command of the Ocean*, p.418.
125 Lavery, *Anson's Navy*, p.35; Wilson, *Empire of the Deep*, p.322.
126 Lambert, *Admirals*, p.141.
127 *Rodger, The Command of the Ocean*, p.418.
128 Lambert, *Admirals*, p.141.
129 Anson, *The Life of Admiral Lord Anson* p.185.
130 Daniel Cunha, 'Coppering the Industrial Revolution History, Materiality and Culture in the Making of an Ecological Regime', *Journal of World-Systems Research*, Vol. 26. 1, Winter/Spring 2020, pp.40-69.

norms – wholly unsuitable for detached duties onboard ship. This confusion and disso-
nance was not just a result of bureaucratic rigour and entrenched administrative systems,
but reflected a simple truth: the lack of a singular vision of what Marines were *for*, and
what they were to *do*.[131] Indeed, Britt Zerbe articulates no fewer than three institutional
visions, and each of those likely had numerous derivatives within the Army, Royal Navy
and Parliament respectively.[132] None of this was helped by the core of new Marine regiments
typically being drawn from existing regiments of foot and officers on half pay, bringing with
them their own preconceptions of soldierly duties and an opportunity for colonels to excise
the dross from their own ranks.[133] Moreover, the 'going on board like a marine' was seen as
undignified work for a soldier of the proper school.[134]

Consequently, Anson's first commission with a dedicated Marine force was not a happy
one. In preparation for his expedition to the Pacific, Anson was initially given Colonel
Bland's Regiment and three independent companies of Marines. Yet, in the event, the War
Office allocated 500 Chelsea pensioners of whom only 259 reported for duty, with the shortfall being made up of raw recruits. Similarly, the fleet, ordered to make-up the deficiency
of some 300 trained seamen in his squadron, instead supplied a draft of 98 Marines and
69 sailors, nearly half the latter of whom were sick on shore. Even when those pensioners
who did make it to Portsmouth were found unfit for service, Anson could not discharge
them: he attempted to land 'two invalid officers' at St Helens, but was thwarted by the Lords
Justices.[135] As it was, not a single invalid survived the epic voyage,[136] a cruel fate for men
who had already 'spent the activity and strength of their youth in their country's service'.[137]

The entire episode smacked of bureaucratic intransigence and ignorance of naval matters,
and the dangers of 'allowing officers...to remain at the head of affairs when that energy is
worn out'.[138] Further, the use of Marines as a substitute for sailors hinted at their confusing
purpose; as early as 1720 they were described as a 'nursery for seamen', an attitude that
persisted well in to the 1740s.[139] As hostilities came to a close in 1748, there was one thing
that both army and navy could agree on: the unsuitability of the current establishment of
marines to their allotted task. Consequently, Anson 'advocated for their complete disband-
ment' rather than attempt any reform to the existing structure and administration.[140] Better
to begin from a clean slate.

---

131 Alfred J. Marini, 'Parliament and the Marine Regiments, 1739', in Merrill L. Bartlett (ed.), *Assault form
the Sea: Essays on the History of Amphibious Warfare* (Annapolis: United States Naval Institute, 1983),
pp.39-45.

132 Britt Zerbe, *The Birth of the Royal Marines 1664-1802* (Woodbridge: Boydell Press, 2013), pp.17-42.

133 Harding, *The Emergence of Britain's Global Supremacy*, pp.72-73.

134 Rex Whitworth, *Field Marshal Lord Ligonier: A Story of the British Army 1702-1770* (Oxford:
Clarendon Press, 1958), p.257

135 Anson, *The Life of Admiral Lord Anson*, p.26.

136 Barrow, *The Life of George Lord Anson*, p.24.

137 Anson, *A Voyage Around the World*, p.7.

138 Anson, *The Life of Admiral Lord Anson*, p.26.

139 Josiah Burchett, *A Complete History of the Most Remarkable Transactions at Sea from the Earliest
Accounts of time to the Conclusion of the Last War with France* (London, 1720), p.615, quoted in Zerbe,
The Birth of the Royal Marines, p.25.

140 Zerbe, *The Birth of the Royal Marines*, p.33.

That opportunity arose in March 1755 when, against a backdrop of feverish public specu-lation, the Admiralty was asked to consider re-establishing the Marines. Never again would 'regiments of invalids…be sent to sea.'[141] Within a week, new administrative processes, officers, formations and structures were submitted and approved by the Court of St James on 3 April 1755, authorising the raising of 5,000 marines in 50 companies to be stationed at Chatham, Portsmouth and Plymouth.[142] As the war continued, the Parliament voted repeat-edly to increase the Marines, reaching a zenith of some 19,000 men in 135 companies.[143] It would be another 20 years before the full structures, including barracks, were in place, but the foundations had been laid: a peacetime establishment was maintained from 1755 onwards, and tactical doctrine and procedures appeared as early as 1763.[144] If today's Corps of Royal Marines owe their existence to any Admiral, it is Anson, not James II: 3 April 1755 rather than 24 October 1664 should be celebrated as their birthday.

Health and Victuals

On Anson's watch, the health of sailors became of paramount importance. This was the responsibility of the Commissioners for Sick and Wounded Seamen, also known as the Sick and Hurt Board, one of the three Boards that reported directly to the Admiralty.[145] The Commissioners were responsible for care of sick personnel either at anchor or ashore; inspection of sick quarters; the selection, retention and appointment of medical personnel; medical supplies and provisioning; and care for prisoners of war.[146] Traditionally, sick seamen would be landed and placed into private residencies to convalesce. On the one hand, this was flexible and cheap: there were no maintenance costs or doctors' fees. On the other, the lack of both and the fact that lodgings were often taverns, meant that once sailors set foot ashore, they either died through inattention, inebriation, or, in the unlikely event that they survived, were sold into service in merchantmen. An improvement to this system was the introduction of contract hospitals in the early 1750s, but these also had their drawbacks: contractors were likely to pocket the fees whilst providing overcrowded and dirty habita-tion.[147] Hospitals had been provided overseas from the early 1740s, yet there the situation was often worse: the New Greenwich hospital in Jamaica was found to have been built 'in the middle of a bog and the most unhealthy part in all the country',[148] whilst the steward of Cobb's Cross hospital in Antigua ran a punch house at the gate.[149] Unfortunately, the Sick

---

141 Lambert, *Admirals*, p.139.
142 Zerbe, *The Birth of the Royal Marines*, p.44.
143 Paul Nicholas, *Historical Record of The Royal Marine Forces* (London: Thomas and William Boone, 1845), p.41.
144 John MacIntyre, *A Military Treatise on the Discipline of the Marine Forces, When at Sea: together with Short Instructions for Detachments Sent to attack on Shore* (London: T Davies, 1763); Nicholas, *Historical Record of The Royal Marines Forces*, p.41; Zerbe, *The Birth of the Royal Marines*, pp.60-62
145 Lavery, *Anson's Navy*, p.114; Rodger, *The Wooden World*, pp.35-36.
146 Lavery, *Anson's Navy*, p.114.
147 Rodger, *The Wooden World*, pp.109-110.
148 Rodger, *The Command of the Ocean*, p.309.
149 Rodger, *The Wooden World*, p.110.

and Hurt Board suffered from the same seasonal contraction as the rest of the Naval estab-lishment; pre-1750, it was a hostilities-only institution.[150]

In 1745, Parliament assented to a new hospital being built at Haslar on the Gosport side of Portsmouth Harbour.[151] It was one of three proposed hospitals, the other two being at Stonehouse in Plymouth, and Chatham, although the latter was not built until much later.[152] Completed in 1761 but with wards operational from 1754, Haslar was an almost unprec-edented expense; at £100,000, it was double the cost of the Admiralty building, and with 2,000 beds it was four-times larger than the private hospital at Guys and St Thomas'.[153] In 1760, it had 60 employees including a 'physician… two surgeons, a dispenser' and 'one nurse to every ten patients'.[154] Plymouth was started later, in 1758, but once it was completed in 1762 its pavilion-style became 'the model and copied all over Europe'.[155] Unfortunately, the modern navy appears to have forgotten the hard-won lessons of its forebears: today, there are no dedicated Naval or Military hospitals in the United Kingdom or its overseas bases.[156]

If effectively treating sick sailors was cure, then prevention was better victuals and clean-living conditions; the experience of 1740 was proof of this need. Whilst scurvy's death-tally has been over-rated, it's impact on sea-time is well observed.[157] In the 1730s, ships struggled to maintain more than a few weeks at sea before men began to fall ill from sickness; by the 1750s, cruises of several months were the norm.[158] Scurvy itself is not necessarily a killer, except in those cases where long voyages prevailed.[159] The human body can store several weeks of Vitamin C; the *Gloucester* did not report the first scorbutic symptoms until a full six months after leaving Spithead, and two months after departing Brazil.[160] The reality is that scurvy left its victims weakened to other diseases such as dysentery or typhus.[161] Maintaining clean air was the standard recommendation, even by James Lind who would eventually make the connection to Vitamin C, especially in the older vessels whose lower gunports could not open.[162] From 1755, cleanliness was the responsibility of the divisional officers: ships were scrubbed with vinegar and ventilated, personnel were issued with clean clothes, and hands were encouraged to bathe where possible. There was a link between dirt and illness, even if it was misunderstood.[163]

150 Lavery, *Anson's Navy*, p.114.
151 Rodger, *The Command of the Ocean*, p.309.
152 Lavery, *Anson's Navy*, p.115.
153 Rodger, *The Command of the Ocean*, p.309.
154 Lavery, *Anson's Navy*, pp.114-115.
155 Rodger, *The Command of the Ocean*, p.309.
156 Andrew Young, '"Left Him Alone with His Glory": Sir John Moore and the Miracle of Corunna', in Timothy G. Heck and Walker D. Mills (eds), *Armies in Retreat: Chaos, Cohesion, and Consequences* (Fort Leavenworth: Army University Press, 2023), p.19.
157 Rodger, *The Command of the Ocean*, p.308.
158 Wilson, *Empire of the Deep*, pp.322-323.
159 Rodger, *The Wooden World*, p.100.
160 Lambert, *Crusoe's Island*, p.71; Anson, *A Voyage Around the World*, p.58.
161 Lambert, *Crusoe's Island*, p.71; Barrow, *The Life of Lord George Anson*, p.39.
162 Lavery, *Anson's Navy*, p.103.
163 Rodger, *The Wooden World*, pp.105-109, 216; Lavery, *Anson's Navy*, p.103.

Beyond keeping personnel clean, it was recognised that quantity and quality of victuals were important for more than just morale.[164] Even if the medical profession did not make the link between fresh victuals and scurvy, seamen sought them out at every opportunity, although their tastes tended to be conservative.[165] Unfortunately, the navy routinely suffered from poor investment in the victualing process; Anson's squadron was a victim of 'sudden mobilisation' combined with a poor harvest.[166] Between 1743 and 1760, the navy slowly expanded its own facilities at each of the major depots (Deptford, Portsmouth and Plymouth), bringing the problem of supply into the hands of the Victualling Board and out of the hands of private enterprise.[167] It was somewhat counter-intuitive: in 1758, the Board was able to feed upwards of 70,000 men for *less* than the cost of feeding 48,000 in 1710, and yet less than one percent of all victuals were condemned. Not only this, but there was an intrinsic link between agricultural markets, the Victualling Board's purchasing power, and the growth of a national and international commerce.[168] The interdependent relationship between state consumers and private producers is one which should be studied by governments today, let alone historians.

Further, the Navy and Victualling Boards experimented with new stores and accepted theories such as Lind's 1753 *Treatise on Scurvy*; the introduction of fresh victuals to ships in port in 1756 reduced scurvy cases.[169] In 1759, worried about the possibility of scurvy amongst the Western Squadron, the Admiralty (with Anson at its head) ordered them to be re-victualled at sea, a 'momentous order' and the 'first adoption on a large scale of the practice of "replenishment at sea" on which modern navies depend.'[170] Not only that, but those ships cruising off the French coast could obtain stores direct from the enemy; the crew of the *Monmouth* captured 20 head of cattle on the island of Beneguet off the Breton coast.[171] The Victualling Board commissioned 14 coasters and barges to supply the fleet. Each vessel, of between 80-100 tons burthen, could transport '20 oxen or 140 sheep plus cabbages, onions and carrots'.[172] Hawke was thus able to maintain the Western Squadron at sea for six months; an unheard-of feat which completely altered the course of the naval conflict.[173] Divorced and quarantined from the rest of humanity, ships at sea soon became bubbles of immunity, even with their cramped conditions on board.[174] On the day of the Battle of Quiberon, Lambert estimates that out of a fleet of 20 battleships, fewer than 20 men

---

164 Wilson, *Empire of the Deep*, p.324; Rodger, *The Wooden World*, p.86.
165 Rodger, *The Wooden World*, p.86.
166 Rodger, *The Command of the Ocean*, pp.305-306.
167 Lavery, *Anson's Navy*, p.114; Wilson, *Empire of the Deep*, p.324.
168 Rodger, *The Command of the Ocean*, pp.306-307; *ibid.*, *The Wooden World*, pp.84-85.
169 Lambert, *Admirals*, p.150; Rodger, *The Wooden World*, pp.85,100-101.
170 Lambert, *Admirals*, p.150; Rodger, *The Wooden World*, p.101.
171 Tim Clayton, *Tars: The Men Who Made Britain Rule The Waves* (London: Hodder & Stoughton, 2008), p.122.
172 David Syrett, *Shipping and Military Power in the Seven Years War* (Exeter: University of Exeter Press, 2008), pp.47-50.
173 Lambert, *War at Sea*, p.120.
174 Rodger, *The Wooden World*, pp.104-105.

were sick.[175] Indeed, James Lind, then serving as a physician at the newly constructed Haslar hospital, remarked upon this:

> It is an observation, I think, worthy of record – that fourteen thousand persons, pent up in ships, should continue, for six or seven months, to enjoy a better state of health upon the watery element, than it can be imagined so great a number of people would enjoy, on the most healthful spot of ground in the world.[176]

This improved state of hygiene and victuals 'enabled the sailors to outfight their rivals.'[177] Hawke maintained a steady correspondence with the Admiralty, informing them of the state of his crews, victuals and ships.[178] Moreover, increased sea time brought by effective victualling had consequences beyond good health. Firstly, naval training is only effective when ships are at sea, with room to practice all points of sailing in formation and sufficient clear range to practice the guns[179]; famously, only the Royal Navy practiced with live rounds rather than squibs. For the French at Brest, the opposite was true: subjected to close blockade, what crews they had wasted and idled their time in harbour unable to train, and often afflicted by typhus.[180]

   Secondly, Britain could now successfully and efficiently embark on that mode of warfare which would become her hallmark: amphibious operations. It is no coincidence that whilst Britain had struggled to project power beyond her own shores in the 1740s, by 1759 she was launching simultaneous strikes on the American, Caribbean, African and European seaboards.[181] One can only project power if the logistical mass and infrastructure exists to do so, something that was not true in 1740. This is testament to the navy that Anson had built; one in which a 'man's first duty was to the good of the Service,' with a 'rigorous devotion to high standards of training and conduct.'[182]

People and Manning

Recruitment, training, selection and retention are perennial questions for any organisation, and the Royal Navy in the eighteenth century was no exception. Then, as now, it was easy enough to build the ships; more significant was finding the right personnel to crew them. Officers were relatively straightforward to recruit, there being only four professions open to the gentry: Army officer; Royal Navy officer; clergyman; or lawyer. Entering into the navy at the tender age of 13 or 14 was a necessary advantage: young boys were hardy and adaptable to the rigours of shipborne life; whilst the requirement to learn a trade precluded the

---

175 Lambert, *Admirals*, p.150.
176 Rodger, *The Wooden World*, p.101.
177 Harding, *Seapower*, p.216.
178 Frank McLynn, *1759: The Year Britain Became Master of the World* (London: Pimlico, 2005), p.360
179 Wilson, *Empire of the Deep*, p.331.
180 Wilson, *Empire of the Deep*, p.333; Jonathan Dull, *The French Navy and the Seven Years War* (Lincoln: University of Nebraska Press, 2005), p.135; Lambert, *War at Sea*, p.119.
181 Andrew Young, 'Amphibious Genesis: Thomas More Molyneux and The Birth of Amphibious Doctrine', in Timothy Heck & B.A Friedman (eds), *On Contested Shores* (Quantico: Marine Corps University Press, 2020), pp.38-54.
182 Rodger, *The Wooden World*, p.31.

expense of university or purchase into a smart regiment, even if influence was still needed. Normally, individuals were taken on as officers' (most likely captain's) servants to learn their trade. Those who did not have influence or could afford some small measure of education might find their way to the Royal Naval Academy at Portsmouth. Primarily for those boys directly under Admiralty patronage, the Naval Academy was a result of the abolition of Pepys' 'King's Letter Boys'. Although it had good intentions, it possessed many disadvantages: entrants required familiarity with Latin; its studies were predominantly theoretical, for a practical profession; and having spent three years in study, graduates entered the fleet absent of the patrons and connections that would further their prospects. At £50-£60 a year, the Academy was not cheap, and nor was it popular, either amongst its trainees or the end customer: the fleet.[183]

However an officer entered the fleet – whether from the servants' quarters, the Academy, from the Warrant or Petty Officers' mess, or indeed from the merchant marine – officers could only obtain a commission after six years' service (with at least two as midshipman or master's mate), having reached the age of 20, and passing the examination for lieutenant.[184] Even so, the examination for lieutenant was hardly the meritocratic ideal one might suppose, and hid many faults:[185] any system is only as good as those that administer it. In the 1740s, that system was creaking, not least because the networks of patronage had singularly failed, as shown in the list of disgraced officers after the Battle of Toulon.[186] Anson set about reforming officer careers and imbuing the corps with a sense of self and pride. First, he formalised arrangements for uniform and commissioned rank equivalency to the Army; common complaints that were quickly rectified.[187] Second, he de-linked promotion beyond lieutenant from political influence.[188] Proven ability and merit would take priority, although personal patronage was still of import; how else would his own officers be advanced?[189] However, whatever the mutterings of officers like Augustus Hervey,[190] the promotion of those who served under Anson in the hard years 1740-44 reads as a 'who's who' of mid-eighteenth century naval commanders: Brett; Saunders; Keppel; Parker; Campbell; Dennis.[191] His reforms to promotion also saw him expand the flag-rank pool – promoting officers too old, infirm or worn out away from frontline commands and into retirement.[192] These so-called 'Yellow Admirals' therefore left vacancies at captain for younger, promising appointees.[193] Similarly, Anson learnt from his own experience of being denied a Commodore's broad

183 Lavery, *Anson's Navy*, pp.54-55; Rodger, *The Wooden World*, pp.60, 145, 265; *ibid., The Command of the Ocean*, p.265.
184 Lavery, *Anson's Navy*, p.54-57; Rodger, *The Wooden World*, pp.60, 262-265; *ibid., The Command of the Ocean*, p.381.
185 Lavery, *Anson's Navy*, pp.54-57.
186 Mahan, *The Influence of Sea Power upon History*, p.268.
187 Lavery, *Anson's Navy*, pp.58-59.
188 Wilson, *Empire of the Deep*, p.333.
189 Lavery, *Anson's Navy*, pp.60-61.
190 Clayton, *Tars*, pp.51-52.
191 Anson, *The Life of Admiral Lord Anson* p.186.
192 Lambert, *Admirals*, p.137-138.
193 Lavery, *Anson's Navy*, p.65.

pennant[194] to formalise procedures for officers temporarily commanding squadrons detached from the main force.[195] Unsurprisingly, this mark of favour advanced Anson's proteges; Augustus Keppel first raised his pennant as a 24-year old in 1749.[196]

Concomitant to this reform to officer selection and promotion, however, Anson reviewed and tightened up the Fighting Instructions.[197] Its twelfth article was explicit:

> Every person in the fleet, who through cowardice, negligence, or disaffection, shall in time of action withdraw or keep back, or not come into the fight or engagement, or shall not do his utmost to take or destroy every ship which it shall be his duty to engage, and to assist and relieve all and every of His Majesty's ships, or those of his allies, which it shall be his duty to assist and relieve, every such person so offending, and being convicted thereof by the sentence of a court martial, shall suffer death.[198]

Whereas a senior officer who 'failed to do his utmost' in 1744 might be cashiered or censured, the 1749 Article would see Admiral Byng executed on his own quarterdeck, leading to Voltaire's infamous quip: 'Dans ce pays-ci, il est bon de tuer de temps en temps un amiral pour encourager les autres'.[199] This was to be a new type of officer corps, one that was incentivised to fight. Pre-1746, too many admirals and captains had been outfought by their French or Spanish counterparts,[200] yet Anson and his proteges (including Hawke) had shown what could be achieved if the fleet was well led: the Western Squadron annihilated French power in 1747, capturing 21 warships at First and Second Finisterre.[201] Under Anson, officers would be held accountable to something greater than political expediency: duty.[202]

That reform went beyond the officer corps to include the seamen but was relatively modest in comparison; there could be limited change without parliamentary consent.[203] The primary concern was how to mobilise the fleet effectively given the perennial scarcity of seamen; Rodger estimates that demand outstripped supply by 2:1.[204] Parliament refused to countenance a voluntary reserve of just 3,000 men in 1749, citing the cost (£10 per man per annum) and the likelihood that individuals would either be 'idle, lazy, indolent' or seek employment in the 'coasting trade or fisheries', and thus not be available for service. Instead, Anson would have to rely on the relatively good peacetime wages enjoyed by sailors, by the volunteer-bounty system, and the impress.[205]

With parliament refusing to countenance a suitable reserve scheme or match wartime merchant marine wage increases, Anson set about increasing the effectiveness of the impress

---

194 Barrow, The Life of George Lord Anson, p.22.
195 Lambert, Admirals, p.138.
196 Lavery, Anson's Navy, p.65.
197 Lambert, Admirals, p.144.
198 Articles of War, as established by an Act of Parliament, 2 December 1749.
199 François-Marie Arouet Voltaire, Candide (1759), Kindle edition, location: 1113.
200 Harding, The Emergence of Britain's Global Naval Supremacy, pp.338-339.
201 Lambert, Admirals, p.137.
202 Wilson, Empire of the Deep, p.321.
203 Lavery, Anson's Navy, p.72.
204 Rodger, The Wooden World, p.149.
205 Lavery, Anson's Navy, p.72; Rodger, The Command of the Ocean, pp.313, 316.

service.[206] In 1755, he stationed tenders in each of the ports to which men pressed ashore could be confined prior to assignment to a ship.[207] This had a secondary effect: by effectively quarantining 'recruits', hopefully any illnesses would run their course before sailors joined their ships, although in the event shore-side illness ran amok in the close confines.[208] Pressing sailors afloat remained the most effective means of manning the fleet.[209] If a naval ship could intercept merchantmen on their inbound voyage, the navy could have their pick of sailors before landfall and exposure to civil society's illnesses and liberties.[210] It was this class of skilled sailors that was in highest demand, and which was most limited. Either way, the impress provided a goodly portion of the navy's recruits, and it needed them in huge numbers: in 1760, over 80,000 men were serving in the Royal Navy, accounting for 67 percent of the nation's available seafarers.[211] Over 184,000 would be recruited over the course of the Seven Years War, with perhaps 15,000 dying from causes other than battle or drowning; approximately one percent of the sea-going total in any given year.[212]

If recruitment was one side of the manning problem, then retention was the other. There appeared to be an average seven percent per annum desertion rate during the Seven Years War, which may be typical of earlier wars, too. As the navy expanded, and as ships' companies underwent the trials and tribulations of loss and churn to the rigours of sea-service, so there was a pressing need to enforce greater cohesion and discipline. If the ship was to operate effectively, then officers and men needed to be acquainted with and trust each other, and to work as a team. With Anson's tacit support, Vice Admiral Thomas Smith popularised, if not invented, the divisional system in 1755. This system went hand in hand with the idea that sailors joined not a navy, but a ship; their loyalty was to the 'officers and shipmates they knew'. The system involved placing lieutenants and midshipman at the administrative heart of a group of sailors, with those parties broken down further and each held accountable for the state of their personal hygiene, clothing, bedding and accoutrements. This was a typically eighteenth-century vision of enlightened leadership, a moral duty that solved a practical problem: sailors content in their shipboard life were less likely to desert or cause discipline problems and insurrection. By the standards of the day, sailors were well paid, well fed, with good conditions of enlistment, and whilst there was use of harsh disciplinary methods, this has often been overstated.[213]

Wartime Vindication

The strength of any armed force can be assessed by its performance, and in Anson's navy we find the clearest example of prior planning and preparation delivering decisive effect.

---

206 Rodger, *The Command of the Ocean,* pp.316-317.
207 Lavery, *Anson's Navy,* p.71.
208 Rodger, *The Wooden World,* pp.107-108.
209 Lavery, *Anson's Navy,* p.72.
210 Clayton, *Tars,* p.161.
211 Rodger, *The Command of the Ocean,* p.319.
212 Lambert, *Admirals,* p.146; Rodger, *The Wooden World,* pp.104-105.
213 Lavery, *Anson's Navy,* p.96; Whitworth, *Field Marshal Lord Ligonier,* p.246; Clayton, *Tars,* p.86; Rodger, *The Command of the Ocean,* pp.316-321; *ibid., The Wooden World,* pp.216-217.

The development and success of an effective maritime strategy (such as Pitt's) was wholly dependent on the organisation and strength of the Royal Navy.[214] With the outbreak of open hostilities with France in 1756, Britain was catapulted into a global conflict she was by and large ill-prepared for.[215] Yet, 'the Seven Years War saw the British perfecting amphibious operations'[216] throughout the globe and becoming the major naval and extra-European power.[217] With campaigns fought on the soil of the American continent, in Europe and in the Indian subcontinent, control of the seas was imperative for the eventual victors and began in the preceding decade with reforms made by Anson.[218]

In 1755, the French navy had 98 warships in service, of which 57 were ships of the line, 31 frigates, and 10 smaller vessels.[219] The issue for the French was not quantity or quality of ships, for these could always be built, but lack of trained sailors to serve them; the French could supply just 52,460 merchant seamen total, of which only 20,000 could be actually called upon.[220] When Britain began snapping up French merchantmen (including 7,500 prime seamen) prior to the outbreak of war, France could do little more than seek compensation.[221] The typhus epidemic in 1757-1758 left a further 10,000 either dead or discharged unfit to serve.[222] For the remainder, poor conditions and pay made desertion a tempting endeavour.[223]

By contrast, even during the peaceful year of 1753 when war seemed far-fetched, the Royal Navy had 67 ships-of-the-line ready for sea compared to the mere 38 they had managed in 1739.[224] By 1755, Britain's navy amounted to over 216 fighting vessels, 117 of which were ships-of-the-line.[225] Whilst French naval architecture was nominally superior to British shipwrights, French vessels carried heavier but less well-made ordnance.[226] Contrast this to the advances in metallurgy and gun design brought on by the industrial revolution and Anson's re-fitting of the fleet.[227] Further, Britain enjoyed a larger availability in manpower due to her merchant and fishing fleets; the Royal Navy expanded from just 10,000 seamen to 75,000 by 1759, achieving the first 30,000 with ease.[228] Britain did not owe naval superiority to weapon technology alone. As the historian Jeremy Black sums it up, 'The greater effectiveness of the British Navy was largely due to the fact that it had more ships, to its extensive

---

214 Kennedy, *The Rise and Fall of British Naval Mastery*, pp.101-102.
215 Young, 'Amphibious Genesis', pp.40-42. For further discussion of the geostrategic headwinds into which Britain sailed in 1755, see Daniel Baugh, *The Global Seven Years War* (London: Routledge, 2014); Brendan Simms, *Three Victories and a Defeat* (London: Penguin, 2008). See also Joseph Krulder's chapter in this volume, 'Ships Wanting in the Whole'.
216 McLynn, *1759*, p.171.
217 Young, 'Amphibious Genesis', pp.38-54.
218 Mahan, *The Influence of Sea Power upon History 1660-1783*, p.329; Harding, *Seapower*, p.291.
219 Harding, *Seapower*, p.291.
220 Lavery, *Anson's Navy: Building a Fleet for Empire 1744 to 1763*, p.146; Harding, *Seapower*, p.205.
221 Dull, *The French Navy and the Seven Years War*, p.38.
222 Lambert, *War at Sea in the Age of Sail 1650 -1850*, p.116.
223 Harding, *Seapower*, p.209.
224 Wilson, *Empire of the Deep*, p.322.
225 Harding, *Seapower*, p.291.
226 Lambert, *War at Sea in the Age of Sail 1650 -1850*, p.116.
227 Harding, *Seapower*, p.203.
228 Harding, *Seapower*, p.210.

and effective administrative system, to the strength of public finances and to good Naval leadership.'[229]

Anson had created the largest fleet, and in the best condition, that Britain had ever taken to war. His unexciting, economical and careful administrative developments trod the 'golden mean between undue cost and ruinous parsimony'.[230] His ability to view the unfolding conflict as an attritional battle for global dominance cemented his key position in the War Cabinet. Taking direction from Prime Minister Pitt, Anson and Field Marshal Ligonier set about destroying French power through economic and expeditionary warfare on targets as wide ranging as India, the Americas, Africa and the coast of Europe. Britain began the Seven Years War with distinct disadvantages. Yet she developed such a successful *modus operandi* that by 1761 she was able to simultaneously strike at strategic fortresses on the very coast of France, at French possessions in the Caribbean and elsewhere, and maintain a quarter of her total army in a European theatre. It was due to the impressive results of these campaigns that Sir Charles Middleton proposed to establish a permanent amphibious task group that would provide a strategic threat to hostile intentions in the North Atlantic.[231]

The successful development of this doctrine was significantly due to Anson.[232] His peacetime selection of commanders based on merit, their understanding of the operational concept and professionalism, was responsible for creating a generation of officers who knew their business. They passed their experience onto their staffs and junior commanders, ensuring that school of thought with a wealth of knowledge continued after the original exponents had retired or died.[233] These commanders were aggressive and dynamic.[234] Much of this aggressive psychology can be traced to the 1755 trial and execution of Admiral Byng. Ordered to the island of Minorca, Byng was later court-martialled and shot 'for failing to do his utmost'; he did not attempt to reinforce the besieged garrison, or to decisively engage the enemy fleet.[235] As a result of Byng's death *pour encourager les autres*, many sea captains redoubled their efforts after 1757, with remarkable determination being shown against superior French forces. Often, French captains expected to be attacked, and 'more than half expected to be beaten'.[236] There was a psychological divide between the French and British on the art of naval war: under Anson, the navy's role was to seek out the enemy fleet and destroy it.[237] For the French, battle at sea was best summed up by the Comte de Maurepas: 'Two squadrons sail from opposite ports, they manoeuvre, they meet, they fire; a few masts are shot away, a few sails torn, a few men killed, a lot of powder and shot wasted – and the

229   Jeremy Black, *Warfare in the Eighteenth Century* (London: Cassell, 2002), p.149.
230   Lambert, *Admirals*, p.144.
231   Young, 'Amphibious Genesis', pp.38-54; Simon Foster, *Hit the Beach!* (London: Cassell, 1998) p.16; David Syrett, 'The Methodology of British Amphibious Operations during the Seven Years and American Wars', *Mariners Mirror*, 58:3, August 1972, p.280.
232   Whitworth, *Field Marshal Lord Ligonier*, p.201.
233   Lambert, *Admirals*, p.155.
234   Wilson, *Empire of the Deep*, p.344.
235   Lambert, *Admirals*, pp.143-144.
236   Rodger, *The Command of the Ocean*, p.272.
237   Corbett, *England in the Seven Years War*, pp.273-274.

sea remains no less salty than before'.[238] Decisive battle at sea was the *sine qua non* of Pitt's maritime, amphibious strategy, precisely because it conferred sea control.[239]

This difference in perspective proved decisive in 1759. First, in an attempt to reinforce the Brest fleet, on 5 August La Clue's Toulon fleet set sail and managed to evade Boscawen's blockade of the Straits.[240] Boscawen's squadron was replenishing in Gibraltar, with no canvas bent on, the majority of the complements ashore, and yet within three hours was pursuing the enemy, who attempted to seek sanctuary in Lagos Bay, Portugal.[241] In the running action that followed, Boscawen's squadron violated Portuguese neutrality:[242] they captured *Centaure*, *Temeraire*, and *Modeste*, whilst La Clue ran *Ocean* and *Redoubtable* aground rather than surrender.[243] Boscawen's victory greatly reduced the threat of invasion, leaving as it did only Conflans' forces in Brest.[244]

Meanwhile, Hawke, with 32 ships-of-the-line in the Western Squadron was blockading the Morbihan and Brest, with up to 20 sail permanently on station whilst the others rotated between refits in Torbay and Plymouth.[245] When Conflans did finally sail on 14 November, heading to the Morbihan to collect his transports, he was forced to run before a gale allowing Hawke, temporarily off station to refit and weather a storm, time to catch him, which he did on the 20th in a rising north westerly gale.[246] Both fleets were short of manpower, but the key difference was in their preparedness for battle: Hawke's fleet had been at sea for many months, honing their craft; Conflans' had been shut up in port.[247] Any confrontation would be a one-sided contest, which Conflans knew all too well.[248] He did not even attempt to form the line of battle, but rather led the desperate escape into Quiberon Bay, not thinking that Hawke would follow into the treacherous channel.[249] That Hawke threw his vessels into the pursuit, despite the risks of setting all sail in a gale, and a lee shore, is remarkable.[250] Whilst he had some knowledge of the waters in Quiberon Bay from a French chart, it was later to be found severely wanting, and whilst acknowledging the risks insisted in personally engaging the French flagship at pistol-shot.[251] The resultant debacle ended in a resounding victory for Hawke and broke French naval power, although one would not know it to read his dispatch: 'had we but two hours more daylight' he lamented, 'the whole had been totally destroyed or taken'.[252] In all, six French vessels were sunk or wrecked on the reefs of Quiberon Bay including the flagship.[253] A further six were bottled up in the Vilaine River having jettisoned

238 Maurepas, quoted in Rodger, *The Command of the Ocean*, p.272.
239 Young, 'Amphibious Genesis', 2020, pp.38-54.
240 Wilson, *Empire of the Deep*, p.333.
241 Rodger, *The Command of the Ocean*, p.277.
242 Lambert, *Admirals*, pp.149-150.
243 Wilson, *Empire of the Deep*, p.334.
244 Lambert, *Admirals*, p.150.
245 Wilson, *Empire of the Deep*, p.330.
246 Lambert, *War at Sea*, p.120.
247 Rodger, *The Command of the Ocean*, p.277.
248 Wilson, *Empire of the Deep*, p.339.
249 Rodger, *The Command of the Ocean*, p.282.
250 Kennedy, *The Rise and Fall of British Naval Mastery*, p.102.
251 Rodger, *The Command of the Ocean*, p.280; Wilson, *Empire of the Deep*, p.341.
252 Lambert, *War at Sea*, p.121; Wilson, *Empire of the Deep*, p.342.
253 Dull, *The French Navy and the Seven Years War*, p.162.

their ordnance, whilst eight managed to escape to Rochefort.[254] French casualties amounted to more than 2,500, most of them Bretons drowned in the appalling seas.[255] Hawke lost two vessels to grounding and 400 men.[256]

Conclusion

What can we take today from the career of Anson? For Anson, duty came first. He inspired loyalty in his subordinates by risking his own career on their behalf and led by example in all that he did. He took interest in all matters, mastering his profession and successfully melding his political and naval careers to the navy's benefit. He did not simply use the existing system, but streamlined it, making the good more efficient and discharging the irrelevant. He selected and promoted the best, rewarding proven ability early, and built ships that were able to power project and influence globally. He established the Marines as a permanent fixture, overhauled all administrative processes, and ensured that the Admiralty became the centralised intersection for all naval business, from political to routine management. He elevated the art of the admiral beyond mere chartwork; he understood clearly that navies have an importance and effect that extends beyond the coastline. He took naval power and made it global, strategic and political.

These acts bequeathed to Britain an Empire and an example of Naval strategic leadership that was taught to Fisher's Royal Navy some 150 years later. Ships built to project power around the globe, manned by professionals who put duty first resulted in a navy whose collective knowledge and cultural maturity was his legacy, one founded on victory. It is no coincidence that this was the name given to the most successful first-rate ever built, laid down in 1759, the *Annus Mirabilis* (the Year of Victories), and that *Hearts of Oak* was penned to celebrate Minden, Quebec, Lagos, and Quiberon. These victories spawned a ship whose presence and name is a daily echo of his dedication and professionalism, of an ethos and culture based on 'the determination to fight and win': HMS *Victory* lies at the heart of Portsmouth Naval Base, a constant reminder to current and future generations of naval personnel.[257] No officer before or since has matched his supreme example as a politician, a strategist, a leader, and a manager. George Anson was not merely a man who used a fleet; he was the giant who built one.

---

254 Rodger, *The Command of the Ocean*, p.280; Wilson, *Empire of the Deep*, p.341.
255 Dull, *The French Navy and the Seven Years War*, p.162.
256 McLynn, *1759*, pp.365-381.
257 This remains the foundation principle of the Royal Navy's Ethos, Values and Standards today: 'The enduring spirit derived from our people's loyalty to their ship, unit or team, sustained by high professional standards and strong leadership that gives us courage in adversity and the determination to fight and win'. Royal Navy, BRD 3 Naval Personnel Management, Ch21, Section 7, Annex H at <https://www.royalnavy.mod.uk/-/media/royal-navy-responsive/documents/reference-library/br-3-vol-1/br3d-vol-1-feb-2022/ch21_compressed.pdf?la=en-gb&rev=f5f58aae983445c6866b361974d90e5e&hash=E359BD0CD4A4ACBB603322081AA68C27> (Accessed 5 March 2023).

Select Bibliography

Published Primary Sources

Anson, George, *A Voyage Around the World in the Years 1740-1744*, Richard Walter ed. (London: John and Paul Knapton, 1748).

Secondary Sources

Barrow, John, *The Life of George Lord Anson* (London: John Murray, 1839).
Lambert, Andrew, *Admirals: The Naval Commanders who Made Britain Great* (London: Faber & Faber, 2008).
Lavery, Brian, *Anson's Navy: Building a Fleet for Empire 1744 to 1763* (Barnsley: Seaforth, 2021).
Rodger, Nicholas, *The Wooden World* (London: Penguin Press, 1988).

10

'Ships wanting in the whole:' Naval Dysfunctions at the Beginning of the Seven Years War

Joseph Krulder

Benjamin Keene, Britain's ambassador to Spain, wrote home to the Southern Secretary, Henry Fox in early May 1756. Keene relayed to Fox the Spanish King's view of the British Royal Navy. For some two years, tensions between France and Great Britain had substantially increased, a factor European powers warily heeded. Keene's job required his preventing Spain from joining forces with France in what would quickly emerge as the Seven Years War. 'As to the Court of Spain', wrote Keene, 'it will appear Extraordinary, that the Catholick King has been wishing for His Majesty's Squadron, and is as uneasy at its Retardment.'[1] Ever the diplomat, Keene's words carried a double meaning. 'Retardment' could mean 'late' in regard to time, or it could signify deficiencies, holding a possibility that the said 'squadron' was not all that good. In this case, both factors were true. The Royal Navy had dispatched a small, undermanned, and ill-fitted fleet toward the Mediterranean which, in fact, arrived too late to prevent France from landing 15,000 troops on the Island of Minorca. With the squadron en route, George II declared war on France (17 May 1756), and on 20 May, a sea battle between France and Britain proved inconclusive. Just over a month later, the British troops at Fort St Philip, the last stronghold on Minorca, surrendered, and the island fell to the French.

However, King Ferdinand VI's concern with the status of Britain's Royal Navy as the Seven Years War erupted should not be deemed extraordinary by modern scholars of that era. Indeed, the Royal Navy was as the Spanish king observed; ill-equipped, undermanned, and in some disrepair when the war officially commenced. This chapter will attempt to uncover the readiness of the Royal Navy as it went to war with France in the beginning throes of the Seven Years War. Through intensive archival research the navy's inauspicious start to the war can be shown to fall into three major categories. First, naval engagements from the previous year; Boscawen's Canadian intercept, the Channel campaign against French maritime interests, and others damaged the readiness of the fleet. Second, a cumbersome supply

---

1   Keene to Fox, 11 May 1756, British Library (BL), ADD MS 43437, f.63.

system certainly failed to keep pace with naval demands; shortages in slops, bedding, and uneven quality in sailcloth and ropes hampered the navy's ability to meet Admiralty expectations. More ominous, perhaps, were the sorry state of shipyard facilities at Portsmouth, Chatham, and Nore, but also overseas facilities within the growing British Empire. Third, the Admiralty's 1755 request to raise 30,000 sailors fell significantly short of the mark. An outbreak of disease stymied naval operations throughout the year. By 1756, filling shipboard billets became a shell game of transfers from one ship to another in a losing bid to send readied fleets to meet the enemy and defend the realm.

Further, a deep study of these Royal Navy's missteps during the opening salvos of the Seven Years War can then become a sort of template. The development of empire-building is a story of ineluctable ocean-going conflicts with others. But the archival evidence in this chapter also reveals that 'empire' consisted of severe domestic constraints. This chapter, therefore, offers an opportunity to reattach military and naval history with those of internal social, cultural, and political points of view.

1755, Royal Navy Operations the Year Prior

> Vice Admiral Boscawen is now under sail with the squadron under his command, except the *Dunkirk* which will follow this evening. As there is a fine breeze of wind easterly, I am in hopes they will get clear of the Wight before night.[2]

Three major naval operations combined in 1755 to place significant strain on the future material readiness of the Royal Navy as the Seven Years War approached. The first of these began in April of 1755. Vice Admiral Edward Boscawen sailed with 19 warships attempting to intercept a French fleet carrying soldiers, weapons, and supplies for their reinforcement of Canada. The second Royal Navy operation began in late July, a sizeable fleet under the command of Vice Admiral Edward Hawke attacked French maritime vessels returning to France on seasonal trade winds. Last, throughout all of 1755, transporting recently impressed men, whether at sea or from distant northern ports to naval bases in the south, placed stress on tenders, the usual transport vessels assigned to such jobs. Additionally, fear of a French invasion upon the British archipelago appeared as a predominate motivator among political elites at Westminster to keep ships anchored and at the ready at various home ports.

Of these 1755 operations, the most well-known is the plight of Boscawen's intercept fleet. Edward Boscawen's reputation as a 'fighting admiral' bound the Admiralty to send him and a fleet to intercept a French troop and supply convoy in late April 1755.[3] Eleven French ships of the line under *Chef d'Escadre* Emmanuel-Auguste de Cahideuc, Comte Dubois de la Motte, and *Chef d'Escadre* Antoine-Alexis Périer de Salvert sailed from Brest to reinforce Canada, gutting their cannons to make room for four battalions or 3,650 men. Jean-Baptist

---

2   Hawke to Clevland, 21 April 1755, The National Archives (TNA), ADM 1/919.
3   Tom Pocock, *Battle for Empire: The Very First World War, 1756-63* (London: Michael O'Mara Books, 1998), p.87.

MacNemara guarded this *en flûte* flotilla with six warships.[4] Crossing the Atlantic to engage the French fleet, Boscawen called for daily gun drills.[5] Initially, Boscawen's 19 ships appeared ready, trained, and led by reputable admiral.

Yet the mission failed. For the second time in his career (the first occasion having been in 1748 off Pondicherry, India) Boscawen critically misjudged a difficult situation. On 8 June, in dense fog off Newfoundland, three of the 17 French ships were spotted. The rest of the French reinforcement fleet were not to be seen. Boscawen's mission was to attack the totality of the enemy. Instead, Boscawen bore down and captured the *Alcide* and *Lys*; the third ship escaped, and the bulk of French reinforcements and supplies made it to Canada. Needless to say, this outcome was not what the Admiralty had hoped for. Captain Augustus Hervey noted in his journal that Boscawen's taking of the two French ships 'made great noise everywhere', as by virtue of the attack, 'war was inevitable'. However, Erskine, the editor of Hervey's journal, stated that Boscawen's actions off Newfoundland placed Britain in moral ambiguity 'without any compensating military advantage'.[6] Diplomatically, Britain appeared as the failed aggressor as the two nations vied for allies in an anticipated war between them.

However, the cost of the mission was more than failed diplomatic ventures. Militarily, Boscawen lost nearly a third of his fleet. The Admiralty expected Boscawen to return to Portsmouth in early September 1755. The admiral, however, chose to leave six of his 19 ships in Halifax, Nova Scotia. Simply put, there were not enough sailors to return the full fleet after the botched attempt at preventing France from resupplying Canada. When Boscawen did arrive in Portsmouth in mid-November, he relayed to the admiralty that sickness ran through his fleet and took some 2,000 lives (more on this below). The loss of men and ships thwarted the Royal Navy's billeting needs and reduced its ability to properly fit out ships for future deployments.

Adding to the navy's vulnerability to either manpower or material readiness is the lesser known but perhaps more important Channel campaign. In July 1755, the Admiralty ended its debate about pre-emptively striking French maritime vessels. Using examples derived from Francis Drake, all three of the seventeenth-century Dutch Wars, and the pre-emptive strikes Britain made against Spain on the eve of the War of Spanish Succession, precedence demonstrated that an attack on French shipping in the Atlantic could go forward ancillary to proper justifications.[7] Vice Admiral Edward Hawke then received a series of orders to ready a sizable fleet, the success of which became one of Britain's greatest naval-led pre-emptive strikes in its history.[8] A total of 353 French merchant vessels were captured in an

---

4   Jonathan R. Dull, *The French Navy and the Seven Years' War* (Lincoln: University of Nebraska Press, 2005), p.25.

5   N.A.M. Rodger, *The Wooden World: An Anatomy of the Georgian Navy* (New York: W.W. Norton, 1996), p.42.

6   David Erskine (ed.), *Augustus Hervey's Journal: The Adventures Afloat and Ashore of a Naval Casanova* (London: Chatham Publishing, 2002), pp.182-183.

7   Julian S. Corbett, *England in the Seven Years' War: A Study in Combined Strategy*, vol. 1 (London: Longmans, Green, and Co., 1907), pp.50-51.

8   It has been argued that Britain's pre-emptive attack on French warships at Mers-el-Kébir in 1940 may equal or surpass the 1755 Channel Campaign's success. Brett C. Bowels, "'La Tragédie de Mers-el-Kébir" and the Politics of Filmed News in France, 1940–1944', *The Journal of Modern History*, vol. 76,

Atlantic and Mediterranean plunder of commercial trading routes and the blockading of important French port towns and cities. Captured French maritime vessels were sent into 'England, Gibraltar, Leghorn, South Carolina, Virginia, Boston, Nova-Scotia and Jamaica' as possible prizes.[9] Diplomacy kept the French ships, its cargo, and its men in limbo. George II, through the Treasury Department, enticed his counterpart, Louis XV, to agree to new peace terms to avoid conflict. Only when the Seven Years War became officially declared (17 May 1756), did the Treasury Department allow the captured ships and cargo to be sold as prizes.

However, the success of the Channel campaign came at a price.[10] Like Boscawen's intercept fleet, disease ran through Hawke's Channel fleet with alarming alacrity. According to historian Stephen Gradish, approximately 4,000 men were sent to various hospitals through the south of England, with 1,000 dead or permanently incapacitated.[11] By the end of September 1755, Hawke called it quits.[12] Admiral John Byng replaced Hawke and took charge of a mostly fresh set of ships to continue plundering French maritime interests beginning mid-October. Though the reports of diseases did abate alleviating local portside hospitals of the crushing numbers of sick sailors, Byng's fleet fell victim to foul weather. November storms pummelled Byng's Channel squadron. Although the weather had turned, the admiral remained on station prompting naval historian Daniel Baugh to emphasize Byng's 'dogged' effort toward the success of the campaign.[13] On 22 November, Byng gave orders for the fleet to return to Portsmouth. Byng sent a dispatch to the Admiralty detailing the damage incurred: the *Buckingham*, *Trident*, *Orford*, *Lyme*, and *Eagle* fell victim to rough seas and heavy gales and were heavily damaged. 'Upon the whole', he wrote, 'I looked upon the Squadron as in a great measure disabled and not fit to remain as Cruisers'. The *Revenge*, one of the ships that later sailed with Byng in the attempt to save Minorca, had its main mast cracked and splintered, and the 'Tallents of the Rudder fetched way as far down as they could see'.[14] Nineteen of 24 ships within Byng's Channel fleet needed refitting once the

---

no. 2 (June 2004), pp.347–88; Philippe Lasterle, 'Could Admiral Gensoul Have Averted the Tragedy of Mers el-Kébir?' *The Journal of Military History*, vol. 67, no.3 (July 2003), pp.835–844; Martin Thomas, 'After Mers-el-Kébir: The Armed Neutrality of the Vichy French Navy, 1940–43', *The English Historical Review*, vol. 112, no. 447 (June 1997), pp.643–670.

9   Prize Commissioners to Treasury Board, 19 October 1764, TNA, T 1/436/94.

10   The Admiralty initially envisioned the attack on French maritime interests to take place off the coast of France, but once word got out, Royal Navy captains in North America, the Caribbean, as well as the Mediterranean joined in. Early on, the Admiralty sometimes referred to the preemptive strike as 'a Channel Campaign' and connected the task toward preventing a French invasion, but it quickly expanded beyond that task and geographic location.

11   Stephen Gradish, *The Manning of the British Navy during the Seven Years War* (London: Royal Historical Society, 1980), p.32.

12   *London Evening Post*, 27 September 1755.

13   Daniel Baugh, *The Global Seven Years War, 1754–1763* (London: Routledge, 2014), pp.142–146. On the weather, confirmation comes from Thomas Turner, a deacon at his church in South Hoathly, noted that on 25 November 1755, the 'night has been a very remarkable windy night and a great quantity of rain . . .' David Vaisey (ed.), *The Diary of Thomas Turner, 1754–1765* (Oxford: Oxford University Press, 1984), p.18.

14   Byng to Clevland, 22 November 1755, TNA, ADM 1/88. Ironically, the *Revenge*'s rudder had just been repaired at Port Mahon, Minorca, in the Mediterranean some months before. Three of those ships: *Buckingham*, *Trident*, and *Revenge* would sail with Byng to Minorca four months and a week later. See,

admiral finally pulled back into Portsmouth.[15] To further show the extent of damage, Navy Treasurer George 'Bubb' Dodington wrote to the exchequer in financial terms. Wear and tear for just 'one Months Course of the Navy ending 30th Novem 1755 [cost] £58,392 · 3 · 0'.[16] Weather ended the Channel Campaign but left a wake of damaged ships that needed immediate repairing. When Byng sailed for the Mediterranean the following April, half of his ships remained in some state of disrepair.

For the Royal Navy, various other operations reduced material readiness and worsened already precarious manning issues. Illustrative to this were the eight warships, fully manned, sent to India under two admirals, George Pocock and Charles Watson. For the first time in its history, the Royal Navy escorted East India Company merchant ships beyond the Atlantic into the Indian Ocean. Once their escort duties were fulfilled, Pocock and Watson remained and patrolled the coasts of the Indian subcontinent, unavailable therefore to tend to military necessities elsewhere.[17]

Additionally, the Admiralty ordered 12 transports to 'Stade in the Elbe' to retrieve Hessian and Hanoverian foot and horse regiments. The Navy office requested from the Victualling Office to prepare the necessaries for boarding and transporting Hessians numbering 3,457 men and 204 horses.[18] Byng left for Minorca in the Mediterranean two days later having been denied transports by the Admiralty. Transporting recently impressed men also stressed the Royal Navy's readiness and manning issues. Here, too, weather played a role in damaging transports and sloops. Several vessels also experienced mutinies and were run aground. The *Tasker* tender, in fact, fell to mutiny twice, in early May off Liverpool, and then again, a month later off Beaumaris, Wales. Near Hull, a mutiny took control of a tender and killed its captain. One hundred and thirty escaped after they ran the tender into the banks of the Trent.[19] Invasion fears also taxed the Admiralty in preparing ships and fleets needed elsewhere for the expected war effort.[20] Despite ministerial apprehensions of a French invasion on British soil, George Anson thought such an invasion as 'not very strong'[21]. Recent history likely drove ministerial and therefore naval policy. Within living memory, Britain witnessed its sovereignty breached by France in two major (1715 and 1745) and two minor (1708 and 1719) attempts. The Admiralty Office chose, perhaps reluctantly, to keep dozens of ships at the ready and close to home shores.

Byng to Clevland, 12 November 1755, TNA, ADM 1/88.

15   Papers Relating to the Army and Navy, BL, ADD MS 33047, f. 24.

16   Dodington to the Treasury, 22 April 1756, TNA, T 1/366/8.

17   Admiral Charles Watson Papers of the India Office Records collections at the BL, MSS EUR D1079.

18   Navy Office to Victualling Office, 5 April 1756, NMM, ADM C 542. Hired German mercenaries were used to protect England's southern coast from a possible French invasion.

19   Court Martial records and newspapers reveal a string of mutinies throughout 1755. On the first *Tasker* mutiny see Hawke to Clevland, 2 June 1755, TNA, ADM 1/920. See also, *Newcastle Courant*, 31 May 1755; *Bodley's Bath Journal*, 2 June 1755; and the *Newcastle Journal*, 31 May-7 June, and 7 June-14 June 1755.

20   John Gordon to Newcastle, 3 October 1755, BL, ADD MS 32859, f. 350. Almon charged that 'The bug-bear fears of an invasion engrossed all the attention of the ministry' well into 1758. See, John Almon, *An Impartial History of the Late War* (London: J. Johnson and J. Curtiss, 1763), pp.91–92.

21   Anson to Holderness, 9 May 1755, BL, MS Egerton 3444, f.42.

This decision manifested in a human shell game, the Admiralty directing ships' billeting needs from London. One example occurred the following March when Admiral Byng was sent orders to head to Portsmouth to fit out a fleet destined to protect Minorca. Yet, once he arrived, the admiral discovered a new set of London-based orders waiting. Byng was to fill the billets of home and channel fleets first, ahead of his Mediterranean-bound ships.[22] As it were, the admiral whisked off 50 supernumeraries just recently assigned to the *Cambridge* prior to his embarkation. Byng would have taken more, but fresh arrivals of impressed men had been sent to the *Blenheim*, the Royal Navy's hospital ship anchored at Portsmouth.[23]

These combined major and minor operations equated to a story of the Royal Navy that attempted to do too much with too little. The effect on naval readiness spilled out into the following year.

Inadequate Supplies and Port Facilities

> The Sugar's extremely black, coarse and ready to run into Molasses; and the fruit in general, mouldy and so mash'd and clotted, that it is scarce possible to determine what was put up for it; full of dust and musty. The Cinnamon very coarse & having neither spicy taste nor flavor... of Shalots and Garlick Stipulated by contract, there is in each Box a few ounces of Chocolate, no way adequate, as to usefulness...[24]

Vice Admiral Edward Hawke ordered officers to conduct a survey of victuals sent to temporary hospital ships that recently anchored at Spithead in late April 1755. A fresh bout of illnesses had sent hundreds of sailors to nearby Haslar Hospital soon overflowing with sick jacktars. Foodstuffs were rowed out to these temporary hospital ships, but the quality of the victuals were found to be insufficient. Hawke then advised the Admiralty to make inquiries of both the local Portsmouth Victualling Office and local contractors.[25] Yet, victuals were the least of Hawke's problems. As the officer overseeing operations at Portsmouth, Hawke encountered a bevy of issues that hampered his and, therefore, the Royal Navy's ability to prepare needed warships for an expected war against France. Indeed, in the same letter complaining of the quality of food, Hawke also criticised 'sheets so patched & darn'd, that is impossible to make a roller of a yard long out of them'.[26] This segment of the chapter explores both the shortcomings of the Royal Navy's supply system and its port facilities as it prepared for the outbreak of what would become the Seven Years War.

As 1755 began, the Admiralty planned to ready 95 additional ships and recruit 30,000 additional seamen for expected actions against France. The previous year ended with the

---

22   Gradish, *The Manning of the British Navy during the Seven Years War*, pp.36-37.
23   Osborn to Clevland, 9 April 1756, TNA, ADM 1/921. Supernumeraries were usually recently impressed men that had arrived at a naval port but not yet assigned to a ship.
24   Hawke to Clevland, 27 April 1755, TNA, ADM 1/919.
25   It should be noted that N.A.M. Rodger suggests that errors in providing the Royal Navy with victuals was astonishingly low as less than '1 per cent' of it was ever condemned. N.A.M. Rodger, *The Wooden World: An Anatomy of the Georgian Navy* (New York: W. W. Norton & Co, 1996), p.85.
26   Hawke to Clevland, 27 April 1755, TNA, ADM 1/919.

Royal Navy's payroll at about 10,000. Quadrupling the number of men was extremely ambitious, yet Parliament's 'Committee on Supply' projected that 40,000 would serve in His Majesty's Navy by the end of 1756.[27] Despite orders to raise men and add ships, by the end of February 1755 apprehensions abounded that the supply system the navy relied upon was already months behind.[28]

The transition from peace time to war can be seen in newspaper advertisements. On 2 January 1755, London's *Public Advertiser* reprinted a Navy Office advertisement seeking blockmakers. Naval yards at Chatham and Sheerness were 'ready' to sign contracts with persons willing to supply the Royal Navy with 'blockmakers wares'. Yet, three weeks later, the Privy Council issued its first of many orders for 'Warrants for impressing Seamen.'[29] Within a month, those in charge of yards throughout southern England bitterly complained of navy gangs absconding with workers waiting for entry at their respective yard gates. At Portsmouth, a master jointer fell into the hands of impressment gangs waiting for gates to open.[30] The Navy Office wrote to the Admiralty that yardmen at Chatham were in short supply. Due to such shortages, the office relayed news that the *Bedford* as well as the '*Orford, Essex, Kingston, Falmouth* and *Rochester*' could not be brought in for 'want of hands'.[31] Just days later, the Admiralty received notice that a contractor who provided both Portsmouth and Plymouth naval facilities with hemp rope also lost men to navy gangs. Mr Henry Schiffner shut down the business claiming he was 'disabled from Complying with his Contract' unless 25 men taken were released back to him.[32] In the coming months, yardmen continued to be in short supply. In mid-October, Vice Admiral Henry Osborn, who by then had replaced Hawke as commander-in-chief at Portsmouth, refused Admiralty orders to send out needed tenders for the Channel campaign. Osborn informed the Admiralty that his sailors were busy rigging out ships in place of yard workers; the latter usually performed such duties. The tenders would have to wait.[33]

The dearth of yardmen to work and prepare warships for service plagued the Royal Navy's vision of quickly recommissioning ships. Investigators were sent to make 'a strict enquiry to know why the Rigging, Cables, and Boats for the Ships... were not timely provided'[34] in English ports. The Commissioner, Captain Fredrick Rogers, told the Navy Board that, in Portsmouth alone, there appeared to be a six-month lag in preparing warships for sea-going ventures. On 7 March 1755, Rogers alerted the board that Portsmouth ropemakers were to have completed 54 ships 'by which only Eighteen were Enter'd' as delivered.[35] The pace of

27   Holderness and 'Revenue Documents', 1756, British Library (BL), ADD MS 32857, ff. 8–34. See also Gradish, *The Manning of the British Navy*, p.32.
28   Hawke to Clevland, 23 February 1755, TNA, ADM 1/919. See also, Gradish, *The Manning of the British Navy*, p.156.
29   List of Orders and Directions Issued by the Privy Council, 23 January 1755, TNA, PC 1/13/76/1.
30   Hawke to Clevland, 23 February 1755, TNA, ADM 1/919.
31   Navy Office to Clevland, 12 May 1755, National Maritime Museum (NMM), ADM/B/150; see also see also Gradish, *The Manning of the British Navy*, p.32.
32   Navy Office to Clevland, 16 May 1755, NMM, ADM/B/150.
33   Osborne to Clevland, 19 October 1755, TNA, ADM 1/920.
34   Commissioner Rogers to the Navy Board, 7 March 1755, NMM, ADM/B/150.
35   Commissioner Rogers to the Navy Board, 7 March 1755, NMM, ADM/B/150.

naval refitting crept so frustratingly slow. The Royal Navy had yet to sail and already operations to ready fleets for wartime service were botched, confused, and in disarray.

Supply issues also added numerous woes to the navy's vision of a quick call up of decommissioned ships. By the end of March, port facilities at Chatham, the Nore, and Portsmouth reported severe shortages of slops and bedding for newly recruited sailors.[36] Hawke complained that his personal directives for the immediate delivery of slops and bedding had gone unheeded for weeks. 'I found no Beding in store…I have been made to expect their coming, but none are Yet arrived'. He demanded that the Admiralty Office investigate the delay in supplies.[37] Rear Admiral Temple West, stationed at Chatham, also griped about slops and bedding. West stated his sailors were 'lying about without Beds' and that he has 'made frequent application' without success. The 'supply', wrote West, 'has not answer'd the Demand'.[38]

Illnesses, in the meantime, sent afflicted sailors from Portsmouth Harbour to nearby Haslar Hospital. Bedding and attire there, too, were in short supply. The contractor, Mr Ward, tussled for months over the hospital's efficacy with Vice Admiral Hawke, but the pressing issue that united them were supply shortages. Ward informed Hawke that when it came to bedding, 'it will be impossible for me to say exactly when the Beddng can be got'. Ward blamed, as Hawke did, the London suppliers as the cause of inadequate amounts of blankets and sheets.[39]

The quality of the supplies delivered also caused consternation among naval officers. Captains complained to Hawke of defective slops. After an investigation, Hawke concluded that the situations was 'much worse' than his captains had been letting on. In early June, Hawke informed the Admiralty that not only were supplies still short but those that did arrive were, in some cases, useless. 'The leather of the shoes is so extremely bad,' he explained, that 'in Quality so very Ill drest and so slightly sewed that they …must be absolutely unserviceable. The Slops delivered to the *Lancaster* a very bad course Linnen'.[40] A rather extensive survey of a mainsail, delivered to Portsmouth by a London manufacturer, also found occasion for numerous negative remarks: seams sewn with two threads instead of the required three; errors in the table and reef bands, as well as shoddy bowline pieces, bolt ropes, leech ropes, cringles, linings, and other defects so numerous as to make the sails unusable.[41] Vice Admiral Edward Boscawen added that he was 'sorry to complain, but I can't help doing it when I see such constant and repeated roguery.' He added that 'Sheets are still the same, rotten, and made out of Rags and Patches taken off the Dunghill, to be sure'.[42]

If the lack of yardmen and the quality of supplies weren't enough, the navy had to put up with the poor conditions of their port facilities. For example, at Portsmouth, a wall near the boathouse had fallen in December of 1752 crushing six boats that were never replaced.

---

36   Navy Board to Clevland, 10 March 1755, NMM, ADM/B/150; Navy Office to Clevland, 22 March 1755, NMM, ADM/B/150.
37   Hawke to Clevland, 8 March 1755, TNA, ADM 1/919.
38   Navy Office to Clevland, 22 March 1755, NMM, ADM/B/150.
39   Ward to Hawke, 31 March 1755, TNA, ADM 1/919.
40   Hawke to Clevland, 2 June 1755, TNA, ADM 1/919.
41   'An Account of a Survey of a Main Topsail for an Eighty Gun Ship made by Mr. Thomas Turner of London by Contract taken at Portsmouth,' 18 April 1755, found in ADM 1/919.
42   Boscawen to Clevland 27 April 1756, NMM, MRF/117.

Reports to the Navy Board from commissioners at Portsmouth in May of 1755 claimed that it was the lack of these boats that was responsible for the neglect of tending to Royal Navy ships in the harbour and those anchored at Spithead.[43] In January the following year, Osborne complained yet again over the lack of these necessary yard boats:

> The want of these is the cause why Ships are not sooner dispatched at Spithead, and the want of Craft in general at the Dock, as the Gunwarf, and Victualing Office, is evident to all the Captains, who have been obliged to wait for their Stores, and Provisions from each of those places, who are repeatedly complaining to me they loose a great deal of time for want of them.[44]

Portsmouth harbour had also become clogged with captured French merchant vessels. The Royal Navy's pre-emptive attack on French shipping prior to the war's commencement had achieved success beyond the expectations of the Admiralty, or that of the two admirals who led it, Hawke and Byng. In early October 1755, when Captain Dennis of the *Medway* came to Portsmouth for an overdue cleaning of its hull, Byng had to inform the Admiralty that the ship could not 'come into the Harbour there being no Mooring clear for her until … some other Ship goes out.'[45]

Decrepit yard conditions, shoddy supplies, and a lack of men to afford either certainly preceded and followed the departure of Boscawen's fleet from Spithead on 21 April 1755.[46] His orders stated that his fleet of 19 ships was to intercept a French squadron sent to reinforce Canada. The failure of Boscawen to disrupt those French designs may have a basis in the faulty transitioning of the Royal Navy from peacetime to war.

'Dangerously Ill of Fevers'

> July 1755 Monday 14th
> …the number of sick sent on shore was 241, five died immediately on land.[47]

William Bayne, a lieutenant aboard the *Torbay*, maintained his logbook with laconic regularity. On 14 July 1755, Bayne logged what soon became a five-day-long procession where sick and often dead sailors were transferred to a hospital at the colonial port of Halifax. The third-rate, 74-gun warship served as Vice Admiral Edward Boscawen's flagship. Of the 19 total ships assigned to his fleet, the *Torbay* seemed to have taken the brunt of a mysterious disease that swept through the entirety of his squadrons. Thirty-three sailors aboard the flagship lost their lives during its transatlantic crossing, but the worst was yet to come. Once in Nova Scotia, a consistent historical estimate exists where 2,000 dead or incapacitated sailors fell victim to a malignant disease which swept through all of Boscawen's

---

43   Rogers to the Navy Board, 7 March 1755, NMM, ADM/B/150.
44   Osborn to Clevland, 8 January 1756, TNA, ADM 1/921.
45   Byng to Clevland, 7 October 1755, TNA, ADM 1/88.
46   Hawke to Clevland, 21 April 1755, TNA, ADM 1/919.
47   Logbook entry 14 July 1755, Lieutenant William Bayne, HMS *Torbay*, NMM, ADM/L/T/169.

Canadian intercept fleet. Further, the Admiralty Office expected Boscawen and his fleet to return to Portsmouth by early September. However, the sickness that decimated his fleet had Boscawen pulling into Spithead nearly two months late and six warships short. The lack of healthy men forced Boscawen to leave six men-of-war behind in Halifax.[48]

However, before Boscawen embarked on this mission, there were warning signs. Hawke, three weeks before Boscawen's departure, notified the Admiralty Office of a pernicious disease. Hawke, then in charge of Portsmouth operations, reported 'four hundred and thirty one sick' filling every bed at nearby Haslar Hospital. When the hospital could hold no more, sick men were sent back to the ships that had dispatched them to Haslar in the first place. Hawke begged commissioners to send additional bedding to both the hospital and to ships as 'the Squadron has already suffered greatly'.[49] Portsmouth, though, was not the only naval port affected by strange illnesses. Several ships at Chatham and the Nore, under the command of Rear Admiral Temple West, experienced similar ailments. West complained to the Navy Office which, in turn, informed the Admiralty that many of the newly raised men 'onboard the Ships at Chatham and Nore, are dangerously ill of Fevers,' thinking that the illness was due to a failure of delivered bedding.[50] To make matters worse, shipboard surgeons and surgeon mates remained absent through the early few months of the January 1755 callup to recommission 95 ships and recruit 30,000 men. Full hospitals, lack of naval physicians, plus multiple naval commanders reporting illnesses were not enough to halt the departure of the Canadian intercept fleet in April, or the Channel campaign which set out in early September.[51]

In this glaring light of such manning deficiencies, it is reasonable to ask what were the afflictions that plagued the Royal Navy in 1755? Consensus among historians and scholars remains fleeting. Julian Corbett, in volume one of *England in the Seven Years War*, claimed that the 'malignant fever, apparently typhoid', had swept over Boscawen's fleet. Christopher Lloyd and Jack Coulter changed the diagnosis to typhus when they published *Medicine and the Navy* in 1961. Michael Duffy backed that claim adding that the same malady was likely the culprit which swept through such fleets as far back as 1740.[52] While these theories do attempt to expose the severity of the illnesses experienced by the Royal Navy in 1755, they do so with a limited view. These contributions fail to take into account the totality of British society which fed the Royal Navy its seamen. If scholars begin to consider the socio-economic picture which then prevailed within the British archipelago at the moment of an intensive nationwide naval impressment, such theories can and should be reassessed. In other words, the disease may not have originated within the navy, but within the recent haul of men collected by navy gangs.

48   Gradish, *The Manning of the British Navy*, p.32.
49   Hawke to Clevland, 6 April 1755, TNA, ADM 1/919.
50   Navy Office to Clevland, 22 March 1755, NMM, ADM/B/150.
51   State Papers and Admiralty papers confirm the beginning and end dates of the campaign. See Hawke to John Mordaunt, 7 September 1755, TNA, SP 42/100/28 and Byng to Clevland, 22 November 1755, TNA, ADM 1/88.
52   Julien S. Corbett, *England in the Seven Years' War: A Study in Combined Strategy* (London: Longmans, Green, and Co., 1907), Vol.1, p.57; Christopher Lloyd and Jack L. S. Coulter, *Medicine and the Navy, 1200–1900* (Edinburgh: E. & S. Livingstone, 1961), Vol.III, p.112; Michael Duffy, 'The Establishment of the Western Squadron as the Lynchpin of British Naval Strategy', in Richard Harding (ed.), *Naval History, 1680–1850*, reprinted (Farnham: Ashgate, 2006), p.104.

What is odd about the disease, however, is scant evidence of it anywhere in the nation's populace. While the number of sick and dying seamen ballooned, civilian death tolls remained stable. Disease-riddled deaths experienced in London during the winter of 1754-1755 do not appear deviant or beyond the norm. London newspapers, for several months prior to Boscawen's departure, were devoid of significant mortality spikes. The tri-weekly *London Evening Post* listed, on average, about 59 deaths per week within the Metropole due to 'fever'[53] These numbers are in line with observations made from historian Charles Creighton who wrote that 'fever' in London, since the time of Thomas Sydenham, was a 'steady item from year to year, seldom falling below a thousand deaths' per year.[54]

If the search, however, is shifted away from London toward provincial England, Wales, Cornwall, and Scotland, documentation then becomes inordinately scarce. The rarity of archival sources in the provinces concerning outbreaks of localised diseases, though, can be juxtaposed against a Royal Navy first. In its pursuit to raise 30,000 men by the end of 1755, navy gangs not only struck at the usual river and port cities and towns but also ventured inland in search of bodies to man the fleets. Thomas Turner noted in his diary that navy press gangs had issued warrants to the magistrates of Hastings and Battle. Pressing men at Hastings made sense, the town sat on the sea. Experienced fisherman and smugglers could become first-rate seamen for His Majesty's Royal Navy. Battle, on the other hand, housed a gunpowder mill and lay six miles inland from Britain's southern coastline. The absurdity of pressing men from Battle likely caused Turner to jot down the occurrence.[55]

However, the present author would argue that it is in Battle, and other interior industries within provincial Britain, where investigations should refocus and assess how the navy came to experience such a terrible outbreak of diseases while such malignancies remained outside of any of the nation's major urban centres. Though the evidence remains scattered, elusive, and uncertain, there exist enough fragmentary pieces to stitch together a good theory as to where, how, and why an epidemic-like disease appeared in the navy, but not in the general populace. The sickness that mired Hawke's fleet, Temple West's ships at Chatham, and Boscawen's fleet sailing toward Halifax likely found origins in the socio-economic conditions of England's putting out system or cottage industries, and interior magistrates who hoped to clear their gaols of riffraff.

It should be noted that Britain in 1755 was about to experience a nationwide food shortage. Two back-to-back overly wet years (1755 and 1756) led to failed crops causing a dearth in foodstuffs. Damages to crops piled up followed by a concomitant rise in prices: Britain's ability to feed its own began to falter. Historian Nicholas Rogers suggests that the 'product of dearth and war' led to one crisis after another during the years from mid-1755 until the end of 1757.[56] Perhaps historian John Bohstedt put it best, dearth mixed with wartime anxi-

---

53   The *London Evening Post*, for example, listed 'Diseases and Casualties this Week' on their stock prices page. Data collected from September 1754 to the end of March 1755 consistently arrived at an average of 59 deaths per week due to 'fever.'

54   Charles Creighton, *A History of Epidemics in Britain* (London: Frank Cass & Co., 1965), Vol.2, p.13.

55   Turner resided in East Hoathly, some 25 miles from Battle. See entry for 3 April 1756, David Vaisey, (ed.), *The Diary of Thomas Turner, 1754–1765* (Oxford: Oxford University Press, 1984), 37.

56   Nicholas Rogers, *Crowds, Culture, and Politics in Georgian Britain* (Oxford: Oxford University Press, 1998), p.81.

eties held a 'potency' that waxed strong.[57] Nothing brings problems and prejudicial conclusions to a head than starvation. By October 1756, much of England and portions of Wales had succumbed to the largest and most intense food riots heretofore then seen by Britain.[58] But the outbreak of riots had much to do with the previous year when food prices nearly doubled and relief to people who laboured in rural cottage industries appeared forgotten.

A turn toward social and economic histories becomes necessary to understand a new theory as to how the navy suffered from an outbreak of diseases while the populace did not.[59] Dating back to pre-Tudor administrations, enclosures had proceeded slowly and disruptions to an entrenched tenurial system began. Under Elizabeth I, however, the rate of enclosures accelerated which prompted severe migrations of rural peasantry to larger towns and cities. By 1600, under Elizabethan rule, one in 10 villages ceased to exist. Gregory Clark surmises that 'the amount of common [agricultural] waste to which even the formally landless poor had access' was likely no more than five percent of all arable land.[60] The progression of enclosures continued, particularly after William III acceded to the throne. Between the ascension of William and Mary and the outbreak of the Seven Years War, definitive lasting structural changes took place to the nation's economy and society: 'shedding labour from the countryside', 'rapid urban growth', 'expanded domestic consumption of non-necessities', 'stimulated manufacturing', and 'the commercialisation of English society', all of which pre-dated the Industrial Revolution.[61] By the mid-eighteenth century, larger and more agriculturally productive lands already supported juvenescent interior industrial centres; Manchester, Birmingham, Leeds, and Sheffield – and were then linked to important dockyard towns; Liverpool, Glasgow, Bristol, Plymouth, and Newcastle – quite possibly with labour that enclosures had shed over the centuries.[62] English poor laws helped to absorb the brunt of these land reallocations and forced migrations so that, comparatively, the English were 'quite easily separated' from the medieval traditions of open and common lands.[63] Thus, by 1700 propertied men held a cultural view that enclosures benefitted the greater

57   John Bohstedt, *The Politics of Provisions: Food Riots, Moral Economy, and Market Transition in England, c. 1550–1850*, paperback (London: Rout-ledge, 2010), p.1.

58   A two-year deluge of wet weather diminished crop yields and ended a near nine-decade long constancy in grain prices. Bohstedt suggests that the price of wheat in London jumped over 35 percent in 1756; pricing jumped in certain industrial centres of provincial England perhaps even more, 50 percent to 80 percent. See Bohstedt, *The Politics of Provisions*, p. 112; Andrew Charlesworth (ed.), *An Atlas of Rural Protest in Britain, 1548–1900* (Beckenham: Croom Helm, 1993), p.86.

59   The theory alludes to consumption or tuberculosis as the culprit that struck the navy in 1775, yet admits that more research is needed. See Joseph J. Krulder, *The Execution of Admiral John Byng as a Microhistory of Eighteenth-Century Britain* (London: Routledge, 2021), pp.145-152.

60   Gregory Clark and Anthony Clark, 'Common Rights to Land in England, 1475–1839', *The Journal of Economic History*, vol. 61, no. 4 (December 2001), p.1034; Steve Hindle, 'Dearth, Fasting and Alms: The Campaign for General Hospitality in Late Elizabethan England', *Past & Present*, vol. 172 (August, 2001), p.62.

61   Lee Davison, Tim Hitchcock, Tim Keirn, and Robert Shoemaker (eds), *Stilling the Grumbling Hive: The Response to Social and Economic Problems in England, 1689–1750* (New York: St. Martin's Press, 1992), pp.xvi–xvii.

62   Davison, *et al* (eds), *Stilling the Grumbling Hive*, pp.xix–xxi.

63   Peter M. Solar, 'Poor Relief and English Economic Development before the Industrial Revolution', *The Economic History Review*, New Series, vol. 48, no. 1 (February 1995), p.9.

good. The number of Parliamentary Acts from 1760 to 1800 (around 1,800 of them) merely placed the exclamation point to enclosure processes centuries in the making.[64]

This quick trip through urban and rural enclosure history points out that England's bottom rung of the tenurial system continually and consistently migrated over the centuries to port towns and cities and then to newly emerging industrial or service sector regions interior of the country.[65] Politically, urban-based guilds worked tirelessly to protect themselves which also contributed to the growth in provincial 'putting out' or cottage industries. This rural-based system employed the poor to convert raw materials into manufactured pieces and goods. However, societal problems emanated as this rural-based put-out system grew more common, and the nature of countryside paternalism changed. The early eighteenth-century upsurge of cottages and putting-out industries located away from urban centres left workers isolated. The poor that worked these cottages could not depend on the manufacture that merely dropped off materials and picked up finished goods, nor could they rely on the rural gentry for support during a crisis. In 1755, such a crisis emerged. Extreme wet weather decimated crops. Geographically secluded, cottages throughout the English, Welsh, and Scottish interiors faced a surprising and sudden scarcity of food followed by a rise in prices.[66] A century-long pattern of food transactions was about to be tested. At the state level, Tudor and early Stuart dynasties responded to food shortages by fixing prices, replete with ceremonial concern towards the lower orders. By the mid-eighteenth century, however, price-fixing shifted to become a responsibility of local magistrates: a regional rather than state concern. However, the state under Georgian rule had accustomed itself to encourage the export of grain.[67] Paternal ideals, especially in the provinces, suddenly butted up against the persistent reality of food in short supply. As Hoppit put it, those 'reciprocal duties and interdependencies' between rich and poor were about to be tested.[68] The emergence of a growing food shortage began to expose the fragility of county-based paternal systems. Bohstedt argues that the previous five decades had stuck a blow to the hoary traditions of paternal oversight. Newer modes of trade had sent agricultural products further and further away from the localities in which they were produced.[69]

Despite these transformative economic changes, grain prices remained relatively stable from about 1690s to 1740s when the War of Austrian Succession briefly caused fluctuations in food imports. Grain price stability did return after 1748. However, the deluge of

---

64   Julian Hoppit, *A Land of Liberty? England 1689–1727* (Oxford: Oxford University Press, 2000), pp.358–359.

65   Patrick Karl O'Brien, 'Path Dependency, or Why Britain Became an Industrialized and Urbanized Economy Long before France', *The Economic History Review*, New Series, vol. 49, no. 2 (May 1996), p.239.

66   On London watchmaker guilds see, Peter Linebaugh, *The London Hanged: Crime and Civil Society in the Eighteenth Century* (Cambridge: Cambridge University Press, 1992), pp.226–228. On seclusion of cottages and concomitant results see, Richard Sheldon, 'Practical Economics in Eighteenth-Century England: Charles Smith on the Grain Trade and Corn Laws, 1756–72', *Historical Research*, vol. 81, no. 214 (November 2008), pp.638–639.

67   R. B. Outhwaite, *Dearth, Public Policy and Social Disturbance in England, 1550–1800* (Cambridge: Cambridge University Press, 1991), p.48.

68   Hoppit, *A Land of Liberty?*, p.76.

69   Bohstedt, *The Politics of Provisions*, pp.144–149.

wet weather beginning in 1755, lasting for two-years, significantly diminished crop yields. Prices in grain began to rise. Some studies suggest that the price of wheat in London jumped over 35 percent in 1756; pricing jumped in certain industrial centres of provincial England perhaps even more, 50 percent to 80 percent.[70] Isolated cottages were often the last to see relief from such inflationary spikes. Local lords and magistrates were slow to fix prices on foodstuffs if they could be found at all.

High food prices and the scarcity of grains took a toll on the rural poor who worked in isolation through the cottage system. By the middle of the eighteenth century, medical practitioners connected the labouring poor's crowded and ill-ventilated working and living conditions to occasional outbreaks of diseases. 'Gaol fever' or 'ship fever' reflected the reality of crammed workhouses, poorhouses, jails, and maritime ships, a breeding centre of contagions which then swept through a populace at the lower rungs of society: mostly ill-paid and thus often nutritionally deficient.[71] Looking over past parish records, Doctor Robert Robertson was convinced that:

> [F]ever was every where essentially the same – the difference of the symptoms arising merely from the constitution of the patient; from the accidental state of the body when it was infected; from the various circumstances they unavoidably then lived under.[72]

Such studies continued. *Observations on the Low Contagious Fever* told of a typhus epidemic that remained specific to remote boroughs of Lancashire: only the cotton mills and textile production centres witnessed the disease, and the fever spread no further than Lancaster and Backbarrow near Ulverston.[73] If there existed any hiccups in food distribution, or if harvests had been low yielding or had outright failed, then 'nervous fevers' were likely to afflict primarily the poor, and 'especially during winter season', which appears, on the face of it, to be about the time the sick started filling up Haslar Hospital near Portsmouth.[74] The resulting combination of poor nutrition coupled to poor work and living conditions occasioned sporadic and quite isolated pockets of disease outbreaks. Here, we can merge these socio-economic histories to military necessity: navy gangs, for the first time in Royal Navy history, visiting, with warrants in hand, interior centres of the country likely retrieved malnourished and sickly recruits. Only two months after the order had been given to send press gangs inland for men, the sickbeds at Haslar Hospital at Gosport were full.

By the end of 1755, the sick and dead that were no longer able to be of service to the Royal Navy numbered over 6,000. Boscawen lost 2,162 sailors, either dead or unfit to serve.

---

70   Bohstedt, *The Politics of Provisions*, p.112.
71   Guenter B. Risse, 'Typhus Fever in Eighteenth-Century Hospitals: New Approaches to Medical Treatment', *Bulleting of the History of Medicine*, vol. 59, no. 2 (Summer 1985), pp.176–179.
72   Robert Robertson, *Observations on the Jail, Hospital, or Ship Fever* (London: J. Murray, 1783), p.4.
73   On *Observations*, Christopher Johnson spoke before a meeting of surgeons in 1869 Manchester and conferred upon the writings of Dr Campbell of Lancaster, who, in 1785 published the following pamphlet; Christopher Johnson, *Remarks on an Epidemic of Typhus, Which Prevailed in the Cotton Districts of Lancashire and was Described by Dr. Campbell of Lancaster in the year 1785* (Lancaster: G.C. Clark, 1869), p.2.
74   Risse, 'Typhus Fever in Eighteenth-Century Hospitals', p.146.

The Channel campaign sent an estimated 4,000 more to hospitals in port cities throughout Southern England. Gradish placed a conservative tally of just over 11 percent of the navy's recruitment drive permanently lost to disease in 1755, and the Seven Years War had yet to be declared. Sickness retarded recruitment efforts to such a degree that Royal Navy manning levels would not meet expectations until 1758.[75]

Conclusion

In 1743, Stephen Hales reported before the Royal Society that 'noxious Air in Ships' had been one of the 'greatest Grievances' concerning the health of sailors in British maritime, including the Royal Navy. Hales, at the same gathering, also reported that Sweden and France had moved toward installing ventilators on some (France), if not all (Sweden) of their warships.[76] The Royal Navy did experiment with ventilators installing one aboard the *Captain* during the War of Austrian Succession. However, as the Seven Years War approached, only one Royal Navy vessel utilized a ventilator to circulate fresh air below decks, the first-rate *Royal George*. Though the technology was available, and that other nations began the process of installing ventilators aboard their warships, the British Royal Navy chose not to outfit their fleets claiming 'the Labour and Difficulty of working' them.[77]

That decision raises a hypothetical: had the British Royal Navy installed ventilators aboard some or all of their ships, would the dead and permanently incapacitated of 1755 been less, much less? Adverse to counterfactuals, the question nonetheless may have an answer. Vice Admiral Boscawen, whose 1755 intercept fleet lost some 2,000 men to a pernicious disease, wrote to the Admiralty comparing the status of the crew aboard the *Royal George* and similar ships without ventilators at Portsmouth. Based on Boscawen's recommendation, beginning in the summer of 1756, the Royal Navy ordered ventilators installed on ships with 20 guns or more.[78] The *Namur*, a 90 gun second-rate (completed in late 1756) sailed as Boscawen's flagship in 1758 with a functioning ventilator. Sailing from Portsmouth for Louisbourg, a muster taken off the island of Madeira revealed only one sailor out of 800 unable to report above deck due to illness.[79] By the end of the Seven Years War, ventilators were attached to the Royal Navy's regimentation toward cleanliness having been installed on most of its ships.

---

75   Gradish, Manning the British Navy, 33.

76   Stephen Hales, *A description of ventilators: whereby great quantities of fresh air may with ease be conveyed into mines, goals [sic] hospitals, work-houses and ships, in exchange for their noxious air. An account also of their great usefulness in many other respects. As in preserving all sorts of grain dry, sweet, and free from being destroyed by weevels, both in grainaries and ships, and in preserving many other sorts of goods. As also in drying corn, malt, hop, gun-powder, &c.; and for many other useful purposes / Which was read before the Royal Society in May, 1741* (London: Unknown Publisher, 1743), pp.v-xv.

77   Hales indicated that the navy's complaint was 'frivolous and groundless'. Hales, *A Description of Ventilators*, p.34.

78   *Daily Advertiser*, 20 August 1756; see also Rodger, *The Wooden World*, pp.106-107.

79   Ernest Heberden, 'Correspondence of William Heberden, F.R.S. with the Reverend Stephen Hales and Sir Charles Blagden', *Notes and Records of the Royal Society of London*, vol. 39, no. 1 (April 1985), p.181.

As to the condition of port facilities, tax expenditures (or a lack of them) may have lent a hand. However, despite the existence and thorough historiography accounting for the rise and maintenance of the fiscal British military state during the long eighteenth century, most of it focuses on revenues rather than expenditures. Thus, charging that the British government allowed its military to deteriorate under a lack of funds between two wars becomes problematic. However, focusing on the land tax and how it evolved from its conception to the beginning of the Seven Years War does reveal a distinct pattern, at least on the revenue side. During the British Civil Wars, Parliament employed the land tax, but its implementation was impermanent. Not until William III and its near coinciding of the creation of the Bank of England did the land tax find permanency. When the land tax became perennially annual beginning in 1698, government financiers quickly realized that short-term loans could be raised on the basis of its incoming proceeds. In fact, the bigger buyer of bonds issued by the Bank of England during the Seven Years War were the landed gentry who purchased these government loans based on the land taxes they paid. See, for example, Henry Fane's letter to the Duke of Newcastle where he declared such arrangements 'schemes' but nonetheless indicated that such loans by the bank would be readily 'filled'.[80] P.G.M. Dickson equated such schemes as tax relief 'in the guise of a national debt.'[81] This 'flower of funds' – as Geoffrey Holmes called it – proved indispensable to Britain during the eighteenth century, preferable to the excise tax after the crises of the 1730s. In short, the land tax was a 'coming of age' moment of Britain's financial revolution. By the end of the Nine Years War, England's wealthy had come to view land tax as an investment in Protestantism and the liberty to pursue property. William III and Queen Anne had successfully laid the fiscal foundation of Great Britain's empire. Further, at the George I's reign, between a third to forty percent of the treasury's revenue emanated from the land tax.[82] What William and Mary and then Queen Anne set up, the Hanoverians reaped. The land tax became a fiscally conservative basis, overtly predictable which led British governments to borrow against its anticipated income, particularly in times of war.

However, the land tax evolved. By the end of the eighteenth century, despite the wars in America and then against France, the land tax contributed a mere 20 percent of the treasury's revenue.[83] Indirect taxes, such as the excise, imposed a greater slice of the government's incoming revenue stream. Warfare and peace adjusted the land tax pursuant to the goals of the emerging British empire. In times of peace, the land tax was almost always cut in half of what it was during wartime.[84] But, even when Britain was at war, landowners

80   Fane to Newcastle, 22 August 1756, BL, ADD MS 32867, f.20.
81   P.G.M. Dickson, The Financial Revolution in England: A Study in the Development of Public Credit, 1688-1756 (New York: St. Martin's Press, 1967), pp.10-11.
82   J.C.D. Clark, English Society 1660-1832, 2nd ed. (New York: Cambridge University Press, 2000), p.56; Geoffrey Holmes, The Making of a Great Power: Late Stuart and Early Georgian Britain, 1660-1722 (London: Longman, 1993), pp.268-269; Ian Gilmour, Riots, Risings and Revolutions: Governance and Violence in Eighteenth-Century England (London: Pimlico, 1993), p.44; Philip Brien and Matthew Keep, 'The Public Finances: a historical overview,' in Briefing Paper, no. 8265, (House of Commons Library, 22 March 2018), p.16.
83   John Rule, The Vital Century: England's Developing Economy, 1714—1815 (London: Longmans, 1992), 289; see also Gilmour, Riots, Risings and Revolutions, p.85.
84   Brien and Keep, 'The Public Finances: a historical overview,' p.4.

grumbled at the price of taxation and the necessity of figuring out how 'we not pay' the typical four shillings on the pound based on land value estimates.[85] Notwithstanding of the pattern of land tax alterations during the first half of the eighteenth century, staking a claim that cuts to the land tax had anything to do with the degradation of port facilities throughout the empire needs more work. True, the land tax was cut in half soon after the War of Austrian Succession came to a conclusion, two shillings to the pound instead of four. In 1756, with the Seven Years War commenced, landowners were once again asked to pay four shillings. Additionally, past works demonstrate that the tax itself was based on land valuations in 1692. Throughout the entire eighteenth century, reassessments of land prices did not take place. Enclosures ballooned throughout the countryside early- to mid-century which clouded true accountings of worth. Several counties purposely kept recently enclosed land prices artificially low so that the burden of taxation on landowners was 'light and diminishing' as the century bore on.[86] Perhaps the best or most honest assessment of the land tax is that elites found means to lessen the burden by mid-century. As to whether the halving of the tax in between two wars led to less spending on military upkeep, there is as of yet no direct line.

However we do know that when Admiral Byng's fleet pulled into Gibraltar in May of 1756, his expectations of utilising its port facilities to make quick repairs to faulty warships within his fleet soon dissolved. Commodore Edgcumbe introduced Byng to Milburn Marsh, a certified shipwright who had just recently evacuated Port Mahon when France invaded Minorca. Gibraltar was then the navy's secondary Mediterranean port, Port Mahon its primary. But the reduction of government funds since the last war (upwards of 75 percent) to maintain military facilities was certainly known to Byng and other officers. Byng asked Marsh to assess the condition of stores and maintenance facilities at Gibraltar. Marsh's report shocked Byng. Gibraltar's mast house, boat house, pitch house, cable shed, and smith's shop were not only decayed, but in some instances tumbling down. Stores were little to none, short on caulking, canvas, pitch and tar, lanterns and oil. The dockyards a 'monument to … complacency and neglect, service corruption, bureaucratic lethargy and dry rot.'[87] The conditions of Gibraltar exceeded the sorry state of Portsmouth's facilities. Two weeks later Byng's limped fleet faced off against a newly built and recently launched French fleet in the Battle of Minorca.

The details of this chapter point out that Royal Navy's ability to establish, extend, and protect the British Empire were restrained by domestic realities. There exists a historical tendency to pin 'Empire' as a function of political, economic, and militaristic machinations. More than three decades ago, arguments that the roots of empire ought to be sought in politics rather than social structures was emphasized.[88] Yet, this chapter demonstrates

---

85   Lady Orford to James Sharpe, July 1756, BL, ADD MS 34728, f.44.
86   Rule, *The Vital Century*, p.87 and 290. See also, P. Mathias and P.K. O'Brien, 'Taxation in England and France, 1715-1810', in *Journal of European Economic History*, 5 (1976), p.616.
87   Dudley Pope, *At 12 Mr Byng Was Shot* (Philadelphia: Lippincott, 1962), pp.106-107; Krulder, *The Execution of Admiral John Byng*, p.158.
88   See, for example, Thomas A. Brady, Jr., 'The Rise of Merchant Empires, 1400-1700: A European counterpoint', in James D. Tracy (ed.), *The Political Economy of Merchant Empires: State Power and World Trade, 1350-1750* (Cambridge: Cambridge University Press, 1991), pp.120-123.

that contingent social and cultural conventions – protean in nature – often affected and indeed hampered policymakers along a dependent path. In January of 1755, Britain's privy council envisioned the call up of 30,000 men to outfit 95 ships in expectation of war. This vision, though, was dependant on social and cultural conditions. When Boscawen sailed to intercept a French fleet bound for Quebec, and when Hawke and Byng began seizing French merchant vessels, the Royal Navy was dealt a severe blow in the form of rampant diseases. This yet unknown bout of ailments shorted the Admiralty's need for sailors by 20 percent. The decision to pluck landmen from interior Britain (a first for the Royal Navy) impinged on longstanding social structures, particularly with the invasion of press gangs upon cramped living and working quarters of the nearly isolated cottage industries. The navy paid a price. Conscription of yard workers combined with less-than-stellar port facility conditions added to severe delays in outfitting Britain's wartime navy. The bottleneck of captured French maritime ships in England's southern ports only exacerbated the situation. Policymakers had learned to alleviate tax burdens in between wars, and the landed elites had learned ways to skirt the burdens even further. Military upkeep may have suffered. This is raised as a cultural issue and the author recognises that much more investigation is necessary.

Byng's fleet was, as the Spanish king indicated, 'retarded.' The late arrival of Byng in the Mediterranean had to do with the previous year's naval exploits and the damage it did to both men and material readiness. The inability to make repairs to some of the ships in Byng's fleet had at its root port facilities that were in disrepair and clogged with hundreds of captured French ships. The Royal Navy at the beginning throes of the Seven Years' War, despite January 1755 orders to refit, remained ill-equipped, understaffed, struggling to make repairs. Small and successful skirmishes took place between French and British navies. At the Battle of Quiberon Bay in late 1759, the results there demonstrated that the Royal Navy had finally overcome its inauspicious start to the Seven Years War.

Select Bibliography

Archives
British Library, London
    Admiral Charles Watson Papers, MSS EUR D1079
    Keene Papers, ADD MS 43437.
    Leeds Papers, MS Egerton 3444.
    Newcastle Papers, ADD MS 32857.
    Newcastle Papers, ADD MS 32859.
    Newcastle Papers, ADD MS 32867.
    Papers relating to the Army and Navy, ADD MS 33047.
    West Papers, ADD MS 34728.
The National Archives (TNA), London
    ADM 1/919-921: Admiralty: Correspondence and Papers.
    ADM 1/88: Admiralty: Letters from Flag Officers, Channel Fleet
    PC 1/13/76: List of Orders Issued by the Privy Council.
    SP 42/100/28: Secretaries of State: State Papers Naval.
    T 1/366: Treasury Board Papers: In Letters.
    T 1/436/94: Treasury Papers: Miscellaneous.
National Maritime Museum, Greenwich Royal Museums Greenwich, England (NMM)
    Board of Admiralty: In-Letters, ADM/B/150.

Letters from Admiral of the Blue Edward Boscawen to John Clevland, MRF/117.
Navy Board: Lieutenants' Logs, ADM/L/T/169.
Victualling Board: In-Letters, ADM/C/542.

Newspapers
Bodley's Bath Journal, 2 June 1755.
Daily Advertiser, 20 August 1756.
London Evening Post, 27 September 1755.
London Evening Post, September 1754 – March 1755
Newcastle Courant, 31 May 1755.
Newcastle Journal, 31 May-7 June.
Newcastle Journal, 7 June-14 June 1755.

Published Primary Sources
Erskine, David, (ed.), *Augustus Hervey's Journal: The Adventures Afloat and Ashore of a Naval Casanova.* (London: Chatham Publishing, 2002).
Johnson, Christopher. *Remarks on an Epidemic of Typhus, Which Prevailed in the Cotton Districts of Lancashire and was Described by Dr. Campbell of Lancaster in the year 1785.* (Lancaster: G.C. Clark, 1869).
Robertson, Robert, *Observations on the Jail, Hospital, or Ship Fever* (London: J. Murray, 1783).
Vaisey, David (ed.) *The Diary of Thomas Turner, 1754–1765* (Oxford: Oxford University Press, 1984).

Published Sources
Baugh, Daniel, *The Global Seven Years War, 1754–1763* (London: Routledge, 2014).
Bohstedt, John, *The Politics of Provisions: Food Riots, Moral Economy, and Market Transition in England, c. 1550–1850* (London: Routledge, 2010).
Clark, J.C.D., *English Society 1660-1832*, 2nd ed. (New York: Cambridge University Press, 2000).
Dickson, P.G.M., *The Financial Revolution in England: A Study in the Development of Public Credit, 1688-1756* (New York: St. Martin's Press, 1967).
Duffy, Michael, 'The Establishment of the Western Squadron as the Lynchpin of British Naval Strategy', in Harding, Richard (ed.), *Naval History, 1680–1850* (Farnborough: Ashgate, 2006).
Dull, Jonathan R., *The French Navy and the Seven Years' War* (Lincoln: University of Nebraska Press, 2005).
Gilmour, Ian, *Riots, Risings and Revolutions: Governance and Violence in Eighteenth-Century England* (London: Pimlico, 1993).
Gradish, Stephen, *The Manning of the British Navy during the Seven Years War* (London: Royal Historical Society, 1980).
Krulder, Joseph J. *The Execution of Admiral John Byng as a Microhistory of Eighteenth-Century Britain* (London: Routledge, 2021).
Linebaugh, Peter, *The London Hanged: Crime and Civil Society in the Eighteenth Century* (Cambridge: Cambridge University Press, 1992).
Lloyd, Christopher and Coulter, Jack L.S., *Medicine and the Navy, 1200–1900* (Edinburgh: E. & S. Livingstone, 1961).
Outhwaite, R.B., *Dearth, Public Policy and Social Disturbance in England, 1550–1800* (Cambridge: Cambridge University Press, 1991).
Pocock, Tom, *Battle for Empire: The Very First World War, 1756-63* (London: Michael O'Mara Books, 1998).
Pope, Dudley, *At 12 Mr Byng Was Shot* (Philadelphia: Lippincott, 1962).
Rodger, N.A.M., *The Wooden World: An Anatomy of the Georgian Navy* (New York: W.W. Norton, 1996).
Rogers, Nicholas. *Crowds, Culture, and Politics in Georgian Britain* (Oxford: Oxford University Press, 1998).
Rule, John. *The Vital Century: England's Developing Economy, 1714—1815* (London: Longmans, 1992).

11

War and Peace: Trends in Royal Navy Courts Martial, 1812-1818

Andrew Johnston

The close of the Napoleonic Wars in 1815 brought an abrupt return to peacetime normalcy for the nearly 150,000 officers, sailors, and marines of the Royal Navy. For most, peace inevitably meant unemployment as ships and men were paid off, and officers who just a few years prior may well have expected rapid promotion found themselves languishing on half pay. From an administrative viewpoint, this immense social and logistical restructuring made way for significant changes regarding how contemporaries viewed questions of crime and punishment in the navy. However, official change would be a long time in coming. The 1749 Articles of War had remained largely unaltered for over a century, and it would not be until the passage of the Naval Discipline Act in 1860 – 50 years after the end of the Napoleonic Wars – that the state of crime and punishment in the Royal Navy became a subject of major parliamentary focus.[1] Even by the early twentieth century, the more negative understandings of naval law led Winston Churchill to infamously describe the 'traditions of the navy' as 'rum, buggery, and the lash', painting a somewhat dismal view of naval discipline which has persisted in the academic and popular consciousness ever since.[2] Stories of running the gauntlet, floggings 'round the fleet, and hangings from the yardarm, such as those described in Nordhoff and Hall's *Mutiny on the Bounty*, depict a very harsh understanding of the naval legal code. Even Nicholas Rodger, in his far less pejorative analysis of mid-eighteenth-century naval society in *The Wooden World*, describes law in the navy as a 'largely organic response to the nature of life at sea, overlaid with a ramshackle legal structure.'[3] And this is a generally fair overview of the nature of discipline in the Royal Navy for much of the eighteenth century. In an era when any convicted felon in a civilian court was, at least in theory,

---

1   Andrew Johnston, '"Arbitrary and cruel punishments": Trends in Royal Navy courts martial, 1860–1869', *The International Journal of Maritime History*, 33:3 (2021), p.541.

2   See Eugene Rasor, *Reform in the Royal Navy* (Hamden, CT: Archon Books: 1976) and Christopher Lloyd, *The British Seaman 1200-1860* (London: Collins, 1968), p.283.

3   N.A.M. Rodger, *The Wooden World: The Anatomy of the Georgian Navy* (London: Collins, 1986), p.229.

expected to receive a sentence of death, the brutal nature of naval punishment was simply seen as a necessary evil to temper a hard existence at sea.

Despite these hardships, numerous authors have emphasised the general acceptance that many sailors had of such draconian punishments, so far as they were used to a degree deemed fair. The sociologists Michael Hechter, Steven Pfaff, and Patrick Underwood emphasise that in the vast majority of eighteenth and early nineteenth-century mutinies, structural grievances, such as harsh discipline as defined by the Articles of War, were only rarely responsible for organised uprisings against naval authority. Rather, incidental grievances, such as incompetent officers, disease outbreaks or perhaps, most infamously, particularly sadistic commanders, proved far more likely to result in widespread discontentment, or even violent mutiny. Exceptions certainly exist in a broad sense, most famously in the Great Mutinies of Spithead and the Nore in 1797. But no specific complaint against punishment was voiced in the demands of the peaceful Spithead mutineers, and sustained and widespread rebellion against the more violent aspects of naval punishment simply did not exist for much of the eighteenth century.[4] When combined with the general conservatism of the British state and Admiralty during the Revolutionary and Napoleonic Wars, it is of little surprise that systemic change in the trends of Royal Navy courts martial did not occur until after peace was signed. What *is* remarkable, however, is the rate by which this change *did* occur once the wars were over, especially given the few legislative changes of the period. Greater proportions of offences coming to court martial and reductions in both executions and extreme floggings were the hallmarks of the early courts martial of the *Pax Britannica*, emphasizing a growing focus on legal reform by officers at all levels of naval hierarchy.

Tracing the historical record of crime and punishment in the Royal Navy requires some basic familiarity with contemporary criminal law, as many of the officers serving on naval courts would have been familiar with these traditions, and the Articles of War themselves often made reference to relevant civilian precedent.[5] When using legal sources for historical analysis, it is important to ask why such sources were created in the first place. As argued by Simon Devereaux regarding the Old Bailey Proceedings, the substance and detail provided by that publication changed dramatically over the eighteenth and nineteenth centuries as it transitioned from a simple report of the goings-on of London's central criminal court to a more substantial transcript of criminal trials of the nineteenth century.[6] The increasing popularity of the Proceedings also coincided with a shifting public morality, which saw the self-censorship of certain cases, particularly sodomy, rape and murder, becoming more prevalent as time went on.[7] Devereaux particularly emphasised the increasing length of the Proceedings during the late eighteenth century. However, such simple quantitative analysis does not alone suggest anything substantial regarding trends in crime and punishment. As

4   Michael Hechter, Steven Pfaff, and Patrick Underwood, 'Grievances and the Genesis of Rebellion: Mutiny in the Royal Navy, 1740-1820', *American Sociological Review*, 81:1 (2016), pp.165-189.

5   John Byrn, *Crime and Punishment in the Royal Navy, Discipline on the Leeward Islands Station 1784-1812* (Southampton: Camelot Press, 1989), p.6.

6   Simon Devereaux, 'The City and the Sessions Paper', *The Journal of British Studies*, 35:4 (1996), p.468. Also, see Robert Shoemaker, 'The Old Bailey Proceedings and the Representation of Crime and Criminal Justice in Eighteenth-Century London', *The Journal of British Studies*, 47:3 (2008), pp.559-580.

7   Devereaux, 'The City and the Sessions Paper', p.491.

noted at the time, an increase in the number and volume of legal records by no means proves 'the increase in vice; it indicates also an increased population, and extended commerce, and improved police.'[8] Similar trends make themselves shown in the legal records of the early nineteenth-century Royal Navy, but it is also important to avoid drawing too many comparisons between these sources. The Proceedings increased in length as the length and complexity of criminal trials grew over the nineteenth century, a trend that was finally quantified in the project 'Datamining with Criminal Intent' in 2011, which developed tools that scholars to query the entirety of the Proceedings to study long-term trends.[9]

No similar trend is particularly evident in the Court Martial Returns from 1812 through 1818. These records were meant to be a quick-reference guide to the full minutes of the court martial proceedings, so extremely brief summaries of charges and sentences are quite common. Nearly 20 percent of charges were five words or less, with 13 percent being only a single word. However, these varied dramatically based on the charge in question. Instances of drunkenness, desertion, theft, and other relatively minor charges were almost always summarised in a single word, whereas trials for the loss of a ship, assault, or charges against senior officers often went on for pages.[10] With so many outliers, it becomes impossible to draw any sort of significant conclusion from the length of the Returns, even if, on average, both charges and sentences increased in detail over the nineteenth century as formal policy regarding the maintenance of court records matured. Regardless, as it is clear from the documents stored at the National Archives that the Admiralty clearly only retained the full trial minutes for cases of particular significance, these summaries are likely all that remain for many thousands of the more mundane naval courts martial of the nineteenth century.

As many historians have emphasised, the increasing population of nineteenth century Britain was one of the most important factors influencing many trends present in legal records as shown by Old Bailey Proceedings. Whatever the length of individual trial accounts, the vast growth of total trials by the early-nineteenth century inevitably produced a more extensive collection of Proceedings. In contrast to the steadily increasing civilian population, however, the size of the nineteenth-century Royal Navy varied dramatically. Determining the exact size of the navy at any given moment during the eighteenth or nineteenth century is extremely difficult due to numerous discrepancies between the numbers of men voted, mustered and borne, let alone those who died through disease or combat, deserted, or were simply discharged. Interestingly, Christopher Lloyd acknowledged the role that computational analysis would play in such a study decades before digital research methods were widely used.[11] Allowing for these difficulties, the numbers collated by several other naval historians allow for an approximation of the navy's growth and decline during the eighteenth and nineteenth centuries, and extrapolating from these numbers can give a rough indication of many of the periods not as comprehensively catalogued. Despite the comprehensive naval legal records which were preserved, there are still several issues when using such documents for historical analysis. Among the most obvious is the simple fact

---

8   As quoted in Devereaux, 'The City and the Sessions Paper', p.466.
9   Dan Cohen, Tim Hitchcock, *et al*, 'Data Mining with Criminal Intent' Final White Paper (2011), <www.oldbaileyonline.org/static/API.jsp> (accessed 21 September 2023).
10   As displayed in TNA ADM 194/42, 194/180, 194/181.
11   Lloyd, *The British Seaman*, p.121.

that, by their very nature, courts martial only record those who were caught or charged with offences. Those whose crimes went unreported, for whatever reason, do not show up in the records. Still, instances of some offences can be theoretically determined through other methods. Desertion, for example, is relatively unique in that 'successful' instances can be determined by analysing ships' muster books, although as previously mentioned this would be a nearly insurmountable task to achieve for the whole of the Royal Navy.

The few scholars to have looked at the subject have been cautious in making too direct a comparison between civilian courts and naval courts martial.[12] The two had functional differences obvious even to contemporaries, but the theoretical purpose of both naval and criminal law also had evident similarities. The obvious deterrent goals of both the 1661 and 1749 Articles of War were mirrored in the brutally draconian legislation of the 1723 Black Acts, which specified over 40 capital offences that would exist for the next century, causing significant public outcry against them, regardless of the relatively few convictions under their statutes.[13] Despite the appearance of such apparently strict legislation, historians of both naval and criminal law emphasise that, given ample use of the pardon, few of these numerous capital offences ever saw the death sentence deployed. A quick search of the legal database *The Digital Panopticon* shows that less than 30 percent of the approximately 5,500 capital convicts sentenced at the Old Bailey from 1750–1850 were actually put to death.[14] Barring extreme circumstances, such as the aftermath of the 1797 Fleet Mutinies, the death sentence was even rarer in the Royal Navy. Although execution was still used, as Voltaire famously stated, '*pour encourager les autres*', even in instances of major offences such as murder, mutiny, and sodomy, the Royal Navy had a very practical reason to avoid the death penalty wherever possible: shortage of manpower. The professionalization of both the officer corps and seamen of the mid-to-late eighteenth-century navy had a decided impact on both capital and corporal punishments, especially when compared to the army of the same period. Unlike the average foot soldier, seen as easily replaceable, able seamen were skilled labourers in every sense of the word, and the mutual respect that existed between such sailors and their officers would often preclude such horrific punishments.[15] Many authors echo such a social contract, arguing that the harsh punishments meted out by both captains and courts martial were accepted, provided that the officers respected the professional capabilities of the seamen.[16]

These realities are certainly obvious when looking at patterns in courts martial records in the final years of the Napoleonic Wars. Nearly 1,200 trials are listed in the Court Martial Returns from 1812–1818, with nearly 1,000 of those taking place during the war or the months immediately thereafter. The overwhelming majority of these trials ended in one of two ways – with a sentence of flogging or an acquittal. Despite the infamy of being 'hanged

---

12   See Byrn, *Crime and Punishment in the Royal Navy*; Markus Eder, *Crime and Punishment in the Royal Navy of the Seven Years' War, 1755-1763* (Aldershot: Ashgate Publishing, 2004).

13   Douglas Hay, Peter Linebaugh, John Rule, E.P. Thompson and Cal Winslow, *Albion's Fatal Tree: Crime and Society in Eighteenth-Century England* (London: Verso, 2011), p.63.

14   'Search Builder', *The Digital Panopticon*, <https://www.digitalpanopticon.org>, (accessed 29 November 2019).

15   A.N. Gilbert, 'The Changing Face of British Military Justice', *Military Affairs*, 49:2 (1985), p.83.

16   Richard Woodman, *A Brief History of Mutiny* (London: Robinson, 2005), p.100.

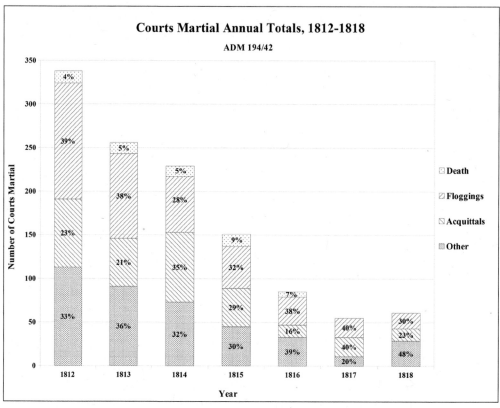

Data collated from TNA: ADM 194/42. Note the total absence of death sentences following 1816, and the sharp decline in annual courts martial years before the end of the war.

from the yardarm,' death was only very rarely used as a deterrent punishment during this time and was carried out even less frequently – the vast majority of death sentences being pardoned, conditionally or otherwise. The category of 'other' contains sentences which were proportionately less common during this period, including dismissal from one's ship or from the service entirely, monetary fines including the 'mulcting' of one's pay, terms of imprisonment and penal servitude, and, usually reserved for officers, 'admonishment to be more careful in future'. From this figure a clear decline in the number of naval courts martial immediately following the war is clear. However, a very different picture is shown when these numbers are considered against the navy's population. The years of the Napoleonic Wars routinely saw more courts martial per year than any year until the 1860s, but the past 25 years of war had seen the navy grow to an unprecedented size, and relatively few trials actually took place *per capita*. There was a general decline in both naval manpower and annual courts martial from 1812 until 1818, but the actual percentage of those tried rose substantially during the same period.

Several factors are ultimately responsible for this phenomenon. One was an, admittedly understandable, reluctance to organise courts martial on fleets or foreign stations under threat of attack. The other, related, reason was the geographic spread of a navy conducting

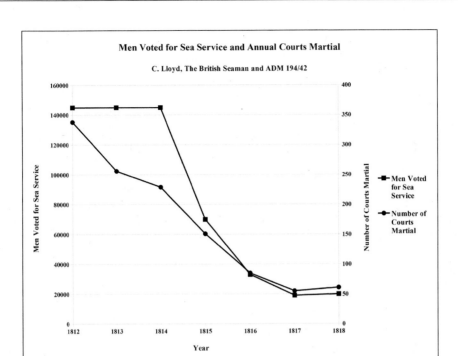

Data collated from C. Lloyd, *The British Seaman*, and TNA: ADM 194/42. Note the constant decline in annual courts martial, contrasted against the sharp decline in naval manpower.

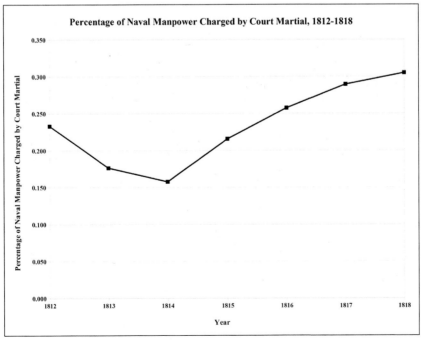

Data collated from C. Lloyd, *The British Seaman*, and TNA: ADM 194/42.

economic warfare against nearly the entirety of Europe, which meant that captains were far more likely to take matters of discipline into their own hands, even when legally forbidden from doing so. From the time of Charles II individual captains were barred from sentencing their subordinates to death, but the *King's Regulations and Admiralty Instructions* also forbade captains from summarily inflicting more than a dozen lashes – a provision often ignored for reasons of convenience and practicality during the wars against France. This provision was actually lifted in 1806, but was swiftly followed by the introduction of standardised punishment returns, a practice later expanded more thoroughly to courts martial as well, and by the end of the war circular orders requiring the justification of extreme punishments by officers were introduced – clear evidence of increasing Admiralty oversight on matters of discipline.[17] Although it would be decades still until use of the lash became formally regulated with the Naval Discipline Act of 1860, these changes show a substantial social shift which occurred throughout this period – a growing revulsion of corporal punishment, and a recognition that less capable officers were as much, if not more, to blame for ill-discipline as the men they commanded. At a basic level, however, questions regarding at what point infractions against discipline were no longer the responsibility of the vessel's commander and instead drew the attention of a formal naval court were known to contemporaries. The punishments captains were empowered to summarily inflict changed dramatically from the sixteenth century, when Francis Drake's trial and execution of Thomas Doughty set a precedent that allowed naval commanders to summarily try subordinates and condemn them to death. This changed by the reign of Charles II, as the 1661 Articles of War and every iteration explicitly restricted a single officer's ability to capitally convict, stating that:

> ...no Court martial where the pains of death shall be inflicted shall consist of less then Five Captains; at least the Admiral's Lieutenant to be as to this purpose esteemed as a Captain and in no case wherein [the] sentence of death shall pass by virtue of the Articles aforesaid or any of them (except in case of mutiny) there shall be execution of such Sentence of Death without the leave of the Lord High Admiral if the offence be committed within the Narrow Seas. But in case any of the Offences aforesaid be committed in any Voyage beyond the Narrow Seas whereupon Sentence of Death shall be given in pursuance of the aforesaid Articles or of any of them then Execution shall not be done but by Order of the Commander in Chief of that Fleet or Squadron wherein [the] Sentence of Death was passed.[18]

Barring these few examples, the changing culture of crime and punishment in the late Napoleonic Royal Navy occurred without formal legislation. In fact, it is somewhat surprising how little the written law changed from the passing of the 1661 Articles of War until comprehensive revision two centuries later in 1860. Passed shortly after the Restoration, the 1661 Articles were the first consolidation of a traditional system of naval justice which dated back to before the days of the Elizabethan navy. Consistent and unwavering focus on

---

17   Rodger, *Command of the Ocean: A Naval History of Britain 1649-1815* (New York: Penguin Books, 2004), p.493.

18   13 Cha. II c. 9, Article 34. Spelling modernised by author.

the penalty of death was the hallmark of these early Articles, as their goal of deterrence was firmly rooted in the jurisprudence of their day – as was their framing of crime as a moral failing, offences against God. Unlike later iterations of the Articles, when the concept of legal mercy had firmly taken root in the naval justice system, the 1661 Articles made no explicit allowance for the Royal Pardon, even going so far as to explicitly forbid it in cases of sodomy. In total, 20 of the 32 listed offences have death as a potential punishment, and officers were no less exempt from this than ordinary sailors – Articles 11 through 14 make specific reference to the conduct of officers to their superiors and against the enemy, all of which promise death.[19]

Despite their severity, the 1661 Articles remained unchanged until 1749, when Admiral Anson introduced 'An Act for amending, explaining and reducing into one Act of Parliament, the Laws relating to the Government of His Majesty's Ships, Vessels and Forces by Sea' which formally abolished earlier legislation in favour of this new expression of justice in the Royal Navy. The 1749 Act repealed and amended several other pieces of naval legislation passed during the reigns of William and Mary, and George I, relating to crime, punishment, courts martial, and piracy. Most of the articles of the 1749 Act remained unchanged from 1661, although an emphasis on legal mercy was now explicitly included, and the provision against pardon in cases of sodomy was removed, at least in writing. Perhaps most notably, the 1749 Articles are far clearer regarding the formal procedure and limits of naval courts martial, explicitly defining the limits of naval court's jurisdiction, and including several provisions clearly taken from contemporary civilian law, such as Article 25, protection from double jeopardy.[20]

The 1749 Articles remained one of the most infamous pieces of legislation relating to discipline within the Royal Navy for the next century. Under their provisions Admiral Byng was executed for 'failing to do his utmost,' Richard Parker and several dozen others were hanged for 'black, bloody mutiny,' and countless other officers, sailors and marines were tried against them during the latter half of the eighteenth century. Several contemporary legal commentators spoke against the Articles' perceived harshness,[21] and even twentieth and twenty-first century media view them with a sort of morbid fascination, perhaps most notably in the film adaptations of C.S. Forester's *Horatio Hornblower* novels. But this is only half the story. Although focus is inevitably placed on the executions, the floggings, and the scandals of naval discipline, the vast majority of those tried received far lighter sentences. As in civilian courts, the majority of those sentenced to death were pardoned, and, of course, the legal records say nothing of the hundreds of thousands of officers and sailors per year who never saw court martial – only the few hundred who did.

In addition to the Articles of War, discipline in the Royal Navy was maintained by the *King's Regulations and Admiralty Instructions*. Much more than a simple disciplinary manual, the Regulations were a guidebook that listed the duties and governed the actions of each member of His Majesty's Navy. Commanding officers were solely authorised to punish

---

19   13 Cha. II c. 9.
20   22 Geo. II c. 33.
21   See W.J. Neale, *History of the Mutiny at Spithead and the Nore* (London: Bradbury and Evans, 1842) and Sir Charles Cunningham, *A Narrative of Occurrences that Took Place During the Mutiny at the Nore* (Chatham: William Burrill, 1829).

their subordinates, although such punishments were often restricted by the Regulations. On a basic level, the distinction between the offences listed in the Articles of War and those outlined in the Regulations was the same that distinguished felonies and misdemeanours in the criminal law. Felonies were defined as 'crimes, conviction for which resulted in an automatic forfeiture of all the felon's property to the Crown... "venomous" offences which cost a man his property... and his life.'[22] By the turn of the nineteenth century nearly all felonies carried the sentence of death, although the liberal use of pardon ensured that relatively few executions actually took place. Misdemeanours, on the other hand, were 'lesser crimes,' for which punishments included fines and various forms of corporal punishment, transportation overseas, and, by the late eighteenth century, short terms of imprisonment. This distinction between felonies and misdemeanours was, at least in part, shared in the Royal Navy; as the Crown protected its power to sentence felons to death, so too did the Admiralty uphold such a right amongst its sailors and officers.

That said, intent was as difficult to ascertain in the nineteenth century as it is today. The distinction between murder and manslaughter was not defined until late into the nineteenth century, and in the accident-prone environment of a ship of war, many 'murders' could easily have been the result of unfortunate circumstances, just as seemingly accidental deaths may have had more malicious causes. The 1749 Articles of War make no explicit distinction between murder and manslaughter, or any such 'greater' and 'lesser' offences, instead judging such charges 'according to the laws and customs in such cases used at sea.'[23] Therefore, without intent, acquittal was the only outcome in cases of loss of life. For example, when charged with the murder of Marine Private William Thomas following a 'scuffle' in 1812, Private Marine Richard Potter was fully acquitted as there 'appeared to be no marks of violence on the body of the deceased [and] the Court was of opinion that though the death ... might have been the result of the scuffle ... there was clearly no intention of murder whatever, and they therefore acquitted the prisoner.'[24] However, this is not to suggest an acceptance by naval courts of loss of life at sea – the court martial of Ship's Corporal Francis Ansell in 1815 for the 'wilful murder of William Thompson, Corporal of Marines' found him guilty, and he was hanged.[25]

Social class, which in the case of the Royal Navy often went hand-in-hand with rank, also had a significant effect of the charges and sentences handed out by naval courts martial. This is a focus shared by many historians of civilian law, and many have emphasised a very class-centric view of the criminal law that has provoked a strong backlash in some circles, arguing that the dual use of 'terror and mercy' allowed the criminal law to function in society.[26] Yet even if this approach has since been deemed insufficient so far as civilian law as concerned, rank and social class are much more important when discussing crime and punishment in the navy. The Returns clearly show that certain charges were far more likely

22   David Bentley, *English Criminal Justice in the Nineteenth Century* (London: The Hambledon Press, 1998), p.2.
23   22 Geo. II c. 33, Article 36.
24   TNA: ADM 194/42, Trial of Private Marine Richard Potter, 15 July 1812.
25   TNA: ADM 194/42, Trial of Francis Ansell, 27 October 1815.
26   Peter King, *Crime, Justice and Discretion: Law and Social Relations in England, 1740-1820* (Oxford: Oxford University Press, 2000), p.373.

to be brought against those of a particular rank, and officers enjoyed certain protection from aspects of the Articles of War – for example, officers were not permitted to be flogged, and petty officers only for mutiny.[27] Execution of officers, although exceedingly rare, was to be carried out via firing squad rather than hanging, as seen in Admiral Byng's 1757 example.[28] Proportionately, officers were much more likely to receive acquittals or to be 'adjudged to be more careful in future'. However, the Admiralty was not above severely punishing those whom they deemed to be dangerous or detrimental to the service, whatever their rank or status. In most listed cases, such offences consisted of disobedience to superiors, especially when combined with violent or insulting language, or, rarely, actual violence. This was the case in 1813, when Marine Lieutenant John Delap was publicly and disgracefully cashiered and drummed out of his Divisional Headquarters for:

> …taking the money of an Officer killed in action & appropriating it for his own use, neglecting to deliver up the same on the demand of the widow of the afore-said Officer, for contempt & disrespect to his superior Officer Lt. General Elliot, for lifting a weapon & offering violence to Lt. Gen. Elliot …and for absence without leave from any Officer competent to give such leave, thereby deserting.[29]

Drunkenness, one of the most common charges regardless of rank, usually resulted in the dismissal of the convicted officer from his ship when proved, with repeated charges or convictions often resulting in dismissal from the service entirely.[30]

As the members that made up naval courts were, by law, exclusively officers, there was no pretence whatsoever of a trial by one's peers for the average sailor, much to the chagrin of contemporary legal commentators.[31] As the largely meritocratic Napoleonic-era officer corps gave way to a far more stagnant social hierarchy during the nineteenth century, class became increasingly important for promotion and opportunity in the navy, and it is there-fore important in the discussion of crime and punishment. The ratio of officers to men fell from 1:28 in 1813 to 1:3 in 1817, displaying the oversaturation of the post-Napoleonic Navy List.[32] In addition, as the only officially accepted method of promotion, seniority ensured that the vast majority of officers were well past their prime by the time they reached command rank. For example, the 1836 Navy List contains one lieutenant whose commission dated from 1 December 1778, 58 years previous, and also lists hundreds of other officers who had not been promoted in decades.[33] Yet in spite of this, the navy remained somewhat merito-cratic in the selection of its officers. Systems of patronage ensured that senior officers would show favouritism only to those who would enhance their reputation, and the standardised lieutenant's examination ensured that prospective officers maintained at least some level

---

27   22 Geo. II c. 33, Articles 19 and 20, and TNA: ADM 194/42.
28   Not one officer from 1812 to 1818 received a sentence of death.
29   TNA: ADM 194/42, Trial of Second Lieutenant John Delap, 14 June 1813.
30   TNA: ADM 194/42, Trial of Lieutenant Robert Dunn, 6 July 1812.
31   Neale, *History of the Mutiny at Spithead and the Nore*, p.8.
32   Lloyd, *The British Seaman*, p.268. These figures include those officers on half-pay.
33   *The NAVY LIST corrected to 20 December 1836* (London: John Murray, 1837), p.19.

of professional competency.[34] That said, in the case of Lieutenant William Bligh of *Bounty* infamy, navigational excellence did not necessarily result in good leadership abilities, although his command ability has been severely underrated by much modern scholarship.[35]

Despite the lasting infamy of being 'hanged from the yardarm' and the – often assumed – inflexibility of both iterations of the Articles of War and the numerous articles which called for execution upon conviction, the hangman's noose was used every bit as strategically in the navy as it was in civilian society. Twenty-one of the 36 offences contained in the 1749 Articles of War list death as a potential punishment, of which 10 list death as the *only* punishment. These include Article Three, providing intelligence to the enemy; Articles 10, 12, and 13, respectively, failure to engage the enemy, cowardice before the enemy, and failure to pursue the enemy; Article 15, desertion to the enemy; Article 19, mutiny; Article 22, striking a superior officer, particularly with a weapon; Article 25, arson; Article 28, murder; and Article 29, sodomy.[36] Many other articles listed death as a *potential* sentence, but generally unless the offence was an immediate and direct violation of discipline, struck directly at the fighting capabilities of the navy *while in action*, or was an offence seen as particularly abhorrent, at least some degree of formal leeway in sentencing was permitted by the Articles.

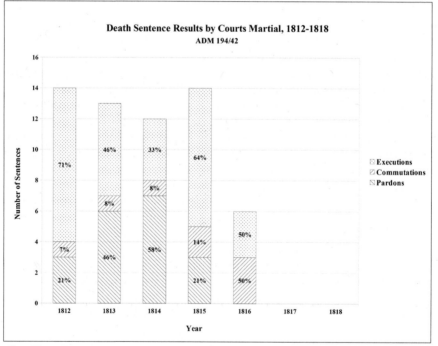

Data collated from TNA: ADM 194/42. Note the sharp decline in death sentences following peace, and the complete absence in 1817 and 1818.

34   Arthur Herman, *To Rule the Waves* (New York: Harper Collins, 2004), p.427.
35   Woodman, *A Brief History of Mutiny*, p.95.
36   22 Geo. II c. 33.

As has been emphasised time and again by scholars of both military and civilian law, however, just because an offence carried the sentence of death did by no means ensure that the sentence was always, or even often, carried out. Of the offences listed above, only a few were likely to be met with the death sentence, whatever the wording of the articles. This included murder; sodomy; the striking, assault, or wounding of a superior officer; and desertion to the enemy. A total of 59 naval courts martial resulted in sentences of death from 1812–1818, of which all occurred between 1812 and 1816. As shown, 27 of these were ultimately pardoned in full or in part, or commuted to a lesser sentence such as transportation. Thirty-two resulted in execution. By charge, the breakdown is as follows:

Table 1: Naval Court Martial Death Sentences by Charge, 1812–1818

Charge	Executions	Pardons
Sodomy	10	3
Striking Superior	6	15
Mutiny	3	5
Murder	5	1
Desertion to the enemy	7	3
Running away with a prize	1	0
Total	32	27

Collated from TNA: ADM 194/42. Several charges of mutiny were paired with charges of striking superiors. As 'violent mutiny' would remain a capital offence until late into the nineteenth century, these have been categorised as charges of mutiny. Additionally, assault resulting in death was treated by naval courts as effectively instances of murder, and hence have been categorised as such here.

From 1812 until 1818 the capital offence to see the fewest number of pardons was sodomy – a trend mirrored in civilian courts, as shown by databases such as the *Old Bailey Proceedings Online* and *The Digital Panopticon*.[37] Convicted murderers were also very unlikely to receive 'His Majesty's most Gracious pardon', but, with relatively few exceptions, all trials for the causing of death between 1812 and 1818 were unable to prove intent. One of those so acquitted, Seaman Jonathan Bartrin, tried in August 1814, even received His Majesty's pardon, 'owing to the favourable circumstances in his case', emphasizing the extreme danger of life at sea, and the accidental deaths that unfortunately occurred.[38]

Despite these and the numerous other offences which, upon conviction, called for execution, pragmatism often stayed the hand of courts during the war years, and the declining need for deterrent public spectacles thereafter meant that relatively few prisoners were ultimately subject to this fate. Legislative changes during this period ensured that the discretion of naval courts had some legal backing. A 1779 amendment to the 1749 Articles of War ensured that no court would find their hands tied as tightly as those of Admiral Byng's several decades earlier, legally empowering the court to 'inflict such other Punishment as the Nature and Degree of the Offence shall be found to deserve' in cases 'attended with

---

37   Also see A.N. Gilbert, 'Buggery and the British Navy, 1700-1861', *Journal of Social History*, 10 (1976), p.72.
38   TNA: ADM 194/42, Trial of Jonathan Bartrin, 2 August 1814.

great Hardship and Inconvenience'.[39] Another act, passed within a year of Waterloo, greatly streamlined the process by which those sentenced to death could receive conditional pardons, further expanding the discretionary powers available to naval courts.[40] Overall, between 1812 and 1818 the sentence of death was sparingly used in the Royal Navy, but for one key exception.

In December 1815 and January 1816, 16 members of the crew of the frigate *Africane* were tried for violations of the second and 29th Articles of War, respectively pertaining to 'scandalous Actions' and 'the unnatural and detestable Sin of Sodomy'.[41] This was during a period when sodomy and other 'unclean acts' were very much still perceived as a hanging offence in civilian courts, and the navy was of similar opinion.[42] Seven of those tried were hanged, the others receiving other forms of serious punishment including upwards of 300 lashes. One James Bruce was sentenced:

> ...to be dismissed from His Majesty's Service, rendered incapable and unworthy of ever serving His Majesty, His Heirs and Successors, in any capacity, to have their uniform coats publicly stripped off their backs on the Quarter deck [of the *Africane*], and to be imprisoned in solitary confinement in the Marshalsea Prison for the term of two years.[43]

B.R. Burg goes into much greater detail on these trials, in which he notes that the *Africane* was infamous within the navy of the time, colloquially known as the 'man-fucking ship'.[44] No amount of punishment appeared capable of deterring the actions of its crew, and not even the ship's decommissioning and breaking-up later in 1816 was capable of putting an end to its infamous reputation.[45] Allowing for this one exception, however, both confirmed and pardoned death sentences declined in number quite dramatically following peace with France, a trend which continued until the Naval Discipline Act of 1860 dramatically reduced the number of capital offences contained in the Articles of War and introduced lesser charges which did not necessarily carry the sentence of death.

Although the sentence of death was rarely used by naval courts, especially after the Napoleonic Wars, the lash was commonplace until well towards the end of the nineteenth century. From the late-eighteenth century onwards, calls for humanitarianism and the abolition of or reduction in the use of the lash began to grow, and although significant reduction in punitive flogging in civilian society occurred, this was not the case in the Royal Navy. It would not be until the Naval Discipline Act of 1860 that naval courts martial were

---

39   19 Geo. III., cap. 17.
40   56 Geo. III., cap. 5.
41   22 Geo. II c. 33, Articles 2 and 29. The *Africane* had a crew of approximately 300, meaning that over five percent of its compliment were tried in that month.
42   Peter King, *Crime and Law in England*, 1750-1840 (Cambridge: Cambridge University Press, 2006), p.176.
43   TNA: ADM 194/42, Trial of James Bruce, 6 January 1816.
44   B.R. Burg, *Boys at Sea: Sodomy, Indecency and Courts Martial in Nelson's Navy* (London: Macmillan, 2007), p.157.
45   See B.R. Burg, *Boys at Sea*, *passim*, and 'HMS AFRICAINE Revisited: The Royal Navy and the Homosexual Community', *Journal of Homosexuality*, 56:2 (2009), pp.173-194.

limited to 48 lashes, and another two decades still until flogging in the navy was formally suspended. As previously shown, flogging was overwhelmingly the most common sentence passed by courts martial during periods of both war and peace, accounting for approximately one-third of all trial outcomes, and this of course says nothing about any summary lashes imposed by captains on their own authority, or pseudo-official practices such as 'starting.' Throughout this entire period, the occasional sentence saw a certain number of lashes inflicted in conjunction with a term of imprisonment, but naval courts would prove far more resistant to the acceptance of long-term prison sentences as a standard punishment when compared to their civilian equivalents, and it would not be until mid-century that imprisonment finally overtook flogging as the most common punishment sentenced by naval courts. The coming of peace in late 1815 seems to have had only a minor effect on the number of naval courts sentencing any number of lashes, as by 1818 approximately 31 percent of courts martial resulted in a sentence of flogging, down only nine percent from 1812.

Although the overall proportion of courts martial to result in flogging did not significantly change with the coming of peace, the number of lashes for a given sentence most certainly did. Neither of the most infamous examples of naval corporal punishment, flogging around the fleet or running the gauntlet, were once referenced in the court records examined. The latter was made illegal by Admiralty order in 1806, but many occurrences of flogging were still quite horrific. Sentences ranged from a few dozen to many hundreds of lashes, the latter fortunately occurring only quite rarely. Of the 419 sentences of flogging passed from 1812 until 1818, 32, or approximately eight percent, consisted of over 400 lashes total. Overwhelmingly, these punishments were reserved for offences that would otherwise receive a sentence of death, such as desertion during action, striking or assault on a superior, or mutiny. As only two such sentences took place after 1815, it is quite clear that naval courts were hesitant to flog to such an extent without active warfare providing a pressing, deterrent need.[46] It was a very different case during the war years, but even still very few trials saw such extreme sentences. One of the rare exceptions occurred in June 1814, when Private Marine Charles Collins was convicted of stabbing his superior officer with a bayonet and sentenced to receive 600 lashes, the largest single such sentence of this period.[47]

Overwhelmingly, the most common single offence punished with flogging was desertion, accounting for 176 of the 419 courts martial resulting in flogging from 1812–1818, almost exactly 42 percent. To reiterate, this was despite the clear guidance of the Articles of War promising death to captured deserters, although, as numerous scholars have emphasised, a navy starving for manpower would hardly have routinely condemned able-bodied sailors to death for desertion alone – every death sentence passed for desertion was specifically for desertion *to the enemy*, and even three of those cases were pardoned. Not a single instance of desertion under any other circumstances was punished by death during or after the war years, despite the 16th Article of War permitting such a sentence.[48] Of course, the chronic

---

46   The two instances in question were both for deserting while on sentry, and theft. See TNA: ADM 194/42, Trials of Samuel Peach, 25 April 1817, and of Joseph Comer, 3 August 1818.

47   TNA: ADM 194/42, Trial of Charles Collins, 10 June 1814.

48   Note that Article 16 of the 1749 Articles states: 'Every Person in or belonging to the Fleet, who shall desert or entice others so to do, shall suffer Death, *or such other Punishment as the Circumstances of*

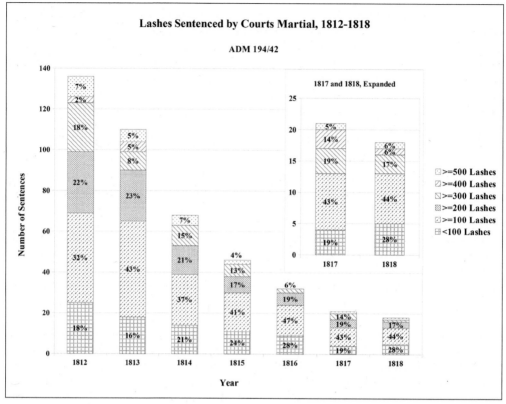

Data collated from TNA: ADM 194/42. Note the decline in sentences of over 300 lashes, but proportionate stability of lesser sentences.

shortage of manpower during the war years meant that, although not punished with death, captured deserters were hardly treated leniently, but sentences tended to lessen once peace was signed. Private Marine Michael Burke, for example, was sentenced to six months' solitary confinement in Cold Bath Fields Prison in 1818, whereas just four years prior Seaman David Edwards received 200 lashes for the same offence.[49]

The fixation on the 'cat' to deter desertion would decline in the years after the war so far as the navy was concerned, but it remained a hotly contested topic among the wider British military. As Peter Burroughs notes regarding attempts to quell desertion from the British Army in North America in the post-Napoleonic decades, there was significant tension between competing disciplinary views. Lord Howick at the War Office used increasingly humanitarian attempts to encourage soldiers to remain, from pay bonuses for good behaviour, alternative leisure activities, or educational programs, whereas the Commander-in-Chief at Horse Guards, Lord Hill, retained staunchly traditionalist disciplinary views.

---

the *Offence shall deserve.*' Neither Article 15 (desertion to the enemy), nor any of the 1661 Articles, make any such allowance for alternative punishments.

49   TNA: ADM 194/42. Trials of Michael Burke, 5 October 1818, and David Edwards, 20 January 1814.

Ultimately the efforts of both were in vain, and the British Army continued to haemorrhage manpower in North America through the mid-nineteenth century.[50] In the Royal Navy, desertion continued to be a significant problem for the remainder of the century, although perhaps not to the degree of the army in North America. Further legislation ensured that fines and lengthy prison sentences awaited captured naval deserters long into the nineteenth century, although following the end of the Napoleonic Wars the lash came under significant scrutiny and within a few decades was all but abandoned for the punishment of most deserters.[51]

Other common offences that resulted in flogging included disobedience, assault, and theft, as well as virtually every serious offence which did not result in a sentence of death – including, interestingly enough, *attempted* desertion. Sentences up to several hundred lashes were uniformly reserved for the most serious such offenses, such as striking superiors, serious assaults regardless of rank, desertion before the enemy, and mutinous actions or language, but sentences of these magnitudes swiftly decreased in likelihood following peace with France, with sentences of 200 or greater declining swiftly once the need for deterrent punishment began to lessen. The decline in lashes inflicted also appears to have occurred proportionately for each offense. Of course, certain offences were far less common or entirely absent from the peacetime court records, such as desertion to the enemy or cowardice during action. However, even fairly serious offences that still appear in these later records, such as disobedience, striking superiors, or absence without leave, still received far more lenient sentences after 1815. Certainly, some individuals still received large numbers of lashes, such as Seaman Morgan Thomas, who received 300 lashes for several charges of 'insolent and mutinous language' in July 1816, but the majority received far fewer – see, for example, the trial of Seaman James Cook, who two years later received 'only' four dozen lashes for virtually the same offence.[52] The post-war navy and the legislative changes of the past half-century clearly allowed a significant degree of discretion on the part of courts martial, and the trial records make it clear that this discretion was often used to both extremes by the various officers of the day.

One final category that calls for additional attention are trials for loss of ship. Courts martial for such cases were relatively unique, as the hearings they entailed were more along the line of inquiry courts than criminal trials. Additional charges could, of course, take root from these hearings, and often did if any of the surviving officers and crew were found guilty of 'failing to do their utmost' to prevent the loss of the ship, whether to enemy action, poor conditions, or otherwise. In addition, ill-discipline among sailors during such times were often punished far more harshly than they would be otherwise. Disgruntled sailors often took the opportunity of such a disaster to attempt desertion, and those who were unsuccessful or later apprehended often received very severe sentences. In the case of the loss of the *Penelope*, a troop ship whose surviving crew came before court martial in July 1815, 47 of the crew deserted, and 'Walter Howell a seaman was guilty of drunkenness and

50   See Peter Burroughs, 'Tackling Army Desertion in British North America', *The Canadian Historical Review* (1980), pp.28-68 and 'Crime and Punishment in the British Army, 1815-70', *The English Historical Review*, 100:396 (1985), pp.545-571.
51   23 &24 Vict., 123. *The Naval Discipline Act, 1860.* Article 46, subheading 7.
52   TNA: ADM 194/42, Trials of Morgan Thomas, 7 July 1816, and James Cook, 29 July 1818.

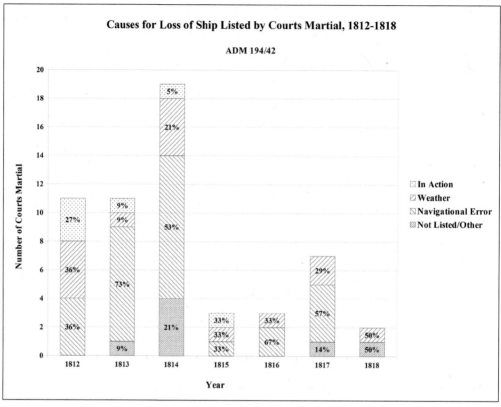

Causes for Loss of Ship Listed by Courts Martial, 1812-1818

ADM 194/42

Data collated from TNA: ADM 194/42. Note the few ships lost in action, even during the war years, when compared to those lost due to poor weather or navigational error.

disobedience... and sentenced to receive five-hundred lashes.'[53] Fifty-six hearings for the loss of ships were recorded as taking place between 1812 and 1818, although only six list enemy action as the cause for the ship's loss.

What is particularly noteworthy of the examined courts martial for ships lost in action is that only in a single instance – for the loss of the *Emulous* in 1812 – were any of the surviving ships' companies censured or in any way reprimanded for their actions. In that case, Captain William Mulcaster was 'only admonished' due to a 'zealous motive...to fall in with the enemy', and Lieutenant Fowle, officer of the watch, and John Wilson, Master, were severely censured for their failure to take proper care when the ship gained soundings.[54] In all other cases, the surviving officers and crew of ships lost in action were 'fully and honourably acquitted,' whether due to their desire to prevent the ship's capture by the enemy, in the case of Lieutenant Pascoe's grounding of the *Daring* gun brig in 1813, or a desire to save the lives of the crew, such as in the case of the loss of the *Biter* in 1814, run aground

---

53   TNA: ADM 194/42, Trial for loss of the *Penelope* troop ship, 21 July 1815.
54   TNA: ADM 194/42, Trial for loss of *Emulous* sloop, 19 October 1812.

after taking on significant water from enemy fire.[55] The loss of the *Peacock* on the North American Station in 1813 provides a far more questionable example.[56] As in all other cases barring that of the *Emulous*, the *Peacock*'s entire compliment were honourably acquitted. However, 'the Court was of opinion that the loss of the said Sloop was owing to the want of skill in directing the fire in consequence of the crew not *having practised the use of the guns for three years*.'[57] Given the threat of American attacks in North American waters during that stage of the War of 1812, it seems that a competent commander would have taken it on himself to prepare his crew for the relatively likely occurrence of combat. Instead, as was the case for several trials for loss of ship over the next century, it is likely that individual negligence went unpunished to protect the reputation of the entire service.[58]

By far the most trials for loss of ship took place in 1814, as Napoleon's initial defeat resulted in the repatriation of many captured crews from British ships, with their hearings only taking place upon their return to England. Even among these cases, the vast majority of vessels lost during this period appear to have been due to poor weather or uncharted waters, particularly along enemy coasts, and in most cases the surviving officers and crew were fully acquitted. Specific charges against officers in these trials overwhelmingly were the result of ignoring common sense or sound navigational advice from their subordinates. If not acquitted, such officers often saw sentences ranging from minor admonishment to outright dismissal. More than any other major charge, trials for loss of ship seem to have fundamentally changed the least during the transition to peace. Both before and after 1815, weather and navigational error, rather than enemy action, led to the loss of nearly every warship, and no significant change in sentencing procedure appears to have taken place with the coming of peace.

While capital and corporal punishments often receive the lion's share of attention in studies of both civil and military law, over half of those tried by court martial during any given year from 1812 until 1818 were either acquitted or received some other, lesser sentence. Often these 'other sentences' were extremely dependent on rank, seniority, or peculiar circumstances unique to the case at hand. The most common such sentence was dismissal, either from one's ship or His Majesty's Service entirely, although specific circumstances varied greatly. Dismissal from one's ship was a common sentence for cases of drunkenness, minor disobedience, and contemptuous language or behaviour to superiors, especially if the accused was themselves an officer. Repeated offences usually saw dismissal from the service entirely, although due to want of manpower this was seldom done during the war years. Reprimands, of varying degrees of severity, were the standard sentence for most convicted officers, carrying with such a sentence the threat of harsher consequences for repeated failings. Both imprisonment and monetary punishments were relatively rare from 1812 until 1818, although both would become increasingly more common as the century continued and they became more publicly palatable than the lash.

---

55   TNA: ADM 194/42, Trials for loss of *Daring*, 2 April 1813, and of *Biter*, 5 June 1814.

56   For more, see Nicholas Kaizer's chapter in this volume, "Unprepared and Unaccountable: The loss of His Majesty's Sloops *Peacock*, *Boxer*, and *Epervier* in the War of 1812".

57   TNA: ADM 194/42, Trial for loss of *Peacock*, 6 June 1813. Author's emphasis.

58   Such as the infamous loss of the *Orpheus* off the coast of New Zealand. TNA: ADM 194/180, Trial of Lieutenant Charles Hill *et al* of the *Orpheus*, 27 April 1863.

Despite the large numbers of trial records referenced in this study, it is important to remember that those sailors punished to such extremes formed a very small proportion of the total manpower of the navy. As noted by Daniel Baugh, naval officers usually did not record normalcy in their logs and dispatches, and therefore histories of naval administration are often a chronical of what went wrong.[59] Additionally, as with any study of historical crime and punishment, inherent limitations exist. Regarding his study of criminal law in early nineteenth-century Essex, Peter King notes that undetected offences, unreported offences, and any offences dealt with outside the formal trial procedure form a 'dark figure of crime', which will likely never be knowable to historians of the subject.[60] In the naval example, many such cases are contained not within the court martial indices, but rather within the enormous collection of unexamined logs and defaulters' books contained in the National Archives, emphasizing the continued legal authority that individual officers were still able to maintain throughout this period, in spite of growing proportions of offences coming before court martial.

While the changing trends in naval courts martial from 1812–1818 may appear subtle, they underpin larger changes taking place concurrently within the Royal Navy and British society that, in the former case, would eventually culminate in the passing of the 1860 Naval Discipline Act. Falling rates of capital convictions and increasing numbers of pardons, declining numbers of lashes inflicted for even the most serious offences, and the slow increase in alternative sentences, such as imprisonment, hint at a growing humanitarianism in naval punishment, enabled for the first time by a period of sustained peace. What legislation that was passed during the war years also emphasised a growing interest in legal matters by the Admiralty, or at the very least an increasing acceptance that such matters were ultimately their responsibility, imposed or otherwise. The decades following peace with France saw growing numbers of sentences that were directly modified by the Admiralty or local commanders-in-chief, and even a few cases where commanders were censured or removed from their commands for the inflicting of 'arbitrary and cruel punishments.'[61] Although it would be quite a few decades until Winston Churchill's or Nicholas Rodger's descriptions of eighteenth-century naval discipline would be truly overwritten by a much more formal understanding of crime and punishment, changes were already underway from the moment of Napoleon's defeat.

Select Bibliography

Archival Sources

The National Archives, Kew (TNA)
    ADM 194/42, Courts Martial Indices, 1812-1855
    ADM 194/180, Courts Martial Returns, 1855-1864
    ADM 194/181, Courts Martial Returns, 1865-1872

---

59   Daniel Baugh, *British Naval Administration in the Age of Walpole* (Princeton: Princeton University Press, 1965), p.2.
60   King, *Crime, Justice, and Discretion*, p.133.
61   TNA: ADM 194/180, Admiralty Memorandum dated 14 January 1862.

Parliamentary Statutes:

Act for the Establishing Articles and Orders for the regulating and better Government of His Majesties Navies Ships of Warr & Forces by Sea, 1661 (13 Cha. II, cap. 9)

An Act for amending, explaining and reducing into One Act of Parliament, the Laws relating to the Government of His Majesty's Ships, Vessels and Forces by Sea, 1749 (22 Geo. II, cap. 33)

An Act to explain and amend an Act made in the Twenty-second Year of the Reign of His late Majesty King George the Second, intituled "An Act for amending, explaining, and reducing into One Act of Parliament the Laws relating to the Government of His Majesty's Ships, Vessels, and Forces by Sea", 1779 (19 Geo. III, cap. 17)

An Act to extend the Powers of an Act of the Thirty-seventh Year of His present Majesty, for enabling His Majesty more effectually to grant conditional Pardons to Persons under Sentence of Naval Courts-martial, and to regulate Imprisonment under such Sentences, 1816 (56 Geo. III, cap. 5.)

The Naval Discipline Act, 1860 (23 & 24 Vict., cap. 123)

Published Sources

Baugh, Daniel, *British Naval Administration in the Age of Walpole* (Princeton: Princeton University Press, 1965).

Burg, B.R., *Boys at Sea: Sodomy, Indecency and Courts Martial in Nelson's Navy* (London: Macmillan, 2007).

Byrn, John., *Crime and Punishment in the Royal Navy, Discipline on the Leeward Islands Station 1784-1812* (Southampton: Camelot Press, 1989).

Devereaux, Simon, 'The City and the Sessions Paper', *The Journal of British Studies* 35:4 (1996), 466-503.

Eder, Markus, *Crime and Punishment in the Royal Navy of the Seven Years' War, 1755-1763* (Aldershot: Ashgate Publishing, 2004).

Gilbert, A.N., 'The Changing Face of British Military Justice', *Military Affairs*, 49:2 (1985), pp.80-84.

Hay, Douglas, Linebaugh, Peter, Rule, John, Thompson, E.P., and Winslow, Cal, *Albion's Fatal Tree: Crime and Society in Eighteenth-Century England* (London: Verso, 2011).

Hechter, Michael, Pfaff, Steven, and Underwood, Patrick, 'Grievances and the Genesis of Rebellion: Mutiny in the Royal Navy, 1740-1820', *American Sociological Review* 81:1 (2016), pp.165-189.

Johnston, Andrew, '"Arbitrary and cruel punishments": Trends in Royal Navy courts martial, 1860–1869', *The International Journal of Maritime History*, 33:3 (2021), pp.525-544

King, Peter, *Crime, Justice and Discretion: Law and Social Relations in England, 1740-1820* (Oxford: Oxford University Press, 2000).

King, Peter, *Crime and Law in England, 1750-1840* (Cambridge: Cambridge University Press, 2006).

Lloyd, Christopher, *The British Seaman 1200-1860* (London: Collins, 1968).

Rodger, N.A.M., *The Command of the Ocean: A Naval History of Britain 1649-1815* (New York: Penguin Books, 2004).

Rodger, N.A.M., *The Wooden World: The Anatomy of the Georgian Navy* (London: Collins, 1986).

Part IV

Naval Social and Cultural History

The social history of the Royal Navy is focused upon the lives and lived experience of officers, seamen, and other maritime professionals. The wider field, and approach, of social history has now become firmly established in the academic world. If operational history deals with how states employed sea power, and the field of administrative history deals with how states created the conditions to successfully wield sea power (or the conditions to squander that sea power), social history deals with the realities of the men – and women – who actually carried out that necessary work. It is a field which is most interested in the lives, careers, and culture of those associated with the Royal Navy, but one which necessarily examines and analyses the operational and administrative realities which formed so much of the world in which the men lived. Here there are three chapters examining the experiences and careers of three very different sorts of maritime professionals.

First, Jim Tildesley examines the career of John Mitchell, who although not a navy-man and not a member of the Royal Navy nonetheless played an important role in helping to keep the ever-expanding and manpower-hungry navy afloat. As a Consul to Norway, Mitchell had a hand in naval recruitment and in supporting British semen displaced by privateering and other acts of warfare. Tildesley also highlights the role played by Mitchell in intelligence gathering. His was a varied and valuable career, although one that became lost in the bureaucracy of the Admiralty. Mitchell, having died in poverty, did not receive his due credit in life but has received a very favourable assessment here.

Andrew Lyter then explores the careers of men also overlooked by the Admiralty and by naval history: the black mariners who served as pilots for British ships in the War of 1812. He explores the wartime careers of Edward Godfrey, King George, Jeremiah Primrose, and Peter Wood, all previously enslaved in the Chesapeake Bay region, and how they furthered British naval interests through service aboard HMS *Poictiers*, during her blockade duties in the War of 1812. Lyter explores how these men used their maritime expertise not only to obtain their freedom but also to carve out new identities as dependable and non-expendable maritime professionals in the face of adversity and a staunch racial hierarchy.

Finally, Callum Easton presents a thorough social history of the pensioners of the Greenwich Naval Hospital. Here, Easton examines the naval professionals who manned the fleet during the long eighteenth century, but doing so largely after the conflicts of that era had ended. His work offers a new perspective of the British maritime workforce, and examines both the careers of these sailors as well as the way in which society viewed them, from the stereotypes of drunken jak tars in the early nineteenth century to the way in which society lionized and idealized these same men in their elder years.

Part IV

Naval Social and Cultural History

12

Seamen, Safe Houses, and Secret Service: A British Consul's Recruiting for the Navy, 1795-1808

Jim Tildesley

With the outbreak of the Revolutionary War with France in 1793, the British Royal Navy, as had happened at the beginning of every war in the eighteenth century, found itself with insufficient ships readily available, with only 140 of a total of 458 having enough seamen. Their crews were made up of volunteer, experienced seamen as the navy did not operate the impress service during peacetime. Initially, the navy sought to acquire skilled seamen willing to volunteer and become the crews of some of the vessels held 'in ordinary'. A standard national bounty of £5 for an able-bodied seaman, £2-10s for an ordinary seaman and £1 for a landsman was offered to all volunteers. Individual towns or areas topped up the national bounty by up to two guineas. The Impress Service secured 62,800 volunteers by January 1795, 50 percent being able-bodied seamen mostly already employed in the merchant fleet. Although recruitment brought substantial numbers of additional seamen into the navy with a greater than fourfold increase, the numbers were still insufficient. The navy re-established the press to bring men into the navy forcibly. The men targeted by the press were skilled seamen who were physically fit. Much has been written about the press, which was a contentious issue during the eighteenth century and remains so with historians to this day. However, finding conclusions based on detailed statistical analysis is relatively rare.

Dancy's analysis of 81 muster books of the period shows that 41 percent of the recruits were volunteers, and 42 percent were 'turned over' from existing naval vessels being decommissioned.[1] Initially, this would have meant that over 80 percent of the men were volunteers, with that percentage reducing over time. By 1801, the impress service had provided nineper-cent of the crews. The figures in this study do not take into account the number of seamen pressed at sea from merchant vessels.[2] By 1795 the Admiralty had a force of 528 men based at Dover, Deal and the other Cinque Ports solely to replace men from merchant vessels whose

---

1   Jeremiah R. Dancy, 'British Naval Manpower during the French Revolutionary Wars, 1793-1802' (Unpublished PhD Thesis University of Oxford 2012), p.58.

2   Dancy, 'British Naval Manpower', p.217.

crew members had been pressed on approaching the Downs. They would ensure cargoes were safely brought into London and the Thames.[3]

Naval crew numbers were constantly degraded primarily through sickness, although desertion was significant. Deaths from enemy action were consistently low. The navy wished to increase the number of vessels in the fleet and needed more crews without crippling Britain's merchant fleet, which was vital to the economy. In 1797 Parliament voted funds for a naval force of 120,000 men, a remarkable increase from the 17,000 seamen at the outbreak of war.[4] In 1795 and 1796, the government legislated a series of Quota Acts requiring individual ports, towns and country-wide local authorities to provide a set number of men for the navy. These acts brought an additional 30,000 men, but probably only one-sixth had sea-going experience. Dancy's analysis suggests that the Quota Acts contributed five percent of the navy's seamen.[5] Even with these measures, the navy's requirement for seamen remained on a knife edge.[6]

The British government recognised that the merchant navy was a training ground for potential naval seamen. Legislation had been passed to assist merchant seamen if they were shipwrecked abroad or found themselves destitute, and that assistance was provided through British Consuls. One aspect of the essential duties of a Consul was to provide relief for shipwrecked British mariners as required by the Relief of Shipwrecked Mariners Act 1736 and later amendments. Consuls were required to assist seamen who had been shipwrecked, captured, or arrived in their area through any other unavoidable accident. From 1793 assisting Naval vessels became a more significant aspect of the work of consuls, facilitating repairs, sourcing supplies, negotiating hospital care and arranging local pilots to assist in navigating naval vessels. In some locations, the Consulate paid local enforcement officers to apprehend British stragglers and deserters.[7]

The expectation during the eighteenth century was that a British Consul would be a resident businessman or trader in a foreign city, usually a port. They would be well known amongst the business community and respected by other businessmen. The primary role of any British Consul focused on assisting British merchants and businesses but also included assistance for British personnel. They were not diplomats, nor were they paid a salary.[8] The effectiveness of a consul at this date depended to a certain extent on how their home country was perceived by the country in which they worked. The protection of British citizens and the provision of advice followed from these original functions. The balance of work depended on the consul's location, the priorities as perceived by the individual consul and the time required to undertake their own private business.[9] The Foreign Office, which co-ordinated the work of consuls, was not formed until 1782, and it was not consid-

---

3   R.K. Sutcliffe, 'Bringing forward shipping for government service: the indispensable role of the transport service, 1793 to 1815' (Unpublished PhD Thesis University of Greenwich 2013), p.184.
4   Dancy, 'British Naval Manpower', p.iii.
5   Dancy, 'British Naval Manpower', p.282.
6   N.A.M. Rodger, *The Command of the Ocean: a Naval History of Britain, 1649-1815* (London: Allen Lane, 2004), pp.442-4.
7   The National Archives (TNA) FO 17/16: Consuls' Accounts 1790-1825.
8   Quincy Wright, 'The Legal Position and Functions of Consuls', *The American Journal of International Law* Vol. 26, No. 1, Supplement: Research in International Law (1932), pp.193-449.
9   David Bayne Horn, *The British Diplomatic Service 1689-1789* (Oxford: Clarendon Press, 1961), p.238

ered necessary to codify the work of consuls. For much of the nineteenth century, no one consulate had a single purpose or identical operational instructions.[10] Some of the specific functions delegated to consuls had been built up over time with the Merchant Shipping Acts requiring consuls to assist and protect British Masters and seamen and provide business intelligence. One aspect of the duties of a consul was to provide relief for shipwrecked British mariners. The overarching Act had become law in 1757, and an amended Act was enacted in 1792. Both Acts required consuls to assist seamen who had been shipwrecked, captured, or arrived in the area for which the consul was responsible through any other unavoidable accident. The 1792 Act increased the sum the consuls could pay for assisting seamen from six pence per man per day to nine pence.[11]

Additionally, consuls ensured that British naval vessels could water their ships and made provision for pilots to assist naval vessels in navigating local coastal waters. The consuls provided the local contacts or arranged for repairs to naval vessels. In ports used by the navy, together with large numbers of merchant vessels, consuls were used by the navy to assist with the identification and return of deserters. The Deputy Consul in Portugal paid Portuguese enforcement officers to apprehend British stragglers and deserters; the same officers had the power to search merchant ships for deserters. The Admiralty refunded the payments for this work. The most significant payment followed a visit to Lisbon by Admiral Jervis' squadron as 77 seamen failed to return to their ships before they sailed and were rounded up by the enforcement officers. The more unusual jobs dealt with by consuls were the requirement for the consul in Naples to provide a large house suitable for a British Naval Hospital. The hospital was in use in time to receive men from HMS *Vanguard* after the Battle of the Nile.

An examination of the Consuls' records and returns shows that some locations offered few opportunities to assist in naval recruitment; others indicate that the consul was not proactive in areas other than those that assisted British business. However, one location and one consul stand out in the early years of the Revolutionary War as exceptional in the level and extent of assistance provided. John Mitchell was appointed British Consul, based in Kristiansand, Norway, in 1784, one of a number representing British Interests in the Kingdom of Denmark-Norway.[12] Mitchell had consular responsibility for both Kristiansand and Christiania (Oslo). A deputy consul was appointed locally at each location to represent Mitchell in his absence. Mitchell was a successful merchant and would become the leading importer of potatoes from Britain to Norway. His commercial interests took him to Denmark, Sweden and Hamburg, all of which were ideal locations to further his business and represent the interests of the British government. It has been suggested that Mitchell was the first British Consul to be appointed and sent to a location rather than already being a merchant resident in the foreign location.[13] Mitchell only refers to his appointment in a letter of 1799, saying, 'It was in consideration of my correspondence with His Majesty's

10   D.C.M. Platt, 'The Role of the British Consular Service in Overseas Trade, 1825-1914' *The Economic History Review, New Series*, Vol. 15, No. 3 (1963), pp. 494-512; see in particular p.495.

11   31 Geo. II 1757; 32 Geo. III 1792.

12   TNA FO 90/10: King's Letter Books, Denmark.

13   Halvard Leira & Iver B. Neumann, 'Consular representation in an emerging state: The case of Norway', *The Hague Journal of Diplomacy*, 3 (2008) pp.1-19, quoting p.13.

Minister during the American War that Sir Morton Eden, Mr Elliot and Mr Fraser then under secretary of state recommended me to the Consulship in 1783.'[14]

The volume of trade passing to and from the Baltic through the Kattegat between Sweden and Denmark and into the North Sea was vast. The British Consul at Elsinore, Nicholas Fenwick, closely watched the number and nationality of the ships passing through these restricted waters. Over 10,000 ships per annum were recorded by the beginning of the 1790s. Fenwick's figures for 1791 revealed a total of 10,452 ships passing through the Sound, with just over a third being British.[15] The hazardous rocky coastline of southern Norway and its proximity to this major shipping route resulted in Mitchell regularly assisting shipwrecked seamen. In 1793 a total of 143 shipwrecked seamen were cared for and returned to Britain from Southern Norway. The men were provided with food and lodging for between 40 and 102 days. During the winter, the harbours were subject to long periods of ice, preventing vessels from using the ports and requiring extended periods of subsistence for some of the seamen awaiting return to Britain. It required 27 different vessels to return the men. Many were small (four were lobster smacks) and could only carry a few passengers. Mitchell paid for subsistence for every seaman returned. If Norwegian vessels carried seamen, there was a passenger fee of either 8/- or 10/-. Mitchell's claim for the cost of the return and subsistence for the 143 shipwrecked seamen was in excess of £500.

With the outbreak of the French Revolutionary War at the beginning of February 1793, Denmark-Norway chose to remain neutral, and their coastlines remained open to the vessels of all belligerents.[16] In 1794 the customs records for Kristiansand and Flekkefjord (the next customs port to the west of Kristiansand) recorded a total of 824 merchant vessel movements in the two ports.[17] The French government encouraged privateers to disrupt British trade as far as possible. French privateers operated in sectors with significant numbers of British merchant vessels operating and minimal support of those vessels by the British navy. Privateers also preferred locations with plentiful secluded creeks and harbours in which to berth. Southern Norway was an ideal location with numerous islands, creeks and harbours. It was also an area of minimal British naval activity. The British Navy's primary areas of concern were the English Channel, Western Approaches and the Mediterranean. In these areas, the navy could observe and restrict any aggressive activities of the French navy. Only after the French occupied Holland and took control of the Dutch navy did Britain establish a North Sea Fleet to monitor and restrict the Dutch from leaving their anchorage at Texel and joining forces with the French fleet sheltering in Brest. Even then, the North Sea Fleet's operations were centred on the southern part of the North Sea. British naval activity in Norwegian waters was restricted to convoy escorts.

---

14   TNA FO 33/17. Eden had been British Minister to Copenhagen from 1779–1782 and Dresden from 1783–1791. William Fraser was Under-Secretary of State for Foreign Affairs in 1783. Hugh Elliot represented Britain in Copenhagen from 1782–1791.

15   Atle L. Wold, *Privateering and Diplomacy, 1793–1807: Great Britain, Denmark-Norway and the Question of Neutral Ports* (London: Palgrave Macmillan, 2020), p.11.

16   TNA ADM 17/15: Consuls' Accounts 1790-1825.

17   Historisk infrastruktur Database <https://databaser.tidvis.no/callList/callListPrimaryPlaces.jsp> (accessed 21 September 2023).

It has been suggested that British merchant ship losses between 1793 and 1814 exceeded 11,000. While seemingly a large number, that figure is only 2.25 percent of the British merchant fleet.[18] During the early years of the Revolutionary War, French privateers were most active in the seas off the coast of Norway. As a result, Consul Mitchell dealt with men captured by privateers and left in Southern Norway by their captors. French privateers also sold the cargoes of the vessels they had captured and the vessels themselves in Norway. There were no prize courts in Norway, and the prize court function was filled by French Consuls. During the second half of the eighteenth century, the accepted protocol had been for countries to issue letters of marque to privateers and then set up prize courts in ports of the country issuing the letter of marque or their colonial territories. The British contention was that the French were blatantly circumventing the accepted international rules for the operation of privateers in Norway. The formal complaints were made by the senior British diplomats in Copenhagen. The British diplomats were provided details of individual incidents from around the Norwegian coast by John Mitchell, who worked assiduously to provide information: 'I considered the approbation of His Majesty's mission at Copenhagen, of what I had done, as not only an authorisation but as imposing upon me a duty to persist and do all that existing circumstances put in my power to provide for the safety of the trade and property of His Majesty's subjects during the war.'[19]

As Mitchell had worked both in Kristiansand and Christiania, travelling between the two locations would have given him a working knowledge of part of the southern coast of Norway. He had also mastered the native language, although not to a standard he found acceptable. In 1793 Mitchell had taken on his own initiative to visit 'on this Coast from the Frontiers of Sweden to the Confines of Bergen in all 21 Sea Ports, and an immense number of Harbours & Creeks.'[20] This is well over 1,000 kilometres of coastline. During these visits, Mitchell started building his primary network of contacts and informants. Significantly there were several Norwegian pilots with whom Mitchell developed a rapport. All were seamen who would effectively gain and pass information by sea, the fastest method available in Norway. Pilots were the local men whose income was most affected by the operation of privateers, substantially reducing the numbers of merchant vessels requiring the services of the pilots and were supportive of Mitchell's efforts to eliminate privateers' use of Norwegian ports. The information from this network frequently resulted in the British diplomats in Copenhagen having a far more detailed account of the activity of privateers than the Danish government with whom they were negotiating.[21] It would take until July 1799 before the Danish Government enacted legislation that closed Norwegian ports to privateers.[22]

From 1793 until the implementation of the Danish legislation in 1799, Mitchell cared for and returned to Britain any captured seamen left in Norway by privateers. Their numbers dwarf the number of shipwrecked seamen, with a total of 541 captured men passing through the Consul's hands in the first year, 1793. He notes a number that 'were ill-treated

18   Patrick Crowhurst, *The French War on Trade: Privateering 1793-1815* (Aldershot: Scolar Press, 1989), p.31.
19   Wold, *Privateering and Diplomacy*, p.87, quoting TNA, FO 22/44.
20   Wold, *Privateering and Diplomacy*, pp.85-87.
21   Wold, *Privateering and Diplomacy*, pp.88-89.
22   Wold, *Privateering and Diplomacy*, pp.53-54.

by their captors' and required medical treatment and clothing.[23] Three of the men died, and Mitchell paid for their burial. The total cost of returning 538 seamen to British ports was £2372-1s. Mitchell or his agents also dealt with men landing in other Norwegian ports. The French Consul in Kristiansand made it his business to record those arriving in that port. He insisted that John Mitchell provide a document stating that an equal number of French seamen held captive in Britain would be returned to France. Eighty-five men were identified as exchange prisoners of war. The French Consul was not made aware of any others arriving in other Norwegian ports.[24]

There was a step change in the use of the Norwegian southern coast anchorages when France invaded Holland and created the Batavian Republic in 1795. Dutch privateers and navy vessels also deposited their captured seamen within Mitchell's area. Three Dutch naval brigs made their operational base the Flekkerøy Island anchorage. John Mitchell sent a report to Lord Grenville:

> Dutch Brigs *Echo* of 18 guns, *de Gier* of 14 and the *Mercury* of 16 arrived in the latter part of August 1795 … they fixed their Rendezvous at Fleckeroe – they have only ventured out when they have sighted defenceless British Merchant Ships … they go out in the evening & return by the morning with their prizes.[25]

During 1796 escaped prisoners of war started to arrive in Norway – 176 men being listed by Mitchell. The majority reported that they had been imprisoned in France, but 20 men had escaped from Holland, having been captured in Amsterdam by invading French forces when ice had prevented them from sailing back to Britain. The group escaped on a Prussian vessel from the Dutch port of Harlingen. Of those imprisoned in France, one group of nine had escaped in Brittany and made their way to Lorient, where they claimed that they easily passed as American seamen until they were able to join a vessel heading for Norway. Mitchell does not record the place of imprisonment for 69 seamen or their escape routes. However, his accounts submitted to the Admiralty provide details of the vessels on which they were captured, the French vessels making the capture and the vessels on which they were returned to Britain together with the port to which they were returned.[26]

On 11 December 1794, the Danish Ship *Helina* arrived at Christiansand from Saint-Brieuc on the north coast of Brittany. On board were Robert Mckay, William Perth, John Sutton and William Robertson, British prisoners who had escaped from French imprisonment in Vannes and walked over 100 kilometres to reach Saint-Brieuc. All four seamen had been part of the crew of the *Lucy Ann*, an Aberdeen vessel captured by a squadron of French ships of the line. They had been landed in Brest and sent to Vannes[27]. The four men spent 57 days in Norway before being put on a vessel heading for Peterhead, leaving Norway on 5 February 1795. John Mitchell's expenses claim for the four men was £13-0-7d for subsistence and £2-16s for their return passage.

---

23   TNA FO 22/27: Foreign Office General Correspondence before 1906, Denmark, 1797 Jan–Apr.
24   TNA FO 22/27: Foreign Office General Correspondence before 1906, Denmark, 1797 Jan–Apr.
25   TNA FO 22/27: Foreign Office General Correspondence before 1906, Denmark, 1797 Jan–Apr.
26   TNA ADM 17/15: Consuls' Accounts 1790-1825.
27   TNA ADM 17/15: Consuls' Accounts 1790-1825.

When escaping prisoners were dealt with entirely by his agents in other ports, the men's names were not always recorded. Five British seamen landed in Mandal on 1 January 1795. They had been on merchant ships from Cork and Liverpool captured by French privateers in March 1794. They had made their escape from Brest on a Swedish vessel. Mitchell's agent Fredrik Giertson looked after the men for 38 days and used one of his merchant vessels to deliver them to Belfast. He did charge a guinea each for the men's passage and provisions on board.[28] One group of three seamen who had been prisoners of war for nine months joined the French Privateer *Vengeance* after discovering that it would operate in northern waters. They deserted from the privateer when it arrived in Norway. Mitchell kept the men concealed until he could secure a passage for them on a vessel sailing to London. The seamen had informed Mitchell that they had been captured by the French when they took the *Royal Charlotte* sailing from Malaya to London. Although there was an East Indiaman of that name at that date, the French never captured it. However, the Bristol-based slaver, *Royal Charlotte*, was captured by the French in 1794 on its way to West Africa with orders to buy 394 slaves and transport them for sale in Jamaica.[29]

As part of his remit as a British Consul, John Mitchell cared for and returned to Britain an average of 850 seamen per annum. However, Mitchell uniquely went beyond his Consular responsibilities to obtain additional men specifically for the navy. He had identified an opportunity to obtain seamen, was willing to underwrite the initial cost and knew he had an infrastructure in the south of Norway to capitalise on his idea. There is no record of any other Consul seeking to recruit seamen for the navy in a similar fashion. French privateers and Dutch naval vessels used Kristiansand and the nearby sheltered anchorages. A small number of potential deserters had approached Mitchell's office in early September 1795 to say that they wished to desert from a Dutch frigate if they could have protection and assistance to reach a British ship. They indicated that up to 60 men from their squadron would desert if they had the opportunity. The squadron consisted of the frigate *Argo* and four brigs. At first, Mitchell attempted to ensure that the Danish government would not object to him assisting seamen to desert from foreign warships. He approached the Danish government through the senior British diplomat in Copenhagen. The Danish response was clear. They had made it a rule to 'deliver up all deserters without regard to what nation they belonged or to the circumstances under which they might have been shipped.'[30]

Mitchell had received seven British deserters from the Dutch frigate before being aware of the negative response of the Danish government. The men had claimed that they had been forced into Dutch service in the port of Rotterdam following the French invasion of the country. Mitchell was not going to return them to the Dutch navy and used his intelligence-gathering network in Southern Norway to spirit the seven men away without them being discovered and without incurring sanctions from the Danish Authorities. Without a British ship in the area, he transported them to Britain in Norwegian merchant vessels. His accounts show that he paid for 'concealment' and a guide to take the men from Kristiansand

28   TNA ADM 17/15: Consuls' Accounts 1790-1825.
29   TNA ADM 17/15: Consuls' Accounts 1790-1825, Society of Merchant Venturers' archive <discoveringbristol.org.uk/browse/slavery/note-about-ship-taken-by-french/> (accessed 14 August 2022).
30   TNA FO 22/24: Foreign Office General Correspondence before 1906, Denmark 1795.

to the small harbour of Mandal to join the Norwegian ships, a 50-kilometre journey by foot, although there is a strong possibility that the journey was made by sea.

British naval vessels would regularly use Norwegian anchorages. However, their length of stay was always short, which required Mitchell to have a local infrastructure to keep the men safe and hidden until they could be moved on board a British vessel. The exact size of his organisation is difficult to establish, but he required safe houses or locations for as many as 30 seamen. He needed reliable local assistants to provide food to the safe houses and act as guides for the night delivery of the deserters to British vessels anywhere along the coast of southern Norway. He utilised his mainly Norwegian business contacts in other ports to assist both in receiving deserters and providing the required accommodation and provisions. Within a year of setting up his 'deserter' network, Mitchell dealt with deserters from Stavanger to Fredrickstad, some 500 kilometres of the Norwegian coastline. Mitchell had 23 agents divided nine to the west of the Naze of Norway and 14 to the east. The seamen not transferred to naval vessels were dispatched by British or Norwegian merchant ships to thirty-one different ports in the British Isles, of which 25 were on the country's eastern side. The sheer number of different ports is indicative of the scale of British trade with Scandinavia and the Baltic.[31]

Many seamen would take an opportunity to drink in some of the many Kristiansand alehouses. Here Mitchell saw another opportunity to encourage any unhappy with their current vessel or commander to desert to the British Navy. He established a partnership with two alehouse keepers, whom he named as Dodd and Wolff. They would receive a guinea for each Dutch or French seamen they persuaded to desert to British vessels.[32]

Following the desertion and escape of the initial seven British seamen, there appears to have been a regular flow of deserters seeking Mitchell's assistance. The whole of the captain's boat crew from the brig *Gier* deserted together on 19 September; three English and five Dutch. They were also taken to Mandal at night to make their escape from Norway. Six more British seamen deserted from the same Dutch brig on 5 October and were given their passage on a British merchant ship whose destination was Dundee.[33]

On 6 December 1795, 11 men, all deserters from the Dutch Frigate *Argo*, arrived at Mitchell's office at night. Four were Dutch, the rest British with one being a soldier. Mitchell's report to the Admiralty explains his actions, 'The *Coromandel* was the only King's Ship then on the station, and her commander, Captain Inglis, was at that time undetermined whither he, in an inactive, mastless vessel should take on board Dutch deserters'. For Mitchell dealing with such a large number of deserters appearing simultaneously, their removal to *Coromandel* would have been an ideal solution. However, Captain Inglis was not confident that the deserters would stay with his ship. Mitchell had to provide their board and lodging for 21 days before he could send them to Sunderland on 'Mr Sanderson's vessel.'[34]

It was not until 3 February that Captain Inglis changed his mind about accepting Dutch deserters. In a letter to Mitchell, Inglis said, 'there cannot be a more effective method of weakening the Dutch Vessels than by taking their men'. As Mitchell was authorised to grant

31   TNA ADM 17/15: British Consuls' Accounts.
32   TNA ADM 17/15: British Consuls' Accounts.
33   TNA ADM 17/15: British Consuls' Accounts.
34   TNA ADM 17/15: British Consuls' Accounts.

an encouragement for those purposes, Inglis would 'take on as many as you can possibly provide me'. In a report to the Admiralty, Mitchell noted that although Inglis would take the deserters, he would offer no financial reward to them. Five men came directly from Mr Dodd's hostelry, and Mitchell paid Dodd a guinea for each man he sent to the *Coromandel*.[35]

From 7 September 1795 to 31 December 1796, Mitchell was instrumental in 130 seamen from foreign warships deserting to join the British Navy. In that year, Dodd and Wolff had secured 30 seamen as their payment of 30 guineas is included in Mitchell's accounts. Mitchell does not note the nationality of all the deserters, but 74 were British and 49 Dutch.[36] There were more desertions than those Mitchell listed. For instance, he notes that between 2 and 4 February, when he was responsible for 15 deserters from the Dutch ships *Echo* and *Argo* being sent to HMS *Brilliant,* others deserted to *Brilliant* without going through Mitchell. The 40 volunteers appeared in the musters of British naval ships anchoring in the vicinity of Christiansand and Flekkerøy between October 1795 and March 1796.[37] The musters give no indication as to how they arrived if they were deserters from foreign naval vessels, privateers or merchant vessels, but, logically, the bulk had arrived from the Dutch vessels. One was clearly not a deserter as the muster states that he was from Christiansand, and he was rated as a landsman, a man with no sea-going experience. The musters provide their age, how they were rated by the British Navy and the location they declared as their original home. The graphs below provide the detail.

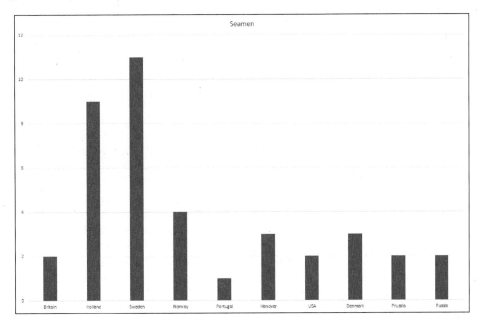

35   TNA ADM 17/15: British Consuls' Accounts.
36   TNA ADM 17/15: British Consuls' Accounts.
37   The four vessels were HMS *Hawke, Coromandel, Reunion* and *Brilliant.* TNA ADM 36/13823, ADM 36/11303, ADM 36/11427, 36/13113.

There are seamen from 10 countries, but such a range was not unusual in European or American naval and merchant vessels. For example, the French privateer *Sans Souci* captured in the North Sea in 1810, had a crew from France, Holland, Germany, Sweden, Norway and the USA.[38] N.A.M. Rodger noted that earlier in the century, 'there were men from every nation under heaven in the Navy.'[39]

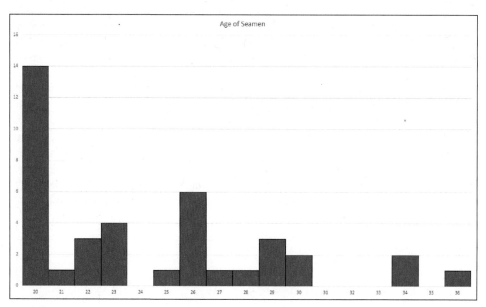

Just as the seamen's nationality confirms the expected pattern for the period, so does the age range. A study of 20,000 seamen from this period showed that 70 percent were 29 or younger, and 44 percent were under the age of 25.[40]

The subsequent naval record of this group of men also reflects the navy as a whole. Three had been promoted from Ordinary Seamen to Able Seamen by July 1796. Within three months of leaving Norway, one had fallen overboard at sea and drowned. One had been sent to sick quarters in Sheerness by May 1796. Twenty-four had fought at the Battle of Camperdown, including four from Holland; one Swede was killed in the action. This is despite their vessel being involved in the Nore mutiny five months earlier. Having fought at the Battle of Camperdown, one deserted in Chatham four months after the action. He had approached a coxswain of a frigate and asked to join that ship. He gave a false name (assuming the name he gave in Norway was not false) and was paid the bounty for joining. He was later identified as a deserter and court-martialled for desertion and claiming a second bounty. His only defence was that he was a foreigner and did not understand English

38   Julian Foynes, *East Anglia against the Tricolor, 1789-1815: An English Region against Revolutionary and Napoleonic France* (Lowestoft: Poppyland Publishing, 2016), p.166.
39   Rodger, *The Wooden World*, p.158.
40   Dancy, 'British Naval Manpower', pp.79-80.

sufficiently to realise he had committed a crime. His mitigation was partially accepted, and he was sentenced to 100 lashes and loss of pay.[41]

In 1795 Mitchell's first full year of operation, 1,001 seamen were returned to Britain, including released prisoners and deserters from foreign vessels. With one seaman incurring no charges the costs associated with the return of 1,000 seamen was not small at over £4,000 per annum.[42] However, considering the national need for large numbers of seamen and the costs associated with recruitment, including bounties, they were not exceptional. Mitchell was well aware of what the Admiralty required, and his scheme should be seen in that context.

Mitchell's schemes to attract deserters from foreign vessels were clearly working. The most significant number of deserters were from a Dutch warship group of a frigate and four brigs. Through Kristiansand social gatherings, which included the Dutch and French Consuls and the Dutch naval captains, Mitchell established that some officers were loyal to the exiled Prince of Orange, particularly the captain of the frigate *Argo* Arnold Christian Dirckinck.[43] Mitchell wrote to the Foreign Minister, Lord Grenville, on 17 October 1795:

> I am of the opinion that I could at a moderate expense persuade them to proceed to England. Money and not the service is the only object of the Dutch officers who command these vessels, particularly the Captain of the Argo; and they are all in some measure devoted to their former governments, or at any rate ill pleased with the present system.[44]

Grenville's reply indicates that the government saw considerable benefits if Mitchell could deliver the Dutch squadron to Britain. The British government saw the potential of a propaganda coup with several Dutch naval vessels deserting to the British, reducing the fleet under French control and adding to that of the British. If John Mitchell thought it was possible at no great cost, then it was worth pursuing.[45]

The authorities wanted any response to be confidential, and, as Mitchell had no access to current cyphers, the response was sent to Mitchell's superior, James Craufurd, the British representative in Denmark.[46] The instruction to Craufurd was explicit: 'the enclosed letter to Mr Mitchell is of a secret nature, I have directed it to be written in cypher but as that gentleman is in possession of no cypher I have to desire that you will decypher it, and send a copy to Mr Mitchell by the first secure private conveyance that may occur.'[47]

---

41   TNA ADM 1/5344: Courts Martial Papers 1798.
42   TNA ADM 17/15: British Consuls' Accounts.
43   All of the correspondence between Mitchell and the Admiralty refers to him as von Dirking or van Dirking. Arnold Christian Dirckinck was 32 and had been in the Dutch navy for 18 years.
44   TNA FO 22/24 Foreign Office Correspondence: Political and Other Departments: General Correspondence before 1906, Denmark.
45   TNA FO 22/24. Foreign Office Correspondence: Political and Other Departments: General Correspondence before 1906, Denmark.
46   Norway was still part of Denmark at this period.
47   TNA FO 22/24: Foreign Office Correspondence: Political and Other Departments: General Correspondence before 1906, Denmark.

After this first response, naval vessels were used to carry the dispatches between Mitchell and Lord Grenville. Captain Hale of the sloop *Hawke* was the officer selected to be the message carrier between Grenville and Mitchell; he was also given instructions on how he should deal directly with the Dutch Commander. A secret letter of 5 November 1795 gave him unambiguous instructions:

> You are at liberty to offer a gratuity to the commanders of the said ships and vessels... to quit the service of the Republic, and to bring their said vessels with their crews to this Country promising at the same time employment to them during the War, under the same conditions, in point of Rank and emolument as they now derive from the Government of Holland.[48]

If it proved difficult to bring the ships to Britain, Captain Hale was ordered to ensure that they were sunk or destroyed and that any gratuity offered to the Dutch Commander was not to exceed the value of the ships. If negotiations only led to the officers wishing to leave, he could also offer every Dutch seaman a bounty as long as it did not exceed the British seamen's current bounty for their respective qualifications. Hale was given the power, in conjunction with Mitchell, to draw bills on the Navy Board for the agreed sum if the ships were destroyed and to pay the men a bounty in advance as their ships sailed if that was found to be necessary. The Admiralty concluded the letter with a reminder that their preference was to get the Ships and men to Britain, and Hale was to assure the Dutch that they would receive their gratuity as soon as they arrived in Britain.

The Under Secretary at the Foreign Office, George Hammond, wrote from Downing Street to Evan Nepean, Secretary to the Admiralty, on 23 November 1795 to tell him that Mitchell's agent, John Riggs, had acknowledged receipt of the first payment of £3,000 for the use of Captain Dirckinck. He was to agree to Dirckinck's request to have his vessels intercepted by a superior British force at the location he had specified. The force would consist of the 50-gun HMS *Leopard*, two frigates and a cutter.

By the end of December 1795, Lord Grenville was looking for some progress. The response he had from Mitchell was a more detailed understanding of Dirckinck's reasoning in offering up his vessels to the British, together with an explanation of some of the difficulties he was having to deal with the other commanders in his squadron. Mitchell's letter sent in cypher on 6 January stated that he had met with Captain Dirckinck the day before and received a number of assurances as to the good faith of the Dutch naval captain. He was still loyal to the exiled Prince of Orange and had only remained in the Dutch navy after the revolution of January 1795 for two reasons. Firstly, he felt he may still have an opportunity to serve the Prince, and secondly, his pay was considerably in arrears, and he still hoped to receive it. He went on to say that if a method of putting the squadron he commanded into the hands of the British could be devised, he would readily do so but warned that Captain Kile of the *Echo* and the other captains of the brigs strongly supported the new regime in Holland and he had to be very careful not to alarm them. Kile, who had commanded the squadron before Dirckinck, might challenge Dirckinck's orders and

---

48   TNA ADM 2/1349: Admiralty Out-Letters Secret Correspondence 1795.

was clearly suspicious of him and his loyalty.[49] Mitchell became directly involved in the conflict between Dirckinck and Kile, reporting to Grenville that, 'I shall try some measures which appear to me practicable to support von Dirking in the Command & to bring Kile to obedience, and shall not fail to inform your Lordship how I succeed.'[50] On 13 January 1796, Mitchell reported to Grenville that he had invited Kile and the other captains of the other two Dutch brigs to dine with him. He found Kile to be 'a violent patriot' who was bitter at the circumstances that had resulted in van Kervell, another of the brig commanders, having seniority over him. Mitchell concluded by saying that he intended to use this particular quarrel to the advantage of Dirckinck. Two weeks later, Mitchell was able to report that he had been invited to an event organised by the Dutch Consul to commemorate 'the restoration of their so called Batavian Liberty.' Also attending were the Dutch naval officers, the Governor, French Consul and principal local inhabitants. Mitchell claimed that he was able to reignite the quarrel between Kile and van Kervell 'and a serious scuffle ensued'. The scuffle allowed Dirckinck the opportunity to order Kile to return to and remain on board his vessel until he received further orders. Dirckinck, in Mitchell's view, had consolidated his authority. However, Dirckinck needed to be sufficiently confident that he could order the Dutch squadron to sail to Britain without the other captains refusing, and he still required a strong British squadron to intercept him when he left Norway.[51]

Dirckinck was now able to make his desertion to Britain even more attractive. He had received orders from Amsterdam to take his squadron to Bergen to escort Dutch East Indies Company Ships with two merchant vessels from the West Indies on the final part of their voyage to Amsterdam. Another group of Dutch naval vessels (a brig of 18 guns, a cutter of 12 Guns & two small brigs of eight guns each) should be anchored at Schuderness and would join the squadron. If Dirckinck was able to bring all of the vessels under his command, he could still follow through with his plan to surrender to a superior British squadron. John Mitchell notified Lord Grenville on 21 February, 1796. He wrote again to Grenville five days later providing him with the detail of the financial arrangements already in place,

> I have granted to the principal concerned my Bill payable immediately in Hambourgh (they refusing Bills on London) £10,000 Sterling, which is little more than one fourth part of the material value according to the estimation of Captain Hale … and I have paid down here to be priorly distributed among the concerned, and which Captain Hale thought necessary, £2,000; and to them for several considerations in facilitating the negotiations £500, together £12,500 sterling.[52]

Mitchell's agent in London had already received the first payment from the secret service budget of £3,000 for the use of Captain Dirckinck.[53] Captain Hale valued the four Dutch

49   TNA FO 22/25: Foreign Office General Correspondence before 1906, Denmark, 1796 Jan–Aug. In some of the letters, Kile is spelt as Kyle.
50   TNA FO 22/25: Foreign Office General Correspondence before 1906, Denmark, 1796 Jan–Aug.
51   TNA FO 22/25: Foreign Office General Correspondence before 1906, Denmark, 1796 Jan–Aug.
52   TNA FO 22/25 Foreign Office Correspondence: Political and Other Departments: General Correspondence before 1906, Denmark 1796.
53   Bodleian Library, University of Oxford, (Bodleian) MS. Eng. c. 7384: Secret Service Papers of Sir Evan

vessels at upwards of £38,000, with the two larger brigs being 'remarkably fine vessels'.[54] Dutch seamen volunteering to join the British navy were to receive a bounty as long as it did not exceed the current British seamen's bounty of £5 for an able seaman. Payments would be made as soon as they arrived in Britain.

As the possibility of Mitchell's plan succeeding drew closer, the Admiralty thought it necessary to inform Mitchell that should the Dutch ships surrender to HMS *Leopard* and her squadron, all the crews involved would be entitled to prize money based on the value of the Dutch vessels. If that was the method of acquiring the vessels, then the Admiralty were only in a position to offer Dirckinck £5,000, although they would also be willing to offer any of the other commanders of the Dutch vessels £2,000 for their part in surrendering their vessels.[55]

On 20 February, 1796, Mitchell provided a nine-point agreement drawn up with Dirckinck in the presence of Captain Hale. It provides for all of Dirckinck's requirements. The key clauses related to the precise location of British vessels to meet and secure the surrender of the Dutch:

> A British Fleet of at least 8 to 10 Sail of the Line and as many Frigates to be dispatched so as to be upon the Dogger Bank, or between the Dogger, the Long Bank, & the Sinking Bank, about the 1st of March if possible; to Cruise from W to E & from E to W in the Latitude 56 or thereabouts, so as to intercept the direct Course or the Course which wind and weather may render most eligible from Kern Island or Schuderness (in some charts called Schotsness) to the Texel. The British Fleet in case of giving alarm, & not to be taken by a NW wind on a Lee Shore, nor should they approach nearer the Naze or Coast of Norway that the Dutch Convoy at or on the Passage from Schuderness may not be alarmed & put into Norway. It will also be necessary that the British Fleet detain all such vessels as they may find at Sea which would carry Information to Holland or Norway.
>
> Every possible precaution should be taken that no Report or Information respecting the destination of the British Fleet transpire, for the Dutch Committee have their Friends & Spies in every Corner.
>
> The British Fleet upon seeing the Dutch Convoy or Squadron should hoist Danish & Swedish colours [word unclear], when so near that the Dutch Squadron cannot possibly avoid a general action nor any of the convoy escape to hoist Russian Colours, and not to show British Colours until engaged. N.B. The Dutch have no orders to attack the Russian Flag.
>
> The Argo Frigate of 36 guns in which will be the Commodore of the Squadron should be attacked by a Force considerably superior to her own because when she strikes the other Dutch Ships will also strike.

Nepean, 1787-1803. Letter from the Agent dated 23 November 1795.

54   TNA FO 22/25 Foreign Office Correspondence: Political and Other Departments: General Correspondence before 1906, Denmark 1796.

55   TNA ADM 2/1350: Admiralty Out-Letters Secret Correspondence. 1796. Letter dated 13 February 1796.

There were also clauses specifying the actions to be taken to protect Dirckinck, 'Commodore von Dirking should be left in safe possession of his Baggage & papers & particularly cared for' and securing the officers who would resist surrendering:

> The first Lieutenant of the Argo, Mr. Ingelbright should be carefully secured with all his Papers & not permitted the use of his papers, nor to return to Holland till further notice, the Captain of the Echo Mr. Veile is to be carefully secured in the same manner as Ingelbright.

A further clause dealt with the possibility that Dirckinck would be joined by Dutch East Indies vessels attempting to return to Holland, having sailed around the north of the British Isles to Bergen to await an escort for the final part of the voyage through the North Sea. The final section considered the method of entering the Texel to capture the Dutch fleet using the Dutch private signals supplied by Dirckinck. This section did not attract any comment from the Admiralty and was never implemented.[56]

During February 1796, there were numerous messages between Mitchell and London as the level and nature of the financial recompense to be agreed with Dirckinck was negotiated. Decisions were being made in Downing Street with Lord Grenville and First Lord of the Admiralty, Lord Spenser. Admiral Duncan, commanding the North Sea Fleet, was consulted, and his advice sought. Duncan also selected the squadrons to patrol in the locations requested by Dirckinck.

The Dutch force made plans to sail on 2 March, then 7 March, and 6 April. They did not sail. On 15 March, Mitchell was able to send a complete set of the Dutch navy's private signals which changed daily. In his accompanying letter, Mitchell reported that Dirckinck had brought his original for Mitchell to copy.[57] The Dutch had not sailed by 10 April, and the reason became apparent when a Danish brig arrived and, during the night, transferred provisions and 101 fresh sailors and two officers for the Dutch squadron. Mitchell's scheme to enlist foreign seamen had been far too successful. Captain Inglis had observed the nighttime transfer of seamen, which, in his view, breached the neutrality agreement. He wrote to Admiral Duncan, having obtained the name of the Danish brig and her captain, 'Do you not think it has been an infraction of the Treaty between Denmark and Britain the bringing out men and stores in a ship under Danish Colours to an enemy of Britain'.[58] Duncan forwarded the information to the Admiralty and subsequently received a reply stating, 'no doubt the Court of Denmark will take proper notice of such a flagrant breach of neutrality.'[59] The Dutch ships finally left Norway on 7 May.

---

56   TNA FO 22/25: Foreign Office Correspondence: Political and Other Departments: General Correspondence before 1906, Denmark.

57   TNA FO 38/1: Foreign Office: Political and Other Departments: General Correspondence before 1906, British Secret Service in Europe 1795-1796.

58   Jim Tildesley, 'I am Determined to Live or Die on Board My Ship'. The Life of John Inglis: An American in the Georgian Navy (Leicester: Matador, 2019), p.349.

59   TNA ADM 2/1350: Admiralty Out-Letters Secret Correspondence. 1796.

John Mitchell regarded Captain Inglis as obstructive and unhelpful, and both complained about the other to Duncan and the Admiralty. Inglis went to the extent of sending copies of all the written exchanges to Duncan with a covering letter explaining that the papers

> …will show my aversion to all illegal acts and will explain what has passed between me and Mr. Mitchell … I refused to comply with Mr. Mitchell's unconditional request contained in his letters 1, 2 & 4 because I thought they were illegal and might be an infraction of the Treaty with Denmark and it appeared to me to be against the 30th Article of that Treaty.[60]

On 8 May 1796, HMS *Sylph* sighted four vessels to the south west and reported the sighting to their commodore on HMS *Pegasus*. They began working towards the vessels, keeping Admiral Duncan informed. They observed the Dutch first hoist Dutch colours and exchange several signals. The Dutch colours were later lowered, and British colours flown, followed by the firing of a single signal gun. None of this matched any agreed signal that the British were expecting. By 12 May, Admiral Duncan decided that he had given the Dutch ships time to surrender and ordered his squadron to close with the Dutch. HMS *Phoenix* closed with Dirckinck's vessel, the *Argo*, and fired a single gun to halt the Dutch ship. The Dutch response was not to stop and surrender but to fire a full broadside. The two vessels exchanged broadsides for a further 25 minutes before the *Argo* struck her colours. The Dutch brigs scattered and headed south with British frigates in pursuit. Two were taken despite one throwing all but two of her 16 guns overboard in an attempt to evade capture. The other two deliberately grounded on one of the West Frisian Islands and were eventually destroyed by the sea. With the Dutch vessels captured, Duncan asked the Admiralty what to do with Dirckinck; Their reply was to treat him along with all of the other Dutch Officers and send him ashore on parole to the designated location, which in Dirckinck's case was Ashford in Kent. He was still there in June 1796 when he wrote to the Admiralty seeking to go to London to see his wife as he believed that she might be pregnant, a request which was granted.[61]

In 1797 Mitchell moved to Hamburg. There is no apparent reason for the move, which at the time, he explained to Grenville that 'Domestic Concerns having obliged me to leave Norway for a few weeks'.[62] A few weeks stretched to years with Mitchell not taking up residence in Norway again. One plausible explanation is that Mitchell became aware that his activities had attracted the attention of Danish Authorities, whose relationship with the British was rapidly deteriorating, and moved to Hamburg for his own safety.[63] The Danes had complained to Lord Grenville about Mitchell exceeding his authority in 1793.[64] Mitchell's attempt to secure the desertion of Dirckinck's squadron would be discovered soon after their capture, as Dirckinck's wife had also been on board *Argo* when it was captured. As his

---

60   Tildesley, '*I am Determined*', p.343.
61   National Maritime Museum, Caird Library (NMM) ADM MT/415: Transport Board, In-Letters from the Admiralty relating to Prisoners of War, Jan-Jun 1796.
62   TNA, FO 22/28: Foreign Office General Correspondence before 1906, Denmark, 1797.
63   TNA, FO 22/16: Foreign Office General Correspondence before 1906, Denmark, 1792 Nov.-1793 Jun. 39–40. Daniel Hailes to Geo Aust Esq., Copenhagen 16 February 1793,
64   Wold, *Privateering and Diplomacy*, pp.110-111.

wife was Anna Holm, the daughter of Peder Holm, the Danish County Governor responsible for the Christiansand area, it would seem to be highly unlikely that the Danish government would not have become aware.[65]

Although Mitchell was no longer resident in Norway in 1797, he continued to liaise with his Norwegian network, appointing the long-standing vice consul at Kristiansand, Christian Höyer, as acting British Consul. In October of the same year, the defeat of the Dutch fleet at Camperdown altered the naval balance in the North Sea and Norwegian waters. The positive effect from Mitchell's perspective was to reduce the number of Dutch and French privateers using Norwegian ports. Höyer was left to administer a somewhat scaled-down version of the system Mitchell had built up in 1793.[66] The accounts for expenses in relation to distressed seamen and other seamen acquired for the navy are incomplete, so it is impossible to provide detailed figures for the period after Mitchell left Norway. There is sufficient to conclude that his system continued to operate. For example, Navy Board files detail a claim made by Mitchell for the 'subsistence and passage of 58 Distressed British Seamen captured by the enemy or otherwise landed in Norway'. The claim covered only January and February 1799 and included subsistence, clothing for some men, boat transport from Arendal and Flekkefjord to Kristiansand and passage with provisions to London. The claim totalled £348.12 and had been sent by Mitchell from Hamburg.[67] Further reimbursement claims from Mitchell to the Admiralty show that his network continued operating, and after 1801 the number of seamen returned to Britain rose from 502 in 1801 to 953 in 1803. There are surviving reimbursement claims for a further five years, although some only appear to cover part of a year.

Over the years following his capture, a better understanding of Dirckinck and his real attitude to both the Dutch Republic and Britain becomes apparent. Many in the Royal Navy were quite willing to believe that he was never wholehearted in his wish to bring all of his ships and men to Britain. Captain Robert Watson, HMS *Isis*, commodore of the vessels delegated to intercept the Dutch squadron and accept their surrender, wrote to Admiral Duncan, 'I am strongly of the opinion that Capt. Van Dorking means to deceive Mr. Mitchell'.[68] Duncan forwarded Watson's letter to the Admiralty. However, at this point, the Lords Commissioners were now less than persuaded and would give no further clear orders to Duncan as to how he should proceed, 'With respect to Captain Von Dorking their Lordships can give no instructions to you upon that subject as any further steps to be taken must depend upon circumstances of which you above are capable of judging.'[69] Equally, Dirckinck may have genuinely wished to desert to the British with his ships but was uncertain that his men and, in particular, his officers would follow him. The discontent of his senior officers is a running theme throughout Mitchell's correspondence.

Letters and reports sent by John Mitchell to the Foreign Office and the Admiralty show that Dirckinck provided intelligence about Dutch forces for several years after his parole and return to Europe. Dirckinck explained in a letter that he had been granted parole on

---

65   Tildesley, 'I am Determined', p.338. The area was then known as Lister og Mandal, now Vest-Agder.
66   Wold, *Privateering and Diplomacy*, pp.91-93.
67   NMM AGC/8/13: Letter to Admiralty from John Mitchell Hamburg 18 Sept 1804.
68   TNA ADM 1/523: Letters from C in C North Sea 1796.
69   TNA ADM 2/1350: Admiralty: Out-Letters Secret Letters 1796.

condition that he did not return to Holland until he had been formally exchanged. He moved to western Prussia and maintained contact with the Dutch navy, forwarding any information to Mitchell in Hamburg. He concluded one letter, 'I hope to God My Lord Spencer will not exchange me'.[70]

After his capture, Grenville refused to honour any further payments. Dirckinck, with Mitchell's support, continued to attempt to claim the monies agreed for the surrender of the Dutch vessels. In October 1799, Lord Spencer and the Foreign Office agreed that Dirckinck was entitled to £7000, which was paid from the Secret Service Budget.[71] Mitchell had previously received £12,600 from the same source, much of which had been paid to Dirckinck in Norway.[72]

There are still aspects of Mitchell's work which remain mysterious, although there can be no doubt about his enthusiastic and energetic support of British interests. His exact status with the British government is unclear. If Leira and Neumann are correct in suggesting that Mitchell had been recruited as Consul when in Britain and not a merchant resident in Norway, it poses the question, why did this unusual selection occur? Could Mitchell have had additional skills that the British government would find valuable? As Mitchell claimed, the recommendations of Sir Morton Eden, Mr Elliot and Mr Fraser might have been sufficient and would not have been unusual in the eighteenth century. The primary sources indicate that he was formally appointed British Consul for Kristiansand and Christiania, which then required a locally recruited deputy for each location. The deputies would act for Mitchell when he was not at one of the locations. During 1786 and 1787, he was away from either location as he was in Stockholm and Copenhagen. In a letter to the Foreign Office, marked private, he asks for reimbursement of £125 and £225 'for gathering intelligence on trade for 9 months previously in Stockholm and Copenhagen following instruction from the Duke of Leeds on October 1786.'[73] The Duke of Leeds was Secretary of State for Foreign Affairs from November 1783 until May 1791. His political memoirs do not exhibit any interest in trade amongst Baltic countries; however, his primary concern was the political situation in Sweden and Denmark and their relationships with France and Russia. The appendix to his memoirs contains the full text of a number of reports on the political situation in Denmark and Sweden in 1784 from Hugh Elliot, the Envoy Extraordinary to Denmark.[74] Elliot held that position from 1782 until 1789, including the period covered by Mitchell's intelligence gathering. There are no reports prepared by Mitchell in the Foreign Office papers that cover the nine-month period when he was gathering intelligence. The lack of documentation and the specific interests of the Duke of Leeds would suggest that Mitchell was gathering information of a sensitive political nature that should remain secret.

---

70   TNA FO 33/18 Political and Other Departments: General Correspondence before 1906, Bremen, Hamburg and Lubeck 1799. Letter from Dirckinck to Mitchell March 1799.
71   Bodleian Ms Eng c7384 Evan Nepean Papers, F54 Most Secret Letter Hammond to Nepean October. 1799.
72   Bodleian Ms Eng c7384 F29; Evan Nepean Papers, F48 Secret Letter Hammond to Nepean Nov. 1796.
73   TNA FO 22/12: Foreign Office General Correspondence before 1906, Denmark, 1790 Jan–Jul.
74   Oscar Browning, *The Political Memoranda of Francis Fifth Duke of Leeds* (London: Camden Society, 1884), pp.235-259.

There is no documentation in Admiralty or Foreign Office papers to indicate that either had sent Mitchell to Hamburg, yet some of his correspondents used the term, Consul. There is certainly no formal appointment as Consul. Hamburg was a neutral location before the French occupation in November 1806. Before that date, it was a mecca for agents from all belligerent nations. From a British perspective, it was the known venue for United Irishman to make contact with French agents willing to work with them. James Craufurd, who had been based in Copenhagen, was appointed British Consul in Hamburg in March 1796. The British government had become very aware of the use of Hamburg by United Irishmen in their negotiations with France, and Craufurd was ordered to keep a close watch on Irish agents, a task he completed with meticulous care. Mitchell's move to Hamburg took place during the following year. Craufurd was aware of his arrival; however, he still found it necessary to contact the Foreign Office. In a private letter to George Hammond, the under-secretary at the Foreign Office, Craufurd wrote, 'May I ask also what Mitchell the Consul at Christiansand is employed about here. I have long known that he is about something, but not exactly what. He is I believe a man of some intrigue.'[75] The author has been unable to locate any response to Craufurd's question. Craufurd's comment is the clearest contemporary remark that indicates that Mitchell was involved in gathering intelligence and not just a Consul working at protecting the business interests of British merchants.

During his period in Norway, Mitchell took the initiative to survey a large number of ports and build a substantial network of mainly Norwegian contacts willing to provide him with intelligence reports and subsequently assist in his scheme to recruit foreign seamen for the British Navy. Such actions were considerably more than those undertaken by any other Consul of the period. Mitchell corresponded directly with the First Lord of the Admiralty and the Foreign Secretary. His views were accepted and acted upon by these senior politicians. He challenged the Danish government and the French and Dutch Consuls over the use of Norwegian ports for the sale of British prizes and their cargoes. Atle Wold identified Mitchell as the central figure in the British action to change Danish policy.[76] Danish senior officials believed that Mitchell had strayed well beyond his remit as a Consul and demanded that he be recalled. James Craufurd, the senior British diplomat at the Danish court, concluded that Mitchell 'may perhaps have gone a little too far in the present instance, but I must in justice to him say that he is active & intelligent, and that he appears to me extremely attentive to the duties of his office'.[77] Craufurd had previously described Mitchell as 'a Man of very good character, active and intelligent and in very decent circumstances'.[78]

Apart from running his business from Hamburg, Mitchell had continued to receive intelligence from Dirckinck; he may also have received information from Dirckinck's brother, Frederick, who had also served in the Dutch navy. Mitchell records payments made to Frederick without noting the reason for the payment. Mitchell made a number of visits to Copenhagen and quite clearly established a relationship with Prince Charles of Hesse, the father-in-law of Crown Prince Frederick, the Danish Regent. Mitchell was not authorised to act for the British government, nor do the records explain how he had established an

---

75   TNA FO 33/18; Craufurd to Hammond April 1799.
76   Wold, *Privateering and Diplomacy*, p.28. Wold provides a detailed narrative of Mitchell's involvement.
77   Wold, *Privateering and Diplomacy*, p.45.
78   Wold, *Privateering and Diplomacy*, pp.106-107.

apparently close contact with a senior member of the Danish Royal family. In this case, his actions were not welcome by the Foreign Office, and Mitchell sent a private letter with an apology and justification. Having said he was sorry, he explained,

> I have travelled on the continent for 22 years and have had the honour to converse with Sovereigns and other Princes amongst whom are the present Princes of Prussia and Sweden. I have the permission to correspond with them on any subject without reserve or etiquette. I have always introduced myself as Mr. Mitchell a private individual travelling for my own affairs. I have always wished without compromising anyone to pass information to the King's Ministers if I believed it to be of value.[79]

In all probability, Mitchell was trying to use his link with Prince Charles to move Denmark into an alliance with Britain, undoubtedly the most ambitious of his efforts to assist the British cause.

Mitchell's reports in 1801 forwarded intelligence to the Admiralty and Foreign Office received from the Dirckinck brothers, his agent in Stavanger and Christiansand, merchant contacts in Copenhagen and Prussia and the British Consul in Elsinore. He was able to report on the armament protecting Gothenburg, the Danish coast, and to send a copy of a French intelligence report on the Danish military presence around the Norwegian coast. He forwarded a paper to the Admiralty entitled, 'Plan or Project of Bonaparte to invade England'. The Admiralty forwarded the report to Admiral Hyde Parker, who had recently been appointed to command the Baltic fleet. Mitchell also sent a copy of the invasion plan direct to Nelson. Besides the wealth of military and naval information, Mitchell could report on a French plan to buy grain exported from Baltic countries and use the Royal Prussian Company to make large purchases of naval timber and hemp. He noted that he had seen the original signed order.[80] Much of the information forwarded would have been of value to Britain. Mitchell also provided intelligence reports to the British military. He wrote to Colonel W.H. Clinton, then military secretary to the Duke of York,[81] in September 1804 concerning his understanding of Napoleon's plans for an invasion of Ireland. He concludes the letter, 'I have been anxious to get information on how prepared the French are as it is always difficult to give any report as a fact but I now believe the crisis is on hand.'[82] The letter sparked an exchange between the Duke of York and 10 Downing Street. It would appear that Mitchell had been a regular provider of intelligence to Clinton.

At some date after 1807, either in Denmark or in a brief return to Christiansand, some action or actions by Mitchell caused him to be arrested. In February 1809, Mitchell gave a detailed account of why:

---

79 TNA FO 33/17: Foreign Office General Correspondence before 1906, Denmark, 1798 Dec.– 1799 March.
80 TNA, ADM 1/3843: Letters from British Consuls 1800-1803.
81 George Byrom Whittaker, *A New Biographical Dictionary, of 3000 Cotemporary Public Characters, British and Foreign, of All Ranks and Professions* (London: Geo. B. Whittaker, 1825), Vol.2, p.369.
82 National Records Scotland (NRS): GD364/1/1138. Papers of the Hope Family of Luffness, East Lothian.

... the Danish government gave me reason to believe that I should be furnished with Passports to enable me to leave as His Majesty's public servant accredited to the court of Denmark. But before I received any such passports the Prince Royal issued an order to arrest me with my family and all those who acted either as my agents or correspondents to the British Consulate Office in Norway.

Mitchell explained that the pretext for his arrest was that his correspondence had tended to aggravate the differences between the two countries (Britain and Denmark). He continued,

Upon the pretext, my property was put under sequester, what was moveable and worth taking away was embezzled by those charged to care for it and the rest sold at a public sale by the King of Denmark's special order... My clerks and servants have been confined in Kongsberg (Denmark). I owe my personal liberty to French General Bernadotte who, upon occupying continental Denmark behaved towards His Majesty's subjects confined in the country with much more military like liberality than the Danes themselves. The French Minister resident in Hamburgh has acted towards us with as much indulgence as he possibly can.[83]

He concluded his letter by saying that he had returned to Norway on parole and continued to assist destitute British seafarers, paying from his own resources and hoped that the British government would reimburse him. Mitchell did not explain the exact date of this event, but Bernadotte did not gain responsibility for Denmark until 1808, although he had governed the Hanseatic towns during the previous year.

In retirement in Edinburgh, Mitchell stated that his papers contained 'many that were most private and confidential exchanges with the Prime Minister, Ministers and august personages on the continent'.[84] They included a source of information that was very close to Napoleon. These papers do not appear to have survived, but his actions show a remarkable initiative, and it is very hard to believe that he acted alone without guidance from the Foreign Office or other senior government officials. One must also question the payment to Mitchell or, on his request, to third parties of substantial sums from the secret service budget if there had not been a material benefit to Britain. Mitchell always justified his actions using phrases like the one included in a letter to Evan Nepean, 'I have no Orders, nor have I any other Motive but merely the Advancement of His Majesty's Service in General'.[85]

Mitchell finally appears in the Edinburgh Archives of 1821 when he is described as formerly of Hamburg, now a resident of Edinburgh. One document records the meeting of his creditors, who were seeking payment of £4241-15-8d. Mitchell said he would pay when he received his outstanding claim of £19,000 from the Navy Board and £3,030 from the Foreign Office. He relied on others to negotiate payments in London as doctors had advised him to avoid mental and physical exertion. The Navy Board wrote to the creditors in 1822,

---

83   TNA ADM 17/15: Consuls' Accounts 1790-1825.
84   NRS CS96/4726: Court of Session: productions in processes. John Mitchell Creditors Reports and Meetings 1821-24.
85   TNA ADM 1/3843: Letters from British Consuls 1800-1803. John Mitchell to Evan Nepean, Hamburg 14 August 1801.

saying they could not pay the claim as insufficient certification had been received. After another year, the Navy Board agreed to a payment of £11,000, which the Creditors accepted. It left Mitchell almost destitute.[86] On 7 May 1823, Mitchell's reimbursement claims for 1797 to 1799 had still not been paid. He died on 15 November 1823. His will, which he signed on 1 August 1822, refers to the death of his wife in January 1819. On his death, his estate would be shared equally between his three daughters, Mary, Georgina and Maria. The specific content of his estate is covered by the phrase:

> …whatever property in money or funds or lands, goods and chattels at the time of my demise possessed of and whatever a debt shall be due to me and likewise my reimbursement from the several departments of His Majesties Government for money or monies disbursed by me as his majesties consul in Norway on the public service and likewise whatever remuneration shall be allowed to me for my service to the public from the year 1784 to 1816.[87]

The failure of John Mitchell to receive the full reimbursement of his expenditure on rescuing and repatriating British seamen, together with funds expended in his efforts to recruit seamen from foreign vessels, hinges on two factors. Firstly, the failure of Mitchell to provide signed documentation relating to each specific item of expenditure. Although his claims were very detailed specific elements of information could not be provided when repatriation was achieved solely by one of Mitchell's agents acting independently. The Admiralty and, no doubt, the Treasury, would not accept the signatures of two prominent Norwegian businessmen as confirmation that the sums listed were the true expenditure for those specific items. The second issue was the fixed sum per day per seaman specified in the Act under which Consuls cared for seamen. Mitchell made it quite clear that the daily sum was wholly unrealistic during the Norwegian winter when basic foodstuffs cost far more than in Great Britain. He was not alone in making such a complaint. As early as November 1795, John Theodore Koster, the British Consul in Lisbon, wrote to the Admiralty saying that with so many released prisoners arriving in the area, he was forced to pay more than nine pence a day as the owners of the Lodging Houses housing the men demanded a greater sum.[88]

This last issue would have even more significance later in the Napoleonic wars when inflation increased prices. The Consul General in the Canary Islands, Gilbert Stuart Bruce, wrote to the Admiralty in February 1813 as he felt it was his duty to inform them of the 'serious injury to the Maritime interests of Great Britain being caused by the inadequate provisions made by the law for the relief of British Seamen in distress in foreign parts.'[89] He goes on to detail the issues,

---

86   NRS CS96/4726: Court of Session: productions in processes. John Mitchell Creditors Reports and Meetings 1821-24.

87   TNA PROB 11/1751/422: Will of John Mitchell, Captain, His Majesty's Consul in Norway of Edinburgh, Mid Lothian. 1829 Feb.

88   TNA ADM 1/3842: Letters from British Consuls 1795–1799.

89   TNA ADM 17/16: Consuls' Accounts 1790-1825.

The stipulated allowance of nine pence per diem is certainly at present as insufficient for a man's subsistence in almost any port in Europe. The French Consuls' allowance for British prisoners was 20d per diem. The American Government have been particularly attentive to the point'... 'British Sailors in distress in foreign ports, being generally provided with American passes or finding little difficulty in obtaining them, very frequently claim the protection & allowance of that government, and thus hundreds of valuable hands are annually & irretrievably lost to Great Britain. The magnitude of this evil and the importance to the country of its being effectually checked cannot fail of calling forth your early representation to government on this subject.

George Foy, British Consul based in Stockholm, had written to the Admiralty in a similar vein.[90]

There is no question that John Mitchell was responsible for the return and recruitment of thousands of seamen for the Royal Navy and British merchant marine. Because of the bureaucratic requirements of the Admiralty, he was never fully reimbursed for this work and died in poverty. His attempt to persuade the commanders of a Dutch naval squadron to desert to Britain was not a complete success. However, the relationship he developed with Captain Dirckinck would continue to provide valuable intelligence for Britain. There is more than enough evidence in primary sources to indicate that Mitchell gained other significant intelligence from numerous sources, all of which he diligently forwarded to the Foreign Office. Mitchell's role as Consul and potato wholesaler would appear to have been a cover for a much broader intelligence gathering operation, the significance of which remains difficult to assess fully.

Select Bibliography

Archival Sources
Bodleian Library, University of Oxford
    MS. Eng. c. 7384: Secret Service Papers of Sir Evan Nepean, 1787-1803
The National Maritime Museum (NMM)
    ADM MT/415: Transport Board, In-Letters from the Admiralty relating to Prisoners of War, Jan-Jun 1796.
    AGC/8/13 Letter to Admiralty from John Mitchell Hamburg 18 Sept 1804.
National Records Scotland
    CS96/4726: Court of Session: productions in processes. John Mitchell Creditors Reports and Meetings 1821-24.
    GD364/1/1138: Papers of the Hope Family of Luffness, East Lothian.
The National Archives, Kew (TNA)
    ADM 1/3842: Letters from British Consuls 1795-1799.
    ADM 1/3843: Letters from British Consuls 1800-1803.
    ADM 1/5344: Courts Martial Papers 1798.
    ADM 17/15: Consuls' Accounts 1790-1825.
    ADM 17/16: Consuls' Accounts 1790-1825.

90   TNA ADM 17/16: Consuls' Accounts 1790-1825.

ADM 2/1349: Admiralty Out-Letters Secret Correspondence 1795.
ADM 2/1350: Admiralty Out-Letters Secret Correspondence. 1796.
ADM 36/11303: Muster Book HMS *Coromandel* 1795 May–1796 Jun.
ADM 36/11427: Muster Book HMS *Reunion* 1795 Oct–1796 Dec.
ADM 36/13113: Muster Book HMS *Brilliant* 1795 Dec–1796 Dec.
ADM 36/13823: Muster Book HMS *Hawke* 1794 Nov–1796 Dec.
FO 22/12: Foreign Office General Correspondence before 1906, Denmark, 1790 Jan. –Jul.
FO 22/16: Foreign Office General Correspondence before 1906, Denmark, 1792.Nov.-1793 Jun.
FO 22/24: Foreign Office General Correspondence before 1906, Denmark 1795 Sept.-Dec.
FO 22/25: Foreign Office General Correspondence before 1906, Denmark, 1796 Jan.-Aug.
FO 22/27 Foreign Office General Correspondence before 1906, Denmark, 1797 Jan–Apr.
FO 33/17: Foreign Office General Correspondence before 1906, Denmark, 1798 Dec.-1799 March.
FO 38/1: Foreign Office: Political and Other Departments: General Correspondence before 1906,
     British Secret Service in Europe 1795-1796.
FO 90/10: Foreign Office King's Letter Books, Denmark. 1760-1797.
HD 1/1 Foreign Office: Expenditure of the Secret Vote Abroad: Correspondence and Papers 1791-
     1803.
PROB 11/1751/422: Will of John Mitchell, Captain, His Majesty's Consul in Norway of Edinburgh,
     Mid Lothian. 1829 Feb.

Published Sources

Browning, Oscar, *The Political Memoranda of Francis Fifth Duke of Leeds* (London: Camden
Society, 1884).
Crowhurst, Patrick, *The French War on Trade: Privateering 1793-1815* (Aldershot: Scolar Press, 1989).
Foynes, Julian, *East Anglia against the Tricolor, 1789-1815: An English Region against Revolutionary and
     Napoleonic France* (Lowestoft: Poppyland Publishing, 2016).
Leira, Halvard & Neumann, Iver B., 'Consular representation in an emerging state: The case of
Norway', *The Hague Journal of Diplomacy* 3 (2008), pp.1-19.
Leira, Halvard & Neumann, Iver B., 'Judges, merchants and envoys; The growth and development of the
     consular institution'. Paper presented at 47th annual ISA convention, San Diego, Ca..
Platt, D. C. M., 'The Role of the British Consular Service in Overseas Trade, 1825-1914' *The Economic
     History Review, New Series*, Vol. 15, No. 3 (1963), pp. 494-512.
Rodger, N.A.M., *The Command of the Ocean: a Naval History of Britain, 1649-1815* (London: Allen Lane,
     2004).
Rodger, N.A.M., *The Wooden World: An Anatomy of the Georgian Navy* (London: Fontana, 1988).
Tildesley, Jim, *'I am Determined to Live or Die on Board My Ship'. The Life of John Inglis: An
American in the Georgian Navy* (Leicester, Matador, 2019).
Weber, Paul, *On the Road to Rebellion–The United Irishmen in Hamburg 1796-1803* (Dublin: Four Courts
     Press, 1997).
Wells, Roger, *Insurrection: The British Experience 1795-1803* (Gloucester: Alan Sutton, 1986).
Whittaker, George Byrom, *A New Biographical Dictionary, of 3000 Cotemporary Public Characters, British
     and Foreign, of All Ranks and Professions* (London: Geo. B. Whittaker, 1825).
Wold, Atle L., *Privateering and Diplomacy, 1793–1807: Great Britain, Denmark-Norway and the Question of
     Neutral Ports* (London: Palgrave Macmillan, 2020).
Wright, Quincy, 'The Legal Position and Functions of Consuls' *The American Journal of International Law*
     Vol. 26, No. 1, Supplement: Research in International Law (1932), pp.193-449.

13

'Discovered Going to the 74 in a Small Boat': Black Pilots and Maritime Opportunity Aboard HMS *Poictiers*, 1812-1813

Andrew J. Lyter

Thursday 22 April 1813 proved to be an ordinary day for the crew working aboard HMS *Poictiers*. Executing a crucial British economic blockade of the Delaware River and Bay in concert with HMS *Belvidera* and HM Schooner *Paz*, *Poictiers* served as the flagship of Commodore John Poo Beresford, and lay at single anchor in the Delaware Bay, with the sails loosed and drying after a rainy evening.[1] For Peter Wood and Jeremiah Primrose, however, this day proved anything but ordinary. These African-American men, born into slavery, endured a life of hardship and adversity since birth. To these enslaved Delawareans, the arrival of this British naval squadron represented the potential for a new life, new opportunities, and a channel in which to navigate their freedom through naval service. By taking a calculated risk and leveraging their maritime knowledge, Peter and Jeremiah would finally break the bonds of their enslavement after rowing across the Delaware Bay towards *Poictiers* and securing their freedom.[2]

In February 1807, the British Parliament passed a bill entitled, 'An Act for the Abolition of the Slave Trade', effectively prohibiting the slave trade in the British Empire. While the trade itself was prohibited, possession of slaves in British colonial holdings remained legal until 1834. This legislation had resounding consequences on both sides of the Atlantic, with social and economic ramifications in the United States, as well as Great Britain and her remaining American colonies. The importation of slaves also became illegal in 1807 in the young American republic, yet this federal law deliberately failed to address the prosperous domestic slave trade within the United States. Maritime service, particularly in times of war, afforded both free and enslaved African-Americans, such as Jeremiah Primrose and Peter Wood, opportunities and freedoms that could not be obtained ashore. Following the

---

1   TNA ADM 51/2694: Captain's Log, HMS *Poictiers*.
2   'Office of the Delaware Statesmen', *Carlisle Weekly Herald*, 7 May 1813.

abolition of the British slave trade, service aboard Royal Naval vessels offered enslaved and free black men further opportunities. These individuals experienced the maritime world in differing capacities, yet working as pilots, especially during wartime, offered perhaps the greatest opportunity.

Pilotage provided these men with opportunities to cultivate new identities, privileges, and the potential to navigate and obtain freedom. Unique to pilots were the additional cultural ramifications that accompanied their post. Unlike the vast majority of sailors who plied the open seas, pilots routinely practiced their trade close to home in local coastal waters. According to historian Kevin Dawson, the area that existed between land-based slave masters and shipmasters at sea served as a 'cultural and political space to invert racial/social valuations and gain uncommon privilege.'[3] Through these coastal waters, black pilots subverted traditional notions of authority by taking command of vessels, all while working towards obtaining personal freedoms and ensuring naval interests.

As stated, providing services as a pilot to the Royal Navy afforded black seamen unparalleled opportunity, and, as evidenced by the men examined in this study, a direct means towards escaping enslavement. These benefits were not part of an altruistic British naval agenda, but were part of an exchange. Some black pilots who sought service with the Royal Navy did so as a means to leverage their maritime familiarity in return for personal freedoms. They would continue to provide such services as long as the reward and opportunities they received were of equal value to the services they were providing. Control and opportunity were key to this exchange. This analysis will be conducted through the lens of HMS *Poictiers,* a standard ship of the line, between the years of 1812 and 1813. By studying this vessel during its wartime service in the War of 1812 on a foreign station, it is possible to identify the unique relationships between black pilots and HMS *Poictiers.* Virginia-born Edward Godfrey, Bermudians James Darrell and King George, and Delawareans Jeremiah Primrose and Peter Wood each provided vital services aboard HMS *Poictiers.* While highlighting the impact that these pilots had on naval operations in return for liberties and privileges, this chapter presents the cultural and social impact of these exchanges in a broader naval context.

Pilots' navigational prowess, seamanship, and uncanny knowledge of the local waters ensured the safe transitioning of both naval and merchant vessels in and out of coastal regions. Maritime tradition shaped the relationship that existed between pilots and inbound and outbound vessels, forging a unique exchange that was counterintuitive to many of the social and military customs of both land and sea.[4] *A Trip to New England*, by Edward Ward, is regularly quoted in discussing the power conferred upon pilots.[5] In Ward's own words, 'A Vessel, whilst the *Pilot* is on Board, is an Emblem of Feeble *Monarchy*; where the *King* has a State-man in his Dominions Greater than himself, That the *Prince* only bears the *Title*, but

---

3   Kevin Dawson, 'Enslaved Ship Pilots in the Age of Revolutions: Challenging Notions of Race and Slavery between the Boundaries of Land and Sea', *Journal of Social History*, 2013, p.2.

4   Dawson, 'Enslaved Ship Pilots', p.8.

5   Simon Finger, 'A Flag of Defiance at the Masthead: The Delaware River Pilots and the Sinews of Philadelphia's Atlantic World in the Eighteenth Century' *Early American Studies*, 8:2 (Spring 2010), p.392; Dawson, 'Enslaved Ship Pilots', pp.4-9.

the other the Command.'[6] Pilots occupied an obscure position in society, yet possessed an exceptionally desirable set of skills.[7] When a vessel entered unfamiliar waters, these ships would raise a signal or fire a gun requesting the services of a local pilot. In response, local pilots would row out, board the vessel, and finally take over the helm, thus ensuring the vessel's safe navigation to its destination. When a pilot boarded a vessel, it was a transformative experience. As stated by Kevin Dawson, pilots ascended from a relegated societal position to the helm of a vessel, and 'overset the social hierarchy.'[8] If white pilots upended societal norms and shipboard hierarchy, the enduring cultural and societal consequences of marginalized black pilots providing that same service cannot be understated.

Prior to arriving on the Delaware Bay, HMS *Poictiers* sailed from England in August 1812, arriving at Halifax, Nova Scotia on 26 September 1812. Soon thereafter, Captain Beresford received orders from Vice Admiral Sir John Warren, the newly appointed commander-in-chief of the North American Squadron, to sail south on 10 October 1812.[9] *Poictiers* was ordered from Halifax to serve as an integral part of a naval blockade that would stretch from Sandy Hook, New Jersey south to Cape Hatteras, North Carolina.[10] *Poictiers*, a 74-gun ship of the line, would be instrumental in ensuring the success of this blockade, with no American frigate capable of defeating such a vessel.

Before sailing south from Halifax, *Poictiers* replenished her stores with provisions for the ensuing voyage and subsequent blockade. The Victualling Board was responsible for both procuring and distributing provisions to Royal Navy vessels in Great Britain prior to sailing to foreign stations. In foreign stations, such as Bermuda and Halifax, provisioning agents were contracted by the board to supplement these victuals with locally acquired food. As stated by historian Daniel Baugh, this provisioning system allowed Royal Naval vessels to 'remain on station, performing the task of seapower.'[11] Per Captain Beresford's log, throughout 9 October 1812 *Poictiers* took on:

> 13 Puncheons of Rum, 23 Tierces of Beef, 35 Barrrells [sic] of Pork, 4 Casks of Suet, 27 Barrells of Flour, 196 each 20 Tierces of Pease, 5 Barrells Each 8 Barrells of Cocoa 14 Barrells of Sugar and 70 Bags of Bread…151 Bags of Bread…26 Quarters of fresh Beef 2495 [?] and 52955 [?] of Vegatables [sic]. Received 11 Butts of Water… Recivd [sic] 350 Loaves of Bread.[12]

6   Edward Ward, *A Trip to New England* (London: Publisher Unknown,1699), p.35.
7   Finger, 'A Flag of Defyance at the Masthead', p.387.
8   Dawson, 'Enslaved Ship Pilots', p.5.
9   'Miscellaneous.' *The Suffolk Chronicle; or Weekly General Advertiser & County Express.* 07 November 1812.
10 Brian Arthur, *How Britain Won the War of 1812: The Royal Navy's Blockade of the United States, 1812-1815* (Suffolk: Boydell Press, 2011), p.72 citing National Maritime Museum, Royal Museums (NMM) HUL/1: Warren's Order Book, order No. 2, Warren to Capt. Sir John P Beresford of HMS *Poictiers*, Halifax, 10 October 1812.
11 Daniel A. Baugh, 'Naval power: what gave the British Navy Superiority?' in L. Esosura (ed.), *Exceptionalism and Industrialization: Britain and its European Rivals, 1688 – 1815* (Cambridge: Cambridge University Press, 2004), p.256. Also in Arthur, *How Britain Won the War of 1812*, p.34.
12 TNA: ADM 51/2694: Captain's Log, HMS *Poictiers*.

The following morning, while running out of Halifax harbour under a cloudy sky with moderate breezes, *Poictiers* 'made signal for a pilot', 'with a gun at 6:15 [a.m.].'[13] At 7:20 a.m., Edward Godfrey boarded *Poictiers*, and immediately 'made sail with Royals and Courses Running out of the Harbour'.[14] Later that day, Edward Godfrey, 'a black pilot',[15] was entered onto *Poictiers*' Muster Book as a *Pilot,* to assist in the navigation of the eastern seaboard.[16] Edward Godfrey had secured his freedom, over 30 years prior, through the Royal Navy. For Edward Godfrey, the Royal Navy represented one of 'freedom's swift-winged angels',[17] as coined by historian Jeffrey Bolster, as he escaped enslavement from Matthew Godfrey of Norfolk, Virginia during the American War of Independence.[18]

At the eruption of the American War of Independence, the Royal Governor of the British Colony of Virginia, Lord Dunmore, recognized that the enslaved population of Virginia was 'ready to join the first that would encourage them to revenge themselves'.[19] On 7 November 1775 while aboard the ship *William* off Norfolk, Virginia, Dunmore issued a proclamation which stated:

> I do hereby farther [sic] declare all indented [sic] servants, negroes, or others (appertaining to rebels) free, that are able and willing to bear arms, they joining his Majesty's troops, as soon as may be, for the more speedily reducing this colony to a proper sense of their duty, to his majesty's crown and dignity [Sic].[20]

In response, enslaved men, women, and children all flocked to Dunmore and his forces for aid and protection. Predominantly living along the coastal regions of Tidewater Virginia, runaways were within close proximity to Dunmore's fleet. Fleeing from the homes of their former masters, these enslaved people almost always escaped in familial units, with Edward Godfrey being no exception.

In 1778, 12-year-old Edward Godfrey responded to Dunmore's proclamation and fled the Norfolk County plantation of Matthew Godfrey, along with three of his family members: Valentine, Bristol, and Kitty Godfrey. In addition to Edward Godfrey's family, in 1785 enslaver Matthew Godfrey filed a claim for the loss of thirty-five 'negroes', 'from the depredations of the Enemy since the commencement of the war'.[21] Following the American War of Independence, over 3,000 black refugees were repatriated from New York to Nova Scotia with a record of each individual's travails and journeys documented in the *Book of*

---

13   TNA: ADM 51/2694: Captain's Log, HMS *Poictiers.*
14   TNA: ADM 51/2694: Captain's Log, HMS *Poictiers.*
15   Loftus, Charles. *My Youth by Sea and Land: From 1809 to 1816* (London: Hurst and Blackett, Publishers, 1876).
16   TNA: ADM 37/3807: Muster Table, HMS *Poictiers.*
17   Bolster, Jeffrey W. Bolster, *Black Jacks-African American Seamen in the Age of Sail* (Cambridge, Massachusetts: Harvard University Press, 1997), p.1.
18   TNA: PRO 30/55/100 10427: Book of Negroes, From Guy Carleton, 1st Baron Dorchester Papers.
19   Alan Taylor, *The Internal Enemy: Slavery and War in Virginia, 1772 – 1832* (New York: W.W. Norton, 2013), p.23.
20   'A Proclamation,' *Rind's Virginia Gazette.* Williamsburg, Virginia. 23 November 1775.
21   'Matthew Godfrey', *Black Loyalists,* DOI: <https://blackloyalist.com/cdc/documents/official/black_loyalist_directory2.htm> (accessed 24 September 2023).

Negroes. On 31 July 1783, 17-year-old Edward Godfrey navigated his freedom as he climbed aboard HMS *Clinton*, sailing from New York City, preparing to sail to the Canadian ports of Annapolis Royal, Nova Scotia, and the nearby St John, on the Bay of Fundy.[22] Over 30 years later, Edward Godfrey once again found himself aboard a Royal Navy ship, not as a refugee, but as a free pilot on the quarterdeck of HMS *Poictiers*.

Norfolk-born Charles Loftus was in Halifax as a member of *Poictiers'* crew after joining as a Midshipman in 1812. Many years after his naval career, Loftus wrote *My Youth by Sea and Land: From 1809 to 1816*, chronicling his time aboard *Poictiers* in great detail. Loftus' memoir builds on the information provided in *Poictiers* Captain's Log, creating a fuller picture of Edward Godfrey's experience aboard this ship of the line. According to Loftus, 'We [*Poictiers*] had taken on board at Halifax a black pilot, who was well acquainted with all the northern and southern coasts of America.'[23] Only one pilot was entered onto the muster book of HMS *Poictiers* while she set sail from Halifax, Nova Scotia, confirming that pilot, was, in fact, Edward Godfrey.[24]

As a black pilot, Godfrey was able to exchange his maritime skills for respect, compensation, and the prospect for new opportunities. Godfrey's name was entered onto *Poictiers* Muster Book in the section for *Supernumeraries for Victuals and Wages*, alongside the names of James Grimes, Jean L'Evegue, John Robinson, John Richards, and Thomas Stretch, all European men who had piloted *Poictiers* prior to crossing the Atlantic.[25] Godfrey was being compensated and listed in the same manner as every other pilot that served before him, regardless of his race. Understanding Godfrey's background and prior relationship with the Royal Navy creates a fuller understanding of the liberating power that naval vessels could represent to enslaved men. On 10 October 1812, Godfrey successfully navigated *Poictiers* out of Halifax Harbour, bound for the safe anchorages of Bermuda.

En route to Bermuda, on Sunday 18 October 1812, *Poictiers* 'saw Strange sail SSE Made sail in chase & cleared Ship for Action… which proved to be the United States Ship of War *Wasp*.'[26] Prior to *Poictiers* arrival, *Wasp* had defeated HMS *Frolic* in a staggering 43-minute single-ship engagement, under the command of Delaware-born Master-Commandant Jacob Jones. As the crew of *Wasp* cleared the deck, repaired, and jury-rigged the newly captured *Frolic*, the larger *Poictiers* was spotted to the windward side on the horizon. As a warning, the superior *Poictiers* fired a shot over *Frolic*, concurrently accepting the surrender of the heavily damaged *Wasp* and retaking *Frolic*. Both vessels would now join *Poictiers* on her journey to Bermuda, with the American crew of *Wasp*, now prisoners of war, aboard *Poictiers*.

Poictiers boasted a crew compliment of 590 sailors, with little fear of an uprising from the much smaller crew of *Wasp*. These 150 captured seamen 'therefore had full liberty to walk about during the day-time, going where they pleased, and at night they were mustered along the main-deck, two sentries being placed over them', according to Midshipman Loftus. Prior to reaching Bermuda, Edward Godfrey ensured British naval success as well as the

---

22   TNA: PRO 30/55/100 10427: Book of Negroes, From Guy Carleton, 1st Baron Dorchester Papers.
23   Loftus, *My Youth by Sea and Land,* p.238 and TNA: ADM 37/3807: Muster Table, HMS *Poictiers*.
24   TNA: ADM 37/3807: Muster Table, HMS *Poictiers*.
25   TNA: ADM 37/3807: Muster Table, HMS *Poictiers*.
26   TNA: ADM 51/2694: Captain's Log, HMS *Poictiers*.

safety of his *Poictiers* shipmates by acting beyond his station as simply a pilot. While on the main deck, he overheard a threatening discussion amongst the American prisoners: 'Remember,' [said one individual,] 'we cut that black fellow's throat the first thing, and when four bells have struck we will be upon them.' Loftus further recalled that Godfrey, in a state of alarm, 'descended to his cabin, seized a pistol which was in the steward's room, and began loading it, but, in ramming down the cartridge, the pistol, which was at full cock, went off.' Responding to this alarm, the boatswain of *Poictiers* called 'All hands ahoy all hands ahoy! Boarders on the quarter-deck! Bring up your cutlasses!' Ascending to the main deck, Charles Loftus witnessed Godfrey, 'standing before the Captain [Beresford] hat in hand. The scene on our quarter-deck at that moment was one of a very striking nature.'[27] Thanks to the vigilance and independent actions of Edward Godfrey, 'the plot had been thus fortunately discovered in time, the American seamen were all made prisoners and bundled down below into the mainhold [sic].'[28] These American prisoners would remain under the strict guard of a complement of marines until *Poictiers* reached Bermuda.

Under the steady navigation of pilot Edward Godfrey, *Poictiers* safely traversed the Atlantic Ocean from Halifax to Bermuda, sailing against the Gulf Stream and approaching Bermuda on 25 October 1812. Loftus recalled the difficulty in reaching Bermuda, a testament to Godfrey's skill: 'Bermuda is a very difficult place to find, lying so low in the water, but very often, when a light breeze is blowing off the land in the evening, one can scent the cedars growing there before he sees them.'[29] Once *Poictiers* reached the treacherous Bermudian waters, Godfrey would turn the helm over to a local pilot, thus ensuring the vessels continued safety.

By the early nineteenth century, Bermuda served Great Britain, specifically the Royal Navy, by helping to fill the void of North American dockyards lost as a consequence of the War of American Independence. Bermuda was strategically located 650 miles off the coast of North Carolina and offered safe anchorages, protecting vessels from the Atlantic. Speaking to its strategic proximity to the United States, Vice Admiral Warren received orders in early 1813 to 'make Bermuda your permanent Station, it is the most centrical Spot within the Limit of your Station.'[30] While this island's temperate climate and geographic location were beneficial to naval operations, the island was very difficult to access and required intricate navigation. A vast network of undersea reefs surrounded the island, and in many cases, merely 500 yards from Bermudian shores.[31] To reach the safety of Bermuda's anchorages, vessels would have to navigate the narrow channels running through these reefs, with some depths measuring less than two fathoms.[32] This elaborate system of reefs that protected the island also created opportunities for entrepreneurial Bermudians.

---

27   Loftus, *Youth by Sea and Land*, p.258-260.
28   Loftus, *Youth by Sea and Land*, pp.260-261.
29   Loftus, *Youth by Sea and Land*, p.238.
30   Arthur, *How Britain Won the War of 1812*, p.43, citing NMM: LBK/2: Warren to Melville, San Domingo, Bermuda, 1 June 1813.
31   Virginia Bernhard, *Slaves and Slaveholders in Bermuda, 1616- 1782* (Columbia: University of Missouri Press, 1999), p.151.
32   Bernhard, *Slaves and Slaveholders in Bermuda, 1616- 1782*, pp.151-152.

The Flatts and its Bridge, Under which is the entrance to Harrington Sound. From an album of original watercolour paintings and sketches of Bermuda by Dr Johnson Savage, c. 1830. (The National Museum of Bermuda, with permission)

By the seventeenth century, Bermudians found their wealth working as wreckers and salvagers with legislation passed later in the century, futilely attempting to restrict such 'wreck fishing'.[33] Bermudians also turned towards the mercantile trade, shipbuilding, and fishing, as well as illicit smuggling. In 1687, Bermuda's Governor Robinson provided a detailed description of the island's inhabitants:

> Generally of quick Growth & of pretty Easie [sic] tempers, [the men were] generally Saylors [sic]…verry [sic] hardy but of unexperienced Courage. [The women were likewise of a large growth & Skillful in Swimming & Pilotting [sic] they are Comonly [sic] Good huswives [sic] & Verry [sic] amorous. [Governor Robinson shared that Bermuda's children had] but little Education their parent… neither Coveting nor affording it.[34]

While Bermudian children lacked a formal education, their uncanny knowledge and education of Bermuda's reef-laden waters could not be questioned, with Bermuda's pilots ensuring the island's vitality. In Bermuda, enslaved and free blacks 'monopolized the profession',[35] and

---

33   Bernhard, *Slaves and Slaveholders in Bermuda*, p.158.
34   Bernhard, *Slaves and Slaveholders in Bermuda*, p.178
35   Dawson, 'Enslaved Ship Pilots', p.1.

found opportunity through their vocation. While practicing law in Bermuda, Connecticut-born Josiah Meigs penned a letter to a friend, praising the reputation of Bermuda's black pilots, stating, 'without skilful pilots who are black fellows educated to the business from childhood it would be impossible to enter any of our [Bermudian] harbours.'[36]

Bermudian pilots did not use charts to guide them in this intricate navigation, nor did they rely upon modern navigational instruments.[37] Instead, as emphasized by historian Kevin Dawson, they mastered the *hydroscope*: 'reading the movement of the surface waters, observing colour variations in reefs, and plumbing the depths with lead-weighted sounding lines, and they navigated ships by lining them up with landmarks.'[38] Through black mariners such as these pilots, 'seamanship became an emblem of black accomplishment.'[39] In return for their seamanship, black pilots were able to gain unprecedented privileges and the potential to achieve freedom while cultivating new identities.

Through their networks, such pilots were crucial in disseminating information across Bermuda and beyond the Atlantic, often pertaining to wartime developments and shipborne traffic. Providing a critical service towards ensuring naval success, Bermudian pilots would also regularly serve aboard Royal Navy vessels in times of war. The importance of Bermuda and its relationship with the Royal Navy grew exponentially following the conclusion of the American War of Independence as British maritime operations expanded and tensions increased with France, and later the United States, respectively. By 1794, British Commander-in-Chief of the North American Squadron, Vice Admiral George Murray, was responsible for 16 British naval vessels.[40] Situated in the Atlantic Ocean off the Eastern coast of the United States, a Royal Naval Dockyard at Bermuda would be integral towards ensuring British naval operations and an enslaved Bermudian pilot, James Darrell, proved to be instrumental in developing that dockyard.

James Darrell personified the opportunity for freedom that could be obtained through pilotage for the Royal Navy. Born into slavery, Darrell's reputation and navigational prowess caught the attention of Lieutenant Hurd, Royal Naval hydrographer, in 1789. Over the next six years, Darrell worked directly for the Royal Navy surveying the craggy reefs of Bermuda's archipelago. With greater familiarity of these waters than many of his peers, Darrell's unrivalled knowledge allowed the Royal Navy to establish this new naval base and, according to historian Kevin Dawson, 'helped shift Bermuda from the backwaters of the British Empire to a colony of strategic importance.'[41]

---

36   Dexter, Franklin Bowditch, (ed.), *Extracts from the Itineraries, and other Miscellanies of Ezra Stiles* (New Haven, Connecticut: Yale University Press, 1916), p.535; Michael, J Jarvis, *In the Eye of All Trade. Bermuda, Bermudians, and the Maritime Atlantic World, 1680-1783* (Chapel Hill: University of North Carolina Press, 2010), p.514. Also referenced in Michael J. Jarvis, 'Maritime Masters and Seafaring Slaves in Bermuda, 1680-1783', *The William and Mary Quarterly*,59:3 (July 2002), p.606.
37   Adrian Webb, 'The Defence of Bermuda: A Maritime and Cartographic Perspective, 1770-1900', in Philip MacDougall (ed.), *Bermuda Dockyard and the War of 1812* (Sussex: Naval Dockyards Society, 2017), p.44.
38   Kevin Dawson, 'The Cultural Geography of Enslaved Ship Pilots,' in Jorge Canizares-Esguerra, Matt D. Childs, and James Sidbury (eds), *The Black Urban Atlantic in the Age of the Slave Trade* (Philadelphia: University of Pennsylvania Press, 2013), p.167.
39   Bolster, *Black Jacks*, p.132.
40   Ann Coats, 'Bermuda Naval Base: Management, Artisans and Enslaved Workers in the 1790s: The 1950s Bermudian Apprentices Heritage', *Mariner's Mirror*, Vol. 95 No. 2 (May 2009), p.151.
41   Dawson, 'Enslaved Ship Pilots', p.83.

The home of pilot James Darrell, St Georges, Bermuda. (Author's photograph)

After the completion of this extensive survey, Darrell judiciously navigated Vice Admiral George Murray's HMS *Resolution* into Bermuda on 15 May 1795.[42] Reading the hydroscope, Darrell helped *Resolution* gracefully traverse the treacherous 'narrows', safely arriving at modern day Murray's Anchorage, St George's, Bermuda. In return for this service, Darrell would escape slavery, with the Governor of Bermuda, James Caruford, purchasing and freeing Darrell.[43] James Darrell also became the first 'King's Pilot', a royally appointed and highly respected position in the maritime hierarchy of Bermuda.[44] Identifying an enormous opportunity, Darrell made a premediated decision and exchanged his mastery as a pilot for his subsequent freedom. His experience directly 'challenged slavery's power relations',[45] yet was accepted as it fulfilled a British need by establishing a crucial naval base in Bermuda. Darrell also received a handsome salary, allowing him to purchase a home in St George's near the adjacent harbour and his own pilot boat. Thus, he became a figure other enslaved and labouring pilots could aspire to as he now represented black maritime success.

42   Dawson, 'Enslaved Ship Pilots', p.13.
43   Dawson, 'Enslaved Ship Pilots', p.13.
44   Dawson, 'Enslaved Ship Pilots', p.83.
45   Bolster, *Black Jacks*, p.132.

Arriving to the archipelago seventeen years following Darrell's celebrated voyage, *Poictiers* continued the tradition of His Majesty's ships employing local experts to guide their vessels to safety – in this case, a black Bermudian pilot. On the morning of 26 October 1812, *Poictiers* followed maritime protocol and fired a gun for a pilot. According to Midshipman Loftus, 'in short time a boat was observed pulling out, manned by four blacks, and with a very dignified-looking personage (also black) sitting in the stern sheets.'[46] Loftus continued, describing *Poictiers'* exchange with this particular Bermudian pilot at length, later ridiculing it as 'most ludicrous.'[47] From this pilot boat emerged a black mariner named 'King George' who boarded *Poictiers* and made a dramatic impact on the members of the crew, as evidenced by the young Loftus.[48] King George was one of two pilots employed in Bermuda at this time to navigate His Majesty's Vessels, the other being 'King Harry.'[49] King George, 'was dressed in a suit of white, with a collar half way up to his ears, and had on his head a large straw hat.'[50] After ascending to the quarterdeck, King George removed his hat to Captain Beresford, 'with a grin on his face', and Captain Beresford turned the command of *Poictiers* over to this pilot on the morning of 26 October 1812.[51]

As King George took the helm, he symbolically adopted the mantle of ship's master, thus commanding respect and deference through sheer skill and competence as a pilot. Like James Darrell, King George had great familiarity with the intricate reef-laden channels and roads leading into Bermuda's safe anchorages. In lieu of modern instruments, pilots like King George, according to Loftus, 'know the route through the different shelvings of the rocks under water — for these rocks are to be seen at a great depth; and when they are not able to see them they take their bearings from points on the land.'[52] King George calmly proved his proficiency through a combination of navigation by landmarks and reading the hydroscope, bringing *Poictiers* to anchor at Murray's Anchorage six hours after taking the helm.

Captain Beresford's willingness to turn the helm of *Poictiers* over to a black Bermudian pilot serves as a testament to the expertise of King George. Ship's masters were open to accepting such temporary reversals of societal norms as long as it ensured the safety of their vessel and furthered their aims.[53] King George was well-familiar with the dangerous channels that ran through Bermuda, and so he excelled at piloting. Demonstrating that familiarity, King George put the helm up and squared the yards, 'every now and then went forward, looked over the bows, and then came back on the quarterdeck with an air of great importance',[54] immediately after taking control of *Poictiers'* helm.

King George's entire exchange with *Poictiers* represented the subversion of societal norms and showcased the freedoms he earned as a pilot. As presented in their thorough analysis

46   Loftus, *Youth by Sea and Land*, p.238.
47   Loftus, *Youth by Sea and Land*, p.239.
48   Loftus explains the role of King George as one of the King's pilots: 'The reader will probably be curious to know who was this King George. In those days there were two pilots employed to take in all the king's vessels – one called King George, and the other King Harry.' Loftus, *Youth by Sea and Land*, pp.238-239.
49   Loftus, *Youth by Sea and Land*, p.239
50   Loftus, *Youth by Sea and Land*, p.238.
51   Loftus, *Youth by Sea and Land*, p.239.
52   Loftus, *Youth by Sea and Land*, p.239.
53   Dawson, 'Enslaved Ship Pilots', p.9.
54   Loftus, *Youth by Sea and Land*, p.239.

of slave clothing and African American culture, Shane White and Graham White state the impact of African-Americans appropriating 'white dress': 'Slaves wearing such clothes was not so much that they were adopting white values, but that they were subverting white authority. Often, it seems, there was a light mocking touch to the activities of slaves.'[55] Black pilots, like King George, took pride in their position and, according to Kevin Dawson, 'used Western material cultural to visually communicate shipboard authority.'[56] King George deliberately dressed in the attire of a gentleman, showcasing his authority and distinguishing his accomplishment, pride, and determination.

Boarding *Poictiers*, King George openly conversed with Captain Beresford before commanding a large crew of 590 Royal Navy seamen and calmly navigating a 74-gun third rate ship of the line, all while representing black achievement in an age of adversity. However, *Poictiers'* time in Bermuda would be short, as she had orders to return to the east coast of the United States.

Departing Bermuda on the 28 October 1812, *Poictiers* sailed under fresh breezes, tasked with daunting orders to assist in the blockade of the expansive American coastline, measuring over 1,900 miles in length. Per the 21 November 1812 orders by Earl Bathurst, Secretary of State for War and the Colonies, the Admiralty was to impose an economic blockade of the American east coast. These instructions included specific orders to place the Delaware Bay and River and Chesapeake Bay under 'a strict and rigorous Blockade.'[57] *Poictiers* was ordered to cruise the Delaware and Chesapeake Bays, as far south as Cape Hatteras. Two thriving port cities sat prominently on the Chesapeake and Delaware Bays, both direct targets of Great Britain's close economic blockade. Baltimore, Maryland, located on the Chesapeake Bay, was a hotbed of American privateer activity and shipbuilding, as well as a thriving port town, eclipsing Boston as America's third largest port by 1797.[58] Located less than 100 miles north on the Delaware River, Philadelphia prospered as America's most successful maritime entrepot and the largest city in the young American Republic. Boasting 111,210 residents in 1810, Philadelphia flourished economically through the re-export trade, with its leading merchants making their fortunes at sea.[59]

Historian Andrew Lambert stated that this specific blockade targeted Republican decision-makers as well as merchants.[60] HMS *Poictiers*, again piloted by Edward Godfrey, reached the Delaware Bay on 14 March 1813, serving as the flagship of this localized blockade. Facing narrow channels, unreliable shoals, and drastic tides, *Poictiers* came to anchor off the coast, mid-channel, adjacent to the town of Lewistown, Delaware. Due to shortages in both seamen and warships, this blockading squadron was smaller than Vice Admiral Warren desired. Warren proposed at least one 74-gun ship and five other vessels

---

55   Graham White and Shane White, 'Slave Clothing and African-American Culture in the Eighteenth and Nineteenth Centuries', *Past & Present*, Aug. 1995, No. 148, p.162.

56   Dawson, 'Cultural Geography of Enslaved Ship Pilots', p.174.

57   Andrew Lambert, *The Challenge: Britain Against America in the Naval War of 1812* (Faber & Faber, 2012), p.109. Lambert is quoting Bathurst to Admiralty, 21 Nov 1812: CO 43/49, pp.153-154.

58   Seth Rockman, *Scraping By: Wage Labor, Slavery, and Survival in Early Baltimore* (Baltimore: John Hopkins University Press, 2009), p.3.

59   Billy G. Smith, *The Lower Sort-Philadelphia's Laboring People, 1750*-1800 (New York: Cornell University Press, 1994), p.64.

60   Lambert, *The Challenge*, p.111.

A 1779 Map of the Delaware River and Bay. (The Lewes Historical Society, with permission)

on each of the major stations, including the Delaware.[61] By March 1813, the blockade of the Delaware only included the 74-gun *Poictiers*, joining 36-gun *Belvidera* and the 10-gun schooner *Paz*. Following the successful implementation of this blockade of the Delaware, Philadelphia would suffer a 90 percent fall in revenue, crippling the maritime port, with the coffers of its mercantile elite drying up.[62] Despite its eventual success, maintaining a blockade was not an easy feat logistically. Facing such a dynamic and treacherous coastline, unpredictable climate, and rapidly diminishing victuals, *Poictiers* would quickly turn to local assistance to ensure the efficacy of their blockade.

In addition to *Poictiers'* 590 men, 274 served aboard the 36-gun *Belvidera,* and 40 men crewed the schooner *Paz*, not including supernumeraries.[63] On 9 March 1813, these 904 seamen sailed their respective vessels from Lynnhaven Bay at the mouth of Chesapeake Bay on a northeast course, returning to the Delaware Bay. Prior to sailing to Halifax, *Poictiers* was victualled with three to six months of basic rations by the Victualling Board, relying on salted meats, butter, beer, and foodstuff that could be preserved in casks for months on end. In Halifax, as we have seen, *Poictiers* took on additional provisions in October 1812, yet the ship's crew, as well as those aboard *Belvidera* and *Paz,* were nearing the end of their supplies by the time they reached Delaware's shores in Spring 1813. On blockade duty *Poictiers* did not have the luxury of the transport ships of the Victualing Board nor provisioning agents providing additional rations. Instead, the onus would fall on Captain Beresford to ensure that his squadron was adequately provisioned, thus ensuring that this economic blockade could be maintained. Instinctively, Beresford attempted to procure victuals locally, contacting local American politicians in the waterfront community of Lewistown, Delaware.

According to his memoir, Midshipman Loftus, after weeks of monotonous duty on the Delaware Bay, climbed the shrouds to 'take a good view of the country from the masthead, and observed with our glasses that there appeared to be several flocks of sheep and herds of cattle grazing inland.'[64] A week after arriving on the Bay, Captain Beresford penned a letter to Delaware Governor Joseph Haslet, offering to pay Philadelphia rates for provisions. As negotiations began to prove fruitless, Beresford threatened, 'If you refuse to comply with this request, I shall be under the necessity of destroying your town.'[65] To this demand, Governor Haslet tersely responded stating: 'A compliance would be an immediate violation of the laws of my country and an eternal stigma on the nation of which I am a citizen; a compliance therefore cannot be acceded to.'[66] Following through on his promise, Captain Beresford and his squadron attacked the community of Lewistown with a naval bombardment between 6 April and 7 April 1813, yet following this futile engagement the naval squadron still lacked the provisions needed to maintain an effective blockade. *Poictiers* would again come to rely upon local black pilots as a means to achieve naval success.

61   Arthur, *How Britain Won the War of 1812*, p.88.
62   Lambert, *The Challenge*, p.111.
63   TNA: ADM 37/ 4223: Muster Table, HMS *Belvidera*; TNA: ADM 37/3807: Muster Table, HMS *Poictiers*; TNA: ADM 37/3753: Muster Table, Schooner *Paz*.
64   Loftus, *Youth by Sea and Land*, p.293.
65   William M. Marine Esq., *The Bombardment of Lewes by the British April 6 and 7, 1813* (Wilmington: Historical Society of Delaware, 1901), pp.14-15.
66   The Collection of the Lewes Historical Society, 1989.1.62, Letter from J.P. Beresford to Lewes, 22 March 1813.

Letter from J.P. Beresford to Lewes, 22 March 1813. Arriving on the Delaware Bay in March 1813, Captain Beresford of HMS *Poictiers* exchanged a series of letters with Lewistown, Delaware attempting to acquire provisions. On 23 March 1813 Beresford's final letter, seen here, threatened 'It is in my power to destroy your town'. A few weeks later, the British naval squadron on the Delaware would bombard Lewistown. (The Lewes Historical Society, with permission)

While *Poictiers* and the rest of the British squadron lay at anchor in the Delaware Bay, Peter Wood and Jeremiah Primrose, enslaved men of nearby Mispillion Hundred, Delaware, would seek their own freedom through *Poictiers*. Enslaved men in coastal communities, such as Mispillion Hundred, often laboured in maritime capacities developing a keen familiarity and confidence working on the water. Through this type of labour these individuals found additional mobility as well as opportunity, allowing them to communicate with enslaved men on neighbouring plantations sharing news – such as the arrival of a British squadron. Utilizing these local networks of communication, recognizing opportunity, and exercising their maritime familiarity, young Wood and Primrose took a calculated risk and rowed over 10 miles across Delaware Bay.

On 22 April 1813, these two men were entered into the Muster Books of *Poictiers* as volunteers.[67] Three days after their escape, the *Carlisle Weekly Herald* reported: 'Many negroes have lately run away from their masters and have been seen going to the British fleet. Two ran away from Col. Wood and Mr. Primrose last week, and were discovered going to the 74 [HMS *Poictiers*] in a small boat.'[68] In his diary, maintained throughout the War of 1812, Lewistown business owner and politician David Rodney too noted their escape: '2 negro men yesterday ran away from Coll. Wood & Primrose to *Poictiers* it is supposed.'[69]

Both Peter Wood and Jeremiah Primrose were previously enslaved in Mispillion Hundred in Kent County, Delaware.[70] Jeremiah Primrose was enslaved under Thomas Primrose and Peter Wood came from one of the largest farms in Mispillion Hundred, enslaved with his parents and sister on John Wood's 655-acre farm.[71] Jeremiah and 19-year-old Peter were just two of over 436 enslaved individuals living in Mispillion Hundred.[72] Historian Gene Allen Smith summarised that 'slaves braved the possibility of being wounded, killed, or captured and punished. They left behind everything they knew for the rumour of freedom.'[73] To enslaved men like Peter and Jeremiah, this risk was worth seeing the 'rumour of freedom' fulfilled. Akin to Lord Dunmore's Proclamation of 1775, in 1813 Earl Bathurst also recognized slavery as a political and military weapon, and offered a similar enticement to America's enslaved populus. Per Bathurst's 1813 orders, he ordered that 'individual slaves who became involved in British operations to be removed from the United States for their own safety and to be given protection and granted freedom.'[74]

---

67   TNA: ADM 37/3807: Muster Table, HMS *Poictiers*. Both men were incorrectly entered onto *Poictiers*' Muster Book as 'Cape May volunteers.' An error as these men joined from the Delaware side of the bay rather than Cape May, lying on the New Jersey side.

68   *Carlisle Weekly Herald*, 7 May 1813.

69   C.H.B. Turner (ed.), *Rodney's Diary and other Delaware Records* (Philadelphia: Allen Lane & Scott, 1911), p.10.

70   Ellen Stanley Rogers and Easter, Louise E. Easter (eds), *1800 Census of Kent County, Delaware* (Bladensburg, Maryland: Publisher Unknown, 1959), p.39.

71   Gary B. Nash and Stanley Miles Albrook, 'The travail of Delaware slave families in the early republic', *Slavery & Abolition*, 40:1, p.15.

72   Nash and Albrook, 'The travail of Delaware slave families', p.10.

73   Gene Allen Smith, *The Slaves' Gamble. Choosing Sides in the War of 1812* (New York: Palgrave Macmillan, 2013), p.95.

74   Smith, *The Slaves' Gamble*, p.88.

After boarding *Poictiers*, Jeremiah Primrose and Peter Wood asserted their value to their new shipmates through their personal familiarity with the dangerous coastline and tributaries of the Delaware. Loftus again shared:

> Our black pilot, who was well acquainted with the Delaware, informed us that, about six or seven miles up the river, on the left bank, there was a large farm house where sheep and bullocks were kept, and that, as a small creek ran up close to the farm, it would be very easy for our boats to land, drive down the stock, and embark them.[75]

On Sunday 25 April 1813, Jeremiah Primrose and Peter Wood led a naval party up the Mispillion Creek to pursue their personal retribution while helping supply the squadron with their much sought after provisions.

Like many enslaved men on the Delaware coast, Peter Wood had a strong working knowledge of the local tides, shoals, and channels of the Delaware, having no problem navigating this landing party back up the Mispillion. 'Having taken, by compass, the bearing of the place where the black pilot had said the stock-farm was situated, they steered away in that direction. In each of our boats were two midshipmen and two marines, and all the men had their cutlasses and pistols, while eight muskets, with their cartridge-boxes, were placed in each boat,' according to Charles Loftus.[76]

The *Carlisle Weekly Herald* further confirmed the British actions of 25 April 1813: 'In the evening, five barges with 150 men landed at the mouth of the Mispillion Creek and took 14 head of cattle; and they killed but three and took the remainder in their barges alive.'[77] Peter Wood had navigated the intricate and shallow Mispillion Creek as a pilot, leading this landing party to the home and farm of his former master, John Wood. After reaching John's Wood's expansive plantation on the Mispillion, 'the marines were landed, and six seamen from each boat, with muskets in hand, were drawn up in line with them on shore. The lieutenant of marines, having left ten men, with a serjeant, as a reserve to fall back upon, advanced towards the house with the officer commanding the expedition, the seamen, and two midshipmen.'[78] Following a brief exchange, the livestock were located grazing in nearby grass meadows as Peter Wood had promised. In addition to the cattle, 60 sheep were procured and distributed throughout the squadron.[79]

Daniel Rodney's diary and The *Carlisle Weekly Herald* both confirm this: 'The Negro that ran away from Col. Wood was seen ashore with the British at the time they were taking the cattle-and it is supposed that he piloted them as it was in sight of his master's house where they landed and took the cattle.'[80] This raid allowed Peter Wood to demonstrate his value to the crew and to obtain his freedom. He successfully navigated the Mispillion Creek, allowing the naval fleet to replenish its provisions and maintain the close economic blockade of the Delaware and Philadelphia.

---

75   Loftus, *Youth by Sea and Land*, p.294.
76   Loftus, *Youth by Sea and Land*, pp.295-296.
77   Loftus, *Youth by Sea and Land*, pp.295-296.
78   Loftus, *Youth by Sea and Land*, pp.296-301.
79   Loftus, *Youth by Sea and Land*, pp.296-301.
80   Loftus, *Youth by Sea and Land*, pp.296-301.

Following such a successful raid, Thomas Primrose endeavoured to have his 'property' returned, and rowed out to *Poictiers* under a flag of truce to retrieve his former slave, Jeremiah, on 5 May 1813.[81] Boarding *Poictiers*, Thomas Primrose was granted the opportunity to speak with Jeremiah, but Captain Beresford made it clear to Thomas Primrose that 'he [Beresford] was authorized to give them up [Peter Wood and Jeremiah Primrose], but if the Primroses [sic] boy was willing.'[82] Contrary to the ethics of Thomas Primrose, Captain Beresford recognized Jeremiah Primrose as an asset to the navy, and per Bathurst's proclamation, was obligated to not give up such runaway slaves. When Primrose and Wood joined *Poictiers*, Captain Beresford was struggling to keep his ship's company at a full complement. On 2 May 1813 *Poictiers* muster book listed 431 men borne with a mere 397 men mustered, therefore, these men were a welcomed addition to his crew. As expected, Jeremiah objected to returning, and remained aboard *Poictiers*, along with Peter Wood, and under the protection of the Royal Navy.

In 'Freedom By Reaching the Wooden World', Historian Thomas Malcolmson shares that following a negative response, 'the white slave owners would have to quietly endure the humiliation of being turned away, snubbed by a person they saw only as a slave.'[83] Thirteen years later, in 1826, an American Congressional Report was created, listing 'slaves stated to have been carried off by the British forces from the State of Delaware, [and as] property transported by the British forces, in violation of the Treaty of Ghent.'[84] This report included 'The Number of the slaves, and amount, conformably to the average values agreed upon and fixed by the Commission', broken down by state, with names of claimants and enslaved individuals listed if available. Over the course of the War of 1812, it is estimated that 5,000 individuals escaped slavery by fleeing to the British.[85] For the state of Delaware, only two claims were made. Thomas Primrose filed a claim for 'Jerry' [Jeremiah], and John Wood filed one for Peter. Despite these efforts, neither Peter Wood nor Jeremiah Primrose would ever return to their former enslavers. Upon leaving the Delaware Bay for Bermuda in the summer of 1813, *Poictiers* still bore the names of two 'volunteers,' on her muster book, Thomas Primrose and Jeremiah Wood. Having proved their value to the Royal Navy, both men were now rated 'seamen' aboard a British ship of the line, and by May 1813 were donning naval slop issue clothing – now fully indoctrinated into the crew. Jeremiah and Peter risked their lives, leveraged their unique skills, and finally attained freedom with the Royal Navy.

There was no single course or trajectory that would ensure black mariners could obtain freedoms through naval service. Each pilot analysed in this piece came from different backgrounds, lived in vastly diverse geographic regions of the Atlantic, and experienced the

---

81   Thomas Malcolmson, 'Freedom by Reaching the Wooden World: American Slaves and the British Navy during the War of 1812', *The Northern Mariner/le marin du nord*, XXII No. 4 (October 2012), p.367. TNA: ADM 51/2694: Captain's Log, HMS *Poictiers*.

82   Turner, *Rodney's Diary*, p.12.

83   Malcolmson, 'Freedom by Reaching the Wooden World', p.367.

84   *American State Papers. Documents, Legislative and Executive of the Congress of the United States from the Session of the First Congress to the Second Session of the Thirty-Fifth Congress, Inclusive: Commencing March 4, 1789 and Ending March 3, 1859* (Washington: Gales & Seaton, 1858), pp.800, 826.

85   Thomas Malcolmson, *Order and Disorder in the British Navy, 1793-1815: Control, Resistance, Flogging and Hanging* (London: Boydell Press, 2016), p.114.

maritime world in unique ways. Despite differences, these individuals shared common experiences and challenges. To obtain sought-after freedoms, they each overcame staggering adversity and sought opportunity by leveraging their maritime skillsets. Through these respective actions, each of these pilots had cultural, social, and military consequences that endure today. By seeking out opportunities through naval service, these men took control of their lives and, in some cases, found lasting freedoms.

Edward Godfrey experienced uncommon privilege serving aboard *Poictiers* as a pilot for five critical months. On 1 March 1813 after reaching the Mid-Atlantic, Godfrey officially joined the crew of *Poictiers* as he was entered onto the muster book as an 'Able Seaman,' a well-respected sailor and member of the ship's company. Having served as a pilot aboard *Poictiers* for roughly five months and another five months as a member of the crew, Godfrey now sought new opportunities. On 10 August 1813, *Poictiers* again returned to Bermuda, and Edward Godfrey ran.[86] *Poictiers* was busy 'getting what stores we required at the dockyard – filling up our casks with water, casks of salt beef, pork, & c., being sent on board, with bags of biscuits—a fresh supply of which had just arrived from Halifax,'[87] as shared by Loftus. With *Poictiers* busy replenishing her stores, Godfrey and his shipmates Philip Vincent of Lisbon, Portugal and John Handy of Fisguard, Wales failed to return from shore leave and deserted naval service.[88] Edward Godfrey had successfully escaped slavery during the American War of Independence, advanced through the Royal Navy, and led a career recognized for his expertise, regardless of his race while still maintaining control over his life. Despite the liberties and livelihood, he had with the Royal Navy, Edward Godfrey now sought out new opportunities in the fluid maritime community of Bermuda, bound to no captain nor enslaver.

Akin to Edward Godfrey, Bermudian King George was recognized for his ability and thus commanded respect. As he boarded *Poictiers* in Bermuda, in his tall straw hat and high-collared white jacket, King George took the helm from Captain Beresford, elevating his own authority and freedom. King George commanded the 590-man crew of *Poictiers* with coolness and precision, demanding the respect afforded to pilots through maritime tradition, and inverting the racial hierarchy through his role and skill. Black men, like King George, behaved in a manner that confused many white sailors who were unable to overcome 'assumptions about black inferiority.'[89] Skilled black pilots stood in stark contrast to the cultural constructs of black subservience. From the moment they ascended the quarterdeck, black pilots dismantled these boundaries of subservience and expanded the margins of opportunity for all blacks. From their attire to their language and authoritative presence, these men executed their role in a carefully curated manner, thus ensuring the greatest opportunity or reward in return for their services.

To previously enslaved men such as Jeremiah Primrose and Peter Wood, the Royal Navy served as a means to achieve their freedom, after they were 'discovered going to the 74 in a small boat.' It presented an opportunity and a future that stood in stark contrast to a life of

---

86   TNA: ADM 37/3807: Muster Table, HMS *Poictiers*.
87   Loftus, *Youth by Sea and Land*, p.25.
88   TNA: ADM 37/3807: Muster Table, HMS *Poictiers*.
89   Bolster, *Black Jacks*, p.139.

enslavement. Once this freedom was secured, these men were able to further demonstrate their value to the Royal Navy, asserting their new identity, not as slaves, but as free men.

Edward Godfrey, King George, Jeremiah Primrose, and Peter Wood each furthered British Naval interests through their service aboard HMS *Poictiers*. Possessing a distinct familiarity for their respective coastal waters, these men ensured both the efficacy of *Poictiers'* blockade of the Delaware as well as her safe traversing of the Atlantic seaboard. In addition to the individual freedoms these men obtained through their service, the cultural ramifications of their collective experiences cannot be understated. These black pilots recognized an opportunity with the Royal Navy, took bold risks to overcome adversity, and navigated their freedom, thus capsizing the racial hierarchy of the period and advancing black maritime identity on both sides of the Atlantic.

Select Bibliography

Archives
The Collection of the Lewes Historical Society, Delaware, United States of America
      1989.1.62, *Letter from J.P. Beresford to Lewes,* 23 March 1813.
The National Archives, Kew (TNA)
      ADM 51/2694: Captain's Log, HMS *Poictiers*.
      ADM 37/3528: Muster Table, HMS *Belvidera*.
      ADM 37/3753: Muster Table, Schooner *Paz*.
      ADM 37/3807: Muster Table, HMS *Poictiers*.
      ADM 37/ 4223: Muster Table, HMS *Belvidera*.
      ADM 53/997: Captain's Log, HMS *Poictiers*.
      ADM 51/2018: Captain's Log, HMS *Belvidera*.
      PRO 30/50/100, 10427: *Book of Negroes,* From Guy Carleton, *1st Baron Dorchester Papers*.
National Maritime Museum
      NMM HUL/1: Warren's Order Book, order No. 2, Warren to Capt. Sir John P Beresford of HMS
          Poictiers, Halifax, 10 October 1812.
      NMM LBK/2: Warren to Melville, San Domingo, Bermuda, 1 June 1813.

Published Primary Sources
American State Papers. Documents, Legislative and Executive of the Congress of the United States from the
      Session of the First Congress to the Second Session of the Thirty-Fifth Congress, Inclusive: Commencing
      March 4, 1789 and Ending March 3, 1859 (Washington: Gales & Seaton, 1858).
Dexter, Franklin Bowditch (ed.), *Extracts from the Itineraries and other Miscellanies of Ezra*
Stiles (New Haven, Connecticut: Yale University Press, 1916)
Loftus, Charles, *My Youth by Sea and Land: From 1809 to 1816* (London: Hurst and Blackett,
Publishers, 1876)
'Miscellaneous', *The Suffolk Chronicle; or Weekly General Advertiser & County Express,* 7 November 1812.
'Office of the Delaware Statesmen', *Carlisle Weekly Herald* 7 May, 1813.
'A Proclamation', *Rind's Virginia Gazette,* 23 November 1775.

Published Sources
Bernhard, Virginia, *Slaves and Slaveholders in Bermuda, 1616- 1782* (Columbia: University of
Missouri Press, 1999).
Bolster, Jeffrey W., *Black Jacks-African American Seamen in the Age of Sail* (Cambridge,
Massachusetts: Harvard University Press, 1997).

Dawson, Kevin, 'The Cultural Geography of Enslaved Ship Pilots,' in. Canizares-Esguerra, Jorge, Childs, Matt D., and Sidbury, James (eds), *The Black Urban Atlantic in the Age of the Slave Trade*, (Philadelphia: University of Pennsylvania Press, 2013), pp. 161-184

Dawson, Kevin, 'Enslaved Ship Pilots in the Age of Revolutions: Challenging Notions of Race and Slavery between the Boundaries of Land and Sea.' *Journal of Social History*, 2013, 71-100.

Finger, Simon, 'A Flag of Defiance at the Masthead: The Delaware River Pilots and the Sinews of Philadelphia's Atlantic World in the Eighteenth Century.' *Early American Studies*. 8: 2, (Spring 2010), pp.386-409.

Jarvis, Michael, J., *In the Eye of All Trade. Bermuda, Bermudians, and the Maritime Atlantic World, 1680-1783* (Chapel Hill: University of North Carolina Press, 2010).

Jarvis, Michael J., 'Maritime Masters and Seafaring Slaves in Bermuda, 1680-1783,'*The William and Mary Quarterly*, Jul., 2002, Vol. 59, No. 3, *Slaveries in the Atlantic World*, 585-622.

Lambert, Andrew, *The Challenge*: Britain Against America in the Naval War of 1812 (London: Faber & Faber, 2012).

Malcolmson, Thomas, 'Freedom by Reaching the Wooden World: American Slaves and the British Navy during the War of 1812,' *The Northern Mariner/le marin du nord*, XXII No. 4 (October 2012), pp.361-392.

Malcolmson, Thomas, *Order and Disorder in the British Navy, 1793-1815: Control, Resistance, Flogging and Hanging* (London: Boydell Press, 2016).

Marine, William M., Esq., *The Bombardment of Lewes by the British April 6 and 7, 1813* (Wilmington, Delaware: Historical Society of Delaware, 1901).

Nash, Gary B. and Stanley, Miles Albrook, 'The Travail of Delaware slave families in the early republic,' *Slavery & Abolition*, 40:1, pp.1-27.

Rockman, Seth. *Scraping By: Wage Labor, Slavery, and Survival in Early Baltimore.* (Baltimore: John Hopkins University Press, 2009).

Rogers, Ellen Stanley and Easter, Louise E. (eds), *1800 Census of Kent County, Delaware* (Bladensburg, Maryland: Publisher Unknown, 1959).

Smith, Billy G., *The Lower Sort-Philadelphia's Laboring People, 1750-*1800 (New York: Cornell University Press, 1994).

Smith, Gene Allen, *The Slaves' Gamble. Choosing Sides in the War of 1812* (New York: Palgrave Macmillan, 2013).

Ward, Edward, *A Trip to New England.* (London: Publisher Unknown, 1699).

14

'Safe Moored': Greenwich Pensioners in Perception and Reality

Callum Easton[1]

For a select few of Britain's maritime labour force, their life cycle ended 'safe moored'[2] at Greenwich Hospital. There they could live out their days, if not in plenty then at least in respectable comfort. Greenwich Hospital's three sets of admission books contain the details of approximately 35,500 admissions.[3] Accounting for readmissions, the number of individuals who called that institution home as resident 'in-pensioners' between 1705 and 1869 is estimated to be in the region of 33,000 men.[4] Due to the wide variety of information recorded in these admission records, the Greenwich pensioners represent one of the best-documented subsets of Britain's maritime labour force available for study. It is reasonable to note that the Greenwich pensioners comprised a relatively small proportion of the hundreds of thousands of men who served on British ships across the eighteenth and nineteenth centuries. Furthermore, admission policies overwhelmingly favoured men with naval service and, to a lesser extent, those who were wounded, so this institution's population cannot be considered entirely representative. Nevertheless, by adopting the viewpoint of the end of a sailor's working life, Greenwich Hospital offers a valuable new perspective of Britain's seagoing workforce and, crucially, one able to provide a holistic assessment of

1   The research on which this chapter is based was completed during a 12-month Caird Research Fellowship at Royal Museums Greenwich (RMG). I gratefully acknowledge the generous support of RMG in the award of this fellowship and of the National Maritime Museum, Greenwich for granting me the use of images from their collections. Martin Wilcox of the University of Hull kindly gave his blessing to my continuing his earlier work on Greenwich pensioners and gave every possible assistance. I could not have completed this work without his invaluable advice and experience.
2   Quoted in Anon., *Greenwich Hospital, A Series of Naval Sketches descriptive of the Life of a Man-of-War's Man by an Old Sailor* (London: James Robins and Co., 1826), p.81. 'Here I am (that is, what's left of me) safe moored in Greenwich, bidding defiance to the dirty sharks of the world.'
3   TNA: ADM73: 36–41 Greenwich Hospital General Entry Books 1704–1846, 36–41; 51–64 Greenwich Hospital Rough Entry Books 1704–1863; 65–69 Greenwich Hospital Entry Books 1764–1865.
4   Unless specified otherwise, whenever this chapter refers to 'Greenwich pensioners' the resident in-pensioners are meant.

their overall career trajectory. This perspective requires a temporal range well beyond 1815 as the lives of naval sailors did not end at the moment peace was signed, while their place in Britain's societal memory far outlived them.

This chapter is divided into three sections. The first outlines the context of Greenwich Hospital itself, including its purpose and operation. The second section examines the changing portrayal of Greenwich pensioners in visual imagery from the late eighteenth century onwards as an indicator of the public perceptions of Greenwich pensioners. It is argued that the visual presentation of Greenwich pensioners evolved from one centred on alcohol-fuelled hedonism in the late eighteenth and early nineteenth centuries to a much more reverential and sentimental portrayal in the second half of the nineteenth century. While highlighting both continuities and differences, this chapter contends that the transformation in the tone of these images reflected contemporary social anxieties and state priorities. Finally, the third section presents preliminary data drawn from a quantitative analysis of a subset of the institution's admission books to begin to chart changes in the relationship between veteran sailors and Greenwich Hospital and to identify disconnects between the popular image of the Greenwich pensioners and the lived reality.[5] It is asserted that the interrelationship between veteran sailors and Greenwich Hospital was more flexible than has been recognised, with each party adapting their behaviour to the changing preferences and policies of the other.

Greenwich Hospital

Greenwich Hospital was founded in 1694 and, between 1705 and 1869, old or wounded seamen resided there in the buildings now known as the Old Royal Naval College. In that time, tens of thousands of Greenwich Pensioners experienced this institution's distinctive welfare regime. This was not a hospital in the modern sense of a place to treat the sick (though from 1769 it did have its own infirmary), but a residential charity where retired sailors could live out their remaining years safe from poverty.

Founded in the reign of William III, partly as a tribute to his wife, the late Queen Mary II, Greenwich Hospital was an ambitious and costly undertaking that quickly dwarfed its older army counterpart, Chelsea Hospital (1682).[6] Across its period of operation, Greenwich Hospital received funding from a variety of sources including Parliamentary grants; the revenues of landed estates that had been gifted to the hospital; unclaimed or forfeited prize money; and compulsory monthly deductions from the wages of naval and merchant seamen.

---

5   'Veteran' is used throughout is in line with the modern usage, meaning anyone having undergone military service regardless of length. However, according to Caroline Nielsen the term carried different connotations at the time (suggesting prolonged service, 20-30 years). See Caroline Nielsen, 'The Chelsea Out-Pensioners: Image and Reality in Eighteenth-Century and Early Nineteenth-Century Social Care' (Unpublished PhD thesis, Newcastle University, 2014), p.xii.

6   Greenwich Hospital was significantly larger than Chelsea Hospital when it came to resident in-pensioners but had fewer out-pensioners. Between 1816-1820 there were approximately 30,000 Greenwich out-pensioners compared to between 40-65,000 Chelsea out-pensioners. See Nielsen, 'The Chelsea Out-Pensioners', pp.258–261; Philip Newell, *Greenwich Hospital, A Royal Foundation 1692–1983* (London: Butler and Tanner Ltd., 1984), p.123.

Greenwich Hospital operated much like an enormous ship. Its governor was assisted by four captains, and discipline was maintained by trusted pensioners, who were awarded the rank of 'boatswain'. Pensioners lived in wards divided into 'cabins' and ate a plentiful but monotonous diet not dissimilar from that served on warships. With their diverse origins, the pensioners reflected the national and international composition of Britain's maritime manpower, while their wounds and illnesses corresponded to the rigours of life at sea. Most entrants were old by the standards of serving sailors, but young men were also admitted, particularly if wounds or illness had made them unsuitable for further service or civilian employment.

The frequent Anglo-French wars of the long eighteenth century (1688–1815) brought significant expansion in fits and starts as resources became available and demand for places grew. From 1763 'out-pensions' were offered in the form of cash payments to non-resident veteran sailors, and these proved especially popular for men with families. The hospital reached its peak after the end of the Napoleonic Wars with approximately 2,800 resident 'in-pensioners'. A long decline followed, slow at first but accelerating through the 1850s, until there were 900 vacancies in 1857,[7] as most men opted for out-pensions rather than resident in-pensions. After an extensive Royal Commission in 1860, no further in-pensioners were admitted after 1865.[8] In 1869, the last remaining in-pensioners left and Greenwich Hospital's tenure as a residential charity ended after 164 years.

With its imposing buildings designed by Sir Christopher Wren, Sir John Vanbrugh, and Nicholas Hawksmoor, and its symbolic location on the banks of the Thames, where the imperial metropole met the world, Greenwich Hospital could not be called utilitarian. So grand was the hospital that, even while it was still under construction, Tsar Peter the Great of Russia, then visiting Britain on one of his fact-finding expeditions, advised King William III to turn St James' Palace over to the veteran sailors and instead take Greenwich for himself.[9] However, in this fine form there was also function. Greenwich Hospital was a declaration to the British people and to a world rich in rivals that Britain's destiny was wedded to control of the seas and the wealth that flowed across them. The apogee of this claim to naval exceptionalism, and a statement of national intent, was the magnificent Painted Hall, where the centrepiece of Sir James Thornhill's painted ceiling depicts William III and Queen Mary crushing King Louis XIV of France and his aspirations to universal monarchy underfoot. Envisioned as the pensioners' dining room, on completion the hall was considered too grand for this quotidian purpose. From 1824 it served as a public gallery to display a growing collection of paintings of sea battles and naval heroes. With Greenwich Hospital performing the role of a naval pantheon, the pensioners themselves played an important part in this civil religion as the living link to naval glory. As such, Greenwich Hospital was simultaneously a symbol of British identity, a tool of national policy, and, primarily, a welfare institution.

To date, histories of Greenwich Hospital have done little to reflect this complexity of purpose. Several works offer a good account of the development of Greenwich Hospital,

---

7   Newell, *Greenwich Hospital*, pp.174–178.
8   Anon., *Report of the Commissioners appointed to inquire into Greenwich Hospital with the Minutes of Evidence and Appendix* (London: George E. Eyre and William Spottiswoode for HM's Stationary Office, 1860).
9   Newell, *Greenwich Hospital*, p.18.

successive stages of building work, and the arrival and departure of hospital governors and other notable individuals, but the lives of the Greenwich pensioners themselves have garnered little attention.[10] This chapter seeks to address this omission. The use of a quantitative methodology allows the identification of the overall contours and trends of the Greenwich Hospital population and the periodisation of the hospital's operation according to changing characteristics of its residents. Far from being the opposite of a microhistorical approach, quantification facilitates the discovery of notable individuals (whether for diverging from general patterns or typifying them) who might otherwise remain entirely absent from the fabric of history. In this respect, the quantitative work reported here forms only the first stage of a multifaceted procedure and serves as a discovery process to establish overarching trends and uncover the most promising avenues for further study, including the use of more qualitative and personal sources.[11] The further addition of visual sources demonstrates the diversity of the Greenwich Hospital archive and the desirability of a hybrid approach. It is to these visual sources that this chapter will turn first.

Greenwich Pensioners in Visual Imagery

With their distinctive appearance and evocative life stories, Greenwich pensioners proved attractive subjects for generations of artists. Consequently, it is no surprise that the portrayal of Greenwich pensioners in visual imagery has a history of its own. It is a history characterised by a transition from an irreverent and light-hearted exhibition of alcohol-fuelled japes to a more sombre and respectful tone with a contemplative, even pensive nature. It is also a history that reflected the changing anxieties of British culture. Through the analysis of a series of examples, drawn from the collections of the National Maritime Museum, Greenwich,[12] this section charts the evolution of the public perceptions of Greenwich pensioners as derived from visual sources.

When looking through images of Greenwich pensioners created in the late eighteenth and the first half of the nineteenth century, it does not take long to identify prominent recurring tropes. The first of these is the strikingly traditional uniform of the Greenwich pensioners consisting of a large blue coat and a black cocked hat.[13] Although the uniform

---

10   See for example, Newell, *Greenwich Hospital*; Pieter van der Merwe, *A Refuge for All, A Short History of Greenwich Hospital* (London: Published by Greenwich Hospital, 2010); C.M. Dawson, *The Story of Greenwich: Palace, Hospital, College* (London: Privately Published, 1977).

11   Promising sources in this respect include Greenwich Hospital Council Minutes, found in TNA ADM67, which functioned as disciplinary records and so include narrative details referring to individual pensioners; and a volume of handwritten poems by Greenwich pensioner, George Hewens, held in the Caird Library of the National Maritime Museum (NMM), see George Hewens, Greenwich Pensioners, Poems on various subjects, NMM LIT/6.

12   The National Maritime Museum holds an extensive collection of images and material culture relating to Greenwich pensioners including the only known surviving examples of Greenwich Hospital uniforms. Greenwich Hospital uniform: pattern 1860, NMM UNI0386 and UNI0387.

13   Today these hats would be called 'tricorne hats', although that term was not current until the mid-nineteenth century.

Figure 1. 'The Greenwich Pensioner Written and composed by Mr Dibdin, for his Entertainment called The Oddities', Caricature by Isaac Cruikshank and S.W. Fores, 25 June 1791. (National Maritime Museum, with permission)

was not entirely unchanging, it was self-consciously old-fashioned,[14] and this tradition continues today with the Chelsea pensioners (army veterans), who continue to wear a red coat and black cocked hat. The second recurring motif is amputation, with a wooden leg, empty sleeve, or both, appearing almost as much a part of the Greenwich pensioner's uniform as the famous blue coat. Double, triple, and occasionally even quadruple amputations are found among the images of Greenwich pensioners. Thirdly, almost ubiquitous in visual portrayals of Greenwich pensioners (and sailors more generally) from this period is the presence or influence of alcohol, which frequently acts as a facilitator of the pensioners' activities. While some of these are physical and boisterous in nature, there is often an underlying strand, the final of our recurring tropes, which is reminiscing, usually fondly, about past service and particularly battles. Throughout this imagery, the tone is generally celebratory and nostalgic. Several examples of images of Greenwich pensioners will now be presented and described in turn. They are then analysed collectively to draw out their common elements, suggest the rationale behind them, and demonstrate the relevance of these sources to wider historical debates.

---

14   See the poems *My Old Cocked Hat* and *The Defunct*, by pensioner, George Hewens. George Hewens, Greenwich Pensioners, Poems on various subjects, NMM LIT/6.

Figure 1 contains all of the elements highlighted above. Created in 1791, this image was made after the French Revolution and some 18 months before the start of almost a quarter of a century of war, but it is a peacetime image. This caricature shows the interior of a tavern with five Greenwich pensioners present in their blue uniforms. In the foreground, one pensioner with a wooden leg and a tankard almost overflowing with beer sings a cheerful song while his friend, who is missing both arms, drinks beer with the help of a maid. The song reminisces sentimentally about the man's time at sea where many dangers were overcome in good spirits. Although in 'the horrors of the fight' his 'precious limb was lopped off', he nevertheless 'went to sea again'. He ends by praising the King by whose beneficence, through Greenwich Hospital, he is able to safely 'lie in Greenwich tier'. Behind him a Greenwich pensioner smokes and seems to doze, while two others pore over a map refighting one of their old battles in the retelling. All five Greenwich pensioners are red faced, while the three in the background are stocky and thick-set: signs of comparative wealth and comfort that would soon be made famous by James Gillray's images contrasting the roast beef and ale of John Bull with the 'soup meagre' of revolutionary France.[15]

While sharing common elements with Figure 1, the scene depicted in Figure 2 is much more raucous. Here 10 Greenwich pensioners, some able bodied, others missing one or more limbs or eyes, riotously commemorate Admiral Nelson's great victory at the Battle of the Nile, while showing little regard for the furniture or decorations. The proprietor looks on, happily more amused than concerned. Alcohol has clearly played a part in the festivities, with goblets and tankards galore, and one of the latter overturned and spilling its contents over the table. As if to emphasise the point, one of the pensioners, sat at the base of the clock, wears the canary yellow punishment coat, usually used to shame men for drunkenness.[16] An almost ghostly portrait of Nelson surveys the scene from the top right corner wearing an expression that it is difficult to read. This print appears to be an homage to William Hogarth's image, *A Midnight Modern Conversation* (1733), which also shows 11 men drinking heavily around a table in similar circumstances.[17]

Finally, Figure 3 shows Greenwich pensioners and two serving sailors playing a game in Greenwich Park. One of them is suspended by a rope from a tree and swings on his wooden 'pins' trying to mark one of his friends with chalk while they haze him with handkerchiefs. The central figure has two wooden legs and several of the other men are missing limbs and an eye. Intriguingly, the man on the left appears to be able-bodied but has his right leg pinned behind him and so sports a wooden leg of his own. The same man's dark and presumably red nose offers the only suggestion of alcohol, which is otherwise absent from this image. Although this picture is dated to circa 1835, it was used to illustrate Matthew Henry Barker's

15   See James Gillray, *French Liberty. British Slavery*, satirical print, British Museum 1868,0808.6253. For a discussion of the portrayal of sailors in caricatures of this period, see James Davey and Richard Johns, *Broadsides, Caricature and the Navy 1756–1815* (Barnsley: Seaforth Publishing in association with the National Maritime Museum, 2012).

16   A note in the Digest of Minutes of the Commissioners of Greenwich Hospital dated 21 April 1715 reads 'Yellow coats ordered for Men under punishment', see TNA ADM67/266. For a painting showing a Greenwich pensioner in the yellow punishment coat see 'Pensioners outside the chapel at Greenwich', NMM BHC1816.

17   See The Metropolitan Museum of Art, New York, USA, 91.1.77, etching by William Hogarth, 1733.

Figure 2. 'The Battle of the Nile', Caricature by George Cruikshank, 1 July 1825. (National Maritime Museum, with permission)

'Nights at Sea; or Sketches of Naval Life During the War', so could be understood to refer back to events that took place during the French Revolutionary and Napoleonic Wars.

These recurring tropes in the presentation of Greenwich pensioners speak directly to several historical debates. Firstly, the bacchanalian portrayal of these men is comparable to the trend identified by Isaac Land whereby sailors were generally presented as noble heroes as long as they were far away but as potentially dangerous and disruptive 'fish out of water' when imposed on civil society on land.[18] There sailors were easily identifiable by their clothing, language, and rolling gait. They were frequently perceived as an unsettling and volatile presence, prone to drunkenness, violence, and disorder.[19] Contemporary caricatures, such as Thomas Rowlandson's 'Portsmouth Point', showed sailors in port drinking, singing, dancing, fighting, and cavorting with prostitutes, with the whole panorama playing out between a tavern and a money lender.[20] Sailors also made their presence strongly felt in many of the most prominent riots and protests to

---

18   Isaac Land, *War, Nationalism, and the British Sailor, 1750–1850* (New York: Palgrave Macmillan, 2009), pp.41, 48–51, 78–88.

19   Catriona Kennedy, *Narratives of the Revolutionary and Napoleonic Wars, Military and Civilian Experiences in Britain and Ireland* (Basingstoke: Palgrave Macmillan, 2013), p.49.

20   See Davey and Johns, *Broadsides, Caricature and the Navy 1756–1815*, p.39.

Figure 3. 'Sling the Monkey', Caricature by George Cruikshank, c.1835. (National Maritime Museum, with permission)

strike eighteenth-century Britain.[21] Tellingly, the term 'strike' for a work stoppage during a labour dispute originates from the act of sailors striking the sails to immobilise their ships while demanding higher pay.[22] The portrayal of Greenwich pensioners in Figures 1–3 shares several of these tropes and this continuity between serving and veteran sailors speaks to the strong occupational identity that Greenwich pensioners were believed to embody. As we will see, the perceptions of sailors and Greenwich pensioners underwent a sea-change during the nineteenth century.

The casual and at times even flippant portrayal of amputation and other war wounds across these images can be interpreted as serving several purposes.[23] Firstly, the presence of these serious and visibly obvious wounds could act as a form of useful shorthand demonstrating that these men were part of the 'deserving poor'. The late eighteenth and early nineteenth centuries were a period of intense concern about welfare provision. This anxiety was informed by a range of factors including the social unrest of the French Revolution, high wartime prices and food riots in Britain during the 1790s, the unexpectedly high rate of population growth revealed by the first three censuses between 1801 and 1821, and the increasing influence of laissez-faire Smithian economics.[24] Perhaps the most famous expression of this thinking was Thomas Malthus' *Essay on the Principle of Population*, published in 1798.[25] Such demographic fears found reflection in the reform of the poor laws in 1834, which sought to replace parish-based 'out relief' with residential welfare centred on workhouses.[26] The identity of 'Greenwich pensioner' was a complex one in societal terms because, on the one hand, these men were considered heroic due to their naval service, but they were also now dependent on welfare or, to put it bluntly, charity cases. In this sense, the instantly recognisable uniform of the Greenwich pensioners could be simultaneously what sociologist Erving Goffman called a 'prestige symbol' and a 'stigma symbol', as it carried both

---

21   George Rudé, *The Crowd in History, A Study of Popular Disturbances in France and England, 1730–1848* (London: Serif, 2005), p.69; Niklas Frykman, *The Bloody Flag, Mutiny in the Age of Atlantic Revolution* (Oakland California: University of California Press, 2020), pp.6–7.

22   Markus Rediker, *Between the Devil and the Deep Blue Sea, Merchant Seamen, Pirates, and the Anglo-American Maritime World, 1700–1750* (Cambridge: Cambridge University Press, 1987), p.205.

23   An exception to this trend can be seen in C.J. Grant's 1834 caricature 'The Way of the World', which shows a Greenwich Pensioner who has lost all four limbs, his nose, and an eye bemoaning his lot to a friend who is 'only' missing an arm and a leg. This seems to present a much darker view of amputation, although it is possible that the improbable severity of the man's injuries, and his friend's response that 'grumble, grumble. You are like the rest of th' World. Never contented', is meant to make this a humorous, farcical image. NMM PAH3318.

24   E.A. Wrigley, 'British population during the "long" eighteenth century, 1680–1840' in Roderick Floud and Paul Johnson (eds), *The Cambridge Economic History of Modern Britain, vol.I, Industrialisation, 1700–1860* (Cambridge: Cambridge University Press, 2004); E.A. Wrigley and R.S. Schofield, *The Population History of England 1541–1871 A Reconstruction* (London: Edward Arnold, 1981), pp.122–126.

25   Thomas Malthus, *An Essay on the Principle of Population* (Oxford: Oxford University Press, 2008).

26   *An Act for the Amendment and Better Administration of the Laws relating to the Poor in England and Wales* (1834). See Boyd Hilton, *A Mad, Bad, & Dangerous People? England 1783–1846* (Oxford: Oxford University Press, 2011), pp.588–600. For a discussion of the perception among some workers that this represented part of a wider class conflict, see the chapter 'Rethinking Chartism' in Gareth Stedman Jones, *Languages of Class: Studies in English Working Class History 1832–1982* (Cambridge: Cambridge University Press, 1984).

positive and negative connotations.[27] In that period, with its concern about the growing cost of welfare provision, the portrayal of visible wounds, and especially amputated limbs, could act to simplify the identity of Greenwich pensioners and present them as deserving objects of charity by conveying at a glance both their sacrifices for their country and their likely (justifiable) inability to provide for themselves or their families through their own labour.

A second interpretation of the portrayal of amputation among Greenwich pensioners can be found in the work of David Turner. Turner argues that such images served to 'disarm the horrors of war' and so sterilise and downplay the risks of military service, while cele-brating the courage of wounded servicemen.[28] He has also identified the importance to mili-tary masculinity of reacting to injury with cheerfulness as seen, for example, in Figure 1 above.[29] It is clear from the images discussed previously that the physical disabilities of the Greenwich pensioners are portrayed as presenting no obstacle to their having the time of their lives, including physical pursuits like drunkenly climbing on tavern tables or 'singing the monkey' in Greenwich Park. In this way, the risks of naval service are trivialised, thereby incentivising men to join the navy. As it transpired, by the time Figures 2 and 3 were produced there would not be another conflict requiring large-scale naval mobilisation until 1914, by which time the required skillset of naval sailors had been utterly transformed, but that is clear only with the benefit of hindsight. The period from 1815 to 1840 was not devoid of crises or war scares where a rapid manning of Britain's wooden warships might have become necessary.[30]

This theme of encouraging naval service connects Greenwich Hospital to historical debates regarding the overarching purpose of welfare provision in eighteenth-century Britain. Joanna Innes and Helen Berry have argued that welfare policies were intended to increase Britain's preparedness for the next bout of warfare,[31] but at first glance this appears inapplicable to Greenwich Hospital as, with few exceptions, its residents were no longer fit for active service. Nonetheless, these views are easily reconciled. Greenwich Hospital's founding charter made clear that the purpose of the institution was both 'the relief and support' of veteran sailors and 'for the encouragement of seaman'.[32] Admiral Sir George Rodney, governor of the hospital from 1765 to 1770, made the connection explicit when he asked 'Who would not be a sailor to live as happy as a prince in his old age?'[33] As such, Greenwich Hospital served the state's purpose of incentivising naval service at one remove: by reassuring men that, after their service, they would be cared for by their grateful country.

---

27   Erving Goffman, *Stigma, Notes on the Management of Spoiled Identity* (London: Penguin, 1990), p.59.

28   David Turner, 'Picturing Disability in Eighteenth-Century England' in Michael Rembis, Catherine Kudlick, and Kim E. Nielsen (eds), *The Oxford Handbook of Disability History* (Oxford: Oxford University Press, 2018), pp.336–339.

29   David Turner, 'Disability history and the history of emotions: reflections on eighteenth century Britain', *Asclepio*, vol.68 (2016), pp.146–158.

30   Hilton, *A Mad, Bad, & Dangerous People?*, pp.289–295, 558–565.

31   Joanna Innes, *Inferior Politics, Social Problems and Social Policies in Eighteenth-Century Britain* (Oxford: Oxford University Press, 2009), pp.3–5, 28–31; Helen Berry, *Orphans of Empire: The Fate of London's Foundlings* (Oxford: Oxford University Press, 2019), pp.6–15, 257–259.

32   Quoted in 'His Majesty's commission for the Royal Hospital for Seamen at Greenwich' (1761), NMM 22671-1001, pp.18–20.

33   Newell, *Greenwich Hospital*, p.88.

This sentiment was reinforced in writing and in images like Figure 1, where the Greenwich pensioner sings the praises of the King for keeping him safe and happy.

As we have seen, the portrayal of Greenwich pensioners in popular imagery across the late eighteenth and early nineteenth centuries was charged with layers of meaning and reflected contemporary social anxieties and state priorities. The same was true of images of Greenwich pensioners from the second half of the nineteenth century onwards, although the context and the illustrations themselves were very different.

After about 1840 the presentation of Greenwich pensioners in images contrasts sharply with what came before. Some of the previous recurring themes remain and are joined by new ones, but the main distinction is in the overall tone of the pictures. Out have gone the energy, the exuberance, and particularly the alcohol, of the older images and in their place is found a solemnity marked by a sentimental Romanticism and an awareness of the passage of time. The medium itself has changed, with the Greenwich pensioners no longer the subject of caricature but of paintings. In part this can be ascribed to the evolving zeitgeist of the Victorian era and the shifting expectations of naval masculinity identified by Joanne Begiato,[34] but it is argued here that changing British national anxieties and insecurities also played a role. Once again, three images that typify this transition will be presented and described in turn and then analysed together to address wider themes and debates.

In Figure 4, two solemn, elderly Greenwich pensioners stand pensively at Nelson's tomb in St Paul's Cathedral.[35] Both are ashen faced and one removes his hat reverentially. The nearer figure has an empty sleeve pinned to the front of his coat, just as Nelson did (although, in his case the right arm), while his companion stands on two wooden legs. The placement of the lantern just below the hero's name and the ethereal trail of smoke from the solitary candle below give this image a sacred, pseudo-religious feel. Two recurring themes remain as continuities from the earlier period: the unmistakable uniform of the Greenwich pensioners and the prominent portrayal of amputation, but they are joined by two new themes. First is the presence or strong association with the totemic embodiment of Britain's naval glory, Horatio Nelson. Second, evident in the advanced age of these men returning to pay their respects to their old commander, is a consciousness of the passage of time and a growing distance between the present and the titanic figures of old. In this respect, Nelson's tomb is presented in terms Pierre Nora would recognise as representing a 'realm' or 'site of memory',[36] and it can be argued that the Greenwich pensioners themselves constituted a living *lieu de memoire*. Poignantly, this image dates from 1868: just one year before the final closure of Greenwich Hospital as a residential charity, and at a point when its fate was already sealed. This further enhances awareness of the passage of time as the gulf separating the British people from the heroics of Nelson's day widened.

---

34   Joanne Begiato, *Manliness in Britain, 1760–1900 Bodies, emotion, and material culture* (Manchester: Manchester University Press, 2020).

35   Holger Hoock has argued that St Paul's Cathedral came to serve as a British military pantheon. See Holger Hoock, *Empires of the Imagination: Politics, War, and the Arts in the British World, 1750–1850* (London: Profile Books, 2010).

36   Pierre Nora (ed.), *Realms of Memory* (New York: Columbia University Press, 1996).

Figure 4. 'Greenwich Pensioners at the Tomb of Nelson', Print after the painting 'Pilgrims to St Paul's' by John Everett Millais, 1868. (National Maritime Museum, with permission)

Figure 5. 'Twas in Trafalgar's Bay', Unknown artist, print after George Fox's painting 'Tales of the Past', c.1882. (National Maritime Museum, with permission).

Figure 5 shows an elderly Greenwich pensioner with a wooden leg explaining J.M.W. Turner's painting the *Battle of Trafalgar* (1822–1824)[37] to a young boy dressed in a sailor suit. The tropes of amputation and the Greenwich pensioner's uniform are again clearly visible: the latter embellished in this case with the addition of some medals and a ship's spyglass placed under the cocked hat. Nelson is present by implication because, while not personally visible in Turner's painting, his choice of depicting the moment the foremast of the *Victory* fell has long been understood to be allegorical of Nelson's own death in the battle. As with Figure 4, the Greenwich pensioner's age emphasises the passage of time. This is further reinforced by the final trope to be identified in these later portrayals of Greenwich pensioners: the juxtaposition of the pensioners and children.[38] This image invokes past, present, and future and represents a 'changing of the guard'. The message conveyed is of the inheritance by one generation from another of the public trust and the intangible secrets of naval glory required to fulfil that trust. In essence it would be possible to compare this image to Turner's most famous painting the *Fighting Temeraire*, with the pensioner in the role of the creaking but majestic hulk and the child as the future-bearing steam tug.

Finally, and perhaps the simplest of these images, Figure 6 depicts a Greenwich pensioner standing in the Painted Hall, saluting a bust of Admiral Nelson, with details of Sir James Thornhill's wall paintings visible in the background. The pensioner stands with evident pride, while the marble pillar on which the bust is resting has been decorated with a laurel wreath and union flag. This image encapsulates the idea that the Greenwich pensioners offered a living link to Nelson and his contemporaries, and so were the last people able to provide personal insights into Britain's greatest epoch of naval achievement. By the time this image was created in 1904, Greenwich Hospital had been closed for 45 years and the long Victorian Age had followed the Napoleonic era into history.

If Figures 4 to 6 have one fundamental sentiment in common then it is nostalgia: nostalgia for the romanticised heroics of the age of sail. For the final two images this is joined by a further sentimentality for (the by then closed) Greenwich Hospital and its colourful occupants. Whereas the pre-1840 images reflected state priorities, and particularly the perennial naval manning problem, it is argued here that Figures 4 to 6 also mirror the societal anxieties of their own period. The fears involved in the prolonged existential struggle against Revolutionary and Napoleonic France, and which lingered for some time afterwards, need not be enumerated here,[39] but long periods of peace could bring insecurities of their own.

---

37   The painting was criticised by many naval men for its lack of historical accuracy, but it has remained a public favourite. See Eric Shanes, *Turner the Life and Masterworks* (London: Parkstone, 2004), pp.166–167.

38   Figure 5 is the only example of this intergenerational trope presented here, but other examples found in the collection of the National Maritime Museum include the print 'Greenwich Pensioner "Well, here was the French, and there was we"' (NMM PAI8796, 1843), which shows a Greenwich pensioner recounting a battle to two well-dressed young boys; and 'The Greenwich Pensioner' print (NMM PAH3306, 1845), which shows a Greenwich pensioner explaining the Battle of the Nile to a young boy in a sailor suit. John Burnet's c.1838 painting, 'Greenwich pensioners commemorating the anniversary of the Battle of the Trafalgar' also shows children listening attentively to Greenwich pensioners. The painting is part of the collection of the Dukes of Wellington at Apsley House, London, accession number WM.1556-1948.

39   Perhaps the most famous expression of these fears can be found in Edmund Burke, *Reflections on the*

Figure 6. 'Saluting the Admiral', Print after the painting by Albert Holden, 1905. (National Maritime Museum, with permission)

For often classically-educated Victorian elites, fears of the degrading impact of decadence, with comparisons to the fall of ancient empires, could be discomforting.[40] Across much of the second half of the nineteenth century, Britannia's hegemony at sea appeared relatively assured, but there were periods of concern. Perhaps most famously, when France launched the world's first ironclad oceangoing warship, *Gloire*, in 1859, Britain appeared suddenly vulnerable.[41] With each passing year the previous victories grew more and more distant. At the same time, the rate of change accelerated. Steam increasingly replaced sails and the celebrated wooden walls of Britain's warships made way for riveted iron.[42] Diplomatically, the industrialisation of the United States and the unification of Italy and Germany created new rivals.[43] An especially dangerous moment came with the end of the Second Boer War (1899–1902), just two years before Figure 6 was created, where Britain found itself diplomatically isolated and 40 percent of volunteer military recruits were rejected as unfit for service.[44] In this context it was perhaps natural to look back with nostalgia on past glories and the men who won them and wonder if the current generation could ever equal such feats of arms.

Against this context the Greenwich pensioners offered a proud and comforting subject for the British public, and this can explain the dramatic shift in how the pensioners were portrayed. They were no longer viewed as drunken and riotous hedonists, but as proletarian elder statesmen, living links to Nelson, and the custodians of the secrets of naval victory: secrets that they must pass on to the next generation if Britain was to retain its leading position among the nations. Isaac Land has identified a wider trend across the nineteenth century whereby nostalgia for the 'Jack Tars' of the vanishing age of sail meant that 'sailors had become respectable at last'.[45] Greenwich pensioners were especially well-placed to benefit from this trend due to their personal links to the victorious navy of yesteryear and their embodiment of tradition.

One area where this was particularly clear was in the uniform of the Greenwich pensioners. Amy Miller has shown that there was a great deal of soul-searching in the late-1820s when new uniform patterns were introduced for naval officers and some in society railed against any perceived deviation from the uniform of '...Duncan, Pellew, Collingwood, Nelson.'[46] As Miller makes clear, however, there had already been repeated bouts of variation in naval uniforms as officers updated their clothing in line with the latest civilian fashions, so that

Revolution in France (Oxford: Oxford University Press, 2009).

40   Duncan Bell has shown how Victorian Britons, concerned by the fall of classical empires, sought to present the British Empire in a different, more progressive light. See Duncan Bell, 'From Ancient to Modern in Victorian Imperial Thought' *The Historical Journal*, vol.49 (2006), pp.735–759.

41   Jesse A. Heitz, 'British Reaction to American Civil War Ironclads', *Vulcan*, vol.1 (2013), pp.56–69.

42   Heitz, 'British Reaction to American Civil War Ironclads', pp.56–69.

43   A.J.P. Taylor, *The Struggle for Mastery in Europe 1848–1918* (Oxford: Clarendon Press, 1957), especially chapters 6, 10, and 17; Richard J. Evans, *The Pursuit of Power, Europe 1815–1914* (London: Penguin Books, 2017), pp.246, 687, 698, 715; Robert Holland, *Blue Water Empire, The British in the Mediterranean since 1800* (London: Allen Lane, 2012), pp.27, 126–128, 163.

44   R.J. Clare, '"Fit to Fight?" How the Physical Condition of the Conscripts Contributed to the Manpower Crisis of 1917–18' *Journal of the Society for Army Historical Research*, vol.94 (2016), pp.225–244; see in particular p.227.

45   Land, *War, Nationalism, and the British Sailor, 1750–1850*, pp.158, 132–136, 148–157.

46   Amy Miller, *Dressed to Kill, British Naval Uniform, Masculinity and Contemporary Fashions, 1748–1857* (London: National Maritime Museum, 2021), pp.96–101.

the uniforms of the mid-1820s were already far removed from anything Nelson would have recognised. Even by 1810 officers' uniforms were notably different from those seen in 1793 when the war began.[47] In the case of the Greenwich pensioners, there was no practical need to update uniforms to reflect the changing requirements of active service and, due to the men's lower social standing, little demand to keep abreast of the latest fashions. Instead, the deliberate traditionalism of their appearance reinforced the social role of Greenwich pensioners as providing a reassuring living link to past glory.

There is evidence that the pensioners themselves were aware of the deliberately anachronistic nature of their uniforms and had mixed feelings about this. One pensioner, George Hewens, left a volume of hand-written poems dating from approximately 1852 to 1869. He dedicates two poems to one of the key elements of the Greenwich pensioner's uniform: the tricorne hat. Across these two poems, entitled *My Old Cocked Hat* and *The Defunct*, Hewens acknowledges that these hats were 'once a symbol of renown' but were by his day 'thou thing uncouth, so antiquated', so that 'oft the yokels flout and jeer' and 'the boys cry out "Old Goose."' Two couplets best summarise Hewens' feelings: 'In such an age thou first could'st stand, O badge of honour, noble, grand', but for his part 'Good riddance, though, my Old Cocked Hat! I never fancied thee – that's flat!'[48] Just as Miller argues for the uniforms of naval officers, the Greenwich Hospital uniform was subject to periodical changes, particularly those aimed at improving comfort or ergonomic issues for the residents, but these did not compromise the overall integrity of the deliberately anachronistic effect.[49] In fact, the most obvious single change (the replacement of stockings with trousers in 1835) was explicitly defended by then Governor, Sir Thomas Hardy, on the grounds that trousers were more customary for sailors.[50]

This desire to emphasise continuity, and especially links to naval victories, also extended to other elements of Greenwich Hospital's operations. For one thing, there appears to have been an element of 'collecting' about the institution's admissions policies, and the institution's public face. As far as it has been possible to establish, Trafalgar veterans and men who served directly under Horatio Nelson appear disproportionately among the hospital's population, or at least in imagery associated with the hospital.[51] State objectives correlated in this regard, with ramifications for how the Greenwich pensioners were 'deployed' in public. Just as the Chelsea pensioners are included in certain state occasions today, the Greenwich pensioners found a place in state ceremonial. On 24 June 1857 Greenwich Hospital received a letter from the Admiralty informing them that 50 pensioners were required 'to attend

---

47   Miller, *Dressed to Kill*, pp.100, 88–95.

48   George Hewens, Greenwich Pensioners, Poems on various subjects, NMM LIT/6.

49   Digest of Minutes of the Commissioners of Greenwich Hospital TNA ADM67/266–67. Changes include altering the kinds of cloth used, replacing the buttons used, and introducing greatcoats.

50   Digest of Minutes of the Commissioners of Greenwich Hospital TNA ADM67/267. A note dated 9 April 1835 reads 'Trowsers substituted for breeches'. See also Newell, *Greenwich Hospital*, p.153.

51   The collections of the National Maritime Museum hold a set of paintings of named individual Greenwich pensioners created in 1832 as studies for John Burnet's painting *The Greenwich Pensioners Commemorating Trafalgar*, which can be seen in the collection of the Duke of Wellington in Apsley House. Men with a connection to Nelson appear to have been prioritised for inclusion including three who served in *Victory* at Trafalgar and Thomas Allen, who had spent a time as Nelson's personal attendant. See NMM BHC2510; BHC3092; BHC2856; and BHC2579.

in Hyde Park at the distribution of the Victoria Cross. Expenses to be paid'.[52] This ceremony occurred two days later with 50 Greenwich and 50 Chelsea pensioners in attendance. Their presence at this, the first ever conferral of the Victoria Cross, was hugely symbolic as these veterans in their traditional uniforms appeared to represent continuity between past, present, and future heroism in such a way as to reassure and encourage the nation. This public parade of Greenwich pensioners was selective. Two years later, a request by the hospital governor for funds to hire a steamer to take pensioners to view Isambard Kingdom Brunel's *Great Eastern* being built on the Isle of Dogs was refused,[53] as was an 1862 request for funds to take pensioners to view the International Exhibition.[54] It appears clear that one role of the Greenwich pensioners was to ease social anxieties about Britain's military strength by presenting a tangible living link to past victories. By embodying the martial virtues of a bygone age, they seemed to promise future success. In these tasks the pensioners' deliberately traditional uniform and the reinvention of their popular portrayal in visual imagery around 1840 both played a pivotal part. As the aims and concerns of the British state and nation evolved over time, so too did the image of the Greenwich pensioners. The final section now turns from artistic portrayal to demographic reality.

Characteristics of the Greenwich Hospital Population

The Greenwich Hospital admission records are exciting in their breadth of detail but daunting in their scale. Perhaps for this reason, there have been few attempts to use these records to chart the demographic contours of the hospital population. The most successful such work is Martin Wilcox's study of resident Greenwich pensioners between 1705 and 1763.[55] Wilcox created a database containing all of the information contained in the admission records about each of the men admitted to Greenwich Hospital during its first 58 years of operation. The end date of 1763 was chosen as marking the end of the first phase of the institution, with that year witnessing significant expansion relating to demobilisation at the end of the Seven Years War and the introduction of non-resident 'out-pensions'. Wilcox's database contains all 8,112 admissions to Greenwich Hospital up to the end of 1763. Of these, full biographical information is available for 3,316 men, who were admitted after 1749.[56] Taking the period 1705 to 1763 as a whole, Wilcox concluded that a typical Greenwich pensioner likely 'came from a poor background', often from the maritime counties of England, the city of London, or the Celtic fringe; generally went to sea at a young age; was 'at considerable risk of injury and disablement'; and was 'more likely than average to be unmarried and childless' at the

---

52   Digest of Minutes of the Commissioners of Greenwich Hospital TNA ADM67/267, note of letter dated 24 June 1857.

53   Digest of Minutes of the Commissioners of Greenwich Hospital TNA ADM67/267, note of letter dated 25 August 1859.

54   Digest of Minutes of the Commissioners of Greenwich Hospital TNA ADM67/267, note of letter dated 25 September 1862.

55   Martin Wilcox, 'The "Poor Decayed Seamen" of Greenwich Hospital, 1705–1763', *International Journal of Maritime History*, vol.25 (2013), pp.65–90.

56   Wilcox, 'The "Poor Decayed Seamen"', p.66.

end of his career.[57] By presenting a range of information from country and region of origin to occupational background and length of naval service, Wilcox provides an unrivalled portrait of the Greenwich Hospital population in its first six decades, with implications for our understanding of Britain's wider maritime labour force.

Whereas Wilcox's work offers a valuable snapshot of the salient features of the population of Greenwich pensioners in the 1750s, this chapter investigates the changes to those features over time. In large part, this reflects our periodisation, as the years 1764 to 1869 witnessed far greater change, including the 'classical' era of the industrial revolution with all of the urbanisation, industrialisation, rapid population growth, and myriad other socio-economic dislocations that this entailed.[58] It was also in this period that Britain's welfare system was overhauled, with the 'Old Poor Law' characterised by parish-based 'outdoor relief' increasingly replaced by 'indoor relief' centred on the workhouse.[59] The reforms of 1834 were long viewed as the key pivot-point in this process, although any impression of a rapid or universal shift in practice has since been heavily challenged from multiple angles.[60]

The findings presented in the remainder of this chapter build directly on the work of Wilcox, with the eventual aim of creating a complete and comprehensive database of all resident Greenwich pensioners.[61] To date, this work rests on a quinquennial study of the remaining 102 years between 1764 and the final admissions to the hospital in 1865. Beginning with 1764, 1769, 1774, and continuing in that fashion until 1864, the present author has extended Wilcox's database by inputting the information on all admissions for every fifth year found in the three sets of admissions books.[62] This has resulted in the addition of a further 6,045 admissions, including readmissions. As will be seen, one of the three sets of admission books ceased to be kept between 1844 and 1849, while in 1864 only one admission book remained, and even that gave little information. Consequently, this chapter is able to present data on some of the features of the Greenwich Hospital population up to 1859 but others only as far as 1844.[63]

It is conceded that, by their incomplete nature, the data and conclusions offered here are necessarily preliminary. It is possible that, once the information from the remaining four-fifths of years is added, different patterns will emerge, or those that are observed will

---

57   Wilcox, 'The "Poor Decayed Seamen"', p.90.

58   For the scale of this dislocation see Roderick Floud, Jane Humphries, and Paul Johnson (eds), *The Cambridge Economic History of Modern Britain vol.I 1700–1870* (Cambridge: Cambridge University Press, 2014 edition), especially chapter two, 'Occupational structure and population change' by Leigh Shaw-Taylor and E.A. Wrigley.

59   Hilton, *A Mad, Bad, & Dangerous People?*, pp.588–600.

60   See for example, Megan Evans and Peter Jones, '"A Stubborn, Intractable Body": Resistance to the Workhouse in Wales, 1834–1877', *Family & Community History*, vol.17 (2014), pp.101–121; Kim Lawes, *Paternalism and Politics, The Revival of Paternalism in Early Nineteenth-Century Britain* (Basingstoke: Macmillan Press, 2000); Nadja Durbach, 'Roast Beef, the New Poor Law, and the British Nation, 1834–63', *Journal of British Studies*, vol.52 (2013), pp.963–989.

61   This completed database is under contract to be published by the List and Index Society in the form of a book joint-authored with Martin Wilcox.

62   General entry books 1704–1846 (TNA ADM73/36–41); Rough Entry Books 1704–1863 (TNA ADM73/51–64); Entry Books 1764–1865 (TNA ADM73/65–69).

63   By 1864 only the Entry Book (TNA ADM73/69) remains available. Between 1849 and 1859 only the Rough Entry Book (TNA ADM73/61–62) and Entry Book (TNA ADM73/69) are available.

be marked with greater certainty. Nevertheless, the provisional dataset is believed to offer a sufficiently robust basis for initial analysis due to the large sample size, the even distribution of years studied between 1764 and 1864, and their inclusion of a range of years of peace, war, mobilisation, and demobilisation. The remaining years yet to be studied could vary markedly from those analysed to date, but there appears to be no *a priori* reason to assume why they would. What follows does not seek to convey all of the information that can be gleaned from the admissions records. Fields such as occupational background and height, which have significant ramifications for debates regarding occupational fluctuations and standards of living during the industrial revolution, are omitted, while place of birth is given on a country rather than regional level. Similarly, factors like number of children and place of last residence are not included here, but offer much potential for future study.

Crucially, the presence of data for one year in five sets limitations that must be acknowledged. In the figures and tables shown below, the year listed is the year of admission, not necessarily the year of a particular event. For example, when considering the manner of discharge from Greenwich Hospital, the data for 1824 shows the proportion of men admitted in 1824 whose time there eventually ended in death, desertion, expulsion etc., *not* the proportion of discharges by each form that took place in 1824 itself. A small proportion of the men admitted in 1824 were discharged that same year (43 out of 345), but for the others their date of discharge ranged over the next 30 years, with the last, James Manjoy, dying on 29 September 1852 after a residence of 28 years and seven months.[64] The current data can be broken down to show, for example, the number of desertions per year, but conclusions could not be drawn from this because, with only one fifth of admissions present in the database, the relationship between the number of desertions currently found in the database for a given year would range to a wild and unpredictable extent from the true picture. Whereas the manner of discharge among the men admitted in 1824 is known for all but one of them, the total number of desertions that took place in 1824 cannot be known until the database contains a complete record of every previous year. While the information based on year of admission is highly valuable in its own right, it is not yet possible to seek to draw causation by, for example, linking an increase in desertions to a change in hospital conditions, such as a decline in food quality or increase in the severity of discipline. Once the database is completed, these questions can be addressed more satisfactorily.

From this quinquennial survey, and the 6,045 admissions that it captures, several arguments are presented here. The first concerns the changing preferences of Britain's veteran sailors and the impact of these on their relationship with Greenwich Hospital. Previous histories of this institution have suggested that introduction of out-pensions from 1763 led to a gradual substitution where fewer men entered the hospital, preferring to take up the out-pension instead.[65] It is argued here that the situation was more nuanced with men using both Greenwich Hospital's residential and non-residential welfare options in a complementary fashion by delaying admission until later in life when medical and other care requirements were likely to be greater. This represents a higher degree of flexibility between veteran sailors and this institution than has heretofore been recognised. Furthermore, this chapter

---

64   Greenwich Hospital General Entry Book 1813–1846, TNA ADM73/40.
65   van der Merwe, *A Refuge for All*, p.16.

contends that the wound profile of the resident Greenwich pensioners was far removed from that presented to the public in the popular imagery analysed in the previous section. These findings mark out Greenwich Hospital as an excellent case study for considering the limitations of traditional views of the changing rationale and practice of British welfare provision in this period and the place of 1834 as a landmark in that process. They also offer useful hypotheses to be tested and retested as the database of resident Greenwich pensioners is expanded towards completion. Several key features of the Greenwich Hospital population will now be discussed in turn through the analysis of a series of tables and figures with particular reference to change over time.

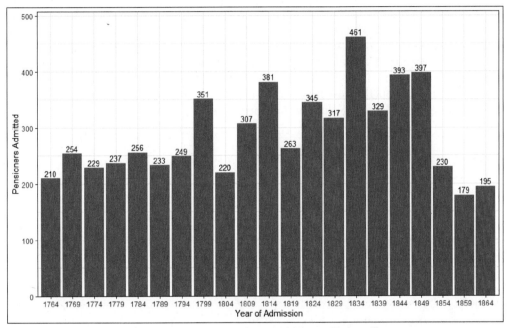

Figure 7. Admissions to Greenwich Hospital by year.[66]

Figure 7 shows at a glance the profile of admissions to Greenwich Hospital for every fifth year between 1764 and 1864. The rate of admission held relatively steady across the second half of the eighteenth century, although several war years, such as 1799, 1809, and 1814 are notably higher. In the case of 1814 the increased rate of admission could be related to demobilisation after the first defeat and exile of Napoleon, although it is interesting to note that 1784 shows a less dramatic increase that could be ascribed to demobilisation after the 1783 Treaty of Paris. Considering the central place that the reforms of 1834 have traditionally held in British welfare history, it is intriguing to note that 1834 saw the highest number of admissions from this sample by a sizable margin (55). This raises the question of whether the

66   Greenwich Hospital General Entry Books 1704–1846, TNA ADM73/36–41.

reforms, particularly the replacement of outdoor with indoor relief,[67] led to a rush of men seeking admission to Greenwich Hospital to ensure they avoided the workhouse. Regarding the traditional view that the provision of the out-pension from 1763 led to a gradual decline in the number of men who chose to become resident in-pensioners, it is perhaps surprising how late the drop in admissions is observed. It is only in 1854, after maintaining an unusually high rate for the previous two years of observation, that a significant drop in admissions is evident. Even then, this drop merely returned admissions to a rate that had been the norm across the whole of the second half of the eighteenth century. There was then a further fall in admissions of just over 20 percent in 1859, but then a slight rally in 1864, at a rate of admission just 15 men fewer than in 1764. Although there is a sharp contrast between the peak years of admission (1824 to 1849) and the last years for which data are here available, it is striking that admissions in these final years (1854 to 1864) were not dramatically different to those sustained across the half-century from 1764. To an extent, taken in isolation, this even brings into question the justifications presented for closing Greenwich Hospital as a residential institution. However, Figures 8 to 10 and Table 1 provide further information that allows us to reconcile these higher than expected admission figures to the unsustainability of Greenwich Hospital's long-term continuation.

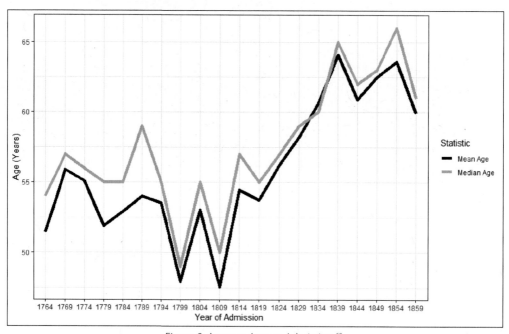

Figure 8. Average Age on Admission.[68]

---

67   As noted above, the scale and uniformity of this change have been repeatedly challenged and qualified.
68   Greenwich Hospital Rough Entry Books 1704–1863, TNA ADM73/51–64; Greenwich Hospital Entry Books 1764–1865, TNA ADM73/65–69.

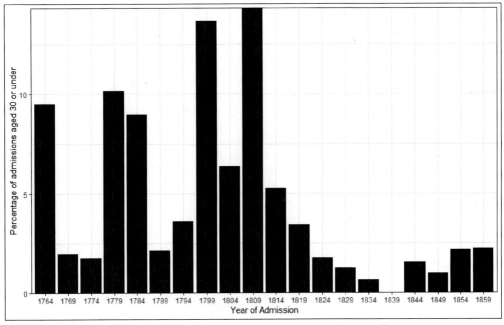

Figure 9. Proportion of Admissions Aged 30 or Younger.[69]

Please note that the tables that follow are expressed as a percentage of admissions in each year. Consequently, where the sum of the data for a given year is less than 100, the shortfall represents individuals for whom the information was not stated, not known, or, in rare cases, illegible.

Table 1: Proportion (%) of Admissions by Duration of Residence in Greenwich Hospital

Year Admitted	< 1 M	1–6 M	7 M–2 Y	2Y1M–10Y	10Y1M–20Y	>20Y
1764	1.90	10.95	12.86	35.71	23.81	13.81
1769	1.57	7.09	16.54	39.76	27.56	7.48
1774	0.44	5.68	12.66	43.67	24.89	12.66
1779	0.42	10.97	12.24	40.08	26.16	9.70
1784	2.34	6.25	8.59	42.97	25.00	14.45
1789	0	5.58	12.88	34.33	32.62	14.59
1794	1.61	6.43	16.06	38.15	24.50	13.25
1799	1.99	11.68	13.39	37.32	19.66	15.67
1804	2.73	10.45	16.82	38.18	21.36	10.45
1809	3.58	13.03	17.92	35.18	18.24	12.05
1814	6.04	9.19	15.75	35.43	22.31	11.02

---

69   Greenwich Hospital Rough Entry Books 1704–1863, TNA ADM73/51–64; Greenwich Hospital Entry Books 1764–1865, TNA ADM73/65–69.

Year Admitted	< 1 M	1–6 M	7 M–2 Y	2Y1M–10Y	10Y1M–20Y	>20Y
1819	4.18	10.27	17.11	40.30	19.01	7.98
1824	2.03	12.75	10.14	39.71	22.32	5.80
1829	0.63	11.67	17.67	46.37	17.67	4.73
1834	1.74	4.77	25.81	40.35	23.64	3.90
1839	3.04	7.29	19.76	45.59	19.15	3.34
1844	1.27	7.12	26.97	40.46	17.56	0.25

(Y= Years, M= Months)

Source: Greenwich Hospital General Entry Books 1704–1846, TNA ADM73/36–41.

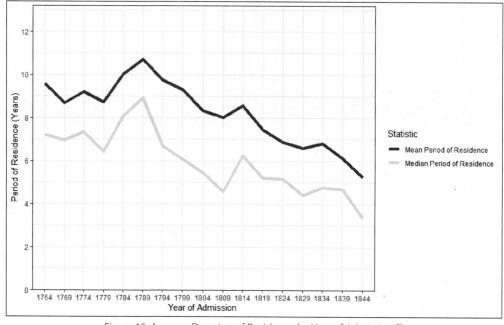

Figure 10. Average Duration of Residence by Year of Admission.[70]

It is possible to argue that, more than simply the decline in admissions after 1849, the main factor that made the continued residential operation of Greenwich Hospital unsustainable was the changing age profile of the men admitted. Figures 8 and 9 are highly telling on this point. In both cases, a clear trend is visible. Periods of warfare had the effect of reducing the average age of men admitted, with a higher proportion of admissions aged 30 or younger. This is associated with younger men falling victim to illness or injury during wartime and then becoming Greenwich pensioners. Figure 8 shows a drop in average age of admissions in 1764, in the immediate aftermath of the Seven Years War; in 1779 and 1784 during and just after the American War of Independence; and during the French Revolutionary and

---

70   Greenwich Hospital General Entry Books 1704–1846, TNA ADM73/36–41.

Napoleonic Wars in 1799 and 1809. Correspondingly, as shown in Figure 9, these same years saw an increase in the proportion of admissions aged 30 or younger. After 1815 the smaller size of the navy and increasing time distance from large-scale warfare resulted in a marked increase in the average age of admissions, while the proportion of admissions aged 30 or younger fell and, after 1819, remained below 2.5 percent. By the 1840s the average age at admission was in the region of a full decade older than it had been in the 1760s and 1770s.

As Table 1 and Figure 10 demonstrate, this increasing age of the men being admitted to Greenwich Hospital had a predictable impact in reducing the average period of residence in Greenwich Hospital by approximately four years between 1764 and 1844. When compared to the peak year of 1799, the average tenure at the hospital fell by almost six years across the following 45 years. Table 1 suggests that, in terms of population distribution by tenure of residence, there was a pronounced decline in those residing at the hospital for over 20 years and one month (until none of the 1844 admissions achieved this tenure), and a marked increase in the proportion of men who resided at the hospital for between seven months and two years. The other categories of period of residence appear to have remained relatively consistent in their share of admissions.

One must be conscious that data on duration of residence could naturally be skewed downwards because later admission dates, coupled with the closure of Greenwich Hospital in 1869, would make it less possible, and at length impossible, to have a long period of residence. A man who entered in 1854, for example, could be there only a maximum of 15 years before closure would have forced him out. This consideration is moot in this case, however, as the data required to calculate duration of residence is only available up to 1844 and so admissions in that year would still have been able to reach the highest category in terms of tenure in the hospital used in Table 1 (at least 20 years and one month). The average age statistics, meanwhile give a clear picture of increased average age on admission. Consequently, this chapter is able to argue with confidence that the reductions in average residence presented here are largely the result of increased average age at admission, and the closure of Greenwich Hospital in 1869 had no impact on the trends in this data.

The trends discussed here reconcile the higher-than-expected rate at which admissions to Greenwich Hospital were maintained with the growing number of vacancies in that institution and its unsustainability of operation. This is because the higher average age on admission and shorter tenures of residence resulted in a faster turnover of residents. Although the number of men admitted to Greenwich Hospital in 1854, 1859, and 1864 was comparable to the rate seen across the second half of the eighteenth century, those men were on average older and spent less time in the hospital before discharge, in most cases on death. As a result, the number of vacancies in the hospital was large and trending upwards by this time,[71] leading to the eventual closure of Greenwich Hospital as a residential charity.

It is argued here that the trends identified in Figures 7 to 10 and Table 1 are indicative of a change in the relationship between Greenwich Hospital and the community of veteran sailors that it was intended to serve. Instead of a straightforward substitution where men increasingly chose the out-pension instead of residency in Greenwich Hospital, there are grounds to suggest that the veteran sailors used both of these options in a complementary

---

71   van der Merwe, *A Refuge for All*, p.16; Newell, *Greenwich Hospital*, pp.174–178.

fashion: increasingly delaying entry to the hospital while enjoying the out-pension until approximately the last two to five years of their lives. By this stage of their life cycle, the men were more likely to be widowers and their children to be married and established in independent households, lessening the veteran sailors' social obligations and connections. At the same time, it is in these final years of life that we would expect their health and mobility issues to be most serious and to require greatest support of a kind that a residential charity like Greenwich Hospital would be best placed to provide. This interpretation finds some anecdotal reflection in a published collection of naval literary sketches:

> Poor fellow! He's an out-pensioner of Greenwich, and picks up what he can in an honest way, to provide for the wants of some half-score of grandchildren that are left orphans. "To be sure", says he, "I might go into the house [Greenwich Hospital] and take care of myself: but then, what's to become of the youngsters, eh?"[72]

Therefore, it would be unwise to consider the out-pension to be mutually exclusive or a direct substitution for residency in Greenwich Hospital. Instead, the veteran sailors appear to have used both in a complementary manner and moved between them with deliberation and care according to their own circumstances and those of their families. These men were active agents who made their own choices in accordance with their best interests as they perceived them at the time. In this way, Greenwich Hospital and the wider community of veteran sailors adapted to each other's policies and preferences and so their relationship should be recognised as one of responsive flexibility. It is important to note that admission to Greenwich Hospital was not entirely the men's own choice to make, as there was a competitive admissions process. However, the hospital officials making admissions decisions could only choose from those who had voluntarily applied in the first place and the admissions process became less competitive with success rates improving as time went on. This is especially true of the later periods (when the trend of increasing age at admission is observed most strongly) until the institution could not be filled to capacity and vacancies grew.[73]

The remainder of this chapter will now turn briefly to several other key features of the Greenwich Hospital population and notable changes over time.

Table 2. Place of Birth as a proportion of Admitted Men (%)

Year of Admission	English	Scottish	Welsh	Irish	Channel Islands or Isle of Man	Overseas Europe	Overseas Americas	Overseas Africa	Overseas Asia	Overseas (any)
1764	50.48	10.95	1.43	26.19	1.43	0.48	0.48	0	0.48	1.44
1769	59.45	16.14	1.18	16.14	0.79	1.18	0.79	0	0	1.97
1774	57.21	15.72	3.06	14.85	0	0.87	1.31	0	0	2.18
1779	56.12	10.55	3.80	15.61	0.42	2.11	0.42	0.42	0	2.95

---

72   Anon., *Greenwich Hospital, A Series of Naval Sketches*, pp.186–187.
73   Newell, *Greenwich Hospital*, especially pp.174–178.

Year of Admission	English	Scottish	Welsh	Irish	Channel Islands or Isle of Man	Overseas Europe	Overseas Americas	Overseas Africa	Overseas Asia	Overseas (any)
1784	41.80	17.58	1.95	12.89	0.39	4.30	2.34	0	0.39	7.03
1789	57.94	10.73	1.72	19.74	0.86	2.15	0.43	0.43	0	3.01
1794	63.86	8.03	0.80	16.47	0	2.01	1.20	0	0	3.21
1799	47.58	8.26	2.28	27.35	0.85	3.70	2.56	0	0.28	6.54
1804	50.00	6.82	4.09	19.55	0.91	2.27	3.18	0	0.91	6.36
1809	43.65	9.77	1.63	24.43	0.33	4.23	3.91	0.33	0.33	8.80
1814	49.61	6.30	3.41	18.90	0.26	2.89	4.72	0.26	0	7.87
1819	42.97	3.80	2.66	15.97	0	1.14	1.90	0	0	3.04
1824	57.97	4.93	1.45	15.65	0.29	1.16	3.19	0	0.29	4.64
1829	64.35	5.68	0.95	13.56	0	1.89	0.95	0.32	0	3.16
1834	65.94	3.90	1.30	11.50	0.22	2.39	1.52	0.65	0.22	4.78
1839	66.26	2.43	1.82	17.02	0	1.82	1.52	0.61	0	3.95
1844	78.63	2.80	0.51	12.72	0.25	2.04	1.53	0.51	0	4.08

Source: Greenwich Hospital Rough Entry Books 1704–1863, TNA ADM73/51–64. An additional five men from this sample were born on board a ship and so are not included here.

Table 3. Proportion of Admissions (%) by Length of Naval Service.

Year of Admission	< 1 Y	1–5 Y	5Y1M–10 Y	10Y1M–15 Y	>15 Y
1764	0.48	15.24	32.86	17.14	30.00
1769	0.79	6.69	25.20	24.80	39.37
1774	0	2.62	20.96	26.20	46.72
1779	2.11	9.70	29.54	17.72	32.07
1784	0	7.81	14.45	9.38	54.69
1789	0	6.87	28.76	24.03	36.91
1794	0.40	6.02	26.51	18.07	42.17
1799	0.85	16.52	17.95	19.66	38.18
1804	0.45	1.36	15.00	22.73	48.64
1809	0.65	9.77	15.31	24.10	39.41
1814	0.26	2.89	9.45	21.00	54.33
1819	0.38	3.42	8.37	16.73	40.30
1824	1.45	4.35	15.65	29.86	34.78
1829	0.32	5.05	12.30	23.03	47.95
1834	0	4.34	22.99	27.55	34.06
1839	0	6.08	27.96	29.79	31.00
1844	0.25	6.36	30.03	36.90	26.46
1849	0.25	6.90	36.95	29.06	26.60
1854	1.30	12.17	25.22	21.30	37.83
1859	1.12	12.85	34.64	16.20	34.08

Source: Greenwich Hospital Rough Entry Books 1704–1863, TNA ADM73/51–64.

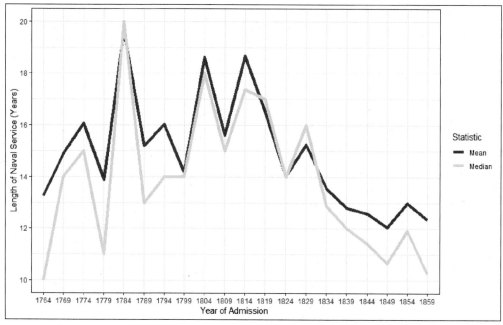

Figure 11. Average Length of Naval Service of Men Admitted to Greenwich Hospital.[74]

Firstly, it must be conceded that Tables 2 and 3 suffer from less complete reporting (as the sum of several of the rows falls far short of 100), but it is interesting that the rates of recording follow an uncannily similar pattern, which perhaps hints at differences according to the practices of the clerk assigned to record this information in the different years of admission.

The main pattern observed from Table 2 is that men born in England always predomi-nated among admissions to Greenwich Hospital, sometimes overwhelmingly so. In all but a few cases, the Irish were the second most numerous group admitted. Perhaps the most interesting fluctuations are in the proportion of admissions who were born overseas, which ranged from a low of 0.6 percent (just one individual) in 1859 to a high of 10.1 percent (31 individuals) in 1809.[75] The average across the whole period between 1764 and 1859 was 4.6 percent, while the average for the years of the French Revolutionary and Napoleonic Wars (1794 to 1814) was 7.4 percent. This is a minimum estimate due to the 156 men admitted in these years for whom no place of birth is recorded.[76] As a proportion of admissions

---

74   Greenwich Hospital Rough Entry Books 1704–1863, TNA ADM73/51–64.
75   For our purposes, 'overseas' or 'foreign-born' men are defined as those whose birth place was outside of the British Isles (including Ireland, the Channel Islands, and the Isle of Man). As such, the category of 'foreigners' includes some men who were British subjects by birth, for example those born in overseas territories, such as Gibraltar or Bermuda.
76   Across this period (admission years 1794, 1799, 1804, 1809, and 1814) a frustrating 10.26 percent of admissions have no recorded place of birth, an unknown number of whom will have been born overseas. As such, the figure of 7.4 percent represents a minimum proportion of foreign-born Greenwich pensioners in these years.

where an identifiable birthplace is given, foreign-born men make up 8.2 percent of new Greenwich pensioners during the war years. This figure closely matches Jeremiah Dancy's estimate of the proportion of foreign-born sailors among Royal Navy crews during the French Revolutionary Wars and also corresponds to the lower end of Sara Caputo's estimate for the period 1793 to 1815. Both of these studies were based on quantitative analysis of ships' muster books, with Dancy choosing a sample of ships serving in British home waters, whereas Caputo concentrated on the most distant naval stations, so it is not surprising that the figures for foreign-born Greenwich pensioners tallies with the lower bound of her estimate.[77] This would suggest that the proportion of foreign-born men admitted to Greenwich Hospital roughly kept pace with the ratio of foreigners serving in the navy at that time. In a sense this is itself surprising as, even in wartime, one would expect an appreciable, though indeterminate, time delay between service and admission whereby Greenwich Hospital admissions would instead reflect the situation in the navy some years earlier.

There are clear peaks to the proportion of admissions born overseas during or just after war years (1784 and 1799–1814), which speaks to the perennial naval manning problem during wartime and the multinational character of the lower decks of British warships in this period. Over time, the clear trend in Table 2 is that an increasing proportion of men admitted to Greenwich Hospital were born in the British Isles (including Ireland). This likely reflects the long period of relative peace after 1815, the concurrently reduced problem of naval manning, and the post-war features of Britain's maritime workforce.[78] Intriguingly, a final wartime peak at 3.5 percent of admissions recording a foreign birthplace in 1854 corresponds to the Crimean War and matches almost exactly Sara Caputo's findings on the proportion of foreign-born sailors in the British Baltic Fleet during that conflict.[79]

Table 3 and Figure 11 are less revealing of changing trends but some suggested arguments can be made. Firstly, years of warfare appear to have seen a greater proportion of admissions with shorter naval careers, which could logically correspond to the admission of younger men recently wounded or suffering from illness, brought to Greenwich straight from active service. In this respect, however, the years 1804 and 1814 seem to be exceptions with relatively few men of short naval service admitted. One explanation would be that these years were affected by wider demobilisation trends, with older sailors having taken advantage of the Peace of Amiens (1802) and the first defeat of Napoleon (1814) to leave the service and

---

77   From a sample of 20,213 men, Dancy finds eight percent of seamen and petty officers were foreign-born between 1793 and 1801, while Caputo has argued that between one in 12 (8.3 percent) and one in seven (14.3 percent) sailors on British warships between 1793 and 1815 was foreign-born. See J. Ross Dancy, *The Myth of the Press Gang, Volunteers, Impressment and the Naval Manpower Problem in the Late Eighteenth Century* (Woodbridge: The Boydell Press, 2018), p.51; Sara Caputo, *Foreign Jack Tars, The British Navy and Transnational Seafarers during the Revolutionary and Napoleonic Wars* (Cambridge: Cambridge University Press, 2022), pp.1–2, 34–36.

78   Simon p.Ville, *English Shipowning During the Industrial Revolution, Michael Henley and Son, London Shipowners, 1770–1830* (Manchester: Manchester University Press, 1987), pp.95–99.

79   Based on a representative sample of five ships from the Baltic Fleet, Caputo found that 3.65 percent of seamen were foreign-born. See Sara Caputo, "'Contriving to Pick Up Some Sailors": The Royal Navy and Foreign Manpower, 1815–1865' in Thomas Dodman and Aurélien Lignereux (eds), *From the Napoleonic Empire to the Age of Empire: Empire after the Emperor* (Basingstoke: Palgrave Macmillan, 2023). I am grateful to Sara Caputo for allowing me to read her chapter prior to publication.

enter Greenwich Hospital. This would also explain the peak in average length of service in 1784 following the Treaty of Paris in 1783. In general, sailors' marketable skills meant that they had better employment prospects than soldiers during periods of demobilisation, but the arrival of peace could still lead to unemployment, hardship, and labour unrest, with the years following the end of the Napoleonic Wars especially difficult.[80] After 1815 the general trend is towards shorter periods of naval service which would seem to reflect the smaller peacetime navy and the growing distance in time from wartime naval mobilisation on the scale seen in previous conflicts from the Seven Years War through to the Napoleonic Wars.

Table 4. Wound Profile of Admissions to Greenwich Hospital (% of men admitted each year)

Year of Admission	No Wound Reported	Lost Multiple Limbs	Lost One Limb	Wounded Limb[s]	Lost Hand/ Foot/ Finger[s]/ Toe[s]	Lost Use of Limb[s]	Sensory Wound	Wounded Private Parts	Other Wounds
1764	71.90	0	2.38	10.00	7.14	0.48	3.33	0.48	4.29
1769	68.50	0	1.97	3.94	3.54	0.79	2.36	0.79	10.63
1774	73.80	0	1.31	10.92	6.11	0.44	2.62	1.31	3.49
1779	42.62	0.42	4.64	21.52	3.80	1.27	4.22	3.38	18.14
1784	35.55	0.39	6.64	20.70	3.91	0.39	8.20	1.56	22.27
1789	50.64	0	2.58	16.31	3.86	1.72	5.15	2.58	17.17
1794	38.96	0	5.62	20.48	1.20	1.61	6.02	4.42	21.69
1799	31.05	0	11.4	21.94	2.28	1.42	6.84	2.85	22.22
1804	43.18	0	3.18	19.55	2.73	3.18	8.64	4.09	15.45
1809	26.06	0.65	8.79	14.33	1.95	7.49	9.12	3.58	28.01
1814	43.83	0.26	1.84	12.07	1.05	1.31	11.81	0.52	27.30
1819	53.23	0	5.70	12.17	1.52	1.14	7.98	1.90	16.35
1824	46.38	0.29	6.09	13.91	4.06	1.45	6.09	2.61	19.13
1829	57.73	0	2.52	16.72	3.47	1.58	3.79	2.52	11.36
1834	63.77	0	1.74	8.89	2.60	0.22	3.04	0.43	19.31
1839	62.01	0	2.13	8.21	2.74	1.82	6.38	0.30	16.41
1844	52.16	0	2.29	18.58	0.76	1.53	4.58	0.76	19.34
1849	63.55	0	3.20	8.13	3.45	0.49	3.94	0.74	18.97
1854	58.70	0	2.17	13.48	1.74	0.43	3.04	0	20.43
1859	53.07	0	2.23	10.61	3.35	0	2.23	0.56	27.93

Sources: Greenwich Hospital Rough Entry Books 1704–1863, TNA ADM73/51–64; Greenwich Hospital Entry Books 1764–1865, TNA ADM73/65–69.

---

80   Evan Wilson, *The Horrible Peace, British Veterans and the End of the Napoleonic Wars* (Amherst: University of Massachusetts Press, 2023).

Table 5. Eventual Manner of Discharge of Admissions to Greenwich Hospital.

Year of Admission	Died	Expelled	Deserted	Discharged to Out Pension	Discharged to Ship or Naval Facility	Discharged Other
1764	76.67	2.38	6.67	3.33	0	1.43
1769	82.28	1.57	6.30	0.39	0.79	8.66
1774	88.65	1.75	4.37	0	0.44	4.80
1779	84.81	2.11	4.64	2.11	0	5.91
1784	82.81	0.78	2.73	4.30	1.17	8.20
1789	87.98	0.86	2.58	1.72	0	6.87
1794	80.72	0.80	5.62	2.01	1.20	9.64
1799	70.37	1.99	4.84	8.26	2.56	11.68
1804	81.82	0.91	5.00	9.09	2.73	0.45
1809	74.92	2.61	5.86	12.70	1.63	2.28
1814	80.58	1.57	2.10	13.12	0.26	2.36
1819	73.00	1.52	4.18	20.91	0	0.76
1824	68.70	1.74	5.22	18.84	0.87	4.35
1829	71.61	0.32	2.52	22.71	0.32	1.58
1834	73.32	0.43	2.39	19.52	0	3.25
1839	75.99	0.61	2.13	16.11	0	3.65
1844	65.90	0.76	3.56	21.37	0	2.29

Source: Greenwich Hospital General Entry Books 1704–1846, TNA ADM73/36–41.

Tables 4 and 5 are the final two included for discussion in this chapter. As mentioned, it is important to remember that the data in Table 5 is arranged by date of admission, not by date of discharge, so the row for 1819, for example, shows the fate of men admitted to the hospital in 1819 whereas the dates of leaving for these men are spread across the succeeding decades.

There are two arguments that arise from Table 4. The first is that there was a change in the way that information on wounds was recorded between 1774 and 1779, and the second is that this data stands at odds with the popular presentation of Greenwich pensioners discussed in the second section of this chapter. Firstly, however, to comment on another significant trend, the proportion of admissions reporting a wound increased markedly during war years. The peaks in 1779 and 1784 correspond with the American War of Independence, and particularly to the stage of that conflict after French and Spanish intervention in 1778 and 1779 respectively, after which point it took on more of a naval dimension. Interestingly, several individuals in the current sample specified that they received wounds in particular engagements in this war, including the Battle of Bunker Hill.[81] The proportion of admissions reporting wounds is also especially high in the war years of 1799, 1804, and 1809,

---

81   For example, Charles Matthews (entry number 15589), admitted on 17 July 1794, reported being wounded in the left leg at 'Bunker Hill America'. John Escott (entry number 15602), admitted on 1 August 1794 also suffered a wounded left leg at Bunker Hill. Greenwich Hospital Entry Books covering 1794, TNA ADM73/38; 54; 65.

whereas after 1815 the trend in the prevalence of wounds is broadly downward, as might be expected from that more peaceful era.

The most startling element of Table 4 is the leap in the proportion of admissions reporting wounds between 1774 and 1779. As discussed, this was a move from a year of peace to one of war, but this alone appears insufficient to explain such a large increase (from 26 percent of admissions reporting a wound to 57 percent).[82] Furthermore, a much higher rate of wounds continued to be reported in every subsequent year, whether war or peace. It is argued here that this sharp divergence in the data was primarily the result of a change in how wound data was recorded in the hospital admission books. While conscious of inconsistencies in the way hospital clerks recorded injuries, Wilcox in his study understood the wound data to refer solely to injuries and ailments that were either permanent (like the loss of an eye), or current at the man's date of admission.[83] That appears to hold true until some point between 1774 and 1779. By 1779, this chapter contends, the practice had changed so that historic wounds were reported as well as current or permanent ones. One interpretation would be that, with increasing competition for places in the hospital, those responsible for admissions decisions were prioritising those who had suffered a wound at any point during their naval career as being more deserving than those who had suffered none.

Several observations lend weight to this argument. Crucially, by combining the information from the three sets of admission records together into one database, a sense of progression can be identified. Together, the sources give information on the wound(s) suffered, the ship in which the wound(s) occurred, and the last ship in which the man served. After 1779 there are many instances where men report wounds that we would consider temporary, such as a broken arm or leg, which occurred in a ship that was not the last ship in which they served. We do not know from this data how many ships (if any) the man served in between the ship where the wound occurred and his final ship before admission to Greenwich Hospital. We can be confident in the vast majority of these cases that these reported temporary wounds would have healed by the date of admission to Greenwich Hospital. The most startling example is of William Stocker, admitted on 20 June 1834, whose entry in the wounds column simply but intriguingly reads 'Struck by lightning'.[84] It would appear safe to assume that this unlucky event did not take place that morning as Stocker was on his way to be interviewed for admission, but instead referred to a historic injury from some point during his naval service, although in this case one might wonder if this would result in some form of permanent or recurring injury.

The second pressing argument derived from Table 4 is that the wound profile of admissions to Greenwich Hospital did not conform to the popular portrayal of Greenwich pensioners in images of the kind discussed in the second section of this chapter. This is especially true when it comes to amputation. Whereas the loss of a limb appeared almost universal in popular portrayals with the loss of two or more limbs far from uncommon, the demographic reality was very different. Across this sample of 6,045 men, the proportion of admissions missing one limb peaked at 11 percent in 1799, while the average across the

---

82   Greenwich Hospital Rough Entry Books 1704–1863, TNA ADM73/51–64; Greenwich Hospital Entry Books 1764–1865, TNA ADM73/65–69.

83   Wilcox, 'The "Poor Decayed Seamen" of Greenwich Hospital', pp.79–83.

84   Greenwich Hospital Entry Book 1833–40, TNA ADM73/68.

years surveyed was just 3.9 percent. Only six men were reported to have lost two limbs — in every case both legs — and none to have lost three or four limbs. These figures are consistent with the findings of a study of 97 skeletons from the cemetery of Greenwich Hospital, of which only five showed signs of likely amputation: in all cases the loss of one leg.[85] In a further challenge to the popular imagery of Greenwich pensioners with wooden legs, 'bone resorption in the amputated limb of all of the lower limb amputees suggested that none of the amputees used the peg leg prosthesis' and other changes to two of the amputee skeletons instead implied 'under arm crutch use'.[86]

Many entries in the two wound columns (one from the Rough Entry Books and the other from the Entry Books) are laconic and only say, for example 'Right leg'. In these cases, it is taken to mean a wound in the right leg and amputation is only inferred if the entry states, for example, 'Right leg lost'. Consequently, it is probable that the proportion of men missing a limb has been underestimated, but likely only slightly and certainly not nearly enough to vindicate the prevalence of amputation seen in the visual sources. Furthermore, comparing the wounded column from the two different entry books acted as a corrective here as whenever one source said, for example, 'Right leg' and the other 'Right leg lost', the amputation was counted. As a result, Table 4 is presented with a suitable degree of confidence.

Finally, Table 5 shows the eventual manner of discharge for the men admitted in each year. Apart from the first and last few years, this information is almost complete for these admission cohorts. Across the entire period death was by far the most common form of discharge, representing a high of 88.7 percent of the men admitted in 1774, but with an average proportion of 77.7 percent across the full sample. Desertion rates tend broadly downwards, but it is difficult to draw conclusions about these or the institutional failings that led men to that recourse until the database is complete. Unsurprisingly, the proportion of men discharged to naval ships, dockyards, and other active facilities is highest during wartime years (1794, 1799, 1804) and almost non-existent otherwise. Finally, the proportion of men discharged to the out-pension grew substantially through the nineteenth century. More research is required on this point before preliminary arguments can be presented, but it will be interesting to investigate whether, since out-pensions had been available since 1763, this increase in the proportion of men leaving Greenwich Hospital to take up the out-pension in the early nineteenth century could have been a response to the growing severity of civil welfare provision with the gradual replacement of outdoor relief with workhouses.

In conclusion, to judge from the disconnect between the popular presentation of Greenwich pensioners in contemporary images and the demographic reality revealed by the admissions books, these men were frequently misrepresented in their own time and have been largely neglected ever since. This is a pity because the level of detail of the Greenwich

85   Ceridwen Boston, Annsofie Witkin, Angela Boyle, and David R.P. Wilkinson, 'Safe moor'd in Greenwich tier': A study of the skeletons of Royal Navy sailors and marines excavated at the Royal Hospital Greenwich (Oxford: Alden Group for Oxford Archaeology Monograph 5, 2008), p.39. For a comparable study of morbidities among North Atlantic merchant seafarers in the late nineteenth century, see Madeleine Mant, 'For those in peril on and off the sea: Merchant marine bodies in nineteenth-century St. John's, Newfoundland', International Journal of Maritime History, vol.32 (2020), pp.23–44.
86   Boston, Witkin, Boyle, and Wilkinson, 'Safe moor'd in Greenwich tier', p.68.

Hospital archives makes the Greenwich pensioners one of the best-recorded subsections of Britain's maritime labour force available for study. In myriad respects, the Greenwich Hospital population is well-placed to shed light both on Britain's crucial seafaring communities and on the course of British welfare provision across this period of unrivalled socio-economic upheaval. This chapter has shown that the relationship between Greenwich Hospital and the veteran sailors it served was one of greater flexibility and pragmatism than had previously been recognised, with each side adapting to the circumstances of the other as well as wider changes in the economic and welfare context. Meanwhile, it has been argued, the visual representation of Greenwich pensioners, while never a particularly accurate impression, reflected state aims and societal concerns, and underwent dramatic change as those aims and anxieties changed in turn. Finally, the perspective offered by the end of a sailor's life cycle, here represented by the veteran seamen of Greenwich Hospital, offers fresh insights into the lives of Britain's maritime workforce and their place in society in war and in peace. For the tens of thousands of sailors who lived out their final days at Greenwich Hospital, that institution was a 'safe mooring' where they could abide free from poverty and refight their battles over again with old shipmates. The findings presented in this chapter represent only a first step towards understanding their lives and experiences.

Select Bibliography

Archives
The National Archives, Kew (TNA)
> Greenwich Hospital Council Minutes, ADM67/119–235
> Greenwich Hospital Digest of Minutes of the Commissioners, ADM67/266–267
> Greenwich Hospital General Entry Books 1704–1846, ADM73/36–41
> Greenwich Hospital Rough Entry Books 1704–1863, ADM73/51–64
> Greenwich Hospital Entry Books 1764–1865, ADM73/65–69
National Maritime Museum, Greenwich (NMM)
> George Hewens, Greenwich Pensioners, Poems on various subjects, LIT/6
> His Majesty's commission for the Royal Hospital for Seamen at Greenwich (1761), 22671-1001

Published Sources
Begiato, Joanne, *Manliness in Britain, 1760–1900 Bodies, emotion, and material culture* (Manchester: Manchester University Press, 2020).
Berry, Helen, *Orphans of Empire: The Fate of London's Foundlings* (Oxford: Oxford University Press, 2019).
Boston, Ceridwen, Witkin, Annsofie, Boyle, Angela, and Wilkinson, David R.P., *'Safe moor'd in Greenwich tier': A study of the skeletons of Royal Navy sailors and marines excavated at the Royal Hospital Greenwich* (Oxford: Alden Group for Oxford Archaeology Monograph 5, 2008).
Caputo, Sara, *Foreign Jack Tars, The British Navy and Transnational Seafarers during the Revolutionary and Napoleonic Wars* (Cambridge: Cambridge University Press, 2022).
Dancy, J. Ross, *The Myth of the Press Gang, Volunteers, Impressment and the Naval Manpower Problem in the Late Eighteenth Century* (Woodbridge: The Boydell Press, 2018) .
Davey, James, and Johns, Richard, *Broadsides, Caricature and the Navy 1756–1815* (Barnsley: Seaforth Publishing in association with the National Maritime Museum, 2012).
Goffman, Erving, *Stigma, Notes on the Management of Spoiled Identity* (London: Penguin, 1990).
Hoock, Holger, *Empires of the Imagination: Politics, War, and the Arts in the British World, 1750–1850* (London: Profile Books, 2010).

Innes, Joanna, *Inferior Politics, Social Problems and Social Policies in Eighteenth-Century Britain* (Oxford: Oxford University Press, 2009).

Kennedy, Catriona, *Narratives of the Revolutionary and Napoleonic Wars, Military and Civilian Experiences in Britain and Ireland* (Basingstoke: Palgrave Macmillan, 2013).

Land, Isaac, *War, Nationalism, and the British Sailor, 1750–1850* (New York: Palgrave Macmillan, 2009).

Miller, Amy, *Dressed to Kill, British Naval Uniform, Masculinity and Contemporary Fashions, 1748–1857* (London: National Maritime Museum, 2021).

Newell, Philip, *Greenwich Hospital, A Royal Foundation 1692–1983* (London: Butler and Tanner Ltd., 1984).

Rudé, George, *The Crowd in History, A Study of Popular Disturbances in France and England, 1730–1848* (London: Serif, 2005).

Turner, David, 'Disability history and the history of emotions: reflections on eighteenth century Britain', *Asclepio*, vol. 68 (2016), pp.146–158.

Turner, David, 'Picturing Disability in Eighteenth-Century England' in Rembis, Michael, Kudlick, Catherine, and Nielsen, Kim E. (eds), *The Oxford Handbook of Disability History* (Oxford: Oxford University Press, 2018).

Wilcox, Martin, 'The "Poor Decayed Seamen" of Greenwich Hospital, 1705–1763', *International Journal of Maritime History*, vol. 25 (2013), pp.65–90.

Wilson, Evan, *The Horrible Peace, British Veterans and the End of the Napoleonic Wars* (Amherst: University of Massachusetts Press, 2023).

Wrigley, E.A., and Schofield, R.S., *The Population History of England 1541–1871 A Reconstruction* (London: Edward Arnold, 1981).

Thesis

Nielsen, Caroline, 'The Chelsea Out-Pensioners: Image and Reality in Eighteenth-Century and Early Nineteenth-Century Social Care' (Unpublished PhD thesis, Newcastle University, 2014).

General Index

Aberdeen 72, 75, 78-80, 86, 270
Admiralty Board 110, 118-121, 126-127, 130, 204, 207-208
Aegean 32-34, 36-37, 39
Aix-la-Chapelle, Treaty of 185
Alcohol: see Drunkenness
Algiers 21, 54, 56, 60-63
Álvarez, *Jefe de escuadra* Cosme 56, 69
American War of Independence 43, 109, 111, 132, 187, 268, 292, 296, 294, 306, 332, 339
Amputation 313, 317-319, 322, 340-341
Anson, Adm. of the Fleet George, Baron 173, 199-211, 213-219, 221-222, 227, 249
Antigua 53, 127, 135, 137, 140, 211
Antwerp 173, 175-178, 184-185, 187-189, 192-193, 196-197
Armata grossa 17, 22, 24-26, 32, 34, 36-37, 39-40
Armata sottile 22, 24, 34, 36-38
Articles of War 174, 242-243, 245, 248-255
Atlantic 18, 20, 45-49, 61, 63, 66, 88, 90-91, 97, 104, 129, 133, 147, 152, 180-181, 183, 187, 190, 219, 225-227, 289, 293-294, 296, 305-308
Azores 48-49, 69

Barbados 135-137, 140-141, 147
Barbary Coast 21, 24, 27, 31, 35-37, 55-56, 60, 62
Barcelona 54-55, 57, 60
Barrier Fortresses 185
Barrington, Rear-Adm. Hon. Samuel 131-133, 135-143, 145-149, 151-152
Bart, *Chef d'escadre* François-Cornil 73, 91, 93, 102-103
Bedford, John Russel, Duke of 200, 204, 207-208, 229
Belgium 178, 183-186, 188-189, 193-194, 196-197
Beresford, Cdre John Poo 289, 291, 294, 298-299, 301-302, 305-307
Bermuda 121-122, 163, 291, 293-299, 305-308

'Black Legend' 42-43, 65
Blyth, Cdr Samuel 159, 166-168, 171
Board of Trade 111, 117
Bonvicini, Fabio 26-27, 36
Boscawen, Vice-Adm. Edward 220, 223-226, 230-233, 236-237, 240-241
Boston 86, 110, 116-119, 126-127, 134, 159, 226, 299, 342
Boulogne 86, 181-182, 190
Brest 88, 91-94, 96-98, 102-103, 105-106, 180-181, 183-184, 186-187, 190, 193, 196, 205-206, 214, 220, 224, 268, 270-271
Britain 25, 43-44, 50-51, 55-56, 58, 60, 64-68, 74, 80, 85, 90, 106-107, 110-111, 113-114, 116-118, 120-122, 128, 133-136, 151-152, 159, 172-173, 175-176, 178-197, 209, 214, 218-219, 221-223, 225, 227, 233-234, 238, 240-241, 244, 261, 266-271, 275-279, 281-282, 284-289, 291, 294, 299, 308-311, 317-319, 322, 324, 326-328, 337, 342-343
Broves, *Chef d'escadre* Jean-Joseph de Rafélis de 139, 145
Buggery 174, 242; see also Sodomy
Burghley, William Cecil, Lord 176, 178, 185, 191
Burrows, Master Commandant William 159-160
Byng, Adm. John 82-83, 201, 216, 219, 226-228, 231, 239-241, 249, 251, 253

Cadiz 48-49, 54, 63, 119, 190
Camperdown, Battle of 274, 281
Canada 111, 172, 224-225, 231
Cape Clear 94, 101-102
Cape Fear 111
Cape Hatteras 110-111, 291, 299
Cape Matapan 36-37, 40
Cape Passaro 42, 60, 62, 64, 201
Cartagena 45-46, 50, 54-57, 62-63, 201, 203-204
Cautionary Towns 176-177

Index of Ships

From Reason to Revolution – Warfare 1721-1815

http://www.helion.co.uk/series/from-reason-to-revolution-1721-1815.php

The 'From Reason to Revolution' series covers the period of military history 1721–1815, an era in which fortress-based strategy and linear battles gave way to the nation-in-arms and the beginnings of total war.

This era saw the evolution and growth of light troops of all arms, and of increasingly flexible command systems to cope with the growing armies fielded by nations able to mobilise far greater proportions of their manpower than ever before. Many of these developments were fired by the great political upheavals of the era, with revolutions in America and France bringing about social change which in turn fed back into the military sphere as whole nations readied themselves for war. Only in the closing years of the period, as the reactionary powers began to regain the upper hand, did a military synthesis of the best of the old and the new become possible.

The series will examine the military and naval history of the period in a greater degree of detail than has hitherto been attempted, and has a very wide brief, with the intention of covering all aspects from the battles, campaigns, logistics, and tactics, to the personalities, armies, uniforms, and equipment.

Submissions

The publishers would be pleased to receive submissions for this series. Please contact series editor Andrew Bamford via email (andrewbamford@helion.co.uk), or in writing to Helion & Company Limited, Unit 8 Amherst Business Centre, Budbrooke Road, Warwick, CV34 5WE

Titles